KEY STUDIES *in*
PSYCHOLOGY

FOURTH EDITION

KEY STUDIES *in* PSYCHOLOGY

FOURTH EDITION

Richard Gross

Hodder & Stoughton
A MEMBER OF THE HODDER HEADLINE GROUP

Orders: please contact Bookpoint Ltd, 130 Milton Park, Abingdon, Oxon OX14 4SB.
Telephone: (44) 01235 827720. Fax: (44) 01235 400454. Lines are open from 9.00 – 6.00,
Monday to Saturday, with a 24 hour message answering service.
You can also order through our website: www.hodderheadline.co.uk

British Library Cataloguing in Publication Data
A catalogue record for this title is available from the British Library

ISBN 0 340 857854

First Published 2003

Impression number   10 9 8 7 6 5 4 3 2
Year   2008 2007 2006 2005 2004 2003

Typeset by Dorchester Typesetting Group Ltd, Dorset
Printed in Great Britain for Hodder & Stoughton Educational, a division of Hodder Headline, 338 Euston Road,
London NW1 3BH by J. W. Arrowsmiths Ltd., Bristol.

Dedication

To the memory of Tim Gregson-Williams, my publisher and friend for thirteen years. The world is just not the same without you.

Contents

INTRODUCTION

As with the three previous editions, the major aim of *Key Studies* is to do what cannot be done in a general, introductory textbook, namely to discuss a number of individual studies in depth. Students very often want to know more about a particular study than can be provided in a general textbook, or by a lecturer in a teaching situation. This means that the student either has to search for, and wade through, the original journal article (which can be difficult and time-consuming), or simply get by with what can be extracted from lecture and textbook.

While it's very important that students (at all levels) get used to reading original sources, it may not be so obvious how to make effective use of that material. The **Background and context** and **Aim and nature of the study** sections that precede each Study, and the **Evaluation** section that follows it, are designed to provide students with a framework for reading *any* original material, so as to make the best use of reading time.

Before reading the Study itself, it's useful to have a theoretical, practical, and/or socio-historical context to put it in. It's also useful to have an idea of the Study's aims, hypotheses, method and design and, where appropriate, the major findings. *After* reading the Study, it can be evaluated in terms of theoretical and methodological issues, subsequent research, applications and implications (both practical and theoretical). The **Evaluation** sub-headings (*Theoretical Issues, Methodological Issues* etc.) usually appear in that order, but sometimes it seemed more appropriate to combine two or more, or to change the order.

Please note that the articles (with the exception of Chapters 2 and 12) aren't reprints of the original, but highly detailed summaries. The aim is to retain the substantial character of the original, but at the same time to reduce unnecessary bulk. So, how have I summarized them?

- I've retained all the section headings as they appear in the original (and in their original order). Not all journals use the same format. For example, some have a summary/abstract at the beginning, others put it at the end, and some don't have one at all.

- Most tables, figures etc. have been retained, but not all.

- I've used a combination of paraphrasing (i.e. rewording) and reproduction of the original. But nothing appears in quotation marks, as this would disturb the continuity and flow of the text.

- I've replaced difficult or obscure language with simpler or more familiar language.

- English English spelling has been used at all times (as opposed to American English), even though most of the studies are published in American journals.

The References given at the back of the book are the sources cited in the ***Background and context/Aim and nature of the study/Evaluation*** sections. It would have been impractical to include all those which appear in the original article.

Although the original article is referred to as 'The Study' throughout, some are, strictly, *not* 'studies' at all, that is, discrete investigations (experiments, questionnaires etc.) conducted by the researchers whose names appear at the beginning of the chapter. For example, Chapter 1 discusses Miller's (1969) Presidential address to the American Psychological Association, Chapter 4 is concerned with Craik & Lockhart's (1972) re-interpretation of memory research, and in Chapter 17, Levinson (1986) proposes a theoretical view of adult development. The 'status' of each 'study' is made clear within each chapter.

Finally, how did I decide which studies should be included? This was definitely the single most difficult aspect of the whole book (especially with the first edition). The main criteria were:

● The need to sample all the major areas of (mainstream, academic) Psychology: cognitive, social, developmental, and so on.

● The need to sample a wide range of empirical methods: experiments (laboratory, field, and natural), correlational studies, case studies, surveys, questionnaire construction, and observational studies.

● The wish to include studies which would (probably) feature in most students' (and some lecturers') 'top ten famous studies of all time' ('classics'), alongside some less well known but equally influential ones (including some that are relatively recent).

Of course, a hundred different authors would choose a hundred different combinations of 33 'key studies'. I hope (and trust) that I've made a selection which will satisfy most readers.

The fourth edition includes all 20 currently prescribed studies in the OCR (AS) specification. These include Loftus & Palmer (1974 : Chapter 5), which replaces Loftus *et al.* (1978) from the previous edition), and Raine *et al.* (1997: Chapter 33), which is new to this edition. Rawlins (1979), Bennett-Levy & Marteau (1984), and Manstead & McCulloch (1981) have been dropped from the previous edition.

The Summary Table which follows shows how the 33 studies relate to each of the four major A level specifications.

Acknowledgements: I'd like to thank Emma Woolf at Hodder for her support and friendship during difficult times. I really do value our friendship, Emma. Thanks too to Jasmine Brown for her handling of the editing of this fourth edition. Also, thanks to Stewart Larking and Jon Berkeley for a brilliant cover.

SUMMARY TABLE SHOWING HOW THE 33 STUDIES RELATE TO THE MAJOR SECTIONS OF THE FOUR A LEVEL SPECIFICATIONS

Study/chapter	EDEXCEL	OCR (AS)	AQA (A)	AQA (B)
Miller (1)	Issues, perspectives & debates (A2)		Perspectives (A2)	Introducing Psychology (AS); Perspectives, Debates & Methods in Psychology (A2)
Deregowski (2)		Cognitive	Cognitive (A2)	Cognitive (AS)
Baron-Cohen et al. (3)		Cognitive	Developmental (A2)	Child Development (A2)
Craik & Lockhart (4)	Cognitive, social & development processes (AS)		Cognitive (AS)	Cognitive (AS)
Loftus & Palmer (5)	Cognitive, social & development processes (AS); Criminal Psychology (A2)	Cognitive	Cognitive (AS)	Cognitive (AS)
Gardner & Gardner (6)		Cognitive	Cognitive (A2)	Cognitive (AS)
Milgram (7)	Cognitive, social & development processes (AS)	Social	Social (AS)	Social (AS)
Haney et al.(8)	Cognitive, social & development processes (AS)	Social	Social (AS)	Social (AS)
Piliavin et al.(9)		Social	Social (A2)	
Festinger & Carlsmith (10)				Social (AS)
Nisbett et al. (11)			Social (A2)	Social (AS)
Tajfel (12)	Cognitive, social & development processes (AS)	Social	Social (A2)	Social (AS)
Samuel & Bryant (13)	Cognitive, social & development processes (AS); Psychology of Education (A2)	Developmental	Developmental (A2)	Child Development (A2)
Bandura et al. (14)	Individual differences, physiology & behaviour (AS)	Developmental	Developmental (A2)	Child Development (A2)
Hodges & Tizard (15)	Child Psychology (A2)	Developmental	Developmental (AS)	Child Development (A2)

Study/chapter	EDEXCEL	OCR (AS)	AQA (A)	AQA (B)
Watson & Raynor (16)	Individual differences, physiology & behaviour (AS)		Individual differences (AS; A2); Perspectives (A2)	Introducing Psychology (AS); Psychology of Atypical Behaviour (A2); Perspectives, Debates & Methods (A2)
Levinson (17)			Developmental (A2)	
Fernald (18)			Cognitive (A2); Developmental (A2)	
Freud (19)	Individual differences, physiology & behaviour (AS)	Developmental	Individual differences (AS); Developmental (A2)	Introducing Psychology (AS); Child Development (A2); Perspectives, Debates & Methods (A2)
Rosenhan (20)	Clinical Psychology (A2)	Individual differences	Individual differences (A2)	Psychology of Atypical Behaviour (A2)
Thigpen & Cleckley (21)	Clinical Psychology (A2)	Individual differences	Individual differences (A2)	Psychology of Atypical Behaviour (A2)
Eysenck (22)	Clinical Psychology (A2)		Individual differences (A2)	Psychology of Atypical Behaviour (A2)
Gould (23)		Individual differences	Developmental (A2)	
Bouchard & McGhue (24)	Individual differences, physiology & behaviour (AS)		Developmental (A2)	
Bem (25)			Developmental (A2)	Introducing Psychology (AS)
Hraba & Grant (26)		Individual differences	Developmental (A2); Perspectives (A2)	
Nobles (27)			Perspectives (A2)	
Schachter & Singer (28)		Physiological	Physiological (A2)	
Dement & Kleitman (29)	Individual differences, physiology & behaviour (AS)	Physiological	Physiological (A2)	
Sperry (30)		Physiological	Physiological (A2)	
Orne (31)				
Blackmore (32)				Contemporary Topics (A2)
Raine et al.(33)		Physiological		Contemporary Topics (A2)

1

Psychology as a means of promoting human welfare

G. A. Miller (1969)

American Psychologist, 24, 1063–75

BACKGROUND AND CONTEXT

According to Murphy *et al.* (1984), Miller's article captures the turmoil that psychology was experiencing during the late 1960s. His paper continues to be cited and many psychologists have endorsed his sentiments, including Shotter (*Images of Man in Psychological Research,* 1975) and Kay in his 1972 Presidential address to the British Psychological Society. More recently, Rappaport & Stewart (1997) have discussed Miller's call to 'give psychology away' in the context of *critical psychology* (see **Evaluation** below).

Murphy *et al.* believe that Miller seems to have drawn attention to two particular issues which had been raised by the radical critics of psychology in the late 1960s, namely, (*i*) the accusation that psychology has created a dehumanizing image of human beings and (*ii*) the accusation that psychology has ignored the real-world setting within which human beings live their lives. The first of these issues is related to the notion of behavioural *control,* discussed at length by Miller. What makes it dehumanizing is that people are capable of *self*-control, controlling their own behaviour, so that imposing a behavioural technology of control removes a basic human freedom, as well as conveying the impression that people are machine-like. This is discussed in detail by Heather (1976).

Control, along with understanding (explanation) and prediction, is usually taken to be one of the major aims of science (including psychology) and is the one emphasized by Skinner, the radical behaviourist. The view of science implicitly guiding most psychological theory and research up to the late 1960s (and often explicitly advocated by psychologists, both behaviourist and cognitive) formed part of what is often called *mainstream psychology* (or what Harré, 1989, calls the 'old paradigm'). This begs fundamental questions regarding the nature of science and the appropriateness of applying the methods of natural science to the study of human beings. These issues will be discussed in the **Evaluation** below.

AIM AND NATURE OF THE STUDY

The article is in fact Miller's Presidential address to the American Psychological Association. In it, he sets out the role which he believes psychology should play in society, namely 'a means of promoting human welfare'. This can and should be achieved by 'giving psychology away': encouraging non-psychologists ('ordinary people') to practise psychology, to be their own psychologists, helping them to do better what they already do through familiarizing them with (scientific) psychological knowledge. Psychology should not be the 'property' of the scientific/professional experts: psychological principles and techniques can usefully be applied by everyone. As he says:

> The techniques involved are not some esoteric branch of witchcraft that must be reserved for those with PhD degrees in psychology. When the ideas are made sufficiently concrete and explicit, the scientific foundations of psychology can be grasped by sixth-grade [12-year-old] children.

This represents a 'policy document' or blueprint for what psychology *ought* to be doing, a prescription for its social function. In the context of mainstream psychology, which claims to be *value-free* (part-and-parcel of the 'objectivity' of science), Miller is explicitly advocating certain values. Although the Presidential address (both in the USA and the UK) has traditionally been an opportunity for taking stock of the discipline of psychology and trying to move it forward, Miller's advocacy of 'giving psychology away' and promoting human welfare was quite a radical thing to be doing in the 1960s.

THE STUDY

The most urgent problems we face today are not produced by nature or imposed as punishment by God but are those we have made for ourselves, and to solve them we must change our behaviour and our social institutions. Psychology is a science directly concerned with behavioural and social processes and so it might be expected to lead the way in the search for new and better personal and social arrangements.

However, psychologists have contributed relatively little of real importance – even less than their rather modest understanding of behaviour might justify. They have not used all the knowledge they do have and the challenge for psychologists is not only to extend and deepen their understanding of mental and behavioural phenomena but to apply this knowledge more effectively to the vast social changes that lie ahead. This doesn't mean that psychologists are failing in the task set them by society or that psychological theories are scientifically invalid. As scientists we are obliged to communicate what we know, but we have no special obligation to solve social problems.

However, psychologists are also citizens, and our obligations as citizens are far broader than our obligations as scientists. Most American psychologists do accept this broader interpretation of their responsibilities and most are engaged full time in trying to solve social problems, and with a certain degree of success.

ROLE OF THE AMERICAN PSYCHOLOGICAL ASSOCIATION

The first article of our Bylaws states that the Association shall have as its object to promote human welfare, a goal that is echoed in our statement of the *Ethical Standards of Psychologists*. But I am very sceptical about how this goal can be translated into objective action for two major reasons.

First, there is the problem of defining human welfare and deciding which group's welfare is being promoted (which may conflict with that of another).

Second, there has been much debate in recent years about the appropriate role for individual psychologists to play in the initiation of social reforms: should they remain expert advisers or should they play a more active part in determining public policy? Those who favour the latter believe that the APA should also become directly involved in advocating particular social policies. However, although the APA's failure to reform society does *not* mean that it approves the social/political status quo, there is relatively little such an association can do and its attitude towards major and urgent human problems is largely irrelevant.

The important question, to my mind, is not what the APA is doing, but what psychologists are doing. What psychology can do as an association depends directly on the base provided by psychology as a science. It is our science that provides our real means for promoting human welfare.

REVOLUTIONARY POTENTIAL OF PSYCHOLOGY

In my opinion, scientific psychology is potentially one of the most revolutionary intellectual enterprises ever conceived by the mind of man. If we were ever to achieve substantial progress toward our stated aim – toward the understanding, prediction and control of mental and behavioural phenomena – the implications for every aspect of society would make brave men tremble.

If this revolutionary potential has been played down in the past, there are probably two major reasons; firstly, the achievements of psychology so far are rather modest: scientific colleagues will admit that psychometric tests, psychoanalysis, conditioned reflexes, sensory thresholds, implanted electrodes and factor analysis are all quite admirable, but they can scarcely be compared to gunpowder, the steam engine, organic chemistry, radio-telephony, computers, atom bombs, or genetic surgery in their revolutionary consequences for society.

However, I do not believe the psychological revolution is still pie in the sky, but that it has already begun.

This leads on to the second reason, namely that we have been looking for it in the wrong place. We have assumed that psychology should provide new technological options, and that a psychological revolution will not occur until somebody in authority exercises these options to attain socially desirable goals. One reason for this assumption, perhaps, is that it follows the model we have inherited from previous applications of science to practical problems. An applied scientist is supposed to provide instrumentalities for modifying the environment; instrumentalities that can then, under public regulation, be used by wealthy and powerful interests to achieve certain goals. The psychological revolution, when it comes, may follow a very different course, at least in its initial stages.

An important difference between applied social science and applied natural science is that:

> when the science is concerned with human beings – not just as organisms but as goal-seeking individuals and members of groups – then it cannot be instrumental in this way [in the way that applied natural science is, by finding a means to an end which is the attainment of human goals], because the object of observation has a say in what is going on and, above all, is not willing to be treated as a pure instrumentality. (Davis, 1966)

More important, however, I believe that the real impact of psychology will be felt, not through the technological products it places in the hands of powerful men, but through its effects on the public at large, through a new and different public conception of what is humanly possible and what is humanly desirable.

I believe that any broad and successful application of psychological knowledge to human problems will necessarily entail a change in our conception of ourselves and of how we live and love and work together. Instead of inventing some new technique for modifying the environment, or some new product for society to adapt itself to however it can, we are proposing to tamper with the adaptive process itself. Such an innovation is quite different from a 'technological fix'. I see little reason to believe that the traditional model for scientific revolutions should be appropriate.

Consider, for example, the effect that Freudian psychology has already had on Western society. It is obvious that its effects, though limited to certain segments of society, have been profound. Yet I do not believe that one can argue that those effects were achieved by providing new instrumentalities for achieving goals socially agreed upon. As a method of therapy, psychoanalysis has had limited success even for those who can afford it. It has been more successful as a method of investigation, perhaps, but even there it has been only one of several available methods. The impact of Freud's thought has been due far less to the instrumentalities he provided than to the changed conception of ourselves that he inspired. The wide range of psychological problems that Freud opened up for professional psychologists is only part of his contribution. More important in the scale of history has been his effect on the broader intellectual community and, through it, on the public at large. Today we are much more aware of the irrational components of human nature and much better able to accept the reality of our unconscious impulses. The importance of Freudian psychology derives far less from its scientific validity than from the effects it has had on our image of man himself.

It may be true that other scientific advances have also changed our conception of man and society (such as Darwin's discovery that our remote ancestors lived in trees) but such new conceptions can have little effect on the way we behave in our daily affairs and in our institutional contexts. A new conception of man based on psychology, however, would have immediate implications for the most intimate details of our social and personal lives.

The heart of the psychological revolution will be a new and scientifically based conception of man as an individual and as a social creature. When I say that the psychological revolution is already upon us, what I mean is that we have already begun to change man's self-conception. If we want to further that revolution, not only must we strengthen its scientific base, but we must also try to communicate it to our students and to the public. It is not the industrialist or the politician who should exploit it, but everyman, everyday.

CONTROL OF BEHAVIOUR

One major message that many scientific psychologists are trying to communicate to the public is the truism that some stimuli can serve to reinforce the behaviour that produces them. The practical significance of this principle is that by controlling the occurrence of these reinforcing stimuli you thereby control behaviour. Since control is the practical pay-off from other sciences, the public is prepared to believe that psychology too is about control.

Closely related to this emphasis on control is the frequently reported claim that living organisms are nothing but machines. Personally, I believe there is a better way to advertise psychology and to relate it to social problems. Reinforcement is only one of many important ideas that we have to offer. Instead of repeating constantly that reinforcement leads to control, I would prefer to emphasize that reinforcement can lead to satisfaction and competence. And I would prefer to speak of understanding and prediction as our major scientific goals.

Understanding and prediction are better goals for psychology and for the promotion of human welfare because they lead us to think, not in terms of coercion by a powerful elite, but in terms of the diagnosis of problems and the development of programmes that can enrich the lives of every citizen.

THE STUDY

PUBLIC PSYCHOLOGY: TWO PARADIGMS

It is possible to identify two alternative images of human nature as influenced by scientific advances in psychology which are similar to McGregor's (1960) Theory X and Theory Y, meant to explain why people work. Theory X (the traditional theory) states that because people dislike work, they must be coerced, controlled, directed and threatened with punishment before they will do it; people have little ambition and want to avoid responsibility and so will tolerate – and may actually prefer – being directed. The alternative Theory Y (based on social science) maintains that work is as natural as play or rest, so that people exercise self-direction and self-control in order to achieve goals to which they are committed: their commitment is a function of the rewards associated with the achievement of their goals. People may actually seek responsibility and many display imagination, ingenuity and creativity, despite the conditions of modern industrial life.

McGregor's theories are rival theories held by industrial managers about how best to achieve their institutional goals. A broader view of the social nature of human beings is taken by Varela, a Uruguayan engineer, who describes two conceptions of man or 'paradigms' (based on Kuhn, 1962). The first of these is a set of assumptions on which our social institutions are currently based:

> All men are created equal, most behaviour is created by economic competition and conflict is inevitable. When things go wrong, there is always someone who is to blame and the guilty person, who is responsible for his own misbehaviour and rehabilitation, must be found and punished.

The second paradigm is based on psychological research and maintains that there are large individual differences between people, both in ability and personality. Human motivation is complex and we never act as we do for any single reason, but positive incentives are generally more effective than threats or punishments. Conflict is not inevitable and can be prevented. A person's perception of the situation is more important to them than 'the true facts' when something goes wrong, and to be able to reason about the situation, their irrational feeling must first be toned down. Social problems are solved by correcting causes, not symptoms, and this can be done more effectively in groups than individually. Teachers and supervisors must be experts in social science because they are responsible for the cooperation and individual improvement of their students or subordinates.

Here, then, is the real challenge: how can we foster a social climate in which some such new public conception of man based on psychology can take root and flourish? In my opinion, this is the proper translation of our more familiar question about how psychology might contribute to the promotion of human welfare.

Part of the answer is that psychology must be practised by non-psychologists. We are not physicians, the secrets of our trade need not be reserved for highly trained specialists. Psychological facts should be passed out freely to all who need and can

THE STUDY

use them. And from successful applications of psychological principles the public may gain a better appreciation of the power of the new conception of man that is emerging from our science.

There are not enough psychologists (including non-professionals) to meet every need for psychological services. Our scientific results will have to be instilled in 'the public consciousness' in a practical and usable form so that what we know can be applied by ordinary people. The people at large will have to be their own psychologists, and make their own applications of the principles that we establish. Of course, everyone practises psychology. I am not suggesting any radical departure when I say that non-psychologists must practise psychology. I am simply proposing that we should teach them to practise it better, to make use self-consciously of what we believe to be scientifically valid principles. Our responsibility is less to assume the role of experts and try to apply psychology ourselves than to give it away to the people who really need it, and that includes everyone. The practice of valid psychology by non-psychologists will inevitably change people's conception of themselves and what they can do. When we have accomplished that, we will really have caused a psychological revolution.

HOW TO GIVE PSYCHOLOGY AWAY

This is no easy matter and there is much resistance to change and new ways of doing things; man's attempts to introduce sound psychological practices into schools, clinics, hospitals, prisons or industries have failed. One problem is that the innovation may be piecemeal, not taking the whole 'culture' of the institution into account. But if you understand the system as a whole, you don't need to control it: relatively minor changes can then have extensive consequences throughout the entire organization. There is no possibility of legislating the changes I have in mind. Passing laws that people must change their 'conceptions' of themselves and others is precisely the opposite of what we need. Education would seem to be our only possibility. This does not mean only education in the schoolroom. I have in mind a more ambitious programme of educating the general public.

In order to get started, we must begin where they are, not assume we know where they should be. If a supervisor is having trouble with his men, perhaps we should teach him how to write a job description and how to evaluate the abilities and personalities of those who fill the job; perhaps we should teach him the art of persuasion or the time and place for positive reinforcement. If a ghetto mother is not giving her children sufficient intellectual challenge, perhaps we should teach her how to encourage their motor, perceptual and linguistic skills. The techniques involved are not some esoteric branch of witchcraft that must be reserved for those with PhD degrees in psychology. When the ideas are made sufficiently concrete and explicit, the scientific foundations of psychology can be grasped by sixth-grade children. Psychological principles and techniques can usefully be applied by every-

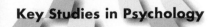

one, not just specialist professionals. We must, however, give people something whose value they recognize, which is valid for them, not give them something which we think is important. Take the example of teaching children to read. The conventional method is for experts to provide teachers with reading schemes which are then used with children. But an alternative method is that developed by Ashton-Warner (1963), a teacher in New Zealand. She begins by asking a child what words (s)he wants and which are bound up with the child's own loves and fears. The words are written on a large card which is given to the child who learns to read them almost immediately: it is *their* word.

These are not dead words of an expert's choosing, but words that live in a child's own experience. Under this regimen, a word is not an imposed task to be learned with reinforcement borrowed from some external source of motivation. Learning the word is itself reinforcing. Each child decides where he wants to start, and each child receives something whose value he can recognize.

This technique for teaching children to read is related to White's (1959) concept of competence motivation – the urge to feel more effective. Psychology can be used to help people feel more effective especially about personal problems in their own life. From this start, some people may want to learn more about the science that helped them increase their competence and then things could become more abstract.

But in the beginning we must try to diagnose and solve the problems people think they have, not the problems we experts think they ought to have, and we must learn to understand those problems in the social and institutional contexts that define them. With this approach we might do something practical for nurses, policemen, prison guards, salesmen – for people in many different walks of life. That, I believe, is what we should mean when we talk about applying psychology to the promotion of human welfare. I can imagine nothing we could do that would be more relevant to human welfare, and nothing that could pose a greater challenge to the next generation of psychologists, than to discover how best to give psychology away.

EVALUATION

What are the appropriate aims of psychology as a science?

Like Skinner (see **Background and context** section above), Cattell has 'carried the torch of science aloft' for 50 years (Kline, 1988). According to Cattell (1981, quoted in Kline, 1988):

> The scientific study of personality seeks to understand personality as one would
> the mechanism of a watch, the chemistry of the life processes in a mammal or

the spectrum of a remote star. That is to say, it aims at objective insights; at the capacity to predict and control what will happen next; and at the establishment of scientific laws of a perfectly general nature.

Kline objects to Cattell's analogy for two main reasons: (a) while there is no disagreement about what a watch is or isn't, this cannot be said of personality, which is a *hypothetical construct*, an abstract term that has no independent existence beyond the mind which constructed it; (b) it is *reductionist*. While it is perfectly possible to study human physiology in an objective, scientific way, this is not the same as studying personality or psychology. There is more to, say, our perceptual experience of the colour red than the neural, biochemical or electrical changes which accompany it: you haven't explained the former by explaining the latter.

While prediction and control may be appropriate aims in engineering, biology and astronomy, this is not true in the case of psychology. As Kline (1988) argues:

> It is clear that the scientific method is unsuited to psychology because the subject matter of psychology is conceptually different from that of the classical sciences for which the method was developed. This is a fundamental problem of the scientific method in psychology.

Miller also sees control as inappropriate. Rather, understanding and prediction are the appropriate aims of psychology. To this extent, he is agreeing with radical critics, such as Shotter and Heather, for whom Skinner represents the ultimate kind of mechanistic, dehumanizing, approach. When you consider that operant conditioning, as applied to people, is based on work with rats and pigeons in the highly controlled environment of the Skinner box, it is little wonder that radical critics should select Skinner as a prime target. Indeed, *self*-understanding is what Miller believes psychology should be striving to provide people with (this is what he means by 'giving psychology away'), and it also relates to psychology's ability to change the way we see ourselves.

Does psychology ignore how people live in the real world?

This is the second of the two issues raised by the radical critics of psychology in the late 1960s which, according to Murphy *et al.* (1984), Miller's article draws attention to (the first issue being its dehumanizing image of human beings: see **Background and context** section above). Miller advocates that we must start with what people themselves believe their problems to be. This is reminiscent of Joynson's (1974) attack on the behaviourists for looking at people as objects, from the outside, while ignoring their experience, and rejecting the validity of their attempts to explain their own behaviour. Radical psychologists would regard any attempt to study people as objects as both unethical and scientifically unsound, since people can and do choose how to act: any theory or system which ignores this feature of human beings must be

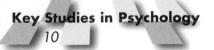

presenting only a partial or inaccurate account. In Davis's (1966) terms, human beings are 'goal-seeking individuals and members of groups'; this makes the subject-matter of psychology *qualitatively* different from that of the natural sciences.

Mainstream psychology and scientism

According to Harré (1989), mainstream psychology (the 'old paradigm') was haunted by 'two unexamined preassumptions', one of which is '*scientism*'. This is defined by Van Langenhove (1995) as:

> . . . the borrowing of methods and a characteristic vocabulary from the natural sciences in order to discover causal mechanisms that explain psychological phenomena.

Scientism maintains that all aspects of human behaviour can and should be studied using the methods of natural science, which represent the sole means of establishing 'objective truth'. This can be achieved by studying phenomena removed from any particular context ('*context-stripping*' exposes them in their 'pure' form) and in a *value-free* way (there is no bias on the part of the investigator). The most reliable way of doing this is through the laboratory experiment, the method that provides the greatest degree of control over relevant variables.

Although much research has moved beyond the confines of the laboratory experiment, the same *positivist* logic is still central to how psychological inquiry is conceived and conducted: method and measurement still have a privileged status (Smith *et al.*, 1995). Similarly, Van Langenhove (1995) believes that, despite vigorous attacks on scientism since the mid-1970s, psychology is to a large extent 'submerged' by the natural sciences model, with the experiment still predominant. (For further discussion of scientism see Gross *et al.*, 1997).

Throughout the article, Miller talks of psychology as a science without ever actually defining what a science is. However, he argues (like Kline) that a science of human beings is qualitatively different from a science of the natural world. Through influencing our image of ourselves and what we think is achievable and important to achieve (changing the goals and not just moving the goalposts!), scientific psychology can help to change the very subject matter it is trying to study! This, surely, means that psychology can never be objective in the way the natural sciences aspire to be, since psychological theories and principles can actually transform the 'things' they are meant to explain. Chemicals are not affected by what chemists say about them, but psychologists are part of their own subject matter, and this is another sense in which total objectivity is impossible.

Miller believes that changing how we see ourselves is a more appropriate model for psychology than developing a technology which has, traditionally, been the measure of the effectiveness of natural science. The latter is more tangible than the former and the effects of applications of Skinner's operant conditioning, for example, may be much easier to quantify than the effects of Freud's view of people as irrational and driven by unconscious forces (see Chapter 19). However, Miller believes that it is precisely the impact on our conception of ourselves and *not* technological applications of psychological principles, which makes psychology (potentially) revolutionary.

Can – and should – psychology be value-free?

As we saw above, a feature of the 'old paradigm's' love affair with natural science is its belief that it is possible for psychologists to be unbiased and value-free, as objective in their study of fellow human beings as physicists are when investigating the physical world. In Lindsay's (1995) Presidential address to the British Psychological Society (BPS) entitled '*Values, ethics and psychology*', he reminded his fellow psychologists that psychology does *not* operate in a social or value-free vacuum:

> I suggest that we must have awareness of the social situation and in particular the values which are predominant in society at any one time.

In McAllister's 1997 Presidential address to the BPS ('*Putting psychology in context*'), she endorses some aspects of scientism but also echoes Lindsay's message. As psychological scientists using empirical research methods, she says, we strive for objectivity. A substantial body of knowledge has been established which contributes to our understanding of the human mind and behaviour. That knowledge is being applied in positive ways to enhance human life and address human problems:

> . . . Yet we need to be aware of the wider socio-political context in which this work takes place. (McAllister, 1998)

According to Prilleltensky & Fox (1997), some *mainstream psychologists* recognise the societal sources of much individual distress, and propose minor reforms of social institutions to help individuals function more effectively. In general, when people become psychologists, they expect to do some good – and often they do. However, *critical psychologists* see the discipline of psychology itself as a mainstream social institution with its own negative consequences. The underlying values and institutions of modern societies (especially, but not exclusively, capitalist societies) reinforce misguided efforts to obtain fulfilment, while maintaining inequality and oppression:

> . . . Because psychology's values, assumptions and norms have supported society's dominant institutions since its birth as a field of study, the field's mainstream contributes to social injustice and thwarts the promotion of human welfare . . . (Prilleltensky & Fox, 1997)

Many critical psychologists agree that certain values are of key importance, including *social justice, self-determination* and *participation, caring* and *compassion, health,* and *human diversity.* While it is not very controversial to list these, individuals and societies in the real world must make choices between competing values, and values need to be advanced in a balanced way. For example, mainstream psychology contributes to value *imbalance* by endorsing *individualism* and deemphasizing values related to mutuality, connectedness, and a psychological sense of community. Not only is this politically and ethically unacceptable, but it misrepresents the nature of human behaviour, which is inherently *social.* As Prilleltensky & Fox (1997) say:

> An individual's behaviour can only be understood in the context of interaction with other human beings within socially created institutions . . . It is this interaction with others throughout our lives that shape our values, our goals, our very views of our selves . . .

In relation to health, psychology attends primarily to those who can afford individual or family/small-group therapy, excluding many with fewer resources:

> . . . By and large, psychologists fit comfortably within a capitalist system that gives lip service to both freedom and equality but in practice supports the freedom of the free market over the equality of distributive justice . . . (Prilleltensky & Fox, 1997)

The particular combination of values needed for human welfare and to create a better society (a 'Good Society') also changes from society to society, culture to culture, group to group, and time to time. Moreover, some values have more potential for transforming society than others, such as feminist efforts (including those of feminist psychologists) to enhance women's power relative to men's through encouraging self-determination.

Giving psychology away

When discussing 'giving psychology away', Miller seems to be talking mainly about helping people to solve their personal – and professional – problems, and so is advocating a problem-centred approach. But doesn't the promotion of human welfare mean more than this? Surely it also involves a much more positive approach, whereby people can realize their potential as human beings (although this will be much harder to achieve when the person faces problems, particularly those to do with basic survival needs – see Maslow, 1954.). However, positive growth may also occur through the process of trying to overcome problems and hardships, and this perhaps deserves more emphasis. Focusing on people's problems is consistent with individualism (see above):

> . . . Encouraging women, people of colour, the poor, and the working class to define their problems as individual ensures that they work to change themselves rather than society . . .' (Prilleltensky & Fox, 1997)

According to Jones & Elcock (2001), being *critically aware*, especially for educational and clinical psychologists, involves recognizing that:

> . . . not all problems can be solved at the level of adjusting the individual. While we, as psychologists, might not feel that it is within our ability to propose changes at a societal level it would, at least, be more honest to admit the limits of our ability to intervene and we can at least suggest, for example, that stress might not be an individual problem but rather a problem of how workplaces and working practices are organized.

However, it is also true that a great deal of psychotherapy is aimed at changing individuals' perception of themselves and increasing their self-understanding. It also aims at increasing autonomy or independence (Lindley, 1987, cited in Fairbairn, 1987), that is, *taking control of one's own life* (a very different aim for psychology than *control* as it is discussed above). To the extent that 'taking control of one's own life is itself an essential part of human flourishing' (Lindley, 1987), much psychotherapy would seem to be based on respect for individuals as persons. This principle is central to the positive evaluation of any changes brought about by psychologists, helping others to make responsible decisions about their lives, 'because taking responsibility for one's own life is at least part of what it is to function fully as a person' (Fairbairn, 1987).

In discussing the 'formulation' of a problem within the context of therapy, Crellin (1998) argues that a basic question is: who holds 'expert knowledge', the client (who is privy to his or her own experiences) or the therapist (who has knowledge of certain theories)? Unless the therapist can put his or her assumptions and presuppositions aside, the client will 'formulate' the problem in terms of the therapist's perspective, rather than their own.

Hawks (1981, cited by Fairbairn & Fairbairn, 1987) believes that prevention rather than cure should be a primary aim of psychology, enabling people to cope by themselves, without professional help, thus 'giving psychology away' to the people (clients), to echo Miller's message.

Outside of a therapeutic context, Jones & Elcock (2001) argue that if the discipline's claims are to be believed, scientific psychology has effectively created a social technocracy:

> . . . where a privileged few are possessed of a body of scientific knowledge that can be used to explain behaviour. However, there is a considerable irony here. By and large, in our own experience, psychologists do not replace their previous everyday psychologizing with their recently gained theoretical knowledge, although they may augment it a little. Often, outside their professional lives psychologists pursue everyday psychology in the same way as everyone else.

'Everyday psychology' refers to the psychological reasoning we all participate in when interpreting and predicting others' behaviour, which in turn creates 'psychological discourses' that represent broad speculation about 'human nature' or the nature of human psychology (see **Exercises**). According to Jones & Elcock (2001), scientific psychology developed partly in response to reservations about the validity of such everyday discourses. But if 'scientific theories' are largely ignored by professional psychologists themselves in their everyday dealings with other people, it is even more likely that the 'rest' of us will do so. As Jones & Elcock say;

> . . . While the replacement of ill-founded claims about human psychology with more rigorous, empirically-based theories is laudable, theories in social psychology have had a limited effect on everyday psychology.

They argue that the discipline of psychology has by and large failed to provide the lay person with the knowledge they need to improve their everyday psychologizing:

> . . . Psychology's concentration on being scientific at the expense of being relevant has meant that Psychology has not had the expected impact on everyday psychologizing. Common sense has not been replaced by a scientific framework, but rather some theories . . . have been incorporated into everyday psychology. Less rigorous approaches . . . have arguably had a greater effect, particularly psychoanalysis . . . (Jones & Elcock, 2001)

Psychoanalysis has achieved its level of popular recognition partly because it addresses people's everyday concerns (i.e. it *is* relevant), even though academic psychologists often consider it to be of marginal importance because of its lack of 'scientific rigour' (see Chapter 19). Scientific psychology needs to produce well-founded theories that will aid people's everyday psychologizing. To achieve this, theories from scientific psychology need to be presented in a way that is accessible and understandable to a lay audience, but which retains scientific rigour. In this way, scientific psychology can close the gap between itself and everyday psychology which is currently occupied by 'popular psychology' (Jones & Elcock, 2001: see **Exercises**).

According to Rappaport & Stewart (1997), Miller's call to 'give psychology away' has a more radical message than merely presenting debriefings and research summaries in non-technical language that lay people can understand. They interpret it to mean that psychologists should share the research *process*, not just the results:

> . . . there is something potentially liberating to be gained from making our work available to the interrogation of "those people" whose circumstances we are trying to change, something for "us" and something for "them". (Rappaport & Stewart, 1997)

Stenner & Brown (1998) ask: what exactly is the nature of this gift (of psychology) and who wants it? They cite Kvale (1992), who claims that new provoking insights about human beings come not from psychology, but from philosophy, literature, art and anthropology. Stenner and Brown add popular science, physics and computing to this list and claim that, stripped of its theoretical context and terminology (the 'rhetoric of scientific method'), so much of mainstream psychological knowledge appears to be no more than common sense.

Exercises

1. In what ways can we all (already) be thought of as psychologists?

2. What are 'demand characteristics' (Orne, 1962), and how do they make experiments using human participants less objective?

3. In the case of psychology, what is 'common sense' knowledge, and how does this relate to 'scientific' (or 'expert') knowledge?

4. Do you agree with Skinner that the major aim of psychology should be the control of behaviour? Or is Miller right when he says the appropriate goals are understanding and prediction?

5. What do you understand by 'popular psychology', and how does it differ from academic/scientific psychology?

2 Pictorial perception and culture

Jan B. Deregowski (1972)

Scientific American, 227, 82–8

BACKGROUND AND CONTEXT

A major advantage of cross-cultural studies is that they act as a buffer against generalizing from a comparatively small sample of the earth's population (Price-Williams, 1966). Unless we study a particular process in *different* cultures, we cannot be sure what the contributory influences are on that process, in particular, heredity and environment. If we find consistent differences between different cultural groups then, unless we have good, independent reasons for believing that these differences are biologically caused, we are forced to attribute them to environmental factors, be they social customs, ecological, linguistic, or some combination of these.

But what exactly do we mean by 'culture'? According to Segall *et al.* (1990):

> Those social stimuli that are the products of the behaviour of other people essentially constitute culture. Briefly, we employ culture – as did Herskovits (1948) – to mean 'the man-made part of the environment'. These products can be material objects, ideas, or institutions. They are ubiquitous, it is rare (perhaps even impossible) for any human being ever to behave without responding to some aspect of culture.

Relating this to perception, cross-cultural studies enable us to discover the extent to which perceiving is structured by the nervous system (and so common to all human beings) and to what extent by experience. These factors are emphasized, respectively, by Nativists and Empiricists.

A common method is to present members of different cultural groups with visual illusions, such as the *Müller–Lyer* and *horizontal–vertical*. The pioneering study by the Cambridge Anthropological Expedition to the Torres Straits (Rivers, 1901) found that, compared with English adults and children, the Murray Islanders were less prone to the Müller–Lyer. This was attributed to the fact that they limited their attention strictly to the task they were asked to perform (judge the length of the arrow shafts), while Europeans tended to regard the figure as a whole (including the arrowheads). By contrast, the horizontal–vertical illusion was *more* marked among the Murray Island men. This, combined with the pronounced character of the illusion in children, led Rivers to conclude that it was due to some physiological condition or, at least, to some simple and primitive psychological condition (Price-Williams, 1966).

A later and more extensive study (Segall, Campbell & Herskovits, 1963) presented illusions to samples of non-European children and adults, mainly African, but including the Philippines. Their findings regarding the Müller–Lyer largely confirmed Rivers's findings (if all the Europeans are compared with all the non-Europeans). However, the horizontal–vertical has a different cultural distribution: the Batoro and Bayankole peoples of Africa, who both live in high open country, are at the top of the susceptibility scale, while the Bete, who live in a jungle environment, are at the bottom. Europeans and Zulus fall somewhere in between.

Allport & Pettigrew (1957) used the *rotating trapezoid illusion*, which is usually reported by Western participants as oscillating to and fro (not revolving in a complete circle, which is objectively what it does), particularly if it is seen through one eye only and from a greater distance. Zulus, however, who are not used to conventional windows and also have a bias towards circularity (not rectangularity) in their culture, are likely to report the illusion less often, especially if it is seen binocularly and from a shorter distance.

One explanation of such cultural differences is Segall *et al.*'s (1966) 'carpentered-world' hypothesis, whereby the visual world of Western culture is largely man-made, consisting of straight lines, and in which there is a bias towards interpreting acute and obtuse angles as right angles extended in space. Since we tend to interpret illusion figures, which are 2-D drawings, in terms of our past experience, we 'add' the third dimension (depth) which is not actually present in the drawing. This misleads us as to the true nature of the stimulus, resulting in what we call an illusion.

> If the [carpentered world] hypothesis is correct, people in industrial urban environments should be more susceptible to illusions such as the Müller–Lyer.
> (Berry *et al.*, 1992).

However, a number of studies failed to support the carpentered-world hypothesis (e.g. Mundy-Castle & Nelson, 1962; Gregor & McPherson, 1965; Jahoda, 1966). Consequently, there was a subsequent move away from environmental or ecological explanations of cultural differences towards considering 2-D pictures as cultural products in their own right. The *interpretation of pictures* came to be seen as an acquired skill of considerable complexity.

AIM AND NATURE OF THE STUDY

The aim of the article is to present a summary of some of the findings from studies of pictorial perception in different cultural groups, including the author's own research and that of others (e.g. Hudson, 1960, 1962). It is unclear when he is referring to his own (and that of his co-workers) rather than someone else's, and it is only through reading other sources (e.g. Serpell, 1976) that this can be achieved.

The overall nature of the studies discussed is *cross-cultural*, since a comparison is being made between the interpretation of 3-D pictures by members of Western cultures (unspecified) and various African countries (e.g. Zambia). However, the method used to actually collect the data is a kind of experiment, in which the *independent variable* is either: (i) the participant's nationality; or (ii) the characteristic of being a 3-D or 2-D perceiver (based on, say, Hudson's picture tests).

In both cases, the investigator is, of course, unable to manipulate the independent variable: it is a characteristic the participant already possesses and is selected accordingly. This method is sometimes referred to as *ex post facto* experimentation (see Coolican, 1999). (Note that cross-cultural studies as such represent *not* a method of collecting data but an overall approach to the study of human behaviour, just as cross-sectional and longitudinal approaches do in developmental psychology. Exactly how data is collected will depend on the purpose of the study, the age of the participants, the kind of behaviour under investigation, and so on: the overall approach may involve the use of experiments, observation or some combination of different methods).

Deregowski also considers some explanations which have been put forward for cultural differences in perception, but no empirical support is provided.

■ T H E ■ S T U D Y ■

> Do people of one culture perceive a picture differently from people of another? Experiments in Africa show that such differences exist, and that the perception of pictures calls for some form of learning.

A picture is a pattern of lines and shaded areas on a flat surface that depicts some aspect of the real world. The ability to recognize objects in pictures is so common in most cultures that it is often taken for granted that such recognition is universal in man. Although children do not learn to read until they are about six years old, they are able to recognize objects in pictures long before that; indeed, it has been shown that a 19-month-old child is capable of such recognition. If pictorial recognition is universal, do pictures offer us a lingua franca for intercultural communication? There is evidence that they do not: cross-cultural studies have shown that there are persistent differences in the way pictorial information is interpreted by people of various cultures. These differences merit investigation not only because improvement in communication may be achieved by a fuller understanding of them but also because they may provide us with a better insight into the nature of human perceptual mechanisms.

Reports of difficulty in pictorial perception by members of remote, illiterate tribes have periodically been made by missionaries, explorers and anthropologists. Robert

THE STUDY

Laws, a Scottish missionary active in Nyasaland (now Malawi) at the end of the nineteenth century, reported: 'Take a picture in black and white and the natives cannot see it. You may tell the natives, "This is a picture of an ox and a dog," and the people will look at it and look at you and that look says that they consider you a liar. Perhaps you say again, "Yes, that is a picture of an ox and a dog." Well, perhaps they will tell you what they think this time. If there are a few boys about, you say: "This is really a picture of an ox and a dog. Look at the horn of the ox, and there is his tail." And the boy will say: "Oh! yes and there is the dog's nose and eyes and ears!" Then the old people will look again and clasp their hands and say, "Oh! yes, it is a dog." When a man has seen a picture for the first time, his book education has begun.'

Mrs Donald Fraser, who taught health care to Africans in the 1920s, had similar experiences. This is her description of an African woman slowly discovering that a picture she was looking at portrayed a human head in profile: 'She discovered in turn the nose, the mouth, the eye, but where was the other eye? I tried by turning my profile to explain why she could only see one eye but she hopped round to my other side to point out that I possessed a second eye which the other lacked.'

There were also, however, reports of vivid and instant responses to pictures: 'When all the people were quickly seated, the first picture flashed on the sheet was that of an elephant. The wildest excitement immediately prevailed, many of the people jumping up and shouting, fearing the beast must be alive, while those nearest to the sheet sprang up and fled. The chief himself crept stealthily forward and peeped behind the sheet to see if the animal had a body, and when he discovered that the animal's body was only the thickness of the sheet, a great roar broke the stillness of the night.'

Thus the evidence gleaned from the insightful but unsystematic observations quoted is ambiguous. The laborious way some of these Africans pieced together a picture suggests that some form of learning is required to recognize pictures. Inability to perceive that a pattern of lines and shaded areas on a flat surface represents a real object would render all pictorial material incomprehensible. All drawings would be perceived as being meaningless, abstract patterns until the viewer had learned to interpret and organize the symbolic elements. On the other hand, one could also argue that pictorial recognition is largely independent of learning, and that even people from cultures where pictorial materials are uncommon will recognize items in pictures, provided that the pictures show familiar objects. It has been shown that an unsophisticated adult African from a remote village is unlikely to choose the wrong toy animal when asked to match the toy to a picture of, say, a lion. Given a photograph of a kangaroo, however, he is likely to choose at random from the array of toys. Yet one can argue that this sample was not as culturally remote as those described above. It is therefore probably safer to assume that utter incomprehension of pictorial material may be observed only in extremely isolated human populations.

Figure 2.1. Pictorial depth perception is tested by showing subjects a picture such as the top illustration. A correct interpretation is that the hunter is trying to spear the antelope, which is nearer to him than the elephant. An incorrect interpretation is that the elephant is nearer and is about to be speared. The picture contains two depth cues: overlapping objects and known size of objects. The bottom illustration depicts the man, elephant and antelope in true size ratios when all are the same distance from the observer.

THE STUDY

Conventions for depicting the spatial arrangement of three-dimensional objects in a flat picture can also give rise to difficulties in perception. These conventions give the observer depth cues that tell him the objects are not all the same distance from him. Inability to interpret such cues is bound to lead to misunderstanding of the meaning of the picture as a whole. William Hudson, who was then working at the National Institute for Personnel Research in Johannesburg, stumbled on such a difficulty in testing South African Bantu workers. His discovery led him to construct a pictorial perception test and to carry out much of the pioneering work in cross-cultural studies of perception.

Hudson's test consists of a series of pictures in which there are various combinations of three pictorial depth cues. The first cue is familiar size, which calls for the larger of two known objects to be drawn considerably smaller to indicate that it is farther away. The second cue is overlap, in which portions of nearer objects overlap and obscure portions of objects that are farther away; a hill is partly obscured by another hill that is closer to the viewer. The third cue is perspective, the convergence of lines known to be parallel to suggest distance; lines representing the edges of a road converge in the distance. In all but one of his tests Hudson omitted an entire group of powerful depth cues: density gradients. Density gradients are provided by any elements of uniform size: bricks in a wall or pebbles on a beach. The elements are drawn larger or smaller depending on whether they are nearer to the viewer or farther away from him.

Hudson's test has been applied in many parts of Africa with subjects drawn from a variety of tribal and linguistic groups. The subjects were shown one picture at a time and asked to name all the objects in the picture in order to determine whether or not the elements were correctly recognized. Then they were asked about the relation between the objects. (What is the man doing? What is closer to the man?) If the subject takes note of the depth cues and makes the 'correct' interpretations, he is classified as having three-dimensional perception. If the depth cues are not taken into account by the subject, he is said to have two-dimensional perception (see Figure 2.1). The results from African tribal subjects were unequivocal: both children and adults found it difficult to perceive depth in the pictorial material. The difficulty varied in extent but appeared to persist through most educational and social levels.

Further experimentation revealed that the phenomenon was not simply the result of the pictorial material used in the test. Subjects were shown a drawing of two squares, one behind the other and connected by a single rod (see Figure 2.2). They were also given sticks and modeling clay and asked to build a model of what they saw. If Hudson's test is valid, people designated as two-dimensional perceivers should build flat models when they are shown the drawing, whereas those designated as three-dimensional perceivers should build a cube-like object. When primary school boys and unskilled workers in Zambia were given Hudson's test and

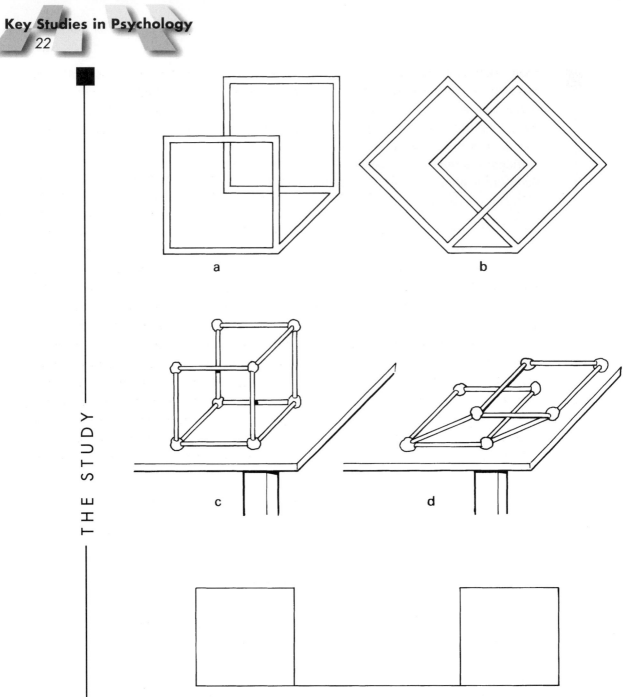

Figure 2.2. Construction-task figures consist of two squares connected by a single rod. Most subjects from Western cultures see the figure (a) as a three-dimensional object, but when the figure is rotated 45 degrees (b), they see it as being flat. Africans from a variety of tribes almost always see both figures as being flat, with the two squares on the same plane.

Stick-and-clay models of figure (a) in the top illustration were made by test subjects. Almost all the three-dimensional perceivers built a three-dimensional object (c). Subjects who did not readily perceive depth in pictures tended to build a flat model (d).

'Split' drawing was preferred by two-dimensional perceivers when shown a model like figure (c) and given a choice between the split drawing and figure (a).

then asked to build models, a few of the subjects who had been classified as three-dimensional responders by the test made flat models. A substantial number of the subjects classified as two-dimensional perceivers built three-dimensional models. Thus Hudson's test, although it is more severe than the construction task, appears to measure the same variable.

The finding was checked in another experiment. A group of Zambian primary school children were classified into three-dimensional and two-dimensional perceivers on the basis of the model-building test. They were then asked to copy a 'two-pronged trident,' a tantalizing drawing that confuses many people. The confusion is a direct result of attempting to interpret the drawing as a three-dimensional object (see Figure 2.3). One would expect that those who are confused by the trident would find it difficult to recall and draw. The students actually made copies of two tridents: the ambiguous one and a control figure that had three simple prongs. To view the figure the student had to lift a flap, which actuated a timer that measured how long the flap was held up. The student could view the figure for as long as he wanted to, but he could not copy it while the flap was open. After the flap was closed the student had to wait 10 seconds before he began to draw. The delay was introduced to increase the difficulty of copying the figure. The results confirmed that the students who were three-dimensional perceivers spent more time looking at the ambiguous trident than at the control trident, whereas the two-dimensional perceivers did not differ significantly in the time spent viewing each of the two tridents.

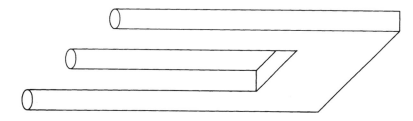

Figure 2.3. Ambiguous trident is confusing to observers who attempt to see it as a three-dimensional object. Two-dimensional perceivers see the pattern as being flat, and are not confused.

Do people who perceive pictorial depth really see depth in the picture or are they merely interpreting symbolic depth cues in the same way that we learn to interpret the set of symbols in 'horse' to mean a certain quadruped? An ingenious apparatus for studying perceived depth helped us to obtain an answer. This is how the apparatus is described by its designer, Richard L. Gregory of the University of Bristol:

> The figure is presented back-illuminated, to avoid texture, and it is viewed through a sheet of Polaroid. A second sheet of Polaroid is placed over one eye crossed with the first so that no light from the figure reaches this eye. Between the eyes and the figure is a half-silvered mirror through which the figure is seen but which also reflects one or more small light sources mounted

THE STUDY

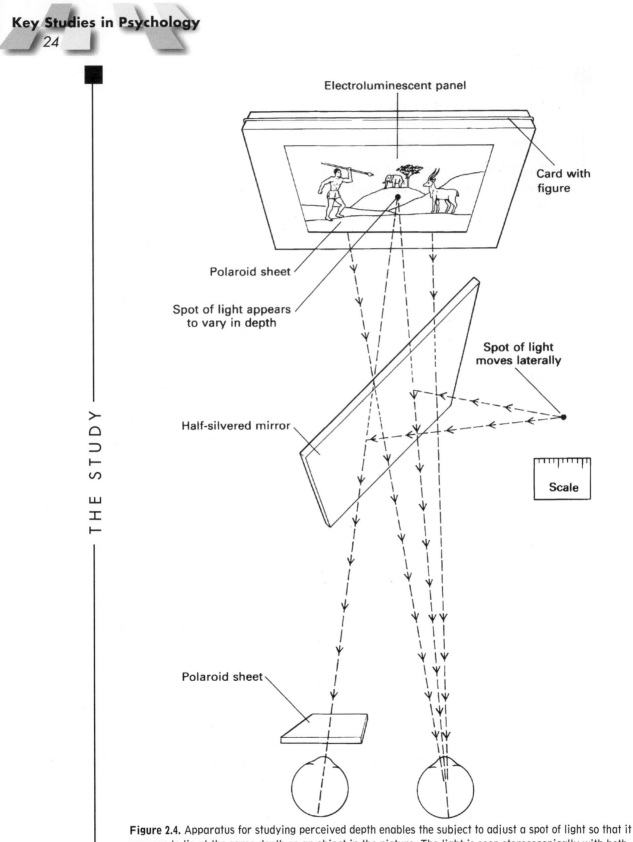

Figure 2.4. Apparatus for studying perceived depth enables the subject to adjust a spot of light so that it appears to lie at the same depth as an object in the picture. The light is seen stereoscopically with both eyes, but the picture is seen with only one eye. Africans unfamiliar with pictorial depth cues set the light at the same depth on all parts of the picture.

on an optical bench. These appear to lie in the figure; indeed, optically they **do** lie in the figure provided the path length of the lights to the eyes is the same as that of the figure to the eyes. But the small light sources are seen with both eyes while the figure is seen with only **one** eye because of the crossed Polaroids. By moving the lights along their optical bench, they may be placed so as to lie at the same distance as any selected part of the figure.

A Hudson-test picture that embodied both familiar-size and overlap depth cues was presented in the apparatus to a group of unskilled African workers, who for the most part do not show perception of pictorial depth in the Hudson test and in the construction test (see Figure 2.4). The test picture showed a hunter and an antelope in the foreground and an elephant in the distance. The subjects set the movable light at the same apparent depth regardless of whether they were asked to place it above the hunter, the antelope or the elephant. In contrast, when three-dimensional perceivers were tested, they set the light farther away from themselves when placing it on the elephant than when setting it on the figures in the foreground. The result shows that they were not simply interpreting symbolic depth cues but were actually seeing depth in the picture.

When only familiar size was used as the depth cue, neither group of subjects placed the movable light farther back for the elephant. The result should not be surprising, since other studies have shown that familiar-size cues alone do not enable people even in Western cultures to see actual depth in a picture, even though they may interpret the picture three-dimensionally.

The fact that depth was seen in the picture only in the presence of overlap cues is of theoretical interest because it had been postulated that a perceptual mechanism for seeing depth cues where none are intended is responsible for certain geometric illusions, for example overestimating the length of the vertical limb of the letter *L*. If the mechanism is the same as the one for the perception of pictorial depth in Hudson's tests, then one would expect a decrease in the perception of geometric illusions in people who have low three-dimensional scores.

Do people who find pictures of the perspective type difficult to interpret tend to prefer pictures that depict the essential characteristics of an object even if all those characteristics cannot be seen from a single viewpoint? Here again the first systematic cross-cultural observations were carried out by Hudson. He showed African children and adults pictures of an elephant. One view was like a photograph of an elephant seen from above; the other was a top view of an elephant with its legs unnaturally split to the sides. With only one exception all the subjects preferred the drawing of the split elephant (see Figure 2.5). The one person who did not prefer the drawing said that it was because the elephant was jumping about dangerously.

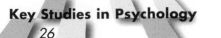

T H E   S T U D Y

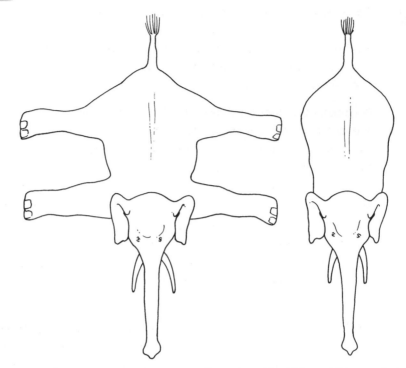

Figure 2.5. Split-elephant drawing (left) was generally preferred by African children and adults to the top-view perspective drawing (right). One person, however, did not like the split drawing because he thought the elephant was jumping around in a dangerous manner.

Other studies have shown that preference for drawings of the split type is not confined to meaningful pictures but also applies to geometric representations. Unskilled Zambian workers were shown a wire model and were asked to make a drawing of it. Only an insignificant proportion of them drew a figure that had pictorial depth; most drew a flat figure of the split type (see Figure 2.2). They also preferred the split drawing when they were shown the model and were asked to choose between it and a perspective drawing. Then the process was reversed, and the subjects were asked to choose the appropriate wire model after looking at a drawing. Only a few chose the three-dimensional model after looking at the split drawing; instead they chose a flat wire model that resembled the drawing. Paradoxically the split drawing had proved to be less efficient than the less preferred perspective drawing when an actual object had to be identified.

Although preference for drawings of the split type has only recently been studied systematically, indications of such a preference have long been apparent in the artistic styles of certain cultures, for example the Indians of the northwestern coast of North America. Other instances of the split style in art are rock paintings in the caves of the Sahara and primitive art found in Siberia and New Zealand. What art historians often fail to note is that the style is universal. It can be found in the drawings of children in all cultures, even in those cultures where the style is considered manifestly wrong by adults.

Perspective drawings and drawings of the split type are not equally easy to interpret. Even industrial draftsmen with a great deal of experience in interpreting engineering drawings, which are essentially of the split type, find it more difficult to assemble simple models from engineering drawings than from perspective drawings.

One theory of the origin of the split style was put forward by the anthropologist Franz Boas. His hypothesis postulated the following sequence of events. Solid sculpture was gradually adapted to the ornamentation of objects such as boxes or bracelets. In order to make a box or a bracelet the artist had to reduce the sculpture to a surface pattern and include an opening in the solid form, so that when the sculptured object was flattened out, it became a picture of the split type. It is possible that this development led to the beginnings of split drawings and that the natural preference of the style ensured its acceptance. There is no historical evidence that this evolution actually took place, however, and it does seem that the hypothesis is unnecessarily complicated.

The anthropologist Claude Lévi-Strauss has proposed a theory in which the split style has social origins. According to him, split representation can be explored as a function of a sociological theory of split personality. This trait is common in 'mask cultures,' where privileges, emblems and degrees of prestige are displayed by means of elaborate masks. The use of these mask symbols apparently generates a great deal of personality stress. Personalities are torn asunder, and this finds its reflection in split-style art.

Both Boas's and Lévi-Strauss's hypotheses ignore the universality of the phenomenon. If one acccepts the existence of a fundamental identity of perceptual processes in all human beings and extrapolates from the data I have described, one is led to postulate the following. In all societies children have an aesthetic preference for drawings of the split type. In most societies this preference is suppressed because the drawings do not convey information about the depicted objects as accurately as perspective drawings do. Therefore aesthetic preference is sacrificed on the altar of efficiency in communication.

Some societies, however, have developed the split drawing to a high artistic level. This development occurs if the drawings are not regarded as a means of communication about objects or if the drawings incorporate cues that compensate for the loss of communication value due to the adoption of the split style. Both of these provisions are found in the art of the Indians of the Pacific Northwest. These pictures were intended to serve primarily as ornaments. They also incorporate symbolic elements that enable the viewer to interpret the artist's intention. Every such code, however, carries the penalty that communication is confined to people familiar with the code. Highly stylized art is not likely to be easily understood outside of its specific culture. Thus whereas the same psychological processes under the influence of different cultural forces may lead to widely different artistic styles, the styles

THE STUDY

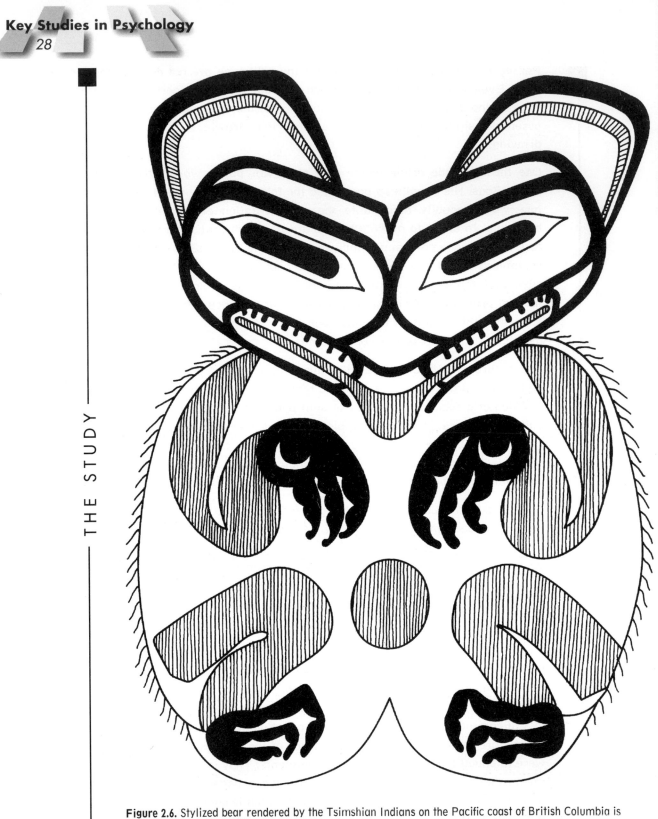

Figure 2.6. Stylized bear rendered by the Tsimshian Indians on the Pacific coast of British Columbia is an example of split drawing developed to a high artistic level. According to anthropologist Franz Boas, the drawings are ornamental, and not intended to convey what an object looks like. The elements represent specific characteristics of the object.

arrived at are not equally efficient in conveying the correct description of objects and evoking the perception of pictorial depth.

What are the forces responsible for the lack of perception of pictorial depth in pictures drawn in accordance with the efficacious conventions of the West? At present we can only speculate. Perhaps the basic difficulty lies in the observers' inability to integrate the pictorial elements. They see individual symbols and cues but are incapable of linking all the elements into a consolidated whole. To the purely pragmatic question 'Do drawings offer us a universal lingua franca?' a more precise answer is available. The answer is no. There are significant differences in the way pictures can be interpreted. The task of mapping out these differences in various cultures is only beginning.

EVALUATION

Theoretical issues

[Before reading on, try to identify *pictorial depth cues* which are missing from the Hudson pictures. What about non-pictorial depth cues? See **Exercises** on page 33.]

One of the things the experienced picture perceiver has learned is the Western artist's use of *relative size* to represent distance. So in Hudson's pictures, a major cue to the relationship between the man, elephant and antelope is their *relative size* against the background knowledge of their normal sizes. Hudson also uses the cues of *overlap* (or *superimposition*) and *linear perspective*. For example, in one drawing the elephant and a tree were shown near the apex of a pair of converging straight lines representing a road. Since the laws of perspective were a late discovery in European art (Gombrich, 1960) and the assumption of parallel edges to a road is promoted by a 'carpentered' environment, it is not too surprising that African children seldom understand this cue. Hudson (1960) found overlap (if noticed) to be the most effective of his three cues (confirmed by Kilbride *et al.* 1968, with a sample of Ugandan schoolchildren).

Also, there is a contradiction between these depth cues and others in the real world, namely *binocular disparity* and *motion parallax*, both of which are missing from Hudson's pictures (and, indeed, from *all* pictures). Also missing is *gradient of density* (or *texture gradient*). Gibson (1950) and Wohlwill (1965) found these all to be more important as depth cues in pictures than in 3-D displays for Western participants over a wide age range.

Serpell (1976) refers to an unpublished report by Kingsley *et al.* in which they got an artist to redraw one of Hudson's pictures adding pebbles on the road and grass in open terrain, each surface showing a gradient of density while everything else remained unchanged. Twelve-year-old Zambian children gave 64% 3-D answers under these conditions compared with 54% on Hudson's original. When colour and haze around distant hills were added, the figure rose to 76%.

Berry *et al.* (1992) point out that texture gradient is a powerful depth cue in photographs but is hardly ever used in stimulus material in cross-cultural studies. To the first-time observer, these pictures may, therefore, display unusual qualities. Another depth cue missing from Hudson's pictures is *elevation* (or *height in the horizontal plane*: the position of a figure higher or lower in the picture). McGurk & Jahoda (1975, cited in Berry *et al.*, 1992) used a test in which elevation was the crucial cue. Using non-verbal responses, participants are asked to place models of people on a response board in similar positions to those occupied by the figures in the stimulus pictures. Using this method, even four-year-olds from Ghana, Hong Kong and Zimbabwe showed evidence of depth perception. All this points to the original Hudson pictures making the perception of depth difficult for non-Western participants.

Hudson's pictures have been criticized in other ways too. Most seriously, there are problems associated with the use of *linear perspective*. In some of the pictures, a horizon is drawn on which all lines converge that represent parallel lines from real space. There has been much debate as to whether this depth cue, which has a very obvious impact on depth perception for Western participants should be seen as an artistic convention (see **Applications and implications** on page 32). More specifically, as used in drawings, linear perspective does not correspond as closely to the 3-D world reality as is usually believed. Parallel lines converge at infinity, but the horizon of our visual field is never at infinity: if we stand on a railway line, for example, the tracks may *appear* to come together at some great distance 'on the horizon', but they *do not* visibly converge into a single point (Berry *et al.*, 1992).

At the same time, under most circumstances, drawings using linear perspective represent the optic array of real space better than drawings constructed not using this principle, and to this extent, linear perspective is not a 'mere' convention.

Methodological issues and other relevant research

Perhaps cultural differences can be attributed not so much to the ability to identify 2-D pictorial representations of the real, 3-D world, but to the conditions under which the recognition of things depicted is made. Specifically:

(*i*)   do the studies Deregowski describes make it difficult for the African participants to give 'correct' responses? Is learning to 'read' pictures as necessary as it appears to be?

(*ii*) could it be that the drawings used by Hudson emphasize certain depth cues while

ignoring others, thus putting non-Western perceivers at a double disadvantage? (This has been dealt with in **Theoretical issues**);

(*iii*) is it also possible that what is taken as a difference in perception is really a matter of stylistic preference? (See **Applications and implications**).

In relation to (*i*), Deregowski *et al.* (1972) studied the Me'en tribe of Ethiopia, living in a remote area and still largely unaffected by Western culture. Members of the tribe were shown drawings of animals and they responded by feeling, smelling, tasting or rustling the paper, showing no interest in the visual content of the picture itself.

However, when the unfamiliar paper was replaced by pictures painted on (familiar) cloth, they responded to the drawing of the animal. These animals were 30cm high (compared with only 5cm on the paper) and, without exception, despite almost certainly not having seen a picture before, seven out of ten correctly identified the first cloth picture as a buck, and ten out of ten the second as a leopard. As Serpell (1976) says:

> Given a sufficiently salient stimulus, with distracting cues removed such as the novelty of paper or the distinct white band of the border, immediate recognition may be possible simply by stimulus generalization, one of the most basic characteristics of learning.

At the same time, several participants misidentified the buck and leopard as other four-legged animals and, in some cases, recognition seems to have been built up gradually, by helping the participant to trace the outline of the animal with a finger. Deregowski *et al.* note the similarity in this respect of their participants' verbal responses to those of young American children in a task presenting successively clearer images for identification, starting with a completely blurred image (Potter, 1966).

Another way of simplifying the task is to ask the participant to recognize an object without having to identify it by name. Deregowski (1968) gave a recognition task to boys and men in a 'relatively pictureless' Bisa community (a region of Zambia remote from main roads). They had to select from an array of 18 model animals the one depicted in a black-and-white photo. Six were commonly seen in the area, the rest were very exotic. The boys were better at finding the strange animals than were the men (they had received more schooling), but the men (mainly hunters) were better with familiar animals. Under optimal conditions, pictures do seem to be recognizable without any prior learning. Unlike words, most pictures are not entirely arbitrary representations of the real world; their arbitrariness:

> . . . lies in what features they choose to stress and what features to leave out and it is these conventions governing this choice which the experienced picture perceiver must learn. (Serpell, 1976).

Applications and implications

Much of the research seems to imply a belief that the Western style of pictorial art represents the real world in an objectively correct fashion: by implication, the participant who does not understand it is 'deficient' in some way. But since 'artistic excellence' is not identical with 'photographic accuracy' (Gombrich, 1960), Serpell (1976) asks if it may be possible that people in different cultures 'reject' Western art forms on *aesthetic* grounds and that all the research has mistakenly described a stylistic preference as a difference in perception.

Hudson (1962) and Deregowski (1969, 1970) found that African people with limited Western education slightly preferred unfolded, 'split', 'developed' or 'chain-type' drawings (as in the left-hand elephant) to 'orthogonal' or perspective drawings (as in the right-hand elephant). Why? Often it is because the latter fails to show some of the important features (recall the African woman shown the photograph by Mrs Donald Fraser).

The importance of artistic convention increases the more symbolic and abstract the art is: the convention is part of the fund of common experience shared by the artist and the audience. Duncan *et al.* (1973) point out that the small lines used by cartoonists to imply motion are the least understood of all the pictorial conventions which have been shown to rural African schoolchildren, and where the artist had drawn a boy's head in three different positions above the same trunk to indicate the head was turning around, half the children thought he was deformed! Likewise, Western observers require guidance from an anthropologist to understand the art forms of American Indians (Boas, 1927) or Nuba personal art in the Sudan (Faris, 1972).

Serpell & Deregowski (1980) describe picture perception as a set of *skills*. A skilled perceiver can deal with a wide variety of cues and use those that are appropriate in a given situation. One such skill is the ability to treat pictures as representations of real space – the Me'en had some initial difficulty with this. Another is interpreting impoverished or ambiguous cues. Berry *et al.* ask if these skills might be hierarchically organized in some way, ranging from general perceptual phenomena to knowledge of specific symbols and conventions:

> Theorizing about picture perception as a set of skills makes clear that cultures differ in the cues that are used and the relative importance attached to each of them . . . culturally specific conditions will determine which skills will develop. In this respect an approach postulating a set of skills does justice to the variations in cross-cultural differences in responses to pictures that from a Western point of view all contain depth cues. (Berry *et al.*, 1992)

Deregowski (1989, cited in Berry *et al.*, 1992), distinguishes between *epitomic* and *eidolic* pictures. The former refer to certain pictures which can be seen as representing an object without creating an illusion of depth (e.g. silhouettes), while the latter refer to pictures which definitely do create the illusion of depth. Some pictures have eidolic qualities even when they cannot be associated with a real object, such as the ambiguous trident and other 'impossible' figures: their eidolic character is so strong that they create an unavoidable impression of an object which cannot exist as a 3-D object in most Western adults (and which also 'doesn't make sense').

While we are aware of epitomic cues (e.g. clouds are perceived as representing faces or animals), we are not usually aware of eidolic cues: we accept them at some unconscious level. This may explain why Western perceivers typically perceive the Müller-Lyer illusion, for example: like other illusion figures, it has eidolic qualities of which we are not consciously aware (thus supporting the carpentered-world hypothesis). Deregowski suggests that on a continuum ranging from epitomic at one end, and eidolic at the other, Hudson's pictures fall closer to the epitomic end, while McGurk and Jahoda's model test (and his own construction-task figures) fall closer to the eidolic end. In turn, this explains why, usually, there are fewer 3-D responses using Hudson's pictures than on the other tasks.

Based on their review of the evidence concerning susceptibility to visual illusions, Segall *et al.* (1999) conclude by stating:

> . . . people perceive in ways that are shaped by the inferences they have learned to make in order to function most effectively in the particular ecological settings in which they live . . . we learn to perceive in the ways that we need to perceive. In that sense, environment and culture shape our perceptual habits.

Exercises

1. Hudson's pictures include the depth cues of relative size, overlap (superimposition) and linear perspective. Deregowski also refers to gradient of density (texture gradient). Serpell says that (*i*) binocular (retinal) disparity and (*ii*) motion parallax are missing. Briefly explain what is meant by each of these.

2. Briefly describe three other depth cues.

3. Most depth cues are both pictorial and monocular. What do you understand by this statement?

4. In Hudson's study, how was 3-D perception operationalized?

5. How was the validity of Hudson's test of 3-D perception established?

6. What kind of validity does this represent?

7. What would be the hypothesis which predicts that Hudson's test is valid (i.e. a one-tailed hypothesis)?

3 Does the autistic child have a 'theory of mind'?

S. Baron-Cohen, A.M. Leslie, and U. Frith (1985)

Cognition 21, 37-46

BACKGROUND AND CONTEXT

Autism was first identified, quite independently of each other, by Kanner in the USA (1943) and Asperger in Austria (1944). It is usually detected from the age of four upwards and diagnosis depends on the presence of characteristic behaviours in accordance with a specific social, affective and cognitive profile (Mitchell, 1997). It is often described as the most severe of all child psychiatric disorders, because, unlike other disorders, people with autism seem to be virtually cut off from other people ('in a world of their own'). This is why it is sometimes categorized as a *psychosis*, implying that it is unlike anything in the normal range of experience (Baron-Cohen, 1995).

The current edition of the Diagnostic and Statistical Manual of Mental Disorders (DSM-IV, 1994), published by the American Psychiatric Association, stresses three fundamental impairments:

- *Qualitative impairments in social interaction*: impaired non-verbal behaviours (especially eye-contact), failure to engage in genuinely social games (such as turn-taking), no attempt to share interests through *joint-attentional behaviours,* and a failure to develop any friendship beyond the most superficial acquaintance. A lack of empathy is often seen as the central feature of the social deficit (Baron-Cohen, 1988; Kanner, 1943).

- *Qualitative impairments in communication*: failure to develop language and communication in the normal way (such as delayed and restricted language development, and inappropriate use of language as a means of communication), and failure to use gesture properly.

- *Repetitive and stereotyped patterns of behaviour, and lack of normal imagination*: an inflexible adherence to specific routines, becoming quite distressed if prevented from performing repetitive rituals, lack of spontaneous make-believe/symbolic play (Leslie, 1987), and engaging in play which is often lacking in creativity and imagination (Baron-Cohen, 1987).

According to Smith *et al.* (1998),

> The challenge for any researcher investigating autism is trying to explain how one syndrome can lead to the specific combination of impairments which typify a person with autism (lack of socialization, communication and imagination); how different people with autism can be affected in markedly different ways; and how it is that people with autism can sometimes have better than average abilities in one or two areas (the 'islets of ability').

The Baron-Cohen *et al.*(1985) study can be seen as meeting the first of these challenges, or at least providing a partial solution.

Despite changes in the form of symptoms with age and a considerbale amount of learning that may be possible, autism seems to be life-long (Frith, 1989). It affects 1–2 individuals per 1000 (about the same as Down's syndrome) and affects 2-4 times as many boys as girls (Frith, 1993). According to Frith (1993), the old image of the autistic child in a glass shell is misleading in several ways. It is incorrect to think that inside the shell is a normal person waiting to emerge, nor is autism a disorder of childhood only. The film *Rain Man*, starring Dustin Hoffman, came at the right time to suggest a new image to a receptive public.

During the 1960s and early 70s, a major theory of autism saw social impairments as secondary to problems of language (Rutter, 1985). However, this lost credibility when it was discovered that children with language disabilities (dysphasias) do not inevitably develop social disabilities, unlike autistic children.

More recent theories see language delay as an entirely independent disability which may co-occur with autism. The most influential current theory maintains that what all autistic people have in common (the core inability) is *mind-blindness* (Baron-Cohen, 1990), a severe impairment in their understanding of mental states and in their appreciation of how mental states govern behaviour (e.g. Baron-Cohen, 1993, 1995). They therefore lack a 'theory of mind', a term originally coined by Premack & Woodruff (1978) based on their work with chimps (including Sarah: see Chapter 6).

The current study is a direct test of the *theory of mind hypothesis* and was itself based on a seminal study by Wimmer & Perner (1983). They devised a *false belief* task, with four, six, and eight-year-olds, involving two small dolls (called Maxi and his mother) who enact a story in which the mother moves Maxi's chocolate from a green drawer (put there by Maxi) to a blue drawer (while Maxi is outside playing). Children are asked *where Maxi would look for the chocolate* when he returned. A *correct answer* ('green drawer') involves attributing to Maxi a *false belief*: the children *know* the chocolate is in the blue drawer, but they also know that Maxi does *not* have this knowledge (so he thinks it is still in the green drawer). An *incorrect answer* ('blue drawer') indicates that children cannot distingush between what they themselves know and what Maxi knows. A correct answer reflects a theory of mind (ToM).

AIM AND NATURE OF THE STUDY

This is essentially a replication of the Wimmer and Perner 'Maxi' study, retaining the vital elements but adapted to make it shorter and simpler and more appropriate in content for older children (Mitchell, 1997). Sally and Anne replace Maxi and his mother, and the story involves transfer of a marble from a basket to a box.

A crucial difference between this and the Wimmer and Perner study is that the latter involved only normal children. Baron-Cohen *et al.* tested:

● 20 autistic children, chronological age (CA) 6-16 (mean 11.11), mean verbal mental age (vMA) 5.5;

● 14 Down's syndrome children, CA 6-17 (mean 10.11), mean vMA 2.11;

● 27 normal children, CA 3-5 (mean 4.5), assumed to have a vMA equivalent to their CA.

Since the children were allocated to experimental conditions by virtue of being autistic, Down's or normal (i.e. non-randomly), and the *independent variable* (their characteristics) could not be manipulated, the method used was a *quasi-experiment*. The *dependent variable* was success or failure on the Sally–Anne test, specifically, on the third of three questions (as used by Wimmer and Perner):

● 'Where is the marble really?' (*Reality question*).

● 'Where was the marble in the beginning'? (*Memory question*).

● 'Where will Sally look for her marble?' (*Belief question*).

As with Maxi, the *correct answer* requires the child to attribute a *false belief* to Sally (she will look in the *wrong place*). The first two questions act as *control* questions, used to ensure (i) that the child has attended to and knows the current location of the marble, and (ii) she remembers where it was before. Since all the children answered the first two questions correctly, any differences in their answers to the crucial Sally question can be taken as indicating differences in the children's ToM abilities.

THE STUDY

ABSTRACT

We use a new model of metarepresentational development to predict a cognitive deficit which could explain a crucial component of the social impairment in child-hood autism. One of the manifestations of a basic metarepresentation capacity is a 'theory of mind'. We have reason to believe that autistic children lack such a 'theory'. If this were so, then they would be unable to attribute beliefs to others and to predict their behaviour. This hypothesis was tested using Wimmer and Perner's puppet play paradigm. Normal children and those with Down's syndrome were used as controls for a group of autistic children. Even though the mental age of the autistic children was higher than that of the controls, they alone failed to attribute beliefs to others. Thus the dysfunction we have proposed and demonstrated is independent of mental retardation and specific to autism.

INTRODUCTION

Childhood autism is a severe developmental disorder. It is a rare condition, affecting about 4 in every 10,000 children. The diagnostic criteria at present are behavioural (American Psychiatric Association, 1980; Kanner, 1943; Ritvo & Freeman, 1978; Rutter, 1978) and the main symptom, which can be reliably identified, is impairment in verbal and nonverbal communication. This impairment is part of the core feature of childhood autism, namely a profound disorder in understanding and coping with the social environment, regardless of IQ. Additional symptoms can occur, in particular mental retardation, islets of ability, and 'insistence on sameness'. Nevertheless, the distinctive feature is failure to develop normal social relationships.

Autistic children find even the immediate social environment unpredictable and incomprehensible. They are often said to 'treat people and objects alike'. Wing & Gould (1979) in their epidemiological study of severely retarded autistic children demonstrate the range of socially impaired behaviour: from total withdrawal through passivity to repetitive pestering. Lord's (1984) review of studies of peer interaction in autistic children highlights improvements due to intervention. A picture of apparently intractable social impairment emerges in the clinical follow-up studies of autism (e.g. Kanner, 1971; Kanner *et al.*, 1972) and in the as yet rare experimental investigations (e.g. Attwood, 1984; Martini, 1980).

Although most autistic children are mentally retarded (DeMyer *et al.*, 1974; Wing *et al.*, 1976), which may account for many of their symptoms (Hermelin & O'Connor, 1970), this in itself cannot be a sufficient explanation for their social impairments. First, there are autistic children with IQs in the normal range, and second, mentally retarded non-autistic children, such as Down's syndrome, are socially competent relative to their mental age (Coggins *et al.*, 1983; Gibson, 1978).

In order to explain the specific impairments of childhood autism it is necessary, then, to consider the underlying cognitive mechanisms independent of IQ (Frith, 1982; Hermelin & O'Connor, 1970; Rutter, 1983). In this paper, we put forward a suggestion which has been derived from a new model of metarepresentational development (Leslie, 1984), which specifies a mechanism underlying a crucial aspect of social skills, namely being able to conceive of mental states (knowing that other people know, want, feel, or believe things); in short, having a 'theory of mind' (Premack & Woodruff, 1978). A theory of mind is impossible without the capacity to form 'second-order representations' (Dennett, 1978; Pylyshyn, 1978). According to Leslie's model this capacity does not appear until the second year of life. While it manifests itself eventually in a theory of mind, Leslie shows that it also accounts for the emergence of pretend play. An absence of the capacity to form second-order representations, then, would lead not only to a lack of theory of mind, with the accompanying social ineptness, but also a lack of pretend play.

Now, it is well known that autistic children, in addition to their social handicaps, also show a striking poverty of pretend play (Sigman & Ungerer, 1981; Ungerer & Sigman, 1981; Wing *et al.*, 1977; Wing & Gould, 1979). An explanation for the lack of pretend play and its curious association with the social impairments typical of autism is not obvious, and again the notion of mental age is not helpful for this purpose. On the one hand, even high IQ autistic children lack pretend play, and on the other hand, severely retarded Down's syndrome children don't (Hill & McCune-Nicolich, 1981). However, if we suppose that autistic children lack second-order representations, then we can make sense of the association of impairments. In order to test this hypothesis we can make the prediction that autistic children will lack a theory of mind. It is of course possible for autistic children to have a theory of mind and still show incompetence, since social competence must depend on many factors. However, if our prediction was proved wrong and autistic children did show evidence of using a theory of mind, then we could rule out a deficiency in second-order representations. Even if our prediction was confirmed, we would still have to establish that this was a *specific* deficit, that is, largely independent of *general* mental retardation. Thus we would have to show (a) that even those rare autistic children whose IQs are in the average range should lack this ability and (b) that non-autistic but severely retarded children, such as Down's syndrome, should possess it.

In a seminal paper, Premack & Woodruff (1978) defined theory of mind as the ability to attribute mental states to oneself and to others. The ability to make inferences about what other people *believe* to be the case in a given situation allows one to predict what they will do. This is clearly a crucial component of social skills. There is growing evidence for the ability to attribute mental states to others, and its development from the second year of life onwards (Bretherton *et al.*, 1981; Mac-Namara *et al.*, 1976; Shantz, 1983; Shultz *et al.*, 1980; Shultz & Cloghesy, 1981). A convincing demonstration that an explicit theory of mind is well within the capacity of normal four-year-olds has been given by Wimmer & Perner (1983), who developed an ingenious paradigm that can be used with very young children based on the case where the child's own belief is different from someone else's belief. In order to succeed on the task the child has to be aware that different people can have different beliefs about a situation. Hence this case provides the strongest evidence for the capacity to conceive of mental states (Dennett, 1978). It is this paradigm that we used in the present study.

M E T H O D

SUBJECTS

Details of the subjects are shown in Table 3.1. The 20 autistic children had been diagnosed according to established criteria (Rutter, 1978). In addition there were 14 Down's syndrome and 27 clinically normal preschool children. The autistic group's mean mental age (MA) was not only higher than that of the Down's syndrome group on a non-verbal scale, but also on the more conservative measure of a verbal scale. We assumed that for the normal group MA would roughly correspond to chronological age (CA). Therefore, their MA was, if anything, lower than that of the handicapped groups. We selected a high functioning subgroup of autistic children in order to enable a stringent test of the specific deficit hypothesis to be made. Thus, the autistic group was of a relatively high mean IQ of 82 (derived from non-verbal MA), mostly in the average and borderline (70–108), with only one subject scoring less than 70. The IQs of the Down's syndrome group were rather lower with a range of 42–89, and a mean of 64.

Table 3.1

MEANS, SDs AND RANGES OF CHRONOLOGICAL AGE (CA) AND MENTAL AGE (MA) IN YEARS;MONTHS

Diagnostics groups	*n*			CA	Nonverbal* MA	Verbal** MA
Autistic	20		Mean SD Range	11;11 3;0 6;1–16;6	9;3 2;2 5;4–15;9	5;5 1;6 2;8–7;5
Down's syndrome	14		Mean SD Range	10;11 4;1 6;3–17;0	5;11 0;11 4;9–8;6	2;11 0;7 1;8–4;0
Normal	27		Mean SD Range	4;5 0;7 3;5–5;9	– 	–

* Leiter International Performance Scale.
** British Picture Vocabulary Test.

PROCEDURE

The procedure is illustrated in Figure 3.1. There were two doll protagonists, Sally and Anne. First, we checked that the children knew which doll was which (Naming Question). Sally first placed a marble into her basket. Then she left the scene, and the marble was transferred by Anne and hidden in her box. Then, when Sally returned, the experimenter asked the critical Belief Question: 'Where will Sally look for her marble?'. If the children point to the previous location of the marble, then they pass the Belief Question by appreciating the doll's now false belief. If however, they point to the marble's current location, then they fail the question by not taking into account the doll's belief. These conclusions are warranted if two control questions are answered correctly: 'Where is the marble really?' (Reality Question); 'Where was the marble in the beginning?' (Memory Question).

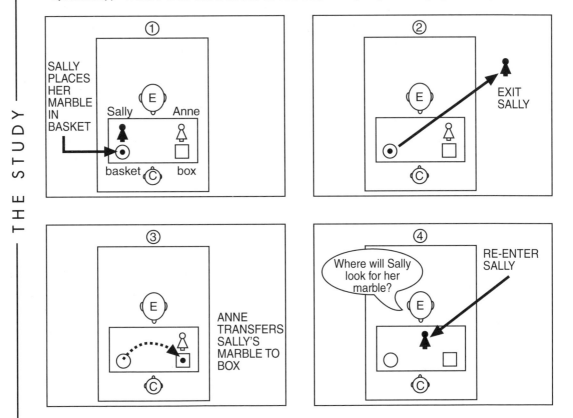

Figure 3.1. Experimental scenario.

The control questions are crucial to ensure that the child has both knowledge of the real current location of the marble and an accurate memory of the previous location. There is no reason to believe that the three questions differ from each other in terms of *psycholinguistic* complexity, but of course we hypothesize that they differ in terms of *conceptual* complexity. The standard scenario was repeated using a new

location for the marble, so that now there were three different locations that the child could point at (basket, box and experimenter's pocket). Correct responses to all three questions for each of the two trials were therefore different.

R E S U L T S

All subjects passed the Naming Question, as well as the Reality and Memory Questions in both trials. The Belief Question for both trials was answered consistently by each child, with the sole exception of one Down's syndrome child who failed trial 1 and passed trial 2. The results for Down's syndrome and normal subjects were strikingly similar: 23 out of 27 normal children, and 12 out of 14 Down's syndrome children *passed* the Belief Question on both trials (85% and 86% respectively). By contrast, 16 of the 20 autistic children (80%) *failed* the Belief Question on both trials. This difference between the groups was highly significant ($\chi_2 = 25.9$, df = 2, $p < .001$). All 16 autistic children who failed pointed to where the marble really was, rather than to any of the other possible locations ($p = .006$, Binomial Test, one-tailed). The four autistic children who passed succeeded on both trials. Their CA ranged from 10;11 to 15;10, their non-verbal MAs were between 8;10 and 10;8 and their verbal MAs between 2;9 and 7;0. Comparison with data in Table 3.1 shows that these children were fairly average on all our available variables. There were certainly other children of equal or greater MA and CA who gave incorrect responses.

D I S C U S S I O N

The fact that every single child correctly answered the control questions allows us to conclude that they all knew (and implicitly believed) that the marble was put somewhere else after Sally had left. The critical question was, 'Where will Sally look?' after she returns. Here a group difference appeared: autistic children answered this question in a distinctly different way from the others. The Down's syndrome and normal preschool children answered by pointing to where the marble was put in the first place. Thus they must have appreciated that their own knowledge of where the marble actually was and the knowledge that could be attributed to the doll were different. That is, they predicted that the doll's behaviour on the basis of the doll's belief. The autistic group, on the other hand, pointed consistently to where the marble really was. They did not merely point to a 'wrong' location, but rather to the marble's actual location. This becomes especially clear on trial 2 where the autistic children never pointed to the box (which had been the 'wrong' location on trial 1), but instead to the experimenter's pocket (that is, again to where the marble really was). This rules out both a position preference and a negativism explanation. Furthermore, the autistic children were not 'contrary' on the Reality or Memory Questions which they always answered correctly. Clark & Rutter (1977, 1979) also found no evidence of alleged negativism in autistic children. The failure on the Belief Question was also not due to random pointing. Nor could it have been due to any failure to understand and remember the demands of the task or the narrative since these children all answered the Naming, Memory and Reality Questions perfectly. We therefore conclude that the autistic children did not appreciate the difference between their own and the doll's knowledge.

Our results strongly support the hypothesis that autistic children as a group fail to use a theory of mind, an inability to represent mental states. As a result, autistic children are unable to attribute beliefs to others and are thus at a serious disadvantage when having to predict other people's behaviour. There is, however, also a suggestion of a small subgroup of autistic childtren who succeeded on the task and who thus may be able to use a theory of mind. These children who nevertheless, by definition (American Psychiatric Association, 1980; Rutter, 1978) show social impairment, would certainly deserve further study. From Leslie's (1984) model we would predict that if they did have the capacity to form second-order representations, then they would also show evidence of an ability to pretend play. Furthermore, we would predict that their social impairments would show a rather different pattern from those autistic children who fail to use a theory of mind.

The ability we have been testing could be considered as a kind of *conceptual* perspective-taking skill (Shantz, 1983). However, it is important to contrast the present task with traditional *perceptual* perspective-taking tasks, such as 'line of sight' or 'three mountains', where a child has to indicate what can be seen from another point of view (Hobson, 1982; Hughes & Donaldson, 1979; Piaget & Inhelder, 1956). Such perceptual perspective-taking tasks can be solved using solely visuo-spatial skills and in no way require attributing beliefs to others (Cox, 1980; Huttenlocher & Presson, 1979). Hobson (1984) has shown that autistic children succeed on perceptual perspective-taking tasks involving dolls as well as can be expected from their MA. According to Hobson, this finding suggests that it is very unlikely that the cognitive abilities reuqired in taking different points of view in perceptual situations are the same as those underlying the autistic child's social disability. The results of the present study confirm this interpretation and point towards a crucial distinction between the understanding of perceptual situations and the attribution of higher order mental states.

We conclude that the failure shown by autistic children in our experiment constitutes a specific deficit. It cannot be attributed to the general effects of mental retardation, since the more severely retarded Down's syndrome children performed close to ceiling on our task. Thus we have demonstrated a cognitive deficit that is largely independent of general intellectual level and has the potential to explain both lack of pretend play and social impairment by virtue of a circumscribed cognitive failure. This finding encourages us to continue with a theoretical framework

THE STUDY

(Leslie, 1984) which can specify the underlying connections betwen pretend play, theory of mind and social skills. Deriving further testable predictions from such a model may lead to a new approach to the cognitive dysfunction in childhood autism (Frith, 1984).

EVALUATION

Theoretical issues

The results show a striking difference between the autistic children and the other two groups on the crucial false belief question. It was as if they had been asked: 'Where is Sally's marble?' They performed much like clinically normal young children do (i.e. children aged below four), but their average CA was just below 12 (Mitchell, 1997). They also performed far worse than the Down's children, despite having a higher mean verbal MA. None of the groups had difficulty answering the reality and memory questions.

According to Leslie (1987, 1994; Leslie & Roth, 1993), underlying ToM is an independent mental module (the *theory of mind mechanism/ToMM*). This is innately determined and begins to mature from about 12/18 months to four years. It processes information in the form of *metarepresentations*: it is specialized for representing *mental* representations ('beliefs about beliefs etc.).

The alternative, domain-*general* account of the child's acquisition of ToM is Piaget's account of *egocentrism* (although the term ToM post-dates his work). Before age seven, children are unable to put themselves in someone else's psychological shoes because they lack reversible thought processes (Bryant, 1998).

In order to choose between these alternatives (domain-specific and domain-general accounts), we need experiments which contrast how children make inferences about other people's beliefs with their success in making very similar inferences which are *not* about beliefs. If the specific modular approach is correct, there should be very little developmental connection between the two types of inference. The little available evidence (e.g. Zaitchik, 1990) suggests the opposite conclusion. There does not appear to be a 'switching on' of a module precisely set to work out what other people know: it is much more likely that young children's difficulties lie in making a clear distinction between what was true in the past and what is true now (Bryant, 1998).

Ironically, both approaches are subject to the same criticism, namely that they see the child as a 'solitary thinker', whose mental abilities develop in a social vacuum. According to Fonagy *et al.*(1997), 'mindreading' does not suddenly develop at three to four years of age, independently of the child's social relationships. Too much happens

between the infant-toddler and its caregiver which is difficult to account for unless we assume a primitive ability to adjust his or her actions in the light of others' assumed mental states. Adults interacting with babies consistently assume that they possess a rudimentary representation of their own and others' minds. This assumption is probably critical to how this capacity actually develops and flourishes between 33-40 months (Bartsch & Wellman, 1995).

The most consistent attempt at making connections between cognitive and social development is the inspiring programme of work by Judy Dunn and her colleagues. She has investigated how children's understanding of mental states is embedded within the social world of the family, with its interactional network of complex and sometimes emotionally charged relationships (Fonagy *et al.*, 1997). Dunn (1994) suggests that the nature of the child's interactions with people intimately involved with them during the time when understanding of minds emerges, may provide important insights into the nature of the conceptual structure that children are acquiring as part of their ToM. One study (of many) supporting this idea is that by Perner *et al.*(1994), which found that three to four-year-olds with siblings are more likely to predict a story character's mistaken (false-belief based) action, compared with only children.

The work of Dunn and Perner *et al.* suggests that the study of *individual differences* in performance on false-belief tasks might be a good way to understand more about the factors involved in acquiring a ToM (Fonagy *et al.*, 1997: see **Subsequent research** below).

Methodological issues

Mitchell (1997) points out two major limitations of the Baron-Cohen *et al.* (1985) study. First, children with autism have difficulty engaging in imaginative activities and make-believe (as we saw in **Background and context** above). Their failure to acknowledge false belief may *not* be due to an impaired theory of mind, but rather to their failure to become immersed in a story requiring them to use their imagination and pretend. If so, the study tells us nothing we did not already know. Second, since Sally is only a doll, she has no mind and, therefore, the question of the content of her beliefs does not arise.

Leslie & Frith (1988) overcame both these problems by incorporating the false-belief task into a real-life interaction. The child was in the company of the two researchers, all three cooperating in putting a penny underneath an upturned cup. Then Frith left. Leslie and the child conspired to transfer the penny to an adjacent upturned cup. When Frith returned, the child was asked the belief question. Under these conditions, most autistic children still gave the wrong answer. Hence, their difficulty in recognizing false belief was *not* confined to a procedure involving mindless dolls (Mitchell, 1997).

Subsequent research

Since Baron-Cohen *et al.*'s (1985) study, researchers from all over the world have replicated and extended the basic findings (one major review being that of Happé, 1994a). Despite the ToM hypothesis being both convincing and powerful, a substantial amount of evidence is accumulating which is undermining it (Mitchell, 1997). Even in successful replications (and in the Baron-Cohen *et al.* study itself), a minority of autistic children reliably succeed in answering the belief question correctly (or acknowledging false belief in some other way).

One attempt to 'rescue' the ToM hypothesis in face of this evidence was Baron-Cohen's (1989) test of *second-order belief*. While the Sally false-belief task involves a *first-order belief* ('I think Sally thinks the marble is in the basket'), a second-order belief involves understanding that someone else can have beliefs about a third person ('I think that Anne thinks that Sally thinks that the marble is in the basket'). Again using a test first devised by Perner & Wimmer (1985) involving Mary and John and an ice-cream van, Baron-Cohen found that *all* the autistic children failed this second-order belief task.

However, some evidence seems to contradict the notion that ToM deficit is a core cognitive deficit in autism. Bowler (1992) found that many autistic adults with generally good intellectual abilities passed a test of second-order belief. However, Bowler's participants were, in fact, diagnosed as having Asperger Syndrome (first identified by Asperger, the co-discoverer, with Kanner, of autism), which shares the social and communicative symptoms of autism but not the history of language delay. Ozonoff *et al.* (1991) also found some adults with Asperger syndrome (or 'high-functioning autism') who passed a second-order belief test.

Baron-Cohen *et al.* (1997) argue that these studies cannot be taken as providing conclusive evidence for an *intact* ToM in such individuals, since such tests can easily produce ceiling effects if used with people whose MA is over six. This is because children with normal intelligence pass such tests at about six (Perner & Wimmer, 1985). It is unfortunate that these tests are often thought of as 'complex', high-level tests of ToM. While they are more complex than first-order tests, the latter are passed by normal four-year-olds: neither first- nor second-order tests are complex tests of ToM, but simply probes for four to six-year-olds respectively.

Happé (1994b) tested adults with autism and Asperger syndrome using an 'advanced' ToM test. This involved story comprehension, where key questions (pitched at the level of normal eight-to-nine-year-olds) concerned either a character's mental states (experimental condition) or physical events (control condition). Her participants had more trouble with mental state stories than matched controls, using fewer appropriate mental state terms in their justifications of why the characters acted as they did.

Baron-Cohen *et al.* (1997) extended Happé's study, using a new *adult* ToM test, which involved looking at photos of the eye region of faces and making a forced choice between which of two words (either basic, such as 'happy' or complex, such as 'arrogant') best described what the person in the photo might be thinking/feeling. This 'Reading the Mind in the Eyes' task could be called a 'mindreading' test (since no assumption is made about any 'theory' the participant may be using), although 'mindreading' and 'ToM' are used interchangeably by Baron-Cohen *et al.* (1997), and by others. Compared with normal adults and those with Tourette Syndrome (characterized by uncontrollable body movements and sounds, including obscenities), those with autism and Asperger Syndrome showed a significant impairment in their mindreading skills (as predicted). Similar results were found using a revised version of the 'Reading the Mind in the Eyes' test (Baron-Cohen *et al.*, 2001).

Similarly, Ruffman *et al.* (2001) found that measuring eye gaze (where children looked when anticipating the return of a story character or an object) tapped social understanding better than a verbal measure (asking a direct question): the eye gaze measure discriminated more effectively between autistic children and those with mild learning difficulties.

Applications and implications

Frith (cited in Gold, 1995) maintains that belief in ToM has practical benefits for teachers, parents and carers of autistic people. It '. . . explains the inexplicable. And it means you can adjust their environment to them, to suit their needs.' For example, it makes sense of the apparent irrational frustration of children trying to communicate using Maketon sign language and who fail to realize that the reason no one is taking any notice of them is that they are signing underneath the table! Similarly, the child whose unprovoked tantrums were explained once his father realized that he pointed at the sweet cupboard and expected to be given sweets even when no one else was in the room to see him pointing!

According to Mitchell (1997), it would be an outstanding breakthrough if we established that autism reduces to an impaired ToM. It would provide a radical new insight, representing a triumph for the cognitive approach, since affective, communicative and social impairments would be seen as *secondary*, all stemming from the *primary* cognitive impairment. If we wanted to plan treatment for the disorder (a cognitive impairment) as opposed to the symptoms (the other impairments), we would need to proceed down the cognitive route. Similarly, with devising better diagnostic tests.

As ToM was first used to describe the mental abilities of chimps (Premack & Woodruff, 1978), it seems appropriate to end by saying something more about non-human species. It would perhaps also be surprising if there were no evidence of mindreading skills in our closest evolutionary relatives. According to Call and Tomasello (cited in

Spinney, 1998), while only humans can distinguish between what they know and what others know, chimps and orang-utans (like three-year-olds who fail the Sally–Anne test) might possess the rudiments of mindreading.

Hauser and Santos (cited in Spinney, 1998) devised a special version of the Sally–Anne test with cotton-top tamarins. They found evidence of understanding that an actor (who is observed looking for an object that has been moved to a different location without the actor's knowledge) cannot know about an event he has not seen.

Deception (an alternative way of testing ToM) has played a crucial role in evolution: when early hominids left their forest habitat to colonize the plains four to five million years ago, they were physically ill-adapted to compete with the highly specialized carnivores already there. However, they had the rudiments of a devious, cunning intelligence: they sharpened their minds to outwit the rest by carving out a unique 'cognitive niche' (Spinney, 1998).

Exercises

1. In the Baron-Cohen *et al.* (1985) study, the autistic children were compared with (a) normal children and (b) Down's syndrome children. Why were these two other groups used? Can you suggest *other* groups that might have been used – and why?

2. In what sense were the reality and memory questions *control questions*? What would have been the effect of not including them?

3. What was the purpose of the naming question?

4. While ToM is very similar to Piaget's concept of *egocentrism*, can you identify any *differences* between them?

5. What type of experimental design was used?

6. In the **Discussion** section, Baron-Cohen *et al.* rule out both a 'position preference' and a 'negativism explanation' when accounting for the autistic children's failure on the Belief Question. What is meant by 'position preference' and 'negativism' in the context of this study?

4 Levels of processing: a framework for memory research

F.I.M. Craik and R.S. Lockhart (1972)

Journal of Verbal Learning and Verbal Behaviour, 11, 671–84

BACKGROUND AND CONTEXT

The view that memory comprises a number of separate stores, between which information passes, has a long history. It was James (1890) who originally distinguished between *primary memory* and *secondary memory*, although Ebbinghaus (1885), one of the pioneers of memory research, would have accepted such a distinction. Hebb (1949), Broadbent (1958) and Waugh & Norman (1965) have also made the distinction, but probably the most discussed and elaborate is Atkinson and Shiffrin's *multistore model* (or 'dual memory' theory, 1968, 1971), so named because it emphasizes short-term memory (STM) and long-term memory (LTM). (These are sometimes referred to as short-term and long-term *stores*: see Table 4.1, page 51). This distinction corresponds to primary and secondary memory respectively.

In the model, STM and LTM are referred to as permanent *structural components* of the memory system, and represent intrinsic features of the human information-processing system. In addition, the memory system comprises relatively transient processes (*control processes*), a major example being *rehearsal*. It serves two main functions: (*i*) to act as a buffer between sensory memory and LTM by maintaining incoming information within STS, (*ii*) to transfer information to LTM.

The levels of processing (LOP) approach represented the first major challenge to the multistore model. While the latter emphasizes the sequence of stages information passes through as it moves from one structural component to another while being processed, Craik and Lockhart's model *begins* with hypothesized processes and sees 'memory' as essentially a by-product of information processing (Parkin, 2000). This is really a reversal of the logic of the multistore model. Again, instead of regarding rehearsal itself as being important, Craik and Lockhart argue that it is what is done with or to the material during rehearsal which determines the durability of memory (or trace persistence). Specifically, memory is a direct function of the depth of processing.

AIM AND NATURE OF THE STUDY

This is a *review paper*, summarizing and discussing the theory and research of other investigators, rather than reporting the findings of the authors' own or most recent research. Its aim is to propose an alternative theoretical framework (LOP) to that which had been dominant during the previous 10–15 years in memory research (the multistore model). The paper represents a landmark in how memory has been conceptualized, and was the stimulus for a great deal of research and theorizing during the 1970s especially. Prior to 1972, psychologists had not really considered the extent to which flexibility in the learning process could affect retention of the material being learnt. But after Craik and Lockhart's paper:

> . . . theorists were acutely aware that processing strategies, imposed or self-generated, were of major importance in determining the outcome of memory experiments . . . (Parkin, 2000)

The multistore model was subsequently overshadowed by LOP (Baddeley, 1999: see **Evaluation** below).

■T■H■E■ ■S■T■U■D■Y■

> This paper briefly reviews the evidence for multistore theories of memory and points out some difficulties with the approach. An alternative framework for human memory research is then outlined in terms of depth or levels of processing. Some current data and arguments are re-examined in the light of this alternative framework and implications for further research considered.

Over the past decade, models of human memory have been dominated by the concept of stores and the transfer of information among them. One major criterion for distinguishing between stores has been their different retention characteristics. The temporal properties of stored information have, thus, played a dual role: besides constituting the basic phenomenon to be explained, they have also been used to generate the theoretical constructs in terms of which the explanation is formulated. The apparent circularity has been avoided by the specification of additional properties of the stores (such as their capacity and coding characteristics), thereby characterizing them independently of the phenomenon to be explained. The essential concept underlying this approach is that of information being transferred from one store to another, and the store-to-store transfer models may be distinguished, at least in terms of emphasis, from explanations which associate different retention characteristics with qualitative changes in the memory code.

In this paper we will (*i*) examine the reasons for proposing multistore models, (*ii*) question their adequacy and (*iii*) propose an alternative framework in terms of levels of processing. The memory trace can be understood as a by-product of perceptual analysis, and trace persistence is a positive function of the depth to which the stimulus has been analysed. Stimuli may also be retained over short intervals by continued processing at a constant depth. These views offer a new way to interpret existing data and provide a heuristic framework for further research.

MULTISTORE MODELS

THE CASE IN FAVOUR

When humans are viewed as information processors (Miller, 1956; Broadbent, 1958) it seems necessary to propose holding mechanisms or memory stores at various points in the system. For example, on the basis of his dichotic listening studies, Broadbent (1958) proposed that information must be held transiently before entering the limited-capacity processing channel; items could be held over the short term by recycling them, after perception, through the same transient storage system and from there, information could be transferred into and retained in a more permanent long-term store. Broadbent's ideas have been extended by Waugh and Norman (1965), Peterson (1966) and Atkinson and Shiffrin (1968). According to the modal model (Murdock, 1967), it is now widely accepted that memory can be classified into three levels of storage: sensory stores, short-term memory (STM) and long-term memory (LTM). These terms will be used to refer to experimental situations, while 'short-term store' (STS) and 'long-term store' (LTS) will be used to refer to the two relevant storage systems.

Stimuli can enter the sensory stores regardless of whether the subject is paying attention to that source (i.e. they are 'preattentive' (Neisser, 1967)). The input is represented in a rather literal form and can be replaced by further inputs in the same modality (Neisser, 1967, Crowder & Morton, 1969). This modality-specific nature, moderately large capacity and transcience of their contents, distinguish the sensory registers from later stores.

Attention to the material in a sensory register is equivalent to reading it out and transferring it to STS, where verbal items are coded in a phonemic way (Schulman, 1971) or in auditory-verbal-linguistic terms (Atkinson & Shiffrin, 1968). STS also has a limited capacity (Miller, 1956; Broadbent, 1958), as indicated by loss of information mainly through displacement (Waugh & Norman, 1965) and by the slower rate of forgetting from STS: 5 to 20 seconds compared with the ¼ to 2-second estimates for sensory storage.

The STS–LTS distinctions are well documented. LTS has no known capacity limit, compared with the limited capacity of STS: verbal items are usually coded phonemically in STS but mainly semantically in LTS (Baddeley, 1966); forgetting from STS is complete within 30 seconds or less while forgetting from LTS is either very slow or material is not forgotten at all (Shiffrin & Atkinson, 1969). In free-recall experiments, the last few items are supposedly retrieved from STS and the early items are retrieved from LTS and it is now known that several variables affect one of these retrieval components without affecting the other (Glanzer, 1972). Further evidence for the STS/LTS distinction comes from clinical studies (Milner, 1970, Warrington, 1971). The differences between the three storage levels are summarized in Table 4.1.

Table 4.1

COMMONLY ACCEPTED DIFFERENCES BETWEEN THE THREE STAGES OF VERBAL MEMORY

Feature	Sensory registers	Short-term store	Long-term store
Entry of information	Preattentive	Requires attention	Rehearsal
Maintenance of information	Not possible	Continued attention Rehearsal	Repetition Organization
Format of information	Literal copy of input	Phonemic Probably visual Possibly semantic	Largely semantic Some auditory and visual
Capacity	Large	Small	No known limit
Information loss	Decay	Displacement Possibly decay	Possibly no loss Loss of accessibility or discriminability by interference
Trace duration	$\frac{1}{4}$–2 seconds	Up to 30 seconds	Minutes to years
Retrieval	Readout	Probably automatic Items in consciousness Temporal/ phonemic cues	Retrieval cues Possibly search process

T H E   S T U D Y

Such multistore models are apparently specific and concrete; information flows in well-regulated paths between stores whose characteristics have intuitive appeal and their properties may be elicited experimentally and described either behaviourally or mathematically. Despite these obvious attractions, when the evidence is examined in greater detail, the stores become less tangible.

THE CASE AGAINST

General critics include Melton (1963) and Murdock (1972). Others have objected to particular aspects, e.g. Tulving and Patterson (1968) argued against the notions of information being transferred from one store to another and, similarly, Shallice and Warrington (1970) presented evidence against the idea that information must necessarily 'pass through' STS to enter LTS. In our view, the criteria listed above do not justify distinguishing between different stores.

CAPACITY

Although limited capacity has been a major feature of the information-flow approach, and especially of STS in multistore models, its exact nature is rather obscure; in particular, is the limitation one of processing capacity, storage capacity or some interaction between the two? In terms of the computer analogy on which such models are based, does the limitation refer to the storage capacity of a memory register or to the rate at which the processor can perform certain operations? The action of a limited-capacity channel (Broadbent, 1958) seems to emphasize the latter while later models (e.g. Waugh & Norman, 1965) seem to emphasize the former; both are present in Miller's (1956) interpretation, although the relationship between them is not explicitly worked out.

Attempts to measure STS capacity have leant towards the storage interpretation, with the number of items being the appropriate scale of measurement, but the research offers a range of values. For example, Baddeley (1970) and Murdock (1972) have found values of two to four words; typically five to nine items are given for memory span (depending on whether the items are words, letters or digits) and if the words in a span list form a sentence, young subjects can accurately reproduce strings of up to 20 words (Craik & Masani, 1969). So, if capacity is a critical feature of STM operation, a box model has to account for this very wide range of capacity estimates.

The most widely accepted explanation is that capacity is limited in terms of chunks and that few or many items can be recoded into a chunk depending on the meaningfulness of the material. But how can a chunk be defined independently of its memorial consequences? And this view sees STS as a very flexible storage compartment which can accept a variety of codes from simple physical features to complex semantic ones.

We see capacity in terms of a limitation on processing: storage limitations are seen as a direct consequence of this more fundamental limitation.

CODING

Based on studies with verbal material, Conrad (1964) and Baddeley (1966) concluded that information in STS is coded acoustically but predominantly semantically in LTS. However, (*i*) STS coding can be either acoustic or articulatory (Levy, 1971; Peterson & Johnson, 1971); (*ii*) even with verbal material, STS can sometimes be visual (Kroll *et al.*, 1970).

Can STS also hold semantic information? When traditional STM paradigms are used, the answer seems to be 'no' (Kintsch & Buschke, 1969; Craik & Levy, 1970), although Schulman (1970, 1972) believes it can.

Coding no longer seems to be a satisfactory basis for distinguishing STS/LTS. Although it could be argued that STS coding is flexible, this position removes an important characteristic by which one store is distinguished from another. We see the coding question as more appropriately formulated in terms of the processing demands imposed by the experimental design and the material to be remembered (see below).

FORGETTING CHARACTERISTICS

If this is to be used as a way of distinguishing STS/LTS, the retention function should be constant across different designs and experimental conditions. But there are cases where this clearly breaks down. For example, in paired-associate learning, STS retention extends over as many as 20 intervening items, while in free-recall and probe experiments (Waugh & Norman, 1965) STS information is lost much more quickly. Again, according to Neisser (1967), the icon (durability of the memory trace for visual stimuli) lasts one second or less, Posner (1969) gives an estimate of up to one to five seconds, while Murdock (1971), Phillips and Baddeley (1971) and Kroll *et al.* (1970) give estimates of six, ten and 25 seconds, respectively. Estimates of recognition memory for pictures are even longer (Shepard, 1967; Haber, 1970). Given that we recognize pictures, faces, melodies and voices after long periods of time, we clearly have LTM for relatively literal non-verbal information, making it difficult to draw a line between 'sensory memory' and 'representational' or 'pictorial' memory.

Whatever the limitations of the multistore model may be, obviously there are some basic findings which any model must accommodate. It seems certain that stimuli are encoded in different ways within the memory system, differently encoded representations seem to last for different lengths of time, and limited capacity at some points in the system seems real enough.

L E V E L S O F P R O C E S S I N G

THE STUDY

Many theorists now agree that perception involves the rapid analysis of stimuli at a number of levels or stages (Selfridge & Neisser, 1960; Treisman, 1964; Sutherland, 1968). Earlier stages are concerned with analysis of such physical or sensory features as lines, angles, brightness, pitch and loudness, while later stages are more concerned with matching the input against stored abstractions from past learning, i.e. pattern recognition and the extractions of meaning. This conception of a series or hierarchy of processing stages is often referred to as 'depth of processing' where greater 'depth' implies a greater degree of semantic or cognitive analysis. After the stimulus has been recognized, it may be further processed by enrichment or elaboration; e.g. a word may trigger associations, images or stores based on the subject's past experience of the word. Such 'elaboration coding' (Tulving & Madigan, 1970) is not restricted to verbal material. We believe that it applies to sounds, sights, smells and so on.

One of the results of this perceptual analysis is the memory trace: its coding characteristics and persistence arise as by-products of perceptual processing (Morton, 1970). Specifically, trace persistence is a function of depth of analysis, with deeper levels of analysis associated with more elaborate, longer-lasting and stronger traces. It is advantageous to store the products of deep analyses since the organism is normally concerned only with extracting meaning from the stimulus.

Highly familiar, meaningful stimuli are, by definition, compatible with existing cognitive structures. So pictures and sentences will be processed to a deep level more quickly than less meaningful material, and will be well retained. Retention is a function of depth, not speed of analysis; various factors such as the amount of attention given to a stimulus, its compatibility with the analysing structures and the processing time available, will determine the depth to which it is processed.

Thus, we prefer to think of memory as tied to levels of perceptual processing; although these levels may be grouped into stages (e.g. sensory analyses, pattern recognition, stimulus elaboration), they are more usefully thought of as a continuum. Similarly, memory is viewed as a continuum from the transient products of sensory analyses to the highly durable products of semantic-associative operations. Superimposed upon this basic memory system is a second way of retaining stimuli, namely through recirculating information at one level of processing, which is otherwise referred to as 'keeping the items in consciousness', 'holding the items in the rehearsal buffer' or 'retention of the items in primary memory'.

We accept Moray's (1967) notion of a limited-capacity central processor which may be used in several different ways. If it is used to maintain information at one level, the phenomena of STM will appear. The processor itself is neutral with regard to coding characteristics and the observed primary memory (PM) code will depend on the processing modality within which the processor is operating. Further, while limited capacity is a function of the processor itself, the number of items held will depend on the level at which the processor is operating: at deeper levels, the subject can make greater use of learned rules and past knowledge, with more efficient handling of material and more material retained. Some types of information (e.g. phonemic features of words) are particularly easy to maintain within PM while others (e.g. early visual analyses – the 'icon') are apparently impossible.

Our notion of PM is identical with that of James (1890) in that PM items are still in consciousness, still being processed or attended to; when attention is diverted, information will be lost at the rate appropriate to its level of processing: slower rates for deeper levels. However, continued processing (i.e. repetition of analyses already carried out – Type I) merely prolongs an item's high accessibility without leading to formation of a more permanent memory trace; Type II processing, by contrast, which involves deeper analysis, should lead to improved memory performance.

EXISTING DATA RE-EXAMINED

INCIDENTAL LEARNING

An important feature of the incidental learning paradigm is that the subject processes the material in a way compatible with, or determined by, the orienting task. Therefore, comparison of retention across different orienting tasks provides a relatively pure measure of the memorial consequences of different processing activities. We agree with Postman (1964) that the instruction to learn facilitates performance only in so far as it leads the subject to process the material in a more effective way than the processing induced by the orienting task in the incidental condition. It is, therefore, possible that with an appropriate orienting task and an inappropriate intentional strategy, learning under incidental conditions could be superior to that under intentional conditions.

So the Levels of Processing approach is interested in systematically studying retention following different orienting tasks within the incidental condition, rather than comparing incidental with intentional learning. Under incidental conditions, the experimenter has a control over the processing the subject applies to the material, which is missing when the subject is merely instructed to learn and uses an unknown coding strategy.

Tresselt and Mayzner (1960) tested free recall after incidental learning under three different orienting tasks: crossing out vowels, copying the words and judging how far the word was an instance of the concept 'economic'. Under the last condition,

THE STUDY

four times as many words were recalled than under the first, and twice as many as under the second condition. Similar results were found by Hyde and Jenkins (1969) and Johnston and Jenkins (1971), who showed that, with lists of highly associated word pairs, free recall and organization resulting from an orienting task requiring the use of the word as a semantic unit, was equivalent to that of an intentional control group with no incidental task, but both were substantially superior to that of an intentional group whose task was to treat the word structurally (checking for certain letters or estimating the number of letters in the word). Again, Mandler (1967) showed that incidental learning during categorization of words produced similar recall level to that of a group who performed the same task but who knew their recall would be tested.

Bobrow and Bower (1969) and Rosenberg and Schiller (1971) found that recall after an orienting task which required processing a sentence to a semantic level was substantially superior to recall of words from equivalently exposed sentences processed non-semantically.

Schulman (1971) had subjects scan a list of words for targets defined either structurally (e.g. words containing the letter 'a') or semantically (e.g. words denoting living things). On an unexpected test of recognition, performance of the 'semantic' group was significantly better than that of the 'structural' group, even though scanning time per word was approximately the same in most cases.

These findings support the general conclusion that memory performance is a positive function of the level of processing required by the orienting task. However, beyond a certain point, how effective a form of processing is depends on how the memory is tested. For example, Eagle and Leiter (1964) found that whereas free recall in an unhindered intentional condition was superior to that of an incidental group and a second intentional group who had also to perform the orienting task, these latter two groups were superior on a test of recognition.

SELECTIVE ATTENTION AND SENSORY STORAGE

Moray (1959) showed that words presented to the non-attended channel in a dichotic listening test were not recognized in a later memory test, and Neisser (1964) found that non-target items in a visual search task left no recognizable trace. So, if stimuli are only partially analysed, or processed only superficially, they do not stay in memory very long. In a neat demonstration of this, Treisman (1964) played the same prose passage to both ears dichotically, but staggered in time with the unattended ear leading: the lag had to be reduced to 1.5 seconds before the subject realized that the messages were identical. When the attended (shadowed) ear led, subjects noticed the similarity at a mean lag of 4.5 seconds. Thus, even though the subjects were not trying to remember the material in either case the further processing required by shadowing was sufficient to treble the durability of the memory trace. She also found that meaningfulness of the material (reversed speech versus normal speech, random words versus prose) affected the lag needed for recognition, but only when the attended channel was leading.

Many studies of sensory memory are also consistent with the Levels of Processing approach. For example, Neisser (1967) concluded that 'longer exposures lead to longer-lasting icons' and studies by Norman (1969), Glucksberg and Cowen (1970) and Peterson and Kroener (1964) all show that non-attended material is lost within a few seconds. Massaro (1970) suggested that memory for an item is directly related to the amount of perceptual processing, but his (1972) claim that echoic memory inevitably lasts only 250 milliseconds is probably an overgeneralization.

THE STS/LTS DISTINCTION

The phenomenon of a limited-capacity holding mechanism in memory (Miller, 1956; Broadbent, 1958) is handled in the present framework by assuming that a flexible central processor can be used at one of several levels in one of several encoding dimensions, and that it can only deal with a limited number of items at a time, i.e. items are kept in consciousness or in PM by continuing to rehearse them at a fixed level of processing. The nature of the items will depend upon the encoding dimension and the level within it: at deeper levels, the subject can make more use of learned cognitive structures, making the item more complex and semantic. The depth of PM will depend both upon the usefulness to the subject of continuing to process at that level and also upon how easily the material can be more deeply processed. For example, if the subject's task is merely to reproduce a few words seconds after hearing them, phonemic analysis will be sufficient, but if the words form a meaningful sentence, deeper levels are needed, and longer units can be dealt with. It seems that PM deals at any level with units or 'chunks' rather than with information (Kintsch, 1970), i.e. we rehearse a sound, letter, word, idea or image in the same way that we perceive objects, not collections of attributes.

Regarding the claimed differences in coding between STS and LTS, we argue that acoustic errors will predominate only in so far as analysis has not proceeded to a semantic level. Much of the data on acoustic confusions in STM is based on material such as letters and digits which have relatively little semantic content, so the nature of the material itself tends to constrain processing to a structural level of analysis, and, not surprisingly, structural errors result.

The finding that presentation rate and word frequency can affect LT but not ST retention (Glanzer, 1972) can be interpreted thus: increasing presentation rate, or using unfamiliar words, inhibits processing to those levels necessary to support LT retention but not ST retention. Conversely, manipulating processing at a structural level (e.g. modality differences – Murdock, 1966) should have transitory, but no long-term, effects.

THE SERIAL POSITION CURVE

In free recall, the recency effect has been taken to reflect output from STS and the primacy effect, output from LTS (Glanzer & Cunitz, 1966). Perhaps the most plausible explanation is that initial items receive more rehearsals and so are better registered in LTS (Atkinson & Shiffrin, 1968; Bruce & Papay, 1970). In Levels of Processing terms, since the subject knows he must stop attending to initial items in order to perceive and rehearse subsequent ones, he subjects the first items to Type II processing, i.e. deeper semantic processing, while late items can survive on phonemic encoding. It would follow that in a subsequent recall test, final items should be recalled least well of all list items (i.e. negative recency) and this has in fact been found (Craik, 1970). But recency items were rehearsed fewer times than earlier items (Rundus, 1971). However, Jacoby and Bartz (1972), Watkins (1972) and Craik (1972) have all shown that it is the type – rather than the amount – of processing which determines the subsequent recall of the last few items in a list.

REPETITION AND REHEARSAL EFFECTS

The effects of repeated presentation depend on whether the repeated stimulus is merely processed to the same level or encoded differently on its further presentations. There is evidence, both in audition (Moray, 1959; Norman, 1969) and in vision (Turvey, 1967) that repetition of an item encoded only at a sensory level, does not improve memory performance. Tulving (1966) has also shown that repetition without intention to learn does not facilitate learning. His experiment, together with one by Glanzer and Meinzer (1967), shows that the suggestion that rehearsal both maintains information in PM and transfers it to LTM (Waugh & Norman, 1965; Atkinson & Shiffrin, 1968) is not necessarily so.

C O N C L U D I N G   C O M M E N T S

The Levels of Processing approach has much in common with that of Cermak (1972), Bower (1967) and Norman and Rumelhart (1970). Similarly, Posner (1969) advocates stages of processing with different characteristics associated with each stage.

If the memory trace is viewed as the by-product of perceptual analysis, an important goal of future research will be to specify the memorial consequences of various types of perceptual operations. Since deeper analysis will usually involve longer processing time, it will be crucial to disentangle such variables as study time and amount of effort from depth.

Our approach does not constitute a theory of memory, but a conceptual framework within which memory research might proceed. Multistore models have been useful but are often taken too literally. Our approach is speculative and incomplete: memory has been looked at purely from the input or encoding end, and no attempt has been made to specify either how items are grouped together and organized or how they are retrieved. Our approach provides an appropriate framework within which these processes can be understood.

EVALUATION

Theoretical issues

According to Eysenck (1984, 1986), LOP was probably the most influential theoretical approach in memory during the 1970s, but it rapidly went out of favour after that. He says that most psychologists believe it contains a grain of truth, but is a substantial over-simplification. We should note, though, that Craik and Lockhart themselves claim (in the final paragraph) that their approach does *not* constitute a theory of memory, but a *conceptual framework* for memory research (and see the title of their article). Earlier in the article they refer to it as offering a new way of interpreting existing data, and as providing a *heuristic framework* for further research (i.e. a strategy, empirical rule or 'rule of thumb' which drastically reduces the amount of 'work' that must be done when trying to solve a problem). However, many people regarded it as a theory (for example, it allows several specific predictions to be made) and, as such, it became the target for criticism (Eysenck & Keane, 2000; Parkin, 2000: see below).

It is basically concerned with the role of coding in learning, and the relationship between how material is processed and the probability that it will subsequently be remembered. As such, it is primarily a theory of LTM (Baddeley, 1999). Craik and Lockhart did not reject the STM/LTM distinction, but they argued that it failed to reveal anything new about human memory; while the multistore model begins with structural components, LOP begins with encoding processes. LOP in fact assumes a primary/STM system that actually does the coding, but details of this are left so unspecified that the 'levels' approach has often, mistakenly, been taken to represent a unitary approach to memory (i.e. there is no STM/LTM distinction) (Baddeley, 1999).

Parkin (1993) points out that Craik and Lockhart were on safe ground in claiming that retention of a stimulus would be a positive function of the depth of processing. During the 1950s and 60s there was considerable interest in *incidental learning*, which makes use of a technique called the *orienting task* (a task requiring a decision about one particular dimension of a stimulus). The point about incidental learning is that participants are not told that they will be asked to remember the presented material (if they were, it would be called *intentional learning*), so that what they in fact remember is a function of the processing involved in the orienting task.

Craik & Tulving (1975) carried out a series of experiments which demonstrated that the deeper the level of processing required by the orienting task, the better the retention. So, for example, being asked, 'Is the word in capital letters? [TABLE/table] represents a *structural* or *orthographic* level of processing, 'Does the word rhyme with wait? [hate/chicken], represents a *phonetic* or *phonemic* level, and 'Is the word a type of food? [cheese/steel] and 'Would the word fit the sentence: 'He kicked the . . . . into the tree'? [ball/rain] both represent a *semantic* level of processing. A consistent finding was that semantic processing produced the best retention, followed by phonetic, with structural producing the poorest, when participants were given an unexpected test of recognition (i.e. a test of incidental learning).

However, Lockhart & Craik (1990) accept that much of their original LOP model was oversimplified. For example:

(*i*)   Originally, Craik and Lockhart saw processing as under the control of a *central processor* with limited but flexible capacity to deal with new information. Retention depended on how the central processor was used during learning (deeper level of processing produces better retention). Embodied in this idea was the *coordinality assumption*, according to which the nature of the processing undertaken in response to an orienting task was directly related to the overt demands of the task. So, if you were asked whether 'TABLE' was in upper or lower case letters, your processing was taken to be *restricted* to the structural or orthographic level. In its extreme form, this assumption is patently wrong. There is abundant evidence that when we look at a word, we are automatically aware of its meaning (Parkin, 2000). The classic demonstration of this is the *Stroop effect* (see **Exercises** below). Although the exact explanation of the Stroop effect is still unclear:

> . . . what we can conclude is that human beings are not able to orient their attention precisely to task demands and that irrelevant information, particularly meaning, is processed regardless of instructions . . . (Parkin, 1993)

Because of phenomena like Stroop, Craik & Tulving (1975) proposed that any stimulus at first undergoes a *minimal core encoding*, which includes a degree of semantic analysis, followed by consciously directed processing appropriate to the task demands. The latter are *effortful* (they depend on some conscious commitment).

(*ii*)   The original model implied that processing takes place in an ordered sequence, from shallower through to deeper. But instead of this continuum, they are now seen as constituting separate 'domains'. This reflected the logical point that it is not possible to pass gradually from, say, structural to phonetic levels, because they contain *qualitatively* different dimensions of information processing which do not overlap in any way (Parkin, 1993).

Methodological issues

Probably the most serious problem with LOP is the difficulty of measuring or defining depth *independently* of the actual retention score: if 'depth' is defined as 'how many words are remembered', and if 'how many words are remembered' is taken as a measure of 'depth', we are faced with a *circular* definition.

Craik & Tulving (1975) were well aware of this problem and they proposed a solution in the form of *processing time*. Based on their observation that semantic orienting tasks always took longer to perform, they devised a non-semantic task that took longer than a semantic one and reasoned that, if processing time were a valid independent measure of depth, the former should produce the best retention. But it did not: despite taking *less* time, the semantic task still produced the best results. Ironically, this was 'good' news for LOP, because if the non-semantic task had proved more effective, it would mean that the relationship between learning and memory is determined merely by how long we spend attending to the stimulus, undermining the whole idea (central to LOP) that memory can be affected by qualitative differences in how information is encoded (Parkin, 1993, 2000).

A different attempt to provide an independent measure of depth was in terms of the kind of orienting task used. Hyde & Jenkins (1973) used five orienting tasks, meant to vary in the amount of processing of meaning involved. These were: (*i*) rating words for pleasantness; (*ii*) estimating the frequency with which the words are used in English; (*iii*) detecting the number of 'e's and 'g's in the words; (*iv*) deciding the part of speech appropriate to each word (noun/verb/adjective/'some other'); (*v*) deciding whether or not the word fitted various sentence frames ('it is the . . .'/'it is . . .'). Hyde and Jenkins defined (i) and (ii) as involving semantic (deep) processing, and (iii), (iv) and (v) as involving non-semantic (shallow) processing. The prediction, of course, was that (i) and (ii) would produce significantly higher retention, and this was, indeed, found. However, the assumption that (i) and (ii) involved thinking of the word's meaning while (iv) did not, has been challenged. If it is no more than an assumption, we are again faced with the lack of an adequate, independent, measure of 'depth' (and, as we saw above when discussing the Stroop effect, we cannot simply equate type of orienting task with the actual processing which takes place). It is impossible to completely control participants' processing activities (Eysenck, 1984, 1986).

Parkin (1979, cited in Parkin, 1993) took up the circularity problem in a series of experiments designed to test whether semantic and non-semantic processing tasks could be distinguished in terms of their ability to evoke associative processing. It is well established that if two words are presented sequentially, identification of the second word is enhanced if it is associatively related to the first (e.g. table-chair). This is called *associative priming*. Semantic tasks should allow this to occur, because they direct conscious processing into the semantic domain (which is where word association 'resides'). Participants were first shown a single word and asked to make either a semantic or non-semantic orienting decision about it. They were then shown a second word, written in coloured ink, which was either an associated or unassociated word, and the task was to name the colour of the ink as quickly as they could. (This second task was, of course, a variant of the Stroop effect.) Participants in the semantic condition took significantly longer to name the colour of the ink when the second word was associated with the first (but association had no influence in the non-semantic condition), indicating that associative priming had taken place. In turn, the associative priming made it easier to identify the second word as well as more difficult to ignore, hence the delay in naming the colour of the ink (*associative interference effect*). Also, recall from the semantic condition was superior. These experiments indicated a solution to the circularity problem, but they have not been followed up (Parkin, 1993).

Subsequent research

Eysenck (1984, 1986) argues that learning and memory are affected by at least four factors: (*i*) nature of the task; (*ii*) the kind of stimulus material used; (*iii*) individual characteristics of the participants (e.g. idiosyncratic knowledge), and (*iv*) the nature of the retention test used to measure memory. In many LOP experiments, several orienting tasks are used, but only one kind of stimulus material (usually words), one fairly homogeneous set of participants, and one kind of retention test (e.g. Hyde & Jenkins, 1973, used only free recall).

However, there are often large *interactions* between the four factors, as demonstrated in a study by Morris *et al.* (1977). They predicted that stored information (whether deep or shallow) will be remembered only to the extent that it is *relevant* to the memory test used. So, deep or semantic information would be of little use if the memory test involved learning a list of words and later selecting words that rhymed with the stored words, while shallow rhyme information would be very relevant. As an initial orienting task, the experimenter read aloud 32 sentences with one word missing from each. Each sentence was followed by vocal presentation of the target word. The participant had to say 'yes' if the target word could appropriately be inserted into the preceding sentence, and 'no' if it couldn't (half the target words could, half could not). For half the sentences, the input-orienting task was semantic, and for the other half it was a rhyme-orienting task. All participants heard all the sentences. Half the participants were given a *standard recognition test* (the 32 original targets were mixed with 32 distractors: participants had to say 'yes' to the targets and 'no' to the distractors), and the other half a *rhyming recognition test* (new words were presented and participants had to say 'yes' to the new words which rhymed with the original targets and 'no' to those that didn't). The usual LOP effect was found (i.e. better retention) in the standard recognition test, but the reverse was true for the rhyming recognition test.

This finding represents an experimental disproof of LOP, specifically the idea that deep processing is *intrinsically* more memorable than shallow processing. The results also demonstrate that how memory is tested must be taken into account when we are trying to predict the consequences of some processing activity: LTM is determined by the relevance of stored information to any given retention test. As Parkin (1993, 2000) puts it, different orienting tasks vary in the extent to which they require participants to regard the stimulus *as a word* (e.g. 'is "tiger" a mammal?' compared with 'does "tiger" have two syllables?'). But retention tests *always* demand that participants remember *words*. Since semantic tasks (by definition) always require attention to be paid to stimuli as words, the superior retention they produce could reflect the bias of the retention test towards the type of information being encoded. Again, a semantic orienting task and a retention test are both concerned with the same kind of information, while a structural or phonetic orienting task and a retention test are not: the former is bound to produce better performance for this reason alone. This is called *transfer-appropriate processing* (Morris *et al.*, 1977) which, since it is rather difficult to dispute, rather deflated the LOP approach (Parkin, 1998).

Another major problem is that LOP is more of a *description* than an explanation: we are not told *why* semantic processing usually produces better retention (Eysenck & Keane, 2000). More recent attempts have been made to extend and modify (or even replace) the original model, using the concepts of *elaboration* and *distinctiveness* (see Eysenck & Keane, 1995).

Eysenck (1984, 1986) believes it is often difficult to choose between LOP, elaboration and distinctiveness because they tend to occur together. It is possible that all three make separate contributions to LTM, but distinctiveness, which relates to the *nature* of processing, is likely to prove more important than elaboration, which is only a measure of the *amount* of processing.

Applications and implications

According to Parkin (1998, 2000), it is quite easy to view the whole LOP idea as something of a blind alley in memory research. As a theory, it proved largely untestable; moreover, it failed to establish any absolute principles of learning. However, this rather dismissive view may not be justified. Before Craik & Lockhart's (1972) paper, memory theorists had paid little attention to the relationship between perception and memory, and to the idea that encoding processes could be flexible (see **Aim and nature of the study** above). LOP showed the enormous variation in encoding that could occur, and all theorizing about memory now takes account of this basic observation. Furthermore, LOP provided the first substantial framework within which one could talk meaningfully of 'encoding deficits' as a reason for memory failure. Finally, the concept of processes, as opposed to systems, and the idea of transfer-appropriate processing, have continued to be influential.

According to Baddeley (1997), although LOP has had limited theoretical power, it was

expected to prove useful as a rule of thumb. Unfortunately, it has so far proved less generally helpful than at first seemed likely. Bower & Karlin (1974) did show that judgements of the honesty of a person in a photograph produced better subsequent recognition than judgement of the person's gender. However, later research indicated that *any* form of coding that induced perception of faces as a whole resulted in slightly better performance than instructions to concentrate on specified physical features. Whether the judgement was apparently deep (such as assessing intelligence or honesty) or shallow (such as merely trying to assess the person's height from the face) made no difference (Winograd, 1976).

Rather more success seems to have come from relating memory deficits in the elderly to depth of processing, but even here things are less clear cut than at first appeared. Similarly, as applied to amnesic patients, LOP's early promise has not been fulfilled (Baddeley, 1997). However, the LOP approach indirectly stimulated research into working memory. As we noted in **Theoretical issues** above, LOP research tended to emphasize factors governing retrieval from LTM. According to Baddeley (1999):

> . . . Short-term memory studies became more closely associated with problems of attention, and with the role of short-term memory in other tasks such as reading and mental arithmetic. This led to the concept of a unitary short-term memory being replaced by that of a multi-component working memory.

Exercises

1. What is the difference between a heuristic and an algorithm?

2. What is the *Stroop effect*?

3. In STM, what other theories of forgetting are there apart from displacement?

4. In LTM, what other theories of forgetting are there, apart from displacement?

5. What is meant by 'chunking' (as a way of increasing STM capacity)?

6. What kind of retention is being tested in
    (*i*) essay-based exams?
    (*ii*) multiple-choice tests?

7. Give two examples of an orienting task used to study LOP.

8. What is the difference between incidental and intentional learning? Why is it important for participants in LOP experiments to be tested under the former conditions?

5 Reconstruction of automobile destruction: An example of the interaction between language and memory

E.F. Loftus and J.C. Palmer (1974)

Journal of Verbal Learning & Verbal Behaviour, 13, 585-589

BACKGROUND AND CONTEXT

The general theoretical framework of Loftus and Palmer's experiment is originally that of Bartlett (1932). In contrast to those models of memory based on stimulus-response theory (associationist models), Bartlett saw memory as involving interpretation and reconstruction of the past. We try to fit past events into our existing *schemata* (mental models or representations of the world), making them more logical, coherent and generally 'sensible', drawing inferences or deductions about what might or should have happened (all this being part of our 'efforts after meaning'). So, rather than human memory being computer-like, with the output matching the input, Bartlett saw it as an active attempt to understand – an 'imaginative reconstruction' of experience.

What is now referred to as 'schema theory' (e.g. Rumelhart & Norman, 1983) regards what we already know about the world as a major influence on what we remember. The use of past experience to deal with new experience is a fundamental feature of the way the human mind works (Cohen, 1993). The knowledge we have stored in memory is organized as a set of schemas, each incorporating all the knowledge of a given type of object or event, acquired from past experience. Schemas operate in a 'top-down' direction to help interpret the 'bottom-up' flow of information from the world. New experiences are not just passively 'copied' or recorded into memory; rather, a memory representation is actively constructed by processes that are strongly influenced by schemas (Cohen, 1993).

Schema theory is not just interesting from an academic perspective. When applied to real-life situations such as eyewitness testimony (EWT), these ideas about the reconstructive and interpretative nature of memory assume critical importance. The greater the unreliability (inaccuracy) of human memory, and the greater the

importance of EWT in cases of crimes and accidents, the greater the likelihood that people will be wrongly accused and convicted (a false positive error) and that the guilty will not come to justice (a false negative error).

Loftus is a pioneer (and still a leading figure) in the field of EWT research, which represents an application of cognitive psychology to real-world, social phenomena. Her basic procedure has been to manipulate the questions participants are asked about a film or slides of an automobile accident (or staged crime), in order to see how these can affect what they remember of the incident. This procedure is an attempt to simulate real-world events in which witnesses are asked questions (often very misleading ones) by police and lawyers.

There is a good deal of support for the reconstructive hypothesis. EWT can easily be distorted, and modified, by information which becomes available *subsequent* to the actual event – even to the extent of 'remembering' things which were not actually seen in the original event. Loftus believes that this new information becomes incorporated into the memory, updating it, and erasing any of the original information which is inconsistent with it (the *substitution hypothesis*). This subsequent information can be presented *either* in the form of *leading questions* (as in the present study), *or* through questions which introduce *after-the-fact information* (as in Loftus, 1975: see **Evaluation** below).

AIM AND NATURE OF THE STUDY

The study was conducted to investigate the influence of the wording of the question used to tap participants' estimates of speed (how fast two cars involved in an accident were travelling) on the actual speed estimate. Loftus and Palmer define a *leading question* as one that, either by its form or its content, suggests to the witness what answer is desired, or leads him/her to the desired answer. So, the leading question represents the *independent variable*, while the speed estimate represents the *dependent variable*. In fact, the study comprises two separate, but related, experiments.

In Experiment 1, 45 students, divided into five groups, watched seven different films of traffic accidents (the films lasting from between 5 and 30 seconds). Following each film, participants were asked a series of specific questions about the accident, the critical question being the one about the speed the cars were travelling. What was manipulated was the verb used to refer to how the cars 'touched'. So, each of the five groups received the same form of the question ('About how fast were the cars going when they —— each other?'), but the missing word was either *contacted, hit, bumped, collided* or *smashed*. The specific verb used in the critical question, therefore, was the *independent variable*. The average (mean) speed estimate given in response to this question was the *dependent variable*.

Loftus and Palmer do not actually state the hypothesis, or state what they expect the results to be (as they do for Experiment 2: see below). But *by implication* they expect that the verbs will produce increasingly higher speed estimates (i.e. *contacted* will produce the lowest and *smashed* the highest).

In Experiment 2, 150 students, divided into three groups, watched a film of a car accident (lasting just four seconds). As in Experiment 1, they were then asked a series of questions, one of which was the critical speed question. But this time, only *hit* and *smashed* were used, with the third group not being asked about speed at all. Again, the specific verb used in the critical question was the *independent variable*.

A week later the participants returned, and without seeing the film again they answered a series of questions about the accident. This time, the critical question was 'Did you see any broken glass?', and participants answered by checking 'yes' or 'no'. Their response to the broken glass question was the *independent variable*.

While there was *no* broken glass in the accident, it is consistent with accidents occurring at high speed. So, Loftus and Palmer expected that participants in the *smashed* group would be more likely to say 'yes' than those in the other two groups. This, therefore, constitutes the hypothesis.

■ T ■ H ■ E ■ ■ S ■ T ■ U ■ D ■ Y ■

How accurately do we remember the details of a complex event, like a traffic accident, that has happened in our presence? More specifically, how well do we do when asked to estimate some numerical quantity such as how long the accident took, how fast the cars were traveling, or how much time elapsed between the sounding of a horn and the moment of collision?

It is well documented that most people are markedly inaccurate in reporting such numerical details as time, speed, and distance (Bird, 1927; Whipple, 1909). For example, most people have difficulty estimating the duration of an event, with some research indicating that the tendency is to overestimate the duration of events which are complex (Block, 1974; Marshall, 1969; Ornstein, 1969). The judgement of speed is especially difficult, and practically every automobile accident results in huge variations from one witness to another as to how fast a vehicle was actually travelling (Gardner, 1933). In one test administered to Air Force personnel who knew in advance that they would be questioned about the speed of a moving car, estimates ranged from 10 to 50 mph. The car they watched was actually going only 12 mph (Marshall, 1969).

Given the inaccuracies in estimates of speed, it seems likely that there are variables which are potentially powerful influences on these estimates. The present research was conducted to investigate one such variable, namely, the phrasing of the question used to elicit the speed judgement. Some questions are clearly more suggestive than others. This fact of life has resulted in the legal concept of a leading question and in legal rules indicating when leading questions are allowed. A leading question is simply one that, either by its form or content, suggests to the witness what answer is desired or leads him to the desired answer.

In the present study, subjects were shown films of traffic accidents and then asked questions about the accident. The subjects were questioned about the speed of the vehicles in one of several ways. For example, some were asked, 'About how fast were the cars going when they hit each other?', while others were asked, 'About how fast were the cars going when they smashed into each other?' As Fillmore (1971) and Bransford & McCarrell (1974) have noted, *hit* and *smashed* may involve specification of differential rates of movement. Furthermore, the two verbs may also involve differential specification of the likely consequences of the events to which they are referring. The impact of the accident is apparently gentler for *hit* than for *smashed*.

E X P E R I M E N T   1

METHOD

Forty-five students participated in groups of various sizes. Seven films were shown, each depicting a traffic accident. These films were segments from longer drivers' education films borrowed from the Evergreen Safety Council and the Seattle Police Department. The length of the segments ranged from 5 to 30 seconds. Following each film, the subjects received a questionnaire asking them first to 'give an account of the accident you have just seen', and then to answer a series of specific questions about the accident. The critical question was the one that asked the subject about the speed of the vehicles involved in the collision. Nine subjects were asked, 'About how fast were the cars going when they hit each other?' Equal numbers of the remaining subjects were questioned with the verbs *smashed, collided, bumped,* and *contacted* in place of *hit.* The entire experiment lasted about an hour and a half. A different ordering of the films was presented to each group of subjects.

RESULTS

Table 5.1 presents the mean speed estimates for the various verbs. An analysis of variance was performed with verbs as a fixed effect, and subjects and films as random effects, yielding a significant quasi-F ratio, F' (5,55) = 4.65, *p* < .005.

Some information about the accuracy of subjects' estimates can be obtained from our data. Four of the seven films were staged crashes; their original purpose was to illustrate what can happen to human beings when cars collide at various speeds.

Table 5.1

SPEED ESTIMATES FOR THE VERBS USED IN EXPERIMENT 1

Verb	Mean speed estimates
Smashed	40.8
Collided	39.3
Bumped	38.1
Hit	34.0
Contacted	31.8

One collision took place at 20mph, one at 30, and two at 40. The mean speed estimates for these four films were: 37.7, 36.2, 39.7, and 36.1 mph respectively. In agreement with previous work, people are not very good at judging how fast a vehicle was actually traveling.

DISCUSSION

The results of this experiment indicate that the form of a question (in this case, changes in a single word) can markedly and systematically affect a witness's answer to the question. The actual speed of the vehicles accounted for little variance in subject reporting, while the phrasing of the question accounted for considerable variance.

Two interpretations of this finding are possible. First, it is possible that the differential speed estimates result merely from response–bias factors. A subject is uncertain whether to say 30 mph or 40 mph, for example, and the verb *smashed* biases his response towards the higher estimate. Second, the question form causes a change in the subject's memory representation of the accident. The verb *smashed* may change a subject's memory such that he 'sees' the accident as being more severe than it actually was. If this is the case, we might expect subjects to 'remember' other details that did not actually occur, but are consistent with an accident occurring at higher speeds. The second experiment was designed to provide additional insights into the origin of the differential speed estimates.

E X P E R I M E N T   2

METHOD

One hundred and fifty students participated in this experiment, in groups of various sizes. A film depicting a multiple car accident was shown, followed by a questionnaire. The film lasted less than a minute; the accident in the film lasted four seconds. At the end of the film, the subjects received a questionnaire asking them first to describe the accident in their own words, and then to answer a series of questions about the accident. The critical question was the one that asked them about the speed of the vehicles. Fifty subjects were asked, 'About how fast were the cars going when they smashed into each other?' Fifty were asked, 'About how fast were the cars going when they hit each other?' Fifty were not questioned about vehicular speed.

One week later, the subjects returned and without viewing the film again they answered a series of questions about the accident. The critical question here was, 'Did you see any broken glass?' which the subjects answered by checking 'yes' or 'no'. This question was embedded in a list of questions, and it appeared in a random position in the list. There was *no* broken glass in the accident, but, since broken glass is consistent with accidents occurring at high speed, we expected that the subjects who had been asked the *smashed* question might more often say 'yes' to this critical question.

RESULTS

The mean estimate of speed for subjects questioned with *smashed* was 10.46 mph; with *hit* the estimate was 8.00 mph. These means are significantly different, t (98) = 2.00, $p < .05$. Table 5.2 presents the distribution of 'yes' and 'no' responses for the *smashed, hit,* and control subjects. An independence chi-square test on these responses was significant beyond the .025 level, χ_2 (2) = 7.76.

Table 5.2

DISTRIBUTION OF 'YES' AND 'NO' RESPONSES TO THE QUESTION 'DID YOU SEE ANY BROKEN GLASS?'

Response	Verb condition		
	Smashed	Hit	Control
Yes	16	7	6
No	34	43	44

THE STUDY

The important result in Table 5.2 is that the probability of saying 'yes' *P(Y)* to the question about the broken glass is .32 when the verb *smashed* is used, and .14 with *hit*. Thus, *smashed* leads both to more 'yes' responses and to higher speed estimates. It appears to be the case that the effect of the verb is mediated at least partly by the speed estimate. The question now arises: Is *smashed* doing anything else besides increasing the estimate of speed? To answer this, the function relating *P(Y)* to speed estimate was calculated separately for *smashed* and *hit*. If the speed estimate is the only way in which effect of verb is mediated, then for a given speed estimate, *P(Y)* should be independent of verb. Table 5.3 shows that this is *not* the case: *P(Y)* is lower for *hit* than for *smashed*; the difference between the two verbs ranges from .03 for estimates of 1–5 mph to .18 for estimates of 6–10 mph. The average difference between the two curves is about .12. Whereas the unconditional difference of .18 between the *smashed* and *hit* conditions is attenuated, it is by no means eliminated when estimate of speed is controlled for. It thus appears that the verb *smashed* has other effects besides that of simply increasing the estimate of speed.

Table 5.3

PROBABILITY OF SAYING 'YES' TO 'DID YOU SEE ANY BROKEN GLASS?'
CONDITIONALIZED ON SPEED ESTIMATES

	Speed estimate (mph)			
	1-5	6-10	11-15	16-20
Verb	Condition			
Smashed	.09	.27	.41	.62
Hit	.06	.09	.25	.50

DISCUSSION

We have first of all provided an additional demonstration of something that has been known for sometime, namely, that the way a question is asked can enormously influence the answer that is given. In this instance, the question, 'About how fast were the cars going when they smashed into each other?' led to higher estimates of speed than the same questions asked with the verb *smashed* replaced by *hit*. Furthermore, this seemingly small change had consequences for how questions are answered a week after the original event occurred.

As a framework for discussing these results, we would like to propose that two kinds of information go into one's memory for some complex occurrence. The first is information gleaned during the perception of the original event; the second is external information supplied after the fact. Over time, information from these two sources may become integrated in such a way that we are unable to tell from which source some specific detail is recalled. All we have is one 'memory'.

Discussing the present experiments in these terms, we propose that the subject first forms some representation of the accident he has witnessed. The experimenter then, while asking, 'About how fast were the cars going when they smashed into each other?' supplies a piece of external information, namely, that the cars did indeed smash into each other. When these two pieces of information are integrated, the subject has a memory of an accident that was more severe than it actually was. Since broken glass is consistent with a severe accident, the subject is more likely to think that broken glass was present. There is some connection between the present work and earlier work on the influence of verbal labels on memory for visually presented form stimuli. A classic study in psychology showed that when subjects are asked to reproduce a visually presented form, their drawings tend to err in the direction of a more familiar object suggested by a verbal label initially associated with the to-be-remembered form (Carmichael, Hogan, and Walter, 1932). More recently, Daniel (1972) showed that recognition memory, as well as reproductive memory, was similarly affected by verbal labels, and he concluded that the verbal label causes a shift in the memory strength of forms which are better representatives of the label.

When the experimenter asks the subject, 'About how fast were the cars going when they smashed into each other?' he is effectively labelling the accident a smash. Extrapolating the conclusions of Daniel to this situation, it is natural to conclude that the label *smash* causes a shift in the memory representation of the accident in the direction of being more similar to a representation suggested by the verbal label.

EVALUATION

Theoretical issues

As we noted in **Background and context**, Loftus favours the *substitution hypothesis* account of what happens to the original memory when recall has been influenced by misleading information. But does it cause memory to undergo change (so that participants are truly *misremembering*), or is the memorial representation merely being *supplemented* by the additional information contained in the misleading questions? According to the idea of *memory as reconstruction*, the memory itself is transformed at the time of retrieval, so that what was originally encoded changes at the point of recall. This is the most important theoretical issue to emerge from the EWT research, and is relevant to general theories of memory as well as EWT itself (Cohen, 1993). According to Loftus, the false, misleading information displaces or transforms the original accurate information, which is then irretrievably lost.

The main alternative explanation is the *co-existence hypothesis*, according to which *both* the original, true version *and* the false, misleading version of the event are retained in memory. Participants usually give the latter, because this was the more recently presented, making it more accessible. This, of course, implies that the original memory still exists and could, in principle, be recovered. But this is unlikely to be true when the two versions are inconsistent: people would have to believe two contradictory things at the same time. In common with the co-existence hypothesis, the notions of *response bias* (post-event information biases the response given on questioning, such that participants choose the most recently given information) and *demand characteristics* (participants report what they believe is expected of them) imply that both memories exist and are equally retrievable.

The present study appears to support the substitution hypothesis. If the *smashed* participants really saw the accident as more serious than the other groups, then they might also 'remember' details (such as broken glass) that were not actually present but which are consistent with an accident occurring at high speed. The results suggest that the answer to the broken glass question was determined by the earlier question about speed, which had *changed* what was originally encoded when seeing the film.

Does the EWT research lend support to schema theory (see **Background and context** above)? According to Alba & Hasher (1983), it does. But Cohen (1993) believes that Loftus's misled witnesses are not only integrating prior knowledge from internal schemas about car accidents etc. with knowledge derived from recent observed events. They are also combining information from two *different external sources*: the observed event, and subsequent verbal information about the event. Clearly, memories are not simple copies of events, but may sometimes be composites based on different sources of information.

According to Fiske & Taylor (1991), the distinction between *episodic* and *semantic memory* (Tulving, 1972) is useful in understanding EWT. A 'leading' question might refer to things which were not actually present at the scene of the crime (*episodic*), but which would be a quite reasonable inference to make in these circumstances (*semantic*, which includes all our schemas and stereotyped beliefs about the world). It is easy to see how a witness could confuse the mention of something in a question with its actual presence at the scene of the crime, if that something is commonly found in such situations. Similarly, if a witness examines a preliminary identity parade, s/he may later remember having seen one of the suspects before, but *not* distinguish between the identity parade and the scene of the crime: the innocent suspect may be misidentified as the criminal because s/he is familiar! Taking this one stage further back, the suspect in the identity parade could be 'recognized' from an artist's impression or photofit picture of the suspect.

However, not everyone agrees with Loftus that post-event information changes the witness's original memory, never to be retrieved again. A number of studies (e.g. Bekerian & Bowers, 1983; Smith & Ellsworth, 1987) indicate that witnesses merely follow the questioner's suggestions, leaving the original memory intact for retrieval under appropriate conditions (Fiske & Taylor, 1991). According to Baddeley (1995), '. . . the Loftus effect is not due to destruction of the memory trace but is due to interference with its retrieval'. Indeed, some of her own research has shown that witnesses cannot always be misled so easily. Loftus (1979) reports that integration does not happen if the misleading information is 'blatantly incorrect'. In one experiment, participants saw colour slides of a man stealing a red purse from a woman's bag. Ninety-eight per cent correctly remembered the colour of the purse. When they read a narrative description of the event containing a 'brown purse', all but two continued to remember it as red.

Thus, memory for obviously important information which is accurately perceived at the time is not easily distorted. In the above example, the colour of the purse is the focus of the whole incident, not a peripheral detail. Cohen (1993) points out that the experiment also showed that once participants recognized one piece of misleading information as false, they were more distrustful and less likely to be misled by any subsequent false information. Cohen summarizes the findings of several studies by saying that people are more likely to be misled if: (*i*) the false information concerns insignificant details which are peripheral to the main event; (*ii*) the false information is given after a delay, when the memory of the actual event has had time to fade; (*iii*) participants are not aware that they may be deliberately misinformed and so have no reason to distrust the information.

Loftus (1991) herself has suggested that changes in the original memory probably only happen to a limited extent. More important is *misinformation acceptance*: eyewitnesses are often willing to 'accept' misleading post-event information, later regarding it as part of their memory for the original event. This tendency increases as the original memory fades over time (Croyle & Loftus, 1995; Loftus, 1997).

Cohen (1993) also believes that EWT research has concentrated on the *fallibility* of memory, and so gives a rather one-sided picture (see **Applications and implications** below). Also, much of the evidence regarding the distorting effects of post-event information is based on experiments involving fairly trivial details (such as broken glass).

Methodological issues

Cohen (1993) argues that many of the errors found in EWT experiments occur because participants are forced to give 'yes' or 'no' answers to direct questions. In real-life situations, where open-ended questions are used and witnesses can respond with

'Don't know' and 'Not sure', testimony is often much more accurate. Conversely, laboratory studies on the accuracy of face recognition (which show very high accuracy, at least for same-race faces) are contradicted by real-world research on EWT: people often do little better than guess when trying to identify an alleged criminal in an identity parade (Fiske & Taylor, 1991).

There are some fairly obvious, and quite crucial differences between the two settings which can largely account for these conflicting results. In the laboratory, stimuli are not moving, distractions are minimal, emotional arousal and involvement are virtually absent, viewing conditions are unobscured and well-lit, witnesses can take their time and so on. EWT research reverses most of these conditions. In addition, laboratory studies tend to use the same photograph as both stimulus and test item, while under real-life 'conditions', real people are the 'stimuli', whose clothing, facial expressions and perhaps other aspects of their appearance may vary from initial encounter to subsequent identification. When photographs used in experiments show the person from different viewpoints with different expressions, hairstyle, clothing, and under different lighting conditions, recognition memory performance is significantly reduced (Bruce, 1998). Furthermore, crimes against people (whether staged or real) are often very fast, unexpected and confusing. So differences between the results of these two kinds of research are hardly surprising.

One famous case-study of a real crime involved a gun-shop owner who shot and killed the man who stole money and guns from the store (Yuille & Cutshall, 1986). Twenty-one of the much larger number of witnesses were interviewed by the police shortly after the event and 13 of them agreed to take part in a research interview, four to five months later. Included among the researchers' questions, intended to clarify points of detail, were two misleading questions based on Loftus & Zanni's (1975) 'a'/'the' broken headlight technique (see **Subsequent research** below). The sheer volume of accurate detail produced in both the police and research interviews was truly impressive. There was very little invention or 'reconstruction', except when a witness observed the event from a disadvantageous viewpoint, such as a passing car or a considerable distance.

Subsequent research

According to Garry, Loftus & Brown (1994), there are four different kinds of memory-distortion studies:

(a) Those concerned with the effect of leading questions (e.g. the present Loftus & Palmer, 1974 study; Loftus & Zanni, 1975). Loftus & Zanni (1975) showed participants a short film of a car accident. Afterwards, some were asked if they had seen *a* broken headlight, while others were asked if they had seen *the* broken headlight. The latter were far more likely to say 'yes' than the former.

(b) Those in which new items are inserted by suggestion into a previously observed scene (e.g. Loftus, 1975; Loftus & Hoffman, 1989). Loftus (1975) showed participants a short film of a car travelling through the countryside. One group was then asked, 'How fast was the white sports car going when it passed the "Stop" sign while travelling along the country road?' (There *was* a Stop sign in the film). A second group was asked, 'How fast was the white sports car going when it passed the barn while travelling along the country road?' (There was *no* barn). 'The' barn implies that there actually was a barn in the film, which is what makes it misleading. A week later, all the participants were asked, 'Did you see a barn?' Only 2.7% of the 'Stop sign' group said 'yes', compared with 17.3% of the 'barn' group.

(c) Those which manipulate details of an object that appeared in a previously observed scene (e.g. Belli, 1989).

All three types are to do with distorting a memory, or at least the report of a memory, of an event which participants actually witnessed.

(d) Those which attempt a much more radical effect: the suggestion of an entire episode that *supposedly* happened, but which did not in fact occur in the participant's past. This amounts to the creation of a completely *false memory*. One example is the 'shopping mall' study (Garry *et al.*, 1994). Fourteen-year-old Chris was convinced by his older brother, Jim, that he had been lost in a shopping mall as a small child. Chris was given summaries of childhood events (three actual events and the false shopping mall incident) and asked to write about each one. Jim repeatedly provided Chris with false details about the shopping mall. Two weeks later, Chris could 'remember' details, such as the appearance of the elderly man who rescued him. When Chris was debriefed, he expressed dismay. Loftus (1997) refers to a small number of similar studies, involving larger groups of participants, all showing that it is possible to 'implant' false memories. This is related to the *false memory syndrome* debate (see **Exercises** and Chapter 19). A considerable amount of recent research has focused on (a) the EWT of children; and (b) the problems of videowitness testimony. We shall consider some of this below.

Applications and implications

(a) In a review of the evidence, Gathercole (1998) identified three main issues guiding research in relation to children as eyewitnesses: (i) whether there are age differences in the reliability of children's memory for experienced events; (ii) whether there are age differences in children's susceptibility to misleading suggestions made by others; (iii) which are the best methods of obtaining unbiased memories from children.

The evidence suggests that young children do have relatively poor memory representations of events, possibly due to their poor understanding of the causal structure of the events. Using the Loftus 'paradigm' (a memory event is followed by some questions incorporating inaccurate information), it has also been found that children of 6 and below are even more vulnerable to the distorting effects of misleading information than older children or adults.

The implication of these findings is that the integrity of young children's memories for real-life events is unlikely to survive detailed questioning, both in and out of the courtroom. Ceci *et al.* (1994) tried to simulate this by asking children to think, repeatedly, over a 10-week period, about both real events and events that never happened (e.g. 'Think real hard, and tell me if this ever happened to you. Can you ever remember going to hospital with a mousetrap on your finger?'). Fifty-eight per cent of preschoolers gave false narratives and at least one false event description; twenty-five per cent responded with 'memories' to most of the fictionalized event descriptions.

Gathercole (1998) concludes by saying that:

> . . . mere exposure to adults asking you about events that did not take place is clearly sufficient under some circumstances to yield false memories . . .

Ceci *et al.* videotaped the children being given a forensic-style interview about both real and false events. Psychologists specializing in children's testimony were no better than chance at discriminating between their accounts of true or false memories!

If children are really more susceptible to the effects of false, post-event information, one explanation for this might be their failure at *source monitoring* (the ability to distinguish between memories from different sources). One practical implication of this is that the incorporation of source monitoring questions (e.g. 'Did you see that happen, or did somebody tell you that it happened?') into interviews should increase the reliability of children's testimony (Poole & Lindsay, 1995). However, even preschoolers are capable of accurate memories given the right circumstances (such as the biased questioning focusing on the central rather than peripheral features of the original event).

In another review of the evidence, Fundudis (1997) concludes that:

> . . . Despite the greater susceptibility of younger children to the effects of suggestion . . . there would appear to be no evidence to support the hypothesis that children are subject to a false memory syndrome. The indication is that the subtle mental, emotional and motivational processes involved in reconstructing an illusory memory, in the form of a false memory syndrome through the influence of suggestion in adults, are far too sophisticated for the child's mind . . .

Importantly, a resistance to listening to children has been a significant feature of many of the notorious child sex abuse scandals during the last 10 years or so, such as Cleveland in 1987 (Harrower, 1998).

(b) Now that closed-circuit television systems (CCTV) are commonplace in shops, banks and so on, there is an increased chance that an image of a criminal will be captured on videotape. This *seems* to neatly side-step human face-memory: once a suspect has been apprehended (using some combination of eyewitness and other forensic evidence), the person's identity can readily be confirmed by comparison with the security videotape. However, things are rather more complicated than this. Bruce (1998) cites the case of a prosecution based entirely on the evidence of a CCTV image which showed a young black man robbing a building society. The defence used an expert witness (Alf Linney, a medical physicist from University College, London), who helped get the evidence thrown out. Clearly, a CCTV image alone might prove very little about a suspect's precise identity. CCTV images can be very variable in quality. Camera and lighting angles may provide no more than a poorly lit, messy image of the top or back of someone's head. On-going research by Bruce and her colleagues is looking specifically at the question of identifying people shown on videotape: even when the image quality is reasonably high, the process of matching identities across different images may be remarkably error-prone.

While the courts understand that there are dangers posed by video evidence of identity, they may not appreciate that these difficulties may extend to high quality rather than low-grade tape. Based on her own research over more than 25 years, Bruce feels that increased efforts should be made to find automatic/semi-automatic face verification computer software, which can be used reliably to supplement human visual impressions of resemblance. CCTV images may be most helpful in identifying criminals when the faces captured on tape are of someone known to the witness. People who are highly *familiar* are readily identified from CCTV images of a quality that would make identification of an *unfamiliar* face extremely difficult (Bruce, 1998).

Based on evidence like that of Loftus's, the Devlin Report (1976) recommended that the trial judge be required to instruct the jury that it is not safe to convict on a single EWT *alone*, except in exceptional circumstances (such as where the witness is a close friend or relative), or when there is substantial corroborative evidence. In addition, research clearly shows that most people remember faces poorly, and recall details *not* from memory but from stereotypes of criminals (i.e. what they think criminals *should* look like: Harrower, 1998). This is consistent with what we said earlier about schema theory (see **Background and context** above).

In relation to the factors that affect the accuracy of EWT, a useful distinction has been made between factors that are beyond the control of the justice system (such as the greater accuracy of identifying *same-race* others) and those that are within their control (such as instructions to eyewitnesses prior to an identity parade/lineup). The former are called *estimator variables,* and the latter *system variables* (Wells, 1978). System variables have proven particularly useful for linking eyewitness identification research to specific proposals for improving the accuracy of EWT (Wells *et al.*, 1998).

While most EWT research has set out to show its unreliability (Cohen, 1993: see **Theoretical issues** above), one noteworthy attempt to improve witness recall is the *cognitive interview* (Geiselman *et al.*, 1985: see Harrower, 2001). This can be thought of as a system variable, and was designed primarily for use by the police. It maximizes the number of possible retrieval routes by, for example, reactivating the context of the original incident. Most studies which evaluate the use of the cognitive interview have shown that it can elicit more information without any loss of accuracy, compared with the standard interview techniques, and it is most effective when used by specially trained police officers with cooperative adult witnesses (Harrower, 2001). However, it has also proved successful with quite young children, and according to Mcmon (1998).

> The cognitive interview emerges as probably the most exciting development in the field of eyewitness testimony in the last 10 years.

According to Wagstaff (2002), research suggests that the cognitive interview shares a number of characteristics with hypnotic memory facilitation procedures, which probably accounts for much of the alleged effectiveness of hypnosis as an interview procedure. The main limitation of the cognitive interview in practice is that it is very time-consuming, both in terms of time spent interviewing witnesses and interviewer training. Consequently, researchers are now investigating how to streamline the interview by examining the relative contribution of the individual components (Kebbell & Wagstaff, 1999).

Exercises

1. In Experiment 1,
   (a) What kind of experimental design was used?
   (b) Why were the films presented in a different order for each group of participants?
   (c) How might the order of the films for each group have been determined?
   (d) Was there a control condition? If so, what was it? If not, does this necessarily represent a design fault?

2. In Experiment 2, the 'broken glass' question was embedded in a list of 10 questions, and it appeared in a random position in the list. Why was this done?

3. *How* do the different verbs used to denote 'touching' cars influence the subsequent estimates of speed?

4. How might Loftus and Palmer have tried to rule out other possible explanations for their results apart from the substitution hypothesis? (See **Theoretical issues** above.)

5. How useful is the 'shopping mall' study (Garry *et al.*, 1994) for understanding the creation of false memories (especially of child sexual abuse) by suggestion during psychotherapy (the *false memory syndrome* issue)? (See **Subsequent research** above.)

6 Teaching sign language to a chimpanzee

R.A. Gardner and B.T. Gardner (1969)

Science, Vol. 165, (3894), 664–72

BACKGROUND AND CONTEXT

For many psychologists, philosophers and linguists, language is the characteristic which makes humans unique amongst animals: it is what makes us the intelligent species we are. Chomsky (1957, 1965), for example, believes that language is unique to humans (it is *species-specific*) and so cannot be acquired by other species; language learning can only occur in organisms possessing various innate linguistic mechanisms, and only humans possess such mechanisms (a Language Acquisition Device/LAD).

According to Aitchison (1998), to ask if humans are the only 'articulate mammals' has a very serious purpose:

> . . . Some animals, such as dolphins and chimpanzees, have a high level of intelligence. If, in spite of this, we find that language is beyond their capability, then we may have found some indication that language is a genetically programmed activity which is largely separate from general intelligence.

Early attempts to teach chimps to speak were almost totally unsuccessful (Kellogg & Kellogg, 1933; Hayes & Hayes, 1951): their vocal apparatus is unsuited to making speech sounds. But this does not rule out the possibility that they are capable of learning language in some non-spoken form, and it was the Gardners who first attempted to do this using American Sign Language (ASL or Ameslan), as used by many deaf people in the USA.

Major subsequent studies include:

(*i*) Premack (1971), involving a female chimp called Sarah, taught to use small plastic symbols of various shapes and colours, each standing for a word and arranged on a special magnetized board;

(*ii*) Rumbaugh (1977) and Savage-Rumbaugh *et al.* (1980), involving another female chimp, Lana, taught to use a special typewriter (controlled by a computer), with 50 keys, each displaying a geometric pattern representing a word in a specially devised language ('Yerkish') which, when typed, appeared on a screen in front of her;

(*iii*) Patterson (1978, 1980), involving a female gorilla, Koko, taught ASL;

(*iv*) Terrace (1979a), involving a male chimp, Nim (Neam) Chimpsky, also taught ASL.

Whichever particular method has been used, the debate has always been about how to evaluate the findings. To be able to judge a chimp's signing as language clearly depends on how we define language in the first place. The starting point for making such a judgement is Hockett's (1960) criteria for language (or design features), which reflect the *discontinuity theory of language*. According to this view, there are *qualitative* (and not just quantitative) differences between human and non-human animal language.

Based on Hockett, Aitchison (1998) proposes that 10 criteria/design features should be sufficient (not all mentioned by Hockett), and by analysing human and non-human language in terms of all 10, she concludes that four are unique to humans, namely:

(a) *semanticity* (the use of symbols to *mean* or refer to objects/actions)

(b) *displacement* (reference to things not present in time or space)

(c) *structure-dependence* (the patterned nature of language and use of 'structured chunks', such as word order)

(d) *creativity* (the ability to produce and understand an infinite number of novel utterances: what Brown, 1973, calls *productivity*).

Studies like the Gardners' should be evaluated in terms of *these* criteria/design features.

AIM AND NATURE OF THE STUDY

The aim of the study was to help answer the question (a classical problem in comparative psychology): to what extent might another species be able to use human language? One way to approach the problem is to try to teach a form of human language to a non-human animal.

The article describes the first phase of a training project, involving an infant female chimp called Washoe. It is a kind of case-study of a single subject, in which detailed records were kept of Washoe's progress over an extended period of time (32 months). Unlike most case-studies involving human beings (see Chapter 19), there was no problem the participant had for which s/he was receiving help. Instead, this was a deliberate attempt to change the subject's behaviour in a particular way, in order to test a scientific hypothesis. This raises ethical issues not faced by most case-studies (see **Evaluation** below).

To the extent that a deliberate attempt was made to change Washoe's behaviour in a particular way, it can be thought of as an experiment, with the training programme the independent variable, and Washoe's actual use of signs the dependent variable. But unlike most dependent variables, operationalizing them doesn't seem sufficient for determining whether the independent variable has actually had an effect. It is the *interpretation* of the dependent variable which is crucial: does Washoe's use of signs constitute language?

T H E S T U D Y

> The extent to which another species might be able to use human language is a classical problem in comparative psychology. One approach to this problem is to consider the nature of language, the processes of learning, the neural mechanisms of learning and of language, their genetic basis and so on; another is to try to teach a form of human language to an animal. We chose the latter alternative and, in June, 1966, began training an infant female chimpanzee, named Washoe, to use the gestural language of the deaf. Within the first 32 months of training it became evident that we had been correct in at least one major aspect of method, the use of a gestural language; additional aspects of method have evolved in the course of the project. In this article we discuss the considerations which led us to use the chimp as a subject and American Sign Language (the language used by the deaf in North America) as a medium of communication, describe the general methods of training as they were initially conceived and as they later developed during the project, and summarize those results which could be reported with some degree of confidence by the end of the first phase of the project.

P R E L I M I N A R Y C O N S I D E R A T I O N S

THE CHIMPANZEE AS A SUBJECT

Whether or not the chimp is the most intelligent animal after man can be disputed; the gorilla, orang-utan and even the dolphin all have their supporters in this debate. Nevertheless, it is generally agreed that chimps are highly intelligent and, perhaps more importantly, that they are sociable and capable of forming strong attachments to human beings.

However, as affectionate as they are, chimps are still wild animals, in contrast with the animals which have been chosen, and sometimes bred, for docility and adaptability to laboratory procedures. They are also very strong animals: a full-grown chimp is likely to weigh more than 120 pounds, and is estimated to be three to five times as strong as a man, pound-for-pound. This great strength presents serious difficulties for a procedure which requires interaction at close quarters with a free-living animal.

A more serious disadvantage is that human speech sounds are unsuitable as a medium of communication for the chimp. The vocal apparatus of chimps is very different from that of man (Bryan, 1963) and, more importantly, their vocal behaviour is very different. Although they do make many different sounds, generally vocalization occurs in situations of high excitement and tends to be specific to the exciting situations. Undisturbed, they are usually silent. Thus it is unlikely that a chimp could be trained to make refined use of its vocalizations. The intensive work of Hayes and Hayes (1951) with Viki indicates that a vocal language is not appropriate for chimps; they used modern, sophisticated, psychological methods, and yet in six years, Viki learned only four sounds that approximated English words.

Use of the hands, however, is a prominent feature of chimp behaviour; manipulatory, mechanical problems are their forte and, more to the point, even caged, laboratory chimps develop begging and similar gestures spontaneously (Yerkes, 1943). Chimps which have had extensive contact with people have displayed an even wider variety of communicative gestures (Hayes & Hayes, 1951; Kellogg & Kellogg, 1967; Kellogg, 1968). This behavioural evidence that sign language is appropriate to chimps was more influential than the anatomical evidence of similarity between the hands of chimps and humans; although chimps can use tools and mechanical devices made to fit the human hand very skilfully, they seem unable to adapt their vocalizations to approximate human speech. It was reasoned that gestures for chimps should be analogous to bar-pressing for rats, key-pecking for pigeons and babbling for humans, i.e. to instrumentally condition an animal, you must choose responses which are suited to members of that species.

AMERICAN SIGN LANGUAGE

Sign language consists of a set of manual configurations and gestures which correspond to particular words or concepts. Unlike finger-spelling, which is the direct encoding of a spoken language, sign languages have their own rules of usage. American Sign Language (ASL), with certain regional variations, is used by the deaf in North America. It can be compared to pictograph writing in which some symbols are quite arbitrary and some are quite representational or iconic, but all are arbitrary to some degree. For example, in ASL the sign for 'always' is made by holding the hand in a fist, index finger extended (the pointing hand), while rotating the arm at the elbow; this is clearly an arbitrary representation of the concept 'always'. However, the sign for 'flower' is highly iconic: it is made by holding the fingers of one hand extended, all five fingertips touching (the tapered hand), and touching the fingertips first to one nostril, then to the other, as if sniffing a flower. While this is an iconic sign for 'flower', it is only one of several conventions by which the concept 'flower' could be iconically represented and so is arbitrary to some degree. Undoubtedly, many ASL signs which seem quite arbitrary today had an iconic origin that was lost through years of stylized usage. Thus, the signs of ASL are neither uniformly arbitrary nor uniformly iconic but vary in their degree of abstraction. The literate deaf typically use a combination of ASL and finger-spelling. This research avoided finger-spelling as much as possible. A great range of expression is possible within the limits of ASL; technical terms and proper names are a problem when first introduced but it is quite easy for a community of signers to agree on some convention. For example, we render 'psychologist' as 'think doctor' and 'psychology' as 'think science'.

The fact that ASL is in current use by human beings is an additional advantage. The early linguistic environment of the deaf children of deaf parents is in some respects similar to what could be provided for an experimental subject and this should permit some comparative evaluation of Washoe's eventual level of compe-tence. For example, in discussing Washoe's early performance with deaf parents, it seems that many of her variants of standard signs are similar to the baby-talk vari-ants commonly observed when human children sign.

WASHOE

While there may be a critical early age for the acquisition of this type of behaviour, newborn chimps tend to be quite helpless and vegetative and are considerably less hardy than older infants. Nevertheless, we reasoned that the dangers of starting too late were much greater than the dangers of starting too early, so we sought the youngest infant we could find. Newborn laboratory chimps are very scarce, and it seemed preferable to obtain a wild-caught infant, even though it would be at least eight to ten months old before it was available for research.

Washoe was named after Washoe County, the home of the University of Nevada. Her age was estimated to be between eight and 14 months at the end of June, 1966, when she first arrived at the laboratory. They are normally completely dependent until the age of two and semi-dependent until four, full adult growth being reached between 12 and 16 (Goodall, 1965; Riopelle & Rogers, 1965).

Washoe was very young when she arrived; she did not have her first canines or molars, had only rudimentary hand–eye coordination, was only beginning to crawl, and slept a great deal. Apart from making friends with her and adapting her to the daily routine, very little could be done during the first few months.

LABORATORY CONDITIONS

At the outset we were quite sure that Washoe could learn to make various signs in order to obtain food, drink, etc. But we wanted Washoe not only to ask for objects but to answer questions about them and also to ask us questions, i.e. to develop

THE STUDY

behaviour which could be described as conversation. With this in mind, confinement was to be about the same as a human infant, her human companions were to be friends and playmates as well as providers and protectors, and they were to introduce a great many games and activities which would maximize interaction with Washoe.

In practice, such an environment is readily achieved with a chimp. A number of human companions have been enlisted to participate in the project and relieve each other at intervals, so that at least one person would be with her during all her waking hours. Washoe adapted very well to this procedure: apparently, it is possible to provide an infant chimp with affection on a shift basis. All her companions have had to master ASL and use it extensively in her presence, in conjunction with interesting activities and also in a general way, as one chatters at a human infant. Occasional finger spelling has been allowed and, of course, there are lapses into spoken English, as when medical personnel examine her.

However, the environment described here is not a silent one. The humans can vocalize in many ways, laughing, making sounds of pleasure and displeasure, whistles and drums are sounded in a variety of imitation games, and hands are clapped for attention. The rule is that all meaningful sounds, whether vocalized or not, must be sounds that a chimp can imitate.

T R A I N I N G   M E T H O D S

IMITATION

The imitativeness of apes is proverbial, and rightly so:

> Chim and Panzee would imitate many of my acts, but never have I heard them imitate a sound, and rarely make a sound peculiarly their own in response to mine. As previously stated, their imitative tendency is as remarkable for its specialization and limitations as for its strength. It seems to be controlled chiefly by visual stimuli. Things which are seen tend to be imitated or reproduced. What is heard is not reproduced. Obviously an animal which lacks the tendency to reinstate auditory stimuli – in other words to imitate sounds – cannot reasonably be expected to talk. The human infant exhibits this tendency to a remarkable degree. So also does the parrot. If the imitative tendency of the parrot could be coupled with the quality of intelligence of the chimpanzee, the latter undoubtedly could speak. (Yerkes & Learned, 1925)

The Hayes (1952) devised a game with Viki in which she would imitate various actions on hearing the command 'Do this'; once established, this was an effective means of training Viki to perform actions that could be visually guided and the same method should be admirably suited to training a chimp to use sign language. Getting Washoe to imitate us was not difficult, for she did so quite spontaneously, but getting her to imitate on command has been another matter: not until she was

16 months did we achieve any degree of control over her imitation of gestures. Eventually, we reached a point where she would imitate a simple gesture, such as pulling at her ears, or a series of gestures, for the reward of being tickled. However, imitation of this sort has not been an important method for introducing new signs into Washoe's vocabulary.

As a method of prompting, imitation has been used extensively to increase the frequency and refine the form of signs. Washoe sometimes fails to use a new sign in an appropriate situation, or uses another, incorrect sign; at such times we can make the correct sign to Washoe, repeating the performance until she makes the sign herself. (With more stable signs, more indirect forms of prompting can be used, e.g. pointing at or touching Washoe's hand or a part of her body that should be involved in the sign, making the sign for 'sign', or asking a question in signs, such as 'What do you want?' or 'What is it?') Her 'diction' (with both new and old signs) has often been improved by simply repeating, in exaggeratedly correct form, the sign she has just made until she repeats it herself in more correct form. But there are limits to the use of prompting with a wild animal; pressed too hard, Washoe can become completely diverted from her original object, may ask for something entirely different, run away, throw a tantrum or even bite her tutor.

Chimps also imitate, after some delay. A typical example is to do with her bath and the doll she always had to play with (from her second month with us). One day, during the tenth month of the project, she bathed one of her dolls in the way we usually bathed her. She filled her little bathtub with water, dunked the doll in the tub, then took it out and dried it with a towel. She has repeated the entire performance, or parts of it, many times since, sometimes also soaping the doll.

This is a type of imitation which may be very important in the acquisition of language by children. Routine activities – feeding, dressing, bathing, etc. – have been highly ritualized, with appropriate signs figuring prominently in the rituals. Many games have been invented which can be accompanied by appropriate signs; objects and activities have been named as often as possible, especially when Washoe seemed to be paying particular attention to them. New objects and new examples of familiar objects, including pictures, have been continually brought to her attention, together with the appropriate signs. All of this has been done in the hope that she would come to associate the signs with their referents and later make the signs herself. We have reason to believe that she has come to understand a large vocabulary of signs.

Some of Washoe's signs seem to have been originally acquired by delayed imitation. A good example is the sign for 'toothbrush'. A part of the daily routine has been to brush her teeth after every meal; at first, she resisted but gradually came to make less and less fuss until after several months she would even help sometimes to brush her teeth herself. Usually, having finished her meal, Washoe would try to leave her highchair; we would restrain her, signing 'first, toothbrushing, then you can go'. One day, in the tenth month of the project, she was visiting the Gardner home and found her way into the bathroom, she looked at the mug full of toothbrushes and signed 'toothbrush'. At the time, we believed she understood this sign but we had not seen her use it. It is unlikely that she was asking for the toothbrushes, since she could easily reach them or that she was asking to have her teeth brushed. This was the first and one of the clearest examples of Washoe apparently naming an object or event for no obvious motive other than communication.

BABBLING

Because the Hayes were trying to teach Viki to speak English, they were interested in babbling. After early encouragement at the number and variety of spontaneous vocalizations she made, these became fewer and fewer to the point where the Hayes felt that there was almost no vocal babbling from which to shape speech. As far as manual 'babbling' is concerned, the reverse happened: it has increased as the project has progressed. We have been particularly encouraged by the increase in movements which involve touching parts of the head and body, since these are important components of many signs. Also, more and more often, when Washoe has been unable to get something she wants, she has burst into a flurry of random flourishes and arm-waving.

We have encouraged Washoe's babbling by clapping, smiling and repeating the gestures (just as you might repeat 'goo goo' to a baby). If the babbled gesture has resembled a sign in ASL, we have made the correct form of the sign and tried to engage in some appropriate activity.

Closely related to babbling are certain gestures which seem to have appeared independently of any deliberate training on our part and which resemble signs so closely that they could be incorporated into Washoe's repertoire with little or no modification. Almost from the first she had a begging gesture: an extension of her open hand, palm up, toward one of us. She made this gesture in situations in which she wanted aid or in which we were holding something she wanted. The ASL signs for 'give me' and 'come' are very similar to this, except that they involve a prominent beckoning movement; gradually Washoe incorporated a beckoning wrist movement into her use of the sign ('come–gimme' in Table 6.1).

INSTRUMENTAL CONDITIONING

It seems intuitively unreasonable that the acquisition of language by human beings could be strictly a matter of repeated instrumental conditioning; that a child acquires language in a similar way to a rat which is conditioned, first to press a lever for food in the presence of a stimulus, then to turn a wheel in the presence of another stimulus, and so on until a large repertoire of discriminatory responses is acquired. Nevertheless, the so-called 'trick vocabulary' of early childhood is probably acquired in this way, and this may be a critical stage in children's language acquisition. Besides, a main objective of the project was to teach Washoe as many signs as possible, by whatever methods we could enlist, including conventional procedures of instrumental conditioning.

There is no doubt that tickling is the most effective reward that we have used with Washoe. In the early months, when we paused in our tickling Washoe placed her hands against her ribs or around her neck, indicating unmistakably that she wanted more tickling. It was decided to shape an arbitrary response which she could use for requesting more tickling; we noticed that, when being tickled, she tended to bring her arms together to cover the place being tickled. The result was a very crude approximation of the ASL sign for 'more' (see Table 6.1), so we would stop tickling and then pull Washoe's arms away from her body. When we released her arms and threatened to resume tickling, she tended to bring her hands together again, in which case we would tickle her again. Occasionally, we would stop tickling and wait for her to put her hands together by herself. At first, any approximation to the 'more' sign, however crude, was rewarded; later, closer approximations were required, and imitative prompting was introduced. Soon, a very good version of the 'more' sign could be obtained but it was quite specific to the tickling situation.

In the sixth month of the project, Washoe signed 'more' for a new game which consisted of pushing Washoe across the floor in a laundry basket; imitative prompting was used from the start. It then began to appear as a request for more swinging (by the arms), again after first being elicited by imitative prompting. From this point on, Washoe transferred the 'more' sign to all activities including feeding, usually spontaneously, when there was some pause in a desired activity or when some object was removed. Often we ourselves were not sure that Washoe wanted 'more' until she signed to us.

T H E   S T U D Y

R E S U L T S

VOCABULARY

Early on we were able to keep fairly complete records of Washoe's daily signing behaviour, but as the amount of signing behaviour and number of signs increased, trying to keep exhaustive records became too cumbersome. So, during the sixteenth month, we settled on the following procedure. When a new sign appeared, we waited for it to be reported by three different observers as having occurred in an appropriate context and spontaneously (i.e. with no prompting other than a question such as 'What is it?' or 'What do you want?'). The sign was then added to a checklist in which its occurrence, form, context, and the kind of prompting needed were recorded. Two such checklists were filled out each day, one for each half of the day.

A reported frequency of at least one appropriate and spontaneous occurrence each day over a period of 15 consecutive days was taken as the criterion of acquisition. Table 6.1 shows 30 signs which met this criterion by the end of the 22nd month of the project. Four others have been listed ('dog', 'smell', 'me' and 'clean') which were judged to be stable, despite the fact that they had not met the stringent criterion by the end of 22 months; however, they had been reported to occur appropriately and spontaneously on more than half of the days in a period of 30 consecutive days.

During the 22nd month, 28 of the 34 signs were reported on at least 20 days and the smallest number of different signs reported for a single day was 23, with a median of 29. Four new signs appeared during the first seven months, nine during the next seven and 21 during the next seven. Clearly, if Washoe's rate of acquisition continues to accelerate, we will have to assess her vocabulary on the basis of sampling procedures.

Differentiation. Column 1 of Table 6.1 lists English equivalents for each of Washoe's signs. However, this equivalence is only approximate, since (*i*) equivalence between ASL and English, as between any two human languages, is only approximate and (*ii*) Washoe's usage differs from that of standard ASL. Although to some extent her usage is indicated in the 'Context' column of Table 6.1, the definition of any given sign must always depend upon her own vocabulary which has been continually changing. For example, when she had very few signs for specific things, Washoe used 'more' for a wide class of requests, but this declined as she acquired signs for specific requests until she was using the sign mainly to ask for repetition of some action that she could not name, such as a somersault. (Perhaps 'do it again' is the best English equivalent of her current use of the sign.)

Differentiation of the signs for 'flower' and 'smell' is further illustration of usage depending on size of vocabulary. As the 'flower' sign became more frequent, it occurred in several inappropriate contexts which all seemed to include odours; for example, opening a tobacco pouch or entering a kitchen with cooking smells. Gradually, through passive shaping and imitative prompting, she came to make the appropriate distinction, although 'flower' (in the single-nostril form: see Table 6.1) continues to occur as a common error in 'smell' contexts.

TRANSFER

In general, when introducing new signs we have used a very specific referent for the initial training: a particular door for 'open', a particular hat for 'hat'. But Washoe has always been able to transfer her signs spontaneously to new members of each class of referents (see the examples of 'more' above). The sign for 'flower' is a particularly good example of transfer, because flowers occur in so many varieties indoors, outdoors and in pictures, and she uses the same sign for all. She also transferred the 'dog' sign to the sound of barking of an unknown dog.

THE STUDY

Table 6.1

SIGNS USED RELIABLY BY CHIMPANZEE WASHOE WITHIN 22 MONTHS OF THE BEGINNING OF TRAINING (THE SIGNS ARE LISTED IN THE ORDER OF THEIR ORIGINAL APPEARANCE IN HER REPERTOIRE; SEE TEXT FOR THE CRITERION OF RELIABILITY AND FOR THE METHOD OF ASSIGNING THE DATE OF ORIGINAL APPEARANCE)

Signs	Description	Context
Come–gimme	Beckoning motion with wrist or knuckles as pivot.	Sign made to person or animals, also for objects out of reach. Often combined: 'come tickle', 'gimme sweet', etc.
More	Fingertips are brought together, usually overhead. (Correct ASL form: tips of the tapered hand touch repeatedly.)	When asking for continuation or repetition of activities such as swinging or tickling, for second helpings of food, etc. Also used to ask for repetition of some performance, such as a somersault.
Up	Arm extends upward and index finger may also point up.	Wants a lift to reach objects such as grapes on vine, or leaves, or wants to be placed on someone's shoulders or wants to leave potty-chair.
Sweet	Index or index and second fingers touch tip of wagging tongue. (Correct ASL form: index and second fingers extended side by side.)	For dessert, used spontaneously at end of meal. Also when asking for candy.
Open	Flat hands are placed side by side, palms down, then drawn apart while rotated to palms up.	At door of house, room, car, refrigerator, or cupboard, or containers such as jars, and on faucets.
Tickle	The index finger of one hand is drawn across the back of the other hand. (Related to ASL touch.)	For tickling or for chasing games.
Go	Opposite of come–gimme.	While walking hand-in-hand or riding on someone's shoulders.

THE STUDY

Signs	Description	Context
		Washoe usually indicates the direction desired.
Out	Curved hand grasps tapered hand; then tapered hand is withdrawn upward.	When passing through doorways, until recently used for both 'in' and 'out'. Also when asking to be taken outdoors.
Hurry	Open hand is shaken at the wrist. (Correct ASL form: index and second fingers extended side by side.)	Often follows signs such as 'come–gimme', 'out', 'open' and 'go', particularly if there is a delay before Washoe obeyed. Also used while watching her meal being prepared.
Hear–listen	Index finger touches ear.	For loud or strange sounds: bells, car horns, sonic booms, etc. Also for asking someone to hold a watch to her ear.
Toothbrush	Index finger is used as brush, to rub front teeth.	When Washoe has finished her meal, or at other times when shown a toothbrush.
Drink	Thumb is extended from fisted hand and touches mouth.	For water formula, soda pop, etc. For soda pop often combined with 'sweet'.
Hurt	Extended index fingers jabbed toward each other. Can be used to indicate location of pain.	To indicate cuts and bruises on herself or on others. Can be elicited by red stains on a person's skin or by tears in clothing.
Sorry	Fisted hand clasps at shoulder. (Correct ASL form: fisted hand is rubbed over heart with circular motion.)	After biting someone, or when someone has been hurt in another way (not necessarily by Washoe), when told to apologize for mischief.
Funny	Tip of index finger presses nose, and Washoe snorts. (Correct ASL form: index and second fingers used, no snort.)	When soliciting interaction play, and during games. Occasionally when being pursued after mischief.

THE STUDY

Signs	Description	Context
Please	Open hand is drawn across chest. (Correct ASL form: fingertips used and circular motion.)	When asking for objects and activities. Frequently combined 'please go', 'out please', 'please drink'.
Food–eat	Several fingers of one hand are placed in mouth. (Correct ASL form: fingertips of tapered hand touch mouth repeatedly.)	During meals and preparation of meals.
Flower	Tip of index finger touches one or both nostrils. (Correct ASL form: tip of tapered hand touch first one nostril, then the other.)	For flowers.
Cover–blanket	Draws one hand toward self over the back of the other.	At bedtime or naptime and on cold days when Washoe wants to be taken out.
Dog	Repeated slapping on thigh.	For dogs and for barking.
You	Index finger points at a person's chest.	Indicates successive turns in games. Also used in response to questions such as 'Who tickle?', 'Who brush?'.
Napkin–bib	Fingertips wipe the mouth region.	For bib, for washcloth, and for Kleenex.
In	Opposite of 'out'.	Wants to go indoors or wants someone to join her outdoors.
Brush	The fisted hand rubs the back of the open hand several times. (Adapted from the ASL 'polish'.)	For hairbrush, and when asking for brushing.
Hat	Palm pats top of head.	For hats and caps.
I–me	Index finger points at or touches chest.	Indicates Washoe's turn when she and a companion share food, drink, etc. Also used in phrases such as 'I drink' and in reply to questions such as 'Who

Signs	Description	Context
		tickle?' (Washoe: 'you'), 'Who I tickle?' (Washoe: 'Me').
Shoes	The fisted hands are held side by side and strike down on shoes or floor. (Correct ASL form: the sides of the fisted hands strike against each other.)	For shoes and boots.
Smell	Palm is held before nose and moved slightly upward several times.	For scented objects: tobacco, perfume, sage, etc.
Pants	Palms of the flat hand are drawn up against the body towards waist.	For diapers, rubber pants, trousers.
Clothes	Fingertips brush down the chest.	For Washoe's jacket, nightgown, and shirts, also for our clothing.
Cat	Thumb and index finger grasp cheek hair near side of mouth and are drawn outward (representing cat's whiskers).	For cats.
Key	Palm of one hand is repeatedly touched with the index finger of the other. (Correct ASL form: crooked index finger is rotated against palm.)	Used for keys and locks and to ask us to unlock a door.
Baby	One forearm is placed in the crook of the other.	For dolls, including animals, such as a toy horse and duck.
Clean	The open palm of one hand is passed over the open palm of the other.	Used when Washoe is washing, or being washed, or when a companion is washing hands or some other object. Also used for 'soap'.

To improve her manual dexterity, Washoe was allowed to practise with padlock keys which opened many cupboards and doors in her quarters. Once she mastered this skill, it transferred to all kinds of locks and keys, including ignition keys. At about the same time, we taught her the 'key' sign using the original padlock keys as a referent. She came to use this sign both to name keys presented to her and to ask for the key to various locks when no one was in sight. She readily transferred the sign to all varieties of keys and locks.

COMBINATIONS

No deliberate attempts were made to elicit combinations or phrases, although we may have responded more readily to strings of two or more signs than to single ones. As far as we can judge, Washoe's early use of strings was spontaneous. Almost as soon as she had eight to ten signs in her vocabulary, she began to use two or three of them at a time, and this tendency has increased in line with her vocabulary, so that it is now a common mode of signing. We, of course, usually signed to her in combinations but if Washoe's use of combinations has been imitative, then it must be a generalized sort of imitation, since she has invented several combinations, e.g. 'gimme tickle' (before we had even asked her to tickle us) and 'open food drink' (for the fridge, which we have always called the 'cold box'). Four signs ('please', 'come–gimme', 'hurry' and 'more') used with one or more other signs account for the largest share of Washoe's early combinations; they function mainly as emphasizers, as in 'please open hurry' and 'gimme drink please'. Five others ('go', 'out', 'in', 'open' and 'hear–listen') accounted for most of the remaining combinations until recently. Typical examples include 'go in'/'go out' (when at some distance from a door), 'go sweet' (for being carried to a raspberry bush), 'open flower' (to be let through the gate to a flower garden), 'open key' (for a locked door), 'listen eat' (at the sound of an alarm clock signalling mealtime) and 'listen dog' (at the sound of the barking of an unseen dog). All but the first and last of these six examples were Washoe's inventions. More recently, Washoe learnt 'I–me' and 'you' so that combinations which resemble short sentences have begun to appear.

CONCLUDING OBSERVATIONS

It is very difficult to answer questions such as 'Do you think that Washoe has language?' or 'At what point will you be able to say that Washoe has language?', because they imply a distinction between one class of communicative behaviour that can be called language and another class that cannot. This in turn implies a well-established theory that could provide the distinction; if the objectives of our research had required such a theory, we would certainly not have been able to begin it as early as we did.

We have been able to verify the hypothesis that sign language is an appropriate medium of two-way communication for the chimp. Washoe's intellectual immaturity, the continuing acceleration of her progress, the fact that her signs do not remain specific to their original referents but are transferred spontaneously to new referents and the emergence of rudimentary combinations, all suggest that significantly more can be achieved by Washoe. Subsequent problems will be to do with the technical business of measurement; we are now developing a procedure for testing Washoe's ability to name objects in which an object or picture of an object is placed in a box with a window. An observer, who does not know what is in the box, asks Washoe what she sees through the window; however, this method is currently limited to items which can fit in the box. The ability to combine and recombine signs must be tested; our hope is that Washoe will eventually be able to describe events and situations to an observer who has no other source of information.

Washoe's achievements will probably be exceeded by another chimp, because it is unlikely that the training conditions have been optimal in this first attempt. Theories of language that depend upon the identification of aspects of language that are exclusively human must remain tentative until a considerably larger body of intensive research with other species becomes available.

EVALUATION

Theoretical issues

It seems almost indisputable that Washoe displayed *semanticity*: after four years of intensive training (based on reports subsequent to the 1969 paper) she had acquired 132 signs. She had no difficulty in understanding that a sign 'means' a certain object or action (Aitchison, 1998). She was also able to generalize from one situation to another (e.g. 'open', 'more'), and sometimes *over*generalized (e.g. 'hurt'). There is also some limited evidence of *displacement*, as when she asked for absent objects or people (e.g. 'all gone cup'/'more milk'). Once she had learned eight to ten signs, she spontaneously began to combine them (showing *creativity*), for example, 'gimme tickle' (come and tickle me), 'go sweet' (take me to the raspberry bushes), 'listen eat' (listen to the dinner gong), 'listen dog', 'Roger come', 'open food drink' (open the fridge), 'hurry gimme toothbrush' and 'Roger Washoe tickle'.

Although she combined some signs in a consistent order (e.g. 'baby mine' rather than 'mine baby'/'tickle me' rather than 'me tickle'), she did not always seem to care about

sign order (e.g. she was as likely to sign 'go sweet' as 'sweet go'). So, the evidence for *structure-dependence* is much weaker. Why?

Aitchison (1998) suggests four reasons:

(*i*)   the Gardners' overeagerness may have led them to reward her every time she signed correctly (regardless of order), so that the idea that order was important may never have been learnt;

(*ii*) it may be easier with words to preserve order than with signs: deaf adults are also inconsistent in their word order;

(*iii*) this may have been a temporary, intermediate stage before she eventually learnt to keep to a fixed order. The Gardners claim (1971, 1975, 1978, 1980) she did so;

(*iv*) she did not and could not understand the essentially patterned nature of language.

This inconsistent pattern is largely confirmed by the other studies involving Sarah, Lana, Koko, and Nim Chimpsky, who showed a statistical preference for putting certain words in a certain order but no evidence of understanding any *rules*.

Methodological issues

It is worth looking at Terrace's study of Nim more closely because the data were analysed more carefully than in any other study (Aitchison, 1998), and it is the most 'scientific' of all the studies (Eysenck, 1984). Approximately half of Nim's 20,000 recorded signs were two-sign combinations, and 1,378 were different. They *seemed* to be structured; for example, of the two-sign utterances including 'more', 789 had 'more' at the beginning, and of those involving a transitive verb (one taking an object), 83% had the verb before the object. But he simply had a *statistical preference* for putting particular words in certain places, while there was no such preference for other words (e.g. 'more' at the beginning, 'Nim' at the end, and any foods at the beginning too). Many other words had a random distribution (e.g. 'eat'). Petitto & Seidenberg (1979) conclude that 'repetitive, inconsistently structured strings are in fact characteristic of ape signing'. Nim's longest recorded utterance is: 'Eat drink, eat drink, eat Nim, eat Nim, drink eat, drink eat, Nim eat, Nim eat, me eat, me eat'.

Even semanticity, which seems to be the one generally agreed criterion of language, is problematical. Is the correct use of signs to refer to things a sufficient definition? The toothbrush example (Washoe) seems to be the use of a sign in order simply to *name* something. But not only is this a very isolated example when compared with how language is used by young children, Savage-Rumbaugh *et al.* (1980) seriously doubt whether any of the apes (including their own, Lana) used the individual elements in their vocabularies as words. Terrace (1987) suggests that a strong case can be made for the hypothesis that the deceptively simple ability to use a symbol as a name required a cognitive advance in the evolution of human intelligence at least as significant as the advances that led to grammatical competence.

Much of a child's initial vocabulary of names is used to inform another person that s/he has noticed something (MacNamara, 1982); often, the child refers to the object spontaneously, showing obvious delight from the sheer act of naming. It is precisely this aspect of uttering a name which has *not* been observed in apes. Could any amount of training produce an ape with such ability? MacNamara thinks not, for the simple reason that the act of referring is not learnt, but is a 'primitive of cognitive psychology' (and is a necessary precursor of naming). By contrast, chimps usually try to 'acquire' objects (approach it, explore it, and so on), and show no signs of trying to communicate the fact that it has noticed an object as an end in itself (Terrace, 1987).

According to Brown (1986), a major difference between children's language development and Nim's use of signs concerns Mean Length of Utterance (MLU). Children initially produce utterances containing an average of 1½ words (MLU = 1½), but this quickly rises to MLU=4. By contrast, Nim's MLU did not rise at all but held steady at 1.1 to 1.6 signs, suggesting that the symbol combinations being produced are *not* constructions, but merely strings of single (unrelated) signs. Young children's longest construction is for several years around the mean, but Nim's longest unbroken string (see above) is unrelated to MLU and far exceeds it. This suggests that MLU does not reflect complexity, and so reinforces the impression that Nim's strings are *only* strings ('Give orange me give eat orange me eat orange give me eat orange give me you'). Clearly, the information transmitted does not increase with increase in MLU.

A frame-by-frame analysis of videotapes revealed that Nim seldom signed spontaneously (about 10% of the time) on his own initiative, but almost always required human prompting to sign at all, and when he signed with a teacher his signs were very often complete or partial imitations of those produced by the teacher (about 40% of all utterances). By contrast, in children just beginning to talk, under 20% of their utterances are imitations of parents' speech and approximately 30% are spontaneous (Eysenck, 1984); this proportion quickly approaches zero (i.e. nearly all are spontaneous). In fact, Nim's rate of imitations actually increased as he got older (Aitchison, 1983). Also, over 70% of Nim's utterances began while his teacher was still signing, so Nim interrupted his teacher much more often than children typically interrupt their parents (Eysenck, 1984). This suggests he was not interested in having a genuine conversation (see Chapter 18).

Positive factors of Terrace's study included the use of videotapes, his circulation of progress reports to experts (who could analyse them for themselves), and his calculation of MLU (standard in child language research). However, Nim had instruction from 60 different signers ('babysitters'), and much of it was done in a classroom (not 'home'). Despite the fact that several trainers were with him for long periods (especially Petitto and Terrace himself), the Gardners (1980), Patterson and Fouts see Nim as an underprivileged chimp, subject to routine drills, not reared like a child at all (which all their subjects were), and for these reasons his ASL performance was below that of Washoe and the others. The Gardners go so far as to claim that he was highly disturbed, insecure, and maladjusted, and a computer analysis of chimp utterances which takes no account of the actual context is bound to give odd results.

The very status of ASL as language is itself questionable. Eysenck (1984) points out, for example, that signs in ASL are defined in terms of four parameters – hand configurations, movement, orientation and location – but the Gardners consistently focused on just one (hand configuration). Brown (1986) states that it is not related to spoken English, and is very unlike English in grammatical structure. Nevertheless, it is capable of expressing any meaning whatsoever: it is language in a *manual–visual* (as opposed to vocal–auditory) modality. However, while ASL when used by humans is undoubtedly a language, we cannot just *assume* that it is so when used by chimps. While there is the danger of *anthropomorphizing* here, we must also beware of excluding signing as language just because it is chimps and not humans moving their hands (Brown, 1986).

Subsequent research

While Patterson (1978) claims that 'language is no longer the exclusive domain of man', and Rumbaugh (1977) argues that 'neither tool-using skills nor language serve qualitatively to separate man and beast any more', Chomsky (1980) believes that the higher apes 'apparently lack the capacity to develop even the rudiments of the computational structure of human language'. Aitchison (1998) agrees by saying:

> . . . even though intelligent animals seem *capable* of coping with some of the rudimentary characteristics of human language, they do not seem *predisposed* to cope with them . . .

And again;

> The apparent ease with which humans acquire language, compared with apes, supports the suggestion that they are innately programmed to do so . . .

Eysenck (1984) concludes that 'as of now . . . language in its complete form is unique to man'. Similarly, Carroll (1986) maintains that:

> . . . although these chimps have grasped some of the rudiments of human language, what they have learned and the speed at which they learn it . . . is qualitatively different from those of human beings.

All of these criticisms and conclusions (both 'pro' and 'con' non-human language) have been based on *production-based* training: putting the chimp through rote learning of symbols, starting from scratch and gradually building up a vocabulary, one symbol at a time. Cearly, this is *not* how children usually acquire language, so perhaps any comparison between children and chimps is simply invalid and tells us very little about the fundamental question: is language unique to human beings?

According to Rumbaugh & Savage-Rumbaugh (1994), the studies we have considered so far (including their own) made a crucial omission: they only taught the apes to 'speak', not to listen (*production* vs. *comprehension*). This represents a fundamental error, since children understand speech *before* they can produce it, yet the apes were expected to generate language before they had a basis from which to comprehend it. It is not surprising, therefore, that these studies revealed little more than sophisticated signalling.

Starting in the 1980s, at the Yerkes Primate Centre and Georgia State University, Savage-Rumbaugh has been working with chimps in a way which is much more like how children acquire language. Instead of being production-based, it is based on the principle that language is first acquired through *comprehension*, from which production then flows. This new approach was applied on a limited scale with Austin and Sherman, two common chimps (*Pan troglodytes*). But it really got going with pygmy chimps (*Pan paniscus*) or bonobos, which are slightly smaller than common chimps but more vocal and more communicative through facial expressions and gestures.

Matata (born in the wild and introduced to the research at age five) was the first bonobo involved, starting in 1981. Instead of ASL, Savage-Rumbaugh used an extensive 'lexigram', a matrix of 256 geometrical shapes and symbols, on a board, each representing verbs and nouns. Whenever a symbol is touched, the English sentence is simultaneously spoken. Matata was a slow learner, but her six-month-old 'kidnapped' son, Kanzi, spontaneously learnt whatever symbols Matata knew. That stimulated an even greater effort to place language learning in a naturalistic context.

By age 10 (1991), Kanzi had a vocabulary of some 200 words, but it is their apparent meaning, and his grasp of certain syntactical rules and complexities of spoken English, rather than the size of his vocabulary, that is really impressive. He was the first to demonstrate that *observational exposure* is sufficient to provide for the acquisition of lexical and vocal symbols. This exposure takes place in the context of routines which emerge out of daily life as it has been constructed for the chimps, such as social play, visits to interesting places, structured testing time, nappy changing, bathing, riding in the car, looking at a book, and so on.

Kanzi learned the rule that 'action precedes object' in two-word utterances, similar to young children, who move from an initial random ordering to an order preference in word pairs. Kanzi was using a basic *lexical syntax*: children use such a syntax spontaneously and Kanzi seemed to be doing the same. He also invented a rule for combining a gesture and a symbol: the lexigram always came first (e.g. the symbol for 'chase'), followed by pointing to someone. The rules Kanzi uses might be called 'protogrammar', a term which should also be applied to children's early utterances (Rumbaugh & Savage-Rumbaugh, 1994).

Savage-Rumbaugh *et al.* (1993) compared Kanzi's comprehension of human speech with that of a child, Alia, who had also learned to use the keyboard. They were tested on over 400 novel sentences, which required some rather unusual actions to be performed (such as putting elastic bands on balls) or referred to unpredictable places or situations (such as 'get the telephone that's outdoors' – when there was one within sight indoors!). At age nine, Kanzi scored 74% correct, and Alia (aged 2½) 65%.

Clearly, Kanzi demonstrated language comprehension, as well as production, without formal training: he had simply responded to the communication going on around him. As with a child, his responses were not pure imitation, but showed an understanding of the use of symbols. Control chimps (raised without exposure to the lexigram) failed to develop an understanding of speech, despite later exposure, because it had not been made available to them through a narrative in which they could participate. This suggests a *critical period* in chimps for language acquisition (Clamp & Russell, 1998).

Rumbaugh & Savage-Rumbaugh (1994) also report findings for Panzee (a common chimp) and Panbanisha (a bonobo), who were raised in the same 'language-rich' environment. Within two years they had both clearly 'picked up' language without any formal, explicit, language training, with Panbanisha proving to be much more competent.

Savage-Rumbaugh believes that the difference between human and chimp grasp of language is merely *quantitative* (one of degree only). Referring to criticisms by Terrace (1987) that Kanzi still only uses his symbols *instrumentally* (to get things done, to ask for things, and so on) rather than to share his perception of the world, Savage-Rumbaugh acknowledges that Kanzi does use symbols for these purposes, but so do young children. While Kanzi's percentage of such symbol use may be higher:

> . . . he can reliably tell you some things, such as when he is going to be 'good' or 'bad', when he has just eaten or where he is headed while travelling. Terrace has consistently refused to acknowledge this. (Savage-Rumbaugh, quoted in Lewin, 1991)

Applications and implications

According to Anderson (1995),

> It is hard to know what to make of the part successes and part failures of the attempts to teach apes language. It is not really a matter of their being inferior to humans. They are different in many ways that have nothing to do with linguistic ability. Therefore, one should not expect their linguistic learning (or, indeed, any other learning) to be identical to human learning . . . learning manifests itself according to the unique characteristics of each species.

When Washoe was five years old, she was sent away with Roger and Deborah Fouts to a primate station in Oklahoma (she had grown so large and potentially dangerous). The Gardners next saw her 11 years later: when they unexpectedly entered the room Washoe was in, she signed their name, then 'Come, Mrs G.', led her to an adjoining room, and began to play a game with her which she had not been observed to play since she left the Gardners' home (Singer, 1993).

Observations like this, as well as supporting the argument that non-humans really are capable of language, also raise some important *ethical* questions, in particular:

(*i*)   how justifiable is the whole attempt to study language in non-humans, whether through production-based or more naturalistic methods, since either way they are removed from their natural habitat in which they do not spontaneously use language?

(*ii*) what happens to the chimps (and other non-humans) when they have served their purpose as experimental subjects?

While the Gardners' claims that Nim Chimpsky was underprivileged and emotionally disturbed are quite exceptional, and while these studies in general are not usually the target for attacks against cruel treatment of animals in psychological research, they nonetheless involve animals which have not chosen to become involved. But perhaps it is the fact that they are great apes, and not just 'other animals', which makes these ethical questions so fascinating and so important.

This relates directly to *The Great Ape Project*, which is (a) the title of a book (subtitle: *Equality beyond humanity*, edited by Singer and Cavalieri), (b) an idea, radical but simple, namely to extend the 'community of equals' beyond human beings to all the great apes: chimpanzees (including bonobos), gorillas and orang-utans, and (c) an organization, comprising 34 academics and others, set up to work internationally for the immediate inclusion of the great apes within the community of equals. This refers to the moral community within which we accept certain basic moral principles and rights as governing our relationships with each other, and which are enforceable at law. The central tenet of the Great Ape Project is that it is ethically indefensible to deny the great apes the basic rights of (1) the right to life; (2) protection of individual liberty, and (3) prohibition of torture. (Collectively, these constitute the 'Declaration of Great Apes'.) Members include Jane Goodall, Roger and Deborah Fouts, Francine Patterson, and Richard Dawkins.

Singer (1993) argues that recognition of the rights of intellectually disabled people (1971 UN Declaration on the Rights of Mentally Retarded Persons/1975 Declaration on the Rights of Disabled Persons) serves as a political and ethical pointer to what might be possible with the great apes. Their inability to stand up and defend their own rights is no barrier to our recognition of those rights: there are mechanisms for overcoming our difficulty in deciding what is in the best interests of those who cannot tell us, in so many words, just what they want. The Anti-Slavery Society can also serve as

a model for the liberation of the great apes. 'It is time to put the slavery of the apes behind us. The great apes need more than humane treatment. They need equality' (Singer, 1993).

Exercises

1. What is the difference between language and communication?

2. What does 'anthropomorphize' mean (see end of **Methodological issues**)?

3. Throughout the **Evaluation**, comparisons have been made between children and chimps. Can you identify some important *differences* between Washoe and children acquiring language under normal circumstances?

4. Can you think of a more valid comparison group for the 'experimental group chimps' than 'normal children'?

5. Does it matter that different studies have used different training methods involving different kinds of language?

6. How reliable are the reports of Washoe's acquisition of new signs? Are the criteria strict enough?

7. Is there anything ethically wrong with the way Washoe was 'acquired' for the study? What do you think about the very attempt to teach her what is 'unnatural'?

7 Behavioural study of obedience

Stanley Milgram (1963)

Journal of Abnormal and Social Psychology, 67, 371–8

BACKGROUND AND CONTEXT

In a very real sense, it is the horrific events of the Nazi concentration camps which form the background to the study. Milgram was originally attempting to test 'the Germans are different' hypothesis, used by historians to explain the systematic destruction of millions of Jews, Poles and others in the 1930s and 1940s. This maintains that (*i*) Hitler could not have put his evil plans into effect without the cooperation of thousands of others; and (*ii*) the Germans have a basic character defect, namely a readiness to obey without question, regardless of the acts demanded by the authority figure, and that it is this readiness to obey which provided Hitler with the cooperation he needed. It is the second part of this hypothesis which Milgram was trying to test.

He had originally planned to take the experiment to Germany, and the New Haven experiment was really intended as a 'pilot', a dummy run. The results clearly made this unnecessary: the 'Germans are different' hypothesis had clearly been shown to be false.

AIM AND NATURE OF THE STUDY

The article describes an experimental study of obedience which has become one of the most famous (and infamous) in the whole of social psychology (indeed, in the whole of psychology). According to McGhee (2001), Milgram's obedience studies are:

> . . . probably the most…disturbing, most discussed, most criticized, and most notorious in the history of psychology . . .

He also believes that we cannot legitimately say that we have thought about social psychology unless we have thought thoroughly about Milgram's studies of 'destructive obedience'. Reactions have been quite emotional, and Milgram has been severely criticized, both on ethical and methodological grounds. Indeed, McGhee (2001) maintains that they – and the controversy that followed them – illustrate many general principles relevant to understanding the nature of ethics in social psychological research as a whole (see **Evaluation** below).

The present study should be understood in the context of a whole series of experiments, of which this was the original. It represents a kind of baseline situation, with subsequent experiments systematically varying different variables, intended to throw light on the findings of the original. This initial experiment came to be called the 'remote-victim' experiment, and produced an obedience rate of 65% (obedience being defined as the percentage of participants that went on giving shocks up to the maximum 450 volts). The second experiment in the series (the 'voice-feedback' experiment) produced an obedience rate of 62.5%, and it is this latter figure with which the obedience rates in these later studies are usually compared (Milgram, 1974). It should be stressed that this series was *not* planned: Milgram was as shocked as anybody by the original findings, which were totally unexpected, but which had to be explored further.

Within the 1963 study, the experimental situation was the same for all participants: there were no experimental and control conditions as such, but the experimenter's 'prods and prompts' to carry on giving shocks for wrong answers by the 'learner' (an actor pretending to be another naive participant) could be considered an *independent variable*, with the degree of obedience (measured by how far up the shock scale the participant went) constituting the *dependent variable.*

The study might be more accurately described as a *controlled observational study* than an experiment. Indeed, observation is used as a technique for collecting data within the overall experimental design. Milgram states that tape recorders and photographs were used to record participants' unusual behaviour (sometimes by additional observers via one-way mirrors). Later studies also made film records of the proceedings, and all participants were interviewed immediately after the experiment. All these techniques generate *qualitative* data (such as participants' emotional response to the situation, and things they said about what they were being asked to do), which complement the *quantitative* data (the number of participants continuing to shock up to different shock levels).

The subsequent series of studies involved the manipulation of different variables thought to influence obedience: considered in this context, the present study is like one condition of a complex experiment (there were 18 studies altogether, including this one: see **Evaluation** below).

■ T H E ■ S T U D Y ■

Obedience is as basic an element in the structure of social life as one can point to. Some system of authority is a requirement of all communal living, and it is only the man living in isolation who is not forced to respond, through defiance or submission, to the commands of others. Obedience, as a determinant of behaviour, is of particular relevance to our time. It has been reliably established that from 1939 to 1945 millions of innocent persons were slaughtered on command; gas chambers were built, deathcamps were guarded, daily quotas of corpses were produced with the same efficiency as the manufacture of appliances. These inhumane policies may have originated in the mind of a single person, but they could only be carried out on a massive scale if a very large number of persons obeyed orders.

Obedience is the psychological mechanism which links individual action to political purpose, the dispositional cement which binds men to systems of authority. Facts of recent history and observation in daily life suggest that, for many people, obedience may be a deeply ingrained behaviour tendency, indeed, a pre-potent impulse overriding training in ethics, sympathy and moral conduct. C.P. Snow (1961) points to its importance when he writes:

> When you think of the long and gloomy history of man, you will find more hideous crimes have been committed in the name of obedience than have ever been committed in the name of rebellion. If you doubt that, read William Shirer's *Rise and Fall of the Third Reich*. The German Officer Corps were brought up in the most rigorous code of obedience . . . in the name of obedience they were party to, and assisted in, the most wicked large-scale actions in the history of the world.

While the particular form of obedience involved in the present study has its antecedents in these episodes, it must not be thought that all obedience entails acts of aggression against others; it may also be ennobling and educative and refer to acts of charity and kindness, as well as to destruction.

GENERAL PROCEDURE

Milgram (1961) devised a procedure which consists of ordering a naïve subject to administer electric shocks to a victim. A simulated shock generator is used, with 30 clearly marked voltage levels ranging from 15 to 450 volts; the instrument bears verbal designations that range from 'slight shock' to 'danger: severe shock'. The responses of the victim, who is a trained confederate of the experimenter, are standardized. The orders to administer shocks are given to the naïve subject in the context of a 'learning experiment', ostensibly set up to study the effects of punishment on memory. As the experiment proceeds, the naïve subject is commanded to administer increasingly more intense shocks, even to the level marked 'danger: severe shock'. Internal resistances become stronger, and, at a certain point, the subject refuses to go on with the experiment; behaviour prior to this is considered 'obedience', in that the subject complies with the commands of the experimenter. A quantitative value is assigned to the subject's performance based on the maximum intensity shock he is willing to administer before he refuses to participate further. The crux of the study is to systematically vary the factors believed to alter the degree of obedience to the experimental commands.

(margin, vertical text) THE STUDY

The technique allows important variables to be manipulated at several points in the experiment, including aspects of the authority figure, content and form of command, instrumentalities for its execution, target object, general social setting, etc. So the problem is not one of designing increasingly numerous experimental conditions but of selecting those which best illuminate the *process* of obedience from the sociopsychological standpoint.

R E L A T E D   S T U D I E S

The investigation bears an important relation to philosophical analyses of obedience and authority (Arendt, 1958; Friedrich, 1958, Weber, 1947), an early experimental study of obedience by Frank (1944), studies in 'authoritarianism' (Adorno, Frenkel-Brunswik, Levinson & Sanford, 1950; Rokeach, 1961), and a recent series of analytic and empirical studies in social power (Cartwright, 1959). It owes much to the long concern with *suggestion* in social psychology, both in its normal forms (e.g. Binet, 1900) and in its clinical manifestations (Charcot, 1881). But it derives primarily from direct observation of the ubiquitous and indispensable fact of social life that when people are commanded by a legitimate authority, they usually obey.

M E T H O D

SUBJECTS

The subjects were 40 males aged 20 to 50, drawn from New Haven and the surrounding communities, obtained by a newspaper and direct mail advertisement which asked for volunteers to participate in a study of memory and learning at Yale University. They represented a wide range of occupations, including postal clerks, high-school teachers, salesmen, engineers and labourers. Their education ranged from one who had not finished elementary school to those who had doctorates and other professional degrees. They were paid $4.50 for their participation in the experiment but they were told that payment was simply for coming to the laboratory, regardless of what happened after they arrived.

PERSONNEL AND LOCALE

The experiment was conducted on the grounds of Yale University in the elegant interaction laboratory. (This detail is relevant to the perceived legitimacy of the experiment; in further variations the experiment was dissociated from the university, with consequences for performance.) The role of experimenter was played by a 31-year-old high-school biology teacher; his manner was impassive and his

Table 7.1

DISTRIBUTION OF AGE AND OCCUPATIONAL TYPES IN THE EXPERIMENT

Occupations	20–29 years *n*	30–39 years *n*	40–50 years *n*	Percentage of total (occupation)
Workers skilled and unskilled	4	5	6	37.5
Sales, business and white collar	3	6	7	40.0
Professional	1	5	3	22.5
Percentage of total (age)	20	40	40	
Total *n* = 40				

appearance somewhat stern throughout, and he was dressed in a grey technician's coat. The victim was played by a 47-year-old accountant, trained for the role, of Irish–American stock, whom most observers found mild-mannered and likeable.

PROCEDURE

One naïve subject and one victim (an accomplice) performed in each experiment. A cover story was invented in order to justify the administration of electric shock by the naïve subject; after a general introduction on the presumed relation between punishment and learning, subjects were told:

> But actually, we know *very little* about the effect of punishment on learning, because almost no truly scientific studies have been made of it in human beings.
>
> For instance, we don't know how *much* punishment is best for learning, and we don't know how much difference it makes as to who is giving the punishment, whether an adult learns best from a younger or an older person than himself, or many things of that sort.
>
> So in this study we are bringing together a number of adults of different occupations and ages. And we're asking some of them to be teachers and some of them to be learners. We want to find out just what effect different people have on each other as teachers and learners, and also what effect *punishment* will have on learning in this situation.
>
> Therefore, I'm going to ask one of you to be the teacher here tonight and the other one to be the learner.
>
> Does either of you have a preference?

Subjects then drew slips of paper from a hat to determine who would be the teacher and who the learner; it was rigged so that the naïve subject was always the teacher and the accomplice always the learner (both slips contained the word 'teacher'). The teacher and learner were immediately taken to an adjacent room and the learner was strapped into an 'electric chair' apparatus. The experimenter explained that the straps were to prevent excessive movement while the learner was being shocked; the effect was to make it impossible for him to escape from the situation. An electrode was attached to the learner's wrist and electrode paste was applied 'to avoid blisters and burns'. Subjects were told that the electrode was attached to the shock generator in the adjoining room.

In order to improve credibility, the experimenter declared, in response to a question by the learner: 'Although the shocks can be extremely painful, they cause no permanent tissue damage'.

LEARNING TASK

The lesson administered by the subject was a paired-associate learning task; the subject read a series of word pairs to the learner and then read the first word of the pair along with four terms. The learner had to indicate which of the four terms had originally been paired with the first word. He communicated his answer by pressing one of four switches in front of him, which in turn lit up one of four numbered quadrants in an answer box, located above the shock generator.

SHOCK GENERATOR

The instrument panel consisted of 30 lever switches set in a horizontal line. Each switch is clearly labelled with a voltage designation ranging from 15 to 450 volts. There is a 15 volt increment between switches going from left to right. In addition, the following verbal designations are clearly indicated for groups of four switches: 'slight shock', 'moderate shock', 'strong shock', 'very strong shock', 'intense shock', 'extreme intensity shock', 'danger: severe shock'; (two switches after this are simply marked XXX).

When a switch is depressed, a pilot light corresponding to each switch is illuminated in bright red, an electric buzzing is heard, an electric blue light ('voltage energizer') flashes, the dial on the voltage meter swings to the right and various relay clicks are sounded. The upper left-hand corner of the generator is labelled 'Shock Generator, Type ZLB, Dyson Instrument Company, Waltham, Mass. Output 15 volts–450 volts'.

The generator was very authentic in appearance and no subject suspected it was merely simulated.

SAMPLE SHOCK

Each naïve subject is given a sample shock on the generator of 45 volts, applied by pressing the third switch; it has its source in a 45-volt battery wired into the generator. This further convinces the subject of the authenticity of the generator.

SHOCK INSTRUCTIONS

The subject is told to administer a shock to the learner each time he gives a wrong answer. Moreover – and this is the key command – he is told to 'move one level higher on the shock generator each time the learner flashes a wrong answer'. Also, he must announce the voltage level before administering a shock, intended to continually remind subjects of the increasing intensity of shocks administered to the learner.

PRELIMINARY AND REGULAR RUN

Pre-tests revealed that the procedure of reading words and administering shocks requires some practice before it can be handled smoothly. A preliminary series of ten words is therefore read to the learner, with seven producing incorrect answers and hence shock, the maximum shock being 105 volts (moderate shock). The regular run involves a second list, using the same procedure, except that the subject is told: 'When you get to the bottom of the list, repeat it over again and continue giving shocks, until the learner has learned all the pairs correctly; start from 15 volts and increase the shock level one step each time the learner gives a wrong answer.'

FEEDBACK FROM THE VICTIM

In all conditions the learner gives a predetermined set of responses to the word-pair test, based on a schedule of approximately three wrong answers to one correct answer. In the present experimental condition no vocal response or other sign of protest is heard from the learner until shock level 300 is reached, when he pounds on the wall of the room and this can be heard by the subjects. From this point on, the learner's answers no longer appear on the panel, and subjects usually turn to the experimenter for guidance. He instructs the subject to treat the absence of a response as a wrong answer and to shock the learner according to the usual schedule, allowing five to ten seconds before considering no response as a wrong answer. The pounding on the wall is repeated after the 315-volt shock but subsequently he is not heard from, and answers do not reappear on the panel.

T H E   S T U D Y

EXPERIMENTER FEEDBACK

At various points during the experiment the subject may turn to the experimenter for advice on whether he should continue administering shocks, or he may indicate that he does not wish to go on. The experimenter's responses were standardized in the form of a number of 'prods', using as many as necessary to bring the subject into line.

Prod1: 'Please continue' or 'Please go on'
Prod2: 'The experiment requires that you continue'
Prod3: 'It is absolutely essential that you continue'
Prod4: 'You have no other choice, you *must* go on'

The prods were always made in sequence: only if Prod 1 was unsuccessful could Prod 2 be used etc. If the subject continued to disobey after Prod 4, the experiment was terminated. The experimenter's tone of voice was always firm, but not impolite. The sequence was begun anew each time the subject balked or showed reluctance to follow orders.

If the subject asked if the learner could suffer permanent physical injury, a special prod ('Although the shocks may be painful, there is no permanent tissue damage, so please go on') was used (followed by Prods 2, 3 and 4 if necessary). If the subject said that the learner did not want to go on, another special prod was used ('Whether the learner likes it or not, you must go on until he has learned all the word pairs correctly. So please go on'), followed by Prods 2, 3 and 4 if necessary.

DEPENDENT MEASURES

The primary dependent measure for any subject is the maximum shock he administers before refusing to go any further. In principle this can vary from 0 to 450; a subject who breaks off at any point prior to the highest shock level is called a *defiant* subject, while one who obeys up to 450 volts is called an *obedient* subject.

FURTHER RECORDS

With few exceptions, experimental sessions were recorded on magnetic tape; occasional photographs were taken through one-way mirrors. Notes were kept on any unusual behaviour, sometimes by additional observers. The latency and duration of shocks were measured by accurate timing devices.

INTERVIEW AND DEHOAX

Following the experiment, subjects were interviewed; open-ended questions, projective measures and attitude scales were used. It was ensured that the subject would leave the laboratory in a state of well-being; a friendly reconciliation with the victim was arranged and an attempt was made to reduce any tensions that arose as a result of the experiment.

R E S U L T S

PRELIMINARY NOTIONS

It is useful to consider how others predicted that the subjects would perform. Fourteen Yale psychology majors were asked to reflect carefully on the experimental situation and predicted that only an insignificant minority of '100 Americans of diverse occupations, and ranging in age from 20 to 50 years' would go through to 450 volts (the estimates ranging from 0 to 3 per cent, with a mean of 1.2 per cent). When the author's colleagues were asked informally, most said that few, if any, subjects, would go beyond 'very strong shock'.

RESULT OF EXPERIMENT 1

Subjects accept situation. With few exceptions, subjects were convinced of the reality of the situation, that they were administering shocks to another person and the most potent shocks were extremely painful. In the post-experimental interview, subjects were asked: 'How painful to the learner were the last few shocks that you administered to him?'. On a printed 14-point scale ranging from 'not at all painful' to 'extremely painful', the modal response was 14 ('extremely painful'), with a mean of 13.42.

Signs of extreme tension. Many subjects showed signs of nervousness and especially when giving the more powerful shocks. In many cases, the degree of tension reached extremes rarely seen in sociopsychological laboratory studies: subjects sweated, trembled, stuttered, bit their lips, groaned, dug fingernails into their flesh, and these were typical, not exceptional, responses. Quite a common sign of tension was nervous laughing fits (14 out of 40 subjects) which seemed entirely out of place, even bizarre. Full-blown, uncontrollable seizures were observed for three subjects. On one occasion, a subject had such a violently convulsive seizure that the experiment had to be halted; the 46-year-old encyclopaedia salesman was extremely embarrassed. Subjects took pains to point out that they were not sadistic types, and that the laughter did not mean they enjoyed shocking the victim.

Distribution of scores. As can be seen from Table 7.2, the obtained distribution of scores deviates radically from the prediction. No subject stopped before administering a shock level of 300 volts (at which point the victim kicks on the wall and no longer gives answers to the teacher's questions). Of the 40 subjects, five refused to obey beyond 300 volts, four more gave one further shock before refusing, two broke

THE STUDY

Table 7.2

DISTRIBUTION OF BREAK-OFF POINTS

Verbal designation and voltage indication	Number of subjects for whom this was maximum shock
Slight shock	
15	0
30	0
45	0
60	0
Moderate shock	
75	0
90	0
105	0
120	0
Strong shock	
135	0
150	0
165	0
180	0
Very strong shock	
195	0
210	0
225	0
240	0
Intense shock	
255	0
270	0
285	0
300	5
Extreme intensity shock	
315	4
330	2
345	1
360	1
Danger: severe shock	
375	1
390	0
405	0
420	0
XXX	
435	0
450	26

off at the 330-volts level and one each at 345, 360 and 375 volts. A total of 14 subjects, therefore, defied the experimenter. It is instructive to reproduce their remarks at the point of defiance as transcribed from the tape recordings:

subject no.[0124]   I think he's trying to communicate, he's knocking . . . Well it's not fair to shock the guy . . . these are terrific volts. I don't think this is very humane . . . Oh, I can't go on with this, no, this isn't right. It's a hell of an experiment. The guy is suffering in there. No, I don't want to go on. This is crazy. [Subject refused to administer more shocks.]

subject no.[0123]   He's banging in there. I'm gonna chicken out. I'd like to continue, but I can't do that to a man . . . I'm sorry I can't do that to a man. I'll hurt his heart. You take your check . . . No really, I couldn't do it.

These subjects were often highly agitated and even angry sometimes, verbal protest was sometimes at a minimum and the subject simply got up from his chair and indicated that he wished to leave the laboratory. Even the 26 subjects who obeyed right up to 450 volts often did so under extreme stress; some expressed reluctance to administer shocks beyond the 300-volt level, and displayed fears similar to those who defied the experimenter – yet they obeyed. After the maximum shock had been delivered, and the experimenter called a halt to the proceedings, many obedient subjects heaved sighs of relief, mopped their brows, rubbed their fingers over their eyes or nervously fumbled for cigarettes. Some shook their heads, apparently in regret; some had remained calm throughout the experiment and showed only minimal signs of tension from beginning to end.

D I S C U S S I O N

Two surprising findings were (*i*) the sheer strength of obedient tendencies shown. Despite having learned from childhood that it is a fundamental breach of moral conduct to hurt another person against his will, 26 subjects abandon this principle in following the instructions of an authority who has no special powers to enforce his commands; no punishment or material loss would result from disobedience. It is clear from the remarks and outward behaviour of many subjects that in punishing the victim they are often acting against their own values; despite their deep disapproval of shocking a man who objects and its denouncement by others as stupid and senseless, the majority complied with the experimenter's commands. The serious underestimation of obedience by the 14 Yale students can be explained by their remoteness from the actual situation, and the difficulty of conveying to them the concrete details of the experiment. But the results were also unexpected to people observing the experiment through one-way mirrors; they often expressed disbelief at what they were witnessing, despite being fully acquainted with the details of the situation; and (*ii*) the extraordinary tension and emotional strain generated by the procedure. One observer related:

> I observed a mature and initially poised businessman enter the laboratory smiling and confident. Within 20 minutes he was reduced to a twitching, stuttering wreck, who was rapidly approaching a point of nervous collapse. He constantly pulled on his earlobe, and twisted his hands. At one point he pushed his fist into his forehead and muttered: 'Oh God, let's stop it'. And yet he continued to respond to every word of the experimenter, and obeyed to the end.

Any understanding of the phenomenon of obedience must rest on an analysis of the particular conditions in which it occurs. The following features of the experiment go some way to explaining the high amount of obedience observed in the situation.

1. The experiment is sponsored by and takes place on the grounds of an institution of unimpeachable reputation, Yale University. It may be reasonably presumed that the personnel are competent and reputable. The importance of these factors is now being studied by conducting a series of experiments outside of New Haven, without any visible ties to the university.

2. The experiment is, on the face of it, designed to attain a worthy purpose: advancement of our knowledge about learning and memory. Obedience occurs not as an end in itself, but as an instrumental element in a situation which the subject construes as significant and meaningful; at least he may assume that the experimenter sees its full significance.

3. The subject perceives that the victim has voluntarily submitted to the authority system of the experimenter. He is not (at first) an unwilling captive but has taken the trouble to come to the laboratory, presumably to aid the experimental research. That he later becomes an involuntary subject does not alter the fact that, initially, he consented to participate without qualification and so has an obligation to the experimenter.

4. The subject has also entered the experiment voluntarily and perceives himself as having an obligation to the experimenter.

5. This sense of obligation to the experimenter is strengthened by the fact of being paid for coming to the laboratory. However, this is partly cancelled out by the experimenter's statement that: 'Of course, as in all experiments, the money is yours simply for coming to the laboratory. From this point on, no matter what happens, the money is yours' (43 undergraduates at Yale acted as subjects without payment and the results are very similar to those obtained with paid subjects).

6. From the subject's standpoint, the fact that he is the teacher and the other man the learner is a purely chance occurrence (determined by drawing lots), i.e. they both had equal chance of being assigned the learner role. So the learner cannot complain on this count.

7. There is, at best, ambiguity regarding the respective rights of a psychologist and his subjects; it is unclear what a psychologist may require of his subject and when he is overstepping the mark. Because the experiment occurs in a closed setting, the subject is unable to remove these ambiguities by discussion with others; there are few standards which seem directly applicable to this situation which is a novel one for most subjects.

8. Subjects are assured that the shocks are 'painful but not dangerous', and so assume that the victim's discomfort is momentary, while the scientific gains from the experiment are lasting.

9. The victim continues to provide answers on the signal box right up to 300 volts and subjects may construe this as a sign that the victim is still willing to 'play the game'.

These features help to explain the high amount of obedience and many of the arguments raised can be reduced to testable propositions.

The following features of the experiment concern the nature of the conflict faced by the subject.

1. The subject is placed in a position where he must respond to the competing demands of two people: the experimenter and the victim; satisfaction of their demands is mutually exclusive. Also, the resolution must take the form of a highly visible action, either continuing to shock or breaking off the experiment. The subject is forced, therefore, into a public conflict for which there is no completely satisfactory solution.

2. While the demands of the experimenter carry the weight of scientific authority, the demands of the victim spring from his personal experience of pain and suffering. The two claims need not be seen as equally pressing and legitimate, since the experimenter seeks an abstract scientific datum, while the victim cries out for relief from physical suffering caused by the subject's actions.

3. The experimenter gives the subject little time for reflection: it is only minutes after the experiment begins that the victim begins his protests. Moreover, the first protests are heard after the subject has only gone through two thirds of the shock levels, implying that the conflict will be persistent and may well become more intense as increasingly powerful shocks are given. This may well be a source of tension to the subject.

4. More generally, the conflict stems from the opposition of two deeply ingrained behaviour dispositions: first, the tendency not to harm other people, and second, the tendency to obey those whom we perceive to be legitimate authorities.

EVALUATION

Theoretical issues

Milgram's obedience studies are just as likely (if not more so) to be discussed in relation to the *ethics* of psychological research (see **Aim and nature of the study** above) as in the context of the social psychological processes that Milgram himself was interested in (and which led him to carry them out in the first place). The ethical implications will be discussed at length in **Applications and implications** below.

However, the studies raise fundamental issues about human behaviour, such as accepting responsibility for our actions and how this forms part of our overall self-concept, the power of social situations to make us act in uncharacteristic ways, the influence other people have over our actions, how we are socialized into playing both submissive and authority roles, and the different valuations we put on different kinds of social influence (such as obedience *versus* conformity). Many of these issues are also raised by the Prison Simulation Experiment (see Chapter 8).

Milgram's findings are extremely unsettling: how can it be that 'ordinary', law-abiding, non-sadistic Americans in the 1960s deliver electric shocks to an undeserving fellow American severe enough to make him unconscious – or even kill him? Surely they must have been acting or pretending in some way: in other words, the results aren't what they seem (see **Methodological issues** below). Alternatively, Milgram is to blame for exposing his unsuspecting participants to such an emotionally distressing experience: they weren't 'responsible' for their actions. But for Milgram, this is precisely the point: rather than claiming that they weren't responsible (they obeyed) because they were so distressed, Milgram would argue that they were distressed because they ceased to feel responsible!

Under certain circumstances, namely when we are told what to do by someone in authority (whom we perceive as having greater *power* than ourselves in that situation), we lose our usual sense of being in charge of what we do ('responsible') and this can be disturbing (especially when the orders conflict with our normal sense of 'justice' and what is morally acceptable). Milgram believes that he is holding up a mirror to us, so that his participants' behaviour reflects how we *all* would behave under those same circumstances. We don't always like what we see!

Moghaddam (1998) cites Turnbull's (1972) study of the Ik, a traditional hunter-gatherer people now living in Uganda, near the Kenya border. Social life involves extreme selfishness and total concern with personal survival, to such an extent that parents deprive children of food, and children even refuse water to aged parents. Cheating and stealing food is common. Why? The explanation seems to lie in the terrible conditions they live in. Formerly hunter-gatherers roaming freely in search of game, they were forced by modernization and national boundaries to live in a confined territory with very limited natural resources. Life became a fierce struggle for survival to the extent that they seemed to have completely abandoned the value we associate with human social life. Such extreme conditions, similar to those in the Nazi concentration camps, where many of the values we normally associate with 'human nature' disappear, underline the power of the situation to shape behaviour:

> . . . our behaviour, it seems, is much more dependent on the social context than the dominant Western model of 'self-contained individualism' assumes. (Moghaddam, 1998)

Methodological issues

A central methodological dilemma faced by social psychologists in particular is how to make their experiments have maximum impact on participants without sacrificing control over the situation (Aronson, 1988). Aronson & Carlsmith (1963) distinguished between two kinds of realism:

(*i*) if an experiment has an impact on the participants, forces them to take the situation seriously, and involves them in the procedures, it has achieved *experimental realism*;

(*ii*) the similarity of the laboratory experiment to the events which commonly happen to people in the real world is referred to as *mundane realism*.

Aronson (1988) believes that a confusion between these is often responsible for the criticism that experiments are artificial and worthless, because they do not reflect the world. He claims that Milgram's experiments are high in (*i*) but lower in (*ii*). There is no doubt that it was taken very seriously by participants (and Baumrind's *ethical* condemnation testifies to this: see **Applications and implications** below). However, Milgram believes it also has great mundane realism. He argues that the essential process involved in complying with the demands of an authority figure is the same, whether the setting is the contrived one of the laboratory, or a naturally occurring one outside the laboratory (see **Subsequent research** below).

A major critique of the methodology of Milgram's experiments was made by Orne & Holland (1968), in a paper entitled *On the ecological validity of laboratory deceptions*. They in fact use the term 'ecological validity' to cover what Aronson (1988) calls *experimental* and *mundane realism*. While Aronson argues that Milgram's experiments are high on the former but lack the latter, Orne and Holland claim that Milgram's experiments are lacking in *both* respects.

As far as *experimental realism* is concerned, they claim that participants do not take the experimental situation at face value, in particular, they fail to believe that the learner is receiving painful shocks. But Milgram (1972, 1992) argues that there is abundant evidence:

(*i*)   In the current (1963) article, we are told that on a 14-point scale, with 14 denoting 'extremely painful' and 1 'not at all painful', when participants are asked, 'How painful to the learner were the last few shocks that you administered to him?' the modal response was 14 and the mean, 13.42. In the later Voice-Feedback experiment, the mean was 11.36 (within the 'extremely painful zone').

(*ii*) The obvious tension and distress shown by participants makes Orne and Holland's suggestion that they were *pretending* to sweat, tremble and stutter so as to please the experimenter 'pathetically detached from reality'. The whole of Baumrind's attack on the *ethics* of the experiment (see **Applications and implications** below) is, of course, based on the reality of that distress.

(*iii*) In the follow-up questionnaire one year after participation, one item dealt with shocks given to the learner. The fairest summary of these results is that 80% believed they were giving painful shocks ('I fully believed . . .'. 56.1; 'Although I had some doubts, I believed the learner was *probably* . . .' 24.0). Only 2.4% were 'certain the learner was not . . .', with 11.4% expressing doubt but leaning on the side of 'not'. Finally, 6.1% 'just weren't sure'.

An interesting replication by Rosenhan (1969) included steps to try to ensure that the post-experiment interviewer was seen as independent of the study itself and interested in the participants' true beliefs about what had gone on (e.g. 'You mean you really didn't catch on to the experiment?'). A full 68.9% of his high-school student sample thoroughly accepted the experiment's authenticity.

Orne and Holland point out what they believe is a major incongruity about the experiment, which is bound to have made participants suspicious: why was the participant being asked to give the shocks when the experimenter could so easily have done it himself? Surely this 'gave the game away'? But the answer is provided in the present (1963) article, as part of the experimental instructions (see page 107).

If Orne and Holland were right, then, says Milgram, all they would need to do is put naïve participants in the position of the victim: no technical illusion is required here, because they cannot now deny the genuineness of what is happening! Ironically, Orne has himself carried out such studies (in the context of hypnosis: see Chapter 31) and reports extreme compliance to the experimenter when told to carry out stupid, tedious, noxious tasks; indeed, he could not find any tasks which people would refuse to do! Milgram refers to studies by Turner & Solomon (1962) and Shor (1962), where participants willingly accepted near-traumatizing shocks, and by Kurdika (1965) where people agreed to eat large numbers of crackers soaked in quinine!

Orne and Holland drew on Orne's (1962) concept of *demand characteristics*, according to which participants look for clues and cues as to how they are meant to behave in the experimental situation, and how they can best perform their participant role. They argued that Milgram's participants were responding to demand cues: the experimenter's instructions ('you must go on' etc.) were interpreted as making the experimental situation no different '. . . from the stage magician's trick where a volunteer from the audience is strapped into the guillotine and another volunteer is required to trip the release lever'. However, when applied to the obedience experiment, wouldn't this mean that people believe they should *break off the experiment*?

As far as *mundane realism* is concerned, Orne and Holland argue that the experimental situation is unique as a context for eliciting behaviour, and so we cannot generalize from it. When people agree to participate, this agreement implies giving the experimenter a free hand to ask virtually anything of them for a limited time and, in return, that no harm will befall them (although there may be some discomfort and inconvenience). The willingness of participants in an obedience experiment to carry out seemingly destructive orders reflects this implicit trust in the experimenter, and does not tell us about how they will behave outside the experimental situation. Milgram's (1977, 1992) response is to argue that:

> The occasion we term a psychological experiment shares its essential structural properties with other situations composed of subordinate roles. In all such circumstances the person responds not so much to the content of what is required but on the basis of his relationship to the person who requires it. Indeed . . . where legitimate authority is the source of action, *relationship overwhelms content*. That is what is meant by the importance of social structure and that is what is demonstrated in the present experiment.

It is ironic that Orne's (1962) paper on demand characteristics is *On the social psychology of the psychological experiment* . . . One of his main arguments there is that, first and foremost, experiments are social situations in which experimenter(s) and participant(s) interact, regardless of the details of the particular investigation. This seems to be, in essence, what Milgram himself is saying: either experiments in general (including Milgram's) have structural properties in common with other social situations, or they don't, but Orne seems to make the obedience experiment an exception to this general rule.

Subsequent research

As noted in **Background and context** above, the 1963 study was the inspiration for a series of experiments (18 in total), which are described in Milgram (1974). Several *cross-cultural* replications of the obedience paradigm have been conducted, including Germany (Mantell, 1971), Australia (Kilham & Mann, 1974), the UK (Burley & McGuiness, 1977), and Holland (Meeus & Raajimakers, 1986). The obedience rates in these studies have ranged from 16% (female students in Kilham and Mann's study) to 92% in Meeus and Raajimakers' study (a sample of the general population).

However, it is very difficult to compare these studies, because of methodological discrepancies between them (Smith & Bond, 1998). For example, different types of stooges are used (e.g. a 'long-haired student' in Kilham and Mann's study), some of

whom may have been perceived as more vulnerable or more deserving of shocks than others. In the Meeus and Raajimakers study, the task involved participants having to harass and criticize someone who was completing an important job application. While Milgram (1974) found no gender difference in obedience rate, the Australian female students were asked to shock a *female* learner (but the learner was always male in Milgram's experiments). Also, with the exception of Jordan (Shanab & Yahya, 1978), all the countries studied have been advanced industrial nations, so we should be cautious about concluding that we have identified a universal aspect of social behaviour. However, Smith & Bond (1998) suggest that:

> . . . in none of the countries studied is obedience to authority the kind of blind process that some interpreters of Milgram's work have implied. Levels of obedience can and do vary greatly, depending on the social contexts that define the meaning of the orders given. The importance of changes in this social context may also vary from country to country.

Bickman (1974) got confederates to dress as either a guard (like a US policeman, but without a gun), milkman or civilian and approach people on the street, asking them to pick up a paper bag, give a dime to a stranger, or move away from a bus-stop. People obeyed the guard more than the other two. Similarly, someone in a firefighting uniform was obeyed more often than a civilian, even though the request (to give someone a dime) had nothing to do with the authority role in question (Bushman, 1984). What both these studies illustrate is that culture teaches us to be more obedient to people in certain roles. Conversely, culture also teaches people in certain roles to expect to be obeyed by others (Moghaddam, 1998).

Applications and implications

As we have noted, the obedience experiments have been condemned on ethical grounds. This is ironic in view of the fact that part of the idea for them was to try to make Asch's earlier classic conformity experiments 'more humanly significant' (Milgram, 1992). An appendix in Milgram's *Obedience to Authority* (1974) is devoted to the ethical criticisms, and Milgram's defence and the following points are taken from that appendix.

Baumrind (1964), one of Milgram's harshest critics, expressed concern for the welfare of the participants. Were adequate measures taken to protect them from the undoubted stress and emotional conflict which they experienced? Milgram argues that this presupposes that the outcome of the experiment was expected: she (Baumrind) is confusing the (unanticipated) outcome with the basic experimental procedure. The production of stress was *not* an intended and deliberate effect of the manipulation: the procedure was discussed with colleagues beforehand, and none anticipated the reactions that occurred. You cannot know your results in advance! Milgram maintains that:

Understanding grows because we examine situations in which the end is unknown. An investigator unwilling to accept this degree of risk must give up the idea of scientific inquiry.

In addition, there was every reason to believe that participants would refuse to obey beyond the point where the victim protested. Milgram asks whether the criticism is based as much on the nature of the (unanticipated) findings as the procedure itself (see **Theoretical issues** above). Aronson (1988) asks if we would question the ethics if none of the participants had given shocks beyond the 'moderate shock level'. Apparently not. It seems that individuals' ratings of the 'harmfulness' of the procedure varies according to the type of outcome they believe to have occurred.

Could it be that underlying the criticism of Milgram is the shock and horror of the 'banality of evil' (the subtitle of Hannah Arendt's book on the Israeli trial of Adolf Eichmann, the Nazi who was in charge of the deportation of the Jews to the death camps)? To believe that 'ordinary people' could do what Eichmann did (or what Milgram's participants did) is far less acceptable than that Eichmann was an inhuman monster, or that experimental participants were put under immorally high levels of stress by an inhuman psychologist!

A very thorough debriefing ('de-hoax') was carefully carried out with all participants during which:

(*i*)   they were reunited with the unharmed actor–victim;

(*ii*)   they were assured that no shock had been delivered;

(*iii*) Milgram and the participant had an extended discussion. Obedient participants were assured that their behaviour was entirely normal and that their feelings of conflict and tension were shared by others, while defiant participants were supported in their decision to disobey the experimenter. All were told they would receive (and did) a comprehensive report when all the experiments were over detailing the procedure and the results, and they were also sent a follow-up questionnaire regarding their participation. There was a 92% response rate. Nearly 84% said they were glad or very glad to have participated, while fewer than 2% said they were sorry or very sorry. Eighty per cent felt that more experiments of this kind should be carried out, and 74% had learned something of personal importance.

Milgram points out that the debriefing and assessment were carried out as a matter of course, and *not* stimulated by the participants' (unexpected) distress. One year following the completion of the experiments, an impartial psychiatrist interviewed 40 participants, several of whom had experienced extreme stress. None showed any signs of having been psychologically harmed, or having suffered any traumatic reactions.

In reply to Baumrind's criticism that the experimenter *made* the participant shock the victim, Milgram states that he started with the belief that every person who came to the

laboratory was free to accept or reject the dictates of authority. Far from being a passive creature, participants are active, choosing adults. Criticism also comes in a play called '*The Dogs of Pavlov*' by Dannie Abse (1971), in which the obedience experiment is a central theme. Kurt, the main character, condemns the experimenter for treating him as a guinea-pig. In the play's introduction, Abse criticizes the illusion used in the experiment, but at the same time seems to admire its dramatic quality. Milgram's reply is included in the foreword to the play. Just as illusion is necessary in theatre and is accepted by the audience, so it is in the experiment:

> The central moral justification for allowing a procedure of the sort used in my experiment is that it is judged acceptable by those who have taken part in it. Moreover, it was the salience of this fact throughout that constituted the chief moral warrant for the continuation of the experiments.

He goes on to say that any criticism of the experiment which does not take into account the tolerant reactions of the participants is hollow. 'Again, the participant, rather than the external critic, must be the ultimate source of judgement.'

However, Milgram (1977, 1992) also acknowledges that the use of 'technical illusions' (a term he prefers to 'deception' because of its moral neutrality) poses ethical dilemmas for the researcher. By definition, the use of such illusions means that participants' *informed consent* cannot be obtained, and he asks whether they can be justified. Clearly, he says, they should never be used unless they are 'indispensable to the conduct of the inquiry', and honesty and openness are the only desirable bases of transactions with people in whatever context. He gives examples of professional occupations in which there exist exemptions from general moral principles, without which the profession could not function (e.g. a male gynaecologist being permitted to examine the genitals of female patients). The justification is that the profession is beneficial both to individual patients and society in general. But what about psychology? If anyone is likely to benefit from 'exemptions', it will not be individual participants, but 'people in general'.

He also proposes two compromise solutions to the dilemma of not being able to obtain informed consent because this will 'spoil' the whole purpose of experiments like his obedience experiments:

(*i*)   *Presumptive consent* (of 'reasonable people') involves obtaining the views of a large number of people about the acceptability of an experimental procedure. These people would not participate in the actual experiment (they would no longer be naïve), but their views could be taken as evidence of how people in general would react to participation.

(*ii*) *Prior general consent* could be obtained from people who might, subsequently, serve as experimental participants. Before volunteering to join a pool of volunteers to serve in psychological research, people would be explicitly told that sometimes participants are misinformed about the true purpose of the study and sometimes experience emotional stress. Only those agreeing in the light of this knowledge would be chosen for a particular study. Such a procedure might reconcile the technical need for misinformation ('deception') with the obligation to obtain informed consent. But people would only be agreeing in a very general way, since they would not know in advance the specific manipulations involved in the particular experiment in which they participated.

However much we may condemn Milgram's obedience experiments on ethical grounds, we should remember that in the early 1960s most of the ethical principles which we now take for granted (such as informed consent, use of deception only as a last resort, and others which Milgram himself discusses) were less clearly documented and enforced. Indeed:

> . . . to some extent contemporary ethics codes are a direct consequence of the public and academic debates that followed Milgram's research . . . (McGhee, 2001)

So, part of Milgram's legacy is a set of ethical principles, which, ironically, are used to judge (usually negatively) Milgram's research itself. But not everyone condemns him. For example, Erikson (1968) praises Milgram for making:

> . . . a momentous and meaningful contribution to our knowledge of human behaviour . . . To engage in such studies as Milgram has requires strong men with strong scientific faith and a willingness to discover that to man himself, not to 'the devil' belongs the responsibility for, and the control of, his inhumane actions.

Etzioni (1968) believes the experiments are of major significance, and that they combine 'meaningful, interesting humanistic study' with 'accurate, empirical, quantitative research'. Finally, Elms (1972) rates the experiment as 'some of the most morally significant research in modern psychology'.

Exercises

1. Which variables in the experimental situation were varied in subsequent experiments in order to determine precisely what accounts for such high levels of obedience? (Milgram mentions one himself, but you will need to consult other sources for this information.)

2. Does the importance of the experiment outweigh the moral objections (assuming, of course, that you accept the moral criticisms)?

3. What kind of a sample were Milgram's participants?

4. (*i*)   What is the difference between conformity and obedience?
     (*ii*)   What do they have in common?

8 A study of prisoners and guards in a simulated prison

Craig Haney, Curtis Banks, and Philip Zimbardo (1973)

Naval Research Reviews 30 (9), 4–17

BACKGROUND AND CONTEXT

The present study appears in the *Naval Research Reviews Journal* which, at first, may seem to have little to do with psychology in general or the psychology of imprisonment in particular.

Brown (1985) observes that Western governments and military authorities were shocked by, and totally unprepared for, attempts at mass indoctrination by the Chinese during the Korean war in the early 1950s. This 'thought reform' (from the Chinese word for the psychological techniques used by Chinese Communists to bring about changes in political attitudes and self-concept) was used on United Nations prisoners of war (Korea), as well as Chinese intellectuals and Western civilians living in China. This represented a totally new method of warfare. Instead of merely 'containing' enemy soldiers, the Communists were actively trying to convert them to their 'side'. It also raised questions about loyalty, treason, and the preparation of soldiers for captivity and, in turn, freedom.

As a result, returning prisoners were extensively studied by military psychologists and psychiatrists, and a great deal of subsequent research was undertaken in the USA, Britain and elsewhere, often financed by the military authorities. (Although not prisoners of war, Western hostages, including Brian Keenan, John McCarthy and Terry Waite, underwent a 'debriefing' period by military doctors and psychologists following their release and before their 're-entry' into 'normal' life. Recognition of the need for psychological preparation for life as a non-captive/prisoner is one of the outcomes of the post-Korean research referred to above.)

Brown (1985) also points out that research by Hebb *et al.* (1952) into the disorientating effects of sensory and sleep deprivation (a technique much used in 'thought reform') was carried out on behalf of the Defence Research Board in Canada. Similarly, when discussing the ethics of the study (see **Evaluation** below) Zimbardo (1973) refers to approval being officially sought and received in writing from the sponsoring agency, the Office of Naval Research (ONR). This explains the appearance of the current article in the *Naval Research Reviews Journal*. From such research, lessons have been learnt on how to resist indoctrination and the stresses of captivity. Some of these lessons have been incorporated into military training (Brown, 1985). So, part of the impetus for the present study was a very practical, military concern with the effects of thought control and indoctrination, together with the wish to train soldiers to withstand such pressures and influences from the enemy.

The article itself focuses exclusively on the need to understand why prisons make their populations (staff and inmates) behave in such destructive, dehumanizing, and pathological ways. Only then will it become possible to make them more humanitarian places. Just what is it about prisons that induces such behaviour, and what essential characteristics had to be created in Haney *et al.*'s 'mock' prison to make it a functionally accurate simulation, will be discussed in **Evaluation** below.

AIM AND NATURE OF THE STUDY

This is one account (of several) of what is generally agreed to be one of the most famous and controversial studies in social psychology, if not in the whole of psychology. Emotional reactions to it have been strong, just as they have been to Milgram's obedience studies (see Chapter 7), and these two studies are often discussed together.

One interesting (and potentially confusing) aspect of the 'Prison Simulation Experiment' as it is usually called, is the sheer number of different sources describing it. The 'norm' is that there is a single reference for a particular study (with other references for subsequent studies). But here we have several references for the same single study. In addition to the current reference (Haney *et al.*, 1973), there are:

(*i*) Zimbardo, P. (Oct. 25, 1971) *The psychological power and pathology of imprisonment*. Statement prepared for United States House of Representatives Committee on the Judiciary: Sub-Committee No. 3: Hearings on Prison Reform San Francisco, California.
       This is cited by Aronson (1992), and I have not come across it elsewhere. In case you are confused by the 1971 reference, the study was in fact carried out between August 14–21, 1971 (Murphy *et al.*, 1984).

(*ii*) Zimbardo, P., Banks, C., Haney, C. and Jaffe, D. (1973) A Pirandellian prison: The mind is a formidable jailor. *New York Times Magazine*, April 8, 38–60. (Incidentally, Craig is sometimes given instead of Haney, and sometimes the names are given in a different order, e.g. Zimbardo, Haney, Banks and Jaffe.)

(*iii*) Haney, C. and Zimbardo, P. (1973) Social Roles, role-playing and education: on the high school as a prison. *Behavioural and Social Sciences Teacher, 1*, 24–45.

(*iv*) Haney, C., Banks, C. and Zimbardo, P. (1973) Interpersonal dynamics in a simulated prison. *International Journal of Criminology and Penology, 1*, 69–97.

These accounts are not identical, and certain details differ from source to source. But the essential details, as well as the basic aims and outcomes of the study, are common to all. (Note that as Zimbardo is the 'senior' investigator, the study is normally referred to as 'Zimbardo's Prison Simulation Experiment', whichever source is being cited. He is the 'author' referred to as playing the 'Superintendent' role.)

The basic hypothesis being tested is the *dispositional hypothesis*, the claim that the 'deplorable condition of our penal system and its dehumanizing effects upon prisoners and guards' is due to the 'nature' of the people who administrate it, or the 'nature' of the people who populate it, or both. More specifically, guards are 'sadistic, uneducated and insensitive', which is, presumably, why they are attracted to the job in the first place, while the antisocial attitudes and behaviour of prisoners will prevail whether they are living 'in society' or 'in prison', so force is needed to keep them under control.

By attributing these characteristics to prisoners and guards, it would follow that nothing needs to be done about prisons themselves. If it is the people in them who are responsible for everything that is wrong (a *dispositional* or *internal attribution*), then changing conditions inside prisons will not make any difference. Haney *et al.* expected to find evidence which would allow them to *reject* the dispositional hypothesis in favour of the view that it is the conditions (physical, social and psychological) of prisons which are to blame, not the people in them (a *situational* or *external attribution*: see Chapter 11) and this is, indeed, what they found. (However, their interpretations of the findings have been made: see **Evaluation** section below). Haney *et al.* point out that:

> . . . the dispositional hypothesis cannot be critically evaluated directly through observation in existing prison settings, because such naturalistic observation necessarily confounds the acute effects of the environment with the chronic characteristics of the inmate and guard populations.

In order to separate these two sets of factors, a 'new' prison must be constructed,

> . . . comparable in its fundamental social psychological milieu to existing prison systems, but entirely populated by individuals who are undifferentiated in all essential dimensions from the rest of society.

In other words, if you control for the characteristics of the individuals by deliberately selecting only non-criminal, non-sadistic, psychologically well-adjusted (in this case) young men, then any negative, pathological behaviour can be attributed to the 'prison'. This assumes that the 'mock' prison captures accurately the *functional* (as opposed to the literal) characteristics of a real prison.

The study is an experiment, in which participants are randomly assigned to one of two 'conditions': the prisoner role or the guard role, in order to observe the resulting pattern of behaviour. The specific hypothesis being tested was that:

. . . assignment to the condition 'guard' or 'prisoner' [will] result in significantly different reactions on behavioural measures of interaction, emotional measures of mood state and pathology, attitudes towards self, as well as other indices of coping and adaptation to this novel situation.

It is also a *simulation*: a prison-like environment was specially created, combining some of the characteristics of a real prison with an environment (milieu) designed and constructed by the experimenters (thus resembling a laboratory situation). Detailed *observation* of the behaviour of prisoners and guards is a critical feature of the study as a whole, providing essential *qualitative* data, using video, audiotape and direct observation.

THE STUDY

After he had spent four years in a Siberian prison, the great Russian novelist Dostoevsky commented surprisingly that his time in prison had created in him a deep optimism about the ultimate future of mankind because, as he put it, if a man could survive the horrors of prison life he must surely be a 'creature who could withstand anything'. The cruel irony which Dostoevsky overlooked is that the reality of prison bears witness not only to the resilience and adaptiveness of the men who tolerate life within its walls, but also to the 'ingenuity' and tenacity of those who devised and still maintain our correctional and reformatory systems.

Nevertheless, in the century which has passed since Dostoevsky's imprisonment, little has changed to render the main thrust of his statement less relevant. Although we have passed through periods of enlightened humanitarian reform, in which physical conditions within prison have improved somewhat, and the rhetoric of rehabilitation has replaced the language of punitive incarceration, the social institution of prison has continued to fail. On purely pragmatic grounds, there is substantial evidence that prisons really neither 'rehabilitate' nor act as a deterrent to future crime – in America, recidivism rates upwards of 75 per cent speak for themselves. And, to perpetuate what is also an economic failure, American taxpayers alone must provide an expenditure for 'corrections' of 1.5 billion dollars annually. On humanitarian grounds as well, prisons have failed: our mass media are increasingly filled with accounts of atrocities committed daily, man against man, in reaction to the penal system or in the name of it. The experience of prison creates undeniably, almost to the point of cliché, an intense hatred and disrespect in most inmates for the authority and the established order of society into which they will eventually return. And the toll it takes in the deterioration of human spirit for those who must administer it, as well as for those upon whom it is inflicted, is incalculable.

Attempts to provide an explanation of the deplorable condition of our penal system and its dehumanizing effects upon prisoners and guards, often focus upon what might be called the *dispositional hypothesis*. While this explanation is rarely expressed explicitly, it is central to a prevalent non-conscious ideology: that the state of the social institution of prison is due to the 'nature' of the people who administer it, or the 'nature' of the people who populate it, or both. That is, a major contributory cause to despicable conditions, violence, brutality, dehumanization and degradation existing within any prison can be traced to some innate or acquired characteristic of the correctional and inmate population. Thus on the one hand, there is the claim that violence and brutality exist within prison because guards are sadistic, uneducated and insensitive people. It is this 'guard mentality', a unique syndrome of negative traits which they bring into the situation, that brings about the inhumane treatment of prisoners. On the other hand, it is argued that prison violence and brutality are the logical and predictable results of the involuntary confinement of a collection of individuals whose life histories are, by definition, characterized by disregard for the law, order and social convention and a concurrent tendency towards impulsivity and aggression. It seems to follow logically that these individuals, having proven themselves incapable of functioning satisfactorily within the 'normal' structure of society, cannot do so either inside the structure provided by prisons. To control such men, the argument continues, whose basic orientation to any conflict situation is to react with physical power or deception, force must be met with force, and a certain number of violent encounters must be expected and tolerated by the public.

The disposition hypothesis has been embraced both by supporters of the prison *status quo* (blaming conditions on the evil in the prisoners), and its critics (attributing the evil to guards and staff with their evil motives and deficient personality structures). The appealing simplicity of this argument locates the source of prison riots, recidivism and corruption in these 'bad seeds' and not in the conditions of the 'prison soil'. Such an analysis directs attention away from the complex matrix of social, economic and political forces that combine to make prisons what they are – and what would require complex, expensive, revolutionary actions to bring about any meaningful change. Instead, rioting prisoners are identified, punished, transferred to maximum security institutions or shot, outside agitators sought, and corrupt officials suspended – while the system itself goes on essentially unchanged, its basic structure unexamined and unchallenged.

However, the dispositional hypothesis cannot be critically evaluated directly through observation in existing prison settings, because such naturalistic observation necessarily confounds the acute effects of the environment with the chronic characteristics of the inmate and guard populations.

To separate the effects of the prison environment *per se* from those attributable to the assumed dispositions of its inhabitants requires a research strategy in which a 'new' prison is constructed, comparable in its fundamental social psychological milieu to existing prison systems, but entirely populated by individuals who are undifferentiated in all essential dimensions from the rest of society.

Such was the approach taken in the present empirical study, namely, to create a prison-like situation in which the guards and inmates were initially comparable and characterized as being 'normal-average' and then to observe the pattern of behaviour which resulted, as well as the cognitive, emotional and attitudinal reactions which emerged. Thus, we began our experiment with a sample of individuals who were in the normal range of the general population on a variety of dimensions we were able to measure. Half were randomly assigned to the role of 'prisoner', the others to that of 'guard', neither group having any history of crime, emotional disability, physical handicap or even intellectual or social disadvantage.

The environment created was that of a 'mock' prison which physically constrained the prisoners in barred cells and psychologically conveyed the sense of imprisonment to all participants. Our intention was not to create a *literal* simulation of an American prison, but rather a functional representation of one. For ethical, moral and pragmatic reasons we could not exercise the threat and promise of severe physical punishment, we could not allow homosexual or racist practices to flourish, nor could we duplicate certain other specific aspects of prison life. Nevertheless, we believed that we could create a situation with sufficient mundane realism to allow the role-playing participants to go beyond the superficial demands of their assignment into the deep structure of the characters they represented. To do so, we established functional equivalents for the activities and experiences of actual prison life which were expected to produce qualitatively similar psychological reactions in our subjects – feelings of power and powerlessness, of control and oppression, of satisfaction and frustration, of arbitrary rule and resistance to authority, of status and anonymity, of machismo and emasculation. In the conventional terminology of experimental social psychology, we first identified a number of relevant conceptual variables through analysis of existing prison situations, then designed a setting in which these variables were operationalized. No specific hypotheses were advanced other than the general one that assignment to the condition 'guard' or 'prisoner' would result in significantly different reactions on behavioural measures of interaction, emotional measures of mood state and pathology, attitudes towards self, as well as other indices of coping and adaptation to this novel situation. What follows is a discussion of how we created and peopled our prison, what we observed, what our subjects reported, and finally, what we can conclude about the nature of the prison environment and the psychology of imprisonment which can account for the failure of our prisons.

M E T H O D

OVERVIEW

The effects of playing the role of 'guard' or 'prisoner' were studied in the context of an experimental simulation of a prison environment. The research design was a relatively simple one, involving as it did only a single treatment variable, the random assignment to either a 'guard' or 'prisoner' condition. These roles were enacted over an extended period of time (nearly one week) within an environment that was physically constructed to resemble a prison. Central to the methodology of creating and maintaining a psychological state of imprisonment was the functional simulation of significant properties of 'real prison life' (established through information from former inmates, correctional personnel and texts).

The 'guards' were free within certain limits to implement the procedures of induction into the prison setting and maintenance of custodial retention of the 'prisoners'. These inmates, having voluntarily submitted to the conditions of this total institution in which they now lived, coped in various ways with its stresses and its challenges. The dependent measures were of two general types:

(i) transactions between and within each group, recorded on video and audiotape as well as directly observed;

(ii) individual reactions on questionnaires, mood inventories, personality tests, daily guard shift reports and post-experimental interviews.

SUBJECTS

The 22 subjects who participated were selected from an initial pool of 75 respondents, who answered a newspaper advert asking for male volunteers to participate in a psychological study of 'prison life' in return for payment of $15 per day. Each respondent completed an extensive questionnaire concerning his family background, physical and mental health history, prior experiences and attitudinal tendencies with respect to sources of psychopathology (including their involvements in crime). Each respondent was also interviewed by one of two experimenters. Finally, the 24 subjects who were judged to be most stable (physically and mentally), most mature, and least involved in antisocial behaviours were selected to participate in the study. On a random basis, half the subjects were assigned the role of 'guard' and half the role of 'prisoner'.

The subjects were normal, healthy, male college students who were in the Stanford area during the summer. They were largely of middle-class socioeconomic status and Caucasian (with the exception of one Oriental subject). Initially they were strangers to each other, a selection precaution taken to avoid the disruption of any pre-existing friendship patterns and to mitigate any transfer into the experimental situation of previously established relationships or patterns of behaviour.

The final sample of subjects were administered a battery of psychological tests on the day prior to the start of the simulation, but to avoid any selective bias on the part of the experimenter-observers, scores were not tabulated until the study was completed.

THE STUDY

Two subjects who were assigned as 'stand-by' in case an additional 'prisoner' was needed were not called, and one assigned as 'stand-by' guard decided against participating just before the simulation phase began – thus, our analysis is based upon 10 prisoners and 11 guards in our experimental conditions.

P R O C E D U R E

PHYSICAL ASPECTS OF THE PRISON

The prison was built in a 35-foot section of a basement corridor in the psychology building at Stanford University. It was partitioned by two fabricated walls; one was fitted with the only entrance door to the cell block and the other contained a small observation screen. Three small cells (6 × 9ft) were made from converted laboratory rooms by replacing the usual doors with steel barred, black painted ones, and removing all furniture.

A cot (with mattress, sheet and pillow) for each prisoner was the only furniture in the cells. A small closet across from the cells served as a solitary confinement facility; its dimensions were extremely small (2×2×7 ft), and it was unlit.

In addition, several rooms in an adjacent wing of the building were used as guards' quarters (to change in and out of uniform or for rest and relaxation), a bedroom for the 'warden' and 'superintendent', and an interview testing room. Behind the observation screen at one end of the 'yard' (small enclosed room representing the fenced prison grounds) was video recording equipment and sufficient space for several observers.

OPERATIONAL DETAILS

The 'prisoners' remained in the mock prison 24 hours per day for the duration of the study. Three were arbitrarily assigned to each of the three cells; the others were on stand-by call at their homes. The 'guards' worked on three-man, eight-hour shifts; remaining in the prison environment only during their work shift and going about their normal lives at other times.

ROLE INSTRUCTIONS

It was made explicit in the contract that those assigned the prisoner role should expect to be under surveillance (have little or no privacy) and to have some of their basic civil rights suspended during their imprisonment, excluding physical abuse. They were given no other information about what to expect nor instructions about behaviour appropriate for a prisoner role; once assigned, they were informed by

THE STUDY

phone to be available at their place of residence on a given Sunday when we would start the experiment.

The 'guards' attended an orientation meeting on the day prior to the induction of the prisoners. There they were introduced to the principal investigators, the 'superintendent' of the prison (the author) and an undergraduate research assistant who assumed the administrative role of 'warden'. They were told that we wanted to try to simulate a prison environment within the limits imposed by pragmatic and ethical considerations. Their assigned task was to 'maintain the reasonable degree of order within the prison necessary for its effective functioning', although the specifics of how this duty might be implemented were not spelt out. They were made aware of the fact that, while many of the contingencies with which they might be confronted were essentially unpredictable (e.g. prisoner escape attempts), part of their task was to be prepared for such eventualities and to be able to deal appropriately with the variety of situations that might arise. The 'warden' instructed the guards in the administrative details, including; the work-shifts, the mandatory daily completion of 'critical incident' reports which detailed unusual occurrences, and the administration of meals, work and recreation programmes for the prisoners. In order to begin involving the guards in their roles even before the first prisoner was incarcerated, the guards assisted in the final phases of completing the prison complex – putting the cots in the cells, signs on the walls, setting up the guards' quarters, moving furniture, water coolers, refrigerators etc.

The guards generally believed that we were primarily interested in studying the behaviour of the prisoners. Of course, we were as interested in the effects which enacting the role of guard in this environment would have on their behaviour and subjective states.

To optimize the extent to which their behaviour would reflect their genuine reactions to the experimental prison situation and not simply their ability to follow instructions, they were deliberately given only minimal guidelines for their guard role. An explicit and categorical prohibition against the use of physical punishment or physical aggression was, however, emphasized by the experimenters. Thus, with this single notable exception, their roles were relatively unstructured initially, requiring each 'guard' to carry out activities necessary for interacting with a group of 'prisoners', as well as with other 'guards' and the 'correctional staff'.

UNIFORMS

In order to promote feelings of anonymity in the subjects, each group was issued identical uniforms. For the guards, the uniform consisted of plain khaki shirts and trousers, a whistle, a police night-stick (wooden baton), and reflecting sunglasses which made eye contact impossible. The prisoners' uniform comprised a loose-fitting muslin smock with an identification number on front and back, no under-clothes, a light chain and lock around one ankle, rubber sandles and a cap made from nylon stocking. Each prisoner was also issued a toothbrush, soap, soap-dish, towel and bed linen. No personal belongings were allowed in the cells.

The outfitting of both prisoners and guards in this manner served to enhance group identity and reduce individual uniqueness within the two groups. The khaki uniforms were intended to convey a military attitude, while the whistle and night-stick were symbols of control and power. The prisoners' uniforms were designed not only to deindividuate the prisoners but to be humiliating and serve as symbols of their dependence and subservience. The ankle chain was a constant reminder (even during their sleep when it hit the other ankle) of the oppressiveness of the environment. The stocking cap removed any distinctiveness associated with hair length, colour or style (as does shaving of heads in some 'real' prisons and the military). The ill-fitting uniforms made the prisoners feel awkward in their movements; since these 'dresses' were worn without undergarments, the uniforms forced them to assume unfamiliar postures, more like those of a woman than a man – another part of the emasculating process of becoming a prisoner.

INDUCTION PROCEDURE

With the cooperation of the Palo Alto City Police Department, all of the 'prisoners' were unexpectedly 'arrested' at their residence. A police officer charged them with suspicion of burglary or armed robbery, advised them of their legal rights, handcuffed them, thoroughly searched them (often as curious neighbours looked on) and carried them off to the police station in the rear of the police car. At the station, they went through the standard routines of being fingerprinted, having an identification file prepared and then being placed in a detention cell. Each prisoner was blindfolded and subsequently driven by one of the experimenters and a guard to our mock prison. Throughout the entire arrest procedure, the police officers involved maintained a formal, serious attitude, avoiding answering any questions of clarification as to the relation of their 'arrest' to the mock prison study.

Upon arrival at our experimental prison, each prisoner was stripped, sprayed with a delousing preparation (a deodorant spray) and made to stand alone naked for a while in the cell yard. After being given their uniform and having an ID picture taken ('mug shot'), the prisoner was put in his cell and ordered to remain silent.

ADMINISTRATIVE ROUTINE

When all the cells were occupied, the warden greeted the prisoners and read them the rules of the institution (developed by the guards and the warden). They were to be memorized and to be followed. Prisoners were to be referred to only by the number on their uniforms, also in an effort to depersonalize them.

THE STUDY

The prisoners were to be served three bland meals per day, were allowed three supervised toilet visits, and given two hours daily for the privilege of reading or letter-writing. Work assignments were issued for which they were to receive an hourly wage to constitute their $15 daily payment. Two visiting periods per week were scheduled, as were movie rights and exercise periods. Three times a day prisoners were lined up for a 'count' (one on each guard work-shift). The initial purpose of the 'count' was to ascertain that all prisoners were present, and to test them on their knowledge of the rules and their ID numbers. The first perfunctory counts lasted only about ten minutes, but on each successive day (or night) they were spontaneously increased in length until some lasted several hours. Many of the pre-established features of administrative routine were modified or abandoned by the guards, and some privileges were forgotten by the staff over the course of the study.

R E S U L T S

OVERVIEW

Although it is difficult to anticipate exactly what the influence of incarceration will be upon the individuals who are subjected to it and those charged with its maintenance, especially in a simulated reproduction, the results of the present experiment support many commonly held conceptions of prison life and validate anecdotal evidence supplied by articulate ex-convicts. The environment of arbitrary custody had great impact upon the affective states of both guards and prisoners as well as upon the interpersonal processes taking place between and within those role-groups.

In general, guards and prisoners showed a marked tendency toward increased negative emotions, and their overall outlook became increasingly negative. As the experiment progressed, prisoners expressed intentions to do harm to others more often. For both the prisoners and guards, self-evaluations were more disapproving as the experience of the prison environment became internalized.

Overt behaviour was generally consistent with the subjective self-reports and affective expressions of the subjects. Despite the fact that guards and prisoners were essentially free to engage in any form of interaction (positive or negative, supportive or openly insulting, etc.), the characteristic nature of their encounters tended to be negative, hostile, insulting and dehumanizing. Prisoners immediately adopted a generally passive response mode while guards assumed a very active initiative role in all interactions. Throughout the experiment, commands were the most common form of verbal behaviour and, generally, verbal exchanges were strikingly impersonal, with few references to individual identity. Although it was clear to all subjects that the experimenters would not permit physical violence to take place,

THE STUDY

varieties of less direct aggressive behaviour were often observed (especially on the part of the guards). Instead of physical violence, verbal insults were used as one of the most frequent forms of interpersonal contact between guards and prisoners.

The most dramatic evidence of the impact of this situation upon the particpants was seen in the gross reactions of five prisoners who had to be released because of extreme emotional depression, crying, rage and acute anxiety. The pattern of symptoms was quite similar in four of the subjects and began as early as the second day of imprisonment. The fifth subject was released after being treated for a psychosomatic rash which covered portions of his body. Of the remaining prisoners, only two said they were not willing to forfeit the money they had earned in return for being 'paroled'. When the experiment was terminated prematurely after only six days, all the remaining prisoners were delighted by their unexpected good fortune. In contrast, most of the guards seemed to be distressed by the decision to stop the experiment and it appeared to us that they had become sufficiently involved in their roles that they now enjoyed the extreme control and power which they exercised and were reluctant to give it up. One guard did report being personally upset at the prisoners' suffering and claimed to have considered asking to change his role to become one of them but never did so. None of the guards ever failed to come to work on time for their shift, and indeed, on several occasions guards remained on duty voluntarily and uncomplaining for extra hours – without additional pay.

The extremely pathological reactions which emerged in both groups of subjects testify to the power of the social forces operating, but still there were individual differences in styles of coping with this novel experience and in degrees of successful adaptation to it. Half the prisoners endured the oppressive atmosphere, and not all the guards resorted to hostility. Some guards were tough but fair ('played by the rules'), some went far beyond their roles to engage in creative cruelty and harassment, while few were passive and rarely instigated any coercive control over the prisoners.

REALITY OF THE SIMULATION

At this point it seems necessary to confront the critical question of 'reality' in the simulated prison environment: were the behaviours observed more than the mere acting out of assigned roles convincingly? To be sure, ethical, legal and practical consideration set limits upon the degree to which this situation could approach the conditions existing in actual prisons and penitentiaries. Necessarily absent were some of the most salient aspects of prison life reported by criminologists and documented in the writing of prisoners. There was no involuntary homosexuality, no racism, no physical beatings, no threat to life by prisoners against each other or the guards. Moreover, the maximum anticipated 'sentence' was only two weeks and, unlike some prison systems, could not be extended indefinitely for breaking the internal operating rules of the prison.

In one sense, the profound psychological effects we observed under the relatively minimal prison-like conditions which existed in our mock prison made the results even more significant, and force us to wonder about the devastating impact of chronic incarceration in real prisons. Nevertheless, we must contend with the criticism that our conditions were too minimal to provide a meaningful analogue to existing prisons. We need to demonstrate that the participants transcended the conscious limits of their preconceived stereotyped roles and their awareness of the artificiality and limited period of imprisonment. We feel there is abundant evidence that virtually all the subjects, at one time or another, experienced reactions which went well beyond the surface demands of role-playing and penetrated the deep structure of the psychology of imprisonment.

Although instructions about how to behave in the roles of guard or prisoner were not explicitly defined, demand characteristics in the experiment obviously exerted some directing influence. Therefore, it is enlightening to look to circumstances where role demands were minimal, where the subjects believed they were not being observed, or where they should not have been behaving under the constraints imposed by their roles (as in 'private' situations), in order to assess whether the role behaviours reflected anything more than public conformity or good acting.

When the private conversations of the prisoners were monitored, we learned that almost all (a full 90 per cent) of what they talked about was directly related to immediate prison conditions, that is, food, privileges, punishment, guard harassment etc. Only 10 per cent of the time did their conversations deal with their life outside the prison. Consequently, although they had lived together under such intense conditions the prisoners knew suprisingly little about each others' past history or future plans. This excessive concentration on the changes of fortune in their current situation helped to make the prison experience more oppressive for the prisoners because, instead of escaping from it when they had a chance to do so in the privacy of their cells, they continued to allow it to dominate their thoughts and social relations. The guards, too, rarely exchanged personal information during their relaxation breaks – they either talked about 'problem prisoners', other prison topics, or did not talk at all. There were few instances of any personal communication across the two role groups. Moreover, when prisoners referred to other prisoners during interviews, they typically expressed disapproval, seemingly adopting the guards' negative attitude.

From post-experimental data, we discovered that when individual guards were alone with solitary prisoners and out of range of any recording equipment, as on the way to or in the toilet, harassment was often greater than it was on the 'yard'. Similarly, videotaped analyses of total guard aggression showed a daily escalation even after most prisoners had ceased resisting and prisoner deterioration had become visibly obvious to them. Thus, guard aggression was no longer elicited, as it was initially, by perceived threats, but was emitted simply as a 'natural' consequence of

THE STUDY

being in the uniform of a 'guard' and asserting the power inherent in that role. In specific instances we noted cases of a guard (who did not know he was being observed) in the early morning hours pacing the yard as the prisoners slept – vigorously pounding his night stick into his hand while he 'kept watch' over his captives. Or another guard who detained an 'incorrigible' prisoner in solitary confinement beyond the duration set by the guards' own rules and then conspired to keep him in the hole all night while attempting to conceal this information from the experimenters who were thought to be too soft on the prisoners.

In passing we may note an additional point about the nature of the role-playing and the extent to which actual behaviour is 'explained away' by reference to it. Remember that many guards continued to intensify their harassment and aggressive behaviour even after the second day of the study, when prisoner deterioration became clearly visible and emotional breakdowns began to occur (in the presence of the guards). When questioned after the study about their persistent insulting and harassing behaviour in the face of prisoner emotional trauma, most guards replied that they were 'just playing the role of a tough guard', although none ever doubted the magnitude or validity of the prisoners' emotional response. To what extremes may an individual go, how great must be the consequences of his behaviour for others, before he can no longer rightfully attribute his actions to 'playing a role' and thereby abdicate responsibility?

When introduced to a Catholic priest, many of the prisoners referred to themselves by their prison numbers rather than their first names. Some even asked him to get a lawyer to help get them out. When a public defender was summoned to interview those prisoners who had not yet been released, almost all of them strenuously demanded that he 'bail' them out immediately.

One of the most remarkable incidents of the study occurred during a parole board hearing when each of five prisoners eligible for parole was asked whether he would be willing to forfeit all the money earned as a prisoner if he were to be paroled (released from the study). Three of the five said 'yes', they would be willing to do this. Notice that the original incentive for participating in the study had been the promise of money, and they were, after only four days, prepared to give this up completely. And, more surprisingly, when told that this possibility would have to be discussed with the members of the staff before a decision could be made, each prisoner got up quietly and was escorted by a guard back to his cell. If they regarded themselves simply as 'subjects' participating in an experiment for money, there was no longer any incentive to remain in the study and they could have easily escaped this situation which had so clearly become aversive for them by quitting. Yet, so powerful was the control which the situation had come to have over them, so much a reality had this simulated environment become, that they were unable to see that their original and singular motive for remaining no longer obtained, and they returned to their cells to await a 'parole' decision by their captors.

The reality of the prison was also attested to by our prison consultant who had spent over 16 years in prison, as well as the priest who had been a prison chaplain, and the public defender, all of whom were brought into direct contact with our simulated prison environment. Further, the depressed affect of the prisoners, the guards' willingness to work overtime for no additional pay, the spontaneous use of prison titles and ID numbers in non-role-related situations all point to a level of reality as high as any other in the lives of all of those who shared this experience.

PATHOLOGY OF POWER

Being a guard carried with it social status within the prison, a group identity (when wearing the uniform), and above all, the freedom to exercise an unprecedented degree of control over the lives of other human beings. This control was invariably expressed in terms of sanctions, punishment, demands, and with the threat of manifest physical power. There was no need for the guards to justify rationally a request as they did in their ordinary life; merely to make a demand was sufficient to have it carried out. Many of the guards showed in their behaviour and revealed in post-experimental statements that this sense of power was exhilarating.

The use of power was self-aggrandizing and self-perpetuating. The guard power, derived initially from an arbitrary and randomly assigned label, was intensified whenever there was any perceived threat by the prisoners and this new level subsequently became the baseline from which further hostility and harassment would begin. The most hostile guards on each shift moved spontaneously into the leadership roles giving orders and deciding on punishments. They became role models whose behaviour was emulated by other members of the shift. Despite minimal contact between the three separate guard shifts and nearly 16 hours a day spent away from the prison, the absolute level of aggression, as well as more subtle and 'creative' forms of aggression manifested, increased in a spiralling function. Not to be tough and arrogant was to be seen as a sign of weakness by the guards, and even those 'good' guards who did not get as drawn into the power syndrome as the others, respected the implicit norm of *never* contradicting or even interfering with an action of a more hostile guard on their shift.

After the first day of the study, virtually all prisoner rights (even such things as the time and conditions of sleeping and eating) came to be redefined by the guards as 'privileges' which were to be earned by obedient behaviour. Constructive activities such as watching movies or reading (previously planned and suggested by the experimenters) were arbitrarily cancelled until further notice by the guards – and were subsequently never allowed. 'Reward' then became granting approval for prisoners to eat, sleep, go to the toilet, talk, smoke a cigarette, wear eye-glasses, or the temporary reduction of harassment. One wonders about the conceptual nature of 'positive' reinforcement when subjects are in such conditions of deprivation, and the extent to which even minimally acceptable conditions become rewarding when experienced in the context of such an impoverished environment.

We might also question whether there are meaningful non-violent alternatives as models for behaviour modification in real prisons. In a world where men are either powerful or powerless, everyone learns to despise the lack of power in others and oneself. It seems to us that prisoners learn to admire power for its own sake – power becoming the ultimate reward. Real prisoners soon learn the means of gaining power, whether through ingratiation, informing, sexual control of other prisoners or development of powerful cliques. When they are released from prison, it is likely they will never want to feel so powerless again and will take action to establish and assert a sense of power.

THE PATHOLOGICAL PRISONER SYNDROME

Various coping strategies were used by our prisoners as they began to react to their perceived loss of personal identity and the arbitrary control of their lives. At first they exhibited disbelief at the total invasion of their privacy, constant surveillance, and atmosphere of oppression in which they were living. Their next response was rebellion, first by the use of direct force, and later by subtle divisive tactics designed to foster distrust among the prisoners. They then tried to work within the system by setting up an elected grievance committee. When that collective action failed to produce meaningful changes in their existence, individual self-interests emerged. The breakdown in prisoner cohesion was the start of social disintegration which gave rise not only to feelings of isolation, but deprecation of other prisoners as well. As noted before, half the prisoners coped with the prison situation by becoming 'sick' – extremely disturbed emotionally – as a passive way of demanding attention and help. Others became excessively obedient in trying to be 'good' prisoners. They sided with the guards against a solitary fellow prisoner who coped with his situation by refusing to eat. Instead of supporting this final and major act of rebellion, the prisoners treated him as a troublemaker who deserved to be punished for his disobedience. It is likely that the negative self-regard among the prisoners noted by the end of the study was the product of their coming to believe that the continued hostility toward all of them was justified because they 'deserved it' (following Walster, 1966). As the days wore on, the model prisoner reaction was one of passivity, dependence, and flattened mood. Let us briefly consider some of the relevant processes involved in producing these reactions.

LOSS OF PERSONAL IDENTITY

For most people identity is conferred by social recognition of one's uniqueness and established through one's name, dress, appearance, behaviour style, and history. Living among strangers who do not know your name or history (who refer to you

THE STUDY

only by number), dressed in a uniform exactly like all other prisoners, not wanting to call attention to oneself because of the unpredictable consequences it might provoke – all led to a weakening of self-identity among the prisoners. As they began to lose initiative and emotional responsiveness, while acting even more compliantly, indeed, the prisoners became de-individuated not only to the guards and the observers, but also to themselves.

ARBITRARY CONTROL

On post-experimental questionnaires, the most frequently mentioned aversive aspect of the prison experience was that of being subjected to the patently arbitrary, capricious decisions and rules of the guards. A question by a prisoner as often elicited derogation and aggression as it did a rational answer. Smiling at a joke could be punished in the same way that failing to smile might be. An individual acting in defiance of the rules could bring punishment to innocent cell partners (who became, in effect, 'mutually yoked controls'), to himself, or to all.

As the environment became more unpredictable, and previously learned assumptions about a just and orderly world were no longer functional, prisoners ceased to initiate any action. They moved about on orders and when in their cells rarely engaged in any purposeful activity. Their zombie-like reaction was the functional equivalent of the learned helplessness phenomenon reported by Seligman and Groves (1970). Since their behaviour did not seem to have any contingent relationship to environmental consequences, the prisoners essentially gave up and stopped behaving. Thus the subjective magnitude of aversiveness was manipulated by the guards, not in terms of physical punishment, but rather by controlling the psychological dimension of environmental predictability (Glass & Singer, 1972).

DEPENDENCY AND EMASCULATION

The network of dependency relations established by the guards not only promoted helplessness in the prisoners but served to emasculate them as well. The arbitrary control by the guards put the prisoners at their mercy for even the daily, commonplace functions like going to the toilet. To do so required publicly obtained permission (not always granted) and then a personal escort to the toilet while blindfolded and handcuffed. The same was true for many other activities ordinarily practised spontaneously without thought, such as lighting a cigarette, reading a novel, writing a letter, drinking a glass of water, or brushing one's teeth. These were all privileged activities requiring permission and necessitating a prior show of good behaviour. These low level dependencies brought about a regressive orientation in the prisoners. Their dependency was defined in terms of the extent of the domain of control over all aspects of their lives which they allowed other individuals (the guards and prison staff) to exercise.

THE STUDY

As in real prisons, the assertive, independent, aggressive nature of male prisoners posed a threat which was overcome by a variety of tactics. The prisoner uniforms resembled smocks or dresses, which made them look silly and enabled the guards to refer to them as 'sissies' or 'girls'. Wearing these uniforms without any under-clothes forced the prisoners to move and sit in unfamiliar, feminine postures. Any sign of individual rebellion was labelled as indicative of 'incorrigibility' and resulted in loss of privileges, solitary confinement, humiliation, or punishment of cell mates. Physically smaller guards were able to induce stronger prisoners to act foolishly and obediently. Prisoners were encouraged to belittle each other publicly during the counts. These and other tactics all served to bring about in the prisoners a lessened sense of their masculinity (as defined by their external culture). It followed then, that although the prisoners usually outnumbered the guards during line-ups and counts (nine vs. three) there never was a direct attempt to overpower them. (Interestingly, after the study was brought to an end, the prisoners expressed the belief that the basis for assignment to guard and prisoner groups was physical size. They perceived the guards as 'bigger', when, in fact, there was no difference in average height or weight between these randomly determined groups.)

In conclusion, we believe this demonstration reveals new dimensions in the social psychology of imprisonment worth pursuing in future research. In addition, this research provides a paradigm and information base for studying alternatives to existing guard training as well as for questioning the basic operating principles on which penal institutions rest. If our mock prison could generate the extent of pathology it did in such a short time, then the punishment of being imprisoned in a real prison does not 'fit the crime' for most prisoners – indeed, it far exceeds it! Moreover, since both prisoners and guards are locked into a dynamic, symbiotic relationship which is destructive to their human nature, guards are also society's prisoners.

EVALUATION

Theoretical issues

In the **Background and context** section above, we asked (a) what exactly is it about prisons that induces destructive, dehumanizing and pathological behaviour, and (b) what are the essential characteristics which Haney *et al.* had to create in order to make their 'mock' prison a functionally accurate simulation. One way of answering these questions is to draw on Goffman's concept of 'total institutions' and Bettelheim's descriptions of 'extreme situations'.

Based largely on his study of psychiatric hospitals, Goffman (1968) defined a total institution as:

> . . . a place of residence and work where a large number of like-situated individuals, cut off from the wider society for an appreciable period of time, together lead an enclosed and formally administered round life.

A central feature of such institutions is the breakdown of the 'normal' boundaries between living, work and leisure. This allows high levels of psychological control over inmates, since all aspects of their lives are controlled. However, a regime can be both total and non-coercive at the same time, as demonstrated by kibbutzim and communes; these are democratic and egalitarian, and membership is (or can be) voluntary.

According to Goffman, the basis of the coercive power of staff is the creation and maintenance of the *inequality and social distance* between inmates and staff. On admission, inmates are robbed of their 'identity kit': personal possessions, clothes, and one's name. Being put into uniforms, which are the same for all inmates, helps create a loss of personal identity (or *de-individuation*), which is reinforced by the use of numbers instead of names. Inmates are systematically degraded and mortified through the physical environment and the behaviour of the staff. Inmates may be deprived not only of their freedom, but control over the structuring of their daily life: when to eat, sleep, go to the toilet, what work to do, and so on. The net effect of all these characteristics of total institutions is that the self which existed prior to entering the institution loses its significance, and a new institutional identity is created in its place. The inmates are regarded as a group, who can be understood almost entirely in terms of their common experiences as members of that institution. The basis for this view lies in the idea of institutions as 'people-processing' factories (Cohen & Taylor, 1972). This represents an extreme *situationalist* approach (in contrast with the dispositional hypothesis which Haney *et al.* are trying to refute), namely that situational variables are the *only* significant influences on behaviour.

However, some institutions are 'more total' than others. For both ethical and practical reasons, the 'mock' prison lacked the racism and enforced homosexuality of most real prisons. In turn, prisons for criminals in the USA or the UK, for example, are somewhat more humanitarian than those experienced by prisoners of war in Korea or Nazi concentration camp inmates during the 1930s and 40s. While having many basic features in common (those which make them all 'total'), the differences may be seen in terms of how 'extreme' is the deprivation suffered by the inmates. Describing conditions in Dachau and Buchenwald concentration camps, where he was an inmate, Bruno Bettelheim (1960) states:

> It is now common knowledge that prisoners suffered extreme deprivation and were deliberately tortured . . . prisoners were clothed, housed and fed in total inadequacy; they were exposed to heat, rain, and freezing temperatures for as long as 17 hours a day, seven days a week. Despite extreme malnutrition, they had to perform hardest labour. Every single moment of their lives was strictly

regulated and supervised. They had no privacy whatsoever, were never allowed to see a visitor, lawyer or minister. They were not entitled to medical care; sometimes they got it, sometimes not, but if they did it was rarely administered by medically trained persons. No prisoner was told why he was imprisoned, and never for how long. All of which may explain why I speak of them as persons finding themselves in an 'extreme situation'.

Bettelheim's previous training and experience as a psychoanalyst helped him to protect himself against the disintegration of his personality which he so dreaded, and which he observed in so many fellow inmates:

What happened in the concentration camps suggests that under conditions of extreme deprivation, the influence of the environment over the individual can become total . . . it was the senseless tasks, the lack of almost any time to oneself, the inability to plan ahead because of sudden changes in camp policies, that was so deeply destructive. By destroying man's ability to act on his own or to predict the outcome of his actions, they destroyed the feeling that his actions had any purpose, so many prisoners stopped acting. But when they stopped acting, they soon stopped living. (Bettelheim, 1960)

In Bandura's terms (1986), extreme situations destroy a person's sense of *self-efficacy*, inducing a sense of *learned helplessness* (Seligman, 1975), and this is what makes them so harmful. Could this account for the pathological behaviour of the prisoner-participants? If so, we would still need a different explanation of the guards' behaviour.

Methodological issues

While not everyone would accept an extreme *situationalist* approach, it offers a means of identifying what different institutions have in common, including psychiatric hospitals, prisons, boarding schools and so on. In this way, we can begin to explain how the institution affects the behaviour of the people within it. The 'mock' prison clearly had many of the features of a total institution (see **Exercises** below).

One fundamental issue is the interpretation of the findings. Haney *et al.* are quite confident that they have found sufficient evidence to be able to 'reject' the dispositional hypothesis in favour of the situational explanation, although we should note that this is based only on qualitative data: there is no statistical analysis presented at all. According to Zimbardo (1973), it is:

. . . one of the most convincing demonstrations of the pathological impact of a prison-like environment on human behaviour. Not that anyone ever doubted the horrors of prison, but rather it had been assumed that it was the predispositions of the guards ('sadistic') and prisoners ('sociopathic') that made prisons such evil places. Our study holds constant and positive the dispositional alternative and reveals the power of social, institutional forces to make good men engage in evil deeds.

So, ordinary people can readily be induced to perform abusive and anti-social acts if they are put in a situation where they can feel relatively anonymous, and where such behaviour is expected of them (Zimbardo, 1975: see **Applications and implications** below).

However, is this the only – or the most valid – interpretation?

According to Banuazizi & Mohavedi (1975), the behaviour of both guards and prisoners may have arisen from the *stereotyped expectations* of how guards and prisoners behave. These expectations were held prior to becoming involved in the experiment, and so their behaviour in the experiment cannot be wholly attributed to their actual experiences in the roles to which they were allocated. These 'mental sets', or 'culturally conditioned images' were brought to the situation and influenced their response to the simulated prison environment, that is, they were 'merely' role-playing. How can role-playing ever constitute a 'real' experience, and is it a suitable methodology for testing the dispositional hypothesis?

(*i*)   One reply to this criticism is to ask at what point 'mere' role-playing becomes a 'real' experience? According to Zimbardo (1971, quoted in Aronson, 1992):

> At the end of only six days we had to close down our mock prison because what we saw was frightening. It was no longer apparent to us or most of the subjects where they ended and their roles began. The majority had indeed become 'prisoners' or 'guards', no longer able to clearly differentiate between role-playing and self. There were dramatic changes in virtually every aspect of their behaviour, thinking and feeling.

This strongly suggests that their experiences were all too real, and that even if they were 'merely' role-playing at the outset, they were very soon taking their roles very seriously indeed.

(*ii*)   Even if the role-playing argument has some validity in relation to the guards, it seems very difficult to justify in relation to the prisoner role: just how *are* prisoners meant to act? Brown (1985) believes that if you asked people to describe how prisoners feel and behave, very few would have anticipated their extreme reactions (and by the same logic, she asks if Banuazizi and Mohavedi would attribute the obedience of Milgram's participants [see Chapter 7] to their stereotypes of teachers?). Besides, even if they were role-playing, were they in this respect any different from individuals who actually enter these roles for the first time? They too bring with them expectations regarding appropriate behaviour and then attempt to put these expectations into practice (Thayer & Saarni, 1975, cited in Baron & Byrne, 1991).

(*iii*) It follows from (*ii*) that those participants allocated to the prisoner role would have been less well prepared psychologically, compared with both the guards and hardened criminals. If their stereotyped expectations of their role were much less clear and if their first knowledge of having been allocated to that role was when they were 'arrested' by the Palo Alto police (something they genuinely did not know was going to happen), isn't it highly likely that they experienced much greater stress than a hardened criminal?

In many ways these middle-class, law-abiding students are very much like their counterparts in the concentration camps described by Bettelheim (1960). He identified social class background and political sophistication, together with previous imprisonment, as major influences on how a prisoner coped with the initial shock of being placed in the camp. The non-political middle-class prisoners coped least well, being utterly unable to understand what had happened to them, and why. They often believed that a terrible 'mistake' must have been made, and what most upset them was being treated like 'ordinary criminals'. They disintegrated as individual persons, losing their sense of self-respect, often becoming depressed in an agitated way, and being the most likely of all the prisoner groups to commit suicide. By comparison, political prisoners expected to be arrested sooner or later, Jehovah's Witnesses (conscientious objectors) had their rigid religious beliefs to support them, and the criminals were the least traumatized of all, since they were now on equal terms with high-status individuals, including, in some cases, the judges who sentenced them!

So, if the prisoner participants were likely to be more distressed by their experience than real prisoners, doesn't this invalidate the findings, at least to the extent that the results cannot be generalized to real prisons? Perhaps. But another possibility is that we normally underestimate the distress of real prisoners. If the 'mock' prison did not allow physical brutality, racism, and involuntary homosexuality and, in addition, all the prisoners knew the study had to end after two weeks, but well-adjusted students still reacted in such an extreme, pathological, way, then:

> How terrible must be the psychic costs exacted of real prisoners in their struggle to adjust and adapt in an environment far harsher and more cruel than any we could have simulated, and who, unlike our student-prisoners, live with absolute uncertainty as to their eventual deliverance from it. (Haney & Zimbardo, 1973, quoted in Hollander, 1981)

According to Shaver (1987), the findings can be interpreted by reference to the concept of *de-individuation*, which refers to a loss of personal identity, associated with a lowering of inhibitions against behaving in socially undesirable ways, and a decreased concern for social evaluation (either self-evaluation or evaluation of the self by others: Zimbardo, 1969). Some of the possible influences on de-individuation are anonymity, diffusion of responsibility in a large group, and altered states of consciousness (induced by drugs, stress, or lack of sleep). Whatever the particular behaviour induced by de-individuation, it tends to be irrational, impulsive and atypical of the person concerned.

According to Shaver (1987), given the random allocation to the roles of prisoner or guard, the impossibility of predicting the extreme reactions and the 'freedom' to leave the experiment at any time:

> . . . its results suggest how truly awesome the de-individuating effect of a real prison – or, for that matter, any institution in which a person becomes his or her role – might be.

Haney *et al.* themselves refer to a loss of personal identity, and they use the term 'de-individuate' (in relation to the prisoners' uniform), but they do so in passing. Brown (1985) believes that the concept of *role*, which relates actual behaviour to prior expectations of what is appropriate in a given context, is much more useful in accounting for the startlingly different behaviour of prisoners and guards.

Applications and implications, and subsequent research

Zimbardo (1975) sees the study as confirming the fragility of our individual agency and morality:

> Individual behaviour is largely under the control of social forces and environmental contingencies rather than personality traits, will power . . . Thus we create an illusion of freedom by attributing more internal control to ourselves, to the individual, than actually exists. We thus underestimate the power and pervasiveness of situational controls over behaviour because: a) they are often non-obvious and subtle, b) we can often avoid entering situations where we might be so controlled, c) we label as 'weak' or 'deviant' people in those situations who do behave differently from how we believe we would.

While the power of social roles to influence our behaviour and experience is clearly great, Zimbardo, in line with the predominant social psychological thinking of his day, frames this power in terms of environmental contingencies and situational controls. According to Burr (2002), although the self-contained, rational and moral individual is being portrayed as weak and easily undermined, Zimbardo is retaining the concept of the *pre-social individual.* He does this by making the distinction between the individual and the social, and presents the very pessimistic view that our behaviour is determined by factors of which we are unaware while still believing that we have free will. Burr argues that to reduce social roles to a set of environmental contingencies does a disservice to the richness of the concept as an analytic tool.

Haney also points out that our personal characteristics and beliefs may not guarantee that we always behave as we would hope:

> Individual differences matter very little in the face of an extreme situation . . . Institutional settings develop a life of their own independent of the wishes and intentions and purposes of those who run them. (Haney, in O'Toole, 1997)

The second part of this quote suggests that we perhaps should not look for isolable variables residing in the situation, but should raise our sights to the level of the collectivity, to the patterns of relationships existing between people in institutions, sub-cultures and other groups (Burr, 2002).

The study has provoked almost as much controversy regarding its ethics as Milgram's did (see Chapter 7). Zimbardo (1973) himself believes that the ethical concerns are even more pronounced in the prison study:

> Volunteer prisoners suffered physical and psychological abuse hour after hour for days, while volunteer guards were exposed to the new self-knowledge that they enjoyed being powerful and had abused this power to make other human beings suffer. The intensity and duration of this suffering uniquely qualify the Stanford prison experiment for careful scrutiny of violations of the ethics of human experimentation.

One of the fiercest critics of the study is Savin (1973) who argues that the benefits resulting from the experiment do not justify the distress, mistreatment and degradation suffered by the participants: the end does not justify the means. Besides, the experimenter is the one most likely to benefit (in terms of professional advancement and so on) without having to experience the harm which the participants have to suffer.

Zimbardo (1973) defends the experiment in a variety of ways:

(*i*) The only deception involved was to do with the arrest of the prisoners at the start of the experiment. They weren't told this would happen partly because final approval from the Palo Alto police wasn't given until minutes before they decided to participate, and partly because the researchers wanted the arrests to come as a surprise. 'This was a breach, by omission, of the ethics of our own informed consent contract', which told participants of everything that was going to happen to them (as far as this was predictable), and was signed by every one of them, thus giving their permission for invasion of privacy, loss of civil rights, and harassment. When it was realized just how intense and extensive these were (in a way that was totally unexpected), the experiment was abandoned (six days into a two-week study).

(*ii*) Approval was officially sought, and received in writing, from the Office of Naval Research, the Psychology Department, and the University Committee of Human Experimentation. This Committee did not anticipate the extreme reactions that were to follow.

(*iii*) An alternative methodology was considered which would prevent possible distress to participants, but at the same time yield the desired information. However, nothing suitable could be found.

(*iv*) Group and individual debriefing sessions were held, all participants returned post-experimental questionnaires several weeks, then several months later, then at yearly intervals. Many submitted retrospective diaries and personal analyses of the effects of their participation.

> We are sufficiently convinced that the suffering we observed, and were responsible for, was stimulus-bound and did not extend beyond the confines of that basement prison.

(v) Finally:

> The upset generated by a Milgram or Zimbardo, both from the public and from their colleagues, in part, stems from ethical concerns. But another part of their power lies precisely in their demonstration of how strong situational determinants are in shaping behaviour. No resort to a correlation between 'those' people who do 'evil' things is allowed: the subjects were randomly assigned . . . Milgram's and Zimbardo's studies evoke public outcry in part because, through shaming dramatizations, they remind us just how fragile our ethical independence and integrity really are.

In other words, if we don't like what psychological research reveals about ourselves, then we tend to criticize the research and the researchers.

Significantly, the study was ended prematurely because someone else (neither Zimbardo nor any of the other researchers) challenged the ethics of what was taking place. Christina Maslach had just received her psychology doctorate from Stanford University, and had agreed to interview the participants (although she was not part of the research team). However, she was involved in a romantic relationship with Zimbardo at the time. She came to the basement prison on the evening of the fifth day, in order to familiarize herself with the experiment ahead of the interviews the following day. When Zimbardo asked her what she thought of it, she started to have '. . . this incredible emotional outburst. I started to scream, I started to yell, "I think it is terrible, what you are doing to those boys!" I cried. We had a fight you wouldn't believe, and I was beginning to think, wait a minute, I don't know this guy. I really don't, and I'm getting involved with him?' (Maslach, in O'Toole, 1997). Zimbardo was shocked and upset by her reaction, but eventually that night he acknowledged what she was saying, and realized what had happened to him and the other researchers. At that point, he decided to call the experiment off:

> She challenged us to examine the madness she observed, that we had created and had to take responsibility for. (Zimbardo, in O'Toole, 1997)

But what exactly had happened to him?

> I allowed myself to play the dual roles of principal researcher, who should be . . . removed from the situation, and superintendent of the prison whose function is maintaining the day-to-day, moment-to-moment survival of the system of the prison, maintaining its 'law and order'. I was trapped in the duality of that role. So, very often I would make decisions . . . completely based on what a

governor of a prison would do and not on what a psychologist would do.
Clearly, that was wrong. I should have had someone else playing that role whilst
I should have just been the outside observer-evaluator . . . (Zimbardo, in
McDermott, 1993)

Maslach and Zimbardo married in 1972. But with hindsight, does he believe the
experiment should never have been allowed to happen? Can the ethical criticisms be
justified in terms of the benefits that have resulted from it?

Zimbardo has testified before legislative bodies, courts and military corrections
authorities. He is pleased that testimony about the prison study influenced Congress to
change one law, whereby juveniles accused of federal crimes cannot be placed before
trial with adult prisoners, because of the likelihood of violence against them. *Quiet
Rage*, a video that he produced from footage of the experiment, continues to be used
in colleges, as well as by civil, judicial, military and law enforcement groups to
enlighten and arouse concern about prison life. But the experiment has not brought
about the changes in prisons, or even in guard training, that he would have liked. In
fact, prisons in the US have been radically transformed in the last 25 years to make
them *less* humane, and Zimbardo views prisons as 'failed social-political experiments'
that continue to bring out the worst in relations between people:

> . . . They are just as bad for the guards as the prisoners in terms of their
> destructive impact on self-esteem, sense of justice and human compassion.
> (Zimbardo, in O'Toole, 1997)

For Zimbardo, the prison experiment has led to research on a range of social
situations that generate pathological conditions. These include the social psychology
of madness and cults, shyness as a kind of self-imposed prison, and time perspective –
how people come to be controlled by their overuse of past, present or future
timeframes.

He rejects the view that psychology – and knowledge in general – would be better off if
experiments like the prison study and Milgram's obedience studies were never done.
They throw light on 'a dark side' of human nature, which, given the current ethical
restraints on research, could not be done (or could it? – see below). Of course, there
must be safeguards for participants. Indeed, he advocates that students or
representatives of whatever population is being studied should sit on the University
Ethics Committee, which should send an observer to a pilot session of any potentially
unethical research. Also, there should be a 'meta-experimenter' acting as an unbiased
observer to monitor the impact of research on both participants and experimenters.
S/he should have the authority to intervene at any time on the participants' behalf. All
psychologists should also be vigilant of colleagues' research which appears to violate
basic principles of 'human rights, dignity and ethics'. However:

> . . . to not allow in advance any ethically sensitive research to be done or any
> monitored pre-testing that empirically evaluates its impact on the subjects, simply

means that there are areas of human nature we will never know about.
(Zimbardo, in McDermott, 1993)

He believes the pendulum has swung too far in the direction of protecting human participants at the expense of new knowledge that could benefit society. One of the subtle dangers arising from this concern with the ethics of experiments is that it gives social psychologists an easy 'out'. Behavioural experiments are time-consuming and labour-intensive, and the easier option is to replace them with 'as if', pencil-and-paper self-reports. If you could discover the same things about human nature from asking people to *imagine* how they would behave in a situation, instead of observing what they do, there's clearly no point doing the latter. The Milgram experiments highlight the difference between what people *predict* will happen in particular situations and what *actually* happens (see Chapter 7). For Zimbardo, one of the major legacies of the prison study is to show the strength of the *fundamental attribution error* and the extent of our underestimation of the power of external situational influences (see **Exercises** and Chapter 11). As he says (in McDermott, 1993):

. . . There's no way until you are in it [the situation], that you begin to feel and become entrapped in the power of that situation.

In the light of this discussion about the ethics and value (scientific and social) of his experiment, it might be difficult to guess how Zimbardo would react to *The Experiment*, the BBC's version of the prison study. This was carried out during December 2001, and was screened in April 2002. A newspaper advert appeared under the heading, 'Do you really know yourself?', appealing for volunteers to take part in a 'university-backed social science experiment to be shown on TV'. It warned that successful candidates would be exposed to 'exercise, tasks, hardship, hunger, solitude and anger'. No financial incentive was offered, nor was it implied that involvement would, as in most reality TV shows, be a short cut to celebrity. Instead, the BBC promised that participation would 'change the way you think' (Brockes, 2001).

According to Reicher (one of the social psychologists in charge, from St. Andrews University), the motivation for the study is to ask:

. . . What are the conditions under which people accept oppression or act against it? We want to study how social systems work. (Reicher, in Brockes, 2001)

A studio at Elstree, Hertfordshire, was converted into a 'social environment', within which the 15 volunteers were randomly allocated to the roles of oppressors and oppressed, and encouraged through a system of 'privileges' and 'punishments', to resent each other. Reicher plays down the prison analogy. It works just as well, he says, as an office or a school, where one set of people have power over another. But the creative director describes it as 'more of a detention centre or a prisoner-of-war camp'.

The Exeter University Ethics Committee gave it the green light of approval, and one aspect that Zimbardo would also approve of is the 24-hour monitoring of the participants by a group of independent clinical psychologists. They were given the power to 'pull the plug' on the experiment if they felt it was damaging the participants. Similarly, an independent ethics panel was appointed to monitor the whole experiment, and was empowered to withdraw participants or stop the experiment if this was judged to be appropriate.

In fact, *The Experiment,* due to last 10 days, was ended after only eight or nine. According to Wells (2002), the independent psychologists became concerned that the participants' emotional and physical well-being was in danger of being compromised. Nevertheless, Reicher and Haslam (the other main research psychologists involved, from Exeter University) were overjoyed with the results, which they feel will prove scientifically important. Far from producing an explosion of aggression, some of the participants felt that 'peacenik' tendencies were dominant. According to Haslam, filming stopped a day early because the research had progressed so smoothly and had produced a wealth of data that would take months to process. This was *not* an attempt to replicate Zimbardo's study, but to extend his research and look at what drives positive group behaviour. While there were 'some moments of profound, positive forms of social behaviour', Haslam acknowledges that there were also 'darker sides' to the study (Farrar, 2002).

Zimbardo's reaction to *The Experiment* was initially one of horror, followed by a more qualified concern, and, if it wasn't for the TV element, possible support. He is amazed that British University psychology departments would become involved (Brockes, 2001: see **Exercises**).

Exercises

1. Identify some of the characteristics of the 'mock' prison which make it a 'total' institution.

2. The data presented are *qualitative*. What does this mean and how is it different from *quantitative* data?

3. The *dispositional hypothesis* sees the behaviour of people in prisons as attributable to their personal characteristics (as opposed to the conditions in the prison). What kind of *attributional bias* does this demonstrate?

4. When Haney *et al.* say that 'naturalistic observation [in existing prison settings] necessarily confounds the acute effects of the environment with the chronic characteristics of the inmate and guard populations' (see page 128, penultimate paragraph), what do they mean?

5. What are the independent and dependent variables?

6. What does 'mundane realism' mean? What is another term for it?

7. What experimental design is being used?

8. What is the major advantage of using video/audio recordings compared with direct observation?

9. What were the (*i*) scientific and (*ii*) ethical reasons for choosing participants who were strangers at the beginning of the experiment?

10. How *scientifically valid* can a TV programme such as *The Experiment* be?

9 Good Samaritanism: an underground phenomenon?

Irving M. Piliavin, Judith Rodin, and Jane Allyn Piliavin (1969)

Journal of Personality and Social Psychology, 1 (4), 289–99

BACKGROUND AND CONTEXT

The major inspiration for bystander intervention research was the real-life murder of Kitty (real name Catherine) Genovese in the Queens district of New York in 1964. The first studies, carried out by Latané and Darley in 1968, were laboratory experiments, and it is ironic that Piliavin *et al.* wanted to take the research out of the laboratory (where the victim was only heard and only other participants were seen) and into the real world, where it had all begun. Not only was Kitty Genovese heard but she and her murderer were also seen.

For more than half an hour, 38 respectable, law-abiding citizens in Queens watched a killer stalk and stab a woman and did not call the police. After she was stabbed the first time she screamed, 'Oh, my God, he stabbed me! Please help me! Please help me!' After the murderer had first grabbed her, lights went on in the ten-storey apartment block and windows were opened. From one of the upper windows in the apartment house, a man called down: 'Let that girl alone'. He walked off a little way up the street; lights went out. He returned to stab her a second time. 'I'm dying,' she shrieked, 'I'm dying.' Windows were opened again, lights went on in many apartments. The assailant got into his car and drove off. He returned to stab her a third time, this time fatally. It was all over by about 3.30 a.m., but the first call to the police was recorded at 3.50 a.m. Witnesses had watched from behind their curtains: one couple pulled up chairs to the window and turned the light out to see better. The caller was a man who did not want to 'get involved'.

This information, from the *New York Times* (March 27th, 1964), suggests that there was no doubt that people knew a serious crime was taking place (*defining the situation*). The repeated stabbings must have conveyed to any witnesses that no one else had gone for help, making *diffusion of responsibility* a difficult justification for not intervening themselves. The actual caller's not wanting to get involved suggests that *the cost of intervention* might be the key variable. Other reasons given by witnesses for their inaction included: 'We thought it was a lovers' quarrel', 'Frankly we were afraid' and 'I was tired'. It would seem that 'bystander apathy' (Latané & Darley, 1970) is too simple a label to attach to the inaction of the 38 witnesses.

Perhaps the whole situation is far more complex than this. A number of important variables are related to life in large cities, and these may have played their part in the failure of the 38 witnesses to act. A common reaction to the Kitty Genovese murder is to say, 'this could only have happened in a large metropolis like New York – it wouldn't have happened in a small town or village', the implication being that people who live in cities are much less caring (whether because city life makes them like this or because uncaring people are attracted to city life). In other words, the focus is on people and their dispositions, rather than on the situational forces which influence people's behaviour. It is all too easy to 'blame' the 38 witnesses for Kitty's murder, perhaps because the need to explain such a horrific event is overwhelming, and the *fundamental attribution error* represents the easiest and least complex explanation we can find (see Chapter 11). These issues will be discussed further in the **Evaluation** below.

AIM AND NATURE OF THE STUDY

This is a *field experiment*, which set out to test certain aspects of bystander intervention (a form of helping behaviour) in the natural setting of a subway (tube) train. The main focus was the effect of type of victim (drunk or ill) and race of victim (black or white) (the *independent variables*) on speed of helping, frequency of helping, and race of helper (*dependent variables*).

It was also concerned with the impact of modelling (another independent variable) in emergency situations, that is, the effect on others of seeing someone go to the help of the victim. A final aim was to examine the relationship between size of the group and frequency and latency of helping, with a victim who was both seen and heard.

Up until 1969, most of the studies of altruism had been laboratory experiments, so the New York subway experiment represents a major landmark in this research area. Although the main method used is an experiment (manipulation of an independent variable), the study also involved *participant observation*.

▮ T H E ▮ S T U D Y ▮

A field experiment was performed to investigate the effect of several variables on helping behaviour, using the express trains of the New York 8th Avenue Independent subway as a laboratory on wheels. Four teams of students, each comprising a victim, model and two observers, staged standard collapses in which type of victim (drunk or ill), race of victim (black or white) and presence or absence of a model were varied. Data recorded by observers included number and race of observers, latency of the helping response and race of helper, number of helpers, movement out of the 'critical area', and spontaneous comments. Major findings were that (*i*) an apparently ill person is more likely to receive aid than one who is apparently drunk, (*ii*) race of victim has little effect on race of helper except when the victim is drunk, (*iii*) the longer the emergency continues without help being offered, the more likely it is that someone will leave the area of the emergency and (*iv*) the expected decrease in speed of responding as group size increases ('diffusion of responsibility' effect found by Darley and Latané) does not occur in this situation. Implications of this difference between laboratory and field results are discussed, and a brief model for the prediction of behaviour in emergency situations is presented.

Since the murder of Kitty Genovese in Queens [New York], a rapidly increasing number of social scientists have turned their attentions to the study of the Good Samaritan's act and an associated phenomenon, the evaluation of victims by bystanders and agents. Some of the findings of this research have been provocative and non-obvious. For example, there is evidence that agents, and even bystanders, will sometimes derogate the character of the victim's misfortune, instead of feeling compassion (Berscheid & Walster, 1967; Lerner & Simmons, 1966), and under certain circumstances, instead of 'safety in numbers', there is 'diffusion of responsibility'. Darley and Latané (1968) found that among bystanders hearing an epileptic seizure over earphones, those who believed other witnesses were present were less likely to seek assistance for the victim than were bystanders who believed they were alone. Latané and Rodin (1969) confirmed this finding for response to a victim of a fall, and also suggested that assistance from a group of bystanders was less likely if the group members were strangers than if they were prior acquaintances. Field experiments by Bryan and Test (1967) support the common sense expectation that one is more likely to be a Good Samaritan if one has just observed another individual performing a helpful act.

Much of the work on victimization to date has been performed in the laboratory, which gives greater control, while field studies are more realistic; the present study was designed to provide more information from the latter setting.

The primary focus of the study was on the effect of type of victim (drunk or ill) and race of victim (black or white) on speed of responding, frequency of responding and the race of the helper. Based on the large body of research on similarity and liking as well as that on race and social distance, it was assumed that an individual would be more inclined to help someone of the same than of a different race. As far as type of victim was concerned, the expectation was that help would be offered more often and more quickly to the apparently ill victim. Why? Firstly, it was assumed that people who are regarded as partly responsible for their plight [i.e. drunk] would receive less sympathy and, consequently, help than people seen as not responsible (Schopler & Matthews, 1965). Secondly, it was assumed that whatever sympathy individuals may experience when they observe a drunk collapse, their inclination to help will be dampened by the realization that the victim may become disgusting, embarrassing and/or violent. This realization may not only constrain helping but also lead observers to leave the scene of the emergency.

THE STUDY

The present study also sought to investigate the impact of modelling in emergency situations. Several investigators have found that an individual's actions in a given situation lead others in that situation to engage in similar actions and these situations include those involving Good Samaritanism (Bryan & Test, 1967). A final concern of the study was to examine the relationship between size of group and frequency and latency of helping, with a victim who was both seen and heard. In previous (laboratory) studies (Darley & Latané, 1968, Latané & Rodin, 1969), increases in group size led to decreases in frequency and increases in latency of responding. In these studies, however, the emergency was only heard, not seen; since visual cues are likely to make an emergency much more arousing for the observer, it is not clear that, given these cues, such considerations as crowd size will be relevant determinants of the observer's response to the emergency. Visual cues also provide clear information as to whether anyone has yet helped the victim or if he has been able to help himself. Thus, in the laboratory studies, observers lacking visual cues could rationalize not helping by assuming assistance was no longer needed when the victim ceased calling for help. Staging emergencies in full view of observers eliminates the possibility of such rationalization.

To conduct a field investigation of the above questions under the desired conditions required a setting which would allow the repeated staging of emergencies in the midst of reasonably large groups which remained fairly similar in composition from incident to incident. It was also desirable that each group retain the same composition over the course of the incident and that a reasonable amount of time be available after the emergency occurred for Good Samaritans to act. To meet these requirements, the emergencies were staged during the approximately 7½ minute express run between the 59th Street and 125th Street stations of the 8th Avenue Independent (IND) branch of the New York subways.

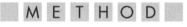 M E T H O D

SUBJECTS

About 4450 men and women who travelled on the 8th Avenue IND in New York City, weekdays, between 11 a.m. and 3 p.m. during the period April 15th to June 26th, 1968, were the unsolicited participants. The racial composition of a typical train, which travels through Harlem to the Bronx, was about 45 per cent black and 55 per cent white. The mean number of people per compartment during these hours was 43 and the mean number of people in the 'critical area' where the incident was staged was 8.5.

FIELD SITUATION

The A and D trains were selected because they make no stops between 59th and 125th Streets; so, for about 7½ minutes there was a captive audience who, after the first 70 seconds of their journey, became bystanders to an emergency. A single trial was a non-stop, 7½-minute journey in either direction. Trials were run only on the old subway carriages since these had two-person seats (rather than extended seats), and the critical area was the end section of any compartment whose doors led to the next compartment. There are 13 seats and some standing room in this area on all trains (see Figure 9.1).

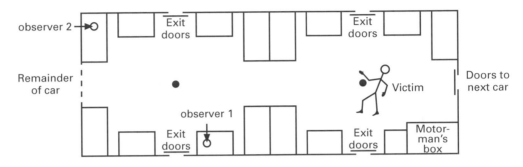

Figure 9.1. Layout of adjacent and critical areas of subway car.

P R O C E D U R E

On each trial, a team of four Columbia General Studies students, two males and two females, boarded the train using different doors. Four different teams, whose members always worked together, collected data for 103 trials. Each team varied the location of the experimental compartment from trial to trial. The female confederates sat outside the critical area and recorded data as unobtrusively as possible during the journey, while the male model and victim remained standing. The victim always stood next to a pole in the centre of the critical area (see Figure 9.1). As the train passed the first station (approximately 70 seconds after departing), the victim staggered forward and collapsed. Until receiving help, he remained supine on the floor, looking at the ceiling. If he received no help by the time the train slowed to a stop, the model helped him to his feet. At the stop, the team got off and waited separately until other passengers had left the station before proceeding to another platform to board a train going in the opposite direction for the next trial. Six to eight trials were run on any given day and all trials on a given day were in the same 'victim condition'.

VICTIM

The four victims (one from each team) were males, aged between 26 and 35, three white, one black, all identically dressed in Eisenhower jackets, old slacks and no tie. On 38 trials the victims smelled of liquor and carried a liquor bottle wrapped tightly in a brown bag (drunk condition), while on the remaining 65 trials they appeared sober and carried a black cane (cane condition). In all other aspects, victims behaved identically in the two conditions, and each victim participated in drunk and cane trials. (Not only were there more cane than drunk trials but they were unevenly distributed across black and white victims. This is because Team 2 violated their instruction to alternate the conditions across days because they 'didn't like' playing the drunk!)

MODEL

Four white males (aged 24 to 29) assumed the role of model in each team, all casually, but not identically, dressed. There were four different model conditions used across both drunk and cane victim conditions:

1. *Critical area – early:* model stood in critical area and waited until passing the fourth station before assisting the victim (approximately 70 seconds after the collapse).
2. *Critical area – late:* model stood in critical area and waited until passing the sixth station before assisting the victim (approximately 150 seconds after the collapse).
3. *Adjacent area – early:* model stood in middle of the compartment, adjacent to critical area and waited until passing the fourth station.
4. *Adjacent area – late:* model stood in adjacent area and waited until passing the sixth station. When the model provided assistance, he raised the victim to a sitting position and stayed with him for the remainder of the trial. An equal number of trials in the no-model condition and in each of the four model conditions were reprogrammed by a random number table.

MEASURES

On each trial one observer noted the race, sex and location of every passenger, seated or standing, in the critical area, together with the total number of passengers and the total number who came to the victim's assistance, plus their race, sex and location. A second observer coded the race, sex and location of all passengers in the adjacent area, plus the latency of the first helper's arrival after the victim had fallen and, on appropriate trials, the latency of the first helper's arrival after the model had intervened. Both observers recorded comments spontaneously made by nearby passengers and also tried to elicit comments from a passenger sitting next to them.

RESULTS AND DISCUSSION

As can be seen from Table 9.1, the frequency of help received by the victims was impressive, at least compared with earlier laboratory studies. The cane victim received spontaneous help (i.e. before the model acted) on 62 out of 65 trials, and even the drunk was helped spontaneously on 19 of 38 trials. The difference cannot be attributed to differences in the number of potential helpers in the compartments; mean number of passengers on cane trials was 45 compared with 40 on the drunk trials.

Table 9.1

PERCENTAGE OF TRIALS IN WHICH HELP WAS GIVEN, BY RACE AND CONDITION OF VICTIM, AND TOTAL NUMBER OF TRIALS IN EACH CONDITION

Trials	White victims		Black victims	
	Cane	Drunk	Cane	Drunk
No model	100%	100%	100%	73%
Number of trials run	54	11	8	11
Model trials	100%	77%	—	67%
Number of trials run	3	13	0	3
Total number of trials	57	24	8	14

In all but three of the cane trials planned to be model trials, the victim received help before the model was scheduled to intervene; this was less likely to happen with the drunk victim, where, in many cases, the early model was able to intervene, and in a few even the delayed model could act.

A direct comparison between the latency of response in the drunk and cane conditions might be misleading, since on model trials one does not know how long it might have taken for a helper to arrive without the stimulus of the model. But omitting the model would drastically reduce the number of drunk trials. Consequently, the trials have been divided into those in which someone helped *before* 70 seconds (the time at which the early model was programmed to help) and those in which no one had helped by this time (including some trials in which people helped the model and a very few in which no one helped at all). (Comparing latencies between cane and drunk non-model trials only, the median latency for cane trials is five seconds and 109 seconds for drunk trials, a difference significant at $p<0.0001$ using the Mann–Whitney U test.)

THE STUDY

Table 9.2

TIME AND RESPONSES TO THE INCIDENT

Trials on which help was offered	Total number of trials		% of trials on which 1 + persons left critical area*		% of trials on which 1 + comments were recorded*		Mean number of comments	
	White victim	Black victim	White victim	Black victim	White victim	Black victim	White victim	Black victim
Before 70 seconds Cane Drunk	52 5	7 4	4% 20%	14% 0%	21% 80%	0% 50%	0.27 1.00	0.00 0.50
Total	57	11	5%	9%	26%	18%	0.33	0.18
After 70 seconds Cane Drunk	5 19	1 10	40% 42%	— 60%	60% 100%	— 70%	0.80 2.00	— 0.90
Total	24	11	42%	64%	96%	64%	1.75	0.82
χ^2 p	36.83 0.001	(a) 0.03	χ^2 time = 23.19 $p < 0.001$ χ^2 cane–drunk = 11.71 $p < 0.001$		χ^2 time = 31.45 $p < 0.001$ χ^2 cane–drunk = 37.95 $p < 0.001$			

(a) Fisher's exact test, estimate of two-tailed probability.

* Black and white victims are combined for the analysis of these data.

It is quite clear from the first section of Table 9.2 that there was more immediate, spontaneous helping of the cane victim than the drunk victim and the effect seems to be essentially the same for the black and white victims.

What of the total number of people who helped? On 60 per cent of the 81 trials on which the victim received help, he received it not from one Good Samaritan, but from two, three or even more. (This analysis only includes data from the non-model trials, since the model's role was to raise the victim to a sitting position and then appear to need assistance, while most real helpers managed to drag the victim to a seat or standing position on their own. Thus the model received rather more help than did real first helpers.) There are no significant differences between black and white victims, or between cane and drunk victims, in the number of helpers, who, subsequent to the first, came to his aid. It would seem, then, that the presence of the first helper has important implications which override whatever cognitive and emotional differences were initially engendered among observers by the victim's characteristics. Perhaps the victim's uniformly passive response to the individual trying to assist him reduced observers' fear about possible unpleasantness in the drunk condition. Another possibility is that second and third helpers were primarily going to the aid of the first helper rather than to the victims.

CHARACTERISTICS OF SPONTANEOUS FIRST HELPERS

On average, 60 per cent of the people in the critical area were males, yet, of the 81 spontaneous first helpers, 90 per cent were males. In this situation, then, men are considerably more likely to help than are women ($\chi^2=30.63$, $p<0.001$).

Of the first 81 helpers, 64 per cent were white, a figure which does not differ significantly from the expected 55 per cent based on racial distribution in the compartments. On the 65 trials on which spontaneous help was offered to the white victims, 68 per cent of the helpers were white which is significantly different ($\chi^2=4.23$, $p<0.05$) from the expected 55 per cent. On the 16 trials on which spontaneous help was offered to the black victim, 50 per cent of the first helpers were white, which represents a slight (non-significant) tendency toward 'same race' helping.

However, when race of helper is analysed separately for cane and drunk conditions, an interesting, though non-significant, trend emerges (see Table 9.3). With both black and white cane victims, the proportion of helpers of each race was consistent with the expected 55 per cent–45 per cent split. But with the drunk, it was mainly members of his own race who came to his aid. Why should this occur? In the case of an innocent victim (i.e. the cane victim), sympathy and trust are relatively uncomplicated by other emotions, and so assistance can readily cut across group lines. But in the case of the drunk (and potentially dangerous) victim, blame, fear and disgust are likely to complicate emotions, especially when the victim is not a

Table 9.3

SPONTANEOUS HELPING OF CANE AND DRUNK BY RACE OF HELPER AND RACE OF VICTIM

Race of helper	White victims			Black victims			All victims		
	Cane	Drunk	Total	Cane	Drunk	Total	Cane	Drunk	Total
Same as victim	34	10	44	2	6	8	36	16	52
Different from victim	20	1	21	6	2	8	26	3	29
Total	54	11	65	8	8	16	62	19	81

White victims: $\chi^2 = 2.11$, $p = 0.16$; black victims, $p = 0.16$ (two-tailed estimate from Fisher's exact probabilities test); all victims = 3.26, $p = 0.08$.

member of one's own group; consequently, help is less likely to be offered. Black and Reiss's (1967) study of the behaviour of white police officers towards apprehended persons tends to support this suggestion: observers noted very little prejudice towards sober individuals, whether white or black, but there was a large increase in prejudice towards drunks, especially if they were black.

MODELLING EFFECTS

There were too few cases of programmed model to allow an analysis. However, while the area variable (critical or adjacent) had no effect on help received, the early model (70 seconds) elicited significantly more help than the late model (150 seconds).

OTHER RESPONSES TO THE INCIDENT

No one left the compartment on any of the trials, but on 21 of the 103 trials, a total of 34 people did leave the critical area. These results are shown in the second section of Table 9.2: people left the area on a higher proportion of trials with the drunk than with the cane victim, and were also far more likely to leave on trials on which help was not offered by 70 seconds than when help was received before that time. The frequencies are too small to make comparisons with each of the variables held constant.

As far as comments of passengers are concerned, content analysis revealed little of interest in the comments themselves. However, far more comments were obtained on drunk than cane trials and most of these were obtained when no one helped until after 70 seconds; this could be due to the discomfort passengers felt in sitting inactive in the presence of the victim, perhaps hoping that others would confirm that inaction was appropriate. Many women, for example, made comments such as 'It's for men to help him' or 'I wish I could help him – I'm not strong enough', 'I never saw this kind of thing before – I don't know where to look', 'You feel so bad that you don't know what to do'.

A TEST OF THE DIFFUSION OF RESPONSIBILITY HYPOTHESIS

In the Darley and Latané experiment it was predicted and found that as the number of bystanders increased, the likelihood that any individual would help decreased and the latency of response increased. Their study involved bystanders who could see neither each other nor the victim. In the Latané and Rodin study, the effect was again found, with bystanders who were face to face but with the victim still only heard. In the present study, bystanders saw both the victim and each other. Did diffusion of responsibility still occur? Two analyses were performed to check this hypothesis. First, all non-model trials were separated into three groups according to the number of males in the critical area (the assumed reference group for spontaneous first helpers). Mean and median latencies of response were then calculated for each group, separately by type and race of victim. No evidence was found for diffusion of responsibility; in fact, response times using either measure were consistently faster for the seven or more groups compared to the one to three groups.

Second, based on an analysis used by Darley and Latané, latencies actually obtained for each size group were compared with a baseline of hypothetical groups of the same size made up by combining smaller groups. (As Darley and Latané pointed out, different-size real groups cannot be meaningfully compared to one another, since, as group size increases, the likelihood that one or more people will help also increases.) To ensure maximum control, the analysis was confined to cane trials with white victims and male first helpers coming from the critical area. Within this set of trials, the most frequently occurring natural groups (of males in the critical area) were three ($n=6$) and seven ($n=5$). Hypothetical groups of three ($n=4$) and seven ($n=25$) were composed of all combinations of smaller sized groups. For example, to obtain the hypothetical latencies for groups of seven, combinations were made of (*i*) all real-size six groups with all real-size one groups, plus (*ii*) all real-size five groups with all real-size two groups etc. The latency assigned to each of these hypothetical groups was that recorded for the faster of the two real groups of which it was composed. Cumulative response curves for real and hypothetical groups of three and seven are shown in Figure 9.2.

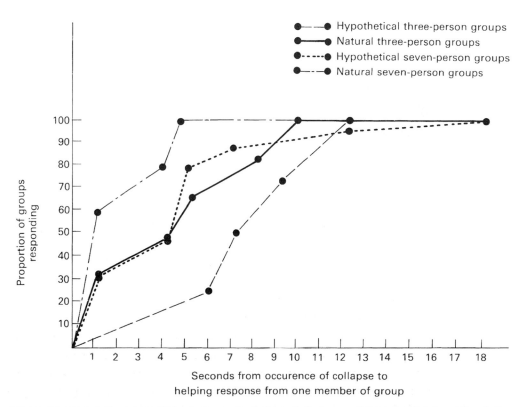

Figure 9.2. Cumulative proportion of groups producing a helper over time (cane trials, white victims, male helpers from inside critical area).

THE STUDY

As can be seen, members of real groups responded more quickly than would be expected on the basis of the faster of the two scores obtained from the combined smaller groups, and these findings do not follow the pattern of findings obtained by Darley and Latané who tentatively conclude that 'a victim may be more likely to receive help . . . the fewer people there are to take action' (Latané and Darley, 1968). How can we explain this discrepancy? (i) As indicated earlier, the fact that observers could see the victim may not only have constrained their ability to conclude there was no emergency but may also have overwhelmed with other considerations any tendency to diffuse responsibility. (ii) Even if diffusion of responsibility is experienced by people who can actually see an emergency, when groups are larger than two, the increment in deterrence to action resulting from increasing the number of observers may be less than the increase in probability that within a given time interval at least one of the observers will take action to help the victim. Clearly, more work is needed in both natural and laboratory settings before we understand the conditions under which diffusion of responsibility will or will not occur.

C O N C L U S I O N S

In this field study, a personal emergency occurred in a public, face-to-face situation, from which it was virtually impossible for the bystander to escape, thus making it different from previous laboratory studies. Some of the major conclusions are:

1. An individual who appears to be ill is more likely to receive help than one who appears to be drunk, even when the immediate help needed is of the same kind.
2. Given mixed groups of men and women, and a male victim, men are more likely to help than are women.
3. Given mixed racial groups, there is some tendency for same-race helping to be more frequent, especially when the victim appears drunk rather than ill.
4. No diffusion of responsibility was found, i.e. help is not less frequent or slower in coming from larger as compared to smaller groups of bystanders; if anything, the effect is in the opposite direction.
5. The longer the emergency continues without help being offered (*i*) the less impact a model has on the helping behaviour of observers, (*ii*) the more likely it is that individuals will leave the immediate area in order to avoid the situation, and (*iii*) the more likely it is that observers will discuss the incident and its implications for their behaviour.

A model of response to emergency situations is briefly presented here as a possible heuristic device, and includes the following assumptions: observation of any emergency creates an emotional arousal state in the bystander, and will be interpreted differently in different situations (Schachter, 1964) as fear, disgust, sympathy, etc. and possibly a combination of these. This arousal state is higher (*i*) the more one can empathize with the victim, i.e. see oneself in his situation (Stotland, 1966), (*ii*) the closer one is to the emergency, and (*iii*) the longer the emergency continues without intervention of a helper. It can be reduced by a number of possible responses: (*i*) helping directly, (*ii*) going to get help, (*iii*) leaving the scene of the emergency, and (*iv*) rejecting the victim as undeserving of help (Lerner & Simmons, 1966). The response that is chosen is a function of the cost–reward matrix that includes costs associated with helping (i.e. effort, embarrassment, possible disgusting or distasteful experiences, possible physical harm, etc.), costs associated with not helping (mainly self-blame and perceived censure from others), rewards associated with helping (mainly self-praise and praise from victim and others), and rewards associated with not helping (mainly those stemming from continuation of other activities). Note that the model implies that the major source of motivation is selfishly to rid oneself of an unpleasant emotional state rather than a positive, altruistic, desire to help. In terms of this model, the following after-the-fact interpretations can be offered:

THE STUDY

1. The drunk is helped less because costs for helping are higher (greater disgust) and costs for not helping are lower (less self-blame and censure because he is partly responsible for his own victimization).
2. Women help less because costs for helping are higher (effort mainly), and costs for not helping are lower (less censure from others; it is not her role).
3. Same-race helping, particularly of the drunk, can be explained by differential costs for not helping (less censure if one is of opposite race) and, with the drunk, differential costs for helping (more fear of opposite race).
4. Diffusion of responsibility is not found on cane trials because costs of helping in general are low, and costs of not helping are high (more self-blame because of possible severity of problem). This suggestion that diffusion of responsibility will increase as costs of helping increase and costs of not helping decrease is consistent with real-life public incidents, in which possible bodily harm to a helper is almost always involved, and with previous research in which either (*i*) it was easy to assume someone had already helped, and thus costs of not helping were reduced (Darley & Latané), or (*ii*) it was possible to think the emergency was minor, which also reduces the costs of not helping (Latané & Rodin).
5. All of the effects of time are also consistent with the model. The longer the emergency continues, the more likely observers are to be aroused and so will have chosen among the possible responses. Thus, (*i*) a late model will elicit less helping since people have already reduced their arousal by one or other method; (*ii*) unless arousal is reduced by other methods, people will leave more as time goes by, because arousal is still increasing; (*iii*) observers will discuss the incident in an attempt to reduce self-blame and arrive at the fourth resolution, namely a justification for not helping based on rejection of the victim.

EVALUATION

Theoretical issues

When discussing the Kitty Genovese murder in the **Background and context** section above, it was suggested that one explanation for the failure of the 38 witnesses to act (before it was too late, anyway) is that people who live in big cities are uncaring. However, Milgram (1970, 1992) and Ross & Nisbett (1991), among others, believe this is an invalid and unhelpful way of understanding what happened. Even if it were true that city dwellers are more callous and indifferent to others' needs, this alone could not account for such incidents where bystanders fail to intervene.

(*i*)   According to Milgram & Hollander (1964):

> Urban friendships and associations are not primarily formed on the basis of physical proximity. A person with numerous close friends in different parts of the city may not know the occupant of an adjacent apartment. This does not mean that a city dweller has fewer friends than does a villager, or knows fewer persons who will come to his aid; however, it does mean that his allies are not constantly at hand. Miss Genovese required immediate aid from those physically present. There is no evidence that the city had deprived Miss Genovese of human associations, but the friends who might have rushed to her side were miles from the scene of the tragedy.

(*ii*)   According to Milgram (1970, 1992), a rule of urban life is respect for other people's emotional and social privacy, perhaps because physical privacy is so hard to achieve. In ambiguous situations (those where a variety of standards are operating), it is much harder to know whether taking an active role is unwarranted interference or an appropriate response to a critical situation. The heterogeneous nature of the city leads to a much greater tolerance regarding behaviour, dress, codes of ethics, etc. compared with the small town, but this diversity also encourages people to withhold their assistance for fear of antagonizing the people involved or crossing an inappropriate and difficult-to-define line. Also, the frequency of demands present in the city result in a norm of non-involvement. As Milgram puts it:

> There are practical limitations to the Samaritan impulse in a major city. If a citizen attended to every needy person, if he were sensitive to and acted on every altruistic impulse that was evoked in the city, he would scarcely keep his own affairs in order.

(*iii*) The 'street' has a symbolic significance for the middle-class mentality, namely, everything that is vulgar and dangerous in life, the very opposite of privacy and the security derived from living among one's prized possessions. As a result, the middle-class person seeks almost automatically to disengage him/herself from the life of the street:

> The tragic drama [Kitty's murder] was taking place on the street, hence hardly relevant to their lives [the 38 witnesses]; in fact, in some ways radically opposed to their outlook and concerns. (Milgram & Hollander, 1964)

(*iv*) Milgram and Hollander also discuss the moral response to the incident, and how this relates to different perspectives and understandings of what took place:

> In our righteous denunciation of the 38 witnesses, we should not forget that they did not commit the murder; they merely failed to prevent it . . .

A related and equally confusing error is to infer ethical values from people's behaviour in concrete situations: did the witnesses remain passive because they thought it was the right thing to do, or *despite* what they felt or thought they should do? We know that people do not always do what they consider to be right. It is highly likely that many of those witnesses, at the level of stated opinions, felt quite as strongly as any of us about the moral obligation to aid a helpless victim. They too, in general (abstract) terms, know what *ought* to have been done. But this has little, if anything, to do with actual behaviour under the 'press of circumstances'. If they had had as clear a grasp of the situation as we have now, the chances are that many of them *would* have acted. Milgram and Hollander cite Bettelheim's *The Informed Heart*, in which he describes the failure of many German Jews during the 1930s to recognize the signs of impending disaster that were all around them.

In March, 1984, a Catherine Genovese Memorial Conference on Bad Samaritanism was held, in which experts could share what they had learned in the 20 years since the tragic event. The *New York Times* again reported the conference:

> It's held the imagination because, looking at those 38 people, we were really looking at ourselves. We might not have done anything either. That's the ugly side of human nature (O'Connor, law professor).

> The case touched on a fundamental issue of the human condition, our primordial nightmare. If we need help, will those around us stand around and let us be destroyed or will they come to our aid? Are those other creatures out there to help us sustain our life and values or are we individual flecks of dust just floating around in a vacuum? (Milgram).

Subsequent research

In their **Conclusions** section, Piliavin *et al.* present a model of response to emergency situations, which was later revised and expanded to cover both emergency and non-emergency helping (Piliavin *et al.*, 1981). According to this *arousal: cost–reward model,*

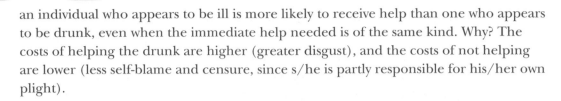

an individual who appears to be ill is more likely to receive help than one who appears to be drunk, even when the immediate help needed is of the same kind. Why? The costs of helping the drunk are higher (greater disgust), and the costs of not helping are lower (less self-blame and censure, since s/he is partly responsible for his/her own plight).

This *cost–reward analysis* constitutes the *cognitive* influence on helping, and refers to the assessment and weighing up of the anticipated costs and rewards associated with both helping and not helping. The other, conceptually distinct but functionally interdependent influence, is *arousal,* which is an emotional response to the needs of others and represents the basic *motivational* construct. A major review of the relevant research was carried out by Dovidio *et al.* (1991: see Gross, 2001). Also see Schroeder *et al.* (1995) for a discussion of the model and relevant research.

The cost-reward analysis is also related to *attribution theory* (see Chapter 11): one of the major determinants of the decision to help or not is the perceived *cause* of the need for help (Weiner, 1992). According to Piliavin *et al.*, the drunk victim is 'partly responsible' for his own plight, but note that they are only proposing this as an 'after-the-fact interpretation'. Is there any evidence that perceived causes are an element of the 'cost–reward matrix'?

A common experimental paradigm is for a student to receive a request for academic assistance from a supposed classmate, with the reasons for the request being manipulated. One early study (Berkowitz, 1969) involved two reasons, experimenter error (*external locus*) or the classmate taking it easy (*internal locus*), with more help being given in the former case. Barnes *et al.* (1979) varied two dimensions of causality independently: (a) *controllability* (the classmate asked to borrow notes either because of low ability [uncontrollable] or lack of effort [controllable]; and (b) *stability.* The uncontrollable cause was much more likely to elicit help, especially if this was seen as a stable characteristic. (Notice that both controllability and stability involve an internal locus, so this was being held constant.) The results suggest, therefore, that it is controllability which is the crucial variable (rather than internal locus).

As applied to the present study, getting drunk is perceived as a controllable cause of a need: people typically are held responsible for their alcohol consumption. When alcoholics are rated along with other stigmatized groups (such as the mentally ill, homosexuals and obese people), they are often seen as the most responsible for their own plight (Weiner, 1992). This is highlighted in campaigns against drink-driving, where, although the driver is clearly not intentionally harming his/her victim, because the harm is a consequence of a freely chosen, controllable act, s/he is held responsible (both legally and morally) for those consequences.

Weiner (1992) sees perceived uncontrollability as making witnesses respond more sympathetically, which, in turn, makes helping more likely, while perceived controllability induces feelings of anger, which make neglect (non-helping) a more likely response. In the present study, the implication is that the ill victim is not responsible because the cause of his need for help is beyond his control, and so he is more likely to receive help for this reason. (In terms of cost–reward, the costs of not helping someone perceived as blameless are far higher than those incurred by not helping someone seen as 'bringing it on themselves'). But are all forms of illness perceived in the same way?

Weiner (1988, cited in Weiner, 1992) asked people to rate 10 stigmas for (a) responsibility and blame, (b) feelings of liking, anger and pity, (c) willingness to give personal assistance and donations to charities. People suffering from Alzheimer's disease, blindness, cancer, heart disease, paraplegia and 'Vietnam War syndrome' were all seen as low on responsibility, high on liking and pity, and were much more likely to be 'promised' help. The reverse picture was true for those with AIDS, drug addictions, obesity, and who committed child abuse.

The degree of responsibility (and hence ratings on all these dimensions) can be altered by providing additional information; for example, someone with heart disease resulting from smoking is much more likely to be blamed. (Note the current debate in the UK about the rights of patients who have already received a liver transplant and who continue drinking heavily to go on the waiting list for another kidney). Similarly, someone who contracted AIDS as a result of a blood transfusion is likely to be judged very differently from someone who contracted it as a result of unprotected sex.

Methodological issues

Given mixed groups of men and women, and a male victim (as in the present study), men are more likely to help than women are. Why? In terms of the arousal: cost-reward model, costs of helping are higher for women (effort mainly), and costs of not helping are lower (less censure from others: 'it is not her role'). So what might have been predicted if the victim were female? According to Eagly (1987), there is good reason to believe the results would not have been very different.

Eagly suggests that helping behaviour is at least as much determined by conforming to gender roles as the demands of the particular situation. Social psychological studies of helping, whether laboratory or field, are confined to short-term encounters with strangers, which seems to increase the chances that men will be the helpers rather than women. This is because such encounters are more consistent with the traditional male gender-role: men are 'heroes', who perform altruistic acts of saving others from harm with some risk to themselves. Related to this is the notion of chivalry (going to the aid of 'helpless females' or the 'damsel-in-distress syndrome'). So, male (*agentic*) helping is often directed towards strangers and women and, in addition, men are expected to be dominant (compared to the submissive female) and assertive, making helping an assertive act of intervention.

Women, by contrast, are expected to place the needs of others (especially family members) before their own. Their orientation is towards listening, sympathizing, showing kindness, and compassion (rather than direct action), and this female (*communal*) type of helping is expressed most readily in the context of long-term relationships. Combined with the female role encouraging avoidance of strangers (particularly men), this means that the sexes should differ in their perception of whether providing aid is likely to lead to danger to themselves as helpers. Especially in situations with an element of risk, men should be more likely to help. Where there is also an audience to witness the helping act and other potential helpers available, this tendency will be even greater. Moghaddam (1998) makes an equivalent distinction between *heroic* (male) and *nurturant* (female) helping.

According to Eagly, the literature (including the present study) by and large confirms these predictions: (*i*) men are more likely to help than women; (*ii*) men are more likely to help women than other men; (*iii*) women help men and other women to an approximately equal extent. But since these findings are largely based on studies that require agentic/heroic helping (including the present study), we cannot draw any general conclusions about sex differences in helping behaviours. Role theory predicts that in other kinds of situations, women will be the greater helpers. Moghaddam (1998) believes that the neglect of communal/nurturant helping reflects a cultural bias in the research.

Interestingly, Piliavin *et al.* found no diffusion of responsibility (as Latané and Darley had found in their laboratory experiments): help was not less frequent or slower in coming from larger groups compared with smaller groups of bystanders. If anything, the effect was in the opposite direction. Why? In the case of the cane victims, the costs of helping are low and those of not helping are high (more self-blame because of possible severity of the problem). It was clearly an emergency, and it was obvious whether help had already been offered, because it happened in full view of the bystanders. No rationalization to the effect that 'someone must have already helped' was possible.

Whatever the advantages of a field experiment like this may be (compared with laboratory studies), an unavoidable feature is that all the participants are unsolicited: they don't know they are participating in an experiment, because they don't know there is an experiment taking place. Nor is it possible to debrief them for obvious, practical, reasons. This raises the *ethical* problem of how to justify putting 'innocent' (non-volunteer) people through what, for some, might be a distressing episode (whether they help or not), when it is not possible to explain to them its false nature and its purpose!

Applications and implications

Given mixed racial groups, Piliavin *et al.* found a tendency for *same-race helping* to be more frequent, especially when the victim appears drunk. Why? The costs of not helping are lower (less censure if one is of the opposite race – at least in a racist society!). But the costs of not helping include the threat to one's self-concept as a fair, non-prejudiced individual, which might explain why, while there was no significant effect of race on helping cane victims, there was a trend ($p = 0.08$) in the drunk condition. Sympathy and trust for the innocent victim are relatively uncomplicated by other emotions, and so assistance can readily cut across race lines. But with the potentially dangerous drunk, blame, fear and disgust do come into play, especially if he is of a different racial group to oneself.

A rather different explanation for help across ethnic lines is given by Milgram (1972, 1992). He cites an unpublished study by Gaertner and Bickman in which Blacks and Whites, with clearly identifiable accents, telephoned strangers (through a 'mis-connection'), giving them a plausible story about how they were stranded on a motorway. They asked the stranger to do them the favour of calling a garage, as they had run out of change for the 'phone. White callers had a significantly better chance of receiving help than the black callers from the white strangers:

> This suggests that ethnic allegiance may well be another means of coping with overload: the city dweller can reduce excessive demands and screen out urban heterogeneity by responding along ethnic lines; overload is made more manageable by limiting the 'span of sympathy. (Milgram, 1972, 1992)

Moghaddam (1998) identifies several models of helping behaviour, placing them on a continuum that runs from 'assumes least self-centredness' at one extreme to 'assumes most self-centredness' at the other. The arousal: cost-reward model comes very close to the 'selfish' end of this scale, with sociobiological accounts (such as Rushton's, 1991) coming at the very end (see Gross, 2001; Schroeder *et al.*, 1995). At the 'unselfish' end comes the *empathy-altruism model* (Batson, 1991, 1995), according to which, when people feel empathy, they become motivated to act, with the ultimate goal of benefiting the person for whom empathy is felt. This contradicts the commonly held view within psychology that all motivation is ultimately directed toward the egoistic goal of increasing our own welfare, and the underlying assumption that human nature is fundamentally self-serving (as made by the arousal: cost-reward model).

To test the empathy-altruism hypothesis, a series of studies have used the tactic of varying the ease with which witnesses of another person in distress can escape (Batson, 1987). If participants' motivation is simply to avoid arousal at the lowest personal cost, they should opt to escape without offering help. Typically, they witness a 'worker' (described as either having similar or dissimilar values to themselves: high and low empathy respectively) receiving electric shocks. Help can be given by participants taking the shocks themselves. They are told either that if they don't help they will not observe the worker take any more shocks (escape possible), or that they will (no escape). As predicted, participants in the high empathy condition tended to help, even when escape was possible. This suggests that there is more to helping than just self-interest.

These and other experiments have led to a move away from *universal egoism*, according to which behaviour that *appears* altruistic always turns out to be self-interest in disguise. According to Batson (2000):

> . . . it is not true that everything we do is directed towards the ultimate goal of benefiting ourselves. It seems that we are capable of being altruistic as well as egoistic.

According to Moghaddam (1998), cross-cultural research shows that the pessimistic explanations offered by the 'selfish' theories do *not* fit what we know about human behaviour. Rather than selfishness being biologically determined (as claimed by sociobiological theories), Moghaddam believes that *culture* is the major source of the great variety of motives (from absolute egoism to true altruism) underlying human prosocial behaviour. However, it is essential when making cross-cultural comparisons to distinguish between help given to *in-group/out-group* members. Under some conditions, people in the USA, for example, tend to be *more* helpful than those in traditional societies to out-group members. This may be because the higher mobility and individualism in the USA (and other Western cultures) lead Americans to interact with out-group members and be both dependent on, and helpful towards, strangers generally. In less mobile, more collectivist, non-Western societies, interactions with outsiders is less common, and less help is offered (Moghaddam, 1998).

Finally, Moghaddam discusses the *meaning* of help:

> Culture provides the rules and norms by which people go about using prosocial behaviour as part of a larger system for managing social relations. Such rules and norms tell us when and how it is appropriate to seek and offer help . . . if the objective were merely to maximize material benefits, then people should take help whenever it is offered, irrespective of the characteristics of the donor. But this is not the case, since the meaning of help is critical for those involved . . .

For example, older people (in certain Western countries, anyway) tend to be particularly sensitive about independence and being able to cope alone (with 'help' often being perceived by them as 'charity'). Women both seek more help than men and receive more offers of help, but as we have seen (see **Methodological issues** above) these findings are based on studies involving mainly *agentic/heroic* helping.

Compared with field studies, laboratory experiments show much lower rates of help-*seeking*. This is because the latter often involve undergraduates who see themselves as in a 'testing' situation, being observed by their lecturers. They do not want to be seen to be needing others. Also, the *social* function of help-seeking (i.e. creating relationships) is missing: people are there briefly, with anonymous others, so there seems little point in trying to extend one's social relationships in such a context (Moghaddam, 1998). This discussion of the meaning of help-giving and seeking underlines the crucial link between *methodology* and research *findings*: the findings of any study cannot be interpreted properly without taking the methodology into account.

Exercises

1. What are the independent and dependent variables in the study?

2. Briefly describe *two* advantages and disadvantages of field experiments compared with laboratory experiments.

3. Name two other kinds of experiment.

4. Why is the Chi-squared (χ^2) test used?

5. What is Fisher's exact probability test?

6. In the **Conclusions** section, Piliavin *et al.* describe their model of helping as a 'possible heuristic device'. What do you understand by this term?

7. What is meant by 'pluralistic ignorance'?

8. How was participant observation used in the study?

9. Distinguish between (a) prosocial behaviour; (b) helping behaviour; and (c) altruism.

10. What are the specific ethical principles being breached by field experiments such as this?

10 Cognitive consequences of forced compliance

Leon Festinger and James M. Carlsmith (1959)

Journal of Abnormal and Social Psychology, 58, 203–10

BACKGROUND AND CONTEXT

According to Festinger's (1957) *cognitive dissonance theory,* whenever an individual simultaneously holds two cognitions (which can be a belief, an idea, awareness or memory of some aspect of our behaviour, or an attitude) which are psychologically inconsistent, s/he experiences *dissonance* (a negative drive state, a state of 'psychological discomfort or tension'). This motivates the individual to reduce dissonance by achieving consonance. A major way of achieving this is through changing one of our cognitions, as in attitude change.

According to the principle of *cognitive consistency* (which is fundamental to the theory), human beings are internally active information processors, who sort through and modify a large number of cognitive elements in order to achieve some kind of cognitive coherence. It is really a part of human nature, a basic human need, thus making cognitive dissonance theory not just a theory of *attitude change,* but also a theory of human *motivation.* Two other major theories of cognitive consistency are Osgood & Tannenbaum's (1955) congruity theory, and Heider's (1958) balance theory.

To appreciate why cognitive dissonance theory was regarded as so innovative and became so influential in social psychology, it needs to be seen in the context of the particular period in the history of psychology as a whole when it first appeared. 1957 was a time when the dominance of behaviourism in America was waning, and the cognitive revolution was gaining momentum (Moghaddam, 1998). It challenged at least two fundamental tenets of behaviourism: (i) that 'mental life' has no place in psychology; and (ii) that behaviour is shaped by reinforcements.

Researchers were beginning to look for alternative sources of inspiration for experimental studies, and in a few years dozens of studies had been carried out. One of the earliest – and still one of the most famous – is the present one. The theory has been tested under three main headings:

(*i*) dissonance *following a decision* (post-decisional dissonance, e.g. having to choose between two equally attractive alternatives, with the prediction that we will devalue the alternative we have rejected);

(*ii*)   dissonance *resulting from effort* (e.g. deciding to put yourself through an embarrassing or stressful situation, only for it to turn out to be trivial and not warranting the embarrassment/stress, with the prediction that the situation will be judged as more important and worthwhile the greater the embarrassment, etc.), and

(*iii*)   engaging in *counter-attitudinal behaviour*, which is where the present ('$1–$20') experiment fits in.

AIM AND NATURE OF THE STUDY

The aim of the study is to test Festinger's (1957) cognitive dissonance theory through a controlled laboratory experiment. Specifically, the two related hypotheses being tested are:

1.   A person induced to do or say something contrary to his private opinion will tend to change his opinion so as to bring it in line with what was done or said.

2.   The larger the pressure to elicit the overt behaviour (beyond the minimum needed to elicit it), the weaker will be the above-mentioned tendency.

The experiment involves three groups/conditions: control, $1 and $20 (which is why the study is often referred to as the '$1–$20' experiment).

THE STUDY

What happens to a person's private opinion if he is forced to do or say something contrary to that opinion? Only recently has there been any experimental work related to this question; two studies by Janis and King (1954, 1956) clearly showed that, at least under certain conditions, the private opinion changes so as to bring it into closer correspondence with the overt behaviour the person was forced to perform. Specifically, they showed that if a person is forced to improvise a speech supporting a point of view with which he disagrees, his private opinion moves toward the position advocated in the speech. The observed opinion change is greater than for persons who only hear the speech, or who read a prepared speech with emphasis solely on elocution and manner of delivery. Janis and King explain the results by proposing that, through mental rehearsal and thinking up new arguments, the subject convinces himself. They present some not totally conclusive evidence to support this explanation which will be discussed later in this report.

Kelman (1953) reasoned that if the person is induced to make an overt statement contrary to his private opinion by the offer of some reward, then the greater the reward offered, the greater should be the subsequent opinion change. However, his data did not support this hypothesis; he found instead that a large reward produced less subsequent opinion change than a smaller reward. In fact, Kelman's finding is consistent with the theory outlined below, but not perfectly so; one reason is that not all subjects in the experiment actually complied, i.e. made an overt statement contrary to their private opinion in order to obtain the reward; another is that, as one might expect, the percentage of subjects who complied increased as the size of the reward increased.

Recently, Festinger (1957) proposed a theory of cognitive dissonance which makes certain predictions about opinion change following forced compliance. The reasoning is as follows:

Let us consider a person who privately holds opinion X but has, as a result of pressure brought to bear on him, publicly stated that he believes 'not X'.

1. This person has two cognitions which, psychologically, do not fit together: one of these is the knowledge that he believes X, the other the knowledge that he has publicly stated that he believes 'not X'. If no factors other than his private opinion are considered, it would follow, at least in our culture, that if he believes X he would publicly state X. Therefore, his cognition of his private belief is dissonant with this cognition concerning his actual public statement.

2. Similarly, the knowledge that he has said 'not X' is consonant with those cognitive elements corresponding to the reasons, pressures, promises of rewards and/or threats of punishment which induced him to say 'not X'.

3. In evaluating the total magnitude of dissonance, we must take into account both dissonances and consonances. If we think of the sum of all the dissonances involving some particular cognition as D, and the sum of all the consonances as C, then we might think of the total magnitude of dissonance as being a function of D divided by D plus C.

   With everything else held constant, the total magnitude of dissonance experienced by the person who believes X but says 'not X' would decrease as the number and importance of the pressures which induced him to say 'not X' increased. From this point on, as the promised rewards or threatened punishments become larger, the magnitude of dissonance becomes smaller.

4. One way of reducing dissonance is for the person to change his private opinion so as to bring it into line with what he has said. One would therefore expect to observe such opinion change after a person has been forced or induced to say something contrary to his private opinion. Furthermore, since the pressure to reduce dissonance will be a function of the magnitude of the dissonance, the observed opinion change should be greatest when the pressure used to elicit the overt behaviour is just sufficient to do it.

The present experiment was designed to test this hypothesis under controlled, laboratory conditions. The amount of reward used to force subjects to make a statement contrary to their private views was varied; the prediction (from **3** and **4** above) is that the larger the reward given to the subject, the smaller will be the subsequent opinion change.

PROCEDURE

THE STUDY

Seventy-one male students in the introductory psychology course at Stanford University were used. In this course, students are required to spend a certain number of hours as subjects (*Ss*) in experiments; they choose among the available experiments by signing their names on a sheet posted on the bulletin board which states the nature of the experiment. The present experiment was listed as a two-hour experiment dealing with 'Measures of Performance'.

During the first week of the course, when the requirement of participating in experiments was announced and explained to the students, the instructor also told them about a study that the psychology department was conducting. He explained that, since they were required to serve in experiments, the department was conducting a study to evaluate these experiments in order to be able to improve them in the future. They were told that a sample of students would be interviewed after having served as *Ss* and they were urged to cooperate in these interviews by being completely frank and honest. This enabled us to measure the opinions of our *Ss* in a context not directly connected with our experiment and in which we could reasonably expect honest expressions of opinion.

When the *S* arrived for the experiment on 'Measures of Performance', he had to wait for a few minutes in the secretary's office. The experimenter (*E*) then came in, introduced himself to the *S*, and together they entered the laboratory room where *E* said:

> This experiment usually takes a little over an hour but, of course, we had to schedule it for two hours. Since we have that extra time, the introductory psychology people asked if they could interview some of our subjects. (*Offhand and conversationally*) Did they announce that in class? I gather that they're interviewing some people who have been in the experiments. I don't know much about it. Anyhow, they may want to interview you when you're through here.

With no further introduction or explanation, *S* was shown the first task, which involved putting 12 spools onto a tray, emptying the tray, refilling it with spools and so on. He was told to use one hand and to work at his own pace. He did this for half an hour. *E* then removed the tray and spools and placed before *S* a board containing 48 square pegs which he was to turn a quarter turn clockwise, then another quarter turn and so on. Again he was to use one hand and to work at his own pace; this took another half hour.

While *S* was working at these tasks, *E* sat, stopwatch in hand, busily making notes; this was to convince *S* that it was the tasks and *S*'s performance on them which comprised the total experiment. In reality, the experiment had hardly begun. The hour spent working on the repetitive, monotonous tasks were meant to provide for each *S* an experience about which he would have a rather negative opinion.

After the hour was over, *E* conspicuously set the stopwatch back to zero, put it away, pushed his chair back, lit a cigarette and said:

> OK. Well, that's all we have in the experiment itself. I'd like to explain what this has been all about, so you'll have some idea of why you were doing this. (*E pauses*) Well, the way the experiment is set up is this. There are actually two groups in the experiment. In one, the group you were in, we bring the subject in and give him essentially no introduction to the experiment. That is, all we tell him is what he needs to know in order to do the tasks, and he has no idea of what the experiment is all about, or what it's going to be like, or anything like that. But in the other group, we have a student that we've hired that works for us regularly, and what I do is take him into the next room where the subject is waiting – the same room you were waiting in before – and I introduce him as if he had just finished being a subject in the experiment. That is, I say:

> 'This is so-and-so, who's just finished the experiment, and I've asked him to tell you a little of what it's about before you start.'

> The fellow who works for us then, in conversation with the next subject, makes these points: (*E then produced a sheet headed 'For Group B' which had written on it: 'it was very enjoyable', 'I had a lot of fun', 'I enjoyed myself', 'it was very interesting', 'it was intriguing', 'it was exciting'. E showed this to S and then proceeded with his false explanation of the purpose of the experiment*). Now, of course, we have this student to do this, because if the experimenter does it, it doesn't look as realistic and what we're interested in doing is comparing how these two groups do on the experiment: the one with this previous expectation about the experiment, and the other, like yourself, with essentially none.

Up to this point, the procedure was identical for *Ss* in all conditions but from this point on they diverged. There were three conditions, Control, $1 and $20, run as follows:

CONTROL CONDITION

E continued:

> Is that fairly clear? (*Pause*). Look, that fellow (*looks at watch*) I was telling you about from the introductory psychology class said he would get here a couple of minutes from now. Would you mind waiting to see if he wants to talk to you? Fine. Why don't we go into the other room to wait? (*E left S in the secretary's office for four minutes. He then returned and said:*) OK. Let's check and see if he does want to talk to you.

$1 AND $20 CONDITIONS

E continued:

> Is that fairly clear how it is set up and what we're trying to do? (*Pause*) Now, I also have a sort of strange thing to ask you. The thing is this. (*Long pause, some confusion and uncertainty in the following, with a degree of embarrassment on E's part, which contrasted strongly with the preceding unhesitant and assured false explanation of the experiment. The point was to make it seem to S that this was the first time E had done this and that he felt unsure of himself.*) The fellow who normally does this for us couldn't do it today – he just phoned in, and something or other came up for him – so we've been looking around for someone that we could hire to do it for us. You see, we've got another subject waiting (*looks at watch*) who is supposed to be in that other condition. Now Professor . . ., who is in charge of this experiment, suggested that perhaps we could take a chance on your doing it for us. I'll tell you what we had in mind; the thing is, if you could do it for us now, then of course you would know how to do it, and if something like this should ever come up again, that is, the regular fellow couldn't make it, and we had a subject scheduled, it would be very reassuring to us to know that we had somebody else we could call on who knew how to do it. So, if you would be willing to do this for us, we'd like to hire you to do it now and then be on call in the future, if something like this should ever happen again. We can pay you $1 ($20) for doing this for us, that is, for doing it now and then being on call. Do you think you could do that for us?

If *S* hesitated, *E* said things like, 'It will only take a few minutes; the regular person is pretty reliable; this is the first time he has missed' or 'if we needed you, we could phone you a day or two in advance; if you couldn't make it, of course we wouldn't expect you to come'. After *S* agreed to do it, *E* gave him the 'For Group B' sheet of paper and asked him to read it through again. *E* then paid the $1 or $20, and made out a handwritten receipt form for *S* to sign. He then said:

> OK, the way we'll do it is this. As I said, the next subject should be here by now. I think the next one is a girl. I'll take you into the next room and introduce you to her, saying that you've just finished the experiment and that we've asked you to tell her a little about it. And what we want you to do is just sit down and get into a conversation with her and try to get across the points on that sheet of paper. I'll leave you alone and come back after a couple of minutes. OK?

E then took *S* into the secretary's office, where he had previously waited and where the next *S* was waiting. He introduced the girl and *S* to one another, saying that *S* had just finished the experiment and would tell her something about it. He then left, saying he would return in a couple of minutes. The girl, an undergraduate hired for this role, said little until *S* made some positive remarks about the experiment and then said she was surprised because a friend of hers had taken the experiment the week before, and had told her it was boring and that she ought to try to get out of it. Most *Ss* responded by saying something like, 'Oh, no, it's really very interesting. I'm sure you'll enjoy it'. After this, the girl listened quietly, accepting and agreeing to everything *S* told her. The discussion between *S* and the girl was recorded on a hidden tape recorder.

After two minutes, *E* returned, asked the girl to go into the experimental room, thanked *S* for talking to the girl, wrote down his phone number to continue the fiction about calling on him again in the future and then said, 'Look, could we check and see if that fellow from introductory psychology wants to talk to you?'

From this point on, the procedure for all three conditions was once more identical. As *E* and *S* started to walk to the office where the interviewer was, *E* said: 'Thanks very much for working on those tasks for us. I hope you did enjoy it. Most of our subjects tell us afterward that they found it quite interesting. You get a chance to see how you react to the tasks and so forth'. This short persuasive communication was made in all conditions in exactly the same way; theoretically, the reason for doing it was to make it easier for anyone who wanted to persuade himself that the tasks had, indeed, been enjoyable.

When they arrived at the office, *E* asked the interviewer if he wanted to talk to *S*, which, of course he did. *E* shook hands with *S*, said goodbye, and left. The interviewer was always unaware of which condition *S* was in. The interview comprised four questions, on each of which *S* was first encouraged to talk before rating his opinion on an 11-point scale. The questions were as follows:

1. Were the tasks interesting and enjoyable? In what way? In what way were they not? Would you rate how you feel about them on a scale from –5 to +5, where –5 means they were extremely dull and boring, +5 means they were extremely interesting and enjoyable, and zero means they were neutral, neither interesting nor uninteresting.

2. Did the experiment give you an opportunity to learn about your own ability to perform these tasks? In what way? In what way not? Would you rate how you feel about this on a scale from 0 to 10, where 0 means you learned nothing and 10 means you learned a great deal.

3. From what you know about the experiment and the tasks involved in it, would you say the experiment was measuring anything important? That is, do you think the results may have scientific value? In what way? In what way not? Would you rate your opinion on this matter on a scale from 0 to 10, where 0 means the results have no scientific value or importance and 10 means they have a great deal of value and importance.

4. Would you have any desire to participate in another similar experiment? Why? Why not? Would you rate your desire to participate in a similar experiment again on a scale from –5 to +5, where –5 means you would definitely dislike to participate, +5 means you would definitely like to participate and 0 means you have no particular feeling about it one way or another.

At the end of the interview, *S* was asked what he thought the experiment was about, and was then asked directly if he was suspicious of anything and, if so, what. *S* was then taken back to the experimental room, where *E* was waiting together with the girl who had posed as the waiting *S* (except in the control group). The true purpose of the experiment was then explained to *S* in detail and the *Ss* in the $1 and $20 conditions were asked to return the money; without exception, all *Ss* did this willingly.

The data for 11 of the 71 *Ss* had to be discarded for the following reasons:

1. Five *Ss* (three in the $1 and two in the $20 condition) indicated in the interview that they were suspicious that the true purpose of the experiment was to tell the girl that the experiment was fun.
2. Two *Ss* (both in the $1 condition) told the girl that they had been hired, that the experiment was really boring but they were supposed to say it was fun.
3. Three *Ss* (one in the $1 and two in the $20 condition) refused to take the money and be hired.
4. One *S* (in the $1 condition), immediately after having talked to the girl, demanded her phone number, saying he would call her and explain things, and also told *E* he wanted to wait until she was finished so he could tell her about it.

These 11 *Ss* were run through the total experiment anyway and the experiment was explained to them afterwards. However, their data are not included in the analysis, which consists of 20 *Ss* in each of the three conditions.

RESULTS

Table 10.1

AVERAGE RATINGS ON INTERVIEW QUESTIONS FOR EACH CONDITION

Questions on interview	Experimental condition		
	Control *n* = 20	$1 *n* = 20	$20 *n* = 20
How enjoyable tasks were (rated from −5 to +5)	−0.45	+1.35	−0.05
How much they learned (rated from 0 to 10)	3.08	2.80	3.15
Scientific importance (rated from 0 to 10)	5.60	6.45	5.18
Participate in similar experiment (rated from −5 to +5)	−0.62	+1.20	−0.25

THE STUDY

The major results are summarized in Table 10.1, which lists, separately for each of the three conditions, the average rating given by Ss to each question on the interview; each question was intended to measure different things. In all the comparisons, the control condition should be regarded as a baseline from which to evaluate the results in the other two conditions; it gives us, essentially, the reactions of Ss to the tasks and their opinions about the experiment as falsely explained to them, without the experimental introduction of dissonance.

HOW ENJOYABLE THE TASKS WERE

This was the most important result to the experiment because they are the ones most directly relevant to the specific dissonance which was experimentally created. The control group results confirmed that the tasks were rather boring and monotonous (–0.45) but in the other two conditions, Ss told someone the tasks were interesting and enjoyable. The resulting dissonance could, of course, most directly be reduced by persuading themselves that they were, indeed, interesting and enjoyable. In the $1 condition, since the magnitude of dissonance was high, the pressure to reduce it would also be high; the average rating of +1.35 was significantly different from the control condition at the 0.02 level for a two-tailed test ($t=2.48$).

In the $20 condition, where less dissonance was experimentally created, there is correspondingly less evidence of dissonance reduction, the average rating of –0.05 is not significantly higher than the control condition. The difference between the $1 and $20 conditions is significant at the 0.03 level for a two-tailed test ($t=2.22$). In short, when Ss were induced, by offer of reward, to say something contrary to their private opinions, this private opinion tended to change so as to correspond more closely with what they had said. The greater the reward offered (beyond what was necessary to elicit the behaviour), the smaller was the effect.

DESIRE TO PARTICIPATE IN A SIMILAR EXPERIMENT

This was less directly related to the dissonance that was experimentally created, but the more interesting and enjoyable they felt the tasks were, the greater would be their desire to participate in a similar experiment. In fact, the results are in the same direction, and the size of the mean differences as large as on the first question. However, the difference between the $1 condition (+1.20) and the control condition (–0.62) is significant only at the 0.08 level for a two-tailed test ($t=1.78$), and the difference between the $1 condition and the $20 condition (–0.25) is only significant at the 0.15 level, for a two-tailed test ($t=1.46$).

THE SCIENTIFIC IMPORTANCE OF THE EXPERIMENT

Another way in which the experimentally created dissonance could be reduced would be for S to magnify the importance of the cognition that it was necessary for the experiment that they should say what they did to the waiting girl. The more scientifically important they considered the experiment to be, the less was the total dissonance. The results are weakly in line with what one would expect if dissonance were partially reduced in this way. The difference between the $1 and $20 conditions reaches the 0.08 level of significance for a two-tailed test ($t=1.79$), while that between the $1 and control conditions is not significant ($t=1.21$). The finding that the $20 condition is actually lower than the control conditions is undoubtedly a matter of chance ($t=0.58$).

HOW MUCH THEY LEARNED FROM THE EXPERIMENT

There are only negligible differences between the conditions, which confirms the expectation that the question had nothing to do with the dissonance and could not be used for dissonance reduction.

D I S C U S S I O N

A POSSIBLE ALTERNATIVE EXPLANATION!

Janis and King (1954, 1956) proposed an explanation for their own findings in terms of the self-convincing effect of mental rehearsal and thinking up new arguments by the person who had to improvise a speech. Kelman (1950), in attempting to explain the unexpected finding that the persons who complied in the moderate-reward condition changed their opinion more than in the high-reward condition, also proposed a similar explanation. Can this explanation serve as an alternative to the cognitive dissonance explanation being offered here?

It would mean that, for some reason, *Ss* in the $1 condition worked harder at telling the waiting girl that the tasks were fun and enjoyable, i.e. they may have rehearsed it more mentally, thought up more ways of saying it, may have said it more convincingly and so on. Wouldn't this have been more likely in the $20 condition, since they were paid more?

The conversations between each *S* and the girl were tape-recorded, transcribed and then rated, by two independent raters, on five dimensions (unaware of which condition each *S* was in). The inter-rate reliability ranged from 0.61 to 0.88, with an average of 0.71. The five ratings were:

1. The content of what *S* said *before* the girl remarked that her friend told her it was boring. The stronger *S*'s positive statements about the tasks and the more ways in which he said they were interesting and enjoyable, the higher the rating.
2. The content of what *S* said *after* the girl made the above-mentioned remark. This was rated in the same way as for the content before the remark.

Table 10.2

AVERAGE RATINGS OF DISCUSSION BETWEEN SUBJECT AND GIRL

Dimension rated	Condition		
	$1	$20	*t*-value
Content before remark by girl (rated from 0 to 5)	2.26	2.62	1.08
Content after remark by girl (rated from 0 to 5)	1.63	1.75	0.11
Overall content (rated from 0 to 5)	1.89	2.19	1.08
Persuasiveness conviction (rated from 0 to 10)	4.79	5.50	0.99
Time spent on topic (rated from 0 to 10)	6.74	8.19	1.80

THE STUDY

3. A similar rating of the overall content of what *S* said.
4. A rating of how persuasive and convincing *S* was in what he said, and how he said it.
5. A rating of the amount of time *S* spent discussing the tasks as opposed to digressing.

The mean ratings for the $1 and $20 conditions (based on average ratings of the two raters) are shown in Table 10.2. In all cases, the $20 condition is slightly higher and only in the case of 'amount of time' does the difference even approach significance. We are certainly justified in concluding that *Ss* in the $1 condition did not improvise more or act more convincingly. Hence, the alternative explanation can be ruled out.

 S U M M A R Y

Recently, Festinger (1957) has proposed a theory of cognitive dissonance. Two predictions from this theory are tested here:

1. If a person is induced to do or say something contrary to his private opinion, there will be a tendency for him to change his opinion so as to bring it into line with what was done or said.

2. The larger the pressure to elicit the overt behaviour (beyond the minimum needed to elicit it), the weaker will be the above-mentioned tendency.

A laboratory experiment was designed to test these hypotheses: subjects were subjected to a boring experience and then paid to tell someone that the experience had been interesting and enjoyable. The amount of money paid was varied. The private opinions of the *Ss* concerning the experiences were then assessed. The results strongly support the theory of cognitive dissonance.

EVALUATION

Theoretical issues

One of the strengths of dissonance theory is that the predictions it makes are *counter-intuitive* (i.e. contrary to what 'common sense' would predict). The 'common-sense' prediction of the \$1–\$20 experiment is, surely, that the participants offered the \$20 would be *more* likely to change their attitude towards liking the task than the \$1 group. The results, of course, go in the opposite direction.

These findings have been confirmed by several studies in which children are given either a mild or severe threat not to play with an attractive toy (e.g. Aronson & Carlsmith, 1963; Freedman, 1965; Turner & Wright, 1965). If children obey a *mild* threat they will experience *greater* dissonance, because it is more difficult for them to justify their behaviour compared with children receiving a severe threat. Similarly, the \$1 group experience the *greater* dissonance. How can you *justify* lying about the boring task for a mere \$1? The solution is to see the task as actually being interesting!

What is referred to here as the 'common-sense' view is, essentially, what *incentive theory* proposes (based on the notion of reward: Janis *et al.*, 1965). It seems that *both* theories can be true, but under different conditions, and a key variable is whether or not the counter-attitudinal behaviour is *volitional* (voluntary or when we feel we have acted of our own free will). If we believe we had no 'choice', there is no dissonance and, hence, no attitude change (see **Methodological issues** below).

The role of perceived freedom of choice is also demonstrated by Elkin & Leippe (1986, cited in Zimbardo & Leippe, 1991). The counter-attitudinal (or attitude-discrepant) behaviour involved writing an essay endorsing the introduction of a parking fee for university students; not surprisingly, a preliminary survey revealed strong opposition. Student participants who opposed the plan were told they would be writing an essay about the 'possibility of a parking fee', and the essays would be sent to a university policy-making committee collecting arguments on both sides. In the *low-choice condition*, the experimenter said that the best procedure for obtaining both

viewpoints (pro- and anti-) was simply to assign people to one or other, regardless of how they personally felt. He then proceeded to ask them to write in favour of the parking fee. In the *high-choice condition*, the experimenter stressed the 'voluntary nature of the issue you decide to write on'. Participants could choose pro- or anti-, even though plenty of anti-essays had already been submitted: the committee needed pro-essays. The experimenter then asked these 'high-choice' participants to sign a release form stressing the voluntary nature of their participation.

After writing the pro-essay, all participants completed an attitude scale on which they rated their true attitude towards the issue. As predicted, only those in the high-choice condition shifted towards a more pro-position, since they had more dissonance to reduce:

> Falling for the illusion of choice created by the experimenter, they had no justification for the attitude-discrepant essay. How could they justify writing in favour of paying to park if they were against it? . . . Low-choice subjects experienced little dissonance, because they had been told what to write.
> (Zimbardo & Leippe, 1991)

The ethics of this methodology seem rather dubious: not only were participants being deceived as to the real purpose of the experiment, but those in the high-choice condition were being misled into believing that they were freely choosing which essay they wrote. A case of double deception!

A study by Freedman (1963) brings out the difference between 'voluntary' and 'involuntary' behaviour very clearly, but creates the illusion of choice in the 'voluntary' group in a rather different way from the other studies. He asked participants to perform a dull task after *first* informing them that either (*i*) the data would be definitely of *no* value to the experimenter since his experiment was already completed; or (*ii*) the data would be of *great* value to him. Dissonance theory would predict that group (*i*) would enjoy the task more, because they would experience the greater dissonance (as a result of doing it *knowing* that the data would be of no value). The results supported the dissonance prediction.

However, in a parallel experiment, the information regarding the value of the data to the experimenter was withheld until *after* participants had completed the task. So, here the participants had *no* choice and the results went in the direction predicted by incentive theory. Those in group (*ii*) enjoyed the task much more (rewarded with gratitude), while those in group (*i*) could reason 'If I'd known, I wouldn't have done it', and so experienced no dissonance. The findings were supported by Linder *et al.* (1967).

A major critic of dissonance theory has been Daryl Bem. He claims that dissonance as such is neither a necessary nor sufficient explanation, and he rejects any reference to hypothetical, intervening variables. According to his *self-perception theory* (1967, 1972), any self-report of an attitude is an inference from observation of one's own behaviour and the situation in which it occurs. If the situation contains cues (e.g. offer of a large, $20, incentive), which imply that we might have behaved that way regardless of how we personally felt (we lie about the task being interesting even though it was boring), then we do not infer that our behaviour reflected our true attitudes. But in the absence of obvious situational pressures ($1 condition), we assume that our attitudes are what our behaviour suggests they are. Put another way, the $20 participants could easily make a *situational attribution* ('I did it for the money'), whereas the $1 participants had to make a *dispositional attribution* ('I did it because I really enjoyed it').

Bem tests his theory through *interpersonal simulation*. So-called 'observer' participants are presented with a summary description of the procedure used in some well-known dissonance experiment (e.g. the $1–$20 study). They are told of the participants' agreement to perform the counter-attitudinal act requested by the experimenter, and are then asked to estimate the original participants' final attitudinal response. The observers' estimates usually match the original participants' responses quite closely, showing the predicted effects of different levels of incentive. So, when told that participants were offered $20, observers are less likely to assume a match between the participants' behaviour and their attitude.

Bem reasons that if a non-involved observer (simulator) can reproduce the results obtained with actual experimental participants, then it isn't necessary to believe that any internal, motivational state (i.e. dissonance) is involved in the $1 participants' attitude change. They simply observe their own behaviour, find no obvious situational explanation (they were being offered a mere $1), and so ask themselves, in effect, 'What must my attitude have been in order for me to describe the tasks as enjoyable?' Answer? 'I must have enjoyed it after all' (a dispositional attribution).

The answers given by the actual and observer participants should, according to Bem, be identical, because, in an important sense, they are *all* only observers (Shaver, 1987). However, the former are observers of their *own* behaviour, while the latter are assessing someone else's, and, according to the *actor–observer effect*, the former are more likely to make a *situational* attribution and the latter a *dispositional* attribution!

Although interpersonal simulations show that observer participants are usually able to replicate the findings of the original study, they can only show that the actual participants *could have* inferred their attitudes from their own behaviour, *not* that they *actually* went through such a process of inference (Stroebe & Jonas, 1996). According to Eiser & van der Pligt (1988), self-perception theory has not fulfilled its promise as a general alternative to dissonance theory.

However, Jones *et al.* (1968) and Piliavin *et al.* (1969) pointed out that one crucial piece of information available to a real participant, but unavailable to a simulating one, is his/her initial attitude to the topic in question (i.e. how boring the task is). Under these conditions, self-perception theory is supported. However, when such information *is* provided, simulators gave responses which differed from those of real participants (thus supporting dissonance theory). As Piliavin *et al.* say, it seems that Bem's simulators had given the *right* answers for the *wrong* reasons.

Perhaps, as with dissonance and incentive theories, *both* processes operate, but to different extents in different contexts. For example, dissonance may apply when we behave contrary to our initial attitude (counter-attitudinal behaviour, *outside* our 'latitude of acceptance'), while self-perception may apply better where our behaviour and initial attitude are broadly consistent (attitude-congruent behaviour, *inside* our 'latitide of acceptance': Hogg & Vaughan, 1998). According to Pennington *et al.* (1999):

> . . . To understand *attitude formation* self-perception theory may be very useful, but in looking at *attitude change* the approach seems less productive.

Another general issue is whether what matters is our *own* inferences about the way we behave, or the inferences we feel *others* might draw about us (*impression management theory*). Tedeschi *et al.* (1971) argue that the effects of many dissonance experiments might not reflect genuine cases of 'private' attitude change, but rather an adoption of a public response that protects participants against the possible accusation of insincerity (the need is to *appear* consistent, rather than a drive to actually *be* consistent).

So, participants might pretend they really believed the task was interesting in order to appear consistent: the *apparent* attitude change among the $1 participants is a tactic to feign consistency between behaviour and subsequent attitude expression. Unlike those in the $20 group, these participants were given insufficient reason to tell another participant the experiment was interesting. It follows that participants must believe that the experimenter can connect them to both their counter-attitudinal behaviour *and* their rating of the task on the attitude scale. Significantly, however, participants' final attitudinal responses were elicited by a *different* experimenter (supposedly, a member of the Psychology department who had no direct contact with the original experimenter, and who was unaware of their initial attitudes, actual behaviour, or which condition they were in).

Impression-management theorists (e.g. Schlenker, 1982; Tedeschi & Rosenfeld, 1981) no longer tend to claim that changes in attitude responses are a mere pretence. Instead, much attitude change is seen as an attempt to avoid social anxiety and embarrassment, or to protect positive views of one's own identity. Accordingly, the roots of the 'tension' hypothesized by Festinger may be in people's *social* concerns with how others might evaluate them, and how they should evaluate themselves.

Methodological issues

The Festinger and Carlsmith study is called 'Cognitive consequences of *forced compliance*'. This implies *lack* of choice and, therefore, we would expect incentive theory (and *not* cognitive dissonance) to hold (see **Theoretical issues** above). The title is rather misleading, since lying to the waiting stooge was, in theory anyway, something the participant *chose* to do, albeit as a favour to the experimenter. This is shown by the fact that three participants did, indeed, refuse to take the money and be hired. So the dilemma for the $1 participants was 'I chose to lie for just $1! How can I justify that?'

The crucial point here is that the researchers deliberately created an *illusion of freedom*, by taking advantage of people's insensitivity to subtle situational prods. The real reasons for the participants agreeing to lie about the tasks were contained in the powerful situational trappings of the experiment. Politely, but firmly, an authority figure (the experimenter) asked a favour of the participant (to deceive the next participant, for scientific purposes: Zimbardo & Leippe, 1991). The compliance pressure was very subtle: the participant, who was already involved in the situation in which the favour was to be done, was being asked to 'step in', to fill a role without which the experiment could not proceed. The request to 'lie' to the next participant was, ostensibly, *not part of the experiment.* 'Favour' implies choice, and this is what participants were meant to believe they had, but 'objectively' the situation was 'stacked' against them so that they were highly likely to 'agree'. Having agreed, the size of the inducement to lie then determined the degree of dissonance, and the corresponding degree of attitude change. Stroebe & Jonas (1996) believe that this 'choice' feature was intuitively built into the experimental situation, despite not being specified in the original theory. As we noted above, this has proved to be essential for dissonance arousal.

Given that all the participants were male and the stooge was female, could there be an interaction effect between (*i*) the size of the reward and (*ii*) the gender of the stooge? Perhaps lying to a female is seen (or was in 1957) as more acceptable (by males) than to a fellow male: but much less so for $1 than $20. Holding gender constant, would lying to an *attractive* female be more dissonant than lying to an unattractive one, and how would this interact with size of reward?

Subsequent research

Another variable which influences dissonance (and which interacts with voluntary/involuntary behaviour) is degree of *commitment.* Carlsmith *et al.* (1966) used a procedure similar to the $1–$20 study, and confirmed Festinger and Carlsmith's findings. However, the dissonance effect was only found under conditions where participants lied in a highly committing, face-to-face situation (they had to make an identifiable video recording). Where they merely had to write an essay and were assured of complete anonymity, then an incentive effect occurred. This face-to-face variable was not manipulated in the current study.

Two variables thought to be *necessary* for dissonance to occur are (*i*) anticipating that our attitude-discrepant acts will have certain aversive consequences; and (*ii*) feelings of personal responsibility for those consequences (Cooper & Fazio, 1984). Presumably, only if we believe we have chosen to act the way that produces those consequences will those feelings of responsibility arise. Stroebe & Jonas (1996) consider this to be another feature that Festinger and Carlsmith intuitively built into the experimental situation: since the confederate indicated that she had intended not participating until she was told how interesting the experiment was, the participant's 'lie' misled her into getting involved in something actually very dull.

An objection that can be made to experiments like the $1–$20 study is that the reasoning involved is *circular*: (*i*) the only evidence for the greater dissonance of the $1 participants is the fact that they rated the task as more interesting; and (*ii*) the fact that they rated the task as more interesting is evidence of the greater dissonance. Is there any *independent* evidence for the existence of dissonance? What kind of evidence do we require/would we accept? Croyle & Cooper (1983) found a more persistent increase in physiological arousal as measured by GSR (galvanic skin response) in participants who wrote a counter-attitudinal essay under high-choice as against low-choice instructions, or who wrote an essay consistent with their own opinion.

According to Cooper & Fazio (1984), attitude change will only occur if this physiological arousal is experienced as unpleasant *and* if it is attributed to the inconsistency between attitude and behaviour. Support for this notion comes from a study (Zanna & Cooper, 1974) in which participants wrote a counter-attitudinal essay under instructions which implied either high or low freedom of choice. Consistent with previous findings, the prediction that high-choice participants change their opinions more than low-choice was confirmed. The novel feature of the experiment was that participants were also given a placebo pill, which they were either told would make them feel tense or relaxed, or told nothing about it at all. The dissonance theory prediction was upheld when participants were given no information, and even more strongly when they were told it would relax them. But when they were told the pill would make them feel tense, no difference between the high- and low-choice conditions was found (see **Exercises** section below).

Applications and implications

Totman (1971) gave patients the illusion of choice over the medication they received, which seemed to have beneficial effects: the medicine is more effective because the individual is more committed to it. Although this interesting demonstration of 'mind over matter' goes beyond dissonance theory, these findings are consistent with the prediction from it that individuals committed by their own choice will manifest their beliefs in the medication to a greater extent than those who are less committed (Stephenson, 1996).

Cooper & Axsom (1982) analysed the benefits of psychotherapy in terms of the *justification of effort* (such as embarrassment, financial cost and so on), which is one of the three 'headings' under which dissonance theory has been investigated (see **Background and context** section above). In line with the predictions made from dissonance theory, they showed that riding an exercise bike to the point of exhaustion was as beneficial as 'implosive' therapy in the treatment of phobias, and those given a 'choice' of treatments benefited most of all.

The controversy between dissonance theory, incentive theory and self-perception theory is important. This is not so much because one of the explanations is 'correct' whereas the other two are 'in error', rather, the controversy is extremely valuable as an example of the development of method and theory in social psychology. According to Shaver (1987):

> . . . What begins as a simple statement (that is, dissonance will be produced whenever one cognitive element implies the opposite of another) becomes, through continuous refinement, a more complex but more accurate statement . . . Along the way, new methods are developed (. . . interpersonal simulations . . .), new pitfalls are discovered, and new areas of research grow out of attempts to resolve theoretical controversy. Perhaps the greatest compliment that can be paid to the theory of cognitive dissonance is the recognition of its extensive role in this continuing process.

Both dissonance and self-perception theories see attitudes 'following' behaviour (people often behave in a certain way, then report attitudes consistent with that behaviour), and to this extent they imply that viewing people as 'rational individuals' (as in Fishbein & Ajzen's *theory of reasoned action*, 1975) is limited (Moghaddam, 1998).

Exercises

1. What kind of experimental design was used?

2. What statistical test was used, and is it the only one which could have been used?

3. Both hypotheses are referred to as two-tailed (see **Summary**). However, as it stands, could the second hypothesis be one-tailed? Give your reasons.

4. Why was it important that the interviewer did not (supposedly) know which conditions participants were being tested under?

5. What were the independent and dependent variables?

6. What statistical test is used to measure the reliability of ratings between the two raters of participants' behaviour?

7. Were the participants a biased sample? Give your reasons.

8. How do you explain Zanna & Cooper's (1974) findings? (see page 190)

9. How could the impact of situational pressures towards compliance have been tested?

11

Behaviour as seen by the actor and as seen by the observer

Richard E. Nisbett, Craig Caputo, Patricia Legant, and Jeanne Maracek (1973)

Journal of Personality and Social Psychology, 27 (2), 154–64

BACKGROUND AND CONTEXT

Fiske & Taylor (1991) distinguish between *attribution theory* and *theories*. Attribution theory deals with the general principles which govern how the social perceiver selects and uses information to arrive at causal explanations or judgements for events (i.e. behaviour) in a wide variety of domains (e.g. academic achievement, pro- and anti-social behaviour). Theories of attribution, on the other hand, draw on the principles of attribution theory and make predictions about how people respond in particular life domains. However, attribution theory does not refer to a single body of ideas and research, but to a collection of diverse theoretical and empirical contributions which share several common concerns. According to Fiske & Taylor (1991), six different theoretical traditions form the backbone of attribution theory:

1. Heider's (1958) common sense psychology;
2. Jones and Davis's (1965) correspondent inference theory;
3. Kelley's (1967, 1972, 1973) covariation model and causal schemata;
4. Schachter's (1964) theory of emotional lability (or cognitive labelling theory);
5. Bem's (1967, 1972) self-perception theory; and
6. Weiner's (1979, 1985) attributional theory of emotion and motivation.

Schachter's theory is discussed in Chapter 28, Bem's theory is discussed in Chapter 10 [Festinger & Carlsmith] in relation to cognitive dissonance, and Weiner's theory is discussed in Chapter 9 [Piliavin *et al.*] in the context of helping behaviour. Heider's theory was clearly the spearhead for attribution theory as a whole (Fiske & Taylor, 1991).

Like Asch (famous for his research into conformity and interpersonal perception), Heider emigrated to the USA from Europe, was very much influenced by Gestalt psychology and wanted to apply this theory of physical object perception to the perception of people (social perception). His *The Psychology of Interpersonal Relations* (1958) marked a new era in social psychology (Leyens & Codol, 1988).

For Heider, the starting point for studying how people understand their social world is 'ordinary' people. How do people usually think about and infer meaning from what goes on around them? How do they make sense of their own and other people's behaviour? These questions relate to what Heider called *common sense psychology* or *naïve epistemology* (epistemology being the branch of philosophy concerned with the nature of knowledge). He saw the 'ordinary' person (or lay person) as a *naïve scientist*, linking observable behaviour to unobservable causes.

As well as being influenced by Gestalt principles of perception (in particular, the figure-ground principle: see **Evaluation** below), Heider believed that Brunswick's (1956) 'lens' model of object perception also had much to contribute to an understanding of social perception, especially the idea that the final perception of a stimulus is based on properties of the stimulus itself, the context in which it is perceived, as well as characteristics of the perceiver. If this is true, and the stimulus cannot be seen 'as it really is', in some objective way, how much more true will this be of people compared with physical objects?

Perhaps Heider's major contribution to attribution theory was the identification of two basic, potential sources or causes of behaviour, namely *personal* or *dispositional* (internal) and *situational* or *environmental* (external: Hewstone & Antaki, 1988). Fundamental to the question: why do people behave as they do? is whether the *locus* of causality is *inside* or *outside* the person, and the task of the perceiver is to decide if a given action is due to which kind of cause. Internal causes would include motivation, ability, attitudes, and personality traits, while external causes would include the behaviour of other people, other people's traits and characteristics, the demands of the social situation, and physical aspects of the environment. Understanding which set of factors should be used to interpret another person's behaviour will make the perceiver's world more predictable, and provide a greater sense of control over it. These basic insights provided the blueprint for the theories that followed (Hewstone & Antaki, 1988). According to Fiske & Taylor (1991), Heider's major contribution was:

> . . . to define many of the basic issues that would later be explored more systematically in further theoretical ventures. In particular, his thinking on causality and responsibility gave rise to subsequent theoretical work by E.E. Jones and Davis (1965) and Kelley (1967).

These two theories/models are the ones which have probably generated the most debate and research. All three theories (Heider, Jones & Davis, and Kelley) adopted the perspective of the perceiver as a naïve scientist and, as such, all three tend to see the lay person as a logical and rational thinker, arriving at attributions in much the same way as professional scientists. Indeed, Kelley's original (1967) ANOVA model was presented as a *normative model*: it showed how perceivers *should* make accurate causal attributions. However, the research has shown that perceivers do *not* act like scientists, following such detailed, formal, logical, rules. Rather, they make attributions quickly, using much less information, and showing clear preferences for certain sorts of explanation. We, therefore, need more *descriptive* models, and this has been at least partly achieved by examining the *biases* involved in the attribution process. These biases, of which the *actor-observer effect* (AOE) is a major example, seem to provide a better descriptive analysis of causal attribution than do complex, normative models (Hewstone & Antaki, 1988).

Aim and nature of the study

This article describes three separate but related experiments carried out in order to test different aspects of the AOE (or the *actor-observer divergence or hypothesis*). The overall hypothesis, first proposed by Jones & Nisbett (1971), states that actors tend to perceive their own behaviour as a response to situational cues, while observers tend to perceive the actor's behaviour as a manifestation of a disposition or quality possessed by the actor. Each of the three experiments tests a different aspect of this general hypothesis:

1. Observers tend to assume that actors have a disposition to behave in the future in similar ways to those just observed (here, to volunteer for some further charity work or 'social service task', namely to canvass for the United Fund), while actors don't share this assumption;

2. Actors tend to attribute the cause of their behaviour (choice of girlfriend and college major) to properties of the chosen entity, while they are more likely to attribute their best friend's similar choices to the friend's dispositional qualities;

3. Actors tend to believe they have fewer personality traits than other people do (including others who are similar and different in age, and others who are familiar and unfamiliar to the actor).

In the **Introduction**, Nisbett *et al.* refer to those experiments as 'demonstrational studies' which illustrate the divergent perspective of the actor and observer. In the **Discussion**, they state that:

> The findings of each of the studies undoubtedly could be explained without resort to the hypothesis proposed by Jones and Nisbett (1971), and even taken as a whole, they cannot be said to indicate that the hypothesis generally holds true. The studies should be regarded merely as demonstrations of some interest in their own right, which are consistent with a proposition that is too widely applicable to be either proved or disproved by anything short of a very large and extremely diverse research programme.

Clearly, these studies represent some of the very first to be carried out in relation to this feature of the attribution process, so Nisbett *et al.* are wisely and understandably cautious about the claims that can be made for the general hypothesis based on them alone. Their use of the word 'tend' in each of the three predictions perhaps conveys this cautious approach, together with the fact that all probability levels are based on two-tailed tests.

However, they also state that if a sufficiently large and varied range of tests of the hypothesis were conducted, it could be 'proved or disproved' in the light of such evidence. Two points of caution of our own should be added to theirs: (*i*) if the hypothesis is very general (as a 'theory' usually is), what is likely to occur is that evidence will accumulate to support certain parts (or specific predictions) and not others: we normally only accept or reject very specific hypotheses, not whole 'general' ones like the actor-observer effect, or theories; (*ii*) it is very rare – and dangerous – to use the terms 'prove' and 'disprove', since this implies 'certainty', when in psychology (and indeed science as a whole) we are only dealing with 'probability'. Chance always plays some part in any particular investigation (hence the use of tests of statistical significance to tell us how much 'faith' we can put in our results: how great a part chance played on this occasion). It is always possible that we will obtain a *different* result if we were to repeat the investigation.

THE STUDY

> Jones and Nisbett proposed that actors are inclined to attribute their behaviour to situational causes, while observers of the same behaviour are inclined to attribute it to dispositional qualities – stable attitudes and traits – of the actor. Some demonstrational studies consistent with this hypothesis were described. College student observers were found to (*i*) assume that actors would behave in the future in ways similar to those they had just witnessed (while actors themselves did not share this assumption); (*ii*) describe their best friend's choices of girlfriend and college major in terms referring to dispositional qualities of their best friend (while more often describing their own similar choices in terms of properties of the girlfriend or major); and (*iii*) ascribe more personality traits to other people than to themselves.

The fact that different individuals often have very different views of the causes of a given person's behaviour is a frequent theme of world literature. The diverse perspectives on the behaviour of the central figure himself, the people whom he affects, the author, and the reader play an important role in works as varied as *Rashomon*, *Huckleberry Finn*, the 'Grand Inquisitor' section of the *Brothers Karamazov*, Gide's *The Counterfeiters*, Durrell's *Alexandria Quartet*, and countless mystery novels. Psychologists, however, have for some reason rarely attempted to analyse the differing perspectives of the witnesses of a given act beyond the frequent observation that perception of motive tends to be in line with self-interest.

A pioneering exception to the psychologist's general lack of interest in this question is Heider's (1958) *The Psychology of Interpersonal Relations*. Jones and Nisbett (1971) recently distilled from Heider's writings a very general hypothesis concerning the divergent perspectives of the actor – that is, the individual who performs a given behaviour – and the observer of the behaviour. They proposed that actors tend to perceive their behaviour as a response to situational cues, while observers tend to perceive the behaviour as a manifestation of a disposition or quality possessed by the actor. Evidence supporting this hypothesis, including work by Jones and Harris (1967), Jones *et al.* (1968), and McArthur (1972), is discussed in detail by Jones and Nisbett. The major reason for the divergent perspectives is probably a simple perceptual one. The actor's attention at the moment of action is focused on the situational cues – the environmental attractions, repulsions and constraints – with which his behaviour is coordinated. It therefore appears to the actor that his behaviour is a response to these cues, that is, caused by them. For the observer, however, it is not the situational cues that are salient but the behaviour of the actor. In gestalt terms, action is figural against the ground of the situation. The observer is therefore more likely to perceive the actor's behaviour as a manifestation of the actor and to perceive the cause of behaviour to be a trait or quality inherent in the actor.

A second probable reason for the differential bias of actors and observers stems from a difference in the nature and extent of information they possess. In general, the actor knows more about his past behaviour and his present experiences than does the observer. This difference in information level probably often serves to prevent the actor from interpreting his behaviour in dispositional terms, while allowing the observer to make such an interpretation. For example, if an actor insults another person, an observer may be free to infer that the actor did so because the actor is hostile. The actor, however, may know that he rarely insults others and may believe that his insult was a response to the most recent in a series of provocations from the person he finally attacked. The difference in information available to the actor and observer is, of course, reduced when they know one another well but is always present to a degree.

The present report describes three different demonstrational studies which illustrate divergent perspectives of the actor and observer. The first study indicates that observers tend to assume that actors have a disposition to behave in the future in ways similar to those which they have just observed, while actors do not share observers' assumptions about their own future behaviour. The second study shows that actors tend to attribute the cause of their behaviour – specifically, choice of college major and girlfriend – to properties of the chosen entity, while they are more likely to attribute the similar choices of their close friend to the friend's dispositional qualities. The third study shows that actors tend to believe that they have fewer personality traits than do other people.

STUDY 1

Study 1 presents data collected in the context of a larger experimental investigation of the perception of the causes of behaviour. An attempt was made to elicit or prevent, via differing monetary incentives, actors' cooperation with an experimenter's request. Observers watched all of the interaction between the experimenter and the actor. It was anticipated that observers but not actors would attribute the actor's compliance or non-compliance to a disposition to comply or not to comply with such requests in general and so would expect the actor's behaviour to generalize to other situations. The relevant details are presented below.

 M E T H O D

OVERVIEW

College co-eds were recruited to participate in an experiment on 'decision-making'. Present at each session were two real subjects and two confederates. One subject was randomly selected to be the observer and the other to be the actor. The confederates played the same role as the actor. The confederates and the actor were requested 'before the experiment began' to volunteer some of their time to serve as weekend hostesses for the wives of potential financial backers of a university institute concerned with the learning disabilities of disadvantaged children. The confederates always volunteered, thus serving as models and agents of social pressure. In some experimental sessions, $0.50 per hour was offered as token remuneration for the weekend's work; in others, $1.50 per hour was offered. After the actor had either volunteered or refused to volunteer, both the actor and observer were taken aside and quizzed about their perceptions of the actor's behaviour.

INSTRUCTIONS TO THE OBSERVER

The observer-subject was told that three other girls would be taking part in the experiment:

> They will be asked to make various decisions. You, however, will **not** be asked to make any decisions . . . Your job will be to watch one of the participants carefully throughout the entire session, during which she'll be making various decisions. After a brief introductory session in which the experiment will be explained to the other girls, you'll join the girl you're to watch in another room, where the decision materials have been assembled.

Experimenter 1 (E1) then told the observer that she would be watching the decision-making of the actor (described as the girl who would be sitting in the left-most chair during the introductory session). Finally, the observer was told that she would be introduced as the experimenters' helper, since 'we've found that people tend to feel self-conscious and unnatural if they think a non-participant is watching them'.

THE STUDY

SCENARIO

For the introductory session, the actor and confederates were led into an experimental room and seated in a row facing a desk at which Experimenter 2 (E2) and the observer sat. E2 introduced herself and then introduced the observer as someone who would be helping in a later part of the experiment. E2 briefly described a fictitious decision study procedure which allegedly would take place after the introductory session. E2 then began the request which formed the core of the experiment:

> Before we get started, though, I happen to have sort of a real decision for you to make. The Human Development Institute at Yale is sponsoring a weekend for the corporate board and a lot of their prospective financial backers. As you may know, the Institute is involved in basic research in learning and education. Right now, their focus is particularly on learning among the underprivileged and in minority groups. The institute often works very closely with the psychology department, which is how I happen to be involved with them. Anyway, these supporters will all be coming to town the weekend of (a date two weeks hence) . . . The committee thought that it would be especially appropriate to involve co-eds by putting them in charge of the wives of the businessmen. There will be some separate activities arranged for these women, and they'll probably be interested in seeing Yale from a woman's point of view. So the committee would like girls to volunteer. There will be 16 or 18 hours in all that you could volunteer for.

E2 went on to briefly describe the various activities of the weekend (tours, receptions etc.) and the times they would take place. E2 then delivered the monetary incentive manipulation: 'They have only limited funds to run the weekend, but they can afford to pay girls who volunteer $0.50 ($1.50) an hour'. E2 then asked if the subjects had any questions. One of the confederates asked how long the session lasted on Saturday, and the other asked what date E2 had said the weekend would take place. Actors only rarely asked a question.

E2 then asked the confederate seated to her right if she would care to volunteer. The confederate 'volunteered' for about four hours. E2 then asked the confederate seated next to the actor if she could volunteer; she volunteered for about 12 hours. Finally, the actor was asked if she could volunteer. Following the actor's response, the actor and observer were taken to separate experimental rooms.

Approximately half the subjects were exposed to a slightly different version of the above scenario, intended as a low-social-pressure variation which might produce lower compliance rates among actors. In this variation, confederates left 'to go to their separate experimental rooms', after announcing their willingness to volunteer, and on a pretext, the experimenter and observer left the actor alone to indicate on a card how many hours she was willing to volunteer. This variation did not in fact have a significant effect on compliance rate, and data were, therefore, pooled for purposes of analysis.

THE STUDY

ASSESSMENT OF PERCEIVED REASONS FOR VOLUNTEERING

The actor was interviewed by E1, whom she had not previously met. E1 began:

> Before we start in with the rest of the decisions, I'd like to ask you a few questions about the decision you just made. We decided to use the Institute's recruiting appeal as one of our experimental decisions, since it's so much like the kind of decision that you run into every day, as opposed to the sort that the rest of the session will be dealing with.

The actor was given 'a list of the reasons that people give us for volunteering for this task' and asked to decide how big a part each reason had played in her decision to volunteer. The list of reasons had proved in pre-tests to be virtually exhaustive. Subjects were asked to rate the importance of each of the following reasons on a 0–8 scale:

1. I wanted to help the University and the Human Development Institute.
2. The activities sounded as if they would be interesting.
3. It was a chance to earn some money.
4. I thought that meeting the people would be fun.
5. The other girls seemed to be interested in it and that made me think it was probably worthwhile.
6. There was a lot of social pressure to volunteer.

The observer was questioned by E2 about the actor's motives for volunteering, if indeed she had. If the actor had not volunteered, the observer was questioned about the motives of the confederate sitting next to the actor. The same measures were used as those for the actor.

ASSESSMENT OF PERCEIVED DISPOSITION TO VOLUNTEER

Following the assessment of motives, both the actor and observer were asked to estimate how likely they felt it would be that the actor would volunteer for a similar social service task, specifically, to canvass for the United Fund. Subjects responded to the following scale:

How likely do you think it is that you (the girl you watched) would also volunteer to canvass for the United Fund?

0	1	2	3	4	5	6	7	8

not at all likely   neither likely nor unlikely   very likely

SUBJECTS

Subjects were Yale co-eds, some of whom participated for credit in an introductory psychology course and some of whom were paid $1.50 to participate. Altogether, 33 actor-observer pairs participated. However, through an error, disposition-to-volunteer data were not obtained for five of the actors.

R E S U L T S

The monetary incentive offered was a very major determinant of the actors' choice of whether or not to volunteer. Of the 17 actors offered $0.50 per hour, only four (24 per cent) volunteered. Of the 16 actors offered $1.50 per hour, 11 (68 per cent) volunteered. *Among volunteers*, however, the amount of money offered did not much affect the *number* of hours volunteered. Volunteers offered $0.50 per hour promised an average of 5.6 hours, those offered $1.50 promised 6.7 hours ($t < 1$, ns). (All p levels reported are based on two-tailed tests.)

Best indications are that neither volunteers offered $1.50 nor their observers fully realized the importance of money in eliciting actors' cooperation. Volunteers offered $1.50 and their observers were agreed in rating the importance of money lower than they rated the importance of three other reasons – desire to help, the interest of the activities, and the fun of meeting the people. This meant that all groups of actors and observers were free to assume that a disposition to volunteer or not to volunteer for such activities was responsible in part for the actors' behaviour. To the extent that dispositional inferences were made, they should have been reflected in the subjects' predictions about the likelihood that the actor would volunteer for a similar task.

Table 11.1 presents the actors' and observers' estimates of the likelihood that the actor would volunteer to campaign for the United Fund. The left-hand columns present perceived likelihood as a function of whether or not the actor volunteered. The right-hand columns present likelihood estimates as a function of the payment offered. The former are more meaningful, but they suffer from the methodological defect that the volunteering variable is a self-selected one, and the subjects who volunteered might have been selectively different on some dimensions from those who did not. The latter correct this defect but introduce some 'slippage' into the manipulation, due to the fact that not all high-payment actors volunteered and not all low-payment actors failed to volunteer.

Table 11.1 shows that the actors' behaviour prompted the observers to make dispositional inferences. Observers' judgements were uncorrelated with actors' judgements, and the data were accordingly analysed by t tests assuming independence of the two sets of data.

If the actor volunteered, observers saw her as more likely to help the United Fund than if she did not ($t = 2.24$, $p < 0.05$). Moreover, observers of volunteers saw them as more likely to help than did the volunteers themselves ($t = 2.12$, $p < 0.05$), and observers of non-volunteers tended to see them as less likely to help than did the

| Table 11.1 |

ACTORS' AND OBSERVERS' ESTIMATES OF THE PROBABILITY THAT THE ACTOR WOULD VOLUNTEER FOR A SIMILAR TASK AS A FUNCTION OF WHETHER OR NOT THE ACTOR VOLUNTEERED AND AS A FUNCTION OF THE AMOUNT OFFERED FOR VOLUNTEERING

Rater	Actor's behaviour		Amount offered	
	Volunteered	Did not volunteer	$1.50/ hour	$0.50/ hour
Actor	3.31	3.92	3.73	3.38
n	16	12	15	13
Observer	4.27	2.78	4.25	2.71
n	15	18	16	17

non-volunteers themselves ($t=1.63, < p < 0.15$). The interaction between volunteering versus non-volunteering and actor versus observer status is significant at the 0.07 level ($t=1.91$).

Ratings as a function of the payment variable show a similar pattern. Observers of the generally volunteering high-payment actors judged them, as a group, to be more likely to help the United Fund than did observers of the generally non-volunteering low-payment actors ($t=2.35$, $p<0.05$). Among actors, the high-payment group did not differ from the low-payment group ($t<1$). The interaction, however, falls short of significance.

It therefore appears that observers are inclined to make dispositional inferences from behaviour under circumstances in which actors infer nothing about their general inclinations. It might be argued, however, that the dispositional inferences of observers were due solely to aspects of the experimental situation that were artificial and ecologically rare. Observers had never seen the actor before, there was no interaction between actor and observer, and the actor's behaviour was limited to a sentence or two. It might be argued that the actor-observer differences might not be found in less impoverished situations. On the other hand, it is important to note that virtually all the situational stimuli impinging on the actor were also visible to the observer, and that fact should have militated against dispositional interpretation on the observers' part. In many real life situations, we are likely to know more about the actor than did the observers, but we are likely to know less about the stimuli affecting his behaviour. In fact, even when we know the actor extremely well, we may know virtually nothing about the stimuli guiding his behaviour in a particular case. To the extent that this is true, we are thrown back once again on dispositional inferences in order to explain the behaviour.

STUDY II

Study II was conducted in order to determine whether actors and observers would differ in their perception of the causes of behaviour even when the actor is well known to the observer. Male college students were asked to write a brief paragraph explaining why they liked the girl they dated most regularly and another brief paragraph explaining why they had chosen their college major. Subjects were also asked to write similar paragraphs about their best friend's choices of girlfriend and college major. It was anticipated that in explaining their own choices, subjects would emphasize the role of properties of the chosen object, and in explaining their friend's similar choices, they would be more likely to emphasize the role played by dispositions and traits of the choosing individual.

M E T H O D

Subjects were Yale undergraduate males (as they were for Study III also) who were offered $1.50 to participate in 'Person Perception Surveys' in groups of 6–20. Study II subjects had all filled out the personality trait questionnaires of Study III prior to providing data for Study II.

Thirty subjects were requested to write four brief paragraphs describing why they liked the girl they had dated the most frequently in the past year or so, why they had chosen their major, why their best friend liked the girl he had dated most regularly in the past year or so, and why he had chosen his major. In addition, subjects were asked to put themselves in their best friend's position and try to write paragraphs as the best friend might, describing why the *subject* had chosen his girlfriend and major. Order of answering for self, best friend and for self as best friend was counterbalanced. 'Best friend' was defined as 'Your best friend of your own age and sex – if there is more than one candidate, choose the one you have known longest'.

The subjects' paragraphs were scored for the degree to which they stressed 'entity' versus 'dispositional' reasons. Each reason was coded as being either a pure entity reason ('She's a relaxing person'; 'Chemistry is a high-paying field') or as invoking some dispositional property of the actor ('I need someone I can relax with'; 'I want to make a lot of money'). Reasons were coded as being dispositional if they referred in any way to the person doing the choosing, thus including many which could be described as Entity X Disposition interaction reasons e.g. ('We have complementary personalities' or 'We can relax together').

Coding was performed by the investigators. However, protocols were also rewritten by changing all first person statements into third person statements and were given to a coder ignorant of the hypothesis. Results are reported in terms of investigator-coded scores, but these are almost identical to those of the blind coder.

Seven of the 30 subjects (or their best friend) did not have a girlfriend or had not yet chosen their major field. Data for such subjects were excluded, leaving 23 cases for the analyses presented. Conclusions would not be altered, however, if the analysable portions of the data from the seven subjects were included.

R E S U L T S

It was anticipated that subjects would tend to describe their own choices of girlfriend and major field as being due to properties of the chosen entity and to see the comparable choices of their best friend as being due to dispositions possessed by the friend. Table 11.2 shows that this is the case. When explaining why they liked their own girlfriend, subjects gave more than twice as many reasons phrased in terms of their own needs, interests and traits ($t=2.54$, $p<0.02$). In contrast, when explaining why their best friend liked his girlfriend, subjects gave almost equal numbers of reasons referring exclusively to the girl and reasons involving the friends' dispositions ($t<1$, ns). The interaction between answers for self versus friend and entity versus disposition is significant at the 0.05 level ($t=2.23$). When explaining their choice of major, subjects gave an almost equal number of entity reasons and dispositional reasons ($t<1$, ns). In contrast, when explaining their best friend's choice of major, subjects gave almost four times as many reasons involving the friend's dispositions as reasons referring exclusively to the major ($t=3.53$, $p<0.002$). The interaction between answers for self versus friend and entity versus disposition is significant at the 0.10 level ($t=1.79$). The tendency to give relatively more entity reasons for self was found regardless of the order in which subjects wrote the paragraphs.

It is interesting to note that subjects were remarkably capable of adopting the perspective of an outside observer of their own behaviour. When asked to write paragraphs explaining their choices of girlfriend and college major as they thought their best friend would see it, they virtually duplicated the pattern in Table 11.2 for explanations of their friend's choices: for girlfriend choices, 2.65 entity reasons were given versus 2.57 dispositional reasons, while for major field choices, 0.39 entity reasons were given versus 2.22 dispositional reasons.

It is possible that the data in Table 11.2 do not reflect a phenomenal difference in the perception of self versus others but merely a difference due to language usage. For example, people may be in the habit of assuming that their hearers or readers know them personally and so do not feel obliged to describe their own dispositions.

Table 11.2

NUMBER OF ENTITY REASONS AND DISPOSITIONAL REASONS GIVEN BY SUBJECTS AS EXPLANATIONS OF THEIR OWN AND THEIR BEST FRIEND'S CHOICES OF GIRLFRIEND AND COLLEGE MAJOR

Explanation	Reasons for liking girlfriend		Reasons for choosing major	
	Entity	Dispositional	Entity	Dispositional
Own behaviour	4.61	2.04	1.52	1.83
Friend's behaviour	2.70	2.57	0.43	1.70

Note: $n = 23$.

They may take it as understood that they need a warm, relaxing girlfriend but may feel it necessary to point this out about a third person. Of course, the experimenters did not know the subjects any better than they knew the subjects' best friend, but habitual patterns of expression may have prevailed over such rational considerations. Language conventions might have affected the results in a second way. Subjects tended to describe their girlfriend using strings of admiring adjectives and were less likely to do this when describing their best friend's girlfriend. These adjectives produced high scores for entity attribution but may have less to do with the subjects' views of causality than with their use of a rhapsodic convention for describing one's true love. Finally, it may have been that simply writing in the first person versus the third person led in some grammatical or structural way to differentiate focus on the object versus the subject of the sentence. If such a tendency existed, it may have been this, rather than the ability to 'reverse perspective' which caused subjects to duplicate the pattern of results for the best friend's choices when describing their own choices (in the third person) from the friend's point of view.

However, the language usage alternative loses some force in view of the results of a follow-up study in which subjects were asked merely to rate the importance of reasons for dating a girlfriend and for choosing a particular major. A list of 16 reasons for dating, drawn from reasons suggested by Study II, and 12 reasons for choosing a major, drawn mostly from Study I, were given to 31 subjects who rated each reason for themselves and for their best friend, on a 5-point scale. Half of the reasons were worded in entity terms ('she's intelligent') and half in dispositional terms ('I need someone I can relax with'). Alternate forms of the questionnaire were constructed, such that each reason that appeared in entity terms on one appeared in dispositional terms on the other.

THE STUDY

The pattern of responses observed in Study II was not found for all the items in the follow-up questionnaire, but it was found for virtually all the reasons rated by subjects as relatively important. As it happened, the seven reasons for dating a girlfriend most frequently given by subjects in Study II all received average ratings of 3.5 or more in the follow-up and none of the other reasons received ratings as high as 3.5. The former involved the attractiveness, intelligence, relaxedness, naturalness, sexual responsiveness, and the fun-loving and affectionate qualities of the girl or the need for these things on the part of the person doing the choosing. For all seven reasons, subjects endorsed the entity-worded form relatively more strongly for self than for best friend. Four of the reasons for choosing a major received ratings as high as 3.5 (intellectual rewards, freedom of approach, breadth of interests covered, route to understanding of the world). For all except the last of these reasons, subjects endorsed the entity-worded form relatively more strongly for self than for best friend. (As a group these reasons had been only somewhat more commonly listed by Study II subjects than reasons rated as relatively unimportant by follow-up subjects.)

Table 11.3 presents mean importance ratings of the 11 reasons which received overall ratings of 3.5 or higher; it combines ratings of reasons for dating and choosing a major since the results are entirely similar for each of these categories separately. It may be seen that subjects tended to assign greater importance to reasons stated in dispositional terms when answering for their best friend. This interaction is significant at the 0.05 level ($t=2.11$).

Table 11.3

RATINGS OF MOST IMPORTANT REASONS FOR CHOOSING GIRLFRIEND AND MAJOR AS A FUNCTION OF ENTITY VERSUS DISPOSITIONAL WORDING

Choice	Entity wording	Dispositional wording
Own	3.99	3.75
Friend	3.44	3.62

Note: $n = 31$.

The follow-up study does not rule out all possible linguistic explanations of the findings of Study II, but it does speak against explanations in terms of language *production* as an artifact. Subjects stressed entity attributions for themselves and dispositional attribution for their best friend, and this was true both when they described choices in their own words and when they merely rated reasons in language provided by an experimenter. Thus, it is not likely that the findings of Study II merely reflect stylistic or structural constraints due to writing in the first versus the third person.

More importantly, it should be noted that the potential interest of Study II would not necessarily be diminished if it could be shown that the findings were due largely to hidden convention of language usage. Kanouse (1971) has argued persuasively that the language used to describe an event greatly affects subsequent attributions: when a given causal candidate is stressed in speech, it is likely to become more prominent phenomenally. It seems entirely plausible that if people are in the habit of using entity terms to describe their own behaviour and dispositional terms to describe that of others, this linguistic fact would have phenomenal repercussions.

STUDY III

Subjects appear to be inclined to interpret the behaviour of other actors in relatively dispositional terms, whether the behaviour is routine and inconsequential or highly personal and important, and whether they know the actors well or not at all. One possible consequence of this tendency to view others' behaviour in more dispositional terms than those used for one's own behaviour is that each individual may view every other individual as possessing more personality traits than he himself possesses. If everyone views his own behaviour as a response to the situational stimuli he confronts at the moment but perceives more cross-situational stability in the behaviour of others, he should perceive the behaviour of others to be more trait determined than his own. In order to examine the possibility that individuals view themselves as relatively trait free, the following study was undertaken.

▮ M E T H O D ▮

PROCEDURE

Twenty-four subjects filled out questionnaires indicating, for themselves and four other stimulus persons, which of three descriptions best fit the stimulus person: a trait/term, its polar opposite, or the phrase 'depends on the situation'. There were 20 such three-choice items for each of the stimulus persons. Questionnaire booklets were arranged so that for the group of subjects as a whole, the questionnaire for each stimulus person preceded the questionnaire for every other stimulus person equally often. On a final questionnaire, subjects rated the desirability of each of the 40 polar traits on a 7-point scale (−3 to +3).

TRAIT TERMS

The trait terms used are presented in Table 11.4.

An effort was made to use trait adjectives that were socially desirable, since it would have been uninteresting to show that people refuse to assign trait descrip-

THE STUDY

THE STUDY

Table 11.4

POLAR TRAIT TERMS USED IN STUDY III

Polar trait terms	
Serious – gay	Sceptical trusting
Subjective – *analytic*	Quiet – talkative
Future-oriented – present-oriented	Cultivated – *natural*
Energetic – relaxed	*Sensitive* – tough-minded
Unassuming – self-asserting	Self-sufficient – sociable
Lenient – firm	Steady – *flexible*
Reserved – *emotionally expressive*	Dominant – deferential
Dignified – *casual*	Cautious – *bold*
Realistic – idealistic	Uninhibited – self-controlled
Intense – *calm*	*Conscientious* – happy-go-lucky

Note: Where trait terms differ in social desirability at the 0.5 level or more, the trait higher in social desirability is in italics.

tions to themselves when both trait alternatives are undesirable. Only two of the 40 terms received a mean rating of less than neutral (tough-minded and deferential). An effort was also made to create trait pairs of equal desirability, so that the factor of desirability would enter as little as possible into the subject's choice. This effort was largely unsuccessful – for about half the pairs, the two trait terms were rated as significantly different in desirability. It was, therefore, necessary to analyse trait parts which differed in desirability separately from those which did not.

STIMULUS PERSONS

The stimulus persons used were self, best-friend, father, an admired acquaintance ('some individual of your own age and sex whom you like, but have known less than three months'), and the television commentator, Walter Cronkite. This sample of stimulus persons was certainly not random or exhaustive, but it did have some useful properties. They had in common the fact that most subjects could be presumed to be favourably disposed toward them. Just as it seemed wise to avoid using trait terms which could be epithets, it seemed wise to avoid using stimulus persons toward whom subjects would be inclined to hurl them. They differed systematically in terms of their similarity to the subject regarding age status (two were the same age as the subject, two were older), and their familiarity to the subject (two were among the people best known to the subject, two were unfamiliar). These differences allowed for an examination of the effects on trait attributions of two variables of some interest.

R E S U L T S

It was anticipated that subjects would attribute fewer personality traits to themselves than to other people. Table 11.5 shows that this was the case. Subjects were significantly more likely to apply the depends-on-the-situation category to themselves than to any other stimulus person. The order in which subjects completed the sheet for self had no effect on the tendency to ascribe more traits to others than to self. Neither familiarity with, nor similarity in age to, the stimulus person, seemed, in themselves, to have much influence on the tendency to ascribe traits, although subjects were somewhat more likely to ascribe traits to Walter Cronkite, the older, unfamiliar stimulus person, than to other stimulus persons. The tendency to attribute more traits to others was as stable across subjects and trait dimensions as it was across stimulus persons. The tendency was reversed for only four of the 24 subjects and for only two of the 20 trait dimensions (reserved–emotionally expressive and cautious–bold).

Table 11.5

MEAN NUMBER OF TRAIT ASCRIPTIONS (OF A POSSIBLE 20) TO EACH STIMULUS PERSON

Item	Stimulus person				
	Self	Best-friend	Father	Acquaintance	Cronkite
Mean trait ascriptions	11.92^a	14.21^{bc}	13.42^b	13.42^b	15.08^c

Note: Means not sharing a superscript differ from each other at the 0.05 level or more; $n = 24$.

The finding that people ascribe more traits to others than to themselves is of considerable interest if it genuinely reflects a tendency to hold a different implicit personality theory for the self than for others. It is of much less interest if it merely reflects a tendency to present the self in a more favourable light than others. Such a tendency could have accounted for the present data in two ways. If subjects had found one or both traits of a given pair to be undesirable, they might have used the depends-on-the-situation category as an 'escape hatch' for themselves but might have been more willing to assign a questionably desirable trait to someone else. Or, a desire to present oneself favourably might have produced the present results if subjects had been using the depends-on-the-situation category as a means of stating that they were neither too much one way nor too much the other but just right. If so, the greater use of the depends-on-the-situation category for self does not reflect a denial of traits but the assertion that the subject occupies the golden mean on trait dimensions.

Evidence is readily available for the possibility that subjects used the depends-on-the-situation category in order to avoid ascribing relatively undesirable traits to themselves. Subjects were asked to rate the desirability of the 40 traits and two subsets of trait dimensions were defined for each subject on the basis of his ratings, (*i*) those where there was no more than one scale point difference between the two, and (*ii*) those where the subject rated one or both the terms negatively or where the discrepancy between the two was greater than one scale point. (For the group as a whole there were almost equal numbers of trait dimensions in the two subsets – 10.21 and 9.79 respectively.) The results of this analysis are incompatible with the self-esteem or self-presentation alternative. The tendency to attribute more traits to others than to self was actually somewhat *more* marked among traits of the first subset (neutral or desirable and about equal in desirability), than among traits of the second subset (undesirable or differed in desirability or both). This indicates that subjects were not merely using the depends-on-the-situation category in order to avoid describing themselves unfavourably. (However, it should be noted that there was a tendency to ascribe more favourable traits to the self. The mean desirability of traits ascribed to self was higher than that for any other stimulus person. This tendency was non-significant for the comparison of self with best friend, of borderline significance for that between self and acquaintance, significant for the comparison with Cronkite, and highly significant for the comparison with father.)

A remaining alternative explanation is that subjects were not denying that they possessed traits but merely asserting that they occupied an ideal middle ground on the trait dimensions. In order to assess this possibility, a follow-up study was needed. This was essentially a replication of the first study, using the best friend as the only stimulus person. However, instead of presenting subjects with a clear choice between two polar trait terms, they were presented with a more conventional 6-point trait continuum, together with the depends-on-the-situation option prominently displayed on the left of the continuum. Subjects were more likely to use the depends-on-the-situation category for themselves than for their friend. Subjects in Study III thus probably checked the depends-on-the-situation alternative not because they wished to present themselves as possessing traits in moderation, but because they perceived themselves as possessing fewer traits.

The follow-up study also provided an opportunity to explore further the effect of familiarity with the stimulus person. Subjects were asked how long they had known their best friend. Answers ranged from a few months to 19 years. The correlation

THE STUDY

between the length of time they had known their best friend and the tendency to ascribe more traits to best friend than to self was −0.45 ($p<0.01$). Thus, subjects were increasingly unwilling to assign traits to their best friend the longer they had known him, and it seems that, at least within a status category, greater familiarity with the stimulus person results in responding to him in the same way as to the self.

D I S C U S S I O N

All three studies provide evidence in support of the hypothesis that actors attribute causality to the situation while observers attribute causality to the actor's dispositions. Observers in Study I presumed that actors would behave in the future in ways similar to those they had just witnessed, while actors did not share this assumption. Subjects in Study II tended to describe their choices of girlfriend and college major in terms referring to the properties of the chosen object but were more likely to describe the similar choices of their friend in terms referring to their friend's dispositional qualities. Subjects in Study III indicated that they believed themselves to have relatively fewer broad behavioural dispositions – traits – than their friends and thus, presumably, to be relatively more likely to behave in accordance with the demands of specific situations.

The findings of each of the studies undoubtedly could be explained without resort to the hypothesis proposed by Jones and Nisbett (1971), and even taken as a whole, they cannot be said to indicate that the hypothesis generally holds true. The studies should be regarded merely as demonstrations of some interest in their own right, which are consistent with a proposition which is too widely applicable to be either proved or disproved by anything short of a very large and extremely diverse research programme.

Actually, genuinely persuasive support for Jones and Nisbett's (1971) proposition is not likely to result from piling up a large number of instances in which it holds true. Much more effective support would be given by studies directly testing the presumed mechanisms on which the proposition rests. An excellent example of such a study was provided by Storms (1973), who demonstrated that the attributional biases of actors and observers are reversed when they are shown videotapes reversing their normal visual perspective. When actors are shown videotapes focusing on their own behaviour and observers are shown videotapes focusing on the actor's situation, actors attribute their behaviour to dispositional causes more than do observers. This reverses the attributional pattern that obtains when actors and observers do not see such videotapes and strongly supports Jones and Nisbett's contention that the individual's perspective channels his causal inferences.

The present framework rests exclusively on mechanisms of information processing and availability. However, a denial of motivational effects on processes of causal inference is not intended. On the contrary, the present view may be easily integrated with the view that motivational factors, such as the desire to maintain self-esteem, or to present oneself in a favourable light, or to denigrate or exonerate other people, sharply affect causal inference. It seems plausible that at least one such motivational factor, probably acting in concert with informational factors, played a role in the present studies. Brehm (1966) has written at some length on the 'reactance' motive, or man's desire to see himself as free and able to control events that are important to him. Such a motive is probably best served when the individual perceives himself to act in accordance with the demands and opportunities of each new situation as it arises. If the individual were to perceive himself as motivated by traits and overriding dispositions he would have to perceive himself as having less freedom and flexibility of action. On the other hand, the individual's sense of freedom should be enhanced to the extent that he perceives *others* to possess broad behavioural dispositions. The more predictable the behaviour of others, the more the individual can perceive the social environment to be stable and understandable and therefore controllable.

EVALUATION

Theoretical issues

In the **Aim and nature of the study** section above, the point is made that the general hypothesis (originally proposed by Jones & Nisbett, 1971) states that actors tend to perceive their own behaviour as a response to situational cues, while observers tend to perceive the actor's behaviour as a manifestation of a disposition or quality possessed by the actor. The second part of this hypothesis (i.e. the *observer*'s bias) is the *fundamental attribution error* (FAE: Ross, 1977). Put another way, the FAE (or *lay dispositionism*: Ross & Nisbett, 1991) is one component of the AOE. Heider's (1958) original theory can account for both 'components' equally well:

> . . . behaviour . . . has such salient properties that it tends to engulf the field rather than be confined to its proper position as a local stimulus whose interpretation requires the additional data of a surrounding field – the situation in social perception.

In other words, the actor represents the 'figure' against the 'ground', constituted by the social situation (just as, say, in the Rubin Vase, when you perceive the vase as figure, the two faces constitute the ground/background). People are active, dynamic, constantly moving and changing, and these properties make them interesting and 'attention-grabbing'. By contrast, the situation is normally fairly static, unchanging, and much less interesting: it is the behaviour which usually stands out from the

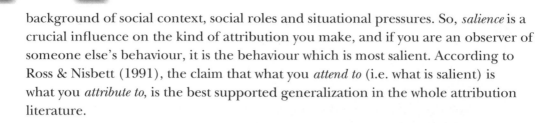

background of social context, social roles and situational pressures. So, *salience* is a crucial influence on the kind of attribution you make, and if you are an observer of someone else's behaviour, it is the behaviour which is most salient. According to Ross & Nisbett (1991), the claim that what you *attend to* (i.e. what is salient) is what you *attribute to*, is the best supported generalization in the whole attribution literature.

However, so far, we have looked at salience exclusively from the observer's perspective (the FAE). What about the actor? In Ross and Nisbett's terms, 'rampant dispositionism is kept in check when it is the self that is in question'. Now what is salient are all the features of the situation which were not attended to by the observer: the observer's 'ground' is the actor's 'figure' (just as the faces can become figure in the Rubin Vase with the vase switching to ground). This, of course, constitutes the 'actor' component of the AOE. How can we account for this? There are two major explanations:

(*i*) the same basic *perceptual-salience* explanation which we have already discussed in relation to the FAE; and (*ii*) the *informational* explanation.

(*i*) In the **Discussion** section, Nisbett *et al.* cite the study by Storms (1973) which has become something of a classic. Two actor participants at a time engaged in a brief, unstructured conversation, while two observer participants looked on. Later, a questionnaire was used to measure the actors' attributions of their own behaviour in the conversation and the observers' attributions of the behaviour of one of the two actors to whom they had been 'matched'. Visual orientation was manipulated by the use of videotapes of the conversation, so that the *no video (control)* group simply completed the questionnaire, the *same orientation* group simply saw a video of what they saw during the original conversation, before completing the questionnaire, and the *new orientation* group saw a video which *reversed* the original orientation, with actors seeing themselves and observers seeing the other actor (again, before completing the questionnaire). As predicted, in the first two groups the usual AOE was found. But, also as predicted, the AOE was *reversed* in the third group: actors made more dispositional attributions than did observers. Visual orientation is an index of perceptual salience, which is a determinant of perceived causality (Brown, 1986).

The fact that it is *possible* (using the artificial means of a video camera) to change the kind of attribution one makes, shows that under 'normal' circumstances,

> . . . attribution is guided to a very substantial degree by one's focus of attention and a primary reason that actors and observers have different causal interpretations is simply because actors and observers typically are attending to different things. (Ross & Nisbett, 1991)

However, as Hewstone & Fincham (1996) point out, person attributions were very high in *all* the conditions of Storms' experiment, and the control condition actually failed to show the normal situational attributions for actors. Also, Storms' findings have not always been replicated. It seems that, while the person in the centre of the visual field *is* rated as more causally important, this weighting does not always have a clear effect on the type of attribution that is made.

But there have been successful replications of the salience effect. For example, participants who could see themselves in a conspicuous mirror assigned more responsibility to themselves than controls who could not (Duval & Wicklund, 1973), and when observers watched a conversation where one participant was made salient by being lit by a bright light, they made more dispositional attributions than for the other participant who was lit by a dim light (McArthur & Post, 1977).

In Study II of the present article, participants had to write five separate paragraphs on (i) why they liked the girl they dated most regularly, (ii) why they had chosen their college major, (iii) why their best friend liked the girl he was dating most regularly, (iv) why their best friend had chosen his college major, and (v) how their best friend would explain the participant's choice of girlfriend and college major. The results of (v) virtually duplicated the pattern of results for (iii) and (iv), showing the ability to 'reverse perspective': participants were 'remarkably capable of adopting the perspective of an outside observer of their own behaviour'. This can be seen as an equivalent finding to that of Storms, but whereas Storms *literally* changed people's perspective by using a video camera, Nisbett *et al.*'s participants changed perspective *mentally* (perceptual versus psychological, respectively).

(*ii*) Also in the **Discussion** section, Nisbett *et al.* state that: 'the present framework rests exclusively on mechanisms of information processing and availability'. This refers to the second of the two major explanations of the AOE.

As an actor, we literally cannot see ourselves behaving, so that what is salient for us are all the situational forces impinging on our behaviour. Similarly (and, as it were, superimposed upon this difference), there is a difference between actors' and observers' *access to information* (Jones & Nisbett, 1971). Actors know how they feel about an event, about their intentions, and about factors giving rise to those intentions (including temporary ones), so they can more appropriately attribute their behaviour to these short-term factors. They also have direct access to their own history, and whether they have behaved in a similar way in the past. Knowing how one can behave differently on different occasions, and in different situations, may discourage the making of dispositional attributions. All of these factors, together with subtle contextual factors, may be inaccessible to the observer. Is there any evidence in the present study which relates directly to this explanation?

Study III is perhaps the most relevant. It was predicted that seeing others' behaviour in more dispositional terms than one's own will result in seeing others as possessing more personality traits than oneself. This was supported and neither familiarity with the stimulus person, nor similarity in age to the stimulus person appeared to influence the outcome. On the face of it, then, there seems to be no evidence to support the informational explanation, since we would expect that the better we know someone, the more access we have to information about that person which an observer under 'normal' conditions (i.e. the observer is a stranger) would *not* have.

However, in the follow-up to Study III, a correlation was found between (a) the length of time participants had known their best friend, and (b) the tendency to attribute more traits to him than to self. The correlation was a significant –0.45, which means that the *longer* they knew him, the *less* likely they were to see him as possessing more traits than self. So, at least within a status category (same-age), greater familiarity with a stimulus person produces attributions which *are* similar to self-attributions, thus supporting the informational explanation.

While Hewstone & Fincham (1996) consider the information explanation to be less interesting and less researched than the salience explanation, Fiske & Taylor (1991) believe that there is supporting evidence, and that both salience and informational factors are probably involved.

Subsequent research

Brown (1986) cites a study by Regan & Totten (1975), which seems to support *both* the salience and informational explanations. Observers were instructed to empathize with one of two women engaged in a real 'get acquainted' conversation. Although they could see both, they were given instructions designed to allow them to adopt the psychological perspective of one or the other of the women. Compared with observers who merely observed one of the two women, the empathizers were much more likely to make *situational* attributions. Instead of attributing causality *to* the actor they most looked at, they attributed causality *in the way the actor did* (i.e. externally). Why?

Brown argues that, normally, observers notice actors' 'gross' behaviour, their 'large muscle movements' and actions: under these conditions, the actions are attributed to the actor. However, in the Regan and Totten study, the observers instructed to emphathize were focusing much more on the actor's expressive behaviour, the finer muscle movements and more subtle aspects of behaviour: effectively, it is the actor's *mental state* which is being observed.

Applying this to Study I, when actors and observers were asked to estimate the likelihood of the actor volunteering in the future for similar social service tasks, the actors 'knew their minds', they knew what did and did not appeal to them about the original request to help, and how much the United Fund resembled it, for them. The observer could not have known any of these things about the actors, who were strangers being observed in a 'non-empathizing' way (in terms simply of the actor's 'gross' decision to volunteer or not to volunteer). The actors also knew what influence the financial incentive had on their decision. But observers believed that volunteering actors would be more likely to canvass for the United Fund than non-volunteering actors, *regardless* of whether they were offered $0.50 or $1.50. They were apparently misled by the actor's behaviour, assuming that it reflected a dispositional tendency (they were making a correspondent inference: Jones & Davis, 1965), as opposed to a suitably compensated 'job opportunity' (Ross & Nisbett, 1991).

A major limitation of the AOE is that it sometimes fails to fit the facts: it is sometimes *reversed* (e.g Chen *et al.*, 1988). If something goes wrong, or we receive negative feedback about something we have done, we typically blame it on the situation (or another person), as the AOE predicts. But what about *positive* feedback and achievements: do we normally want to attribute these to the situation as well? No! We usually want to take the credit for our successes (*self-enhancing bias*), but do not want to accept the blame for our failures (*self-protecting bias*). Together, these are referred to as the *self-serving bias* (Miller & Ross, 1975), which seems to explain certain attributions that actors make which the AOE cannot handle.

An interesting exception to this general rule is the clinically depressed person who believes that when things go wrong, the causes are internal, are stable over time and reflect a global deficiency (Abramson & Martin, 1981: see Chapter 28). An intriguing parallel has been reported in the case of unhappily married couples, who tend to see negative behaviour by their partner as reflecting internal, stable and global causes, while happily married couples make the same attributions for their partner's positive behaviour. Similarly, while happy couples attribute negative behaviours to external, unstable and specific factors, this same attribution is made by unhappy couples to positive behaviours. Bradbury & Fincham (1990) call these patterns *relationship-enhancing* (happy couples) and *distress-maintaining* attributions (unhappy couples).

Buehler *et al.* (1995) have extended the AOE to other kinds of judgement. They examined people's predictions as to how long it would take them to complete various tasks and activities and found evidence of an optimistic bias: people *underestimated* their own completion times. However, when judging *others'* completion times, this bias disappeared (to be replaced by a pessimistic bias). A similar pattern emerged when people were asked to make predictions about the future course of romantic relationships. Thus, differences in perspective are likely to have important and interesting effects on many different types of interpersonal relationship (Hewstone & Fincham, 1996).

Methodological issues

Weiner (1992) believes that the status of the AOE remains uncertain. Part of the problem is that dispositional and situational attributions are not always clearly separable. For example, if female X says that she dates male Y because he is sensitive, does this indicate a situational attribution (he 'causes' her to like him), or a dispositional attribution (she likes sensitive people)?

In Study II, Nisbett *et al.* give as an example of a *pure entity reason* (i.e. situational) for liking the girl they dated most regularly, 'she's a relaxing person', while 'I need someone I can relax with' is given as a *dispositional* example. However, a much more ambiguous example (in relation to choice of college major) is 'I want to make a lot of money' (classified as dispositional because it refers to the person doing the choosing) and 'chemistry is a high-paying field' (situational). They are more ambiguous in the sense that the two statements convey very similar information and, in fact, imply one another (Hewstone & Fincham, 1996).

This distinction is really at the heart of attribution theory, and while it has much intuitive appeal, in practice it is often difficult to achieve. Indeed, some studies have shown that many participants fail to understand the difference, and/or do not find it meaningful. The result is that the reliability and validity of such measures are now challenged rather than assumed (Hewstone & Antaki, 1988).

Applications and implications

According to Zimbardo & Leippe (1991), Western culture stresses the 'cult of the ego':

> It is no wonder that we tend to look for the person in the situation more than we search for the situation that makes the person. Indeed, one of the major lessons of social psychology is that human behaviour is much more under the influence of situational variables than we normally recognize or are willing to admit.

By failing to account adequately for the power of those subtle situational forces (for example, roles, rules, uniforms, symbols and group consensus), we become vulnerable to those very forces, since we *overvalue* our dispositional strength to resist undesirable forces and *undervalue* the situational power to make us comply with them. They cite the case of the 40 psychiatrists whom Milgram asked to predict the outcome of his obedience experiment (see Chapter 7). In predicting that fewer than one per cent would go all the way to 450 volts (and that those few would have to be psychopathic), these 'experts' were making a dispositional attribution which their professional training had caused them to overuse. The whole purpose of Haney *et al.*'s (1973) prison simulation experiment (see Chapter 8), was to test the *dispositional hypothesis* in relation to the pathological behaviour so commonly displayed in such total institutions. Haney *et al.* found the hypothesis to be inadequate.

If Western culture is guilty of the 'cult of the ego', then it is also true that American social psychologists may have been guilty of *ethnocentrism*, or at least a failure to recognize the variability between cultures and sub-cultures with regard to how people make attributions (Ross & Nisbett, 1991). For example, Miller (1984, cited by Ross & Nisbett) found that Hindus were more likely than Americans to explain events in terms of situational or contextual factors, and this applied to both pro-social and deviant behaviours. Could it be that situational factors really do play more of a role in determining behaviour in the East than the West? Indeed, this is a basic assumption made by scholars who contrast *individualistic* (Western) and *collectivist* (Eastern) cultures (see Chapter 27). Ross and Nisbett suspect that the truth involves *both* factors: situational influences in non-Western contexts may actually be more powerful *and* also more salient explanations of behaviour. This and other evidence shows that different cultures construe the world in truly different ways, and suggests that marked cognitive differences may have fundamentally *social* origins.

Smith & Bond (1998) discuss the AOE in the context of communication breakdown between members of different cultural groups. They argue that, until people from different cultures become more knowledgeable about each others' cultural codes, the 'cycle of misattribution' will continue. This cycle will sooner or later result in distressing experiences, which set a 'withdrawal dynamic' into motion.

Exercises

1. In **Background and context**, reference is made to the *Gestalt* psychologists. What does 'gestalt' mean and who are the main figures associated with this school of psychology?

2. In relation to the results of Study I, what does '(t<1, *ns*)' mean?

3. *t*-tests were used throughout for Study I. What does this tell you about the rating scale on which actors and observers estimated the probability of the actor volunteering for a similar task (see Table 11.1)?

4. In the **Discussion** of Study I, 'It might be argued . . . that the dispositional inferences of observers were due solely to aspects of the experimental situation that were artificial and ecologically rare'. What does 'artificial and ecologically rare' mean?

5. Although all the *p* levels are based on two-tailed tests, the wording of the hypotheses suggests *one*-tailed predictions. For example, in Study II, 'It was anticipated that in explaining their own choices, subjects would emphasize the role of properties of the chosen object, and in explaining their friends' similar choices, they would be more likely to emphasize the role played by dispositions and traits of the choosing individual'.
   (*i*)   Which words in particular convey that this may be one-tailed?
   (*ii*) Re-write it so that it is, unambiguously, *two*-tailed.
   (*iii*) What are other terms for 'one-' and 'two-tailed'?

6. In Study I, observers of non-volunteers tended to see them as less likely to help them than did the non-volunteers themselves. The result is given as t=1.63, 0.10<p<0.15. What does this mean?

7. In Study II,
   (*i*) What are the independent and dependent variables?
   (*ii*) What experimental design is used?
   (*iii*) By what method were the paragraphs scored for the degree to which they stressed 'entity' versus 'dispositional' reasons?
   (*iv*) How was 'dispositional' defined?

8. In the Study II follow-up, participants were presented with reasons in a questionnaire. Alternate forms of the questionnaire were constructed (such that for every reason which appeared in entity form on one, there was a dispositional form of that reason on the other, and vice-versa).
   (*i*) What is another name for 'alternate forms'?
   (*ii*) What is it a measure of?
   (*iii*) What other, equivalent measures are there?

9. In Study III, there were 20 three-choice items (trait term/polar opposite/'it depends on the situation') for each of the five stimulus persons (including self). For the group of participants as a whole, the question for each stimulus person preceded the question for every other stimulus person equally often.
   (*i*) What is this arrangement called?
   (*ii*) Why was this arrangement used in this particular case?

10. In Study III, 'The tendency to attribute more traits to others was as stable across subjects and trait dimensions as it was across stimulus persons.'
    What does this mean?

11. In the **Discussion**, reference is made to Brehm's (1966) concept of *reactance*. Do you agree that seeing ourselves as motivated by traits/dispositions makes us *less* free, and that freedom lies in seeing ourselves as acting in accordance with the demands and opportunities of each new situation as it arises?

12 Experiments in intergroup discrimination

Henri Tajfel (1970)

Scientific American, 223, 96–105

BACKGROUND AND CONTEXT

According to Brown (1986), it is quite fitting that the study of *minimal groups* and the subsequent Social Identity theory designed to explain the results of these studies should have occurred in Europe. This is because Europeans have plenty of experience of group conflict. Tajfel himself was a European Jew who, unlike the majority of his fellow-Jews, survived World War II. There is a tragic irony (or perhaps prophesy) to Tajfel's reference in the article to his Slovene friend's description of the stereotype held in Yugoslavia of Bosnians: not only does Yugoslavia no longer exist, but even in that part of Europe with such a long history of ethnic strife, who could have predicted the scale and intensity of hostility between the different ethnic groups, especially the 'ethnic cleansing', perpetrated by Moslems, Serbs and Croatians alike? How can we account for prejudice, discrimination and hostility between groups or between individuals, because they are members of those groups?

One psychological approach is to regard prejudice and out-group rejection as 'residing' within the personality structure of individuals, and probably the most influential example of this approach is Adorno *et al.*'s (1950) theory of the Authoritarian Personality. Because they defer to authority, such people are liable to *conform* to societal norms, and would project their aggression onto out-groups which are already perceived as such in their society (Brown, 1985).

Conversely, if societal norms of prejudice and discrimination are sufficiently powerful, many people may engage in discriminatory behaviour who do not have most or any of the characteristics of the authoritarian personality. So, in practice, cultural or societal norms may be much more important than individual personality in accounting for ethnocentrism, out-group rejection, prejudice and discrimination. Brown (1985) gives the example of Nazi Germany, where many people became overtly anti-Semitic who might well not have held such views, or voiced them or acted upon them in a society where anti-Semitism was not the norm. In other words, discrimination can occur in the absence of prejudice; prejudice is not a *necessary* precondition for discriminatory

behaviour, just as prejudice does not guarantee that discrimination will occur (it is not a *sufficient* condition either).

Since prejudice and discrimination can have their source in cultural norms, as distinct from individual personality, it seems logical to look for specific causes stemming from the relationship which exists between various social groups. This was the approach adopted by Sherif, his wife and other colleagues during the 1950s and the early 1960s (Sherif & Sherif, 1953; Sherif *et al.*, 1955; Sherif *et al.*, 1961). These studies all involved 12-year-old boys at summer camps in America, and the best known of these is the last, the *Robber's Cave* experiment, which Brown (1986) describes as the most successful field experiment ever conducted on intergroup conflict.

These researchers experimentally created what Brown calls 'real ethnocentrism, real stereotypes, and real perceived injustice', by assigning previously unacquainted strangers to groups, allowing them to establish a group identity, and then putting these groups into competition with each other. In this instance, the competition took the form of a 'grand tournament', comprising a number of athletic and other events, with the winners receiving a trophy and four-bladed knives, prizes held in great esteem by these 12-year-old, white, middle-class, American boys. (The research was actually conducted between 1949 and 1953.) What has come to be called *realistic group conflict theory* states that objective competition between groups is a *sufficient* condition for prejudice and discrimination, and this is the conclusion drawn by Sherif *et al.* (1961).

However, even assuming that it is sufficient (and a study by Tyerman & Spencer (1983) involving English boy scouts at annual camp challenges this conclusion), we still need to ask if it is actually *necessary*. In other words, can prejudice and discrimination occur or be created in situations in which there is *no* competition? Another way of asking the question is: does being of one nationality, religion, ethnicity, or class *in and of itself* generate predictable orientations towards members of other nationalities, etc.? (Brown, 1996), and if so, what is the 'minimal case' for producing them? The present study was designed to answer these two important questions.

Rabbie & Horwitz (1969) were, in fact, the first to investigate this. They reasoned that the essential condition for the arousal of group feelings was the perception of interdependence of fate among group members. Schoolchildren who did not know each other were randomly divided into two groups of four, were given ID badges (green or blue), and initially were seated either side of a screen, so that they could only see members of their own group (*control condition*). In the *experimental conditions*, they further experienced a 'common fate' by being given (or deprived of) some new transistor radios.

Subsequently, in all conditions, the screen was removed and the children were asked to stand up and read out some personal biographical details about themselves, while the others rated them on several scales. Only in the experimental conditions were these impressionistic ratings markedly affected by group affiliation: in-group members were consistently rated more favourably than out-group members.

Rabbie and Horwitz concluded that classification into a group *by itself* had little influence on group members' judgements, but when that classification coincided with some common experience of reward or deprivation, then group-related perceptions emerged (Brown, 1996). (They later changed their minds, after conducting a follow-up study: Horwitz & Rabbie, 1982.) Tajfel and his colleagues took this one stage further, claiming that mere categorization *was* sufficient for producing intergroup discrimination.

AIM AND NATURE OF THE STUDY

This article is an early report of laboratory experiments carried out at the University of Bristol by Tajfel and his colleagues into intergroup discrimination. It is not, in fact, a very commonly cited reference, the most common being Tajfel, Billig, Bundy and Flament (1971), *Social categorization and intergroup behaviour,* which appeared in the *European Journal of Social Psychology*. Almost all the subsequent articles first appeared in this journal, and the related Social Identity theory (see **Evaluation** below) is very much a European product (Brown, 1986).

The actual experiments reported here are the same as those reported in the 1971 article. However, the term *minimal group* is never used in either, and yet this is how the experiments are usually referred to. Indeed, Tajfel established a basic procedure for investigating intergroup discrimination and ingroup favouritism (the *minimal group paradigm*), which is the equivalent of the Asch paradigm for investigating conformity and the Milgram paradigm for the study of obedience (see Chapter 7). It represents a modification and extension of the procedure used by Rabbie and Horwitz.

The whole point of the paradigm is to establish the 'baseline conditions' for intergroup discrimination (Schiffman & Wicklund, 1992), that is, the demonstration that merely putting people into groups, however arbitrary and meaningless the allocation may be, is sufficient for people to discriminate in favour of their own group and against members of the other group.

The same hypothesis is tested by two separate experiments, the first involving the task of estimating the number of dots on a screen, the second involving preference for slides of paintings by Klee and Kandinsky. The hypothesis states that:

> . . . discriminatory intergroup behaviour can sometimes be expected even if the individual is not involved in actual (or even imagined) conflicts of interest and has no past history of attitudes of intergroup hostility.

THE STUDY

Intergroup discrimination is a feature of most modern societies. The phenomenon is depressingly similar regardless of the constitution of the 'ingroup' and of the 'outgroup' that is perceived as being somehow different. A Slovene friend of mine once described to me the stereotypes – the common traits attributed to a large human group – that are applied in his country, the richest constituent republic of Yugoslavia, to immigrant Bosnians, who come from a poorer region. Some time later I presented this description to a group of students at the University of Oxford and asked them to guess by whom it was used and to whom it referred. The almost unanimous reply was that this was the characterization applied by native Englishmen to 'coloured' immigrants: people coming primarily from the West Indies, India and Pakistan.

The intensity of discrimination varies more than the nature of the phenomenon. In countries with long-standing intergroup problems – be they racial as in the US, religious as in Northern Ireland or linguistic-national as in Belgium – tensions reach the boiling point more easily than they do elsewhere. In spite of differing economic, cultural, historical, political and psychological backgrounds, however, the *attitudes* of prejudice toward outgroups and the *behaviour* of discrimination against outgroups clearly display a set of common characteristics. Social scientists have naturally been concerned to try to identify these characteristics in an effort to understand the origins of prejudice and discrimination.

The investigative approaches to this task can be roughly classified into two categories. Some workers stress the social determinants of prejudice and discrimination. Others emphasize psychological causation. In *The Functions of Social Conflict*, published in 1956, Lewis A. Coser of Brandeis University established a related dichotomy when he distinguished between two types of intergroup conflict: the 'rational' and the 'irrational'. The former is a means to an end: the conflict and the attitudes that go with it reflect a genuine competition between groups with divergent interests. The latter is an end in itself: it serves to release accumulated emotional tensions of various kinds. As both popular lore and the psychological literature testify, nothing is better suited for this purpose than a well-selected scapegoat.

These dichotomies have some value as analytical tools but they need not be taken too seriously. Most cases of conflict between human groups, large or small, reflect an intricate interdependence of social and psychological causation. Often it is difficult, and probably fruitless, to speculate about what were the first causes of real present-day social situations. Moreover, there is a dialectical relation between the objective and the subjective determinants of intergroup attitudes and behaviour. Once the process is set in motion they reinforce each other in a relentless spiral in which the weight of predominant causes tends to shift continuously. For example, economic or social competition can lead to discriminatory behaviour; that behaviour can then in a number of ways create attitudes of prejudice; those attitudes can in turn lead to new forms of discriminatory behaviour that create new economic or social disparities, and so the vicious circle is continued.

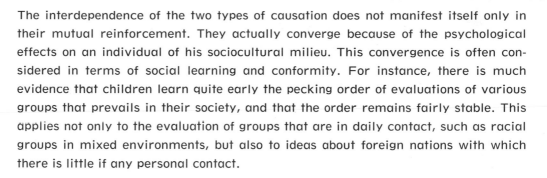

The interdependence of the two types of causation does not manifest itself only in their mutual reinforcement. They actually converge because of the psychological effects on an individual of his sociocultural milieu. This convergence is often considered in terms of social learning and conformity. For instance, there is much evidence that children learn quite early the pecking order of evaluations of various groups that prevails in their society, and that the order remains fairly stable. This applies not only to the evaluation of groups that are in daily contact, such as racial groups in mixed environments, but also to ideas about foreign nations with which there is little if any personal contact.

In studies conducted at Oxford a few years ago my colleagues and I found a high consensus among children of six and seven in their preference for four foreign countries. The order was America, France, Germany and Russia, and there was a correlation of 0.98 between the preferences of subjects from two different schools. As for adults, studies conducted by Thomas F. Pettigrew in the late 1950s in South Africa and in the American South have shown that conformity is an important determinant of hostile attitudes toward blacks in both places (above and beyond individual tendencies toward authoritarianism, which is known to be closely related to prejudice toward outgroups).

These studies, like many others, were concerned with attitudes rather than behaviour, with prejudice rather than discrimination. Discrimination, it is often said, is more directly a function of the objective social situation, which sometimes does and sometimes does not facilitate the expression of attitudes; the attitudes of prejudice may be socially learned or due to tendencies to conform, but they are not a very efficient predictor of discriminatory behaviour. According to this view, psychological considerations are best suited to explaining and predicting the genesis and functioning of attitudes; the facts of intergroup discrimination are best related to, and predicted from, objective indexes of a social, economic and demographic nature.

Although I have no quarrel with this view, I am left with a nagging feeling that it omits an important part of the story. The fact is that behaviour toward outgroups shows the same monotonous similarity as attitudes do, across a diversity of socioeconomic conditions. This apparent diversity may, of course, obscure an underlying common factor of 'rational' conflict, of struggle to preserve a *status quo* favourable to oneself or to obtain an equitable share of social opportunities and benefits. Another kind of underlying regularity is nonetheless common to a variety of social situations and is an important psychological effect of our sociocultural milieu. It is the assimilation by the individual of the various norms of conduct that prevail in his society.

For the purposes of this article I shall define social norms as being an individual's expectation of how others expect him to behave and his expectation of how others will behave in any given social situation. Whether he does or does not behave according to these expectations depends primarily on his understanding of whether or not and how a situation relates to a specific set of expectations. If a link is made

THE STUDY

A

MATRIX 1

−19	−16	−13	−10	−7	−4	−1	0	1	2	3	4	5	6
6	5	4	3	2	1	0	−1	−4	−7	−10	−13	−16	−19

MATRIX 2

12	10	8	6	4	2	0	−1	−5	−9	−13	−17	−21	−25
−25	−21	−17	−13	−9	−5	−1	0	2	4	6	8	10	12

B

MATRIX 3

1	2	3	4	5	6	7	8	9	10	11	12	13	14
14	13	12	11	10	9	8	7	6	5	4	3	2	1

MATRIX 4

18	17	16	15	14	13	12	11	10	9	8	7	6	5
5	6	7	8	9	10	11	12	13	14	15	16	17	18

C

MATRIX 5

−14	−12	−10	−8	−6	−4	−2	−1	3	7	11	15	19	23
23	19	15	11	7	3	−1	−2	−4	−6	−8	−10	−12	−14

MATRIX 6

17	14	11	8	5	2	−1	−2	−3	−4	−5	−6	−7	−8
−8	−7	−6	−5	−4	−3	−2	−1	2	5	8	11	14	17

Figure 12.1. First experiment conducted by the author and his colleagues utilized these six matrices. The numbers represented points (later translated into awards or penalties in money) to be assigned by a subject to other individuals; by checking a box the subject assigned the number of points in the top of the box to one person and the number in the bottom of the box to another person; he did not know the identity of these people but only whether each was a member of his own group or 'the other group'. (The groups had been established by the experimenters on grounds that were artificial and insignificant.) Each matrix appeared three times in a test booklet with each row of numbers labelled to indicate whether the subject was choosing between two members of his own group (ingroup) other than himself, two members of the outgroup or one member of the ingroup and one member of the outgroup. Choices were scored to see if subjects chose for fairness, maximum gain to their own group or maximum difference in favour of the ingroup.

between the one and the other – if an individual's understanding of a situation in which he finds himself is such that in his view certain familiar social norms are pertinent to it – he behaves accordingly.

There is nothing new to this formulation; it is inherent in most studies and discussions of intergroup prejudice and discrimination that stress the importance of conformity. The point I wish to make is broader. Conformity contributes to hostile attitudes and behaviour toward specified groups of people in situations that are usually characterized by a history of intergroup tensions, conflicts of interest and early acquisition by individuals of hostile views about selected outgroups. We are dealing, however, with a process that is more general and goes deeper than the learning of value judgements about a specific group and the subsequent acting out of accepted patterns of behaviour toward that group. The child learns not only whom he should like or dislike in the complex social environment to which he is exposed but also something more basic. An individual constructs his own 'web of social affiliations' by applying principles of order and simplification that reduce the complexity of crisscrossing human categorizations. Perhaps the most important principle of the subjective social order we construct for ourselves is the classification of groups as 'we' and 'they' – as ingroups (any number of them to which we happen to belong) and outgroups. The criteria for these assignments may vary according to the situation, and their emotional impact may be high or low, but in our societies this division into groups most often implies a competitive relation between the groups. In other words, intergroup categorizations of all kinds may

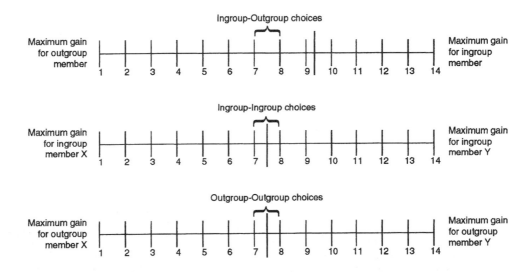

Figure 12.2. Results were scored by ranking the choices from 1 to 14 depending on which box was checked. The end of the matrix at which the ingroup member got the minimum number of points (and the outgroup member the maximum) was designated 1; the other end, giving the ingroup member the maximum, was 14. The mean choices (long vertical lines) are shown here. In the intergroup situation the subjects gave significantly more points to members of their own group than to members of the other group. In the intragroup situations, however, the means of the choices fell at Rank 7.5, between the choices of maximum fairness (brackets).

bring into play what seems to the individual to be the appropriate form of inter-group behaviour.

What this essentially means Is that the need to bring some kind of order into our 'social construction of reality' (a term recently used by Peter L. Berger of the New School for Social Research and Thomas Luckmann of the University of Frankfurt) combines with the hostility inherent in many of the intergroup categorizations to which we are continually exposed to develop a 'generic norm' of behaviour toward outgroups. Whenever we are confronted with a situation to which some form of intergroup categorization appears directly relevant, we are likely to act in a manner that discriminates against the outgroup and favours the ingroup.

If this is true, if there exists such a generic norm of behaviour toward outgroups, several important consequences should follow. The first is that there may be discrimination against an outgroup even if there is no reason for it in terms of the individual's own interests – in terms of what he can gain as a result of discriminating against the outgroup. The second consequence is that there may be such discrimination in the absence of any previously existing attitudes of hostility or dislike toward the outgroup. And the third consequence, following directly from the second, is that this generic norm may manifest itself directly in behaviour toward the outgroup before any attitudes of prejudice or hostility have been formed. If this reasoning is correct, then discriminatory intergroup behaviour can sometimes be expected even if the individual is not involved in actual (or even imagined) conflicts of interest and has no past history of attitudes of intergroup hostility.

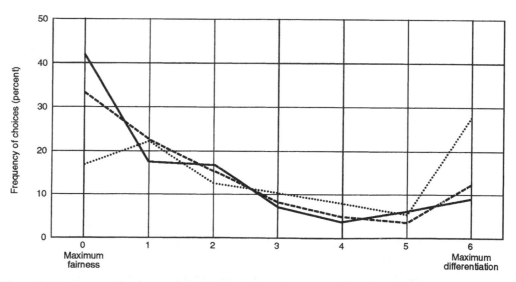

Figure 12.3. Intergroup discrimination was a deliberate strategy in the ingroup-outgroup choices (dotted curve) and fairness a deliberate strategy in the ingroup-ingroup (dashed) and outgroup-outgroup (solid) choices. This is indicated by the fact that the frequencies of intergroup choices differed significantly from those of the intragroup choices only at the extreme points of the distribution, the points of maximum fairness and of maximum discrimination. (For this analysis the two fairest choices in each matrix, the two middle ones, were ranked together as 0 and departures in either direction were scored from 1 to 6.)

At the University of Bristol, in collaboration with Claude Flament of the University of Aix-Marseille, R. P. Bundy and M. J. Billig, I have conducted experiments designed to test this prediction and others that follow from it. The main problem was to create experimental conditions that would enable us to assess the effects of intergroup categorization *per se*, uncontaminated by other variables, such as interactions among individuals or pre-existing attitudes. We aimed, moreover, to look at the behaviour rather than the attitudes of the subjects toward their own group and the other group, to ensure that this behaviour was of some importance to them and to present them with a clear alternative to discriminating against the outgroup that would be a more 'sensible' mode of behaviour.

Perhaps the best means of conveying the way these criteria were met is to describe the procedure we followed in the first experiments and its variants in subsequent ones. Our subjects were 64 boys, 14 and 15 years old from a state, or 'comprehensive', school in a suburb of Bristol. They came to the laboratory in separate groups of eight. All the boys in each of the groups were from the same house in the same form at the school, so that they knew each other well before the experiment. The first part of the experiment served to establish an intergroup categorization and in the second part we assessed the effects of that categorization on intergroup behaviour.

In the first part the boys were brought together in a lecture room and were told that we were interested in the study of visual judgements. Forty clusters of varying numbers of dots were flashed on a screen. The boys were asked to estimate the number of dots in each cluster and to record each estimate in succession on prepared score sheets. There were two conditions in this first part of the experiment. In one condition, after the boys had completed their estimates they were told that in judgements of this kind some people consistently overestimate the number of dots and some consistently underestimate the number, but that these tendencies are in no way related to accuracy. In the other condition the boys were told that some people are consistently more accurate than others. Four groups of eight served in each of the two conditions.

After the judgements had been made and had been ostentatiously 'scored' by one of the experimenters, we told the subjects that, since we were also interested in other kinds of decision, we were going to take advantage of their presence to investigate these as well, and that for ease of coding we were going to group them on the basis of the visual judgements they had just made. In actuality the subjects were assigned to groups quite at random, half to 'underestimators' and half to 'overestimators' in the first condition, half to 'better' and half to 'worse' accuracy in the second one.

Instructions followed about the nature of the forthcoming task. The boys were told that it would consist of giving to others rewards and penalties in real money. They would not know the identity of the individuals to whom they would be assigning these rewards and penalties since everyone would have a code number. They would

be taken to another room one by one and given information as to which group they were in. Once in the other room they were to work on their own in separate cubicles. In each cubicle they would find a pencil and a booklet containing 18 sets of ordered numbers, one to each page. It was stressed that on no occasion would the boys be rewarding or penalizing themselves; they would always be allotting money to others. At the end of the task each boy would be brought back into the first room and would receive the amount of money the other boys had awarded him. The value of each point they were awarding was a tenth of a penny (about a tenth of a US cent). After these instructions were given, the boys were led individually to their cubicles to fill out their booklets.

On each page in the booklet there was one matrix consisting of 14 boxes containing two numbers each. The numbers in the top row were the rewards and penalties to be awarded to one person and those in the bottom row were those to be awarded to another. Each row was labelled 'These are rewards and penalties for member No. — of your group' or '. . . of the other group'. The subjects had to indicate their choices by checking one box in each matrix. On the cover of each booklet and at the top of each page was written: 'Booklet for member of the — group'.

There were six matrices (see Figure 12.1) and each of them appeared three times in the booklet – once for each of three types of choice. There were ingroup choices, with the top and the bottom row signifying the rewards and penalties to be awarded to two members of the subject's own group (other than himself). Then there were outgroup choices, with both rows signifying the rewards and penalties for a member of the other group. Finally there were intergroup, or 'differential', choices, one row indicating the rewards and penalties to be awarded to an ingroup member (other than himself) and the other the points for an outgroup member. (The top and bottom positions of ingroup and outgroup members were varied at random.)

The results for the intergroup choices were first scored in terms of ranks of choices. In each matrix Rank 1 stood for the choice of the term that gave to the member of the ingroup the minimum possible number of points in that matrix; Rank 14, at the opposite extreme of the matrix, stood for the maximum possible number of points. Comparable (but more complex) methods of scoring were adopted for the other two kinds of choice, the ingroup choices and the outgroup ones, and for comparison of these choices with those made in the differential situation.

The results were striking. In making their intergroup choices a large majority of the subjects, in all groups in both conditions, gave more money to members of their own group than to members of the other group. All the results were – at a very high level of statistical significance – above both Rank 7.5, which represents the point of maximum fairness, and the mean ranks of the ingroup and outgroup choices. In contrast the ingroup and outgroup choices were closely distributed about the point of fairness. Further analysis made it clear that intergroup discrimination was the deliberate strategy adopted in making intergroup choices.

A

MATRIX 1

19	18	17	16	15	14	13	12	11	10	9	8	7
1	3	5	7	9	11	13	15	17	19	21	23	25

MJP
MJP
MIP
MD

MIP
MD

MATRIX 2

23	22	21	20	19	18	17	16	15	14	13	12	11
5	7	9	11	13	15	17	19	21	23	25	27	29

B

MATRIX 3

7	8	9	10	11	12	13	14	15	16	17	18	19
1	3	5	7	9	11	13	15	17	19	21	23	25

MIP
MJP
MIP
MJP
MD

MD

MATRIX 4

11	12	13	14	15	16	17	18	19	20	21	22	23
5	7	9	11	13	15	17	19	21	23	25	27	29

THE STUDY

Figure 12.4. Second experiment involved new matrices. Each was presented in four versions labelled (as in Figure 12.5 overleaf) to indicate whether the choice was between members of different groups or between two members of the same group; the intergroup choices sometimes had the ingroup member's points in the top row and sometimes had them in the bottom row. The objective now was to analyse the influence of three variables on the subjects' choices: maximum ingroup profit (*MIP*), maximum joint profit (*MJP*) and maximum difference in favour of the ingroup member (*MD*). These varied according to different patterns in the Type *A* and Type *B* matrices and in the different versions; in some cases the maxima were together at one end of the matrix and in other cases they were at opposite ends. For example, in the ingroup-over-outgroup version of Type *A* matrices the maximum ingroup profit and maximum difference were at one end and the maximum joint profit at the other end (*bold type*); in the outgroup-over-ingroup version of the same matrices the three maxima were together at the right-hand end of the matrices (*ordinary type*). Type *B* ingroup-over-outgroup versions, on the other hand, distinguish the difference in favour of ingroup from the other two gains (*bold*).

Before continuing, let us review the situation. The boys, who knew each other well, were divided into groups defined by flimsy and unimportant criteria. Their own individual interests were not affected by their choices, since they always assigned points to two other people and no one could know what any other boy's choices were. The amounts of money were not trivial for them: each boy left the experiment with the equivalent of about a dollar. Inasmuch as they could not know who

These numbers are rewards for:

member no. 74 of Klee group	25	23	21	19	17	15	13	11	9	7	5	3	1
member no. 44 of Kandinsky group	19	18	17	16	15	14	13	12	11	10	9	8	7

Please fill in below details of the box you have just chosen:

	Amount
reward for member no. 74 of Klee group	21
reward for member no. 44 of Kandinsky group	17

Figure 12.5. Page of booklet, presenting a single matrix, is reproduced as a subject might have marked it. In addition to checking a box, the subject filled in the blanks below it to confirm his choice. The page heading reminded him which group he was in. The awards were made to persons identified only by number and group; the subject did not know who they were but only their group identification.

was in their group and who was in the other group, they could have adopted either of two reasonable strategies. They could have chosen the maximum-joint-profit point of the matrices, which would mean that the boys as a total group would get the most money out of the experimenters, or they could choose the point of maximum fairness. Indeed, they did tend to choose the second alternative when their choices did not involve a distinction between ingroup and outgroup. As soon as this differentiation was involved, however, they discriminated in favour of the ingroup. The only thing we needed to do to achieve this result was to associate their judgements of numbers of dots with the use of the terms 'your group' and 'the other group' in the instructions and on the booklets of matrices.

The results were at a very high level of statistical significance in all eight separately tested groups of eight boys. In view of the consistency of the phenomenon we decided to analyse it further and also to validate it with a different criterion for intergroup categorization. We tested three new groups of 16 boys each, this time with aesthetic preference as the basis of the division into two groups. The boys were shown 12 slides, six of which were reproductions of paintings by Paul Klee and six by Wassily Kandinsky, and they were asked to express their preference for one of the other of these two 'foreign painters'. The reproductions were presented without the painter's signature, so that half of the subjects could be assigned at random to the 'Klee group' and half to the 'Kandinsky group'.

The matrices that confronted the boys subsequently in their individual cubicles were different from those in the first experiment. We were not interested in assessing the relative weights of some of the variables that may have pulled their decisions in one direction or the other. In this experiment we looked at three variables: maximum joint profit, or the largest possible joint award to both people; maximum ingroup profit, or the largest possible award to a member of the ingroup, and maximum difference, or the largest possible difference in gain between a member of the ingroup and a member of the outgroup in favour of the former.

THE STUDY

There were four different matrices (see Figure 12.4). As in the first experiment, there were three types of choice: between a member of the ingroup and a member of the outgroup, between two members of the ingroup and between two members of the outgroup. In the outgroup-over-ingroup version of Type A matrices (that is, where the numbers in the top row represented amounts given to a member of the outgroup and in the bottom row to a member of the ingroup) the three gains – joint profit, ingroup profit and difference in favour of the ingroup – varied together; their maxima (maximum joint profit, maximum ingroup profit and maximum difference) were all at the same end of the matrix. In the ingroup-over-outgroup version, ingroup profit and difference in favour of ingroup went together in one direction and were in direct conflict with choices approaching maximum joint profit. In the Type B matrices outgroup-over-ingroup versions again represented a covariation of the three gains; in the ingroup-over-outgroup versions, difference in favour of ingroup varied in the direction opposite to joint profit and ingroup profit combined.

A comparison of the boys' choices in the various matrices showed that maximum joint profit exerted hardly any effect at all; the effect of maximum ingroup profit and maximum difference combined against maximum joint profit was strong and highly significant; the effect of maximum difference against maximum joint profit and maximum ingroup profit was also strong and highly significant. In other words, when the subjects had a choice between maximizing the profit for all and maximizing the profit for members of their own group, they acted on behalf of their own group. When they had a choice between profit for all and for their own group combined, as against their own group's winning *more* than the outgroup at the sacrifice of both of these utilitarian advantages, it was the maximization of *difference* that seemed more important to them.

Evidence leading in the same direction emerged from the other two types of choice, between two members of the ingroup and between two members of the outgroup: the ingroup choices were consistently and significantly nearer to the maximum joint profit than were the outgroup ones – and this was so in spite of the fact that giving as much as possible to two members of the outgroup in the choices applying solely to them presented no conflict with the ingroup's interest. It simply would have meant giving more to 'the others' without giving any less to 'your own'. This represented, therefore, a clear case of gratuitous discrimination. We also included in the second experiment some of the original matrices used in the first one, with results much the same as before. Again all the results in this experiment were at a high level of statistical significance.

In subsequent experiments we tested the importance of fairness in making the choices, the effect on the choices of familiarity with the situation and the subjects' ideas about the choices that others were making. Fairness, we found, was an important determinant; most of the choices must be understood as being a compromise between fairness and favouring one's own group. We found that discrimination not only persisted but also increased when the entire situation became more familiar to the subjects. With familiarity there was also an increase (when the boys were asked to predict the other subjects' behaviour) in their expectation that other boys were discriminating.

Much remains to be done to analyse the entire phenomenon in greater detail and to gain a fuller understanding of its determining conditions, but some clear inferences can already be made. Outgroup discrimination is extraordinarily easy to trigger off. In some previous studies of group conflict, such as one conducted by Muzafer Sherif at the University of Oklahoma, groups had to be placed in intense competition for several days for such results to occur (see *Experiments in Group Conflict*, by Muzafer Sherif; *Scientific American*, Offprint 454); in other situations behaviour of this kind can occur without direct conflict if it is based on previously existing hostility. Yet neither an objective conflict of interests nor hostility had any relevance whatever to what our subjects were asked to do. It was enough for them to see themselves as clearly categorized into an ingroup and an outgroup, flimsy as the criteria for this division were – even though the boys knew one another well before the experiments, their own individual gains were not involved in their decisions and their actions could have been aimed to achieve the greatest common good.

It would seem, then, that the generic norm of outgroup behaviour to which I have referred does exist and that it helps to distort what might have been more reasonable conduct. This norm determines behaviour – as other social norms do – when an individual finds himself in a situation to which, in his view, the norm applies. Behaviour is never motiveless, but it is a crude oversimplification to think that motives in social situations include no more than calculations of self-interest or that they can be derived from a few supposedly universal human drives such as aggression toward the outsider, the need to affiliate and so on. To behave socially is a complex business. It involves a long learning process; it is based on the manipulation of symbols and abstractions; it implies the capacity for modification of conduct when the situation changes – and social situations never remain static. To behave *appropriately* is therefore a powerful social motive, and attempting to do so means to behave according to one's best understanding of the situation. Judgements of what is appropriate are determined by social norms, or sets of expectations.

It seems clear that two such norms were understood by our subjects to apply to the situation we imposed on them: 'groupness' and 'fairness'. They managed to achieve a neat balance between the two, and one might assume that in real-life situations the same kind of balance would apply. Unfortunately it is only too easy to think of examples in real life where fairness would go out the window, since groupness is often based on criteria more weighty than either preferring a painter one has never heard of before or resembling someone else in one's way of counting dots. Socialization into 'groupness' is powerful and unavoidable; it has innumerable valuable functions. It also has some odd side effects that may – and do – reinforce acute

T H E   S T U D Y

intergroup tensions whose roots lie elsewhere. Perhaps those educators in our competitive societies who from the earliest schooling are so keen on 'teams' and 'team spirit' could give some thought to the operation of these side effects.

EVALUATION

Theoretical issues

In the 1970 article, Tajfel argues that in order to simplify and bring order to our 'social construction of reality', we gradually learn to classify social groups as 'we' and 'they' (in-groups and out-groups). This combines with the hostility which is inherent in many of the group stereotypes to which we are constantly exposed to produce 'generic norms' of behaviour towards out-groups (behaving in ways which discriminate against the out-group and in favour of the in-group). He sees this as a process which is both more general and goes deeper than either the learning of value judgements about a specific group, or conformity. It has three consequences: (*i*) there may be discrimination against an out-group even if there is no reason for it in terms of the individual's own interests (what s/he can gain from any such discrimination); (*ii*) such discrimination may occur in the absence of any previously existing attitudes of hostility or dislike towards the out-group; (*iii*) this generic norm may manifest itself directly in behaviour towards the out-group *before* any prejudice or hostility have developed.

Relating this to Sherif *et al.*'s (1961) Robber's Cave experiment, the usual conclusion drawn is that prejudice and hostility are a *consequence* of the competition between the two groups. So, if Tajfel is correct, then (as we saw in **Background and context** above) competition is *not* necessary for these to arise. Indeed, when the Rattlers first learned of the existence of the Eagles (the names the two groups gave themselves), they immediately expressed the wish to challenge them. This intergroup rivalry occurred *before* the actual intergroup competitions had been announced: just being in one group and becoming aware of a second group seemed to trigger feelings of competitiveness.

This, together with other experimental findings, strongly suggests that, 'conflictual goal relationships are not actually necessary to elicit in-group bias in people's judgements' (Brown, 1988). However, nor can we conclude that *mere* group membership is the crucial variable, since several other variables are also present. In order to establish that the fact of belonging to one group *in and of itself* will affect our attitudes and behaviour towards other groups, we must remove all these other variables as potential influences on attitudes and behaviour. The minimal group paradigm (MGP) is an attempt to create experimental conditions that would enable us to assess the effects of *intergroup categorization* as such, uncontaminated by other variables.

Methodological issues

Schiffman & Wicklund (1992) list the criteria for *minimal groups* as follows:

1. There should be no face-to-face interaction between group members.
2. Complete anonymity of group membership should be maintained.
3. There should be no instrumental or rational link between the criteria for intergroup categorization and the nature of in-group/out-group responses required from participants.
4. The responses should not represent any utilitarian value to the participant.
5. The strategy of intergroup differentiation should conflict with a strategy based on more 'rational' or 'utilitarian' principles.
6. The responses should comprise real decisions about the distribution of concrete rewards (and/or penalties) to others.

How can these criteria be seen in the Tajfel *et al.* experiments?

1. The boys worked on their own in separate cubicles when actually allocating the points (but they had initially assembled as one large group when estimating the dots or choosing between the paintings of Klee and Kandinsky).
2. They only knew of other in-group/out-group members by a code number (e.g. 'member no. 74 of Klee group'): they did not know the personal identity of these group members. The Bristol schoolboys all knew each other well before the experiment began, and very likely were members of the same sports teams, friendship groups and so on. However, according to Brown (1986), 'none of those advance meaningful functioning groups had any connection with the new imposed and arbitrary classification. As underestimators and overestimators the boys had no prior history.' This point is also relevant to (3) below.
3. The groups were in fact determined randomly, although the boys believed that they were placed in one or the other because they were under-/overestimators (in Experiment 1), or because they preferred Klee or Kandinsky (in Experiment 2). The point here is that there is no obvious link between being an overestimator, say, and being given the opportunity to award more points to fellow overestimators than to underestimators (unlike the situation of Rattlers and Eagles in the Robber's Cave experiment, where they were asked to indicate friendship choices from both groups).

This is really the criterion which relates most directly to what 'minimal' means. However, while being an under-/overestimator, or preferring Klee or Kandinsky, might seem rather arbitrary and meaningless as a basis for allocating people to groups, it is possible to get even more minimal. As Brown (1986) points out, there are two grouping factors operating, namely (*i*) explicit group assignment by the experimenter, and (*ii*) the supposed similarity on which that group assignment was supposedly based (so, there was still *some* basis).

Billig & Tajfel (1973) went much further (indeed, as far as it is possible to go in creating arbitrary, artificial, groups). They actually *told* participants that they were being assigned on a purely random basis and, in front of them, tossed a coin or drew lottery tickets which determined their membership of 'As' and 'Bs' or 'Kappas' and 'Phis'. The same results were found as for the 1970/1971 experiments.

4.   The boys could only award points to *others* (either other in-groupers or out-groupers), never to themselves. Also, they were told that their points allocation would in no way affect the number of points they themselves would receive. They would be given the number of points allocated to them by others and they could not know what others would do, or in any way influence how others behaved in order to maximize self-gain.

5.   There were three basic strategies that could be used when awarding points: (*i*) *fairness or even-handedness:* as far as possible, an equal number of points would be awarded to any two individuals, regardless of whether they were both members of the in-group, both members of the out-group, or one of each; (*ii*) *maximum generosity:* awarding points in a way which discriminates in favour of the out-group; (*iii*) *maximum in-group favouritism* (or, differentiation in favour of the in-group/MD): awarding points in a way which favours the in-group compared with the out-group (even if this means sometimes awarding the in-group member *fewer* points than they could be awarded using some other strategy).

It is important to note that different matrices differed according to how 'transparent' they were in relation to these three strategies. In other words, it was sometimes very obvious, and at others much less obvious, just how one could benefit a fellow Klee or overestimator relative to a Kandinsky or underestimator (see **Exercises** below).

The results in all the experiments carried out to date have shown that participants rarely choose extreme positions on any of the three strategies, but the *relative* pulls or strengths of these can be determined by looking at the various kinds of matrices. The norms of fairness and maximum in-group favouritism both operated, with fairness mitigating in-group favouritism (i.e. preventing the latter from taking extreme values). For example, if we take Matrix 3 (B) from Experiment 2, with the top line representing a member of the Klee group and the bottom line a member of the Kandinsky group, if the main goal were to gain as many points as possible for the Klee (*maximum in-group profit/MIP*), Klees should choose the extreme right hand box (19 points is the largest number available to Klees). In doing this, they would earn fewer points than Kandinskys (25 points). But, in fact, boxes towards the left-hand end of the matrix are much more likely to be chosen, which will mean fewer *absolute* points for Klees (e.g. 7 as opposed to 19), but the *difference* is now in favour of the Klees (*maximum differentiation in favour of the in-group/MD*). According to Brown (1986):

One of the most consistent and psychologically telling results in all this research is the preference for a maximal ingroup advantage over the outgroup, even at the sacrifice of total ingroup rewards. It is above all the social *comparisons* between the groups that matters to subjects.

The matrix in this example is less transparent than others used (see **Exercises** below). The results in the 1970 article are summarized in terms of average ranks, with 1 indicating that the in-group member received the minimum and the out-group member the maximum number of points (corresponding to maximum generosity) and 14 indicating the reverse (maximum differentiation in favour of the in-group). When allocating points to members of the *same* group (whether in- or out-group), fairness prevailed (the mean rank was 7.5); when allocating points *between* an in-group and an out-group member, significantly more points were awarded to in-group members (mean of over 9), with fairness preventing it from reaching a more extreme value. So there is a crucial difference in behaviour between *intra*group and *inter*group choices.

A less obvious test of in-group favouritism is to compare *in-group/in-group* choices with *out-group/out-group* choices. Although the same overall mean was found in both cases (7.5, suggesting fairness), the former tend to favour choosing the largest total sums (maximum joint profit/MJP), while the latter tend to favour smaller total sums, thereby indirectly conferring a relative advantage on the in-group.

6. The experimental task is to actually display intergroup *behaviour*: allocate points to be exchanged for money at the end, rather than expressing attitudes (which do not necessarily translate into discriminatory acts).

According to Schiffman & Wicklund (1992), the MGP faces a major problem, namely its exclusion of 'psychological factors'. The individual participant is not attributed with variables normally thought to be important in explaining interpersonal phenomena, such as degree of ego involvement or needs and conflict, which might manifest themselves in the group situation. They argue that underlying the MGP is a 'singularistic-atomistic' approach (Sorokin, 1966), which is related to the analytical method of research: when investigators are faced with vast, complex, sociocultural structures and processes, they often try to resolve them into 'elementary units' or 'components', an approach derived from the physical (natural) sciences. This fundamentally *reductionist* approach has meant that the original research goal (to shed light on the determinants of intergroup discrimination), has not been achieved:

> By excluding psychological variables, *differentiation between groups* was ultimately shown to be dependent on *differentiation between groups*.
> (Schiffman & Wicklund, 1992)

In other words, as it stands, the minimal group experiment really tells us very little – at least nothing we did not already know.

Subsequent research

Much subsequent research has, perhaps inevitably, been concerned with aspects of the methodology of the MGP. For example, could the results be an artifact of the nature of the task? As we saw above, different strategies are, in principle, available to participants for allocating points. But doesn't the standard set-up suggest that discrimination might be the most appropriate strategy, because it does have a kind of *forced-choice* format, in which case, the results may be due to this format rather than categorizing people into groups (Brown, 1986)? Locksley *et al.* (1980) created random minimal groups (with American participants), giving each person five piles of poker chips to distribute (instead of points, thus removing the element of forced choice). Despite this, the same results were obtained as in the earlier studies, using the standard set-up.

A further potential problem, suggesting a further alternative explanation, is to do with *demand characteristics* (Orne, 1962). According to Schiffman & Wicklund (1992), 'The experimental situation is designed in such a way that it demands differentiation between the two groups'. What else can participants do except discriminate? In principle, there is a major alternative (as we have already seen), namely, fairness, but in practice, being told to allot points to fictitious members of two different groups makes it very likely that a discriminating strategy will be adopted (partly, but not completely, to do with the forced-choice nature of the task).

Perhaps schoolboy culture encourages an interest in group membership, so that if they are divided by adults into groups, they will automatically interpret these groups as 'teams' and think in terms of competition (Brown, 1986; Pennington *et al.*, 1999). However, the fact that many different national, cultural and age groups, of both sexes, have all been tested, producing essentially the same results, strongly suggests that 'English schoolboy norms' play very little part in explaining the original findings.

An experiment by St. Claire & Turner (1982) was specifically designed to test the issue of demand characteristics. A control group was tested in the standard way, while a second group was merely asked to predict how the control participants would react. A third group was tested in the standard way, but in addition was told that the study was about prejudice. If the results of groups one and two were similar, this would support the demand characteristics explanation and, consistent with this explanation, group three participants should show even more marked group discrimination than group one. While there was significant in-group favouritism in groups one and three, this was *not* predicted by those in group two. St. Claire and Turner concluded that this showed the demand characteristics explanation to be invalid. However, Schiffman and Wicklund are critical of this kind of 'simulation' and they cite the example of Milgram who asked 40 psychiatrists to predict obedience rates but who drastically underestimated what real participants actually did (see Chapter 7). This kind of simulation fails to capture the actual pressures and demands felt by people involved in the actual situation.

Also, although the expected difference between groups one and three did not occur, only 30% of those in the 'prejudice' condition correctly recalled the title of the study and only 26% seemed aware of the hypothesis (demand cues). This suggests that the differential manipulation of groups one and three had not worked, so that the demand characteristics hypothesis had not been properly tested. If that is so, it cannot be rejected either (Schiffman & Wicklund, 1992). However, when group one participants were later asked what rule, if any, they had used in allocating points, most said that they had followed no rule in particular, or that they had tried to be fair. In fact, they had followed the rule of in-group favouritism 'without realizing it'. They also acknowledged that selfishness would be regarded as the socially undesirable thing to do. These two facts combined (i.e. they knew selfishness was wrong but used this strategy) constitute strong evidence that they were *not* doing what the experimenter expected or what the situation demanded (Brown, 1986).

Given that in-group favouritism using the MGP is a reliable, pervasive phenomenon, can it be generalized to distribution of penalties and aversive stimuli? Hewstone *et al.* (1981) modified the normal paradigm by asking participants to *subtract* money from in-group/out-group members (who had previously been allocated an initial sum). Although there was some evidence of in-group bias, this was less pronounced than in the standard procedure.

Mummendey *et al.* (1993) extended this principle by asking participants to distribute (what they thought would be) durations of an unpleasantly high-pitched tone. This seemed to eliminate completely in-group favouritism, and strategies for equalizing outcomes (fairness) and minimizing the total amount of aversive stimulation were much more common. How can we explain this difference? Perhaps in the relatively 'aseptic' laboratory conditions, there is a strong social desirability norm against harming fellow participants, which would, in turn, raise the threshold for displaying in-group favouritism (Mummendey *et al.*, 1993). Alternatively, it could be that *positive* and *negative* ingroup bias (treating in-groupers less punitively) are controlled by different processes (Brown, 1996).

Applications and implications

Despite all these methodological problems with the MGP, the minimal group data were the starting point for a major *theory* of intergroup discrimination, ethnocentrism and hostility, namely *Social Identity theory* (SIT: Tajfel & Turner, 1979, 1986). Dividing the world into a manageable number of categories does not just help us to simplify and make sense of it, it also serves to help us define who we are. Our sense of identity is closely bound up with our various group memberships (Brown, 1988). A positive social identity is achieved and maintained by:

> . . . favourable comparisons that can be made between the in-group and some relevant out-groups: the in-group must be perceived as positively differentiated or distinct from the relevant out-group. (Tajfel & Turner, 1979)

The driving force behind such processes is the general striving for maintaining and enhancing our self-esteem.

How can SIT account for the results of the minimal group experiments on which it is based? According to Brown (1996), code numbers for group members produce a feeling of anonymity in a meaningless group. The only possible source of identity is the in-group (primitive as it is), and the only way to make it distinguishable in a positive way from the out-group is to allocate more points to in-group members. But if we have to favour the in-group *in order to* distinguish it from the out-group, isn't this the *reverse* of what happens under 'normal' circumstances, whereby groups which we have already identified as 'in' or 'out' (they are already distinguished) are favoured (or not) *because* they are 'in' or 'out'?

The problem here seems to be one that we discussed above, namely, the very 'status' of the MGP. The arbitrary/artificial nature of minimal groups is so far removed from our real-life group memberships, that it can be asked if they have any ecological validity/mundane realism at all. In turn, how valid can SIT be if it derived from the minimal group data?

In their critique of SIT, Schiffman & Wicklund (1992) argue that the MGP implicitly assumes that participants will be content with *any* group to which they are assigned, and that they will eagerly defend their group, no matter how they 'joined' it, and irrespective of all its characteristics. But clearly things are much more complex psychologically than this picture implies: indeed, the implicit assumption is simply false. A related criticism is that participants find themselves allocated to a group based on a criterion chosen by the experimenter, it is not freely chosen, and it has no relationship to existing groups in their background. The so-called 'social identity' that stems from group assignment is, then, nothing more than the fact of having been assigned to a group (Schiffman & Wicklund, 1992).

Despite these problems, SIT, and *self-categorization theory* (Turner, 1985; Turner *et al.*, 1987) which is an extension of it, have been a major influence on European – especially British – social psychology (Pennington *et al.*, 1999). According to Burr (2002), the minimal group experiments and SIT were devised to explain intergroup conflict, and there has been considerable debate regarding the extent to which conflict in the real world can be understood in these terms. But regardless of its relevance to this issue, SIT has much to offer for our understanding of identity:

. . . It is one of the few theories emerging from psychological social psychology to postulate a thoroughly social understanding of the person and to regard the social realm as more than a set of variables which may come to influence the ready-made person. (Burr, 2002)

Exercises

1. How does Tajfel distinguish between prejudice and discrimination?

2. The matrices below are very 'transparent'.
   (*i*)   What does 'transparent' mean here?
   (*ii*) Briefly describe the three basic strategies which it is possible to adopt in the minimal group situation when awarding points.
   (*iii*) Indicate how, for the matrices below, a member of the Klee group could award points according to these three strategies.

No.74 Klee	1	2	3	4	5	6	7	8	9	10	11	12	13	14	
No.44 Kandinsky	14	13	12	11	10	9	8	7	6	5	4	3	2	1	A

No.12 Kandinsky	1	2	3	4	5	6	7	8	9	10	11	12	13	14	
No.50 Klee	14	13	12	11	10	9	8	7	6	5	4	3	2	1	B

(For each matrix, A and B, the Klee member must choose *one* box, e.g. in A, the fourth box from the left, 4/11, would mean 4 points awarded to no. 74 Klee and 11 points awarded to no. 44 Kandinsky.)

3. Explain the difference between *intra*group and *inter*group choices. How do these differ in terms of participants' typical allocation of points?

4. As well as matrices differing in their degree of transparency, the same matrix appeared three times, once for each kind of intra- and intergroup choice.
   (*i*) Why was this done?
   (*ii*) Name the method by which this was done.

13

Asking only one question in the conservation experiment

Judith Samuel and Peter Bryant (1984)

Journal of Child Psychology and Psychiatry, 25 (2), 315–18

BACKGROUND AND CONTEXT

The ability to *conserve* represents one of the major landmarks within Piaget's (e.g. 1950) theory of cognitive development. It marks the end of pre-operational and the beginning of operational thought (at about seven), a major qualitative shift from non-logical to logical thought, albeit still tied to actual, concrete situations.

Piaget's conservation experiments are probably his most famous. Essentially, they involve presenting the child with two identical quantities (say, two beakers of water), whose appearance is changed (transformed) in some way (the water from one beaker is poured into a different size beaker). The child is asked the same question ('Is there the same amount of water in the two beakers?') both before *and* after the transformation. According to Piaget, pre-seven-year-olds reliably fail conservation tasks (they maintain that there is no longer the same quantity following the transformation), because they lack the logical thinking (or 'operations') required (specifically, *compensation* and *reversibility*).

There have been many replications of Piaget's conservation experiments, sometimes with important modifications. For example, Rose & Blank (1974) dropped the *pre-transformation question, and found that six-year-olds often succeeded on a test of number conservation compared with those tested on the standard (Piagetian) version. Significantly, when the children were retested on the standard form of the task a week later, they made fewer errors than the controls. (Other modifications to Piaget's methods are discussed in **Evaluation** below).

The present experiment represents one in a long line of studies which challenge Piaget's conclusions regarding conservation through criticizing his *methods*. The common feature of these studies is their focus on the conditions under which children will display their ability to conserve, rather than whether or not they can conserve at all!

AIM AND NATURE OF THE STUDY

The study is a partial replication of the study by Rose and Blank, in which only the *post-*transformation question in Piaget's conservation experiment was asked. While Rose and Blank used only six-year-olds to study number conservation, Samuel and Bryant used five-, six-, seven- and eight-year-olds to study conservation of mass (or substance) and volume, as well as number. So, the present study is on a much larger scale, and far more wide-ranging, than the former.

It also involves quite a complex experimental design. As well as the manipulation of the form of the task (standard/Piaget or one-judgement):

(*i*)   there is a control condition (fixed-array);

(*ii*) age is an additional independent variable (though not a manipulated one); and

(*iii*) there is a mixed design, such that the four age groups constitute independent samples, with each being randomly split into three (corresponding to (*i*) and (*ii*) above), and within each of these conditions, participants are tested on all three types of conservation (repeated measures).

To the extent that age is an independent variable that is selected for, rather than actually manipulated, that part of the study is not a true experiment, but a quasi-experiment.

▪THE▪STUDY▪

▪INTRODUCTION▪

It is often claimed that young children do not understand the principle of the invariance of quantity. This conclusion is based on the results of the well-known conservation experiments by Piaget and Szeminska (1952), which apparently show that children below seven or eight often wrongly treat a perceptual change as a real one, e.g. simply lengthening a row of counters or squashing balls of plasticine seems to change the child's judgements about their number or volume respectively.

However, one cannot be certain about this conclusion. As Donaldson (1978, 1982) has pointed out, the experimenter might unwittingly force children to produce wrong answers against their better judgement. One of the most powerful empirical demonstrations of the justice of Donaldson's criticism was provided by Rose and Blank (1974). They varied the traditional number conservation experiment slightly by asking one question rather than two. The usual procedure is first to show the child two identical rows of counters side-by-side, and ask him/her whether they are the same number (pre-transformation question) (the answer almost invariably is 'yes'), and then to lengthen or shorten one of the rows and ask the same question once again (post-transformation question). Rose and Blank's variation was to drop the pre-transformation question and to only ask the child to compare the rows after the transformation, a manoeuvre which had a significant effect: children who failed the traditional task often succeeded when one question only was asked.

The result suggests that young children often fail the traditional task for a reason which is quite different to the one suggested by Piaget. Instead, the child may think that the experimenter asks the question the second time because he wants another answer. If this is so, the child's error in the conservation task has nothing to do with the transformation (and, therefore, with the principle of invariance), but is simply a misinterpretation of what the experimenter wants to hear.

Thus the experiment is an extremely important one, but it is also limited: it deals only with number, and involves only one age-group, six-year-old children. We badly need to know whether younger and older children are affected in the same way by being asked one question only, and also whether other versions of the conservation task will produce the same pattern of results.

METHOD

SUBJECTS

In all, 252 boys and girls between the ages of five and eight-and-a-half took part in this experiment. They were all in schools and playgroups in and around Crediton, Devon. They were divided into four age groups of 63 children, whose mean ages were five years three months, six years three months, seven years three months and eight years three months. Each group was divided into three subgroups, which were closely matched in age.

DESIGN AND PROCEDURE

SUBGROUPS AND CONDITIONS

The groups were divided into three subgroups of equal mean age, and each subgroup underwent a different condition. The three conditions were:

(*i*)   standard: the traditional two question conservation task;

(*ii*) one judgement: the conservation task with only one question asked, the post-transformation;

(*iii*) fixed-array control: the child saw no transformation being made but only saw the post-transformation display. The purpose of this third condition was to check that children who answered the post-transformation correctly in the other two conditions did so by bringing over information from the pre-transformation display.

MATERIAL

Three kinds of material were used in different trials. These were:

(a) *Mass*, in which condition (*i*) and (*ii*) children were first shown two equal and identical Playdoh cylinders or two similar but unequal cylinder shapes, one longer than the other; the transformation was to squash one of these into a sausage or a pancake. After this, the children were asked to compare the cylinder and the pancake (or the cylinder and the sausage). The condition (*iii*) children also made this comparison without seeing the first display or the transformation.

(b) *Number*, in which the children in conditions (*i*) and (*ii*) were shown two rows of counters of equal length arranged side by side in one-to-one correspondence. The rows contained either six and six counters or six and five counters. Then one row was spread out or bunched up. The condition (*iii*) saw only the post-transformation displays.

(c) *Volume*, in which the children in conditions (*i*) and (*ii*), were first shown two identical glasses, either with the same or with different amounts of liquid. Then the liquid from one glass was poured into a narrower one or a shallow wider one.

TRIALS

Each child was given four trials with each kind of material, two with equal and two with unequal quantities. The order of these trials, and the order in which the three types of material were introduced, were systematically varied between children.

R E S U L T S

No systematic difference between equal and unequal quantity trials was found, so the results were pooled for the two types of trial.

The results are presented in Tables 13.1 and 13.2. They show the reliability and generality of Rose and Blank's experimental results. The one-judgement task (Rose and Blank's task) was typically easier than the standard conservation task and the fixed-array control. This seems to be generally true of all three types of material and of all four levels. Table 13.1 shows that there are few exceptions to this general pattern, and the statistics suggest that these are chance variations.

Table 13.1

MEAN ERRORS (OUT OF FOUR) IN THE THREE CONDITIONS AND WITH THE THREE TYPES OF MATERIAL

Age (yr)	Material	Standard	One judgement	Fixed array
5	Mass	2.762 (1.109)*	2.095 (1.444)	2.524 (0.906)
	Number	2.524 (1.622)	2.095 (1.540)	2.619 (1.463)
	Volume	3.238 (1.191)	3.048 (1.290)	3.286 (0.825)
6	Mass	1.571 (1.247)	1.286 (1.350)	2.143 (1.082)
	Number	1.809 (1.468)	1.381 (1.759)	1.476 (1.367)
	Volume	2.286 (1.694)	1.667 (1.522)	2.762 (1.230)
7	Mass	0.952 (1.430)	1.000 (1.414)	1.286 (0.983)
	Number	1.143 (1.424)	0.381 (0.844)	1.429 (1.620)
	Volume	1.143 (1.582)	1.000 (1.414)	2.238 (1.151)
8	Mass	0.667 (1.321)	0.381 (0.844)	0.905 (0.868)
	Number	0.429 (0.791)	0.238 (0.610)	0.619 (0.844)
	Volume	0.571 (1.218)	0.667 (1.321)	1.714 (1.314)

* Figures in brackets are standard deviations.

Table 13.2

MEAN ERRORS SUMMED ACROSS MATERIALS (A) AND AGE (B)

	Standard	One judgement	Fixed array
(A) The three conditions and four age groups summed across materials (mean errors out of 12)			
5 yr	8.524 (2.805)*	7.333 (3.427)	8.571 (2.083)
6 yr	5.714 (3.6214)	4.333 (4.075)	6.381 (2.149)
7 yr	3.238 (3.766)	2.571 (3.646)	4.857 (2.965)
8 yr	1.667 (2.494)	1.333 (1.755)	3.333 (2.055)
(B) The three conditions and mass, number and volume summed across age (mean errors out of four)			
Mass	1.512 (1.516)	1.190 (1.427)	1.714 (1.160)
Number	1.476 (1.570)	1.024 (1.488)	1.536 (1.531)
Volume	1.810 (1.769)	1.595 (1.663)	2.500 (1.286)

* Figures in brackets are standard deviations.

A mixed-design analysis of variance was used, in which the main terms were age groups (five-, six-, seven- and eight-year-olds), conditions (standard, one judgement, fixed array), and material (mass, number, volume); the last variable was a repeated measure. This analysis produced significant age differences ($d.f.3,240$, $F=44.53$, $p<0.001$); conditions differences ($d.f.2,240$, $F=8.64$, $p<0.001$) and materials differences ($d.f.2,480$, $F=25.35$, $p<0.001$). There were no significant interactions.

Subsequent Newman-Keuls tests showed the following facts about these differences:

(*i*) age: there was a significant difference between every age group, and the ordering was quite regular, the older groups doing consistently better than the younger;

(*ii*) conditions: the one-judgement task was significantly easier than the other two tasks (Rose and Blank's result). The standard task was also significantly easier than the fixed-array task;

(*iii*) materials: the number task was significantly easier than the mass and the volume tasks. Thus, despite overall differences in the skills of the four groups and in the difficulty posed by the three types of material, Rose and Blank's result held good. Children who failed the traditional conservation task nevertheless succeeded more often when only one question was asked.

DISCUSSION

The consistent superiority of the one-question condition leads inexorably to one conclusion; children who fail the traditional conservation task often do understand the principle of invariance, and make their mistakes for a quite extraneous reason, this being that the experimenter's repetition of the same question about the same material makes them think that they must change their answer the second time.

Any other explanation seems far fetched. The children must have been using their knowledge of invariance when they solved the one-judgement task, because they carried over information from the pre-transformation display, and to do so, they must have realized that nothing had changed. How do we know they carried over this information? Because they did much better than the fixed-array children who never saw the first display. All in all, it does seem that the repetitive questioning of the traditional conservation experiment actively misleads the child.

Once again, as in many other cognitive experiments (Bryant, 1982a,b), we must conclude that the important question is not whether a child possesses an intellectual skill, but how and when he decides to apply that skill. Young children, it seems, often do use the principles of invariance, unless experimenters unwittingly persuade them not to.

■ S U M M A R Y

Rose and Blank have shown that six-year-old children do a great deal better in a conservation-of-number task if they are only asked to make a comparison after the transformation, rather than both before and after seeing the quantity transformed. The present experiment shows that this important result also applies to other materials (mass and volume), and to a wide age range (five to eight years old).

■ ■ ■ ■ ■ ■ ■ ■ ■ ■

EVALUATION

Theoretical issues

Samuel and Bryant found the one-judgement task (post-transformation question only) to be significantly easier than the other two tasks (confirming Rose and Blank's results), and the number conservation to be significantly easier than the mass and volume tasks. This last finding is interesting, because it seems to support Piaget's concept of *horizontal décalage*: conservation does *not* appear all in one go during the concrete operational stage, but in an invariant order during the stage (e.g. number and liquid quantity: six–seven years; substance (or mass) and length: seven–eight years; weight: eight–ten years; volume: 11–12 years). (Note that what Samuel and Bryant call volume is more accurately called liquid/continuous quantity: volume was tested by Piaget through *displacement* of liquid.)

Another alternative to Piaget's method of testing conservation was the famous 'Naughty Teddy' experiment (McGarrigle & Donaldson, 1974), which was concerned with number and length conservation. In the case of number, it proceeded in the normal way up to the point where the child agrees that there is an equal number of counters in the two rows. Then 'Naughty Teddy' (a glove puppet) emerges from a hiding place and sweeps over one of the rows and rearranges it, so that the one-to-one correspondence is disrupted. The child is invited to put Teddy back in his box and the questioning resumes: 'Now, where were we? Ah, yes, is the number in this row the same as the number in that row?' and so on. Fifty out of 80 four- to six-year-olds conserved under the Naughty Teddy condition, compared with 13 out of 80 tested using the standard form. According to Piaget, it should not matter *who* re-arranges the counters (or *how* this happens) – but it seems to be relevant to the child.

However, Light *et al.* (1979) criticized 'Naughty Teddy' on the grounds that the children were, non-verbally and unwittingly, being instructed to 'ignore the rearrangement'. So, in a sense, the task itself may be 'lost'. In other words, they may have been so absorbed by Naughty Teddy's antics and putting him back in his box, that they did not actually notice the perceptual transformation.

A way of testing this hypothesis was designed by Moore & Frye (1986). They distinguished between an *irrelevant* perceptual change (which is what the traditional conservation procedure involves: nothing is added/subtracted) and a *relevant* one (something is actually added/subtracted). They predicted that if Naughty Teddy is, in fact, distracting, then children should do worse when a relevant change occurs (they *added* a counter to one row, so the correct answer is that the two rows are now *unequal*), and better when an irrelevant change occurs. This is, indeed, what they found, thus supporting the criticism of Light *et al.* and so, indirectly, supporting Piaget.

A criticism made by many psychologists, including Margaret Donaldson (1978), is that Piaget focused on the child's understanding of the *physical world* to the exclusion of the *social world*. Intellectual development cannot be properly understood without examining the development of social understanding. By trying to understand cognitive development in isolation, Piaget has systematically *underestimated* children's logical abilities. There is a discrepancy between children's sophistication outside experimental situations, and their inadequacies in them: how can we resolve this discrepancy?

Essentially, Donaldson argues that when children are confronted with a task or problem, they have to decide what is required of them, and they do this from two sources: (*i*) *the words that are spoken*; and (*ii*) *the setting in which the words are spoken*. The former are interpreted in the light of the child's interpretation of the latter. In Piaget's conservation tasks, these two sources of information can *conflict* with each other:

> Before the child has developed a full awareness of language, language is embedded in the flow of events which accompany it. So long as this is the case, the child does not interpret words in isolation, but instead interprets *situations*, more concerned to make sense of what people do when they talk and act than to decide what words mean. After all, the child may not be aware of language, but is keenly aware of other people. (Donaldson, 1978)

The fact that the experimenter asks the child essentially the *same* question twice (once before the transformation and once afterwards) can confuse a child who (*i*) understands that nothing has actually changed (can conserve) but who (*ii*) believes that a *different answer is expected* ('why else would the experimenter ask me the question again?'). This is called the *extraneous reason hypothesis* (see **Subsequent research** below). The child cannot 'dis-embed' the verbal question from the situation as a whole, in which an adult, a stranger to the child and an authority figure, seems to require a particular response (a different answer). While for Piaget social understanding is simply a manifestation of cognitive development, for Donaldson the development of social understanding is both separate and of greater importance (Smith & Cowie, 1992). Smith *et al.* (1998) point out that other investigators have not always replicated McGarrigle & Donaldson's (1974) main findings.

According to Meadows (1995), Piaget implicitly viewed children as largely independent and isolated in their construction of knowledge and understanding of the physical world ('child-as-scientist'). This excludes the contribution of other people to children's cognitive development. The *social* nature of knowledge and thought is a basic proposition of Vygotsky's (e.g. 1962) theory (see Gross, 2001).

Despite these (and other) criticisms, Bee (2000) believes that:

> . . . his [Piaget's] theory sets the agenda for most research in this area for the past thirty years and still serves as a kind of scaffolding for much of our thinking about thinking.

Methodological issues

The Samuel and Bryant study represents a great advance on the Rose and Blank study, because it involves four age groups (five-, six-, seven- and eight-year-olds), three conditions of testing (standard, one judgement and fixed array), and three kinds of conservation task (mass, number and volume). Thus there were three independent variables, with age being selected for (rather than manipulated), and the dependent variable being success on the conservation task.

Where there is more than one independent variable, the design is referred to as a *factorial* design ($4 \times 3 \times 3$ = four age groups $\times$ three conditions $\times$ three conservation tasks), and the appropriate test is the *Analysis of Variance* (ANOVA) test. This is one of the must useful and versatile of all statistics used in psychology today (Solso & Johnson, 1989). It is a parametric test, which calculates from the scores, the proportion of total variance due to each of the independent variables and the interactions between them, plus the proportion due to all other variables (error variance). These are known as F ratios (F = the ANOVA statistic symbol). This produced significant age, condition and materials differences, but no significant interaction.

Note that the experimental design was mixed, with age and conditions constituting an independent-groups (unrelated) design, and the materials constituting a repeated-measures (related) design. As with the parametric *t*-test, there are ANOVAs for related and unrelated designs.

What about the Newman-Keuls tests which were used after the ANOVAs? It is probably the most commonly used post-ANOVA test, a necessary next step used to test for significant differences between the items of each main term. For example, not only did age contribute significantly to the overall variance in the scores (along with conditions and materials), but eight-year-olds did significantly better than seven-year-olds, who did significantly better than six-year-olds and so on.

Subsequent research

A partial replication of the Samuel and Bryant experiment was carried out by Porpodas (1987). Using six- and seven-year-old Greek children, he used the three same conditions as Samuel and Bryant, plus volume and number conservation, and the results by and large confirmed those of both Samuel and Bryant, and Rose and Blank.

However, Porpodas was also interested in testing the *explanation* given by those investigators, namely the 'extraneous reason hypothesis'. According to this, the traditional two-question task may unwittingly force the child to give the wrong answer by essentially asking the same question twice. The superior performance of participants in the one-question condition compared with the fixed-array children seems to indicate that they carry over information from the pre-transformation display: they use their working or short-term memory (STM) to help them realize that nothing changes when the transformation is made. This suggests that in the traditional Piagetian task, the child's failure may be due to interference in its STM, due to the experimenter talking to the child when s/he asks the first (pre-transformation) question. If this hypothesis is correct, then children's difficulty in carrying over information from the pre-transformational display should be observed, even in the one-question condition, if something interferes with the child's STM.

Accordingly, Porpodas selected a different sample of 186 boys and girls, six- and seven-year-olds, who were tested under one of three conditions: (*i*) traditional; (*ii*) one question and (*iii*) one question with interference, again using number and volume conservation. In the latter, the experimenter started a short discussion with the child (irrelevant to the task), during which the transformation was performed in full view of the child, but without referring to it in any way. Children of both age groups under this condition did *worse* than children under both (*i*) and (*ii*) for both number and volume, but significantly more so for the six-year-olds on volume and seven-year-olds with number.

Porpodas concludes from his findings that asking one question does not *guarantee* the child will reveal its understanding of the principle of invariance (so that it will conserve). What is mainly needed is the uninterrupted functioning of the child's STM (which the traditional form of the task prevents!). So this explanation is *additional* to the 'extraneous reason' explanation for failure in the Piagetian task, *not* an alternative to it.

Applications and implications

According to Bryant (1998), despite studies like those of McGarrigle & Donaldson (1974), Light *et al.* (1979), and Rose and Blank (1974) – and, indeed, his own (Samuel & Bryant, 1984) – it would be too hasty to dismiss Piaget's conservation experiments

> . . .as a clumsy manoeuvre whose results are based on a complete
> misunderstanding between the adult experimenters and the children whom they
> test . . .

He points out that in the 'Naughty Teddy' experiment, for example, not all the
children in the 'favourable' (accidental) condition gave the correct answer: there was
an appreciable number of conservation failures which need explaining (see
Theoretical issues above).

In addition, critics of Piaget's methods (and conclusions) take failures in the standard
conservation tasks to be *false negatives*: the children *can* conserve but are being
prevented from displaying this ability by the misleading form of the task. However, the
Light *et al.* (1979) study strongly suggests that McGarrigle & Donaldson (1974) may
have produced *false positives:* the children gave the correct answer (i.e. they displayed
conservation) but, in fact, did not *understand* that nothing had really changed (because
they were distracted by Naughty Teddy, and would probably not have noticed if
anything *had* changed).

What this underlines is the difficulty (if not the impossibility) of trying to 'lay bare' any
human ability (child or adult): a logical operation such as conservation cannot be
understood independently of those methods used to tap it or 'expose' it. So, perhaps
what we need is a *variety* of methods, providing us with several 'takes' on the ability in
question, a chance to observe it from a number of different 'angles'. What is beyond
dispute is that the *social* dimensions of any task are as important as the more logical
ones. As McGarrigle & Donaldson (1974) say:

> It is possible that the achievements of the concrete operational stage are as much
> a reflection of the child's increasing independence from features of the
> interactional setting as they are evidence of the development of a logical
> competence.

Exercises

1. In relation to the order in which each child was tested with the three types of
material, Samuel and Bryant say that these were 'systematically varied' between
children.
   (*i*)   What's another term for 'systematically varied'?
   (*ii*) Why was this necessary?
   (*iii*) How might this have been done?

2. Why was the fixed-array condition used?

3. Give an example of *vertical décalage*. (See **Exercises** for Chapter 17.)

14 Transmission of aggression through imitation of aggressive models

Albert Bandura, Dorothea Ross, and Sheila A. Ross (1961)

Journal of Abnormal & Social Psychology, 63 (3), 575–82

BACKGROUND AND CONTEXT

Albert Bandura is probably the most influential of the Social Learning theorists. While accepting the basic principles of operant (or instrumental or Skinnerian) conditioning (along with those of classical or Pavlovian conditioning), Bandura believes that:

(*i*) conditioning on its own is inadequate as an explanation of the majority of human, social behaviour;

(*ii*) reinforcement is not the all-important influence on behaviour which Skinner claimed for it; and

(*iii*) learning cannot be properly explained without attributing cognitive processes to the learner (the S-O-R approach, as opposed to Skinner's S-R or 'empty organism' approach).

As far as (*i*) is concerned:

> If all learning depended upon the reinforcement of existing responses, it would be difficult for a person to acquire new behaviours. Fortunately, mechanisms for learning exist . . . making it possible for new things to be learned without it being necessary to wait for each activity to be produced by the individual learner. One way to learn is through watching other people behave, and in this way we can acquire habits, skills, and knowledge without having to directly experience the consequences of every single action . . . People are able to learn from what they observe, and they thereby gain access to a much wider range of abilities than would be possible if all learning depended upon the reinforcement of behaviours. (Howe, 1980)

So *behavioural learning* (or *modelling*) represents a major alternative to conditioning as a basic form of human learning. It is much more efficient than trial-and-error learning (the basis of operant conditioning); for example, watching a model perform some skill may prevent us having to painstakingly make mistake after mistake in our attempts to acquire the skill ourselves. Related to this is the fact that the model is demonstrating the 'whole' skill, while, according to Skinner, each component of the overall skill must be learned separately, step by step, and then 'put together' ('chaining') at the end of the process. Again, many complex behaviours (e.g. language) could probably never be acquired unless children were exposed to people who modelled them (even allowing for some kind of inborn language ability or Language Acquisition Device: see Chapters 6 and 18).

As Shaffer (1985) points out, observational learning allows the young child to acquire many novel responses in a large number of settings, where the models are simply 'going about their own business' and not trying to teach the child anything. But this is a double-edged sword: often the modelled behaviour is not what the parents (or society in general) would approve of (e.g. smoking, swearing, and aggression). The point is that children are continually learning a whole range of behaviours (desirable and undesirable) through the same basic process of modelling. This often involves 'no trial' learning (it is acquired 'all at once' rather than gradually, as in trial and error), neither elicited by a conditioned stimulus (as in classical conditioning), nor strengthened by reinforcing consequences (as in operant conditioning).

The present study is a good demonstration of this, as are some of the equally well-known studies carried out later, such as Bandura, Ross and Ross (1963a). Like the present study, children (96 three- to five-year-olds) were tested under three different conditions, after first being frustrated by the removal of the promise of attractive toys and later being observed during a 20-minute period when they played, individually, with toys which included a Bobo doll and a mallet. Instead of a non-aggressive live model, there was a filmed aggressive model. The filmed model produced the most imitative aggression, followed closely by the live model, with the non-aggressive model way back in third place. As in the present study, the imitative aggression was a 'carbon copy' of the model's aggressive acts (illustrating the 'no trial' learning – see above). (Bandura's points *(ii)* and *(iii)* are discussed in the **Evaluation** section below).

According to Baron (1977), Bandura's Bobo-doll experiments constitute the 'first generation' (or 'phase one') of scientific research into the effects of media violence. With the exception of the current (1961) experiment, all the Bobo-doll experiments involved filmed (symbolic) models, usually presented via a TV screen (as opposed to a projector screen). The basic finding was that young children can acquire new aggressive responses not previously in their behavioural repertoire, merely through exposure to a filmed or televised model. If children could learn new ways of harming others through such experience, then by implication, mass-media portrayals of violence might be contributing, in some degree, to increased levels of violence in society (Baron, 1977).

AIM AND NATURE OF THE STUDY

Although aggressive responses are clearly not the only kind of behaviour that is learned through observation, experimental studies of modelling have concentrated upon the influence of aggressive models. According to Howe (1980):

> This is not because the researchers all believe that aggressive responses are more important than other social activities . . . compared with other social behaviours, aggressive actions are easy to discern and convenient to measure objectively. Objective measurement of helping behaviours may be difficult, but it is not difficult to observe one child kicking another!

The article reports a laboratory-based experimental study of imitation in which children (36 boys and 36 girls, age range 37–69 months, mean age 52 months, i.e. 4 years 4 months) are exposed to aggressive or non-aggressive models (the *independent variable*) in order to see how such exposure affects the children's behaviour (imitative learning: the *dependent variable*) in a new situation when the model is not there. It is this last feature which sets the present study apart from earlier ones, which 'provide convincing evidence for the influence and control exerted on others by the behaviour of a model', but:

> . . . a more crucial test of imitative learning involves the generalization of imitative responses to new settings in which the model is absent. (Bandura, Ross & Ross, 1961)

Several hypotheses were being tested:

(*i*) participants exposed to aggressive models will reproduce aggressive acts resembling those of the models to a significantly greater extent than both participants exposed to non-aggressive models and those not exposed to any models at all (control group). (This is the major, overall, hypothesis);

(*ii*) participants exposed to subdued, non-aggressive models will display significantly less imitative aggression than control group participants (this is a secondary hypothesis, which follows from (*i*) and is 'contained' within it);

(*iii*) participants will imitate the behaviour of same-sex models to a greater degree than opposite-sex models,

(*iv*) boys will be more likely to imitate aggression than girls, especially when they are exposed to aggressive male models.

■T H E ■ S T U D Y ■

A previous study, designed to account for the phenomenon of identification in terms of incidental learning, demonstrated that children readily imitated behaviour exhibited by an adult model in the presence of the model (Bandura & Huston, 1961). A series of experiments by Blake (1958) and others (Grosser *et al.*, 1951; Rosenblith,

1959; Schachter & Hall, 1952) have likewise shown that mere observation of responses of a model has a facilitating effect on subjects' reactions in the immediate social influence setting.

While these studies provide convincing evidence for the influence and control exerted on others by the behaviour of a model, a more crucial test of imitative learning involves the generalization of imitative response patterns to new settings in which the model is absent.

In the experiment reported in this paper, children were exposed to aggressive and non-aggressive adult models and were then tested for the amount of imitative learning in a new situation in the absence of the model. According to the prediction, subjects exposed to aggressive models would reproduce aggressive acts resembling those of their models and would differ in this respect both from subjects who observed non-aggressive models and from those who had no prior exposure to any models. This hypothesis assumed that subjects had learned imitative habits as a result of prior reinforcement, and these tendencies would generalize to some extent to adult experimenters (Miller & Dollard, 1941).

It was further predicted that observation of subdued, non-aggressive models would have a generalized inhibiting effect on the subjects' subsequent behaviour, and this would be reflected in a difference between the non-aggressive and the control groups, with subjects in the latter group displaying significantly more aggression.

Hypotheses were also advanced concerning the influence of the sex of the model and sex of subjects on imitation. Fauls and Smith (1956) have shown that preschool children perceive their parents as having distinct preferences regarding sex appropriate modes of behaviour for their children. Their findings, as well as informal observation, suggest that parents reward imitation of sex-appropriate behaviour and discourage or punish sex-inappropriate imitative responses, e.g. a male child is unlikely to receive much reward for performing female-appropriate activities, such as cooking, or for adopting other aspects of the maternal role, but these same behaviours are typically welcomed if performed by females. As a result of differing reinforcement histories, tendencies to imitate male and female models thus acquire differential habit strength. On this basis, one would expect subjects to imitate the behaviour of the same-sex model to a greater degree than a model of the opposite sex.

Since aggression, however, is a highly masculine-typed behaviour, boys should be more predisposed than girls towards imitating aggression, the difference being most marked for subjects exposed to the male aggressive model.

T H E   S T U D Y

THE STUDY

■ M E T H O D

SUBJECTS

The subjects were 36 boys and 36 girls enrolled in the Stanford University Nursery School. They ranged in age from 37–69 months, with a mean age of 52 months.

Two adults, a male and a female, served in the role of model, and one female experimenter conducted the study for all 72 children.

EXPERIMENTAL DESIGN

Subjects were divided into eight experimental groups of six subjects each and a control group of 24 subjects. Half the experimental subjects were exposed to aggressive models and half to models that were subdued and non-aggressive in their behaviour. These groups were further subdivided into male and female subjects. Half the subjects in the aggressive and non-aggressive conditions observed same-sex roles, while the other half in each group viewed models of the opposite sex. The control group had no prior exposure to the adult models and was tested only in the generalization situation.

It seems reasonable to expect that the subjects' level of aggressiveness would be positively related to the readiness with which they imitated aggressive modes of behaviour. Therefore, in order to increase the precision of treatment comparisons, subjects in the experimental and control groups were matched individually on the basis of rating of their aggressive behaviour in social interactions in the nursery school.

The subjects were rated on four 5-point rating scales by the experimenter and a nursery school teacher, both of whom were well acquainted with the children. These scales measured the extent to which subjects displayed physical aggression, verbal aggression, aggression towards inanimate objects, and aggressive inhibition. The latter scale, which dealt with the tendency to inhibit aggressive reactions in the face of high provocation, provided a measure of aggression anxiety.

Fifty-one subjects were rated independently by both judges so as to permit an assessment of interrater agreement. The reliability of the composite aggression score, measured by means of the Pearson product-moment correlation, was 0.89. The composite score was obtained by summing the ratings on the four aggression scales; based on these scores, subjects were arranged in triplets and assigned randomly to one of two treatment conditions or to the control group.

EXPERIMENTAL CONDITIONS

In the first step in the procedure, subjects were brought individually by the experimenter to the experimental room and the model, who was in the hallway outside the room, was invited by the experimenter to come and join in the game. The experimenter then escorted the subject to one corner of the room, which was structured as the subjects' play area. After seating the child at a small table, the experimenter demonstrated how the subject could design pictures with potato prints and picture stickers provided. The potato prints included a variety of geometrical forms; the stickers were attractive multicolour pictures of animals, flowers and western figures to be pasted on a pastoral scene. These activities were selected since they had been established, by previous studies in the nursery school, as having high interest value for the children.

After having settled the subject in his corner, the experimenters escorted the model to the opposite corner of the room which contained a small table and chair, a tinker-toy set, a mallet, and a 5-foot inflated Bobo doll. The experimenter explained that these were the materials provided for the model to play with and, after the model was seated, the experimenter left the experimental room.

In the *non-aggressive condition*, the model assembled the tinker toys in a quiet, subdued manner, totally ignoring the Bobo doll.

By contrast, in the *aggressive condition*, the model began by assembling the tinker toys but after approximately a minute, the model turned to the Bobo doll and spent the remainder of the period aggressing towards it.

Imitative learning can be clearly demonstrated if a model performs sufficiently novel patterns of responses which are unlikely to occur independently of the observation of the behaviour of a model and if a subject reproduces these behaviours in substantially identical form. For this reason, in addition to punching the Bobo doll, a response that is likely to be performed by children independently of a demonstration, the model exhibited distinctive aggressive acts which were to be scored as imitative responses. The model laid Bobo on its side, sat on it and punched it repeatedly in the nose. The model then raised Bobo, picked up the mallet and struck the doll on the head, after which the model tossed the doll up in the air aggressively and kicked it about the room. This sequence of physically aggressive acts was repeated approximately three times, interspersed with verbally aggressive responses such as, 'Sock him in the nose . . .', 'Hit him down . . .', 'Throw him in the air . . .', 'Kick him . . .', 'Pow . . .', and two non-aggressive comments, 'He keeps coming back for more' and, 'He sure is a tough fella'.

Thus in the exposure situation, subjects were provided with a diverting task which occupied their attention and at the same time ensured observation of the model's behaviour in the absence of any instruction to observe or to learn the responses in question. Since subjects could not perform the model's aggressive behaviour, any learning that occurred was purely on an observational or covert basis.

At the end of 10 minutes, the experimenter entered the room, informed the subject that he would now go to another game room, and bid the model goodbye.

AGGRESSION AROUSAL

Subjects were tested for the amount of imitative learning in a different experimental room that was set off from the main nursery school building. The two experimental situations were thus clearly differentiated; in fact, many subjects were under the impression that they were no longer on the nursery school grounds.

Prior to the test for imitation, however, all subjects, experimental and control, were subjected to mild aggression arousal to ensure that they were under some degree of instigation to aggression. The arousal experience was included for two main reasons. First, observation of aggressive behaviour exhibited by others tends to reduce the probability of aggression on the part of the observer (Rosenbaum & deCharms, 1960). Consequently, subjects in the aggressive condition, compared with both the non-aggressive and the control groups, would be under weaker instigation following exposure to the models. Second, if subjects in the non-aggressive condition expressed little aggression in the face of appropriate instigation, the presence of an inhibiting process would seem to be indicated.

Following the exposure experience, therefore, the experimenter brought the subject to an anteroom that contained these relatively attractive toys: a fire engine, a locomotive, a jet fighter plane, a cable car, a colourful spinning top, and a doll set complete with wardrobe, doll carriage and baby crib. The experimenter explained that the toys were for the subject to play with, but, as soon as the subject became sufficiently involved with them (usually in about two minutes), the experimenter remarked that these were her very best toys, and that she did not let just anyone play with them, and that she had decided to reserve these toys for the other children. However, the subject could play with any of the toys that were in the next room. The experimenter and the subject then entered the adjoining experimental room.

It was necessary for the experimenter to remain in the room during the experimental session otherwise a number of children would either refuse to remain alone or would leave before the end of the session. However, in order to minimize any influence her presence might have on the subjects' behaviour, the experimenter remained as inconspicuous as possible by busying herself with paper work at a desk in the far corner of the room and avoiding any interaction with the child.

TEST FOR DELAYED IMITATION

The experimental room contained a variety of toys including some that could be used in imitative or non-imitative aggression, and others that tended to elicit predominantly non-aggressive forms of behaviour. The aggressive toys included a 3-foot Bobo doll, a mallet and peg board, two dart guns, and a tether ball with a face painted on it which hung from the ceiling. The non-aggressive toys included a tea set, crayons and colouring paper, a ball, two dolls, three bears, cars and trucks, and plastic farm animals.

In order to eliminate any variation in behaviour due to mere placement of the toys in the room, the play material was arranged in a fixed order for each of the sessions.

The subject spent 20 minutes in the experimental room, during which time his behaviour was rated in terms of predetermined response categories by judges who observed the session through a one-way mirror in an adjoining observation room. The 20-minute session was divided into 5-second intervals by means of an electric interval timer, thus yielding a total number of 240 response units for each subject.

The male model scored the experimental sessions for all 72 children. Except for the cases in which he served as model, he did not have knowledge of the subjects' group assignments. In order to provide an estimate of interscorer agreement, the performances of half the subjects were also scored independently by a second observer. Thus one or the other of the two observers usually had no knowledge of the conditions to which the subjects were assigned. Since, however, all but two of the subjects in the aggressive condition performed the model's novel aggressive responses while subjects in the other conditions only rarely exhibited such reactions, subjects who were exposed to the aggressive models could be readily identified through their distinctive behaviour.

The responses scored involved highly specific concrete classes of behaviour and yielded high interscorer reliabilities, the product-moment coefficients being in the 0.90s.

RESPONSE MEASURES

Three measures of imitation were obtained;

Imitation of physical aggression. This category included acts of striking the Bobo doll with the mallet, sitting on the doll and punching it in the nose, kicking the doll, and tossing it in the air.

Imitative verbal aggression. Subject repeat the phrases 'Sock him', 'Hit him down', 'Kick him', 'Throw him in the air', or 'Pow'.

THE STUDY

Imitative non-aggressive verbal responses. Subjects repeat, 'He keeps coming back for more', or 'He sure is a tough fella'.

During the pre-test, a number of the subjects imitated the essential components of the model's behaviour but did not perform the complete act, or they directed the imitative aggressive response to some object other than the Bobo doll. Two responses of this type were therefore scored and interpreted as partially imitative behaviour.

Mallet aggression. Subject strikes objects, other than the Bobo doll, aggressively with the mallet.

Sits on Bobo doll. Subject lays the Bobo doll on its side and sits on it, but does not aggress towards it.

The following additional non-imitative aggressive responses were scored:

Punches Bobo doll. Subject strikes, slaps, or pushes the doll aggressively.

Non-imitative physical and verbal aggression. This category included physically aggressive acts directed towards objects other than the Bobo doll and any hostile remarks except for those in the verbal imitation category: e.g. 'Shoot the Bobo', 'Cut him', 'Stupid ball', 'Knock over people', 'Horses fighting, biting'.

Aggressive gun play. Subject shoots darts or aims the gun and fires imaginary shots at objects in the room.

Ratings were also made of the number of behaviour units in which subjects played non-aggressively or sat quietly and did not play with any of the toys at all.

THE STUDY

R E S U L T S

COMPLETE IMITATION OF MODELS' BEHAVIOUR

Subjects in the aggression condition reproduced a good deal of physical and verbal aggressive behaviour, resembling that of the models, and their mean scores differed markedly from those of subjects in the non-aggressive and control groups who exhibited virtually no imitative aggression (see Table 14.1).

Since there were only a few scores for subjects in the non-aggressive and control conditions (approximately 70 per cent of the subjects had zero scores), and the assumption of homogeneity of variance could not be made, the Friedman two-way analysis of variance by ranks was used to test the significance of the obtained differences.

The prediction that exposure of subjects to aggressive models increases the proba-

Table 14.1

MEAN AGGRESSION SCORES FOR EXPERIMENTAL AND CONTROL SUBJECTS

Response Category	Experimental groups				Control groups
	Aggressive		Non-aggressive		
	F model	M model	F model	M model	
Imitative physical aggression					
Female subjects	5.5	7.2	2.5	0.0	1.2
Male subjects	12.4	25.8	0.2	1.5	2.0
Imitative verbal aggression					
Female subjects	13.7	2.0	0.3	0.0	0.7
Male subjects	4.3	12.7	1.1	0.0	1.7
Mallet aggression					
Female subjects	17.2	18.7	0.5	0.5	13.1
Male subjects	15.5	28.8	18.7	6.7	13.5
Punches Bobo doll					
Female subjects	6.3	16.5	5.8	4.3	11.7
Male subjects	18.9	11.9	15.6	14.8	15.7
Non-imitative aggression					
Female subjects	21.3	8.4	7.2	1.4	6.1
Male subjects	16.2	36.7	26.1	22.3	24.6
Aggressive gun play					
Female subjects	1.8	4.5	2.6	2.5	3.7
Male subjects	7.3	15.9	8.9	16.7	14.3

bility of aggressive behaviour is clearly confirmed (see Table 14.2). The main effect of treatment conditions is highly significant, both for physical and verbal imitative aggression. Comparison of pairs of scores by the sign test shows that the obtained overall differences were due almost entirely to the aggression displayed by subjects who had been exposed to the aggressive models. Their scores were significantly higher than those of either the non-aggressive or control groups, which did not differ from each other (Table 14.2).

Imitation was not confined to the model's aggressive responses. Approximately one-third of the subjects in the aggressive condition also repeated the model's non-aggressive verbal responses, while none of the subjects in either the non-aggressive or control groups did so. This difference, tested by means of the Cochran Q test, was significant well beyond the 0.001 level (Table 14.2).

THE STUDY

Table 14.2

SIGNIFICANCE OF THE DIFFERENCES BETWEEN EXPERIMENTAL AND CONTROL GROUPS IN THE EXPRESSION OF AGGRESSION

Response category	$\chi^2 r$	Q	p	Comparison of pairs of treatment conditions		
				Aggressive vs. non-aggressive p	Aggressive vs. control p	Non-aggressive vs. control p
Imitative responses						
Physical aggression	27.17		<0.001	<0.001	<0.001	0.09
Verbal aggression	9.17		<0.02	0.004	0.048	0.00
Non-aggressive verbal responses		17.50	<0.001	0.004	0.004	ns
Partial imitation						
Mallet aggression	11.06		<0.01	0.26	ns	0.005
Sits on Bobo doll		13.44	<0.01	0.018	0.059	ns
Non-imitative aggression						
Punches Bobo doll	2.87		ns			
Physical and verbal	8.96		<0.02	0.026	ns	ns
Aggressive gun play	2.75		ns			

PARTIAL IMITATION OF MODEL'S BEHAVIOUR

Differences in the predicted direction were also obtained on the two measures of partial imitation.

Analysis of variance of scores based on the subjects' use of the mallet aggressively towards objects other than the Bobo doll reveals that treatment conditions are a statistically significant source of variation (Table 14.2). In addition, individual sign tests show that both the aggressive and control groups, relative to subjects in the non-aggressive condition, produced significantly more mallet aggression, the difference being particularly marked with regard to female subjects. Girls who observed non-aggressive models performed a mean number of 0.5 mallet aggression responses as compared to mean values of 18.0 and 13.1 for girls in the aggressive and control groups, respectively.

Although subjects who observed aggressive models performed more mallet aggression (M=20.0) than their controls (M=13.3), the difference was not statistically significant.

With respect to the partially imitative response of sitting on the Bobo doll the overall group differences were significant beyond the 0.01 level (Table 14.2). Comparison of pairs of scores using the sign test reveals that subjects in the aggressive group reproduced this aspect of the models' behaviour to a greater extent than did the non-aggressive ($p=0.018$) or the control ($p=0.059$) subjects. The latter two groups, on the other hand, did not differ from each other.

NON-IMITATIVE AGGRESSION

Analyses of variance of the remaining aggression measures (Table 14.2) show that treatment conditions did not influence the extent to which subjects engaged in aggressive gun play or punched the Bobo doll. The effect of conditions is highly significant ($\chi^2=8.96$, $p<0.02$), however, in the case of the subjects' expression of non-imitative physical and verbal aggression. Further comparison of treatment pairs reveals that the main source of overall difference was the aggressive and non-aggressive groups, which differed significantly from each other (Table 14.2), with the former displaying the greater amount of aggression.

INFLUENCE OF SEX OF MODEL AND SEX OF SUBJECTS ON IMITATION

The hypothesis that boys are more prone than girls to imitate aggression exhibited by a model was only partially confirmed. *t* tests computed for subjects in the aggressive condition reveal that boys reproduced more imitative physical aggression than girls ($t=2.50$, $p<0.01$) but no more imitative verbal aggression.

The use of non-parametric tests, necessitated by the extremely skewed distributions of scores for subjects in the non-aggressive and control conditions, prevent an overall test of the influence of sex of model as such, and of the various interactions between the main effects. Inspection of the means in Table 14.1 for subjects in the aggression condition, however, clearly suggests the possibility of a Sex X Model interaction. This interaction effect is much more consistent and pronounced for the male model than for the female model. Male subjects, for example, exhibited more physical ($t=2.07$, $p<0.05$) and verbal imitative aggression ($t=2.51$, $p<0.05$), more non-imitative aggression ($t=3.15$, $p<0.025$), and engaged in significantly more aggressive gun play ($t=2.12$, $p<0.05$) following exposure to the aggressive male model than the female subjects. In contrast, girls exposed to the female model performed considerably more imitative verbal aggression and more non-imitative aggression than the boys (Table 14.1). The variances, however, were equally large and with only a small *N* in each cell, the mean differences did not reach statistical significance.

Data for the non-aggressive and control subjects provide additional suggestive evidence that the behaviour of the male model exerted a greater influence than the female model on the subjects' behaviour in the generalization situation.

Remember that, except for the greater amount of mallet aggression shown by the control subjects, no significant differences were found between the non-aggressive

THE STUDY

and control groups. The data indicate, however, that the absence of significant differences between these two groups was due, primarily, to the fact that subjects exposed to the non-aggressive female model did not differ from the controls on any of the measures of aggression. With respect to the male model, on the other hand, the differences between the groups are striking. Comparison of the sets of scores using the sign test reveals that, in relation to the control group, subjects exposed to the non-aggressive male model performed significantly less imitative physical aggression ($p=0.06$), less imitative verbal aggression ($p=0.002$), less mallet aggression ($p=0.003$), less non-imitative physical and verbal aggression ($p=0.03$), and they were less inclined to punch the Bobo doll ($p=0.07$).

While the comparison of subgroups, when some of the overall tests do not reach statistical significance, is likely to capitalize on chance differences, nevertheless the consistency of the findings adds support to the interpretation in terms of influence by the model.

NON-AGGRESSIVE BEHAVIOUR

With the exception of expected sex differences, Lindquist (1956) Type III analyses of variance of the non-aggressive response scores produced few significant differences.

Girls spent more time than boys playing with dolls ($p<0.01$). No sex differences were found in use of the other stimulus objects, i.e. farm animals, cars, or tether ball.

Treatment conditions did produce significant differences on two measures of non-aggressive behaviour that are worth mentioning. Subjects in the non-aggressive condition engaged in significantly more non-aggressive play with dolls than either subjects in the aggressive group ($t=2.67$, $p<0.02$), or in the control group ($t=2.57$, $p<0.02$).

Even more noteworthy is the finding that subjects who observed non-aggressive models spent more than twice as much time as those in the aggressive condition ($t=3.07$, $p<0.01$) in simply sitting quietly without handling any of the play material.

D I S C U S S I O N

Much current research on social learning is focused on the shaping of new behaviour through rewarding and punishing consequences. Unless responses are emitted, however, they cannot be influenced. The results of this study provide strong evidence that observation of cues produced by the behaviour of others is one effective means of eliciting certain forms of responses for which the original probability is very low or zero. Indeed, social imitation may hasten or short-cut the acquisition of new behaviours without the necessity of reinforcing successive approximations as suggested by Skinner (1953).

Thus subjects given an opportunity to observe aggressive models, later reproduced a good deal of physical and verbal aggression (as well as non-aggressive responses) largely identical with that of the model. By contrast, subjects who were exposed to non-aggressive models or who had no exposure to any models, only rarely produced such responses.

To the extent that observation of adult models displaying aggression communicates permissiveness for aggressive behaviour, such exposure may serve to weaken inhibitory responses and thereby to increase the probability of aggressive reactions to subsequent frustrations. However, the fact that subjects expressed their aggression in ways that clearly resembled the novel patterns exhibited by the models, provides striking evidence for the occurrence of learning by imitation.

In the procedure used by Miller and Dollard (1941) for establishing imitative behaviour, adult or peer models performed discrimination responses following which they were consistently rewarded, and the subjects were similarly reinforced whenever they matched the leaders' choice responses. While these experiments have been widely accepted as demonstrations of learning by means of imitation, in fact, they simply involve a special case of discrimination learning in which the behaviour of others serves as discriminative stimuli for responses that are already part of the subjects' repertoire. Auditory or visual environmental cues could easily have been substituted for the social stimuli to facilitate the discrimination learning. By contrast, the process of imitation studied in the present experiment differed in several important respects from the one investigated by Miller and Dollard in that subjects learned to combine fractional responses into relatively complex novel patterns simply by observing the performance of social models without any opportunity to perform the models' behaviour in the exposure setting, and without any reinforcers delivered either to the models or to the observers.

An adequate explanation of the mechanisms underlying imitative learning is lacking. Those that have been offered (Logan *et al.*, 1955; Maccoby, 1959) assume that the imitator performs the model's responses covertly. If it can be assumed in addition that rewards and punishments are self-administered in conjunction with the covert responses, the process of imitative learning could be explained in terms of the same principles that govern instrumental trial-and-error learning. In the early stages of the developmental process, however, the range of component responses in the organism's repertoire is probably increased through a process of classical conditioning (Bandura & Huston, 1961; Mowrer, 1950).

The data provide some evidence that the male model influences the subject's behaviour outside the exposure setting to a greater extent than was true for the female model. In the analyses of the Sex X Model interactions, for example, only

THE STUDY

the comparisons involving the male model produced significant differences. Similarly, subjects exposed to the non-aggressive male model performed less aggressive behaviour than the controls, whereas comparisons involving the female model were consistently non-significant.

In a study of learning by imitation, Rosenblith (1959) has likewise found male models more effective than females in influencing children's behaviour. Rosenblith proposed the tentative explanation that the school setting may involve some social deprivation in respect to adult males which, in turn, enhances the males' reward value.

The trends in the data produced by the present study suggest an alternative explanation. In the case of a highly masculine-typed behaviour, such as physical aggression, there is a tendency for both male and female subjects to imitate the male model to a greater degree than the female model. On the other hand, in the case of verbal aggression, which is less clearly sex linked, the greatest amount of imitation occurs in relation to the same-sex model. These trends, together with the finding that boys compared with girls are in general more imitative of physical aggression but do not differ in imitation of verbal aggression, suggest that subjects may be differentially affected by the sex of the model but that predictions must take into account the degree to which the behaviour is sex-typed.

The preceding discussion has assumed that maleness-femaleness, rather than some other personal characteristics of the particular models involved, is the significant variable – an assumption that cannot be tested directly with the available data. It was clearly evident, however, particularly from boys' spontaneous remarks about the display of aggression by the female model, that some subjects at least were responding in terms of a sex discrimination and their prior learning about what is sex-appropriate behaviour (e.g. 'Who is that lady? That's not the way for a lady to behave. Ladies are supposed to act like ladies. . .', 'You should have seen what that girl did in there. She was just acting like a man. I never saw a girl act like that before. She was punching and fighting but no swearing'). Aggression by the male model on the other hand, was more likely to be seen as appropriate and approved by both the boys ('Al's a good socker, he beat up Bobo. I want to sock like Al') and the girls ('That man is a strong fighter, he punched and punched and he could hit Bobo right down to the floor and if Bobo got up he said, "Punch your nose". He's a good fighter like Daddy').

The finding that subjects exposed to the non-aggressive models were more inhibited and unresponsive than subjects in the aggressive conditions, together with the obtained difference on the aggression measures, suggests that exposure to inhibited models not only decreases the probability of occurrence of aggressive behaviour, but also generally restricts the range of behaviour emitted by the subjects.

'Identification with the aggressor' (Freud, 1946) or 'defensive identification' (Mowrer, 1950), whereby a person presumably transforms himself from object to agent of aggression by adopting the attributes of an aggressive, threatening model

THE STUDY

so as to reduce anxiety, is widely accepted as an explanation of the imitative learning of aggression.

The development of aggressive modes of response by children of aggressively punitive adults, however, may simply reflect object displacement without involving any such mechanism of defensive identification. In studies of child-training antecedents of aggressively antisocial adolescents (Bandura & Walters, 1959) and of young hyper-aggressive boys (Bandura, 1960), the parents were found to be non-permissive and punitive of aggression directed towards themselves. But they actively encouraged and reinforced their sons' aggression towards persons outside the home. This pattern of differential reinforcement of aggressive behaviour served to inhibit the boys' aggression towards the original instigators and encouraged the displacement of aggression towards objects and situations eliciting much weaker inhibitory responses.

Moreover, the findings from an earlier study (Bandura & Huston, 1961), in which children imitated, to an equal degree, aggression exhibited by a nurturant and a non-nurturant model, together with the results of the present experiment in which subjects readily imitated aggressive models who were more or less neutral figures, suggest that mere observation of aggression, regardless of the quality of the model-subject relationship, is a sufficient condition for producing imitative aggression in children. A comparative study of the subjects' imitation of aggressive models who are feared, liked and esteemed, or who are essentially neutral figures, would throw some light on whether or not a more economical theory than the one involved in 'identification with the aggressor' can explain the modelling process.

SUMMARY

Twenty-four preschool children were assigned to each of three conditions. One experimental group observed aggressive adult models; a second observed inhibited, non-aggressive models; while subjects in a control group had no prior exposure to the models. Half the subjects in the experimental conditions observed same-sex models and half viewed models of the opposite sex. Subjects were then tested for the amount of imitative aggression performed in a new situation in the absence of the models.

Comparison of the subjects' behaviour in the generalization situation revealed that subjects exposed to aggressive models reproduced a good deal of aggression resembling that of the models, and that their mean scores differed markedly from those of subjects in the non-aggressive and control groups. Subjects in the aggressive condition also showed significantly more partially imitative and non-imitative aggressive behaviour and were generally less inhibited in their behaviour than subjects in the non-aggressive condition.

THE STUDY

Imitation was found to be differentially influenced by the sex of the model with boys showing more aggression than girls following exposure to the male model, the difference being particularly marked on highly masculine-typed behaviour.

Subjects who observed the non-aggressive models, especially the subdued male model, were generally less aggressive than their controls.

The implications of the findings based on this experiment and related studies for the psychoanalytic theory of identification with the aggressor were discussed.

EVALUATION

Theoretical issues

Bandura (1973) sees aggression primarily as a specific form of social behaviour, both acquired and maintained in much the same way as many other forms of behaviour. Other proponents of this Social Learning approach to aggression (which contrasts strongly with both instinct theories, such as those of Freud and Lorenz, and drive theories, notably Dollard *et al.*'s frustration–aggression hypothesis) are Buss (1971) and Zillman (1978).

As far as its acquisition is concerned, Social Learning theory (SLT) maintains that a large and varied range of conditions may be responsible, including direct provocation by others, heightened physiological arousal, environmental stressors, and lasting attitudes and values. But by far the most important is exposure to live or filmed (symbolic) models. According to SLT (in contrast with drive and instinct theories), humans are not seen as constantly driven or impelled towards violence by built-in, internal forces or ever-present external stimuli but, instead, people only aggress under appropriate social conditions which tend to facilitate such behaviour. It also adopts a much more optimistic view of the possibility of preventing or controlling human aggression: since it is *learned* behaviour, it is open to direct modification by altering or removing the conditions which normally maintain it (Baron, 1977).

For Skinner, no reinforcement equals no learning. But Bandura maintains that *learning* may occur without any reinforcement: exposure to a model's behaviour is sufficient for learning to occur. However, reinforcement can influence the likelihood of the learned behaviour actually being *performed* (but is only one of several influences on actual behaviour). What's more, reinforcement may be either *direct* (it is the child who is reinforced for imitating the model) or *vicarious* (it is the model whose behaviour is reinforced or punished), while for Skinner there is only one kind of reinforcement, namely direct.

Subsequent research

So, Bandura introduces the fundamental distinction between *learning* and *performance*, with reinforcement (either direct or vicarious) being unnecessary for the former but playing an important role in the latter (be it direct or vicarious). An early indication of this came in another study by Bandura, Ross and Ross (1963b). Four-year-olds watched one of two films, both involving two men, Johnny and Rocky. In the first film, Johnny is playing with some attractive toys. Rocky asks if he can play too, but Johnny refuses and Rocky becomes very aggressive towards Johnny and his toys, eventually winning them away from Johnny. Johnny sits dejectedly, while Rocky celebrates with food and drink.

In the second film, things begin in the same way as for the first film, but Rocky is beaten up by Johnny. A control group watched no film. Seeing Rocky rewarded (film 1) resulted in the highest number of imitated acts of aggression, while seeing him punished led to the lowest number, with the control group falling midway between the two.

Does this mean that the children actually *learned* more about aggression from watching film 1 than those who saw film 2, or simply that they were more ready to *reproduce* the behaviour they had observed? This, of course, is the learning versus performance issue: does failure to imitate mean that no learning has taken place?

A later study (Bandura, 1965) showed the answer to be 'no'. He tested children under three conditions (model rewarded, model punished and model neither rewarded nor punished) and found, as in the 1963 study, that the first group imitated more than the second group (but no more than the control group). In a second phase of the experiment, children were offered rewards for imitating the model's behaviour and, under those conditions, all three groups produced the *same* number of imitative aggressive acts. So, clearly, in the first phase the children were *performing* differently, but in the second phase, their near identical performance revealed that they had all *learned* equally about aggression from whichever model they saw. In terms of the distinction between vicarious and direct reinforcement, vicarious reinforcement influenced imitation (phase 1) and direct reinforcement influenced imitation in phase 2, *but* neither had any influence over what the children learned about the model's aggressive behaviour.

If learning can take place without being expressed through behaviour, then the question arises as to just what it is that is being learned in observational learning:

> What are children acquiring that enables them to reproduce the behaviour of an absent model at some point in the future – often the distant future?. (Shaffer, 1985).

Bandura's (1977) answer is *symbolic representations* of the model's behaviour, stored in memory, and retrieved at a later date to guide the child's own attempts at imitation.

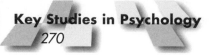

They may take the form of images or verbal labels that describe the behaviour in an economical way. Other cognitive processes relate to the very nature of reinforcement. While Skinner saw reinforcement working in an 'automatic' way to make the behaviour it follows more likely to be repeated, Bandura saw it as providing information, and this applies as much to vicarious as to direct reinforcement. As Mischel (1986), another SL theorist, puts it:

> Information that alters the person's anticipations of the probable outcomes to which a behaviour will lead changes the probability that he will perform the behaviour. Models inform us of the probable consequences of particular behaviours and thus affect the likelihood that we will perform them.

While SLT can say how a child might acquire a particular behaviour pattern, it fails to take account of the underlying developmental changes that are occurring (Bee, 2000). For example, do three-year-olds and ten-year-olds typically learn the same amount or in the same way from modelling? Given Bandura's emphasis on cognitive aspects of the modelling process, a genuinely developmental SLT is possible, but has yet to be proposed (Bee, 2000). Indeed, the importance of cognitive processes is reflected in Bandura's (1986, 1989) re-naming of SLT as *social cognitive theory*.

Methodological issues

As noted in **Background and context** above, one implication of Bandura's research findings was that mass-media portrayals of violence might be contributing to increased levels of violence in society. Bandura (1965) himself warned against such an interpretation in the light of his finding that acquisition does not necessarily mean performance. Nevertheless, the mere *possibility* of such effects was sufficient to focus considerable public attention on his research. However, criticisms of the Bobo-doll 'paradigm' (both then and since) would also suggest that public concern was rather premature:

(i) As far as the films used, they differ in several important ways from standard TV or movie material. They are very brief (3½ minutes being a very common presentation time), often lack a plot, provide no cause or justification for the model's behaviour, and that behaviour is typically quite bizarre (deliberately, so that it is distinctive and so likely to grab the child's attention), but for that reason highly unlikely to appear on TV or anywhere else!

(ii) Similarly, the novelty of the Bobo doll is itself a crucial factor in Bandura's experiments. For example, Kniveton & Stephenson (1970, cited in Cumberbatch, 1995) found that children not familiar with the doll imitated five times more than children with previous exposure to it. Indeed, Nobel (1975, cited by Cumberbatch, 1995) suggests that even young children participating in laboratory experiments understand that they are expected to play a particular role. He quotes one shrewd four-year-old who, on first arriving at the laboratory for a modelling experiment, was heard to point out to his mother: 'Look, Mummy, there's the doll we have to hit'.

(iii) Not only is the exposure time very brief, but the effects (the DV) are demonstrated almost immediately. Can a single exposure have long-term effects, as they might (so it is feared) outside the lab? According to Hicks (1965, 1968, cited in Baron, 1977), it can. He retested children six–eight months following a brief exposure (less than 10 minutes) and found that 40% of the models' aggressive acts could still be reproduced after a single showing of the film.

(iv) The DV is operationalized as aggressive acts directed at an inanimate object (an inflated doll) specifically designed for such treatment. Since no living being is harmed by such actions, should we really describe the behaviour as 'aggression' at all? Wouldn't it be more appropriate to interpret the behaviour as a form of play, especially as the Bobo doll is, essentially, a 'toy' (Klapper, 1968, cited in Baron, 1977)?

Bandura's (1973) response to this is to draw once more on the learning versus performance distinction. Procedures based on attacks against inanimate objects are useful for understanding how such behaviours are acquired, since aggressive responses are often learned in contexts that are far removed from actual harm to others. He gives the examples of boxers in training using punch bags, and hunters practising shooting at inanimate targets. He also gives the example of airline pilots training on simulators: it's a good idea to make your mistakes (especially when they can have such disastrous consequences) in a context that is not 'real'. Baron (1977) claims that, unfortunately, assaults against inanimate objects have often been interpreted as providing evidence about performance as well as acquisition. All that we should claim for the Bobo doll experiments is that they show we can acquire new aggressive responses by observing others; the further claim that exposure to filmed or televised violence may sometimes produce interpersonal aggression does not seem justified solely on the basis of the Bobo-doll studies.

However, Johnson *et al.* (1977, cited in Baron, 1977) found that the amount of play aggression shown by nursery-school children towards a Bobo doll and other toys was significantly related to ratings of general aggression by peers (0.76) and teachers (0.57). This suggests that children's behaviour in such play situations may after all be related to their aggression towards other people. It is possible, however, that they are both related to some third factor (e.g. high level of motor activity). What it also demonstrates is the importance of assessing the child's 'normal' level of aggression before any exposure to a model: the current (1961) study does this by matching children on aggression ratings prior to allocating them to the experimental conditions.

(v) The situation in which the aggression occurs (i.e. the child's imitation of the model) is very permissive: any realistic consequences of aggressive behaviour, such as peer retaliation or adult punishment, are absent (Gunter & McAleer,

1997). But perhaps this criticism is relevant only to the performance side of the learning versus performance distinction.

(*vi*) According to Gunter & McAleer (1990):

> Although we can be quite certain about what occurs in the laboratory, we are left with a great deal of uncertainty concerning how much the process demonstrated in the laboratory accurately reflects what happens in children's lives.

According to Baron (1977), one response to these criticisms was 'phase 2' of the TV-violence research, aimed at (*i*) using more realistic measures of aggression in which behaviour would be directed against other people; (*ii*) exposing participants to more realistic materials; and (*iii*) eliminating the precise similarity between the model's behaviour and the context within which the participants could themselves aggress. One of the leading researchers in this 'phase' was Leonard Berkowitz. (For a thorough review of relevant research, see Berkowitz, 1993.)

However, the role of observational learning in explaining the impact of media violence (as well as pro-social behaviour, gender-role stereotypes and so on) is still considerable, along with arousal, disinhibition and desensitization.

Applications and implications

Although Bandura was intitially more concerned with developing theoretical issues than with applied aspects of the media, his (and Berkowitz's) laboratory based experimental approaches stimulated many others to explore the study of media violence. Perhaps more importantly, their theoretical orientations have helped to shape the way later researchers have conceptualized media effects (Cumberbatch, 1995).

As well as its relevance to symbolic models (TV, cinema etc.), SLT has always had much to contribute in explaining the so-called 'cycle of violence' or, more technically, the 'intergenerational transmission of aggression'. The basic idea is that if you have been the victim of (physical) abuse as a child, you are very much more likely to be an abusing parent than if you haven't. It also increases the chances that you will be a wife (or a husband) batterer. Berkowitz (1993) refers to this early experience as a *risk factor* for the development of adult aggressiveness: it makes it more probable, but is never certain, or inevitable. Why?

Many of the same factors which are proposed to explain the effect of TV violence are relevant here, including desensitization, disinhibition and imitation. One feature of disinhibition is that you learn the 'right' way to act in a given situation by observing what others do. When children see adults fight, they learn that they too can solve their problems by attacking the people who 'get in their way'.

As Berkowitz (1993) points out, you don't have to have been the victim of abuse yourself: *witnessing* violence may be sufficient. However, when you are yourself the victim, you are simultaneously suffering the painful effects *and* witnessing the aggressive behaviour. Physical punishments are demonstrations of the very behaviour which the parents are very often trying to eliminate in their child; ironically, the evidence suggests that the child is likely to become *more*, not less, aggressive!

The term 'copy-cat' violence implies the role of observational learning, and Bandura (1973) claims that documented cases of the contagion of TV/movie violence, although fairly rare, still occur with alarming regularity over time, airline hijackings being one example. Air piracy was unknown in the USA until 1961. Then some successful hijackings of Cuban airliners to Miami were followed by a wave, reaching a peak of 87 in 1969 (Mischel, 1986).

Observational learning also influences emotional responses, through the process of *vicarious (classical) conditioning*: 'by observing the emotional reactions of others to a stimulus, it is possible vicariously to learn an intense emotional response to that situation' (Mischel, 1986). This can help explain the learning of animal phobias in people who have not suffered a traumatic incident with the animal themselves, but *have* witnessed somebody else's fear, which may be quite sufficient. These same basic principles can be used to *remove* phobias, through a form of therapy called *modelling*.

Bandura *et al.* (1969) assigned teenage and adult volunteers, all with intense snake phobias, to one of three treatment conditions (or a non-treatment control). Condition (1) (*systematic desensitization*) involved relaxation training while visualizing progressively stronger fear-arousing snakes; Condition (2) (*symbolic modelling*) involved showing films of fearless children and adults interacting in a progressively bold way, first with plastic snakes, later with real snakes, which were being held and allowed to crawl freely all over them. These volunteers were also trained in relaxation techniques; Condition (3) (*live modelling and guided participation*) involved observing a model, initially through an observation window, then directly in front of them. The model encouraged the volunteers to handle the snake themselves, first with gloves on, then with bare hands, guiding them physically, then gradually allowing the volunteer to 'take charge'. Condition (3) proved to be the most powerful, being almost completely successful in removing the phobia quickly and completely – to the volunteers' amazement. Modelling is also used as part of *assertiveness training*, helping people to overcome shyness and to assert themselves more effectively, and *covert modelling* involves imagining scenes in which a model performs in an assertive way (Mischel, 1986).

According to Newell & Dryden (1991), Bandura's SLT has facilitated a greater acceptance of *cognitive behaviour therapies*, which they claim are defined '. . . by their emphasis on the interaction between the cognitive, behavioural, and physiological systems . . . ' They are *not* specific techniques but:

. . . sets of orientations and models of human experience . . . They . . . share a common view of human response as being based on reciprocal structures, processes and contents, behaviours, and antecedents and consequences of those behaviours in the environment are intimately related in a multidirectional fashion. Thus, cognitions and behaviours are not only shaped by the environment, but shape it, giving to the client an active role in creating future outcomes. (Newell & Dryden, 1991)

According to Kent (1991), Bandura (1986) has been conducting some of the more important work on the relationships between what people believe and what they do. When people believe they have control over their behaviour and can achieve their goals, they have a sense of '*self-efficacy*'. Anxiety is experienced when we perceive ourselves as being ill-equipped to manage potentially painful events/situations. For example, a snake phobic may have a high sense of self-efficacy in most areas of his/her life, but perceives situations involving snakes as beyond his/her control. Behavioural treatments, such as *in vivo* exposure (actually seeing, handling a snake and so on) and modelling have important effects on patients' self-efficacy beliefs. Indeed, Bandura (1986) argues that a variety of therapies may all be effective for the same reason, namely, that they serve to increase a patient's sense of self-efficacy. Whether the aim is to control or change cognition may be less important long term than helping patients become more confident in their ability to deal with situations that previously induced fear and anxiety (see Chapter 22).

Exercises

1. What is the major difference between the current study and earlier studies of modelling?

2. In relation to Hypothesis (*iii*), Bandura *et al.* say that:

as a result of differing reinforcement histories, tendencies to imitate male and female models thus acquire differential habit strength

Put this into your own words to explain what they mean.

3. (*i*) Which experimental design is being used?
   (*ii*) What is the advantage *in this particular case* of using this design?
   (*iii*) What alternative design could have been used?
   (*iv*) How does the design used here affect the choice of statistical test?

4. (*i*) What can you infer about the rating scale used to measure the children's aggression (before the experiment) from the use of the Pearson product-moment correlation coefficient?
   (*ii*) Which alternative test could have been used?

5. Why was it felt necessary to deliberately subject all the children to 'mild aggression arousal' following exposure to the model?

6. In relation to Hypothesis (*i*), the Friedman two-way analysis of variance by ranks was used. What is this test and when is it used?

7. The Cochran *Q* test was used to test for any significant differences between the groups in their imitation of the model's (non-aggressive) verbal responses. What is this test and when is it used?

8. In relation to Hypothesis (*iv*), *t* tests showed that boys are more prone than girls to imitate a model's physical aggression, but not so for verbal aggression. However, the 'extremely skewed distributions of scores' for participants in the non-aggressive and control conditions meant that non-parametric tests had to be used. Why?

9. What is another term for:
  (*i*) 'reward'?
  (*ii*) 'reinforcing successive approximations'?
  (*iii*) 'instrumental trial and error learning'? (See **Discussion**)

10. In the final paragraph of the **Discussion** (before the **Summary**), Bandura *et al.* say:

the mere observation of aggression, regardless of the quality of the model–subject relationship, is a sufficient condition for producing imitative aggression in children.

Does this need to be qualified in the light of subsequent research?

11. Do you consider the study to be ethically sound?

15 Social and family relationships of ex-institutional adolescents

Jill Hodges and Barbara Tizard (1989)

Journal of Child Psychology and Psychiatry, 30 (1), 77–97

BACKGROUND AND CONTEXT

The general context is that of the effect of early experience on later behaviour and development; more specifically, the effect of institutional upbringing on later attachments (both to adults and peers, within and outside the family). Related to this are several interrelated questions, namely:

(*i*)   If the later environment continues to be deprived, you would expect a continuation of deprived behaviour. But if the change in environment is sufficiently great, is there a corresponding change in behaviour?

(*ii*)   Can early deprivation effects be reversed or at least modified?

(*iii*)   Are some aspects of development (e.g. social/linguistic) more vulnerable than others?

(*iv*)   Are there critical or sensitive periods for the development of behaviour?

According to Rutter (1989), over the last 30 years there have been major changes in how the developmental process has been conceptualized:

(a)   During the 1950s, the dominant view was the consistency of personality and the lack of major changes after the first few years of life. Longitudinal studies (like those of Goldfarb, Spitz, and others) sought to chart this early stabilization of personality, and urged that maternal deprivation in infancy caused permanent and irreversible damage (Bowlby, 1951).

(b)   But longitudinal studies failed to show high stability over time, and the claims regarding maternal deprivation were severely criticized (e.g. Yarrow, 1961). It became clear that people changed a good deal over the course of development, and that the outcome of early adversities were quite diverse, with long-term effects heavily dependent on the nature of subsequent life experiences (Clarke & Clarke, 1976). Even markedly adverse experiences in infancy carry few risks for later development – if the subsequent rearing environment is good (Rutter, 1981).

(c)   It was then argued that there is little consistency in psychological development; what there was depended on people's interpretation of their experiences (Kagan, 1984). Mischel (1968, 1969) challenged the very notion of personality traits,

claiming that most behaviour is situation-specific.

(d) In recent years, there has been a limited swing back to a rather complex mix of continuities and discontinuities (Rutter, 1987).

Rutter then goes on to identify and discuss a number of principles and concepts of development directly related to *(d)* above, including:

A *life-span perspective* is necessary because homo sapiens is a social animal, and social development occurs relative to a person's interactions and transactions with the social environment (Erikson, 1963; Bronfenbrenner, 1979; Hinde, 1987; Hinde & Stevenson-Hinde, 1988). Key social experiences, such as marriage and childbearing, tend to happen after childhood, so social development needs to be studied into adult life (see Chapter 17).

The *timing*, as well as the nature, of experiences is likely to influence their impact. For example, very young infants are protected from separation experiences because they have yet to develop strong attachments; older children are protected because they have learned to maintain relationships over time and space. Toddlers are most at risk, because attachments are just becoming established at that age, and therefore they lack the cognitive skills required to maintain a relationship during an absence (Rutter, 1981, 1987). Again, experiences may be felt differently, and/or produce different societal responses if they arise at non-normative times, for example, teenage pregnancy and difficulties in parenting (Hayes, 1987), early marriage and the increased risk of divorce (Otto, 1979), differences in effects between redundancy in middle life and retirement in old age (Warr, 1987), and the psychological consequences of unusually early puberty (Graham & Rutter, 1985).

Both continuities and discontinuities are to be expected (Hinde *et al.*, 1988; Rutter, 1987). The process of development is concerned with *change*, and it is not reasonable to suppose that the pattern will be set in early life. Physiological changes (e.g. puberty) and new experiences will both serve to shape psychological functioning. But also continuities will occur, because children carry with them the results of earlier learning and of earlier structural and functional change.

AIM AND NATURE OF THE STUDY

The article represents the latest in a series of reports on the development of a number of ex-institutional children who subsequently grew up in family situations, and who had been studied since the time they were still in institutions. This 'progress report' is characteristic (though not an inevitable feature) of *longitudinal studies*, in which the same group of people is followed up over a period of time, usually years. By contrast, in *cross-sectional studies* people of various ages are all studied at more-or-less the same point in time.

Like *cross-cultural studies* (see Chapter 2), longitudinal (and cross-sectional) studies represent an overall approach. They are exclusively found in the area of developmental

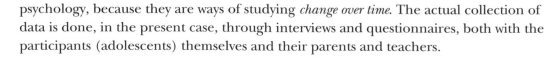

psychology, because they are ways of studying *change over time*. The actual collection of data is done, in the present case, through interviews and questionnaires, both with the participants (adolescents) themselves and their parents and teachers.

Hodges and Tizard also refer to their study as a 'form of natural experiment': some change occurs, in the natural course of events (here the child's environment: the *independent variable*), which can be studied for its effect on some aspect of the child's development (here, social relationships: the *dependent variable*). Those children whose environment is changed are compared with (matched) controls whose environments have not changed, so this represents an independent-groups design. The independent variable has two main 'values' (adoption and restoration), and this allows the two ex-institution groups to be compared with each other (as well as with the control/comparison groups).

Just as importantly, since it is a longitudinal study, the children are being compared with *themselves*: we want to know how the adolescents were behaving at ages four and eight.

T H E   S T U D Y

[This is in fact one of two articles by the above authors, which appeared in the same volume, reporting on different aspects of the same study. The Introduction section of the summary that follows contains some material from the companion article.]

A group of children raised in institutions and experiencing multiple-changing caregivers until at least two years of age, then adopted or restored to a biological parent, have been followed longitudinally into mid-adolescence. Such maternal deprivation did not necessarily prevent them forming strong and lasting attachments to parents once placed in families; but whether such attachments developed, depended on the family environment, being much more common in adopted children than in those restored to a biological parent. Both groups were, however, more oriented towards adult attention and had more difficulties with peers and fewer close relationships than matched comparison adolescents, indicating some long-term effects of their early institutional experiences.

I N T R O D U C T I O N

The classic studies of the effects of early institutionalization saw the ability to make deep relationships as particularly endangered. Bowlby (1951) and Goldfarb (1945) focused on maternal deprivation as the salient aspect of institutional care responsible for this effect. Goldfarb (1943a) found that children with early institutional experience were more emotionally withdrawn in early adolescence, even after years in a foster family, than children who had been in families throughout. He related their incapacity for deep human relationships to their early years when 'strong anchors to specific adults were not established'.

A follow-up study of institutional children has allowed a detailed look at some of these questions.

Earlier studies by Tizard and co-workers (Tizard & Joseph, 1970; Tizard & Tizard, 1971; Tizard & Rees, 1974, 1975; Tizard, 1977; Tizard & Hodges, 1978) followed a group of children who had experienced institutional care for the first years of their lives, most of whom were then adopted, fostered, or restored to their biological parents. The children received good physical care in the institutions, which also appeared to provide adequately for their cognitive development: by four-and-a-half years, the mean WPPSI [Wechsler Pre-School Primary Scale of Intelligence] score of the institution children was 105, and earlier signs of some language retardation were no longer evident. However, staff turnover, and an explicit policy against allowing too strong an attachment to develop between children and the nurses who looked after them, had given the children little opportunity to form close, continuous relationships with an adult. By the age of two, an average of 24 different caregivers had looked after them for at least a week; by age four, the average was 50. This seems to fit Bowlby's (1951) description of maternal deprivation as 'not uncommonly almost complete in institutions . . . where the child often has no one person who cares for him in a personal way and with whom he feels secure'. As a result, the children's attachment behaviour was very unusual. At two, they seemed to be attached to a large number of adults, i.e., they would run to be picked up when anyone familiar entered the room and cry when they left. At the same time, they were more fearful of strangers than a home-reared comparison group (Tizard & Tizard, 1971). By four, 70 per cent of these still in institutions were said by the staff 'not to care deeply about anyone' (Tizard & Rees, 1975). It seems likely that generally the children's first opportunity for a close, reciprocal, long-term attachment came when they left the institutions, and were placed in families, at ages ranging from two to seven years.

Although most formed attachments to their parents, the ex-institution children showed a number of atypical features in social development. At four, they were no longer shy of strangers. About a third were markedly attention-seeking and over-friendly to strangers, and a few were indiscriminately affectionate to all adults. Although these traits were shown only by a minority of the children they did set the ex-institution children off as a group from comparison, non-institution children.

The study is a form of natural experiment, with a fundamental change in the children's environment; usually children from a poor early environment have a poor later one too. This fundamental change allows us to see whether the early environment had a persisting influence, despite very different later experience, and also whether different types of later experience lead to different outcomes. These issues are clearly relevant to questions of child-care policy, especially which kind of placements seem to have the best outcome for the child, and whether adoption is a satisfactory placement option for children past infancy. According to BAAF (British Agencies for Adoption and Fostering) (1984), while the overall number of adoptions by people unrelated to the child has dropped considerably, the proportion of older children adopted has risen (37 per cent over three in 1983, 14 per cent in 1970). However, Bacon and Rowe (1978) found that adoption was still relatively rare for older children in residential care, and Hapgood (1984) suggests there is an unmet need for older child placement.

By eight, the majority of adopted children and some of the restored children had formed close attachments to their parents, despite their lack of early attachments in the institutions. The adoptive parents very much wanted a child, and put much time and energy into building up a relationship. The biological parents, by contrast, were more likely to be ambivalent about having the child back, and to have other children, plus material difficulties, competing for their attention. According to their parents, the ex-institutional children did not present more problems than a comparison group who had never been in care; but according to their teachers, more of them showed problems, notably attention-seeking behaviour, especially from adults, restlessness, disobedience and poor peer relationships; they were quarrelsome and unpopular (as they had been at four). Their earlier over-friendliness also persisted (Tizard & Hodges, 1978). These difficulties are very similar to those reported by Goldfarb (1943, 1945), but whereas he found many other problems in his ex-institutional group, including poorer cognitive and language skills, this was not the case with the present sample, presumably because the care offered in institutions has improved considerably since the 1940s.

So the present study indicated that, on the one hand, early institutional care and the lack of close attachments had not had the drastically damaging effects predicted by Bowlby (1951), but on the other hand there were indications that, despite more adequate institutional care, and despite in many cases the formation of deep and lasting attachments to parents once the children entered families, some of the children still showed lasting effects of their earlier institutional rearing. This raises two major questions:

1   How enduring are these effects of early experience? Could they be reversed after the age of eight? Given the degree to which ex-institutional children had 'normalized' within their families, it seemed possible that further time in the family would reduce still further the remaining effects of early institutional care. At age eight, the children had spent an approximate minimum of 25 per cent of their lives in institutions, reducing to 12 or 13 per cent by age 16. Do the

remaining effects of early institutionalisation reduce similarly, or do they remain?

2 How satisfactory is the outcome for adopted children and families, especially compared with possible alternative placements? At age eight, the adoptive children were doing better in virtually every way than restored children, although still showing more difficulties than children who had never been in care (especially at school). Do adopted children continue to do relatively well? The National Child Development Study (Lambert & Streather, 1980) found that at 11, when their better home circumstances were taken into account, adopted children, as well as illegitimate children were less well-adjusted than legitimate children in similar home circumstances, and that the adjustment of the adopted group had apparently deteriorated relative to that of other children between seven and 11. Further, adolescence is generally thought to be a time of particular potential stress for adopted children and adoptive families (Mackie, 1982), whether the adoption is seen as causing difficulties in itself (Schechter, 1960) or as complicating pre-existing difficulties and normal developmental tasks (Chess, 1953). This in itself would suggest that difficulties might increase rather than decrease during adolescence. To some extent, the same may apply to the small group of restored children, as many had become members of step-families, recognized as a source of difficulty for family members (Robinson, 1980).

However, other studies of adopted children placed in infancy suggests that their earlier difficulties might decrease with age. Bohman and Sigvardsson (1985) found this to be true up to 18, while restored and fostered children showed markedly more difficulties than the adopted group. Raynor (1981) supports the picture of a decrease in problems as adoptees grew older. During adolescence, peer group relationships become more important, and family relationships change as adolescents begin to move towards eventual independence from parents. Because of the ex-institution group's earlier difficulties with peers, it seemed important to look at how they were negotiating this adolescent task, and how far they had become able to form close relationships with peers, as well as deep attachments to parents.

For all these reasons it was decided to trace all the children who had been followed up until the age of eight and reassess them at age 16.

ATTRITION IN THE SAMPLE

Considerable difficulty was experienced in locating the children after eight years without contact, but eventually all were found. However, of the 51 children studied at age eight, nine were not available for study at age 16. These nine, added to the 14 unavailable after age four, mean that the losses over the 12 years (four to 16) amount to 35 per cent. (The NCD study similarly lost approximately one third of its sample by age 11.)

THE STUDY

WHEREABOUTS OF ADOPTED CHILDREN

Of the 28 adopted children seen at age eight, 26 were still in their adoptive homes at age 16. A further child who had been adopted shortly before her tenth birthday was added to the group. Two placements had broken down between eight and 16 (one with new foster parents, one in local authority residential care), and neither of these children was included in the groups analysed for this article. A third adopted adolescent was seen in a residential psychiatric unit, but spent some weekends at home and was included in the adopted group.

The adopted group included three boys who were fostered when seen at age eight in what were intended as permanent placements, and were still in these families at 16. Since there was no possibility of the biological parent reclaiming the child, it was felt that psychologically, if not legally, they should be counted as adoptions.

WHEREABOUTS OF RESTORED CHILDREN

Twelve out of the 13 restored children seen at age eight were still with their parents at 16; the remaining one was currently in a secure unit for disturbed and delinquent adolescents but was included in the restored group. Three others had either spent time in residential units for young people with emotional/behavioural problems, or lived with friends after running away from home. But all three were back with their families.

WHEREABOUTS OF CHILDREN IN RESIDENTIAL OR FOSTER CARE

Only one child had remained in residential care throughout until 16. The rest of those who had been in residential or temporary foster care at age eight had experienced many changes, but five were back in residential care at 16.

NUMBERS SEEN AT 16

Altogether, 17 adopted boys and six adopted girls, six restored boys and five restored girls, three boys and two girls in institutional care were interviewed.

STABILITY OF DIFFERENT TYPES OF PLACEMENT BETWEEN TWO AND 16

A total of 33 children were placed in adoptive families after age two; information is provided about the stability of the placement for 24 of them. A total of 25 children were restored to biological parents after age two; information is provided about 16 of these. As many placements had broken down, at least temporarily, as had not; a much higher proportion than in the case of the adoptive placements. But the greatest amount of instability occurred in the institutional group.

EFFECTS OF ATTRITION AND CHANGES IN PLACEMENT GROUPS UPON CHARACTERISTICS OF SAMPLE

The adopted children unavailable for study at age eight had shown somewhat fewer problems of adjustment at age four, and the restored children somewhat more, than the average of their respective groups. The data do not suggest a systematic loss of children who, as eight-year-olds, presented fewer or more problems at home than those who remained and were studied at 16.

C O M P A R I S O N G R O U P S

A new, matched comparison group was formed to replace the one used in earlier stages of the study. This previous comparison group of 30 London working-class children was set up when the study children were in institutions at age two, and no longer seemed appropriate either for the primarily middle-class adopted group, or for the restored group who often lived in primarily disadvantaged homes. In addition, the majority of ex-institutional children were boys, while the former comparison group had been half boys and half girls.

A comparison 16-year-old was found for each of the adopted and restored adolescents, matched on sex, one- or two-parent family, Registrar General's occupational classification of main breadwinner, and position in family. Any adolescent with a mental or physical handicap, or chronic illness, or who had spent longer than a few weeks away from their family in residential care or hospital at any age, was excluded from the comparison group. For logistical reasons, all the matched comparisons were drawn from the London area, while the study adolescents were scattered throughout the British Isles. The matched comparisons were obtained via General Practitioner medical practices.

Fifty-three practices were approached: eight refused, 22 failed to respond. The final comparison group was obtained from 16 different practices; all families of 16-year-olds in these practices were approached via a letter from the GP asking for cooperation in a study of adolescents and their families. About 30 per cent indicated that they did not wish to be contacted, and the final comparison group was selected from the remainder. A possible source of bias is that the 30 per cent included families with severe difficulties in childrearing.

An additional comparison group was used to assess information obtained from the schools; this comprised study children's same-sex classmate, nearest in age.

▉ A S S E S S M E N T
▉ P R O C E D U R E

The study adolescents and their mothers (fathers too were occasionally present) or careworkers were interviewed by J.Hodges, and their matched comparisons by one of four other researchers, all experienced interviewers. It was not possible, practically, for the authors to interview all the study families themselves, so different groups of subjects were studied by different interviewers. However, this disadvantage is offset by the advantage of having the study families assessed by an interviewer already known to them: some families probably would have refused to be interviewed by a stranger.

Interviews were tape-recorded with the permission of the adolescent or adult being interviewed. Each visit to the house or institution lasted several hours, and occasionally a second visit was needed to complete the assessment. The parent or careworker was interviewed, and also completed the 'A' scale questionnaire (Rutter, Tizard & Whitmore, 1970) on the adolescent's behaviour; the adolescent was interviewed and completed the 'Questionnaire on Social Difficulty' (Lindsay & Lindsay, 1982).

Permission was obtained from both the parents and adolescent to contact the school via a postal questionnaire, comprising the 'B' scale (Rutter, 1967; Rutter *et al.*, 1970), used for comparison with the previous stage of the study, and a questionnaire, devised for the study, focusing on relationships with teachers and peers. Teachers were asked to complete one set for the study adolescent and one for the same-sex classmate next in age (forming the school comparison group).

▉ R E S U L T S

RELATIONSHIPS WITHIN THE FAMILY

Attachments to parents. Figure 15.1 shows the proportion of adopted, restored and comparison children said by the mother to be attached to her at ages eight and 16, and also the proportion of those institutional children said to have a close attachment to an adult. As at eight, the vast majority (17 out of 21) of the adoptive mothers felt that their child was deeply attached to them, and this was true for all their comparisons. Of the four mothers who felt that their child was not closely attached to them, at 16, one had taken the same view when the child was eight; at 16, the relationship seemed mutually rejecting and hostile. The other three had described their eight-year-old as closely attached but now doubted the strength of their attachment.

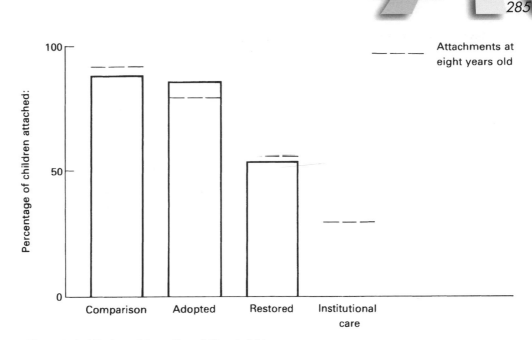

Figure 15.1. Attachment to mother at 16 and eight years.

T H E   S T U D Y

By contrast, only five out of nine restored children were described as deeply attached to their mother (the figure for age eight was six out of 13).

When asked if the child was easy to love, and whether the mother found any of her children easier to love than others, one out of seven of the mothers of restored adolescents who also had other children felt she loved each child equally (compared with six out of eight comparisons); five of the other six restored mothers preferred a sibling to the restored child. Nine out of 14 adoptive parents and 13 out of 16 of their comparisons felt they loved their children equally.

Adopted adolescents were more often said by their mothers to be attached to their father at 16 than the restored group ($p < 0.01$), who, in turn, differed similarly from their comparisons. No adopted or comparison adolescents were said to have become less attached to their father as they grew older, but two out of five restored adolescents were.

Relations with siblings. The comparison adolescents reported fewer marked problems with siblings than the ex-institution group as a whole ($p = 0.03$), and the mothers confirmed this ($p = 0.02$). The restored group got on particularly badly with their siblings, as they had at age eight.

Showing affection. At age eight, the adopted children and those still in institutional care were found to be the most affectionate and cuddly, with restored children strikingly the least cuddly. At 16, mothers were asked how easy it was to be affectionate to them, e.g. giving them a kiss or cuddle. As they grew older, ten out of 22 adopted children had become less demonstrative; as a group, they were not significantly more demonstratively affectionate at 16 than their matched comparisons. However, the restored group were still strikingly less affectionate; less than the adopted group ($p<0.01$), and less than their own matched comparisons ($p<0.01$). There was also a clear (but not significant) tendency for adoptive parents to find it easier to show affection to their adolescents than parents of restored adolescents. The difference was especially marked regarding the father (as perceived by the mothers); fathers of restored adolescents also showed affection less readily than their matched controls, and this, apparently, had also been true at eight.

Confiding and support. A majority of all the groups of mothers believed they knew when their son or daughter was upset, and the adolescents felt the same (see Table 15.1).

Table 15.1

ISSUES RELATING TO CLOSENESS WITH PARENTS, CONFIDING AND SUPPORT

	Adopted	Their comparisons	Restored	Their comparisons
Mother believes adolescent would confide over at least some anxieties	17 (85%)	19 (91%)	8 (80%)	8 (80%)
Mother feels she would realize if adolescent upset	16 (84%)	16 (76%)	5 (56%)	8 (80%)
Adolescent feels parent would realize if upset, at least sometimes	13 (65%)	15 (71%)	8 (80%)	6 (60%)
Parent feels adolescent would ask for support	13 (72%)	14 (67%)	7 (78%)	7 (70%)
Adolescent feels (s)he could ask for support	11 (58%)	12 (57%)	5 (51%)	6 (64%)

Though restored mothers were less certain than others, their children indicated no such doubts. Around 70 per cent of the adolescents would ask the mothers for support or advice over some – but not all – problems (according to the mothers), and over 50 per cent of the adolescents felt they would do so.

The adopted and restored groups did not differ greatly from their comparison groups in the proportion who would turn to a parent if they felt depressed or miserable. A higher proportion of adopted and restored adolescents than their comparisons would not confide in anyone, and fewer, at least of the adoptees, would confide in a peer.

Table 15.2

ADOLESCENTS' VIEWS: WHO WOULD THEY CONFIDE IN? (BASED ON A RANGE OF NINE QUESTIONS)

Confide in	Adopted	Their comparisons	Restored	Their comparisons
Nobody	28%	17%	23%	22%
Parent	44%	39%	43%	35%
Other family member	2%	5%	4%	1%
Outside adult	6%	5%	8%	6%
Peer	16%	30%	17%	33%
N/A (not worried)	3%	4%	5%	3%
(Total number of responses)	(177)	(191)	(96)	(89)

Table 15.2 shows answers to questions about who, if anyone, they would confide in if worried about a range of concerns, namely: (*i*) if they felt very miserable; (*ii*) if anxious about their appearance; (*iii*) if worried that something was wrong with them; (*iv*) if worried about not being liked by the opposite sex; (*v*) if they felt something was wrong with their body; (*vi*) if they were in severe financial difficulty; (*vii*) if they were unhappy over their boy/girlfriend; (*viii*) if they needed to know about contraception; (*ix*) if they became pregnant, or made someone pregnant, without wishing to. They tended to confide in different people depending on the particular anxiety, e.g. 75 to 80 per cent in all groups would turn to a parent over financial difficulty, but only one ex-institution and two comparison adolescents would do so if worried about not being liked by the opposite sex; instead, they would either keep it to themselves, deny it or share it with a peer. Table 15.2 shows a composite score based on pooled responses to all nine kinds of question.

The adopted and restored adolescents were at least as likely to turn to parents as comparisons were, who had always lived in their families, but were less likely to turn to their peers.

Disagreement over control and discipline. Both the adolescents and their mothers believed that disagreements over style of dress or hairstyle were very rare in all groups; disagreements over staying out late, doing homework, helping round the house and pocket money was significantly less frequent in adoptive families than in their comparisons, according to the parents ($p < 0.01$). However, comparison adolescents themselves reported fewer rows than ex-institution adolescents, especially in the case of the restored group ($p<0.02$). Significantly more of the restored adolescents felt their parents were too strict, compared with their own comparisons ($p=0.05$).

PEER RELATIONSHIPS

Overall ratings. Based on the mothers' answers to five open-ended exploratory questions, plus questions about specific difficulties, a rating was made of the adolescents' peer relationships over the last year. Another rating was made based on the interview with the 16-year-olds who also completed a 46-item self-report questionnaire on social difficulty (Lindsay & Lindsay, 1982). The questionnaire sent to teachers also asked them to rate how popular the adolescents were with peers, compared with classmates.

Specific difficulties with peer relations. Overall, the ex-institutional adolescents had poorer peer relationships than their comparisons. Six out of 30 of the former were definitely said to be 'friendly with anyone who's friendly towards him/her' as opposed to 'choosing his/her friends', another seven parents were uncertain if this was so. There were no differences regarding the number of contacts with same- or opposite-sex friends, or whether the 16-year-old currently had a boy/girlfriend (with parents and the adolescents more or less agreeing on this). Ex-institution adolescents reported themselves less often than their matched comparisons as belonging to a 'crowd' of young people who generally went around together ($p<0.02$), and this difference was significant between the adopted group and their matched comparisons ($p<0.01$).

Teachers rated the ex-institution group as more often quarrelsome, less often liked by other children and as bullying other children more than the comparison group.

Special friends. According to the mothers, the ex-institution adolescents were much less likely to have a definite special friend than their comparisons ($p<0.002$) (11/31 compared with 24/31), but there was no difference between adopted and restored. Interviews with the adolescents showed a similar, but not significant, pattern.

Table 15.2 shows that fewer ex-institution adolescents said they would confide in peers on a range of issues; significant differences (compared with comparisons) were found for feeling miserable or unhappy (13 per cent vs. 43 per cent, $p<0.01$), being worried something was wrong with them (3 per cent vs. 19 per cent, $p<0.05$), and being concerned about contraception (14 per cent vs. 39 per cent, $p<0.04$). These differences remained even allowing for the finding that the comparison groups were more likely to have a special friend.

Relationship between attachment and peer relations. Overall ratings of the adolescents' peer relationships were not related to attachment to the mother at 16.

However, the ex-institution children, who at eight were described as closely attached to their mothers, had better peer relationships at 16 than those who were not attached at eight. Also, 16-year-olds who were closely attached to the mother at 16 were less likely to be seen as 'friendly towards anyone who's friendly towards him/her' by peers.

Overfriendly behaviour. Some institutional children at four, had been indiscriminately friendly towards adults; although this had become much less apparent by eight, it was still present in some children. Of the 11 16-year-olds seen as 'over-friendly' at eight, two were still seen as exceptionally friendly, and keen to get attention from an adult (as were two not seen as 'over-friendly' at eight). However, their behaviour was socially acceptable, and did not worry the parent as it usually had done at eight.

Although there was no overall relationship between being 'over-friendly' at eight and friendliness towards strangers at 16, there was a clear tendency for 'over-friendliness' at eight to be associated with parents' rating at 16 that the adolescent was friendly with any peer who was friendly towards them, rather than choosing their friends.

RELATIONSHIPS WITH TEACHERS

As eight-year-olds, the ex-institution children were seen by their teachers as trying more than most to get attention from teachers and from a stranger entering the room. Teachers saw these 16-year-olds as still 'trying to get a lot of attention from adults', more often than the school comparison group ($p<0.05$), but not significantly more than their matched comparisons. The restored 16-year-olds were more often aggressive than the adopted ($p<0.03$) and their matched ($p<0.01$) and school comparisons ($p<0.04$).

D I S C U S S I O N

There is an interesting asymmetry about the findings; while the whole ex-institutional group differs from the comparison adolescents in their peer relationships and with adults outside the family, only the restored group differs from comparisons in their family relationships.

The family relationships of most of the adopted 16-year-olds seemed satisfactory, both for them and their parents, and differed little from non-adopted comparisons who had never been in care. In contrast, the restored group still suffered difficulties and poor family relationships much more often than either the adoptees or their own comparison group. They and their parents were less often attached to each other, and, where there were siblings, their mothers tended to prefer them to the restored child. Restored 16-year-olds showed less affection to their parents than did any other groups (as they had when eight), and their parents, equally, found it difficult showing affection to them; they seemed to identify less with their parents and wanted less involvement in family discussions. Restored adolescents also had more difficulty with siblings than did adoptees, probably because the former had entered their families to find younger siblings already there; the problems remained at mid-adolescence.

Although good relationships were not universal in the adoptive families, these families differed very little from their comparison group, but contrasted greatly with the restored group. Early institutional care had not necessarily led to a later inability to form a close attachment to parents and to become as much a part of the family as any other child. Where the parent wanted the child, and put a lot into the relationship, attachments were encouraged to develop and the adoption was successful; where this was lacking, the adoption situation broke down. This also seems to account for the difference between the adopted and restored groups, and there is no evidence that differences in the children before family placement account for the adopted/restored differences (Tizard, 1977). The adoptive parents differed as a group from the restored parents; they had very much wanted a child, put a lot of time and energy into building a relationship with the child, were often ready to accept very dependent behaviour initially, while the restored parents tended to have fewer resources, more other children and had been more ambivalent about the child living with them, and often expected great independence from their young child (Tizard & Hodges, 1978).

In contrast, the two ex-institution groups showed very similar relationships to peers and adults outside the family. Although the indiscriminate 'over-friendliness' of some eight-year-olds no longer seemed a problem at 16, the ex-institution group was still more often oriented towards adult attention and approval than comparison adolescents; they were also more likely to have difficulties in peer relations, less likely to have a special friend or to see peers as a source of emotional support, and more likely to be friendly to any peer, rather than choosing their friends. Taking all these five characteristics together, ex-institution adolescents are very much more likely to show four to five of them than comparison adolescents. This suggests an ex-institution 'syndrome' which does not seem to be merely a reflection of general behavioural and emotional disturbance. However, it only occurs in half the group, and the behaviour characteristics are *differences* from the comparison group, not necessarily *difficulties*.

The pattern of differences resembled the picture when the children were eight. So is the 'syndrome' permanent and, if so, how will the adolescents be able to make close emotional attachments and sustain love relationships and marriage as they enter adulthood? How can we explain the findings?

(*i*)   Could there be a class-related difference in the child-rearing practices of the

THE STUDY

families of the adopted and restored adolescents compared with their comparison groups? This seems unlikely, since the difference between the adopted and restored parents in their attitudes and child-rearing patterns was more striking than how the two ex-institution groups differed from their comparison groups. For example, adoptive parents spent more time playing with their children, involved in 'educative' pursuits with them, and involved them more in joint household activities than a middle-class comparison group, while the restored parents spent *less* time doing these things than a working-class comparison group.

(*ii*) Lambert and Streather (1980) suggest that the relatively poorer adjustment of adoptees at 11, compared to non-adopted children, may have been based on the adoptive parents' uncertainty about their own reactions, which had communicated itself to the children and made relationships harder for them. If this applies to the present study, how could the uncertainty have operated to produce the differences found?

(*iii*) Clarke and Clarke (1979) have suggested a transactional explanation. While the adoptive parents made great efforts to foster close attachments in their children, they did not put the same sort of effort into helping them get on with peers or teachers, so the difficulties remained in these areas. Furthermore, unlike the highly motivated parents, there was no reason for the ex-institution children's peers, or teachers and other non-family adults, to tolerate or make special efforts towards children who could not already relate reasonably well, or who were attention-seeking; such difficulties would thus be likely to be self-perpetuating.

(*iv*) Another possible transactional hypothesis puts more emphasis on the long-lasting impact of the early institutional experience on development, i.e. what the child has become able to elicit from the environment (rather than what it has to offer). The early insecurity of their relationships with the nurses (assessed at two by running to be picked up when staff entered the room and crying when they left) mirrored the rapid change of nurses who looked after them.

These findings seem to parallel those of La Fremiere and Sroufe (1985) and Waters *et al.* (1979), who view social relationships with peers as an aspect of development particularly vulnerable to difficulties in early attachment. Children who as infants had been seen as having secure attachments to their mother (assessed by Ainsworth's (1978) Strange Situation), managed peer relationships better at three-and-a-half and five than those who had not been securely attached. However, others (e.g. Kagan, 1984; Campos *et al.*, 1983) have proposed alternative interpretations of the link between strange situation behaviour and other behaviour, such as the effect of underlying temperamental variables and cultural influences on socialization.

(*v*) A related hypothesis, which also stresses the direct impact of early experience on the child's development, invokes the concept of developmental

delay. Anna Freud (1966) outlines a detailed 'developmental line', a sequence in which adequate development of the child's relation to parents forms a pre-condition for normal, later peer relationships and others outside the family. The ex-institution children had their first opportunity to develop these close, exclusive attachments at around an age when most children, in their families at birth, have already done so. They may continue to lag somewhat behind these children in the broadening of their social horizons beyond the family and the increase in the emotional importance of peers relative to parents. Some support for this comes in the findings that (a) close attachment to a parent at eight was related to good peer relationships at 16, while attachment at 16 was not so related; (b) close attachment at eight was more strongly linked than attachment at 16 to selectivity in choosing friends; (c) children described as 'solitary through choice' at eight, suggesting less peer involve-ment (and possibly more with parents) than is usual at that age, seemed to have the most satisfactory peer relationships at 16.

There is insufficient data to be able to choose between these theories; indeed, more than one may be needed to account for the findings.

In conclusion, the study suggests that children who are deprived of close and lasting attachments to adults in their first years of life can make such attachments later. But these do not arise automatically if the child is placed in a family, but depend on the adults concerned and how much they nurture such attachments. Yet despite these attachments, certain differences and difficulties in social relationships are found over 12 years after the child joined a family; these are not related to the kind of family, but seem to originate in the children's early institutional experience. Since they affect relationships with peers, as well as adults outside the family, they may have implications for the future adult relationships of these 16-year-olds. Whether these differences are now permanent, or further modifiable, we do not know.

EVALUATION

Theoretical issues

A major source of data regarding the whole continuity–discontinuity debate (especially in the context of adverse early experience) are studies of children who, in the natural course of events, have experienced major changes (for the better) in their environments. This allows us to determine the specific effects of early experiences, as distinct from those of later ones, which has proved difficult because of the strong associations between the two under ordinary circumstances (Rutter *et al.*, 1998). The Hodges and Tizard longitudinal study is a major study of this kind.

Even more dramatic are studies of children who are discovered after having suffered severe and prolonged privation, the most famous cases including Anna (Davis, 1940, 1947), Isabelle (Mason, 1942), the Czech Twins (Koluchova, 1972, 1976, 1991), Genie (Curtiss, 1977), Mary and Louise (Skuse, 1984), and Romanian orphanage children (Rutter *et al.*, 1998). The first four cases are quite well known (see Clarke & Clarke 1976; Gross, 2001). The case of Mary and Louise is not so well known.

In 1977, Mary, almost nine, was referred to the Children's Department at a large post-graduate teaching hospital. During the previous year, she had shown increasingly disruptive behaviour in the small children's hospital where she had lived the previous six years with her sister Louise (14-months older). Their early lives were spent in a remarkably deprived environment, with a mentally retarded and microcephalic mother, who may have also been schizophrenic. Upon their discovery by Social Services, they were described as '. . .very strange creatures indeed'.

Aged 3½ and 2⅓ respectively, they took no notice of anything or anyone, except to scamper up and sniff strangers, grunting and snuffling like animals. Both still sucked dummies, and no attempt had been made to toilet train them (so they were still in nappies). Neither had any constructive play, but picked up objects, handled, smelt and felt them. Mary had no speech at all, and made no hearing responses; she made just a few high-pitched sounds. It later came to light that they had been tied on leashes to the bed, partly as a way their mother could ensure the flat stayed spotless, and partly to ensure they would not fall off the balcony. If they became too noisy or active, they were put onto a mattress and covered with a blanket. They were subsequently taken into care.

Louise made rapid progress in the children's home. With the help of regular speech therapy, her previous unintelligible speech began to resemble natural language. She began half time at local primary school when 5 years 2 months, then full time. She was disruptive at first, easily frustrated and upset. But she was inquisitive, and soon settled in, growing to love school and soon making one special friend. At 5¾, her social skills were 9–15 months below her age level, but she was perceived as pleasant, cooperative and friendly. Over the next few years, her social and academic development proceeded in most respects far more rapidly than Mary's. Her cognitive functioning was at borderline level, and she was educated throughout at a normal school.

By contrast, Mary remained distant and aloof, lacking social responses, failing to initiate interactions with children and adults and having little to do with Louise. She barely responded to verbal/gestural commands; after a trial period she was judged unsuitable for speech therapy. Despite gradual progress in toilet training, she seemed unsuitable, at 4½, for normal school. A year after entering care, she made her first spontaneous attempt to communicate, and she started smiling socially. She showed excellent motor coordination, but often crawled instead of walking. At 5 years, 2 months, she joined the local ESN (M) school, where her main problem remained language: still no spontaneous speech at 5¾. At 7, she could no longer be tolerated by

a local youth group or Brownies, and she was transferred to an Autistic Unit at 7 years, 5 months. A year later she was speaking rather like a deaf child. She showed some remarkable abilities (e.g. at jigsaw puzzles), and concentrated well during IQ testing. She seemed to understand all spoken instructions, was amicable, affectionate and made good eye-contact. But following a visit from Uncle Rupert (her father?) and an occasional home overnight visit, she regressed: her concentration faded, she became enuretic, showed rage for no obvious reason and became very aggressive, even violent, to others, property and herself. She ran away, and was moved to a unit for mentally retarded children within a psychiatric hospital.

What the cases of Louise and the others mentioned above demonstrate is that theories which stress the overriding importance of early experience for later growth (i.e. *critical periods*) are inadequate (Clarke, 1972). Adverse early life experiences may, but not necessarily, have serious lasting effects on development in some circumstances (Clarke & Clarke, 2000; Rutter, 1981). Individuals show great resilience to such events and circumstances, and there is no straightforward connection between cause and effect in most cases.

Hodges and Tizards' results strongly support the view that Bowlby greatly oversimplified the effects of early (de)privation, by over-emphasizing the mother's role in what is a much wider-ranging and more complicated set of relationships and influences. A critical period for development (except arguably for language, but even here it seems doubtful: see **Applications and implications** below) seems *not* to exist, though arguably a *sensitive* one does. The fact that even the adopted children were not 'unscathed' supports the view that the first one-and-a-half to two years is still the optimum time for the development of attachments (but not the *only* time).

Rutter & Rutter (1992) believe that the present data strongly suggest that the lack of depth and selectivity in the adolescents' peer relationships was a consequence of their early institutional experiences, with the lack of selective attachments being the probable key feature. However, while there may seem to be some sort of sensitive period for the development of close friendships in adolescence, we need to know (amongst other things) whether the pattern of relationships in adolescence will persist into adult life (again see **Applications and implications**).

Further, there is an increasing tendency to see children as part of a social system in which they are in a mutually modifying relationship, with the mother no longer playing such a pivotal role (Skuse, 1984). 'Maternal deprivation' is too general and heterogeneous, and its effects too varied, to be of continuing value (Rutter, 1981).

Methodological issues

Hodges and Tizard refer to their study as a kind of natural experiment. This inevitably raises the question as to how it was decided which children would be adopted and which restored to their biological parents. If it was because of certain characteristics of the children themselves (e.g. those who were adopted were seen as more socially responsive), wouldn't this spoil the logic of the 'experiment'? Hodges and Tizard in fact deny this (see **Discussion**).

One of the major problems associated with longitudinal studies is discussed in the study, namely *attrition*. Of the 51 ex-institution children studied at age eight, nine were unavailable: two families of restored adolescents refused contact, as did four adoptive families (all these adolescents were still with their families). The remaining three consisted of one girl who had been in a foster family at eight, but disappeared in between being traced and interviewed, and another two who had left care after eight (one to live with parents abroad and one to live with adoptive parents who did not reply to the original letter). How representative of the original institution sample was the sample of 16-year-olds? How much additional attrition could the researchers afford over, say, a further 20- to 30-year period? (Would this be within the researchers' lifetime? We seem to have discovered another problem with longitudinal studies!)

The data were collected mainly through interviews and questionnaires, and so can only be as reliable and/or valid as those methods. Was there any independent way of checking the accuracy of the answers given? How objective can we be about our own children and parents and, indeed, ourselves? How objective could the teachers be, given that they knew which pupils were ex-institution children?

Subsequent research

As important as case studies such as those of Anna, Isabelle, and the Czech twins may be, the numbers involved are, of course, very small. The opportunity to study the psychological effects of early global deprivation in a systematic way arose from the adoption into English families (following the fall of the Ceaucescu regime) of a large number of children reared in extremely poor conditions in Romanian institutions. A high proportion of such children show severe developmental retardation, growth failure and widespread infections.

Rutter *et al.* (1998) reported their findings from a study of 111 Romanian children who entered the UK before the age of two, and 52 control group children (within-UK adoptees, who had not suffered early privation). Both groups of adoptive parents were educationally and occupationally above general population norms, and were not significantly different from each other. Both groups of children were assessed at age four using the Denver Scales (designed to be used by parents to focus on readily observable attainments), the McCarthy Scales (a general cognitive index which correlates highly with both Binet and Wechsler IQs: see Chapters 23 and 24), and detailed measures of socioemotional and behavioural functioning.

Some of the residential institutions in which the Romanian children had been raised

were officially called 'hospitals', others 'orphanages', but in practice there were few differences between them. Conditions varied from poor to appalling. The children were mainly confined to their cots, there were few, if any, toys or playthings, very little talk from caregivers, no personalized caregiving, gruel was fed by bottles, often left propped up, and the general physical environments, while variable, were sometimes very harsh. As a whole, these children were more severely deprived, physically and psychologically, than almost any other sizeable group of children previously studied. The conditions were, in all respects, incomparably worse than those in the UK or almost any other industrialized country.

At the time of entry to the UK, most of the Romanian children were severely malnourished and suffered from chronic and recurrent respiratory and other infections. In addition:

> . . . considered as a whole, the evidence is entirely consistent in indicating that the Romanian adoptees as a group showed major developmental retardation at the time of entry to the UK, that over half were functioning in the retarded range . . . (Rutter *et al.*, 1998)

By age four, the physical catch-up was very substantial, although they remained (as a group) slightly lighter, shorter and smaller in head circumference than the control group. Their *developmental catch-up* was just as impressive (although those who were adopted *before* six months had an advantage, their catch-up being almost complete by age four). In fact, Rutter *et al.* (1998) claim that, despite their profoundly unpromising start in life (or in view of it?), the degree of cognitive catch-up was 'spectacular':

> . . . This dramatic catch-up following a major change in the circumstances of rearing provides clear evidence that the initial developmental retardation was caused by the profoundly depriving circumstances of their early institutional rearing.

A further follow-up at age six is in progress.

Other Romanian orphans were adopted by Canadian families between the ages of eight months and five-and-a-half years (Chisolm *et al.*, 1995). It seems that some negative impact on the children's relationship with adoptive parents can be attributed to their institutional experiences. For example, their behaviour was often described as *ambivalent* (they simultaneously wanted contact and resisted it). Also, they weren't easily comforted when distressed. Follow-up is needed to see if life in a loving family can eventually overcome this impairment (see **Applications and implications** below). However, based upon their intellectual recovery, there are good reasons for being optimistic (Schaffer, 1998).

Applications and implications

What about long-term personality and social adjustment of those who experience extreme early deprivation? While there is little evidence so far on the adult status of such cases, what there is is encouraging. Hodges and Tizard's research indicates that children who fail to enjoy close and lasting relationships with adults in the first years of life *can* make such attachments later on. The ex-institution children have now been followed up into adulthood (average age 31 years) through postal questionnaires (Hodges *et al.*, in preparation; Jewett, 1998) and interviews using the adult attachment interview (AAI: Main *et al.*, 1985) with a sub-sample of the ex-institution group (Williams, 1999).

There were few significant differences between the ex-institution group and the comparison group, including evidence of psychiatric disorder. However, the former consistently reported difficulties in relationships with friends, partners and children, and significantly greater difficulties in relationships with their families of upbringing. They also reported a tendency to be over-aggressive in their interpersonal relationships, and to be independent and self-reliant. But they also reported *more rewarding* intimate friendships, with higher levels of companionship, and higher self-esteem than the comparison group (these differences *weren't* statistically significant). While acknowledging the small sample size (22 ex-institution, 23 comparison), Hodges (personal communication, 2000) states that:

> . . . the evidence seems to support both the view that the effects of earlier adversity fade given the right later circumstances, and the view that there are some enduring effects producing continuities in personal characteristics.

Koluchova (1976) reported that at 14 (seven years after their discovery), the Czech twins had no psychopathological symptoms or eccentricities. They had gone on to technical school, training as typewriter mechanics, but later went on to further education, specializing in electronics. They both had very good relationships with their adoptive mothers (they were adopted by two women), their adoptive sisters, and the women's relatives. Both were drafted for national service, and later married and had children. At the age of 29, there were described as entirely stable, without abnormalities, and enjoying warm relationships (Koluchova, 1991).

Also relevant here is Quinton & Rutter's (1988) study of women who spent most of their childhood in group (residential) homes. They experienced difficulties in close friendships, sexual/love relationships and parenting, especially if they were institutionalized in infancy and stayed until at least age 16. The considerable turnover of staff in the children's homes at that time (like those in which the present sample of 16-year-olds grew up) makes it likely that many of these women failed to develop normal attachments. According to Rutter & Rutter (1992), the study suggests that '. . . a lack of early selective attachments may predispose to difficulties in all kinds of very close relationships in adult life'. However, while *as a group* the institutionalized women

were less sensitive, supportive and warm towards their children (compared with non-institutionalized controls), there was also considerable variability *within* the instituiton group, and by no means all of them made poor parents. One way of explaining this variability is in terms of *developmental pathways*. For example, some of the women had much more positive school experiences than others, making them three times more likely as adolescents or young adults to make proper plans and choices for their career and marriage partner. As a result, they were 12 times more likely to marry for positive reasons, which in turn increased by five times the chances of their marital relationship being supportive. This itself increased their chance of good social functioning (including being a caring parent) by a factor of three (Rutter, 1989).

This represents a route for escaping early adversity: similar adverse experiences in childhood can give rise to multiple outcomes (Schaffer, 1996b). In other words, the 'same' early experience does not inevitably mean the same consequences later in life. This variation in outcome is partly explained by the positive effects of later experiences (as we have just seen), but also by the specific deprivations and distortions of early experience, *and* the vulnerability of different individuals to such adversity (Skuse, 1984).

Most human characteristics (with the possible exception of language) are strongly 'canalized' (Scarr-Salapatek, 1976), and thus virtually resistant to obliteration by even the most dire early environments (Skuse, 1984). Rutter *et al.*'s (1998) study of the adopted Romanian orphans also supports Skuse's view that, in the absence of genetic or congenital abnormalities or a history of gross malnourishment, victims of such deprivation have an excellent prognosis.

Exercises

1. Briefly describe **three** advantages and **three** disadvantages of the longitudinal, compared with the cross-sectional, approach (*not* including the attrition of the sample in longitudinal studies).

2. Briefly describe **two** ways in which a natural experiment differs from a laboratory experiment.

3. Why was it thought necessary to form a new, matched comparison group for the study of the ex-institution adolescents, and who were they?

4. Why was it necessary to have a comparison group at all?

5. Reference is made to the *Strange Situation*.

   (*i*) Who designed it?
   (*ii*) What is it used for?
   (*iii*) What happens?

16

Conditioned emotional reactions

John B. Watson and Rosalie Rayner (1920)

Journal of Experimental Psychology, 3 (1), 1–14

BACKGROUND AND CONTEXT

J.B. Watson was the founder of *Behaviourism*, the school of thought which claims that behaviour – the overt, observable and measurable aspects of human activity – is the only appropriate subject matter for the scientific discipline of psychology. Watson was reacting against the attempts of the early psychologists, such as Wundt, to study the conscious human mind through *introspection* (inspection of one's own mind) as a way of trying to establish general laws of human thought. Watson saw this as a futile pursuit, since only the individual has access to his/her mind. No one else can inspect it in order to check the accuracy of what the introspections reveal: the mind is 'private', while behaviour is 'public' (accessible to other observers), and this is a basic requirement of all science.

If behaviour is a valid subject matter for psychology, we have to have some way of defining it and analysing it, and Watson found the key in the concept of the *conditioned reflex* (or conditioned response). All behaviour can be broken down into a number of such conditioned responses: however complex it may appear, it is composed of these simple units, all of which, in turn, are based on the three inborn human emotions, namely, rage, fear and love (sex).

The conditioned reflex had been discovered in the first few years of the twentieth century by Pavlov, the Russian physiologist, in his study of the digestive system of dogs. Through associating a stimulus (UCS) which naturally produces a particular response (UCR) with a neutral stimulus which does not (CS), the latter eventually comes to produce the response on its own: when it does, it is referred to as a conditioned response (CR). Watson was the first psychologist to apply this process of classical (or respondent/Pavlovian) conditioning to human behaviour, with 11-month-old Albert B. (better known as 'Little Albert') destined to become one of the most famous children in the whole of the psychological literature (along with Little Hans: see Chapter 19). The study was to become part of social science folklore, and clinched Watson's fame as the father of behaviourism (Simpson, 2000).

AIM AND NATURE OF THE STUDY

The aim of the study is to provide an empirical demonstration of the claim that various kinds of emotional response can be conditioned. The study is a laboratory experiment involving a single participant, Albert B. In some situations, considerations of economy (both of time and effort) lead to the use of just one participant in an experiment (Robson, 1973) and is called the 'single-participant (or subject) design'. This has a long history in psychology, perhaps the most famous example being the pioneering work of Ebbinghaus in the study of memory in the 1880s, the psychologist acting as his own (single) participant. Albert was certainly a desirable participant, because his mother was a wet-nurse in the hospital (Harriet Lane Home for Invalid Children) where Watson and Rayner happened to be working. Far from being an invalid, he was strong, healthy and not easily upset, and this made him especially suitable.

The study also represents a *diary study*, the detailed record of the behaviour of one child over a period of approximately 1½ months (though not on each day during that period). But unlike the diary studies of Darwin and, to some extent, Piaget, it was very specific behaviour which was being observed: (his fear response – or otherwise – to particular animals and objects).

THE STUDY

In recent literature there have been various speculations regarding the possibility of conditioning various types of emotional response, but direct experimental evidence has been lacking. If the theory advanced by Watson and Morgan (1917) is true, i.e., that in infancy the original emotional reaction patterns are few, consisting of fear, rage and love, then there must be some simple method by which the range of stimuli which can elicit these emotions and their compounds is greatly increased. Otherwise, complexity in adult response could not be accounted for. Watson and Morgan proposed that this range was increased by means of conditioned reflex factors, and that the early home life of the child provides a laboratory situation for establishing conditioned emotional responses (CERs). The present authors have recently put the whole matter to an experimental test.

Experimental work so far has been done on only one child, Albert B, reared almost from birth in a hospital environment: his mother was a wet nurse in the Harriet Lane Home for Invalid Children. His life was normal: he was healthy from birth and one of the best developed youngsters ever brought to the hospital, weighing 21 pounds at nine months of age. He was, on the whole, stolid and unemotional; his stability was one of the major reasons for using him as a subject. We felt that we could do him relatively little harm by carrying out such experiments as described below.

At approximately nine months of age, we ran him through the emotional tests that have become part of our routine for determining whether fear reactions can be elicited by other stimuli than sharp noises and the sudden removal of support. Briefly, the infant was confronted suddenly, and for the first time, successively with a white rat, a rabbit, a dog, a monkey, masks with and without hair, cotton wool, burning newspapers, etc. Manipulation was the most usual reaction produced. *At no time did this infant ever show fear in any situation.* These experimental records were confirmed by the casual observations of his mother and hospital attendants; no one had ever seen him in a state of fear and rage, and he practically never cried.

Up to approximately nine months, we had not tested him with loud sounds. When he was eight months, 26 days old, a sound was made by striking a hammer upon a suspended steel bar four feet in length and ¾ inch in diameter. The laboratory notes are as follows:

> One of the two experimenters caused the child to turn its head and fixate her moving hand; the other, stationed back of the child, struck the steel bar a sharp blow. The child started violently, his breathing was checked and the arms were raised in a characteristic manner. On the second stimulation the same thing occurred, and in addition the lips began to pucker and tremble. On the third stimulation the child broke into a sudden crying fit. This is the first time an emotional situation in the laboratory has produced any fear or even crying in Albert.

We had expected exactly these results on account of our work with other infants brought up under similar conditions. However, dropping and jerking the blanket on which Albert was lying was done exhaustively without producing the fear response. This loss of support does effectively produce fear in younger infants but at what age such stimuli lose their potency is not known. Nor is it known whether less placid children ever lose their fear of them; it probably depends on the training the child gets and is quite common in adults.

The sound stimulus, therefore, at nine months, gives us the means of testing several important factors: (*i*) Can we condition fear of an animal, e.g. a white rat, by visually presenting it and simultaneously striking a steel bar? (*ii*) If such a CER can be established, will there be a transfer to other animals or other objects? (*iii*) What is the effect of time on such conditioned emotional responses? (*iv*) If, after a reasonable period, such CER's have not died out, what laboratory methods can be devised for their removal?

1   At first there was considerable hesitation on our part in making the attempt to set up fear responses experimentally. A certain responsibility attaches to such procedure. We decided finally to go ahead, comforting ourselves by the reflection that such responsibilities would arise anyway as soon as the child left the sheltered environment of the nursery for the rough and tumble of the home. We did not begin this work until Albert was 11 months, three days old. As before, we put him through all the regular emotional tests. *Not the slightest sign of a fear response was obtained in any situation.* The steps taken to condition emotional responses are shown in our laboratory notes.

11 MONTHS, THREE DAYS

(*i*)   White rat suddenly taken from the basket and presented to Albert. He began to reach for rat with left hand. Just as his hand touched the animal the bar was struck immediately behind his head. He jumped violently and fell forward, burying his face in the mattress. But he did not cry.

(*ii*)   Just as the right hand touched the rat, the bar was struck again. Again Albert jumped violently, fell forward and began to whimper. In order not to disturb him too seriously, no further tests were given for one week.

11 MONTHS, TEN DAYS

(*i*)   Rat presented suddenly without sound. There was steady fixation but no tendency at first to reach for it. It was then placed nearer, whereupon Albert began to reach, tentatively, with right hand. When the rat nosed his left hand, he immediately withdrew it. He started to reach for the rat's head with forefinger of left hand, but withdrew it suddenly before contact. Thus the two-joint stimulations given the previous week were not without effect. He was tested with his blocks immediately afterwards to see if they shared in the process of conditioning. He began immediately to pick them up, dropping them, pounding them, etc. In the rest of the tests the blocks were given often to quieten him and to test his general emotional state. They were always removed from sight when the process of conditioning was under way.

(*ii*)   Joint stimulation with rat and sound. Started, then fell over immediately to right side. No crying.

(*iii*)   Joint stimulation. Fell to right side and rested on hands, with head turned away from rat. No crying.

(*iv*)   Joint stimulation. Same reaction.

(*v*)   Rat suddenly presented alone. Puckered face, whimpered and withdrew body sharply to the left.

(*vi*)   Joint stimulation. Fell over immediately to right side and began to whimper.

(*vii*)   Joint stimulation. Started violently and cried, but did not fall over.

(*viii*) Rat alone. *The instant the rat was shown, the baby began to cry. Almost instantly he turned sharply to the left, fell over on left side, raised himself on all fours and began to crawl away so rapidly that he was caught with difficulty before reaching the edge of the table.*

This was as convincing a case of a completely conditioned fear response as could have been theoretically pictured. In all, seven joint stimulations were given to produce the complete reaction. If the sound had been of greater intensity, or of a more complex clang character, the number of joint stimulations might have been materially reduced.

2   When a CER has been established for one object, is there a transfer? Five days later, Albert was again brought back into the laboratory and tested as follows:

11 MONTHS, 15 DAYS

(*i*)   Tested first with blocks. He reached steadily for them, playing with them as usual. This shows that there has been no general transfer to the room, table, blocks, etc.

(*ii*)   Rat alone. Whimpered immediately, withdrew right hand, turned head and trunk away.

(*iii*) Blocks again offered. Played readily with them, smiling and gurgling.

(*iv*)   Rat alone. Leaned over to left side as far away from rat as possible, then fell over, getting up on all fours and scurrying away as rapidly as possible.

(*v*)   Blocks again offered. Reached immediately for them, smiling and laughing as before.

This shows that the CER had carried over completely for the five days in which no tests were given. The question of transfer was next taken up.

(*vi*)   Rabbit alone. The rabbit was suddenly placed on the mattress in front of him. The negative reaction was pronounced. He leaned as far away from it as possible, whimpered, then burst into tears. When it was placed in contact with him he buried his face in the mattress, then got up on all fours and crawled away, crying as he went. This was a most convincing test.

(*vii*) The blocks were next given to him, after an interval. He played with them as before. Four people observed that he played far more energetically with them than ever before.

(*viii*) Dog alone. The dog did not produce as violent a reaction as the rabbit. The moment fixation occurred, Albert shrank back and, as it approached, he tried to get on all fours, but did not cry at first. As soon as the dog passed out of his range of vision he became quiet. The dog was then made to approach Albert's head (who was lying down); he straightened up immediately, fell over to the opposite side and turned his head away. He then began to cry.

(*ix*)   The blocks were again presented and he began to play with them immediately.

(*x*)   Fur coat (seal). Withdrew immediately to left side and began to fret. Coat put close to him on the left side, he turned immediately, began to cry and tried to crawl away on all fours.

(*xi*)   Cotton wool. Presented in paper package. At the end, the cotton wool was not covered by the paper. Placed first on his feet. He kicked it away, but did not touch it with his hands. When his hand was placed on it he

THE STUDY

immediately withdrew it but did not show the shock produced by the animals or fur coat. He then began to play with the paper, avoiding contact with the wool itself. He eventually began to lose some of his negativism.

(*xii*) Just in play, Watson put his head down to see if Albert would play with his hair. Albert was completely negative. Two other observers did the same thing but he began to play immediately with their hair. A Santa Claus mask was then presented to Albert, and again he was markedly negative.

11 MONTHS, 20 DAYS

(*i*) Blocks alone. Played with them as usual.

(*ii*) Rat alone. Withdrawal of whole body, bending over to left side, no crying. Fixation and following with eyes. The response much less marked than on first presentation the previous week. It was decided to freshen up the reaction by another joint stimulation.

(*iii*) Just as the rat was placed on Albert's hand, the rod was struck. Violent reaction.

(*iv*) Rat alone. Fell over at once to left side. Reaction practically as strong as on former occasion but no crying.

(*v*) Rat alone. Fell over to left side, got up on all fours and started to crawl away. No crying, but as he moved away, he began to gurgle and coo, even while trying to avoid rat.

(*vi*) Rabbit alone. Leaned over to left side as far as possible. Did not fall over. Began to whimper but reaction not as violent as on previous occasions.

(*vii*) Blocks again offered. Albert reached for them immediately and began to play.

So far, all the tests had been performed on a table with a mattress in a small, well-lit dark room. What would happen if the situation were markedly changed? Before testing this, we freshened up the reaction to both the rabbit and the dog by joint stimulation; this was the first time such joint stimulation had taken place.

(*viii*) The rabbit at first was given alone. The reaction was exactly as in (*vi*) above. When the rabbit was left on Albert's knees for a long time, he began tentatively to reach out and manipulate its fur with forefingers. While doing this, the steel rod was struck, causing a violent reaction.

(*ix*) Rabbit alone. Reaction the same as on trial (*vi*) above.

(*x*) Rabbit alone. Started immediately to whimper, holding hands far up, but no crying. Conflicting tendency to manipulate very evident.

(*xi*) Dog alone. Began to whimper, shaking head from side to side, holding hands as far away from the dog as possible.

(*xii*) Dog and sound. A violent, negative reaction caused. Began to whimper, turned to one side, fell over and started to get up on all fours.

(*xiii*) Blocks. Played with them immediately and readily.

Immediately after the above experiment, Albert was taken into the large, well-lit lecture room belonging to the laboratory. He was placed on a table in the centre of the room immediately under the skylight. Four people were present. The situation was thus very different from the small dark room.

(*i*) Rat alone. No sudden fear reaction at first. But the hands were held up and away, and no positive manipulatory reactions appeared.

(*ii*) Rabbit alone. Fear reaction slight. Turned to left and kept face away, but reaction never pronounced.

(*iii*) Dog alone. Turned away, but did not fall over. Cried. Moved hands as far away as possible, and whimpered as long as the dog present.

(*iv*) Rat alone. Slight negative reaction.

(*v*) Rat and sound. Albert jumped violently, but did not cry.

(*vi*) Rat alone. No negative reaction at first, but when rat placed nearer, he began to draw back his body, raising hands, whimpering, etc.

(*vii*) Blocks. Played with them immediately.

(*viii*) Rat alone. Pronounced withdrawal of body and whimpering.

(*ix*) Blocks. Played with them as before.

(*x*) Rabbit alone. Pronounced reaction. Whimpered, fell over backwards and had to be caught.

(*xi*) Dog alone. At first no pronounced reaction; hands held high over head, breathing checked, but no crying. Just at this moment, the previously quiet dog barked loudly, three times, just six inches away from Albert's face. He immediately fell over and started wailing, stopping only when the dog was removed.

The above results suggest that emotional transfers do take place, and that the number of transfers from an experimentally produced CER may be very large.

3   We have already shown that the CER will continue for a week and, because of Albert's imminent departure from the hospital, it was impossible to make the interval longer than one month. Accordingly, no further experimentation was undertaken for 31 days after the above test. During the month, however, Albert was brought weekly to the laboratory for tests on right–left handedness, imitation and general development.

ONE YEAR, 21 DAYS

(*i*) Santa Claus mask. Withdrawal, gurgling, then slapped at it without touching. When his hand was forced to touch it, he whimpered and cried. This happened on two further occasions. He finally cried at the mere sight of the mask.

THE STUDY

(*ii*) Fur coat. Wrinkled his nose and withdrew both hands, drew back whole body and began to whimper as coat brought nearer. Reached tentatively with left hand, but drew back before making contact. He accidentally touched it while moving to one side and immediately began to cry, nodding his head in a very peculiar way (not seen before). Withdrew both hands as far as possible from the coat. When laid on his lap, he continued nodding and whimpering, withdrawing his body as far as he could, pushing it with his feet, but never touching it with his hands.

(*iii*) Fur coat. Removed from sight and presented again after a minute. He immediately began to fret, withdrawing body and nodding as before.

(*iv*) Blocks: began to play with them as usual.

(*v*) The rat. He allowed it to crawl towards him without withdrawing. He sat very still and fixated it intently. Rat touched his hand, Albert withdrew it immediately, leaned back as far as possible, but did not cry. When rat placed on his arm, he withdrew body and began to fret, nodding head. Rat then allowed to crawl against his chest. He first began to fret, then covered his eyes with both hands.

(*vi*) Blocks. Reaction normal.

(*vii*) Rabbit. Placed directly in front of him. Albert showed no avoidance at first. After a few seconds he puckered up his face, began to nod and then to push rabbit away with feet, withdrawing body at same time. As it came nearer he began pulling his feet away, nodding and wailing 'da da'. After about a minute, he reached out tentatively and touched rabbit's ear with right hand, finally manipulating it. Again he began to fret and withdrew hands. Reached out tentatively with left hand and touched it, shuddered and withdrew whole body. Left hand placed on rabbit. Albert immediately withdrew hand and began to suck thumb. Rabbit put in his lap. He began to cry, covering face with both hands.

(*viii*) Dog. It was very active. Albert fixated it intently for a few seconds, sitting very still. He began to cry but did not fall over backwards as on last contact with dog. When dog pushed closer, he first sat motionless, then began to cry, covering face with both hands.

These experiments would seem to show conclusively that directly conditioned emotional responses, as well as those conditioned by transfer, persist, although with a certain loss of intensity, for over one month. Our view is that they persist and modify personality throughout life. Albert was extremely phlegmatic. Had he been emotionally unstable, both kinds of CERs would probably have persisted through the month unchanged in form.

4   Unfortunately, Albert was taken from the hospital the day the above tests were made. Hence the opportunity of developing an experimental technique for removing the CERs was denied us. We believe that these responses in the home environment are likely to persist indefinitely, unless an accidental method for

removing them is hit upon. Had the opportunity existed, we should have tried several methods: (*i*) constantly confronting the child with those stimuli which produced the responses, in the hope that habituation would occur corresponding to 'fatigue' of reflex when differential reactions are to be set up; (*ii*) trying to 'recondition' by showing objects producing fear responses (visual) while simultaneously stimulating the erogenous zones (tactual), first the lips, then the nipples, and, as a last resort, the sex organs; (*iii*) trying to 'recondition' by feeding him candy or other food just as the animal is shown; (*iv*) building up 'constructive' activities around the object by imitation and putting the hand through the motions of manipulation.

INCIDENTAL OBSERVATIONS

Whenever Albert was emotionally upset, he would continually thrust his thumb into his mouth which instantly made him impervious to the stimuli producing fear. This method of blocking noxious and emotional stimuli (fear and rage) through erogenous stimulation seems to persist from birth onwards, throughout adolescent and adult life. Freud's conception of the stimulation of erogenous zones as being the expression of an original 'pleasure' seeking principle may be turned about and possibly better described as a compensatory (and often conditioned) device for the blockage of noxious and fear and rage producing stimuli.

While in general our results do not conflict with Freudian concepts, we would dispute the Freudian belief that sex (or in our terms, love) is the principal emotion in which CERs arise, which later limit and distort personality. We see fear as much a primal factor as love in influencing personality; it does not gather its potency from love, but belongs to the original and inherited nature of man.

Freudians, 20 years from now, if they come to analyse Albert at that age, will probably tease from him the recital of a dream which will be interpreted as showing that Albert, at three years old, tried to play with his mother's pubic hair and was scolded violently for it. Albert may be fully convinced of the truth of this interpretation of his fear if the analyst has the authority and personality to put it over convincingly.

It is probable that many of the phobias in psychopathology are true CERs either of the direct or transferred type. These may persist only in people who are constitutionally inferior. Emotional disturbance in adults cannot be traced back to sex alone. They must be retraced along at least three parallel lines; to conditioned and transferred responses set up in infancy and early youth in all three of the fundamental human emotions.

EVALUATION

Theoretical issues

Watson believed that the child's unconditioned responses (fear, rage and love) to simple stimuli are only the starting points in 'building up those complicated habit patterns we later call our emotions' (Watson, 1931). For example, the emotion of jealousy is not innate or inevitable, but rather is:

> . . . a bit of behaviour whose stimulus is a (conditioned) love stimulus, the response to which is rage', (e.g. stiffening of whole body, reddening of face, pronounced breathing, verbal recrimination and possibly shouting).

This is a good illustration of the *reductionist* nature of Watson's behaviourism (and of behaviourism in general): complex human emotions are broken down into (reduced to) simple CERs, a whole broken down into its constituent parts (see Gross, 2001). Along with this reductionist approach to the explanation of emotional development, Watson was proposing a *quantitative* view of development: as the child grows up, its behaviour becomes more complex, but it is basically the same kind of behaviour as it was earlier (i.e. a series of CERs which become added and re-combined). The same basic principles are involved at all ages (those of classical conditioning). By contrast, a *qualitative* view (such as that of Freud or Piaget) sees development as passing through a series of distinct stages, with different *kinds* of behaviour involved at each stage.

The case of Little Albert seems to support the general belief that (even) babies are not indifferent to their experiences, and that nasty experiences, especially, may have peculiar after-effects (Walker, 1984). Here, Watson and Freud seem to be in agreement. However,

> In my view, it would be foolish to claim that experiences as extreme as those suffered by Albert are not likely to have some carry-over effects in infants, but even more ridiculous to assume that conditioning is a sufficient explanation for all adult emotions. (Walker, 1984)

Methodological issues

Little Albert is often cited as an example of 'classic research', being reported in every textbook of psychology from generation to generation. But ironically (according to Cornwell & Hobbs, 1976), its 'classic' reputation has resulted in the details of the experiment being obscured, making psychologists less (rather than more) cautious, producing a false impression of familiarity with the details and a 'painting out the warts'.

In *The Strange Saga of Little Albert*, Cornwell and Hobbs argue that the experiment is a classic example of how a piece of research can become *misreported/misrepresented* until it assumes 'mythical' proportions. In 1917, Watson was awarded a grant to do research into the development of reflexes and instincts in infants. As we have seen, he believed that there is a limited number of inborn emotional reactions which are the starting point for building (through the process of conditioning) the complex emotions of adulthood. He began his experiments with Little Albert in 1919, attempting to show how conditioned emotional responses (CERs) come about and how they can be removed, with the results being published in 1920.

Watson and Rayner stressed the limited nature of their evidence. They may have planned to study other children, but were unable to continue their research at the John Hopkins University (Baltimore). In 1920, in a sensationally publicized case, Watson was divorced by his wife, and immediately married Rosalie Rayner. He was forced to resign from his job.

In 1921, Watson and Rosalie Rayner Watson published a second account of Little Albert (in *Scientific Monthly*). In it, they stated that Albert *did* show fear in response to a loss of support (being held and then let go), the opposite of the original paper. Also Watson subsequently referred to this 1921 paper as the original, although the 1920 paper is the one more often cited. A third account was given in some lectures by Watson which were eventually incorporated into his book *Behaviourism* (1924). It is also recounted in other books and articles. Each of these accounts is, at least once, referred to as 'the original'.

In a survey of 76 'general psychology' books at Glasgow University, Cornwell and Hobbs found at least one distortion in 60% of the 30 different reports of the experiment. They ask if all the mistakes are just the result of carelessness. There is no doubt that several accounts seemed to put the experiment in a more favourable light, both methodologically and ethically. For example:

(*i*)   the implication is made that Albert was one of a series of infants studied, that is, a larger sample;

(*ii*) on the assumption that a child will instinctively show fear of rats, the rat is often reported as a 'rabbit', making Albert's initial *lack* of fear seem more plausible, and his conditioned fear more striking;

(*iii*) many accounts claim that the conditioned fear was removed before he left the hospital: indeed, Watson and Rayner knew a month in advance that he would be leaving. Eysenck, for example, gives details of a fictitious extinction involving pieces of chocolate!

This last 'myth' raises two major issues: (a) did Watson and Rayner in fact intend to remove the CER (and even if they did, does this let them off the hook ethically)? and (b) how might they have done it? These are discussed in the **Applications and implications** below.

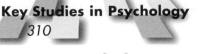

Subsequent research

Not long after the Little Albert experiment, Watson supervised the treatment of Little Peter, a two-year-old living in a charitable institution, who had an extreme fear of rabbits, rats, fur coats, feathers, cotton wool etc. He showed no fear of wooden blocks and similar toys. This was carried out by Mary Cover Jones (1924), who describes the case of Peter as a sequel to that of Little Albert ('... Albert grown a bit older ...'). While the case of Little Albert showed how a fear could be *produced* experimentally under laboratory conditions, Jones used the method of direct *unconditioning* in an attempt to *remove* Little Peter's naturally occurring phobias.

In unconditioning, the feared object is associated with something pleasurable, and exposure to it is gradually increased. The rabbit was put in a wire cage in front of Peter while he ate his lunch in his high chair. At first, the caged rabbit anywhere in the room caused a fear response, but the cage was gradually moved nearer and Peter tolerated this (steps 1–4). At step 6, he could tolerate the rabbit being out of its cage, and by step 13 he could hold it on his lap. He then stayed alone in the room with the rabbit (14), allowed it in the play pen with him (15), fondled it affectionately (16), and, finally, let the rabbit nibble his fingers (17). This is generally regarded as the first reported use of (what is now known as) *systematic desensitization* (the term first used by Wolpe in 1958), a commonly used method for the removal of phobias.

Applications and implications

As we noted above, two unanswered questions concern (a) Watson and Rayner's intention to remove Little Albert's CER; and (b) the method(s) they might have used to do so.

(a)   At the beginning of their paper, they state 'a certain responsibility attaches to such a procedure' (i.e. inducing the CER experimentally), and they were very hesitant about doing so. They eventually decided to go ahead, since '... .such responsibilities would arise anyway as soon as the child left the sheltered environment of the nursery for the rough and tumble of the home'. When they say 'responsibility' they seem to mean 'risk', thus giving a false impression of having grappled long and hard with the ethical issues involved. But what sort of justification is it to say Albert would have acquired the CERs anyway? Is he likely to have encountered rats at all, and is he likely to have encountered any of the other stimuli while his ears were assaulted by the sound of a full-grown man striking a hammer upon a large steel bar immediately behind his head?

The fact that he was stolid and unemotional, and the belief that the experiment could do him relatively little harm, cannot be used in their defence either: some stimulus was needed which would frighten him, otherwise the experiment could not proceed, and so Watson and Rayner were knowingly deciding to cause him distress. The ethics of Watson and Rayner's techniques seemed to draw little open criticism at the time – either from the university administration, or from other psychologists. According to Hulse (cited in Simpson, 2000), 'Times were just different, people were trusted to behave themselves . . . It's only been in the last 20 to 30 years that issues of ethics in science have become profoundly part of the consciousness of scientists'.

(b) They state that they would have tried several methods in an attempt to remove the CER ('had the opportunity existed'):

(*i*) constantly confronting Albert with the feared object sounds like *flooding*, a form of forced reality testing from which there is no escape;

(*ii*) and (*iii*) sound like *systematic desensitization*, whereby the fear is gradually extinguished by exposing the patient to increasingly frightening situations in combination with a pleasurable stimulus (see Little Peter above);

(*iv*) sounds like *modelling* (e.g. Bandura), whereby the patient observes another person (the model) encountering the feared object, but without showing any fear (see Chapter 14).

Jones (1924) states that they *did* intend to uncondition Little Albert's fear. They also wished to discover if removing the fear of one animal/object (such as the rat) would 'spread without further training to other stimuli'. Jones found that this did, indeed, happen with Little Peter.

According to Eysenck & Rachman (1965), Wolpe & Rachman (1960) and other behaviourist psychologists and therapists, the case of Little Albert exemplifies how *all* phobias (abnormal fears) are acquired (i.e. through classical conditioning). Wolpe and Rachman maintain that:

> Any neutral stimulus, simple or complex, that happens to make an impact on an individual at about the time a fear reaction is evoked, acquires the ability to evoke fear subsequently . . . there will be generalization of fear reactions to stimuli resembling the conditioned sttimulus.

While there is evidence showing that *some* phobias are acquired in this way, to claim that all phobias are acquired this way – and *only* in this way – is extreme and indefensible. For example, some phobias are easier to induce experimentally (in people who do not already have them), and it is common knowledge that certain 'naturally occurring' (not deliberately induced) phobias are more common than others. For example, rats, jellyfish, cockroaches, spiders and slugs are consistently rated as frightening, while rabbits, ladybirds, cats and lambs are consistently rated as non-frightening (Bennett-Levy & Marteau, 1984).

These and similar findings are consistent with Seligman's (1970) concept of *biological preparedness*, according to which different species are biologically equipped to acquire certain conditioned responses more easily if they have high survival value. What this implies is that there is more to phobias than the mere process of classical conditioning. Indeed, Rachman (1977) maintains that direct conditioning of any kind accounts for relatively few phobias. Instead, many phobias are acquired on the basis of information transmitted through observation and instruction (such as is involved in *modelling*: see Chapter 14). It is interesting to note that Jones (1924) claims that Little Peter's fear of animals was '. . . probably not a directly conditioned fear. It is unlikely that he had ever had any experience with white rats, for example. Where the fear originated and with what stimulus, is not known . . . '

According to Harris (1997), Albert's fear was difficult to induce, transitory, and the whole experiment a failure (which, he claims, Watson and Rayner themselves recognize!). Yet every available textbook account states how easily they created a rat phobia, which then generalized into a life-long fear of rabbits and other furry, white things. This, of course, is a very similar argument to that of Cornwell and Hobbs, which we considered above. But *why* should textbook authors (including H.J. Eysenck) want to present the study in a more favourable light than it appears to deserve?

Harris (1997) claims that it was serving a celebratory 'origin myth' for behaviourists, who wanted their speciality to have a long and convincing past. Although orthodox and more recent behaviourists portray the study with slightly different details, all versions suggest that Watson had tapped into the power of behaviourism as a theory and technology: the case of Little Albert helps to legitimize the whole behaviourist enterprise!

There is no suggestion that textbook accounts are *deliberately* altered; indeed, many (if not most) textbook authors would not describe themselves as behaviourists and so have no special 'allegiance' to Watson. Also, Cornwell and Hobbs provide us with good reasons as to why these misreportings of the study should have arisen. However, the '*Strange Saga of Little Albert*' (the title of Cornwell and Hobbs' article) can be seen as a case study in the creation of myths, even within a so-called 'science' of psychology. It also demonstrates the importance of reading *original material* whenever possible!

Exercises

1. According to Cornwell and Hobbs (1976), Box 16.1 below contains over 20 mistakes. How many can you spot?

Box 16.1

In the 1920s, J.B. Watson did a series of experiments with children showing how emotional responses can be conditioned and deconditioned. Watson's first subject was an eight-month-old orphan, Albert B, who happened to be fond of rabbits, rats, mice and other furry animals. He appeared to be a healthy, emotionally stable infant, afraid of nothing except loud sounds, which made him cry.

To establish a conditioned fear response in Albert, Watson selected a toy rabbit as a conditioned stimulus. Initially this rabbit evoked no fear in the child. Then the rabbit was displayed to Albert and, half a second or so later, Watson made a sudden loud noise (the unconditioned stimulus) by crashing metal plates together right beside Albert's head. This noise alarmed the infant and he began to cry. Thereafter the sight of the formerly friendly rabbit alone, without the loud noise, was sufficient to elicit crying – a conditioned fear response.

This fear response to the toy rabbit did not die away after a day or two, but continued. Moreover, it spread to other stimuli that bore a resemblance to the rabbit, such as a glove, a towel, a man's beard, a toy and a ball of wool.

Watson did not leave Albert with his conditioned fear. In the second part of the experiment, Alfred's fear response was deconditioned by pairing the rabbit with stimuli that had pleasant associations (such as mother, favourite dessert and so on). By presenting the rabbit at mealtimes, at a distance which Albert could tolerate without whimpering, it was possible to gradually move the animal closer without any open signs of fear in the child.

Eventually Albert was once more able to stretch out his hand to feel the rabbit, and the two were happily reunited.

---

2. How does the single-participant design relate to other kinds of experimental design?

3. What's another word for 'transfer' (of the CR to other, similar, stimuli)?

4. The CER did not transfer to Albert's building blocks. What feature of conditioning does this illustrate?

5. What are the other **two** basic phenomena involved in conditioning (in addition to your answers to **3** and **4** above)?

17

A conception of adult development

Daniel J. Levinson (1986)

American Psychologist, 41(1), 3–13

BACKGROUND AND CONTEXT

As Levinson points out, the study of *adult* development is very recent, although the study of development within the discipline of psychology has a much longer history. Indeed, some of the major figures in psychology as a whole, Freud and Piaget, were largely, if not exclusively, interested in the process of development, but this was seen as being concentrated in the early years of an individual's life.

Freud's theories are very complex and comprise many different interweaving strands, with the five psychosexual stages representing just one of these. However, since repression of childhood memories into the unconscious mind (in particular, the combination of feelings for the parents which make up the Oedipus complex) forms one of the central ideas in the theory as a whole, it seems reasonable to claim that *psychosexual development* is a fundamental characteristic of psychoanalytic theory. This is reflected in another fundamental idea, namely that early experience is crucial in the shaping of adult personality. The deterministic nature of Freud's theory as a whole is perhaps most clearly seen in the belief that 'the child is father to the man', and this has become part of 'common-sense' psychology (see Chapter 19). Although Piaget focused even more closely than Freud on the process of development, his is still considered to be one of the 'big' theories within psychology as a whole. It describes four stages of *cognitive development* (see Chapter 13).

What Freud and Piaget have in common is a view of development as essentially completed by the middle-to-late teenage years. For Freud, because of the psycho*sexual* nature of development, personality development is intimately tied to biological maturation, and the last stage (genital) begins with the biological process of puberty. For Piaget, the formal operational stage begins at about 11 or 12 and ends at about 15; after this, there is no further qualitative change in the individual's intellectual abilities, only an increase in knowledge.

It was Erikson's theory (another of the 'big' theories), which first acknowledged that development does *not* stop at about the time we are becoming physically mature, but continues into adulthood and old age. According to Stevens (1983), Erikson's most original contribution to the study of the ego is his account of the *Eight Ages of Man*, in which he shows that ego development is a process that lasts throughout life (from 'womb to tomb' as his students labelled a series of lectures he gave at Harvard University on the human life cycle, or more commonly, from 'cradle to grave'). Representing a major extension of Freud's psychosexual stages, Erikson first proposed his eight stages of psycho*social* development in *Childhood and Society* (1950). The theory was reworked and elaborated in several subsequent publications, including *Identity and the Life Cycle* (1959).

Largely because of the impetus provided by Erikson, developmental psychology now takes a 'life-span' approach, as opposed to a 'child development' approach. Erikson's 'Eight Ages' correspond to infancy, early childhood, play age, school age, adolescence, young adulthood, maturity and old age, each of which is characterized by a basic issue conceptualized as a pair of alternative orientations or 'attitudes' towards life, the self and other people. While not exclusively concerned with adulthood, Erikson's theory has provided an important stimulus for subsequent thinking and research on adult development, including that of Levinson (Stevens, 1983).

AIM AND NATURE OF THE STUDY

This much-cited article is primarily *theoretical*. Rather than describing the results of some particular investigation, Levinson is putting forward his theory of adult development (*life-structure theory*). Like all theories, this is based on empirical data, including his own (see below), but you would need to consult these earlier publications (particularly *Season of a Man's Life*, published in 1978, and written with Darrow, Klein, E.B. Levinson and McKee) for a first-hand account of how they were obtained.

He makes his primary aims very clear:

(*i*)   to present his *conception of adulthood* and of a developmental process within it; and
(*ii*)   to discuss adult development *as a field of study*.

(It is in terms of these two aims that the article is a theoretical one.)

As far as (*i*) is concerned, the theory originated in the study of men's lives (with the 1978 reference being the most common). But, like most theories, it has evolved since it was first proposed. This has occurred partly because of his research with women (he refers to this as being 'in press', meaning that it is not yet published but is soon to be so. It appeared as *Seasons of a Woman's Life*, written with J.D. Levinson, in 1997: see **Subsequent research** below). The theory includes the following elements: (a) the concept of *life course* and *life-cycle*; (b) the concept of the *individual life structure*; (c) *a conception of adult development*.

As far as (*ii*) is concerned, he discusses six major issues, namely:

1. What are the alternative ways of defining a structural stage or period?
2. What relative emphasis is given to the structures and structure-building periods or stages as compared to the transitional, structure-changing periods?
3. How can we make best use of the distinction between hierarchical levels and seasons of development?
4. Are there age-linked developmental periods in adulthood?
5. What are the relative merits and limitations of various research methods?
6. How can we bring together the developmental and the socialization perspectives?

The two primary aims are clearly overlapping. For example, the concept of the *individual life structure* is central to Levinson's theory. It also relates to the second of the six issues, which refers to the distinction between *structure-building* and *structure-changing* periods, also central to his theory of adult development.

We should note here that Figure 17.1 (see page 325) shows an expanded version of the diagram which originally appeared in the 1978 book. For example, it includes the four eras which constitute the life cycle, namely, pre-adulthood (0–22), early adulthood (17–45), middle adulthood (40–65) and late adulthood (60–?). While none of the age ranges has been changed, the names of some of the periods have: 'Entering the adult world' (22–28) has become 'Entry Life Structure for Early Adulthood', 'Settling Down' (33–40) has become 'Entry Life Structure for Middle Adulthood', and 'Culmination of Middle Adulthood' (55–60) has become 'Culminating Life Structure for Middle Adulthood'.

■THE■STUDY■

Adult development is becoming an important field of study for psychology and other disciplines. Little has been done, however, to conceptualize the nature of adult development and to define the major issues in this field. The concepts of life course, life cycle, life structure are summarized, together with the adult development of the life structure in early and middle adulthood. Six major issues which must be dealt with by every structural approach to adult development are: What are the alternative ways of defining a structural stage or period? What relative emphasis is given to the structures as compared to the transitional periods? How can we make best use of the distinction between hierarchical levels and seasons of development? Are there age-linked developmental periods in adulthood? What are the relative merits and limitations of various research methods? How can we bring together the developmental perspective and the socialization perspective?

The study of adult development is, one might say, in its infancy. It has been taken seriously in the human sciences for only the past 30 years or so, largely due to Erikson's (1950, 1958, 1969) germinal writings. His most obvious contribution was his theory of stages in ego development. Less obvious is the fact that his view of development is deeply grounded in his conceptions of the life cycle and the life course. Each ego stage has its primacy at a particular age level or segment of the life cycle, from infancy to old age. The sequence of age segments and ego stages thus provides a representation of the life cycle as a whole; the meaning of a stage is defined in part by its place in the total sequence. In addition, his developmental concepts arose out of his primary concern with the individual life course: the process of living, the idea of life history rather than case history, the use of biography rather than therapy or testing as his chief research method. Without abandoning the distinction between self (psyche, personality, inner world) and external world (society, culture, institutions, history), he gave first consideration to the life course – the engagement of self with world.

Although a good deal has been learned since the 1950s about specific features of adult life, very little has been done to advance the general theory of adult development. At the same time, various fields of psychology (such as child development, gerontology, personality, social, clinical, and counselling psychology), as well as the social sciences and humanities, are becoming more aware that they need – and lack – an adult development perspective. Adult development is a significant problem for psychology as a discipline and an important link between psychology and other disciplines, including sociology, biology and history.

My first primary aim here is to present my conception of adulthood and of a developmental process within it. My intention is to explicate a theoretical position, not to prove it nor to argue for its superiority over others. The theory originated in my initial study of men's lives (Levinson, 1977/1978). It has evolved over the last few years, particularly through my current research on women's lives (Levinson, in press). It is supported by a number of other studies (e.g. Gooden, 1980; Holt, 1980; Kellerman, 1975; Levinson, 1984; Stewart, 1976) but a great deal must yet be done to test and modify it. It includes the following elements: (a) the concepts of *life course* and *life cycle*, which provide an essential framework for the field of adult development, within which studies of one process or age level can be connected to others but without which we have a miscellany of findings and no integrated domain of inquiry; (b) the concept of the *individual life structure*, which includes many aspects of personality and of the external world but is not identical with any of these and evolves in its own distinctive way; and (c) *a conception of adult development* – the evolution of the life structure in early and middle adulthood. Life structure development is different from, and should not be confused with, the development of personality, social roles, or other commonly studied processes.

Second, I will discuss adult development as a field of study. I will consider six major issues that help to define what the field is about and what work must be done to establish it more securely; the list is not complete, but it provides a useful starting point. Reference will be made to the work of others, but the main goal is to clarify my own position.

THE STUDY

THE STUDY

THE LIFE COURSE

Life course is one of the most important yet least examined terms in the human sciences. It is a descriptive term, not a high-level abstraction, and refers to the concrete character of a life in its evolution from beginning to end.

Course indicates sequence, temporal flow, the need to study a life as it unfolds over the years. To study the course of a life, one must take account of stability and change, continuity and discontinuity, orderly progression as well as stasis and chaotic fluctuation. It is not enough to focus solely on a single moment; nor is it enough to study a series of three or four moments widely separated in time, as is ordinarily done in longitudinal research. It is necessary to examine 'lives in progress' (White, 1952) and to follow the temporal sequence in detail over a span of years.

Life must include all aspects of living: inner wishes and fantasies; love relationships; participation in family, work, and other social systems; bodily changes; good times and bad – everything that has significance in a life. To study the life course, it is necessary first to look at a life in all its complexity at a given time, to include all its components and their interweaving into a partially integrated pattern, then to trace the evolution of this pattern over time.

The study of the life course has presented almost insuperable problems to the human sciences. Each discipline has claimed as its special domain one aspect of life, such as personality, social role or biological functioning, and has neglected the others. Every discipline has split the life course into separate segments such as childhood or old age. Research has been done from such diverse theoretical perspectives as biological ageing, moral development, career development, adult socialization, enculturation, and adaptation to loss or stress, with minimal recognition of their interconnections. The resulting fragmentation is so great that no discipline or viewpoint conveys the sense of an individual life and its temporal course.

The recognition is slowly dawning that the many specialities and theoretical approaches are not isolated entities but aspects of a single field: the study of the individual life course. During the next decade, this study will emerge as a new multidisciplinary field in the human sciences, linking the various disciplines, with the parts becoming less isolated and each part enriching the others.

THE LIFE CYCLE

The idea of the life cycle goes beyond that of the life course. In its origin, it is metaphorical, not descriptive or conceptual. The imagery of 'cycle' suggests that there is an underlying order in the human life course; although each individual life is unique, everyone goes through the same basic sequence. The course of life is not a simple, continuous process. There are qualitively different phases or seasons. The metaphor of seasons appears in many contexts. There are seasons in the year. Spring is a time of blossoming, and poets allude to youth as the spring time of the life cycle. Summer is the season of the greatest passion and ripeness. An elderly ruler is 'the lion in winter'. There are seasons within a single day – dawn, noon, twilight, the full dark of night   each having its counterpart in the life cycle. There are seasons in love, war, politics, artistic creation and illness.

The imagery of the life cycle thus suggests that the life course evolves through a sequence of definable forms. A season is a major segment of the total cycle. Change goes on within each season, and a transition is required for the shift from one to the next. Every season has its own time, although it is part of and coloured by the whole. No season is better or more important than any other. Each has its necessary place and contributes its special character to the whole.

What are the major seasons in the life cycle? Neither popular culture nor the human sciences provide a clear answer to this question. The modern world has no established conception – scientific, philosophical, religious or literary – of the life cycle as a whole or of its component phases. There is no standard language that demarcates and identifies several large segments of the life cycle. The predominant view rarely stated explicitly, divides it into three parts: (a) an initial segment of about 20 years, including childhood and adolescence (pre-adulthood); (b) a final segment starting at around 65 (old age); and (c) between these segments, an amorphous time vaguely known as adulthood.

A good deal is known about the pre-adult years, which for a century have been the main province of the field of human development. The idea is now accepted that in the first 20 years or so all human beings go through an underlying sequence of periods – prenatal, infancy, early childhood, middle childhood, pubescence and adolescence. Yet children grow in infinitely varied ways as a result of differences in biological, psychological and social conditions. In its concrete form, each individual life course is unique. The study of pre-adult development seeks to determine the universal order and the general developmental principles that govern the process by which human lives becomes increasingly individualized.

Historically, the great figures in the study of child development, such as Freud and Piaget, assumed that development is largely completed at the end of adolescence, which meant they had no basis for concerning themselves with the possibilities of adult development or with the nature of the life cycle as a whole. An impetus to change came in the 1950s when geriatrics and gerontology were established as fields of human service and research. Unfortunately, gerontology has not gone far in developing a conception of the life cycle, one possible reason being that it skipped from childhood to old age without examining the intervening adult years. Present understanding of old age will be enhanced when more is known about adulthood;

thus, old age can be connected more organically to the earlier seasons.

There is now very little theory, research or cultural wisdom about adulthood as a season (or seasons) of the life cycle. We have no popular language to describe a series of age levels after adolescence. Words such as *youth*, *maturity*, and *middle age* are ambiguous in their age-linkages and meanings, reflecting the lack of any cultural definition of adulthood and how people's lives evolve within it. Nor is there an adequate conception of the nature of adulthood in the human sciences.

My own view of the life cycle derives from my research and draws on the work of earlier investigators such as Erikson (1950, 1969), Jung, von Franz, Henderson, Jacobi and Jaffe (1964), Neugarten (1968), Ortega Y Gasset (1958) and van Gennep (1960).

ERAS: THE MACRO-STRUCTURE OF THE LIFE CYCLE

I conceive of the life cycle as a sequence of *eras*. Each era has its own biophysical character, and each makes its distinctive contribution to the whole. There are major changes in the nature of our lives from one era to the next, and lesser, though still crucially important changes within eras. They are partially overlapping: a new era begins as the previous one is approaching its end. A *cross-era transition*, which generally lasts about five years, terminates the outgrowing era and initiates the next. The eras and the cross-era transitional periods form the macro-structure of the life cycle, providing an underlying order in the flow of all human lives yet permitting exquisite variations in the individual life course.

Each era and developmental period begins and ends at a well-defined modal age, with a range of about two years above and below this average. The age-linked phases in adult life goes against conventional wisdom. Nevertheless, these age findings have been consistently obtained in the initial research and in subsequent studies. The idea of age-linked eras and periods now has the status of an empirically grounded hypothesis that needs further testing in various cultures.

The first era, *Pre-adulthood*, extends from conception to roughly age 22. During these 'formative years' the individual grows from highly dependent, undifferentiated infancy through childhood and adolescence to the beginnings of a more independent, responsible adult life. It is the era of most rapid biopsychosocial growth. The first few years of life provide a transition into childhood, during which time the neonate becomes biologically and psychologically separate from the mother and establishes the initial distinction between the 'me' and the 'not me' – the first step in a continuing process of individuation.

The years from about 17 to 22 constitute the *Early Adult Transition*, a developmental period in which pre-adulthood draws to a close and the era of early adulthood gets underway. It is thus part of both eras, and not fully a part of either. A new step in individuation is taken as the budding adult modifies her or his relationships with family and other components of the pre-adult world and begins to form a place as an adult in the adult world. From a childhood-centred perspective, development is now largely completed and the child has gained maturity as an adult. The field of developmental (i.e. child) psychology has traditionally taken this view. Taking the perspective of the life cycle as a whole, however, we recognize that the developmental attainments of the first era provide only a base, a starting point from which to begin the next. The Early Adult Transition represents, so to speak, both the full maturity of pre-adulthood and the infancy of a new era. One is at best off to a shaky start, and new kinds of development are required in the next era.

The second era, *Early Adulthood*, lasts from about age 17 to 45 and begins with the *Early Adult Transition*. It is the adult era of greatest energy and abundance and of greatest contradiction and stress. Biologically, the 20s and 30s are the peak years of the life cycle. In social and psychological terms, early adulthood is the season for forming and pursuing youthful aspirations, establishing a niche in society, raising a family, and as the era ends, reaching a more 'senior' position in the adult world. This can be a time of rich satisfaction in terms of love, sexuality, family life, occupational advancement, creativity and realization of major life goals. But there can also be crushing stresses. Most of us simultaneously undertake the burdens of parenthood and of forming an occupation. We incur heavy financial obligations when our earning power is still relatively low. We must make crucially important choices regarding marriage, family, work, and lifestyle before we have the maturity or life experience to choose wisely. Early adulthood is the era in which we are most buffeted by our own passions and ambitions from within and by the demands of family, community, and society from without. Under reasonably favourable conditions, the rewards of living in this era are enormous, but the costs often equal or even exceed the benefits.

The *Midlife Transition*, from roughly age 40 to 45, brings about the termination of early adulthood and the start of middle adulthood. The distinction between these two eras, and the concept of Midlife Transition as a developmental period that separates and connects them, are among the most controversial aspects of this schema. The research indicates, however, that the character of living always changes appreciably between early and middle adulthood (Holt, 1980; Gooden, 1980; Levinson, 1978, 1984, in press). Similar observations, based on different methods and evidence, are given in the work of Jung, Ortega, Erikson and others, noted earlier. The process of change begins in the Midlife Transition (though the forms and degree of change vary enormously) and continues throughout the era. One developmental task of this transition is to begin a new step in individuation, enabling us to become more compassionate, reflective and judicious, less tyrannized by inner conflicts and external demands, and more genuinely loving of ourselves and others. Without it, our lives become increasingly trivial or stagnant.

The third era, *Middle Adulthood*, lasts from about 40 to 65. During this era our bio-logical capacities are below those of early adulthood but are normally still sufficient for an energetic, personally satisfying and socially valuable life. Unless our lives are hampered in some special way, most of us during our 40s and 50s become 'senior members' in our own particular worlds, however grand or modest they may be. We are responsible not only for our own work and perhaps the work of others, but also for the development of the current generation of young adults who will soon enter the dominant generation.

The next era, *Late Adulthood*, starts about age 60. The *Late Adulthood Transition*, from 60 to 65, links middle and late adulthood and is part of both. My speculations regarding this era (and late, late adulthood) are given in Levinson (1978).

THE LIFE STRUCTURE AND ITS DEVELOPMENT IN ADULTHOOD

THE STUDY

My approach to adult development grows out of, and is shaped by, the foregoing views regarding the life course and the life cycle. I am primarily interested in understanding the nature of a person's life at a particular time and the course of that life over the years. Personality attributes, social roles, and biological characteristics are aspects of a life; they should be regarded as aspects and placed within the context of the life.

The key concept to emerge from my research is the *life structure*: the underlying pattern or design of a person's life at a given time. It is the pillar of my conception of adult development. Periods in adult development refer to periods in the evolution of the life structure.

The meaning of the term 'life structure' can be clarified by comparing it with personality structure. A theory of personality structure is a way of conceptualizing answers to a concrete question: 'What kind of person am I?' Different theories offer numerous ways of thinking about this question and of characterizing oneself or others; for example, in terms of traits, skills, wishes, conflicts, defences or values.

A theory of life structure is a way of conceptualizing answers to a different ques-tion: 'What is my life like now?' As we begin reflecting on this question, many others come to mind. What are the most important parts of my life, and how are they interrelated? Where do I invest most of my time and energy? Are there some relationships – to spouse, lover, family, occupation, religion, leisure, or whatever – that I would like to make more satisfying or meaningful? Are there some things not in my life that I would like to include? Are there interests and relationships, which now occupy a minor place, that I would like to make more central?

In pondering these questions, we begin to identify those aspects of the external world that have the greatest significance to us. We characterize our relationship with each of them and examine the interweaving of the various relationships. We find that our relationships are imperfectly integrated within a single pattern or structure.

The primary components of a life structure are the person's *relationships* with various others in the external world. The other may be a person, a group, institution or culture, or a particular object or place. A significant relationship involves an investment of self (desires, values, commitment, energy, skill), a reciprocal investment by the other person or entity, and one or more social contexts that contain the relationship, shaping it and becoming part of it. Every relationship shows both stability and change as it evolves over time, and it has different functions in the person's life as the life structure itself changes.

An individual may have significant relationships with many kinds of others, including an actual person in the individual's current life. We need to study interpersonal relationships between friends, lovers, and spouses; between parents and their adult offspring at different ages; between bosses and subordinates, teachers and students, and mentors and protégés. A significant other might be a person from the past (e.g. Ezra Pound's vital relationship with the figure of Dante) or a symbolic or imagined figure from religion, myth, fiction, or private fantasy. The other might not be an individual but a collective entity such as a group, institution, or social movement; nature as a whole, or a part of nature such as the ocean, mountains, wildlife, whales in general, or Moby Dick in particular; or an object or place such as a farm, a city or country, 'a room of one's own', or a book or painting.

The concept of life structure requires us to examine the nature and patterning of an adult's relationships over the years. These relationships are the stuff our lives are made of. They give shape and substance to the life course. They are the vehicle by which we live out – or bury – various aspects of our selves and by which we participate, for better or worse, in the world around us. Students of the life course seek to determine the character of each relationship, its place within the person's evolving life, and the meaning of this life for the person and his or her world.

At any given time, a life structure may have many and diverse components. But only one or two components – rarely as many as three – occupy a central place in the structure. Most often, marriage, family and occupation are the central components of a person's life, although wide variations occur in their relative weight and in the importance of other components. The central components are those that have the greatest significance for the self-evolving life course. They receive the largest share of the individual's time and energy, and they strongly influence the character of the other components. The peripheral components are easier to change or detach; they involve less investment of self and can be modified with less effect on the fabric of the person's life.

THE STUDY

THE STUDY

In terms of open systems theory, life structure forms a boundary between person-ality structure and social structure and governs the transactions between them. A boundary structure is part of the two adjacent systems it connects, yet is partially separate or autonomous. It can be understood only if we see it as a link between them. The life structure mediates the relationship between the individual and the environment. It is in part the cause, the vehicle, and the effect of that relationship; it grows out of the engagement of the self and the world. Its intrinsic ingredients are aspects of the self and of the world, and its evolution is shaped by factors in the self and in the world. It requires us to think about the self and the world together rather than making one primary and the other secondary or derivative. A theory of life structure must draw equally upon psychology and the social sciences.

DEVELOPMENTAL PERIODS IN EARLY AND MIDDLE ADULTHOOD

In tracing the evolution of the life structure in the lives of men and women, I have found an invariant basic pattern (with infinite manifest variations): evidence shows that life structure develops through a relatively orderly sequence of age-linked periods during the adult years; this is a surprising finding given the absence of similar regularity in ego, moral or career development, and other specific aspects of life.

The sequence consists of an alternating series of *structure-building* and *structure-changing* (transitional) periods. Our primary task in a structure-building period is to form a life structure and enhance our life within it: we must make certain key choices, form a structure around them, and pursue our values and goals within this structure. Even when we succeed in creating a structure, life is not necessarily tranquil. The task of building a structure is often stressful indeed, and we may dis-cover that it is not as satisfactory as we had hoped. A structure-building period usually lasts five to seven years, 10 at the most. Then the life structure that has formed the basis for stability comes into question and must be modified.

A *transitional* period terminates the existing life structure and creates the possibil-ity for a new one. The primary tasks of every transitional period are to reappraise the existing structure, to explore possibilities for change in the self and the world, and to move toward commitment to the crucial choices that form the basis for a new life structure in the ensuing period. Transitional periods usually last about five years. Almost half our adult lives is spent in developmental transitions. No life structure is permanent – periodic change is in the nature of our existence.

As a transition comes to an end, one starts making crucial choices, giving them meaning and commitment, and building a life structure around them. The choices are, in a sense, the major product of the transition. When all the efforts of the transition are done – the struggles to improve work or marriage, to explore altern-ative possibilities of living, to come more to terms with the self – choices must be

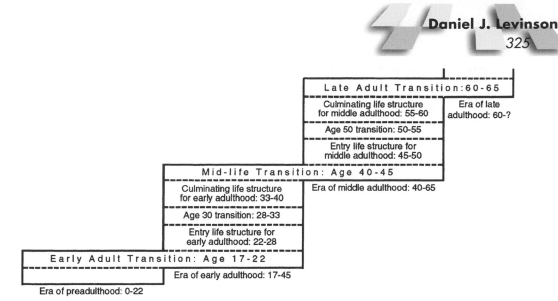

Note: This is an expanded adaptation of an earlier version that appeared in *The Seasons of a Man's Life* (p. 57)) by D. J. Levinson with D.N.Darrow, E.B.Klein, M.H.Levinson and B.McKee, 1978, New York: Alfred A.Knopf, Inc. Copyright 1978 by Alfred A.Knopf, Inc. Adapted by permission.

Figure 17.1. Developmental periods in the eras of early, middle and late adulthood.

THE STUDY

made and bets must be placed. One must decide, 'This I will settle for', and start creating a life structure that will serve as a vehicle for the next step in the journey.

Within early and middle adulthood, the developmental periods unfold as follows (Figure 17.1). Each period begins and ends at a well-defined average age; there is a variation of plus or minus two years around the mean. (For a discussion of the age-linkages, see Issue 4 below.)

1 The *Early Adult Transition* (17–22) is a developmental bridge between pre-adulthood and early adulthood.

2 The *Entry Life Structure for Early Adulthood* (22–28) is a time for building and maintaining an initial mode of adult life.

3 The *Age 30 Transition* is an opportunity to reappraise and modify the entry structure and to create the basis for the next life structure.

4 The *Culminating Life Structure for Early Adulthood* (33–40) is the vehicle for completing this era and realizing our youthful aspirations.

5 The *Midlife Transition* (40–45) is another of the great cross-era shifts, serving both to terminate early adulthood and to initiate middle adulthood.

6 The *Entry Life Structure for Middle Adulthood* (45–50), like 2 above, provides an initial basis for life in a new era.

7 The *Age 50 Transition* (50–55) offers a mid-era opportunity for modifying and perhaps improving the entry life structure.

8 The *Culminating Life Structure for Middle Adulthood* (55–60) is the framework in which we conclude this era.

9 The *Late Adult Transition* (60–65) is a boundary period between middle and late adulthood, separating and linking the two eras.

The first three periods of early adulthood, from roughly 17–33, constitutes its 'novice phase'. They provide an opportunity to move beyond adolescence, to build a provisional but necessarily flawed entry life structure, and to learn the limitations of that structure. The two final periods, from 33–45, form the 'culminating phase', which brings to fruition the efforts of this era. A similar sequence exists in middle adulthood. It, too, begins with a novice phase of three periods, from 40–45. The Midlife Transition is both an ending and a beginning. In our early 40s we are in the full maturity of early adulthood and are completing its final chapter; we are also in the infancy of middle adulthood, just beginning to learn about its promise and its dangers. We remain novices in every era until we have had a chance to try out an entry life structure and then to question and modify it in the mid-era transition. Only in the period of the Culminating Life Structure, and the cross-era transition that follows, do we reach the conclusion of that season and begin the shift to the next. During the novice phase we are, to varying degrees, discovering as we so often do that the era ultimately gives us much more and much less than we had expected.

This sequence of eras and periods holds for men and women of different cultures, classes, and historical epochs. There are, of course, wide variations in the kinds of life structures people build, the developmental work they do in transitional periods, and the concrete sequence of social roles, events, and personality change. The theory thus provides a general framework of human development within which we can study the profound differences that often exist between classes, genders and cultures.

THE FIELD OF ADULT DEVELOPMENT: SIX MAJOR ISSUES

Like Pirandello's (1964) play, *Six Characters in Search of an Author*, the study of adult development might be titled *Dozens of Fragments In Search of an Animating Source and Unifying Plot*. The fragments have to do with personality change and development (cognitive, moral, ego etc.), occupational career development, marriage and family development, adult socialization, biological development, adaptation to stress, and more. Diverse studies deal with one or other of these topics, but they have no obvious connection with each other and no clear place in a larger scheme of things.

It is time we asked more seriously: What do we mean by 'adult development'? What are the main tasks confronting us as we attempt to define and establish it as a field of study? I have attempted to pursue these questions by identifying six fundamental issues. These are important to anyone entering this field, whatever the approach.

I will discuss each issue from the vantage point of my own theory and research. To exemplify the diversity of approaches, comparisons will be drawn between life structure theory and other, more or less structural theories of development. These include the structural stage theories of Kegan (1982), Kohlberg (1969, 1973), Loevinger (1976), Piaget (1970) and Werner (1940). Also relevant are personality theories in which the idea of structure is important but less fully articulated, such as Freud's theory of psychosexual stages, Jung's (Jung, von Franz, Henderson, Jacobi and Jaffe, (1964)) theory of adult individuation, and Erikson's (1950) theory of ego stages.

The most common non-structural approach is to look for age-linked changes in specific variables. A set of 'age curves' showing regular increase or decrease in certain variables with age may be interpreted as evidence for an underlying developmental sequence. This approach tends to be quantitative and variable-centred and to portray development as a continuous, incremental process. The structuralists, in contrast, emphasize patterns rather than single variables, and they look for a series of qualitatively (structurally) different stages rather than continuous, quantitative change. The two approaches are not mutually exclusive but are rarely held in combination. Reaching a more balanced view of their relative merits is an important issue but beyond the scope of this article.

The basic structural model, most clearly articulated by Piaget (1970) and held, with variations by many developmental theorists, is that development in any domain involves the evolution of a structure (cognitive, moral, ego or whatever). The structure develops through a series of stages or periods. Structural theorists generally use the term *stage*. I use the term *period*, partly to avoid the connotation of hierarchical progression so common in the other theories. When I need a very general term referring to a segment (stage, period, era or whatever) within a developmental sequence, I speak of *phase*. In every structural theory, a phase building and maintaining a structure is followed by a phase of transformation or transition, which leads to the formation of a qualitatively different structure. One research problem is to identify a sequence of structures. Another is to understand what happens in a transition: the process by which one structure is transformed into another and the factors that shape this process.

All the various theories have been useful and all reflect the rather primitive stage of psychology as a discipline. We are all groping in the dark, working with imperfect concepts, methods and evidence. In identifying the following issues my intent is to provide an analytic basis on which we can compare various approaches, clarify the similarities and differences among them, and consider the state of this field as a whole.

ISSUE 1

What are the alternative ways of defining a structural stage or period? In the Piagetian tradition, development is a sequence of stages. Each stage is defined in terms of the *structure* that characterizes it. A stage, in this view, *is* a structure, a time of building and maintaining a structure. Other theorists, such as Erikson and Freud, defined a stage in terms of its *developmental tasks*. Erikson identified each ego stage in terms of a polarity (trust vs. mistrust, generativity vs. stagnation or exclusivity). A person is in a stage when that polarity is of central importance in experiencing the self and relating to the world. The primary developmental tasks of a stage are to come to terms with both of its polar opposites and to arrive at some balance or integration of the poles, so that they are no longer entirely opposed. One positive outcome of the developmental work is the formation of a stage-specific virtue, such as fidelity or caring. However, Erikson did not propose a single optimal ego *structure* as the defining characteristic of an ego stage. Rather, he described various kinds of developmental work on the tasks and various kinds of developmental achievement or impairment that may be the products of the stage.

Like Erikson and Freud, I define each period primarily in terms of its developmental tasks. I am also concerned with the kinds of life structures that are formed in every structure-building period, and in that sense I am perhaps more of a 'structuralist' than they. But unlike Piaget, I do not identify a particular structure as the predominant or optimal one for a given period; the life structures generated in any period are infinitely varied.

ISSUE 2

What relative emphasis is given to the structures and structure-building periods or stages as compared to the transitional, structure-changing periods? Piaget focused mainly on the sequence of structures. When he spoke of a stage, he meant a structure. His successive stages in cognitive development form a hierarchical series of cognitive levels or structures. Although recognizing that transitions are required for the shift from one structure to another, he did not study the transitional process. He treated the transitions as lacunae or zones of ambiguity between the structures, rather than as stages in their own right with a distinctive character of their own. By and large, Piaget studied the structures rather than the course of development as a continuing evolution.

In contrast, there is now a growing body of research on transition; for example, periods of change and readjustment following a major life event such as marriage, divorce, the birth of a child, retirement, or the loss of a loved one (Hareven & Adams, 1982; Lowenthal *et al.*, 1975). Indeed, the focus on the process of change is often so strong that little attention is given to the states (structures) which precede and follow it. Much of the recent theory and research on transitions is centred narrowly on adaptation and change stemming from a single event and is generally not based on a theory of adult development and cannot, in itself, generate a theory of adult development (Levinson, 1980).

In studying the development of the life structure, I give equal weight to the structure-building and structure-changing periods. Adults spend almost as much time in the latter as in the former and both play a crucial part in adult development. I am equally concerned with the life structures people form at different ages and with the transitions that lead from one life structure to another. I study the sequence by which individuals build, live within, modify, and rebuild the life structure over a span of many years. The standard methods of cross-sectional and longitudinal research are not adequate for this task; we must develop biographical methods that more fully capture the flow of the life course (see Issue 5, below).

ISSUE 3

How can we make best use of the distinction between hierarchical levels and seasons of development? In the Piagetian approach, the successive stages form a hierarchical progression from lower to higher on a developmental scale; stage 3 is developmentally more advanced than stage 2 and less advanced than stage 4. In other theories such as Freud's, Erikson's and mine, the phases are more like seasons. Phase 3 comes after phase 2 and to some extent builds upon it, but phase 3 is not necessarily more 'advanced'. Each phase has its own intrinsic value, appropriate to its place in the life cycle. The sequence of phases is seen within the framework of the life cycle rather than as a temporal order governed solely by its own internal logic.

This issue is of fundamental importance in the study of adult development. The imagery of a hierarchy of developmental stages is prevalent in the study of childhood, where development takes primarily the form of positive growth. There are generally agreed-upon criteria for judging that one stage represents a 'higher level' than another in pre-adulthood, where we make dramatic advances in body shape and size, cognitive complexity, adaptive capability, and character formation. The variables that show such rapid growth until age 20 or so tend to stabilize in early adulthood and then gradually decline over the course of middle and late adulthood.

Development is not synonymous with growth but has the twin aspects of 'growing-up' and 'growing-down'. Perhaps the best term for the former is *adolescing* (moving towards adulthood), and for the latter, *senescing* (moving toward old age and dissolution). The balance of the two varies from era to era.

In pre-adulthood we are mostly, though not only adolescing. In late adulthood we are mostly senescing, though there is some vitally important adolescing to be done as we come to the culmination of the entire life cycle and attempt to give fuller

THE STUDY

meaning to our own lives, to life and death as ultimate states, and to the condition of being human. At the end of the life cycle, as we engage in the final process of biological senescing, we are also engaged in the final work of psychological senescing, of growing to our full adulthood. It is a costly oversimplification to equate childhood with growth and old age with decline.

In early and middle adulthood, adolescing and senescing coexist in an uneasy balance. Biologically, the forces of senescence come to equal and then gradually to exceed those of adolescence. Psychosocially, there are possibilities for further growth, but these are not guaranteed to occur because of both external constraints and inner vulnerabilities. Simple models of growth do not hold in adulthood. It is inappropriate to study adult development with childhood-centred models. Adulthood has its own distinctive character and must be studied in its own right, not merely as an extrapolation from childhood. Erikson warned us of this long ago, and Jung even earlier, but it is a hard lesson to learn.

We still know very little about the complexities and contradictions of the human life course. When we have learned much more about the kinds of life structures people build at different ages, under different conditions, we may be better able to evaluate, conceptualize, and measure the variations in developmental level among life structures.

It is clearly unrealistic to assume that a person's culmination life structure for early adulthood (in the 30s) will necessarily be more advanced developmentally than the preceding entry life structure (in the 20s). And when we compare the culminating life structure for early adulthood with entry life structure for middle adulthood, we have to take account of the change in eras, which presents new possibilities and new burdens. We need to observe and describe the individual life course as richly as possible and to generate concepts that represent its underlying complexity, order and chaos.

The concept of *satisfactoriness* of the life structure (Levinson, 1978) has, like many of my concepts, both an external and internal reference.

Externally, it refers to the *viability* of the life structure in the external world – how well it works and what it provides in the way of advantages and disadvantages, successes and failures, rewards and deprivations. Internally, it refers to the *suitability* of the life structure for the self. The key questions here are: What aspects of the self can be lived out within this structure? What aspects must be neglected or suppressed? What are the benefits and costs of this structure for the self?

Satisfactoriness is not the same as 'level of adjustment', 'sense of well-being', or 'life satisfaction', as these are usually assessed in questionnaire or brief interview studies. Some people feel quite satisfied with lives that are reasonably comfortable and orderly but in which they have minimal engagement or sense of purpose. Their lives have much viability in the world but little suitability for the self. When the self

THE STUDY

is so little invested in the life, the life in turn can offer little to the self – though many adults settle for this condition. Similarly, people who are passionately engaged in living, and who invest the self freely in the life structure, may experience much turmoil and suffering. They ask more of life than it can readily provide. The intense engagement in life yields more abundant fruits but exacts a different and in some ways greater toll.

Assessing the satisfactoriness of the life structure is thus complex and we cannot do it by means of a few behavioural criteria or questionnaire items. Moreover, the basis for assessment must be different seasons of life.

It is important also to distinguish between the development of the life structure and of the self during the adult years. Psychologists with strong intellectual origins in the study of childhood tend to think of development as growth in various aspects of the self, such as cognition, morality and ego functions. The study of adulthood, and especially of life structure development, takes us beyond the focus on the self: we need to examine the life course in its complexity, to take into account the external world as well as the self, to study the engagement of the self in the world, and to move beyond an encapsulated view of the self.

ISSUE 4

Are there age-linked developmental periods in adulthood? The most common response among psychologists to this controversial finding is disbelief. They claim that it is simply not possible that development should unfold in so orderly a sequence during adulthood – a standard series of periods, each beginning at a well-defined modal age with a range of only four or five years around it. They note that the available evidence goes against the hypothesis of age-linked stages in adult personality development. Moreover, social roles and careers evolve according to institutionally defined timetables that vary widely among institutions and cultures. Instead, they regard adulthood as a series of major life events (such as marriage, loss and retirement) which may bring about changes in individual adaptation or personality and which occur at widely varying ages, making impossible the kind of temporal order I have found.

I agree (1978, 1980, 1981) that neither individual personality nor social roles evolve through a standard sequence of age-linked stages in adulthood. Only Gould (1978) has proposed such a sequence but his hypothesis awaits further testing. Erikson (1950) and Vaillant (1977) proposed a sequence of ego states but were less specific about the age linkages. I also agree that major life events occur at varying ages. It is abundantly evident that, at the level of events, roles, or personality, individual lives unfold in myriad ways.

However, I do propose that there is an *underlying* order in the human life course, an order shaped by the eras and by the periods in life structure development.

THE STUDY

Personality, social structure, culture, social roles, major life events, biology – these and other influences exert a powerful effect on the actual character of the individual life structure at a given time and on its development during adulthood. It is my hypothesis, however, that the basic nature and timing of life structure development are given in the life cycle at this time in human evolution.

My viewpoint is a tentative, empirically based hypothesis, not a fully demonstrated truth. The concept of life structure emerged slowly – and unexpectedly – during the first years of my research into the adult development of men. The discovery of a sequence of alternating, age-linked structure-building and transitional periods came even more slowly. That sequence has been found in the intensive study of many lives: the account of interviews with 40 men (Levinson, 1978) and the 45 women in my current study (Levinson, in press); the accounts of over 100 men and women, from different countries and historical periods, whose lives have been sufficiently portrayed in biographies, novels and plays; a study of women's lives into their 30s by Stewart (1976); a study of Black men by Gooden (1980); biographical studies of Jung (Holt, 1980) and Willi Brandt (Kellerman, 1975); a pilot sample of 30–40 men and women interviewed for my forthcoming project on middle adulthood; and accounts of the life cycle written over 2000 years ago by Confucius, Solon, and the authors of the Talmud (Levinson, 1978). I know of no systematic evidence which disconfirms the hypothesis.

The hypothesis of age-linked periods in life structure development is thus well grounded in empirical evidence, though not in quantitative, large-sample research. A theory of life structure development can be tested adequately only by intensive studies of the individual life course, through which we follow the evolution of the life structure over a span of years.

ISSUE 5

What are the relative merits and limitations of various research methods? The favoured methods in developmental research have traditionally been the cross-sectional and the longitudinal. *Cross-sectional* research is the most efficient and manageable, but it has severe limitations as a means of exploring the process of development.

Longitudinal research has the great advantage of enabling us to study a sample over a span of years, but it has major disadvantages as well. The initial concepts and methods may become outmoded after a few years, but the method requires administration of the same measures at periodic intervals over the course of at least several adult years. The measures may have different meanings and validities at different points in history. Longitudinal studies of adult development usually involve massive testing and interviewing at intervals of 1–10 or more years. The sample means are then used to plot continuous age curves, which may represent development sequences. This method is at its best when we have well-identified variables that stem directly from developmentally important concepts and for which we have measures of established reliability and validity. We are far from this ideal in the field of adult development. Even when interesting age curves are found, we are often uncertain about the validity of the measures, the significance of the variables, and the theory of development for which the findings are relevant. A premature emphasis on quantification often keeps us from exploring the phenomena under study and from generating powerful concepts from which appropriate measures can be derived.

The *biographical* method is an effort to reconstruct the life course by interviewing the person and by using various other sources, much as the biographer does in writing a book-length life story. Like the cross-sectional and longitudinal methods, it is not a single entity but a broad approach, with many variations in research design, techniques and aims. It, too, has inherent limitations, especially in its reliance on memory and reconstruction. But it has certain advantages and ought to be recovered from the limbo to which psychology has for so long been relegated. For the study of life structure development, we have no other method of comparable value. It is the only method which enables us to obtain a complex picture of the life structure at a given time and to delineate its evolution over a span of years. It is well suited for gaining a more concrete sense of the individual life course, for generating new concepts, and, in time, for developing new variables, measures, and hypotheses that are rooted in theory and are relevant to life as it actually evolves.

ISSUE 6

How can we bring together the developmental perspective and the socialization perspective? By and large, psychologists study the development of properties of the person – cognition, morality, ego, attitudes, interests, or psychodynamics. When we find a basic order in the evolution of these properties, the order is assumed to have its origins in the nature of the organism. External conditions influence the specific forms of individual growth and decline and serve to facilitate or hinder the process, but the basic developmental scheme is seen as organismically given. Indeed, a *developmental perspective* in psychology has traditionally meant the search for a maturationally built-in, epigenetic, programmed sequence.

The social sciences, on the other hand, look primarily to the sociocultural world for the sources of order in the life course. They show how culturally defined age grades, institutional timetables, and systems of acculturation and socialization shape the sequence of our lives. What may broadly be called the *socialization perspective* (Clausen, 1972; Hareven & Adams, 1982; Lowenthal *et al.*, 1975; Neugarten, 1968) holds that the timing of life events and the evolution of adult careers in occupation, family and other institutions is determined chiefly by forces in the external world; forces in the individual biology or psyche produce minor variance around the externally determined norms. A balanced approach would draw on both perspectives, an integration which has rarely been attempted.

What about the evolution of the life structure? Is it determined primarily from within or from without, a product more of development or of socialization? The life structure constitutes a boundary – a mediating zone between personality structure and social structure. It contains aspects of both and governs the transactions between them. The life structure is a pattern of relationships between the self and the world, with an inner-psychological and an external-social aspect. The universal sequence of periods in the evolution of the life structure has its origins in the psychobiological properties of the human species, as well as in the general nature of human society at this phase of its evolution (Levinson, 1978). Each individual life structure progresses through the successive periods in its own unique way, influenced by a multiplicity of specific biological, psychological and social conditions.

Because the life structure is neither solely a property of the individual, nor simply a matter of externally imposed events and roles, it is necessary *to create a new perspective that combines development and socialization* and that draws equally on biology, psychology, and social science, as well as on the humanities. New cross-disciplinary boundary systems must be generated if we are to progress in the study of basic individual and social phenomena – not the least of which is the human life course. The study of the life structure and its development is an effort in this direction.

EVALUATION

Theoretical issues

An interesting parallel between Levinson and Erikson (see **Background and context** above) is that while Erikson is probably best known for his ideas about adolescence (*identity versus role confusion*), in particular the notion of an 'identity crisis', Levinson's theory of adult development has helped to popularize the concept of a 'mid-life crisis'. (The term 'mid-life crisis' was coined by Jaques (1965), who claimed that people encounter a crisis as they realize their own mortality and a change in time-frame from 'time since birth' to 'time left to live' (Shek, 1996).) Levinson, in fact, talks about the Mid-Life Transition, between the ages of 40 and 45, but doesn't use the term 'mid-life crisis' as such. However, in describing men at this structure-changing period, Levinson *et al.* (1978) say:

> They question nearly every aspect of their lives and feel that they cannot go on as before. They will need several years to form a new path or modify the old one.

And again,

> It is not possible to get through middle adulthood without having at least a moderate crisis in either the Mid-Life Transition or the Age Fifty Transition . . .

Another parallel between Erikson and Levinson, related to the first, is that crisis (whether in adolescence or middle age) is not only inevitable, but necessary. Erikson talked about the 'normative crisis' of adolescence, meaning that a crisis must be experienced for a sense of identity to be achieved. Similarly, Levinson *et al.* claim that men who do very little questioning or 'soul searching':

> . . . will pay the price in a later developmental crisis or in a progressive withering of the self and a life structure minimally connected to the self.

Is Levinson's view of the 'mid-life crisis' valid?

Although the available data is sparse, Rutter & Rutter (1992) believe that going through middle age in a relatively peaceful, untroubled way is actually a *favourable* indicator of future development: *lack* of emotional disturbance in mid-life predicts *better,* not worse, functioning in the 60s. This is the opposite of what Levinson proposes. While the available evidence is consistent with the view that a degree of self-questioning may well be adaptive and healthy, this does not need to be distressing or disturbing in order for the transition to be managed well. (Similarly, the data on adolescence is largely inconsistent with Erikson's concept of 'normative crisis' and the related concept of 'storm and stress' (*Sturm und Drang*), first introduced into psychology by Hall (1904), one of the pioneers of developmental psychology. In neither case does the life-stage appear to be *inherently* stressful.)

According to Rutter & Rutter (1992), this issue of the necessity of distress is one of three propositions involved in Levinson's concept of *mid-life crisis*. The other two, touched on above, are generally accepted by theorists of all persuasions and are certainly much less controversial than the first:

(*i*) Middle age is associated with a wide range of adaptations in the life pattern, some stemming from role changes that bring with them fairly drastic consequences (such as divorce, remarriage, major occupational change, redundancy, and serious, crippling illness), others which are more subtle, such as children growing up and leaving home (the 'empty nest' syndrome), the ageing (and likely death) of one's parents, and the new role of grandparent. These are all examples of *critical life events* (or *marker* events or *psychosocial transitions*), some being much longer-term processes than others (and so perhaps not appropriately called 'events' at all). For example, children do not usually suddenly leave home (unless they 'run away'), nor do one's parents suddenly grow old. Psychosocial transitions which occur over a relatively short period of time, allowing little opportunity for preparation (e.g. the sudden death of a loved one) are more likely to be distressing and to be the most dangerous, in the sense of commonly preceding the onset of mental illness (Parkes, 1993).

However, those which take place over a much longer time period (such as the increasing dependency needs of ageing parents, or the implications for the parents' marital relationship of children leaving home), still require people to undertake a major revision of their *assumptive world* (the basic expectations and beliefs we have of the world based on our past experience) and have lasting rather than transient implications (Parkes, 1993). Such psychosocial transitions are not confined to the 40s and 50s, but may take place at any time from early adulthood onwards (Rutter & Rutter, 1992).

(*ii*) Middle age brings with it significant changes in the *internal* aspects of a person's life structure. Regardless of the presence or absence of external events, mid-life constitutes a time of reappraisal where we question what we have achieved and still want to achieve (especially in relation to the marital relationship and work life), worries about the future, inability to enjoy leisure time, and a feeling that health is deteriorating (Shek, 1996). The claim that people go through periods of self-doubt and reappraisal of their lives is not, in itself, controversial. What *is* controversial is the focus on issues which apply particularly to middle-class people in the Western world, and the view of self-questioning as being confined to a specific age period. As we noted above, many psychosocial transitions can occur at any time during adulthood (and are not confined to adulthood), and are often, by their nature, unpredictable. Levinson *et al.* acknowledges that tasks of mid-life individuation can arise at other ages. For example, they describe the *age-30 crisis* during the Age-30 Transition (although they did not see this as inevitable, as the later mid-life crisis is, or even necessary). To this extent, they seemed to want things both ways! While crises may be more common in the 40s for men in our culture, self-questioning often takes place *several* times during a person's lifetime (Rutter & Rutter, 1992).

This is demonstrated in a study by Shek (1996) of 1500 married adults, men and women (aged 30–60, divided into six age-groups) in China, giving them a 15-item Mid-life Crisis Scale. While some expressed dissatisfaction with their work and personal achievement, most did not indicate dissatisfaction at a 'crisis level', and there was no significant rise or peak in the levels of concern for those in any particular age-group. If there is a mid-life crisis, it appears not to be a universal phenomenon.

Methodological issues and subsequent research

Levinson *et al.*'s (1978) *Seasons of a Man's Life* was based on extensive interviews with 40 men, producing the inevitable criticism that his theory of adult development may not apply to women. He refers in the current article to the 45 women being interviewed in his current study, the findings of which were published in 1997 (see **Aim and nature of the study** above). Like his original male sample, these women were aged 35–45, comprising 15 homemakers (full-time housewives/mothers), 15 business women, and 15 academics.

The broad pattern of developmental periods as described in the present article have been confirmed, and this applies also to a number of small-scale research projects conducted by female students for their doctoral (PhD) dissertation (cited by Craig, 1992). However, some of the *differences* between the two samples are intriguing and perhaps are more revealing than the similarities. We shall focus on just two of these here: (*i*) the different *dreams* of men and women, and (*ii*) the difference in their relationship with a *mentor*.

(*i*)   Levinson describes the 'gender-splitting' phenomenon in adult development, whereby men tend to have a unified vision of their futures, which is focused on their career, while women are more likely to have split dreams. Many of the women in his sample (both the academics and business women) wanted to combine career and marriage, albeit in different ways. The academics were less ambitious and more willing to forego their careers so long as they could continue intellectually stimulating community involvement after their children were born, while the business women wanted to maintain their careers but on a reduced level. Only the 'homemakers' had a unified dream: to be full-time wives and mothers (much as their own mothers had been).

But trying to integrate career and marriage/family responsibilities proved to be very difficult. Surprisingly, perhaps, the homemakers weren't especially happy either: by age 35–45, only 20% continued to be in a strictly traditional marriage, 30% were divorced, 30% were *feeling* divorced, and 20% were trying to redefine their marriage, often to their husband's displeasure! Bearing in mind the very unrepresentative sample, it seems that women experience a greater degree of *conflict* between their careers and marriage than do men (see Chapter 25).

According to Nicholson (1993), a woman's decision to have children usually results in a significant gap in her career; on average, women in the UK will take seven years out of employment to raise a family. However, Taylor & Taylor (2001) ask if there has ever been a process of social change as rapid and profound as the decline in the fertility rate over the past 40 years. In Sweden, for example, the rate over the past 10 years has declined from 2.1 children per woman (the level needed to maintain a stable population) to 1.5. They say this can be explained by the combination of wealth, superior healthcare, and contraception (but the impact of the feminist movement must also have contributed).

But what is even more striking is the rise in the number of women who are choosing not to have children at all. In the 1940s, only one woman in 10 did not have children: now that figure is almost one in four! Women are also having children later (average age for a first child is nearly 30). According to Taylor & Taylor (2001):

> The growing importance of women's careers may mean that having children today is regarded as a practical option only for those with such low

expectations that they assume they have no career to ruin, or those so well-off they can afford a surrogate family to run things while mother and father are away at work . . .

So, perhaps the evidence presented by Nicholson (1993) for the UK and by Craig (1992) for the US, which can be seen as supporting the concept of gender splitting, is no longer as relevant as it was. Changes in these patterns of having children (whether or not to have them, how many, and when), combined with dramatic increases in the number of women in the workforce (e.g. Kremer, 1998), suggest that gender splitting may be less significant than it was for Levinson's female sample. (But we should also bear in mind the small and unrepresentative nature of this sample, as was his original male sample. So, any generalized conclusions about women's *or* men's development are difficult to draw.)

(*ii*) Levinson found that women enter into a relationship with a mentor less often than men. This is a crucial feature of the Entry Life Structure for Early Adulthood (22–28), since the mentor helps support the novice to realize his/her dream. How can we explain it?

It is partly explained by the fact that there are fewer women available to assume the guiding, counselling role of mentor which, in turn, seems to reflect sexism: 'there can be no doubt that aspiring women professionals . . . have to contend with a formidable barrier of sexual prejudice' (Nicholson, 1993).

For example, in 1991, 7000 men applied to study psychology at Universities in the UK, compared with 18000 women. In 1992, 70% of the student membership of the British Psychological Society (BPS) were women, which figure reduced to 60% for graduate membership. But in the 'higher' categories of membership, only 38% of Associate Fellows and 12% of Fellows were women. Male academics outnumbered female by 7:1 and the number of female Heads of Department was negligible (Jackson, 1992).

At the end of 1979, women represented 10% of the academic staff at British Universities but accounted for a mere 3% of professors. In 1991, the number of women entering medical schools in Britain was higher than men for the first time, but women still constituted less than 1% of consultants and general surgeons (Nicholson, 1993).

In asking 'why do men get all the best jobs?', we can again cite gender splitting. This suggests a fundamental way in which, in addition to sexism, being a woman constitutes a serious obstacle to professional success: while a man can pursue professional success with single-minded determination, a woman usually has to divide her time and energy between her job and her second career: housewife and mother (Nicholson, 1993). But as we saw above, for a growing number of women this may be a conflict that no longer has to be faced – either because they are choosing not to have children, or to have fewer of them later in life, and hence, further into their chosen career.

Applications and implications

The discussion above of the impact of psychosocial transitions (see **Theoretical issues** above) itself raises another fundamental question about theories of adult development which identify stages or periods (or some equivalent term). Levinson recognizes that this is one of the most controversial parts of his theory.

No one disputes that adult life involves a host of stresses, challenges and transitions. But it is one thing to portray adult development as a ladder-like progression through an inevitable, universal series of stages, and quite another to view the process as open to major individual variations. Some of these stem from differences in self-concept, expectations and other aspects of intra-psychic functioning, some from vulnerabilities, strengths and attitudes based on previous life experiences, and still others from key psychosocial transitions/major life events arising in adult life, which serve to close down or open up opportunities, or which change life circumstances in a lasting way (Rutter & Rutter, 1992).

Levinson sees the study of major life events and adaptation to these as the major alternative to his approach, which is to define adulthood as a series of *age-linked periods*. He prefers the term 'period' to 'stage', partly because he wants to avoid the connotation of hierarchical progression, which is so common in other theories (especially Piaget's: Issue 3). He also argues (Issue 4) that studying major life events does not in itself provide a basis for a *theory* of development.

Rutter and Rutter argue against *all* stage theories of development, including Levinson's. They maintain that:

> . . . by concentrating on stages, they imply a mechanical predictability that is out of keeping with the dynamics of change, the extent of the flux over time and the degree of individual variability that seems to be the case.

In other words, stage theories seem to assume that there is just one developmental path which everyone takes. Such theories also portray development as *discontinuous*: the process can be divided into distinct 'chunks', qualitatively different segments, instead of a continuous process of change.

What 'stage' theories clearly do is (over-) emphasize what is *common* to individuals who are located in a particular developmental period and, to this extent, they under-emphasize individual differences. But could this be more appropriate (or less inappropriate) in the case of children than adults? After all, each of us goes through precisely the same stages of pre-natal development, and many of the behavioural changes after birth (particularly during infancy and early childhood, then again at

puberty) can be explained in terms of biological growth or maturation. After adolescence, the role of learning and experience may be relatively more important: the longer we live, the more experience we accumulate and the more divergent individuals' experiences become. It could be argued, then, that children are more similar to each other than adults are to each other, because of the role of learning and experience. It follows from this that *chronological age* may be a more accurate indicator of developmental progress (although still only an approximate guide) in the case of children than adults.

At both early and late stages of life, we equate bodily changes with psychological ones, and we do this *relative* to adulthood. According to Salmon (1985):

> In how we understand and, therefore, constitute our human lives, it is the period of adulthood to which we accord much the greatest power and prestige. Adulthood is the stage towards which we see childhood as climbing, and from which old age is seen as declining.

So, childhood and youth are not only the time when biological growth occurs, but individuals at this time are *acquiring* skills, abilities, achievements, social status and personal relationships. It is a time of positive psychological growth. In contrast, we generally see all these things as being *lost* during old age, reflecting the physical decline which characterizes this time in our lives (Salmon, 1985).

But is this an appropriate way of looking at the life cycle? Both Salmon, and Rutter and Rutter, agree that loss is an inescapable part of life at every phase, but it may be a positive or 'growth' experience. Equally, all sorts of 'gains' may be made at the old-age end of life. So youth does not have a monopoly on positive change, just as the elderly do not have a monopoly on negative change. Levinson himself makes a similar point when distinguishing between *adolescing* (moving towards adulthood) and *senescing* (moving towards old age and dissolution). These correspond to 'growing up' and 'growing down' respectively, twin aspects of development which are both found throughout the life cycle, with the balance between the two shifting at different eras.

So how do biology, age and stage apply to an understanding of adulthood? What does it mean to be an adult (or 'adult'), and is our understanding of what it means changing? According to Craig (1992):

> Changes in adult thought, behaviour and personality are less a result of chronological age or specific biological changes and are more a result of personal, social, and cultural events or forces.

Many theorists define adulthood in terms of *maturity*, a hallmark of which is the ability to respond to change and adapt successfully to new conditions. Positive resolution of contradictions and difficulties is the basis of adult activity. Craig argues that this gradual (re-)structuring of social understanding and behaviour does not lend itself easily to a *stage* theory of development – not all adults progress in the same way or structure their lives in a similar fashion.

Levinson's reply to these arguments is given in Issue 4. He agrees that neither individual personality nor social roles evolve through a standard sequence of age-linked stages in adulthood (as Gould, 1978, proposed), while both Erikson (1950) and Vaillant (1977) were less specific about age linkages in their stage theories of ego development. He also agrees that major life events occur at varying ages. In all these respects, 'individual lives unfold in myriad ways'. But while there is no predictable sequence in the concrete individual life course (the details of a particular individual's life as it unfolds), there is an *underlying* order or sequence in the human life course (the pattern of the human life cycle in general):

> It is my hypothesis . . . that the basic nature and timing of life structure development are given in the life cycle at this time in human evolution. (Levinson, 1986)

Perhaps we can account for this underlying order or sequence in the 'human' life course in a way that attaches greater importance to the role of social and cultural factors than to any biological/maturational influences shared by all human beings. Most (if not all) cultures prescribe the 'right time' for leaving the family home, getting a job, getting married, having children, retiring, and so on. This is Schlossberg *et al.*'s concept of the 'social clock'. (Note that not all cultures will necessarily recognize all of these as marker events.) However, just what the right time is differs from culture to culture.

For example, in Jordan 40% of brides are in their teens, while in Hong Kong this figure is only 3%. In Western Europe, less than 10% of men over 65 remain in the work force, compared with 16% in the USA, 36% in Japan, and 69% in Mexico (Myers, 1998). These variations in the social clock challenge the view of adult development as stage-like, including a mid-life crisis (Myers, 1998).

Just as social clocks are 'set' at different times in different cultures for different life changes, in Western cultures the clock becomes 're-set' over time. For example, 40–50 years ago, a stable job and income could be achieved (by men) by age 21, and so this was seen as the time to 'settle down'. If a woman wasn't married by the time she was 25 she was 'on the shelf' and if still single by 29, she was an 'old maid'. Common beliefs about the appropriate age for child-bearing put pressure on women to become mothers by their early 20s, and pregnancy after 26 was seen as 'late' (Apter, 2001). As we saw above, these patterns are drastically different now: what is fast becoming the norm would have been considered deviant in previous generations (and vice-versa).

As both cause and effect of these changes, our whole understanding of what it means to be adult is changing. In *The Myth of Maturity* (2001), Apter argues that it is taking young people far longer to achieve adult status than it used to. She refers to 18–24-year-olds as 'thresholders', because they are only on the brink of achieving self-

sufficiency, independence and autonomy (commonly cited adult qualities). They are like '. . . apprentices to adulthood. Quite simply, they need to learn the ropes . . .'. This is reflected, for example, in the fact that 58% of 22–24-year-olds and 30% of 24–30-year-olds (still) live with their parents. Leaving home is not a single event but a prolonged process: 40% of female, and 50% of male, thresholders who leave home will subsequently return.

These findings reflect social, cultural and economic changes. Apter says there are a thousand different routes from adolescence to adulthood, each involving uncertainty and risk:

> . . . Entry into adulthood is now less tangible and more individualistic than ever. Each thresholder will advance at her own pace, seek out her own vision, and suffer her own doubts. (Apter, 2001)

According to Blair (in Bedell, 2002), the notion of settling down is faintly ridiculous, when the average British marriage lasts nine years (seven in the USA), and where short-term contracts have taken the place of many (previously permanent) jobs. Richardson (in Bedell, 2002) has published a report (*The Young West: How We Are All Growing Older More Slowly*), whose central thesis is that these days there's no hope of feeling grown-up until our mid-30s. While this used to be the threshold of middle age, it is now merely the beginning of the end of a protracted adolescence. By this age, he says, people in the West have become, psychologically and culturally, what previous generations recognized as fully formed adults. Few of us really get there before that.

Exercises

1. Levinson prefers the term 'period' to 'stage' because this avoids the connotation of hierarchical progression which is so common in other theories (especially Piaget's). What does he mean by *hierarchical progression*?

2. Levinson argues that Piaget focused mainly on the sequence of stages (structures), and did not study the transitional processes by which the child shifts from one structure to another. Piaget treated transitions as lacunae or zones of ambiguity between the structures. What name did Piaget give these lacunae or zones of ambiguity? Give an example (and see Chapter 13).

3. Briefly describe what is involved in (a) *longitudinal* and (b) *cross-sectional* research. What makes the latter 'the most efficient and manageable'?

4. During the era of Middle Adulthood, we are responsible not only for our own work and perhaps the work of others, but also for the development of the current generation of young adults. Which stage of *Erikson*'s theory does this correspond to?

5. Briefly describe how the Social Readjustment Rating Scale (Holmes & Rahe, 1967) relates stress and major life events.

6. What is *gerontology*, and is it a field of psychology (as Levinson classifies it)?

7. What is *geriatrics*?

18 Four-month-old infants prefer to listen to motherese

A. Fernald (1985)

Infant Behaviour and Development, 8, 181–195

BACKGROUND AND CONTEXT

There are two broad approaches to explaining language development in humans, corresponding to the nature-nurture, or heredity-environment debate which recurs throughout psychology. According to one account, associated with Skinner and Bandura, language development can be attributed largely to environmental input and learning (the *nurture* view). According to the other account (the *nature* view), mainly associated with Chomsky, Lenneberg and McNeill, *grammar* (the *structure* of language) is an inherent, biologically determined human capacity, and the process of language development is essentially one of *acquisition* (as distinct from *learning*).

In *Verbal Behaviour* (1957), Skinner applied the principles of operant conditioning to explain children's language development. Essentially, he claimed that adults shape the baby's sounds into words and its words into sentences: correct grammar is reinforced and incorrect grammar is not. Imitation also plays an important role.

Despite the lack of empirical support for Skinner, and despite Chomsky's (1959) attack exposing some of the conceptual weaknesses of an operant conditioning account, the role of environmental factors cannot be dismissed altogether. The environment clearly supplies the *content* of language, imitation must be involved in the learning of accent and vocabulary, and the inborn Language Acquisition Device (LAD: Chomsky, 1965, 1968) must have environmental input to 'work on'.

There is also evidence that children who hear a lot of language develop vocabulary a little faster in the early years than those who are talked to less (e.g. Engel *et al.*, 1975). However, it is not the sheer amount that matters, but rather the *responsive* use of language (talking to the baby when it makes some noise or gesture). Parents who are responsive in this way have children whose later language development is faster (e.g. Clarke-Stewart, 1973; Olson *et al.*, 1986). Beyond some *minimally sufficient* exposure to language, variations in quantity make some small difference (Bee, 2000).

Another facet (beyond sheer quantity) that may be important is the *simplicity* of the language. *Motherese* (so-called because it is more often used by mothers: Snow &

Ferguson, 1977; Schachter & Strage, 1982) is such a form of language and is what Fernald's (1985) study is concerned with.

AIM AND NATURE OF THE STUDY

The study is a laboratory experiment, whose aim is to discover whether babies prefer listening to motherese than to 'normal' adult-adult speech. Forty-eight four-month-olds were tested individually, while sitting on their mother's lap, in a room with two loudspeakers, one on each side. Each speaker could produce either (a) an eight-second burst of a woman talking to her own baby (*motherese*) or (b) an eight-second burst of the same woman talking to another adult (*adult-adult speech*). These two kinds of speech constituted the independent variable (IV).

During four *training trials*, the babies learned that one type of speech sound was to come from one side of the room and another type from the other side: the eight-second burst of speech would be played and the baby would turn towards it (or be turned by the mother swivelling her chair in that direction). In the 15 *experimental trials*, the baby had to turn towards the left or right *before* any speech sound was heard, i.e. turning left or right *caused* motherese or adult-adult speech to be turned on.

The dependent variable (DV) was, therefore, the number of times (out of 15) the baby turned (at least 30 degrees: a 'criterion head-turn') towards the source of motherese or adult-adult-speech. The hypothesis was that the babies would turn more often towards the motherese side.

Because each baby was tested 15 times (there were 15 experimental trials), the design represents a repeated measures design. This meant that two key variables had to be controlled for: (*i*) the side of presentation of motherese/adult-adult speech (left/right); (*ii*) the order of presentation of the two types of speech in the training period (motherese first/second). This was achieved by dividing the babies into four groups of 12, such that:

- group 1 heard motherese on the *left* and heard it *first* in the training period.

- group 2 heard motherese on the *right* and heard it *first* in the training period.

- group 3 heard motherese on the *left* and heard it *second* in the training period.

- group 4 heard motherese on the *right* and heard it *second* in the training period.

Thus, all possible combinations of left/right and first/second were accounted for.

THE STUDY

The speech register used by adults with infants and young children, known as motherese, is linguistically simplified and characterized by high pitch and exaggerated intonation. This study investigated infant selective listening to motherese speech. The hypothesis tested was that infants would choose to listen more often to motherese when given the choice between a variety of natural infant-directed and adult-directed speech samples spoken by four women unfamiliar to the subjects. Forty-eight 4-month-old infants were tested in an operant auditory preference procedure. Infants showed a significant listening preference for the motherese speech register.

The intonation, or prosody, of adult speech to infants and young children is characterized by a higher pitch and wider range than in normal adult conversation (Fernald & Simon, 1984; Garnica, 1977; Menn & Boyce, 1982; Stern *et al.*, 1983). Such exaggerated intonation in parental speech is thought to serve several functions related to language development, including marking turn-taking episodes in mother-infant dialogue (Snow, 1977), helping infants track and parse the speech stream (Fernald & Simon, 1984), and acoustically highlighting new linguistic information (Fernald, 1984b; Fernald & Mazzie, 1983; Gleitman & Wanner, in press). However, for the prelinguistic infant, primary functions of the exaggerated prosody of motherese may be the elicitation and maintenance of the infant's attention and the communication of affect (Fernald, 1984a; Papousek & Papousek, 1981; Sachs, 1977). In fact, mothers' specific use of rising pitch contours to engage an alert infant in social interaction (Stern *et al.*, 1982) and falling pitch contours to sooth a distressed infant (Fernald *et al.*, 1984; Papousek & Papousek, 1984) suggests that maternal prosody may indeed be finely tuned to infant attention and arousal levels. The present study is designed to investigate experimentally infant selective listening to the exaggerated intonation of motherese.

Research on infant auditory preferences has been relatively limited in comparison with the extensive literature on selective visual attention in infancy (Banks & Salapatek, 1983). Methodological constraints associated with differences between looking and listening behaviour may partly account for this imbalance. Visual fixation, a necessary component of visual attention, is a convenient and widely used dependent variable in infant visual-preference research, although its sufficiency as a criterion has been questioned (Haith, 1981; Posner & Rothbart, 1980). For auditory perception, however, orientation to the stimulus source is not essential. Since no easily observable behaviour necessarily accompanies listening, studies of infant auditory preference must rely either on indirect behavioural measures or on operant procedures. Behavioural measures used to assess infant responsiveness to auditory stimuli include smiling (Wolff, 1963), vocalization (Bankiotes *et al.*, 1972; Brown, 1979), and motor quieting (Turnure, 1971). Operant procedures have more

THE STUDY

commonly been used, beginning with Friedlander's (1968) experimental procedure in which infants operate an automated device enabling them to listen to either one of a pair of auditory signals, a technique used successfully with infants from the age of 9 months (Glenn & Cunningham, 1982; Glenn *et al.*, 1981). With younger infants, operant measures used to study selective listening include sucking (DeCasper, 1980; Bertoncini & Barriere, 1978; Mills & Melhuish, 1974), and visual fixation (Colombo & Bundy, 1981; Sullivan & Horowitz, 1983).

Selective listening studies attempt to demonstrate not only that infants discriminate between two auditory stimuli, but also that they are more responsive to one signal than to the other. While research in infant speech perception is focused primarily on the discrimination and categorization of isolated phonetic and prosodic contrasts (see Aslin *et al.*, 1983, for an extensive review), selective listening studies have tended to use longer, continuous speech samples to investigate the relative salience to the infant of dimensions of speech such as voice quality (Bankiotes *et al.*, 1972), normal and distorted speech (Glenn & Cunningham, 1982; Jones-Molfese, 1977; Turnure, 1971), and repetition rate (Friedlander, 1968). Young infants tend to listen more to a female voice than to silence or white noise (Colombo & Bundy, 1981), and they are more responsive to the mother's voice than to a stranger's (Brown, 1979; DeCasper & Fifer, 1981; Mehler *et al.*, 1978; Mills & Melhuish, 1974). The salience of maternal prosody to the infant is displayed by increased attention (Fernald, 1984a, 1984b; Glenn *et al.*, 1981; Sullivan & Horowitz, 1983). Mehler *et al.* (1978) found that 6-week-old infants responded to the mother's voice when she spoke with high inflection but not when she spoke in a monologue. Glenn & Cunningham (1983) found that infants of 9–18 months listened more to their mother's voice when she addressed infants than when she spoke to an adult.

In previous preference studies using continuous motherese speech as an auditory stimulus (Friedlande, 1968; Glenn & Cunningham, 1983), the voice presented was that of the infant's own mother. These studies did not address the question of whether the infant was responding to the familiar caretaking speech of the individual mother or rather to more general acoustic characteristics of the motherese speech register. As auditory stimuli, the exaggerated pitch contours typical of motherese may be highly salient to the young infant, whose perceptual, attentional, and affective responsiveness to certain acoustic dimensions of motherese may predispose it towards motherese vocalizations, relative to other forms of auditory stimulation (see Fernald, 1984a).

In the present study, a new auditory preference procedure was designed using operantly conditioned head-turns as the dependent measure. The hypothesis tested was that 4-month-old infants would show a preference for motherese speech when given the choice between listening to a variety of infant-directed and adult-directed speech samples spoken by four women unfamiliar to the subjects. That is, with the production of two alternative sets of natural speech samples under infant control, infants would make significantly more head-turns in the direction required to produce infant-directed speech (motherese) than in the direction required to produce normal adult speech.

M E T H O D

SUBJECTS

Forty-eight 4-month-old infants (*M* age: 122.5 days ±5), 21 females and 27 males, participated as subjects. An additional 27 infants (*M* age: 121.3 days ±5), 12 females and 15 males, were tested but were excluded because of fussiness (21), experimenter error (3), or equipment failure (3). All were full-term infants with no history of hearing disorders or ear infections.

Four-month-olds were chosen because pilot-testing showed that younger infants were less able to sustain attention for the duration of the testing session, resulting in higher subject attrition.

STIMULI

Tape-recordings were made of 10 adult women as they talked to: (a) their 4-month-old infants, and (b) the adult interviewer. None of these women was the mother of an infant who participated in the study. Recordings were made in a sound-attenuated room. For mother-infant recordings, the infant was placed in an infant seat on a low table, while the mother sat comfortably facing the infant. The microphone was placed slightly above and behind the infant seat, about 62cm from the mother's mouth. The mother's voice was recorded for 5 min while she played with the infant. For mother-adult recordings, the mother sat upright in her chair and spoke with the interviewer for a few minutes about various topics. Again, the microphone was placed about 62cm from the mother's face.

The recordings of four of these women were selected for further editing. Criteria for selection were: (a) overall recording quality, (b) the absence of crying, vocalization, and audible breathing from the infant (who sat near the mother while she spoke with the interviewer), and (c) the presence of intonationally complete phrase groups of both infant-directed and adult-directed speech, each approximately 8 s long, from the same speaker. Care was also taken to select speech samples from a particular talker that differed from each other by no more than 400 ms. When such comparable phrase groups from the infant-directed and adult-directed speech of four different women had been identified, they were dubbed onto a two-track tape loop: the onsets of the two speech samples from a particular talker were precisely aligned on the two tracks of the tape. The resulting stimulus tape consisted of four

THE STUDY

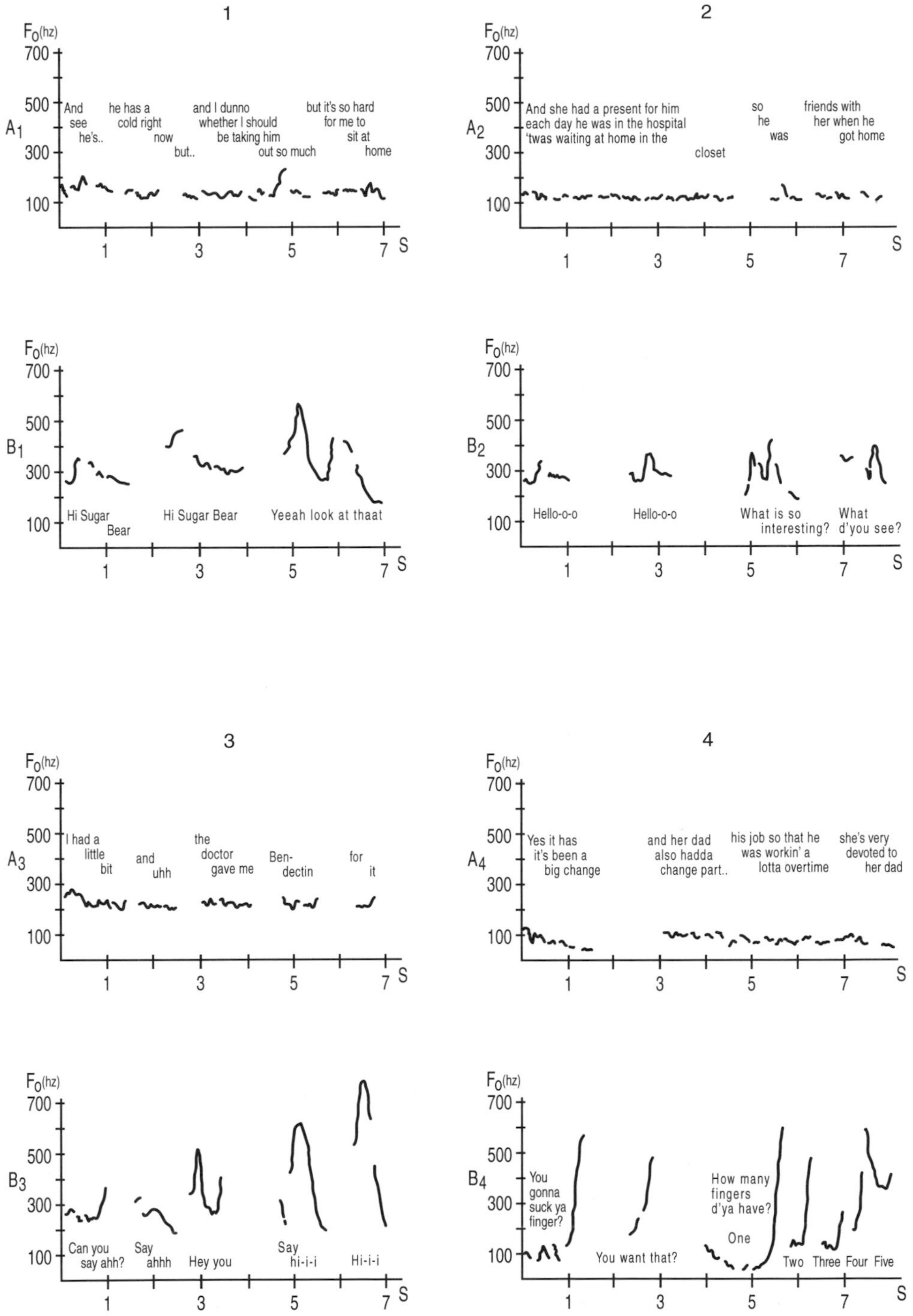

Figure 18.1. Intonation contours from the speech of four women (1–4): (A) Adult-directed speech; (B) Infant-directed speech or motherese. Fundamental frequency (F), measured in hertz (hz), is the acoustic correlate of pitch.

THE STUDY

different samples of natural infant-directed speech, each approximately 8 s long, separated from one another by 2 s silent intervals, recorded on one track. Each of these was aligned with a sample of natural adult-directed speech of comparable duration ($\pm$ 400 ms) from the same talker, on track two.

Appropriate loudness levels for the two sets of stimuli were determined by asking six graduate students in speech science to make loudness-matching judgements. The intonation contours of the four pairs of speech samples used as auditory reinforcers are shown in Figure 18.1.

DESIGN

This experiment used a 2 $\times$ 2 factorial design, with side of presentation of motherese (left vs. right) and training order (motherese first vs. motherese last) as between-subject variables. The dependent measure was the number of trials, out of 15, in which the infant's head-turn was in the direction required to produce motherese. Twelve subjects were assigned randomly to each of the four groups, with the constraint that the distribution of males and females was balanced throughout the groups.

APPARATUS

All testing was conducted in a sound-attenuated room, separated from an adjacent control room by a one-way mirror. A testing booth was constructed, consisting of panels on three sides and open on the fourth side (see Figure 18.2). The mother, with the infant facing forward on her lap, was seated on a swivel chair in the centre of the test booth. To the left and right, slightly behind the infant's head, were mounted two loud-speakers, for which 20 cm circular openings were cut in the side panels and covered with white cloth. Two small, red blinker lights were mounted on the side panels at the level of the infant's eyes but out of the field of its peripheral vision when facing forward. A small green blinker light was mounted at midline on the centre panel, also at eye level. Directly below the green light was a 5 cm circular opening for the lens of a video camera, connected to a video monitor in the control room. Three vertical lines were marked on the screen of the monitor, a centre line indicating the position of the infant's nose when facing directly forward, and two lines to the left and right corresponding to the position of the infant's nose when the infant had made a criterion head turn ($>$30°) to one side or the other. The output of each of the two tape-recorder channels could be presented through either the left or right loudspeaker in the tests booth, depending on the predetermined experimental condition.

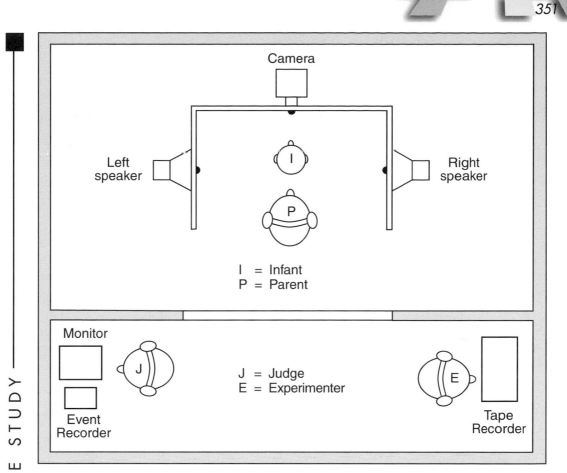

Figure 18.2. Auditory preference technique: Infant testing booth and control-room configuration.

PROCEDURE

The mother and infant were seated in the centre of the test booth. Throughout the experiment, the mother listened through headphones to recorded music to mask the sound of the speech signals presented to the infant. The infant's head position was observed on the video monitor by a judge, who was unaware of which set of speech stimuli was being presented on which side. The judge had to: (a) judge when the infant's eyes were at midline, thus enabling the infant to start a new trial; (b) judge when the first criterion head-turn to the left or right had occurred, after the infant's eyes had returned to midline; (c) record these judgements on three channels of the event recorder, operated by foot pedals; (d) instruct the experimenter when, and on what side, to present a speech sample to the infant; (e) decide, in the case of infant fussiness, if the experiment should be terminated. The experimenter had to: (a) assign each infant randomly to an experimental condition, and (b) to run the tape-recorder, switching to the appropriate channel on the command "left" or "right" from the judge, and stopping the recorder at the end of each 8-s speech sample. The experimenter monitored the sound production on headphones in order to start and stop the tape-recorder at the correct moment.

Two individuals served as judge throughout this experiment. Both were trained extensively in judging criterion head-turns during pilot training. A reliability check was conducted by having the two observers judge in turns independently during the same five testing sessions. Two judgements were considered to be in agreement if they were both in the same direction and occurred within a 2.5-s time window. The two observers showed 93.6% agreement on their head-turn judgements.

Training Trials. The experiment began with a training period in which the infant was familiarized with four of the different speech samples available from the two sides of the booth. The green centre light was turned on to draw the infant's attention to midline. When the judge decided that the infant's eyes were at midline, the green centre line was turned off. The judge then signalled "left" or "right" to the experimenter, depending on the predetermined training order for each subject. The experimenter then switched the tape-recorder to the appropriate channel, presenting one 8-s speech sample to the infant in the test booth, along with the red light on the corresponding side. The training period consisted of four familiarization trials; sound was presented twice to each side, in alternating order, accompanied each time by the red light on the appropriate side. After each sound presentation, the red light was switched off and the green centre light turned on, until the infant's gaze was once again at midline. When the judge decided that the infant's eyes had returned to midline, the green light was turned off, and a new training trial began. During the training period, the mother was instructed to rotate her chair to the appropriate side, if the infant did not spontaneously orient to the sound and light within a few seconds of presentation. Although the mother was unable to hear the stimuli, she was told to use the red light accompanying sound presentation as her cue to turn to the side, and the green centre light as her cue to return to centre. After the four training trials, the mother was instructed to keep her chair exactly centred in the test booth, ensuring that the infant's legs were not shifted to one side or the other.

Test Trials. Following the four training trials, sound presentation was made contingent upon a 30° head-turn by the infant. The green centre light was turned on to attract the infant's attention and turned off when the infant's eyes were judged to be at midline. The first criterion head-turn to the left or right was then rewarded with presentation of one speech sample, accompanied by the red light, on the side to which the infant had turned. The 8-s auditory reinforcer was played to completion, regardless of whether or not the infant turned away. After each sound presentation, the infant had to return to midline in order to initiate the next trial. Completion of 15 test trials was required from each infant for inclusion in the study.

THE STUDY

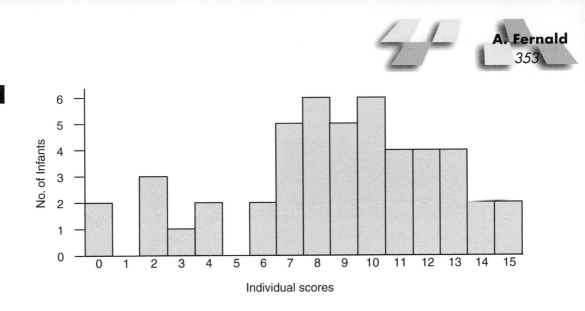

Figure 18.3. Distribution of individual infant scores; each score represents the number of trials out of 15 on which the infant's head turn was in the direction of motherese.

RESULTS

The score for each subject was based on the total number of trials, out of 15, in which the infant turned in the direction required to produce motherese. These data were analyzed in several ways, all showing a significantly greater number of head-turns toward motherese than toward adult-directed speech. A two-tailed t-test, comparing the mean number of head-turns in the direction of motherese (8.73) with an expected chance-performance mean (7.50), showed a significant difference between the means, $t(40) = 2.042$, $p < .05$. Two nonparametric tests were also used. A Wilcoxon matched-pairs, signed-rank tests (Siegel, 1956) performed on the difference scores obtained for each infant by subtracting the number of head-turns toward motherese from the number toward adult-directed speech, revealed a reliable difference, $T = 2.36$, $p < .01$. Considering the data from a slightly different point of view, 33 of the 48 infants turned more often (i.e., $> 50\%$ of the trials) toward motherese than toward adult-directed speech (Figure 18.3). A binomial test showed this proportion to be significantly greater than chance ($p < .01$). These results support the study's major hypothesis, that infants would show a preference for motherese by making significantly more head-turns in the direction required to produce infant-directed than adult-directed speech.

An initial inspection of the data for sex differences in infant listening preference revealed that the performance means are virtually identical, thus sex was disregarded as a factor in subsequent analyses. Two other questions were of interest: Would infants show a response bias toward the right side, as suggested by Kinsbourne (1978)? And would infant performance in this preference task be influenced by training order? That is, would infants who heard motherese as the first speech presentation during the training period perform differently from those hearing

THE STUDY

motherese as the last speech presentation? A 2 × 2 (Side of Presentation of Motherese × Training Order) analysis of variance revealed no significant main effects for side of presentation, $F (1.44) = .01$, $p > .05$, or training order, $F (1.44) = .003$, $p > .25$. However, an unexpected interaction between these two factors emerged as significant, $F (1.44) = 4.50$, $p < .05$. Infants presented motherese on the left side showed a strong preference only when motherese was first in the training order, whereas infants presented motherese on the right side showed a strong preference only when motherese was presented last in the training order. No theoretical explanation for this interaction is apparent. The possibility that this effect could have been due to some procedural error seems unlikely, because the interaction was not replicated in subsequent experiments using the same procedure (Fernald & Kuhl, 1981).

DISCUSSION

Given the choice between listening to a variety of samples of either typical motherese or typical adult conversational speech, 4-month-old infants chose more often to listen to motherese. These results extend previous findings that infants are more responsive to their mother's own voice when she is addressing the infant (Glenn & Cunningham, 1983; Mehler *et al.*, 1978). Since the speech samples used here as auditory reinforcers were produced by four different female speakers, all unfamiliar to the subjects, the results of this study demonstrate an infant preference for motherese rather than for the mother's voice as such.

Certain problems regarding the interpretaion of infant preference studies in general should be mentioned. The assumption that infant "preference", as manifested in two-alternative visual choice experiments, is volitional and in other ways analogous to preference in adults has been questioned by Posner & Rothbart (1980). The technique used in this experiment, however, differs in important ways from the typical visual preference technique, exempting it from some of Posner and Rothbart's main objections. An operant procedure was used here, requiring a presumably volitional head-turn to generate a sound, unlike visual preference procedures, where the infant responds to two visual stimuli which are simultaneously present in the visual field. Furthermore, while visual preference studies often assume the identity of fixation time and visual attention, no theoretical assumptions are made in this study about the relation between the dependent variable and auditory attention. Since speech signals were used here as auditory reinforcers rather than as stimuli presented to gain and maintain attention, the question of "attention-getting" versus "attention-holding" (Cohen, 1972) is not directly addressed.

Another more global objection to common interpretations of infant preference has been made by Haith (1981), who argues that infants should not be characterized "as a multiple-choice, decision-making device". As Haith points out, in a typical visual preference study, infants look at the non-preferred stimulus perhaps only 5–10% less than the preferred stimulus, since both are in fact engaging. In the present study as well, infants showed considerable interest in the nonpreferred stimulus, choosing to listen to adult-directed speech on 43% of the trials. After all, human speech in whatever form is a richly patterned acoustic stimulus, and while motherese may be particularly salient to the infant, that is not to say that normal adult speech is uninteresting. Furthermore, the experience of turning speech sounds on and off with a head-turn was clearly novel and fascinating in itself for most infants, and it was to be expected that head-turns would occur in both directions as the infant explored the possibility of generating different kinds of complex auditiory signals. Haith's (1981) proposal that infant visual behaviour should be seen as continuous rather than as discrete and preferential is relevant to infant listening behaviour as well, despite inherent differences between visual and auditory processing (see Fernald, 1984a). While "preference" is operationalized here as a tendency to choose one kind of auditory stimulus more than another, it should be remembered in the following discussion that the infant's everyday auditory experience does not consist of making such choices but rather of listening with varying degrees of interest to a wide variety of sounds.

Why should the motherese speech register be differentially attractive to infants? Infant-directed speech differs from adult-directed speech along several dimensions that might account for this preference. In addressing infants, adults typically use a simplified lexicon, consisting primarily of monosyllabic and disyllabic words, often with special terms of affection (Ferguson, 1964). Or perhaps the intonation of motherese, with its exaggerated pitch level and range, slower rhythm and tempo, and relatively smooth and simple pitch contours (Fernald & Simon, 1984; Stern *et al.*, 1983), accounts for infants' preference. In fact, Fernald & Kuhl (1983) have found fundamental frequency, or pitch, to be a primary acoustic determinant of infant preference.

Fernald (1984a) has argued that the characteristic pitch contours of motherese are prepotent auditory stimuli for the infant. The infant's early selective responsiveness to motherese may have its origins in innate perceptual, attentional, and affective predispositions to process sound in certain ways, as well as in the infant's experience with the speech patterns used by adults in caretaking and social interaction. For example, the fact that infant auditory sensitivity (e.g. Sinnott *et al.*, 1983) and frequency discrimination abilities (Olsho, 1984) are better in the region of 500 Hz than in the region of 100 Hz suggests that speech at a higher pitch may have some perceptual advantage for the infant. Other psychoacoustic studies of auditory pattern perception in adults (e.g. Bregman, 1978; Divenyi & Hirsh, 1978) suggest that the pitch contours of motherese, simple in form and highly continuous in pitch excursion, may constitute auditory patterns that are more easily processed and remembered by the infant, when compared with the more complex and variable prosodic patterns of normal adult speech.

THE STUDY

THE STUDY

The salience of motherese for the infant may result not only from perceptual predispositions to process certain sounds more readily and effectively than others, but also from the infant's selective affective responsiveness to certain attributes of auditory signals. Several investigators have reported that infants show greater behavioural and cardiac responsiveness to relatively more complex auditory stimuli, such as speech, than to simpler sounds, such as continuous pure tones (e.g. Clarkson & Berg, 1983; Eisenberg, 1976). However, speech sounds are not all alike in their power to engage infant attention. Fernald *et al.* (1984) presented 4-month-old infants with rising and falling intonation contours, with either a wide pitch range as in motherese or a narrow pitch range as in normal adult speech. Infants showed consistently greater heart rate deceleration in response to the motherese pitch contours. These various findings suggest a possible psychophysiological basis for the infant's preference for human speech over other simpler auditory stimuli (Colombo & Bundy, 1981; Glenn *et al.*, 1981) as well as for the infant's preference for the exaggerated intonation of motherese.

Such psychobiological arguments for an adaptive fit between the acoustic characteristics of adult speech to infants and the perceptual and affective processing capabilities of the infant lead to the prediction that motherese is a universal human care-taking behaviour, both within and across cultures. Studies of the speech addressed to infants by fathers (e.g. Menn & Boyce, 1982; Rondal, 1980) and young children (e.g. Sachs & Devin, 1975; Shatz & Gelman, 1973) show that they also use a special register. Future research on motherese should investigate fathers' and siblings' speech to infants and infant responsiveness to prosodic modifications in male as well as female voices.

Cross-culturally, motherese has been widely reported, although its universality is disputed. The use of a prosodically distinctive speech register in adult speech to infants is documented in several European, American, African, and Asian languages (e.g. Blount & Padgug, 1976; Ferguson, 1964; Kelkar, 1964). Schieffelin (1979), however, claims that the Kaluli of Papua, New Guinea, do not use motherese and rarely address their infants directly. Yet Schieffelin also reports that Kaluli mothers commonly hold the infant up to face themselves or other people while speaking "for" the infant in a special high-pitched voice register. Perhaps this Kaluli practice is functionally equivalent to speaking motherese, providing a form of rich and varied auditory stimulation particularly appropriate for the infant. In addition to experimental research, more extensive cross-cultural observations are needed, substantiated by careful acoustic analyses, to increase our understanding of the functions and generality of motherese.

EVALUATION

Theoretical issues

According to Schaffer (1996), motherese (or *baby-talk register)* represents one of several support processes which take place in one:to:one interactions between parents and their baby, helping to move the latter's communication from non-verbal to primarily verbal. Other support processes include adopting 'helpful' speech styles, the use of attention-eliciting techniques, the appropriate timing of verbal input, and involvement in *formats* (Bruner, 1983).

In talking to young children, adults quite automatically adjust the manner of their speech to the child's ability to understand. The term 'motherese' is misleading, because almost *anyone* will adopt it under these circumstances (Eliot, 1999; Schaffer, 1996), including four-year-old playmates of two-year-old learners (Shatz & Gelman, 1973). For this reason, a more scientifically accurate term for 'motherese' is *infant-directed speech* (Bee, 2000). The major characteristics of motherese are as follows:

1. the use of a higher-pitched voice and slower pace than adult-adult speech, with clear pauses at the end of sentences;
2. sentences are short and almost always grammatical (unlike adult-adult speech, which includes many more long, and often ungrammatical, sentences);
3. sentences are grammatically simple, with relatively few modifiers or clauses. The most commonly used measure of grammatical complexity is mean length of utterance/MLU: Smith *et al.*, 1998);
4. speech is highly repetitive, with a tendency to use the same sentences or minor variations of the same sentences over and over. Once children start producing their own speech, adults also repeat these sentences in the form of 'recastings' of the original, making them more grammatical (what Brown, 1965, calls 'imitation with expansion'). According to Bee (2000), children's attention seems to be drawn to recast sentences. For example, Farrar (1992) found that two-year-olds were two to three times more likely to imitate a correct grammatical form after they had heard their mother recast their own sentences than when that same correct grammatical form appeared naturally in the mother's conversation;
5. vocabulary is concrete, almost always referring to objects and people immediately present, intended to focus the listener's attention and getting him/her to act upon, or at least to gaze upon, those objects and people (*action directives*: Shatz, 1978). It is also limited to words the child will understand, such as 'dog', rather than 'collie' or 'animal', i.e. a label of intermediate generality (Blewitt, 1983).
6. as the child's sentences become longer and more complex, adults' language moves ahead in length and complexity, always a notch or two ahead of the child (Phillips, 1973; Stern *et al.*, 1983).

In sum, adults make speech to children simpler, briefer, more repetitive and more attention-worthy (probably its most important characteristic) than adult-adult speech (Schaffer, 1996). It is probably the higher pitch of motherese that is especially attractive and, therefore, attention-grabbing for babies (Bee, 2000). In contrast to vision (where newborns show a distinct preference for simpler stimuli), their hearing preferences are towards the more complex, musical and highly intonated sounds that are characteristic of motherese. This makes it ideally suited to stimulate the baby's sense of hearing. Preference for motherese probably begins to develop in the womb, where the intonation and pitch of the mother's voice are transmitted more clearly than her specific speech sounds. After birth, this preference is reinforced through the affection and attention that typically accompany motherese (Eliot, 1999).

At the same time, children who rarely hear recastings of their own speech still acquire a complex grammar, albeit more slowly. So, while motherese or language feedback may make a child's task easier, it does not seem to be the *cause* of the child's language development (Bee, 2000). While it seems to occur in the vast majority of cultures, it is *not* universal, and it is greatly reduced among depressed mothers in the USA. Nevertheless, children in all cultures, and children of depressed mothers still succeed in acquiring language, suggesting that motherese might be *helpful* without being *necessary* (Bee, 2000).

Fernald's (1985) finding that babies prefer motherese is consistent with the view that it helps the child to actually discover syntactic form (grammatical rules and regularities). But Gleitman & Wanner (1988) believe that it is also consistent with an evolutionary view, according to which mothers and babies have evolved a complementary adaptation. Gleitman and Wanner favour the latter view, describing maternal vocalizations as 'sweet to the ears of the species', facilitating mother-infant interaction. The evolutionary view is, of course, consistent with Chomsky's belief in LAD, while the belief that motherese helps the child to discover syntactic form is consistent with Skinner's emphasis on learning (see **Background and introduction** above).

Subsequent research

Several studies have confirmed Fernald's discovery of a preference for motherese, including those of Cooper & Aslin (1990), Fernald & Kuhl (1985), Pegg *et al.* (1992), and Werker *et al.* (1994). It seems to be the *higher pitch* that they particularly like (Fernald & Kuhl, 1985), and, in keeping with what we noted above (**Theoretical issues**), several studies have found that adults (both male and female) speaking to babies typically raise the pitch of their voice and introduce greater melodic contour compared with talking to other adults (e.g. Fernald, 1989; Shute & Wheldall, 1995). Since women are biologically equipped to produce higher pitched sounds more easily (Durkin, 1995), it may be no surprise that a lot of research (both before and since Fernald's 1985 study) has looked at babies' preference for their mother's voice.

Methodological issues

Even quite young babies show a preference for the human voice over other sounds, although they are less sensitive to lower frequency sounds than are older children or adults. Infants prefer listening to their mother's voice as opposed to a female stranger, as demonstrated by, for example, Mehler *et al.* (1978). They constructed a device enabling one-month-olds to control their own access to audio recordings by altering their sucking rate. If they sucked faster, they heard more of the voice more quickly. For those who heard their mother's voice *after* first hearing a stranger's voice a few times, sucking rate *increased*, while the opposite was true for those who first heard their mother's voice a few times, followed by the stranger's.

This preference is evident as early as 45 hours (less than two days) after birth (Field, 1985), at which age babies would have had only about four hours post-natal contact with their mothers, but considerably more pre-natally! (Durkin, 1995; Eliot, 1999). Indeed, the fetus lives in an auditory environment and is sensitive to sounds from as early as the third month of pregnancy (Slater, 1994).

In order to display a preference (however early or late it appears), the baby must first be able to *discriminate* between its mother's and a stranger's voice. Although this is not a very controversial claim to make about babies' abilities, it is important to note that it is based upon an *inference* from the baby's behaviour (such as sucking faster or slower in Mehler *et al.*'s study described above), *not* a direct observation. Babies cannot *tell* us what they prefer, so researchers must devise alternative means by which they can *show* their preferences.

There are many fewer studies of hearing than of vision. This is because (a) vision is considered to be the primary human sense; and (b) it is much more difficult to measure auditory abilities (Slater, 1994). While visual preferences can be detected in a fairly direct way, through observing the baby's eye-movements (as in the *spontaneous visual preference technique* or preferential looking, as used by Fantz, 1961), measuring sensitivity to sounds is more indirect. As we noted earlier, the baby must be trained to behave in a certain way (such as suck a special nipple, or, in the Fernald study, turn a minimum distance towards the sound source) from which its preference can then be inferred. Using the nipple-sucking technique, Moon *et al.* (1993, cited in Slater, 1994) showed that, remarkably, by only two days after birth, babies prefer to listen to their native language rather than a foreign language!

Applications and implications

Another method used to study infant perception (in all modalities) is *habituation*, in which the baby is repeatedly or continuously presented with a stimulus until it stops responding to it (as if it had been removed). Eimas *et al.* (1971) habituated one-or four-month-olds to a syllable ('pa'), then introduced a new stimulus ('ba'). The babies' attention picked up when the slightly different sound was introduced, with even the younger ones apparently detecting a change.

Other studies have shown that infants are sensitive to at least 50 different speech contrasts (e.g. Aslin, 1987; Mehler & Dupoux, 1994). DeCasper & Spence (1986) had pregnant women read nursery rhymes twice daily during the final weeks of pregnancy. After they had given birth, their two-to-three-day old babies were given dummies which enabled them to control the availability of a passage of speech, and they showed a reliable preference for the familiar nursery rhymes. According to Durkin (1995):

> Clearly, these kinds of findings may have important implications for our understanding of how children acquire language, and most of the research is conducted with this in mind . . . sensitivity to the subtle variations among the vocal productions of other human beings is likely to be useful to someone who will be spending a lot of time in the company of human beings.

As we have seen, motherese is characterized by a number of features, including *prosodic contours* (sound patterns), such as raised pitch, which parents use to capture, then maintain, their baby's attention (Stern *et al.*, 1983). These prosodic contours seem to enable infants to understand the intent of speech before they can identify the meaning of individual words. Infants must also identify individual words in the speech they hear before they can produce words themselves. But how do they reach the point where, like adults, they can distinguish individual words in the speech they hear?

Part of the answer seems to be that mothers stress words in ways that help babies to locate them in speech. For example, they stress words that are especially important and speak loudly at particular points in the 'conversation' (Smith *et al.*, 1998). Messer (1981) found that when parents talk to their 14-month-olds, labels for objects are more likely than any other word class to be the loudest in the utterance, helping infants to identify words for everyday objects in their world. These labels also occurred more often in the *last* part of an utterance, making them more likely to be remembered. Similarly, Fernald & Mazzie (1991) found that mothers gave new words prominence when reading stories to their 14-month-olds. These new words were more likely to be at the end of an utterance, and to be given more emphasis.

According to Smith *et al.* (1998), there are some important unanswered questions about motherese. For example, how short should the mother's MLU ideally be? One answer is longer, but only a little, than the child's MLU. What is needed is analysis of real conversations in naturalistic settings, preferably with representative samples. Another question concerns the ways in which adult-child interaction reflects cultural attitudes and beliefs about children. In Samoa, for example, children are not treated as partners in dialogue, but are spoken 'at' through songs and rhythmical vocalizations, speech is loud and sharp, not simplified. The onus is on the child to make itself clear to the adult, and no allowance is made by adults. Similarly, the Kaluli of New Guinea (cited by Fernald in the **Discussion** section) rarely engage infants in dyadic communicative exchanges. Mothers tend to treat them as 'having no understanding' and so tend not to address them verbally. Even later on they do not use motherese, but rather a highly directive style consisting mainly of 'one-liners' that do not require any verbal response (Schaffer, 1996).

These findings suggest that motherese is *not* universal, and that it is not a 'natural' phenomenon (i.e. one that has developed through human evolution: see **Theoretical issues** above). Nevertheless, children in these cultures learn to speak, and to develop mutual points of focus and joint attention with their parents, as do blind babies in Western culture. Perhaps interactions do not occur according to one particular biologically-designed choreography (Schieffelin & Ochs, 1988).

Exercises

1. Why did Fernald not use the voice of the babies' own mothers?

2. Given the IV and hypothesis, should it make any difference if the voice is male or female?

3. Was operant conditioning actually involved in (a) the *training* trials, and (b) the *experimental* trials? If so, how?

4. Was the hypothesis one-or-two-tailed?

5. (a) By what method were left/right and order of voice presentation controlled?

   (b) Could these have been controlled in any other way?

6. Why was it important to have a 'criterion head-turn' (defined as at least 30 degrees, as seen through the video camera)?

7. Briefly describe the *spontaneous visual preference technique* (as used, for example, by Fantz, 1961). What is the essential difference between this and the method used by Fernald in the experimental trials (see question **3** above)?

19 Analysis of a phobia in a five-year-old boy

Sigmund Freud (1909)

Pelican Freud Library, Vol. 8, Case Histories 1 (1977)

BACKGROUND AND CONTEXT

Freud's work represents many things (often just referred to as 'psychoanalysis'). It is a theory of personality, personality development (hence, a theory of child development, including moral), a theory of motivation and dreams, as well as being an approach to the treatment of (certain kinds of) mental disorder. It is useful to refer to all the theoretical aspects of his work as 'psychoanalytic theory', and to the related method of psychotherapy as 'psychoanalysis'.

The five-year-old boy with whom this case study is concerned is called Hans: hence, 'The case of Little Hans'. This is an important study because of the claims Freud made for it, namely, that it confirms the Oedipal theory already set out in *Three Essays on the Theory of Sexuality* (1905). The case study gave the abstract theory a personality (Ward, 2001). It also demonstrates Freud's explanation of the origin of phobias (in contrast with, say, the learning theory explanation: see Chapters 16, 22 and 30).

Little Hans is also the only child patient which Freud reported on, and this assumes particular significance in the light of a standard criticism of Freud's theorizing, namely, that he built up a whole theory of *child development* around his (almost) exclusive treatment of *adult* patients.

AIM AND NATURE OF THE STUDY

The study reports the findings of the psychoanalytic treatment of a five-year-old boy. In fact, the actual account of the analysis comprises the middle section of the report as a whole, the others being Introduction, in which a great deal of background information is provided, and Discussion. The summary that follows incorporates elements of all three sections.

The kind of study being reported is a *case-study*, sometimes referred to, misleadingly, as a *case history*. The latter is really just the collection of background information as a necessary preliminary to the primary aim of the study, which is to understand and/or treat the 'subject' of the study. Most case-studies take place in a *clinical* context: they are reports of attempts by doctors, psychiatrists, psychologists and others in the caring professions to help those needing professional assistance, due to brain damage/injury, mental disorder, a genetic abnormality, or some other problem. (This is not to be confused with the *clinical interview* as used by, for example, Piaget.)

As important as it may be for the patient concerned, the case-study is usually intended to throw light on the problem under investigation (in this case, phobias as a form of neurotic disorder) or, in the case of brain-damaged patients, certain aspects of normal psychological functioning (e.g. how memory works). The actual collection of data can take place in a number of different ways, such as psychological testing, observation, and even experimentation.

In Freud's case (as in most case-studies), there is no real distinction to be made between the case-study as a form of helping and as a piece of scientific research (a point made by Freud himself in defence of the criticism that the method is *unscientific*: see **Evaluation** section below).

▪T▪H▪E▪ ▪S▪T▪U▪D▪Y▪

[This, in fact, appears in three parts: Introduction, Case History and Analysis, and Discussion. The summary that follows is based on the Discussion, but also includes material from the Introduction, and Case History and Analysis.]

▪P▪A▪R▪T▪ ▪1▪

My impression is that the picture of a child's sexual life presented in this observation of Little Hans agrees very well with the account I gave of it (basing my views upon psychoanalytic examinations of adults) in my *Three essays [on the Theory of Sexuality, 1905d]*. But before going into the details of this agreement, I must deal with two objections which will be raised against my making use of the present analysis for this purpose. The first objection is to the effect that Hans was not a normal child, but (as events – the illness itself, in fact – showed) had a predisposition to neurosis, and was a young 'degenerate'; it would be illegitimate, therefore, to apply to other normal children conclusions which might perhaps be true of him. I shall postpone consideration of this objection. According to the second, and more uncompromising, objection, an analysis of a child conducted by his father, who went to work instilled by *my* theoretical views and infected with *my* prejudices, must be entirely devoid of any objective worth. A child, it will be said, is necessarily highly suggestible, and in regard to no one, perhaps, more than to his own father; he will allow anything to be forced upon him, out of gratitude to his father for taking so much notice of him.

I do not share the view, which is at present fashionable, that assertions made by children are invariably arbitrary and untrustworthy. The arbitrary has no existence in mental life. The untrustworthiness of the assertions of grown-up people is due to the predominance of their prejudice. For the rest, even children do not lie without a reason. If we reject Little Han's statement root and branch, we should certainly be doing him a grave injustice. On the contrary, we can quite clearly distinguish from one another the occasions on which he was falsifying the facts or keeping them back under the compelling force of a resistance, the occasions on which, being undecided himself, he agreed with his father (so that what he said must not be taken as evidence), and the occasions on which, freed from every pressure, he burst into a flood of information about what was really going on inside him and about things which, until then, no one but himself had known. Statements made by adults offer no greater certainty. It is a regrettable fact that no account of a psychoanalysis can reproduce the impressions received by the analyst as he conducts it, and that a final sense of conviction can never be obtained from reading about it, but only from directly experiencing it. But this disability attaches in an equal degree to analyses of adults.

Little Hans is described by his parents as a cheerful, straightforward child, and so he should have been, considering the education given him by his parents, which consisted essentially in the omission of our usual educational sins. It was with the outbreak of illness and during the analysis that discrepancies began to make their appearance between what he said and what he thought; this was partly because unconscious material, which he was unable to master all at once, was forcing itself upon him, and partly because the content of his thoughts provoked reservations on account of his relation to his parents. It is my unbiased opinion that these difficulties, too, turned out no greater than in many analyses of adults.

It is true that, during the analysis, Hans had to be told many things that he could not say himself, that he had to be presented with thoughts which he had so far shown no signs of possessing, and that his attention had to be turned in the direction from which his father was expecting something to come. This detracts from the evidential value of the analysis, but the procedure is the same in every case. For a psychoanalysis is not an impartial scientific investigation, but a therapeutic measure. Its essence is not to prove anything, but merely to alter something. In a psychoanalysis, the physician always gives his patient the conscious anticipatory ideas by the help of which he is put in a position to recognize and to grasp the unconscious material. It is true that a child, on account of the small development of his intellectual systems, requires especially energetic assistance. And yet, even during the analysis, the small patient gives evidence of enough independence to acquit him upon the charge of 'suggestion'.

The first trait in Little Hans which can be regarded as part of his sexual life was a quite peculiarly lively interest in his 'widdler': an organ deriving its name from that one of its two functions which, scarcely the less important of the two, is not to be eluded in the nursery. This interest aroused in him the spirit of enquiry, and he thus discovered that the presence or absence of a widdler made it possible to differentiate between animate and inanimate objects. He assumed that all animate objects were like himself, and possessed this important bodily organ; he observed that it was present in the larger animals, suspected that this was so too in both his parents, and was not detered by the evidence of his own eyes from authenticating the fact in his new-born sister:

> A little later, Hans was watching his seven-day-old sister being given a bath. 'But her widdler's still quite small,' he remarked; and then added, as though by way of consolation, 'When she grows up, it'll get bigger all right'.

One might also say that it would have been too shattering a blow to his '*Weltanschauung*' if he had had to make up his mind to forgo the presence of this organ in a being similar to him; it would have been as though it were being torn away from himself. It was probably on this account that a threat of his mother's which was concerned precisely with the loss of his widdler, was hastily dismissed from his thoughts, and only succeeded in making its effects apparent at a later period.

> When he was 3½, his mother found him with his hand on his penis. She threatened him in these words: 'If you do that, I shall send for Dr A. to cut off your widdler. And then what'll you widdle with?'
>
> *Hans:*   'With my bottom.'

The reason for his mother's intervention had been that he used to like giving himself feelings of pleasure by touching his member: the little boy had begun to practise the commonest – and most normal – form of auto-erotic sexual activity.

The pleasure which a person takes in his own sexual organ may become associated with scopophilia (or sexual pleasure in looking) in its active and passive forms, in a manner which has been very aptly described by Alfred Adler (1908) as 'confluence of instincts'. So Little Hans began to try to get a sight of other people's widdlers; his sexual curiosity developed, and at the same time he liked to exhibit his own widdler. One of his dreams, dating from the beginning of his period of repression, expressed a wish that one of his little girl friends should assist him in widdling, that is, that she should share the spectacle. The dream shows, therefore, that up until then, this wish had subsisted unrepressed, and later in formation confirmed the fact that he had been in the habit of gratifying it. The active side of his sexual scopophilia soon became associated in him with a definite theme. He repeatedly expressed both to his father and his mother his regret that he had never yet seen their widdlers, and it was probably the *need for making a comparison* which impelled him to do this. The ego is always the standard by which one measures the external world; one learns to understand it by means of a constant comparison with oneself. Hans had observed that large animals had widdlers that were correspondingly larger than his; he consequently suspected that the same was true of his parents, and was anxious to make sure of this. His mother, he thought, must certainly have a widdler 'like a horse'. He was then prepared with the comforting reflection that his widdler would grow with him. It was as though the child's wish to be bigger had been concentrated on his genitals.

Thus, in Little Hans' sexual constitution, the genital zone was from the outset the one among his erotogenic zones which afforded him the most intense pleasure. The only other similar pleasure of which he gave evidence was excretory pleasure, the pleasure attached to the orifices through which micturition and evacuation of the bowels are affected. In his final fantasy of bliss, with which his illness was overcome, he imagined he had children, whom he took to the WC, whom he made to widdle, whose behinds he wiped; for whom, in short, he did 'everything one can do with children'. It therefore seems impossible to avoid the assumption that, during the period when he himself had been looked after as an infant, these same performances had been the source of pleasurable sensations for him.

At this juncture, it is as well to emphasize at once the fact that, during his phobia, there was an unmistakable repression of these two, well-developed components of his sexual activity. He was ashamed of micturiting before other people, accused himself of putting his finger to his widdler, made efforts to give up masturbating, and showed disgust at 'lumf' and 'widdle', and everything that reminded him of them. In his fantasy of looking after his children, he undid this latter repression.

In his attitude towards his father and mother, Hans really was a little Oedipus who wanted to have his father 'out of the way', to get rid of him, so that he might be alone with his beautiful mother and sleep with her. This wish had originated during his summer holidays, when the alternating presence and absence of his father had drawn Hans' attention to the condition upon which depended the intimacy with his mother which he longed for. At that time the form taken by the wish had been merely that his father should 'go away', and at a later stage it became possible for his fear of being bitten by a white horse to attach itself directly into this form of the wish. But subsequently (probably not until they had moved back to Vienna, where his father's absences were no longer to be reckoned on), the wish had taken the form that his father should be *permanently* away, that he should be 'dead'. The fear which sprang from this death-wish against his father, and which may thus be said to have had a normal motive, formed the chief obstacle to the analysis.

The most important influence upon the course of Hans' psychosexual development was the birth of a baby sister when he was 3½ years old. That event accentuated his relations to his parents, and gave him some insoluble problems to think about; and later, as he watched the way in which the infant was looked after, the memory traces of his own earliest experiences of pleasure were revived in him.

> At five in the morning, labour began, and Hans' bed was moved into the next room. He woke up there at seven and, hearing his mother groaning, asked, 'Why's Mummy coughing?' Then, after a pause, 'The stork's coming today for certain'. Naturally he has often been told during

the last few days that the stork is going to bring a little girl or a little boy, and he quite rightly connected the unusual sounds of groaning with the stork's arrival.

He was then called into the bedroom. He did not look at his mother, however, but at the basins and other vessels, filled with blood and water, that were still standing about the room. Pointing to the blood-stained bedpan, he observed in a surprised voice, 'But blood doesn't come out of *my* widdler'. Everything he says shows that he connects what is strange in the situation with the arrival of the stork. He meets everything he sees with a very suspicious and intent look, and *there can be no question that his first doubts about the stork have taken root.*

Hans is very jealous of the new arrival, and whenever anyone praises her, says she is a lovely baby and so on, he at once declares scornfully: 'But she's not got any teeth yet'. During the first few days, he was naturally put very much in the background. He was suddenly taken ill with a sore throat. In his fever he was heard saying: 'But I don't *want* a baby sister!'

Affection for his sister might come later, but his first attitude was hostility. From that time forward, fear that yet another baby might arrive found a place among his conscious thoughts. In the neurosis, his hostility, already suppressed, was represented by a special fear, a fear of the bath.

I asked him whether he was afraid and if so, of what.

Hans:	Because of falling in.
I:	But why were you never afraid when you had your bath in the little bath?
Hans:	Why, I sat in that one. I couldn't lie down in it, it was too small.
I:	When you went in a boat at Gmunden, weren't you afraid of falling into the water?
Hans:	No, because I held on, so I couldn't fall in. It's only in the big bath that I'm afraid of falling in.
I:	But Mummy baths you in it. Are you afraid of Mummy dropping you in the water?
Hans:	I'm afraid of her letting go and my head going in.
I:	But you know Mummy's fond of you and won't let go of you.
Hans:	I only just thought it.
I:	Why?
Hans:	I don't know at all.
I:	Perhaps it was because you'd been naughty and thought she didn't love you any more?
Hans:	Yes.
I:	When you were watching Mummy giving Hanna her bath, perhaps you wished she would let go of her so that Hanna should fall in?
Hans:	Yes.

In the analysis he gave undisguised expression to his death-wish against his sister. His inner conscience did not consider this wish so wicked as the analogous one against his father, but it is clear that in his unconscious he treated both persons in the same way, because they both took his mummy away from him, and interfered with his being alone with her.

P A R T   2

THE STUDY

One day, while Hans was in the street, he was seized with an attack of anxiety. He could not yet say what it was he was afraid of, but at the very beginning of this anxiety state, he betrayed to his father his motive for being ill; the gain from illness. He wanted to stay with his mother and to coax with her; his recollection that he had also been separated from her at the time of the baby's birth may also, as his father suggests, have contributed to his longing. It soon became evident that his anxiety was no longer reconvertible into longing; he was afraid even when his mother went with him. In the meantime, indications appeared of what it was to which his libido (now changed into anxiety) had become attached. He gave expression to the quite specific fear that a white horse would bite him.

In the early days of his illness, when the anxiety was at its highest pitch, he expressed a fear that 'the horse'll come into the room', and it was this that helped me so much towards understanding his condition.

The first thing we learn is that the outbreak of the anxiety state was by no means so sudden as appeared at first sight. A few days earlier the child had woken from an anxiety dream to the effect that his mother had gone away, and that now he had no mother to coax with.

But the beginnings of this psychological situation go back further still. During the preceding summer Hans had had similar moods of mingled longing and apprehension, in which he had said similar things, and at that time they had secured him the advantage of being taken by his mother into her bed. We may assume that since then Hans had been in a state of intensified sexual excitement, the object of which was his mother. The intensity of this excitement was shown by his two attempts at seducing his mother (the second of which occurred just before the outbreak of his anxiety).

> Hans, 4¼. This morning Hans was given his usual daily bath by his mother, and afterwards dried and powdered. As his mother was powdering round his penis and taking care not to touch it, Hans said: 'Why don't you put your finger there?'
>
> *Mother*:   Because that would be priggish.
> *Hans*:   What's that? Priggish? Why?
> *Mother*:   Because it's not proper.
> *Hans* (laughing):   But it's great fun.
>
> and he found an incidental channel of discharge for it by masturbating every evening, and in that way obtaining gratification.

We have already described the child's behaviour at the beginning of his anxiety, as well as the first content which he assigned to it, namely, that a *horse* would bite him. It was at this point that the first piece of therapy was interposed. His parents represented to him that his anxiety was the result of masturbation, and encouraged him to break himself of the habit. I took care that, when they spoke to him, great stress was laid upon his affection for his mother, for that was what he was trying to replace by his fear of horses. This first intervention brought a slight improvement, but the ground was soon lost again during a period of physical illness. Hans' condition remained unchanged. Soon afterwards, he traced back his fear of being bitten by a horse to an impression he had received at Gmunden. A father had addressed his child on her departure with these words of warning: 'Don't put your finger to the white horse or it'll bite you'. The words 'don't put your finger to', which Hans used in reporting this warning, resembled the form of words in which the warning against masturbation had been formed. It seemed at first, therefore, as though Hans' parents were right in supposing that what he was frightened of was his own masturbatory indulgence. But the whole nexus remained loose, and it seemed to be merely by chance that horses had become his bugbear.

I had expressed a suspicion that Hans' repressed wish might now be that he wanted at all costs to see his mother's widdler. As his behaviour to a new maid fitted in with this hypothesis, his father gave him his first piece of enlightenment, namely, that women have no widdlers. He reacted to this first effort at helping him by producing a fantasy that he had seen his mother showing her widdler. This fantasy, and a remark made by him in conversation to the effect that his widdler was 'fixed in, of course', allow us our first glimpse into the patient's unconscious mental processes. The fact was that the threat of castration made to him by his mother some 15 months earlier was now having a deferred effect upon him. For his fantasy that his mother was doing the same as he had done was intended to serve as a piece of self-justification; it was a protective or defensive fantasy.

Having partly mastered his castration complex, he was now able to communicate his wishes in regard to his mother. He did so, in what was still a distorted form, by means of the fantasy of the two giraffes.

Hans: In the night there was a big giraffe in the room and a crumpled one, and the big
               one called out because I took the crumpled one away from it. Then it stopped
               calling out, and then I sat down on top of the crumpled one.

I (puzzled):   What? A crumpled giraffe? How was that?

Hans: Yes. (*He quickly fetched a piece of paper, crumpled it up and said:*) It was
               crumpled like that.

I: And you sat down on top of the crumpled giraffe? How? (*He again showed me
               by sitting down on the ground.*)

I: Why did you come into our room?

Hans: I don't know myself.

I: Were you afraid?

Hans: No, of course not.

I: Did you dream about the giraffe?

Hans: No, I didn't dream. I thought it. I thought it all. I'd woken up earlier.

I:	What can it mean: a crumpled giraffe? You know you can't squash a giraffe together like a piece of paper.
Hans:	Of course I know. I just thought it; of course there aren't any really and truly. The crumpled one was all lying on the floor, and I took it away – took hold of it with my hands.
I:	What? Can you take hold of a big giraffe like that with your hands?
Hans:	I took hold of the crumpled one with my hand.
I:	Where was the big one meanwhile?
Hans:	The big one just stood further off.
I:	What did you do with the crumpled one?
Hans:	I held it in my hand for a bit, till the big one had stopped calling out. And when the big one had stopped calling out, I sat down on top of it.
I:	Why did the big one call out?
Hans:	Because I'd taken away the little one from it.

His father recognized the fantasy as a reproduction of the bedroom scene which used to take place in the morning between the boy and his parents; and he quickly stripped the underlying wish of the disguise which it still wore. The boy's father and mother were the two giraffes.

The giraffe fantasy strengthened a conviction which had already begun to form in my mind when Hans expressed his fear that 'the horse'll come into the room', and I thought the right moment had now arrived for informing him that he was afraid of his father because he himself nourished jealous and hostile wishes against him. In telling him this, I had partly interpreted his fear of horses for him – the horse must be his father – whom he had good internal reasons for fearing. Certain details of which Hans had shown he was afraid, the black on horses' mouths and the things in front of their eyes (the moustaches and eyeglasses which are the privilege of a grown-up man), seemed to me to have been directly transposed from his father onto the horses.

By enlightening Hans on this subject, I had cleared away his most powerful resistance against allowing his unconscious thoughts to be made conscious, for his father was himself acting as his physician. The worst of the attack was now over, there was a plentiful flow of material; the little patient summoned up courage to describe the details of his phobia, and soon began to take an active share in the conduct of the analysis.

It was only then that we learnt what the objects and impressions were of which Hans was afraid. He was not only afraid of horses biting him – he was soon silent upon that point – but also of carts, of furniture vans, and of buses (their common quality being, as presently became clear, that they were all heavily loaded), of horses that started moving, of horses that looked big and heavy, and of horses that drove quickly. The meaning of these specifications was explained by Hans himself: he was afraid of horses *falling down*, and consequently incorporated in his phobia everything that seemed likely to facilitate their falling down.

It was at this stage of the analysis that he recalled the event, insignificant in itself, which immediately preceded the outbreak of the illness, and may no doubt be regarded as the precipitating cause of its outbreak. He went for a walk with his mother, and saw a bus horse fall down and kick about with its feet. This made a great impression on him. He was terrified, and thought the horse was dead; and from that time on he thought that all horses would fall down. His father pointed out to him that when he saw the horse fall down he must have thought of him, his father, and have wished that he might fall down in the same way and be dead. Hans did not dispute this interpretation, and a little while later he played a game consisting of biting his father, and so showed that he accepted the theory of his having identified his father with the horse he was afraid of. From that time forward, his behaviour to his father was unconstrained and fearless, and in fact a trifle overbearing. Nevertheless, his fear of horses persisted; nor was it yet clear through what chain of association the horse's falling down had stirred up his unconscious wishes.

Quite unexpectedly, and certainly without any prompting from his father, Hans now began to be occupied with the 'lumf' complex and to show disgust at things that reminded him of evacuating his bowels.

We learn that, formerly, Hans had been in the habit of insisting upon accompanying his mother to the WC, and that he had revived this custom with his friend Berta, at a time when she was filling his mother's place, until the fact became known and he was forbidden to do so. In the end, his father went into the lumf symbolism, and recognized that there was an analogy between a heavily loaded cart and a body loaded with faeces, between the way a cart drives out through a gateway and the way in which faeces leave the body, and so on.

> Without any warning, as it were, Hans produced a new fantasy. Later on, he began: 'Daddy, I thought something: *I was in the bath, and then the plumber came and unscrewed it. Then he took a big borer and stuck it into my stomach*'.

Henceforward, the material brought up in the analysis far outstripped our powers of understanding it. It was not until later that it was possible to guess that this was a remoulding of a *fantasy of procreation*, distorted by anxiety. The big bath of water, in which Hans imagined himself, was his mother's womb, the 'borer' which his father had, from the first, recognized as a penis, owed its mention to its connection with 'being born'. The interpretation that we are obliged to give to the fantasy will of course, sound very curious: 'With your big penis you "bored" me (i.e. "gave birth to me") and put me in my mother's womb'. For the moment, however, the fantasy eluded interpretation, and merely served Hans as a starting point from which to continue giving information.

Hans showed fear of being given a bath in the big bath, and this fear was once more a composite one. One part of it escaped us as yet, but the other part could at once be elucidated in connection with his baby sister having her bath. Hans confessed to having wished that his mother might drop the child while she was being given her bath, so that she should die. His own anxiety while he was having his bath was a fear of retribution for this evil wish, and of being punished by the same thing happening to him. Hans now left the subject of lumf, and passed on directly to that of his baby sister. We may well imagine what this juxtaposition signified – nothing less, in fact, than that little Hanna was a lumf herself – that all babies were lumfs, and were born like lumfs. We can now recognize that all furniture vans, drays and buses were only stork-box carts, and were only of interest to Hans as being symbolic representations of pregnancy, and that when a heavy or heavily loaded horse fell down, he can have seen in it only one thing: a childbirth, a delivery. Thus, the falling horse was not only his dying father, but also his mother in childbirth.

And at this point Hans gave us a surprise. He had noticed his mother's pregnancy and had, at any rate after the confinement, pieced the facts of the case together; without telling anyone, it is true, and perhaps without being able to tell anyone. All that could be seen at the time was that, immediately after the delivery, he had taken up an extremely sceptical attitude towards everything that might be supposed to point to the presence of the stork. *But that – in complete contradiction to his official speeches – he knew in his unconscious where the baby came from and where it had been before*, is proved beyond a show of doubt by the present analysis; indeed, this is perhaps its most unassailable feature.

The most cogent evidence of this is furnished by the fantasy of how Hanna had been with them at Gmunden the summer before her birth, of how she had travelled there with them, and of how she had been able to do far more then than she had a year later, after she had been born. All of this was intended as a revenge upon his father, against whom he harboured a grudge for having misled him with the stork fable. It was just as though he had meant to say: 'If you really thought I was as stupid as all that, and expected me to believe that the stork brought Hanna, then in return I expect *you* to accept *my* inventions as the truth'.

There are not many more mysteries ahead of us now. What remains are just such confirmations on Hans' part of analytical conclusions which our interpretations had already established. Another symptomatic act, happening as though by accident, involved a confession that he had wished his father dead, for, just at the moment his father was talking of this death-wish, Hans let a horse that he was playing with fall down; knocked it over in fact. Furthermore, he confirmed in so many words the hypothesis that heavily loaded carts represented his mother's pregnancy to him, and the horse's falling down was like having a baby.

We have already considered Hans' two concluding fantasies, with which his recovery was rounded off. One of them:

The plumber came, and first he took away my behind with a pair of pincers, and then gave me another, and then the same with my widdler. He said: 'Let me see your behind!' and I had to turn round, and he took it away; and then he said: 'Let me see your widdler!'

Hans' father grasped the nature of this wishful fantasy, and did not hesitate a moment as to the only interpretation it could bear.

I: He gave you a *bigger* widdler and a *bigger* behind.

Hans: Yes.

I: Like Daddy's; because you'd like to be Daddy.

Hans: Yes, and I'd like to have a moustache like yours and hairs like yours (*he pointed to the hairs on my chest*).

This was not merely a repetition of the earlier fantasy concerning the plumber and the bath. The new one was a triumphant, wishful, fantasy, and with it, he overcame his fear of castration. His other fantasy:

April 30th. Seeing Hans playing with his imaginary children again. 'Hallo', I said to him, 'are your children still alive? You know quite well a boy can't have any children'.

Hans: I know. I was their Mummy before, *now I'm their Daddy.*

I: And who's the children's Mummy?

Hans: Why Mummy, and you're their *Grandaddy.*

I: So then you'd like to be as big as me and be married to Mummy, and then you'd like her to have children.

Hans: Yes, that's what I'd like, and then my Lainz Grandmummy (my mother) will be their Grannie.

This did not merely exhaust the content of the unconscious complexes which had been stirred up by the sight of the falling horse and which had generated his anxiety. It also corrected that portion of those thoughts which was entirely unacceptable; for, instead of killing his father, it made him innocuous by promoting him to a marriage with Hans' grandmother. With this fantasy, both the illness and the analysis came to an appropriate end.

EVALUATION

Theoretical issues

One of the most serious problems faced by much of Freud's theory in general, and the case of Little Hans in particular, is that of *alternative explanations.* Is Freud's interpretation of Hans's phobia the only reasonable, feasible one? Amongst those who offer alternative interpretations are two very eminent psychoanalysts, Erich Fromm and John Bowlby.

According to Fromm (1970), Freud wanted to find support for the theory of sexuality based on adults by directly reviewing material drawn from a child. Regarding Hans's parents' treatment of him is concerned, was this as positive as Freud claims? According to Freud:

> His parents were both among my closest adherents, and they had agreed that, in bringing up their first child, they would use no more coercion than might be absolutely necessary for maintaining good behaviour. And, as the child developed into a cheerful, good natured and lively little boy, the experiment of letting him grow up and express himself without being intimidated went on satisfactorily.

He adds:

> Considering the education given by his parents, which consisted essentially in the omission of our usual educational sins, [undoubtedly they] were determined from the very beginning that he was neither to be laughed at nor bullied.

But what about the threat of castration from the mother, her threats not to come back, the lies they told (such as those about the stork, and the mother telling Hans she too has a penis, which was confirmed by the father)?

According to Fromm, Freud had a 'blind spot': he was a liberal, rather than a radical, critic of bourgeois society. He wanted to reduce and soften the degree of severity in educational methods, but he did not go so far as to criticize the basis of bourgeois society, namely the principle of force and threat. His original belief that his adult patients had all been victims of incest as children ('Seduction Theory') was later changed (to become the 'Oedipus Complex') in line with this same, non-radical attitude. Emphasizing the child's incestuous desires is a way of defending the parents; for example, weren't there cases of his mother actively seducing him? (see **Applications and implications** below).

While Freud claims that the dread of castration came from 'very slight allusions', Fromm believes that there were clear, strong threats made by the mother! Nor does the dream about the plumber necessarily suggest the fear of castration is focused on the father, nor even that it expresses fear of castration at all. It is at least as probable that the dream manifests Hans's desire to have a penis as large as his father's, and to be able to exchange his small one for a larger one: the wish to be grown up (as opposed to a fear of castration). In fact, this seems to be the interpretation which Hans's father actually provides! Freud himself makes the point that:

> . . . his painful expectations were given a happier turn. Yes, the Doctor *did* come, he *did* take away his penis – but only to give him a bigger one in exchange for it.

According to Mitchell (1974), by realizing that one day he would be a father in his own right, Hans more or less resolved his infantile fear of castration.

Freud's extreme patriarchical attitude prevented him from conceiving that the woman *could* be the main cause of fear. Fromm (1970) maintains that:

> . . . clinical observation amply proves that the most intense and pathogenic fears are indeed related to the mother; by comparison, the dread of the father is relatively insignificant.

It would appear that Hans needed his father to protect him from a menacing mother. Fromm believes that the successful outcome of the therapy was due not so much to the interpretations made of Hans's fear, as the protective role of the father and the 'super-father' (Freud).

Fromm believes the fear of horses has two origins:

(*i*)   fear of the mother (due to her castration threat); and
(*ii*) fear of death (he had witnessed the funeral at Gmunden, and then later the fallen horse which he thought was dead). To avoid both fears, he developed a fear of being bitten, which protects him both from horses and from experiencing both types of anxiety.

According to Freud, the boy's incestuous desire for the mother is 'endogenous' (*not* the result of maternal seduction). But is it as intense, exclusive and spontaneous as Freud believed? Fromm points out that Hans's mother liked to have him in bed with her, and to take him with her to the bathroom. But Hans wanted to sleep with Maried (their landlord's 13-year-old daughter), and once said he preferred her company to his mother's.

Finally, Fromm suggests that Hans's hostility is aimed at his *mother* (based on her castration threats, her 'treason' at giving birth to Hanna, and his desire to be free from fixation on her), rather than his father (as the Oedipus theory claims). Referring to a fantasy about a horse he took out of the stable:

Father:	You took it out of the stables?
Hans:	I took it out because I wanted to whip it.
Father:	Which would you really like to beat? Mummy, Hanna or me?
Hans:	Mummy.
Father:	Why?
Hans:	I should just like to beat her.
Father:	When did you ever see someone beating their Mummy?
Hans:	I've never seen anyone do it, never in all my life.
Father:	And yet you'd just like to do it?
Hans:	With a carpet-beater. (*His mother often threatened to beat him with it.*)

There is much evidence of great warmth and friendship in Hans's relationship with his father. Fromm concludes that:

> . . . this was a slight phobia, such as occurs in many children, and it would probably have disappeared by itself without any treatment, and without the father's support and interest.

Bowlby (1973) reinterprets the case of Little Hans in terms of attachment theory. He asks whether Hans's anxiety about the availability of attachment figures played a larger part than Freud realized. Agreeing with Fromm, Bowlby argues that most of Hans' anxiety arose from threats by the mother to desert the family. The main evidence comes from:

(*i*)   the sequence in which the symptoms developed and statements made by Hans himself; and

(*ii*) evidence in the father's account that the mother was in the habit of using threats of an alarming kind to discipline Hans, including the threat to abandon him.

The symptoms did not come out of the blue; Hans had been upset throughout the preceding week. They began when Hans had woken up one morning in tears. Asked why he was crying, he said to his mother:

> When I was asleep I thought you were gone, and I had no Mummy to coax with. ('coax'=cuddle).

Some days later, his nursemaid had taken him to a local park, as usual. But he started crying in the street, and asked to be taken home, so he could 'coax' with his mother. During that evening, he became very frightened and cried, demanding to stay with his mother. The next day, his mother, eager to find out what was wrong, took him to Schönbrunn, when the horse phobia was first noticed. But the week preceding the onset of the phobia was *not* the first time Hans had expressed fear his mother might disappear. Six months earlier, he made remarks such as:

> Suppose I was to have no Mummy. Suppose you were to go away.

When Hanna was born, Hans was kept away from his mother. The father states that Hans's 'present anxiety, which prevents him leaving the neighbourhood of the house, is in reality the longing for [his mother] which he felt then'. Freud endorses this by describing Hans's 'enormously intensified affect' for his mother as 'the fundamental phenomenon in his condition'.

Thus, both the sequence of events leading up to the phobia and Hans's own statements make it clear that, distinct from and preceding any fear of horses, Hans was afraid that his mother might go away and leave him (Bowlby, 1973). Did she actually threaten, implicitly or explicitly, to leave the family? She certainly does use rather alarming threats:

(*i*)   To cut off his widdler (or 'wi-wi-maker').

(*ii*)   A year later, when the phobia was first reported, she was still trying to break him of the habit (of masturbating). She 'warned him' not to touch his penis, but no details are given of the warning.

(*iii*) Three months later, Hans came into his father's bed one morning and told him:

> Hans: When you're away, I'm afraid you're not coming home.
> Father: And have I ever threatened you that I shan't come home?
> Hans: Not you, but Mummy. Mummy's told me she won't come back.
> Father: She said that because you were naughty.
> Hans: Yes.

(*iv*)   Even the fear of being bitten by a horse is consistent with the view that fear of the mother's departure is the main source of anxiety. During the summer holiday of the previous year, Lizzi, a little girl staying in a neighbouring house, had gone away. The luggage was taken to the station in a cart pulled by a white horse. Lizzi's father was there and had warned her:

> Don't put your finger to the white horse or it'll bite you.

So, fear of being bitten was closely linked in Hans's mind to someone's departure. Table 19.1 summarizes the different interpretations of Freud and Bowlby.

Gay (1988) refers to an article by an American psychoanalyst, Slap, entitled *Little Hans' Tonsillectomy* (1961), in which he offers an intriguing *complementary* interpretation of his fear of horses. In February 1908, in the second month of the neurosis, Hans had his tonsils out, at which point the phobia worsened and, shortly after, he explicitly

Table 19.1

DIFFERENCES OF INTERPRETATION BETWEEN FREUD AND BOWLBY

Item	Freud	Bowlby
Hans's insistent desire to remain with his mother	Expression of sexual love for mother, having reached extreme 'pitch of intensity'	Anxious attachment ('separation anxiety')
Dreams that she had gone away and left him	Expression of fear of punishment for incestuous wishes	Expression of fear that she'd carry out threat to desert family
White horse will bite	Wish that father would go away	Fear of mother's desertion
Mother's displays of affection and allowing him to come into her bed	Action which might have encouraged Hans' Oedipal wishes	Natural and comforting expression of motherly feelings

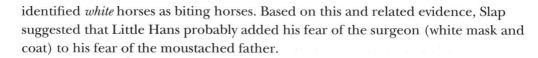

identified *white* horses as biting horses. Based on this and related evidence, Slap suggested that Little Hans probably added his fear of the surgeon (white mask and coat) to his fear of the moustached father.

This extra fear is most easily explained in terms of the acquisition of a conditioned fear response through classical conditioning (see the case of Little Albert: Chapter 16), and strongly suggests that a psychoanalytic explanation may be quite compatible with one derived from learning theory. But Eysenck (1985), probably Freud's most outspoken critic (see Chapter 22), wants to *substitute* Freud's account with an explanation based on classical conditioning. Eysenck refers to an evaluation of the case of Little Hans by Wolpe & Rachman (1960), two eminent behaviour therapists, who propose that the incident which Freud refers to as merely the 'exciting cause' (i.e. trigger) of Hans's phobia, was, in fact, the cause of the *entire* disorder, namely, the moment when the horse collapsed in the street:

> *Hans:* No. I only got it [the phobia] then. When the horse and the bus fell down, it gave me such a fright, really! That was when I got the nonsense.
>
> *Father:* All of this was confirmed by my wife, as well as the fact that the anxiety broke out immediately afterwards.

Hans's initial fear response generalized to all horses, horse-drawn buses and vans, and features of horses such as muzzles and blinkers. He was more afraid of large vehicles than small ones (the original incident involved a large bus), and these were also the *last* aspects of the phobia to disappear. All of this, they argue, is consistent with the conditioned fear explanation.

All these (apparently conflicting) explanations of Hans's phobia can (ironically) be accommodated within the psychoanalytic account of phobias. According to Freud, phobias (child or adult) typically represent the conscious manifestation of *several* unconscious sources of anxiety, which become focused on/compressed into the single phobic object or situation (through *condensation, transformation,* and other unconscious processes: Ward, 2001). So, fear of castration by his father (Freud), fear of his mother's threats to castrate him (Fromm), fear of being abandoned by his mother (Bowlby), and fear of horses as a generalized conditioned fear response (Wolpe and Rachman) can *all* be seen as condensed into the single fear of being bitten by a horse. Freud's account of phobias in general is, arguably, the only one that is broad enough to explain how these different elements could all form part of the 'same', specific, fear. What Freud saw in Hans was a little boy full of many fears, albeit castration anxiety was the predominant one (Ward, 2001).

Methodological issues

Freud is aware of the methodological objections which could be raised to the fact that Hans was being analysed by his father (Max Graf, an eminent music critic and one of the early members of the psychoanalytic society). His wife (Hans's mother) had been treated by Freud before her marriage to Hans' father: how could the father be objective in his observations and psychoanalyse someone with whom he was so emotionally involved? Also, the child will be susceptible to his father's suggestions. Doesn't this immediately invalidate the case-study as an *independent* confirmation of Freud's Oedipal theory?

Freud himself seems to agree with this criticism by saying that Hans's father did have to put into words things Hans could not himself say, be presented with thoughts which he had not previously shown signs of possessing, and so on. However (and this is perhaps the critical point), although this 'detracts from the evidential value of the analysis', the 'procedure is the same in every case' (i.e. with adult patients too):

> For a psychoanalysis is not an impartial scientific investigation, but a therapeutic measure. Its essence is not to prove anything but merely to alter something.

While this may meet the immediate criticism outlined above, doesn't it at the same time condemn the whole of Freud's work to the realm of 'non-science', since his theories are all constructed on the basis of his work with neurotic patients? Isn't the consulting room his 'laboratory', his patients the 'participants', and what they say about themselves (especially their childhood) the data?

This point is answered by Storr (1987), a leading popularizer of psychoanalytic theory and himself a trained psychoanalyst. Storr claims that, although some of the hypotheses of psychoanalytic theory can be tested scientifically (they are refutable), this applies only to a minority: the majority are based on observations made in the course of psychoanalytic treatment, which cannot be regarded as a scientific procedure. Such observations are inevitably contaminated by the subjective experience and prejudice of the observer, however detached s/he tries to be, and so cannot be regarded in the same light as observations made during, say, a chemistry or physics experiment. Although it is certainly possible to study human beings as if they were objects merely responding to the stimuli impinging on them (as in experimental psychology), it is *not* possible to conduct psychoanalysis (or any form of psychotherapy) in this way.

So, do we have to accept Storr's conclusion that psychoanalytic theory can never be thought of as scientific? One defence of Freud may be that to study people as objects responding to stimuli is not truly scientific, because that is not what people are actually like, and so to study them in this way is not only unethical but inaccurate. Perhaps Freud is much closer to treating people *as* people and, to that extent, *more* of a scientist than most experimental psychologists!

If, as Freud claims, the case of Little Hans shares with all case-studies (i.e. all psychoanalytic treatments) the characteristic of being a 'therapeutic measure' rather than 'an impartial scientific investigation', it still has some rather distinctive features:

(*i*) it was conducted not by the therapist author (in this case Freud) but by a second party (the father) who acted as an intermediary between Freud and the patient (Hans): Freud had met Hans twice, once for a 'therapeutic session', once to take him a birthday present (Gay, 1988);

(*ii*) very little was said in the case-study about technique (*how* the psychoanalysis was conducted). One interesting exception is when Freud points out that the father was pushing Little Hans too hard:

> He asks too much and investigates in accord with his own presuppositions instead of letting the little boy express himself. (quoted in Gay, 1988)

This is ironic in view of the criticisms made of Freud that he already saw Little Hans as a 'little Oedipus' before any therapy began (a case of the pot calling the kettle black?).

> By its nature, then, however broad its theoretical implications, 'Little Hans', with its most unorthodox technique, hardly recommended itself as an exemplar. It must remain unique. (Gay, 1988)

On the positive side, Gay argues that the case of Little Hans demonstrates what all psychoanalytic therapy has in common (the 'excavation' of childhood foundations of adult neurosis). But because of Little Hans's age, compared with adult therapy, there was relatively little 'digging' that needed to be done.

Freud's father died in 1896 and it is widely accepted that this had a profound effect on him personally as well as on the development of his theory. His reflection, through self-analysis, on his relationship with his father was partly responsible for his emphasis on the Oedipus complex. But according to Gay (1988), what matters is *not* whether Freud had, or imagined he had, an Oedipus complex, but whether his claim that everyone passes through such a complex can be empirically substantiated.

However, Freud 'did not regard his own experiences as automatically valid for all humanity' (Gay, 1988). His work demonstrates an ambivalence he felt towards recognition of the individual on the one hand, and universal features of the human psyche on the other:

> . . . his famous case histories eloquently reflect his simultaneous commitment to individuality and generality; each depicts an unduplicable patient who at the same time belongs to a category of cases. (Gay, 1988)

A similar point is made by Jacobs (1992):

> Freud's case histories read like individual stories; but he used them to put forward more general hypotheses, in his wish to be regarded as a serious scientist.

This relates to the *idiographic-nomothetic* debate in psychology which, in turn, is part of the more general debate about the nature of science (see **Exercises** for Chapter 27 and Gross, 2003).

Applications and implications

As noted in **Background and Context** above, the case of Little Hans is intended to support Freud's Oedipal theory which, in turn, (largely) replaced the earlier Seduction theory of neurosis (or, more accurately, the sexual abuse theory of hysteria: Mollon, 1998). Whereas the Seduction theory (1896) claimed that adults' neurotic symptoms are the result of (actual) incest and sexual abuse experienced in childhood, according to the Oedipal theory (1905) what his patients claimed were memories of abuse, were, in fact, merely fantasies.

Freud has been condemned in recent years for this retraction of the original theory, which recognized abuse as real. Alice Miller (1986), for example, holds the Oedipal theory partly responsible for society's reluctance to acknowledge the extent of incest and sexual abuse in general, and Masson (1992) has accused him of cowardice: he compromised the truth because he could not tolerate isolation from the Viennese medical establishment. More seriously:

> . . . fantasy – the notion from Freud that women invent allegations of sexual abuse because they desire sex – continues to play a role in undermining the credibility of victims of sexual abuse. (Masson, 1992)

In his defence, Jacobs (1992) and Mollon (1998) point out that Freud didn't totally abandon the Seduction theory: it lost its emphasis as he developed his theory of infantile sexuality, but at various points in his career he acknowledged that abuse does take place. What Freud rejected was the Seduction theory as a general explanation of how all neuroses originate (Gay, 1988).

More seriously, according to Esterson (1998, 2001), Israels & Schatzman (1993), and others, Masson's account of the seduction theory (which originally appeared in *Assault on Truth,* 1984) is *mistaken,* based on a fundamental misconception. In Freud's theory, the fantasies are *unconscious* and so must be analytically uncovered by the therapist: reports of child sexual abuse (CSA) that the patient had always remembered *don't fall into this category.* The cornerstone of Masson's (1984) account of Freud's abandonment of the 'truth' (that most of his female patients told him they had been sexually abused in early childhood, usually by their father) is contradicted by the contemporary documentary evidence (Esterson, 1998, 2001).

Freud has not only been pilloried by Masson and many feminists for concealing the truth about CSA (thus making it more difficult for psychodynamic therapists to recognize the truth of their patients' accounts of CSA), but he has also been seen as

responsible for so-called *false memory syndrome* (FMS). In 1993, false memory *societies* were established, both in the UK and the USA, providing support and information for people (typically parents) who believed they had been falsely accused of sexually abusing their now adult children. The latter typically 'recovered' memories of CSA during the course of psychotherapy, and therapists were accused by the parents of having 'implanted' these (false) memories into their vulnerable patients.

Once again, however, it seems that Freud has been hard done by. According to Mollon (1998), the Freud who has been so vilified (especially by American critics such as Crews, 1997) seems to be a Hollywood caricature:

> . . . Indeed, the truth seems the very opposite of this current myth – Freud highlighted the unreliability and reconstructive nature of memory . . .

An interpretation or reconstruction along the lines of 'your father then sexually abused you' has no psychoanalytic meaning (even if factually true). Mollon argues that:

> . . . To assume that psychoanalysts search for buried memories, analagous to lost video-recordings, is to misunderstand profoundly the analytic endeavour. Psychoanalysis is the study of mental life – the psychoanalyst observes the mind which expresses itself (in words and behaviour) in the consulting room . . .

Mollon concludes by saying that the accusation that Freud invented 'recovered memory therapy' has no legitimate place in any discussion of Freud.

Freud believed passionately that all children's questions should be answered honestly, including (and perhaps particularly) those about sexual matters (such as 'Where do babies come from?'), from as early an age as possible. He recognized, of course, that children will always interpret what they are told in terms of their current phantasies and 'theories' (Mitchell, 1974; Ward, 2001), but:

> . . . In the collective denial of children's sexuality and phantasy life, we abandon them to solve these momentous problems on their own– and we fail to relieve the anxieties which lie at the heart of the child's sexual life . . . (Ward, 2001)

Freud believed that if the child wants to know where babies come from, it is because s/he wants to know where *this particular baby* comes from – the one who may take away his/her mother's love and threatens his/her whole existence (for Hans, this was Hanna).

There is a fascinating postscript to the case-study (Freud, 1922) which tends to support various aspects of both Fromm and Bowlby's interpretation (see **Theoretical issues** above). He lost touch with Hans after 1911.

> The publication of this first analysis of a child had caused a great stir and even greater indignation, and a most evil future had been foretold for the poor little boy, because he had been 'robbed of his innocence' at such a tender age and had been made the victim of psychoanalysis. But none of these apprehensions

had come true. Little Hans was now a strapping youth of 19. He declared that he was perfectly well, and suffered from no troubles or inhibitions. Not only had he come through his puberty without any damage, but his emotional life had successfully undergone one of the severest of ordeals. His parents had been divorced, and each of them had married again. In consequence of this, he lived by himself, but he was on good terms with both of his parents, and only regretted that, as a result of the breaking-up of the family, he had been separated from the younger sister he was so fond of.

It seemed that he had gone with his father, when the parents first split up. When he heard his case history, he failed to recognize himself: he could remember nothing. The analysis had not preserved the events from amnesia, but had been overtaken by amnesia itself. 'Little Hans' became Herbert Graf, a well-known producer and director of operas.

Exercises

1. Why is the case-study considered to be the least scientific of all empirical methods used by psychologists?

2. Quite apart from any of your answers to **1**, is there anything about the case of Little Hans which makes it less scientific than it might otherwise have been?

3. The kind of data Freud presents is *qualitative*. What is the difference between this and *quantitative* data?

4. Is it possible – or necessary – to choose between Freud's, Fromm's and Bowlby's interpretations? Can they all be (partially) true?

20 On being sane in insane places

D.L. Rosenhan (1973)

Science, 179, 250–8

BACKGROUND AND CONTEXT

The whole attempt to classify mental illness is an integral part of the *medical model* of mental disorder (or psychological abnormality). This is the view of mental disorder on which traditional psychiatry is based. Psychiatrists, as medical doctors, are trained to regard mental illness as comparable to other kinds of (physical) illness, but the symptoms are behavioural and cognitive rather than bodily. (However, any hard-and-fast distinction between these two broad categories soon begins to break down: many symptoms of anxiety, for example, take a physical form, such as vomiting, sweating, goose-flesh, and headaches and, conversely, physical illness will usually make us feel tired, depressed, lower our self-esteem, cause us anxiety, and so on).

The vocabulary used by psychologists and other non-psychiatrists, as well as the lay person, to refer to mental disorder is borrowed from medical terminology: deviant behaviour is referred to as *psychopathology*, is classified on the basis of *symptoms*, the classification being called a *diagnosis*, the methods used to try to change the behaviour are called *treatments* or *therapies*, and these are often carried out in psychiatric *hospitals*. If the deviant behaviour ceases, the *patient* is said to be *cured* (Maher, 1966). It is the use of such vocabulary which reflects the pervasiveness of a 'sickness' model of psychological abnormality (together with terms such as 'syndrome', 'prognosis' and 'in remission'). We tend to think about abnormal behaviour *as if* it were indicative of some underlying *illness*.

All systems of psychiatric classification stem from the work of Emil Kraepelin (1913), who claimed that certain groups of signs and symptoms occur together sufficiently often to merit the designation 'disease' or syndrome; he then described the diagnostic indicators associated with each syndrome. Kraepelin's classification is embodied in the 1959 Mental Health Act, although the latter is much broader and, in fact, is concerned with mental *disorders* (which includes mental *illness*).

One of the two major classification systems currently used in the UK is the Mental Disorders Section of the Tenth Revision of the International Classification of Diseases (ICD-10) published by the World Health Organization in 1992. There is considerable overlap between ICD-10 and the system used in the USA, namely, the American Psychiatric Association's Diagnostic and Statistical Manual of Mental Disorders (DSM), originally published in 1952, revised in 1968 (DSM-II) and again in 1980 (DSM-III), with a minor revision in 1987 (DSM-III-R). It is currently in its fourth edition (DSM-IV, 1994).

However, the systems differ as regards the number of major categories they use. For example, ICD-10 has a single category for Schizophrenia, Schizotypal States and Delusional Disorders, which correspond to three separate DSM-IV categories, namely Schizophrenia, Delusional Disorders, and Psychotic Disorders not elsewhere classified.

AIM AND NATURE OF THE STUDY

The study is an experimental test of the hypothesis that psychiatrists cannot reliably tell the difference between people who are sane and those who are insane. According to Rosenhan, if the hypothesis is supported it follows that the classification system being used to make such a diagnosis cannot be valid (since reliably differentiating the sane from the insane is a minimum requirement of a particular diagnostic label, such as schizophrenia, actually describing a patient's mental disorder).

The hypothesis was tested in two different ways:

(*i*)   the major experiment (what most of the article is devoted to describing and discussing, and the one usually cited by others) involved pseudo-patients trying to get admitted to various hospitals in different parts of the USA, complaining of hearing voices (auditory hallucinations). Pretending to hear voices was the manipulated *independent variable* (though this pretence was dropped once admission had been gained), and the *dependent variable* was whether or not psychiatrists admitted the pseudo-patient on the strength of a particular diagnostic label (in 11 out of 12 cases this was schizophrenia, the other being manic-depressive);

(*ii*)   a secondary experiment involved misinforming various members of staff at a research and teaching hospital, that they could expect one or more pseudo-patients to try to gain admission during the next three months (based on accurate information concerning the first experiment). So, this false information was the manipulated *independent variable*, and the *dependent variable* was the number of patients which staff subsequently suspected of being pseudo-patients (remember, all patients were genuine). Since both parts of the study took place in actual psychiatric hospitals, the study is primarily a *field experiment*.

It also involves a large measure of *participant observation*: once admitted, the pseudo-patients kept written records of how the ward as a whole operated, as well as how they personally were treated. One of the ironies of the findings is that it was (other) patients who suspected them, not the staff. Although they did not disclose their true identity (they did not 'blow their cover'), they did begin to behave as normally as possible (including saying they did not hear the voices any longer) and, to this extent, they were not 'fully participant'. However, the very nature of the findings meant that, at least as far as the *staff* were concerned, they were treated identically to other patients. This enabled them to experience the ward from the patient's perspective while also maintaining the degree of objectivity required in a scientific investigation.

THE STUDY

If sanity and insanity exist, how shall we know them?

The question is neither capricious nor itself insane. However much we may be personally convinced that we can tell the normal from the abnormal, the evidence is simply not compelling. It is commonplace, for example, to read about murder trials in which eminent psychiatrists for the defence are contradicted by equally eminent psychiatrists for the prosecution regarding the defendant's sanity. More generally, there are a great deal of conflicting data on the reliability, utility, and meaning of such terms as 'sanity', 'insanity', 'mental illness' and 'schizophrenia' (Ash, 1949; Beck, 1962; Boisen, 1939; Kreitman, 1961; Kreitman *et al.*, 1961; Schmitt & Fonda, 1956; Seeman, 1953). As early as 1934, Benedict suggested that normality and abnormality are not universal; what is viewed as normal in one culture may be seen as quite aberrant in another. Thus, notions of normality and abnormality may not be quite as accurate as people believe they are.

To raise questions about normality and abnormality is in no way to question the fact that some behaviours are deviant or odd. Murder and hallucinations are deviant. Nor does raising such questions deny the personal anguish often associated with 'mental illness'; anxiety, depression and psychological suffering exist. But normality and abnormality, sanity and insanity, and the diagnoses which flow from them may be less substantive than many believe them to be.

At its heart, the question of whether the sane can be distinguished from the insane (and whether degrees of insanity can be distinguished from each other) is a simple one: do the salient characteristics that lead to diagnosis reside in the patients themselves or in the environments and contexts in which observers find them? From Bleuler, through Kretschmer, through the recently revised *Diagnostic and Statistical Manual* of the American Psychiatric Association, there has been a strong belief that patients present symptoms which can be categorized and, implicitly, that the sane are distinguishable from the insane. But more recently, based on theoretical, anthropological, philosophical, legal and therapeutic considerations, the view has grown that psychological categorization of mental illness is, at best, useless and, at worst, harmful, misleading and pejorative. Psychiatric diagnoses are seen as being in the minds of the observers, and are not valid summaries of characteristics displayed by the observed (Becker, 1963; Braginsky *et al.*, 1969; Crocetti & Lemkau, 1965; Goffman, 1961, 1964; Laing, 1960; Phillips, 1963; Sarbin, 1972; Scheff, 1966; Schur, 1969; Szasz, 1963).

A way of deciding between these views is to get normal people (i.e. people who do not have, and have never suffered, symptoms of serious psychiatric disorders) admitted to psychiatric hospitals, and then determining whether they were discovered to be sane and, if so, how. If the sanity of such pseudo-patients were always detected, there would be prima-facie evidence that a sane individual can be distinguished from the insane context in which he is found, since it is carried within the person. But if the pseudo-patients' sanity were never detected, serious difficulties would arise for those who support traditional modes of psychiatric diagnoses. Assuming that the hospital staff were not incompetent, that the pseudo-patient had been behaving as sanely as he had been outside the hospital, and that it had never been previously suggested that he belonged in a psychiatric hospital, such an unlikely outcome would support the view that psychiatric diagnosis betrays little about the patient, but much about the environment in which he is observed.

This article describes such an experiment. Eight sane people gained secret admission to 12 different hospitals. (Data from a ninth pseudo-patient are not included because, although his sanity went undetected, he falsified aspects of his personal history, and so his experimental behaviours were not identical to those of the others.) Too few psychiatrists and psychologists, including those who have worked in psychiatric institutions, know what the experience is like of being a patient, and while there have been occasional reports of researchers submitting themselves to psychiatric hospitalization (Barry, 1971; Belkuag, 1956; Candill *et al.*, 1952; Goldman *et al.*, 1970), these researchers have commonly stayed in the hospitals for short periods of time, often with the knowledge of the hospital staff. How much were they treated like patients and how much like research colleagues? Their reports about the inside of the psychiatric hospital have been valuable. This article extends those efforts.

PSEUDO-PATIENTS AND THEIR SETTINGS

The eight pseudo-patients comprised a psychology graduate student in his 20s, three psychologists, a paediatrician, a psychiatrist, a painter and a housewife (three women, five men). All used pseudonyms, in case their alleged diagnoses embarrass them later. Those in the mental health professions claimed other occupations in order to avoid the special attentions which might be accorded by staff, as a matter of courtesy, or caution, to ailing colleagues. Apart from myself (I was the first pseudo-patient, and my presence was known to the hospital administrator and chief psychologist and, as far as I can tell, to them alone), the presence of pseudo-

patients and the nature of the research program were unknown to the hospital staffs.

In order to generalize the findings, admission into a variety of hospitals was sought. The 12 hospitals in the sample were located in five different states on the East and West coasts. Some were old and shabby, some quite new, some were research orientated, others not, some had good staff–patient ratios, others were quite understaffed. Except for one private hospital, all were state or federal funded or, in one case, university funded.

After calling the hospital for an appointment, the pseudo-patient arrived at the admissions office complaining that he had been hearing voices. Asked what the voices said, he replied that they were often unclear, but as far as he could tell they said 'empty', 'hollow', and 'thud'. The voices were unfamiliar and were of the same sex as the pseudo-patient. These symptoms were chosen partly because of their apparent similarity to existential symptoms, which are alleged to arise from painful concerns about the perceived meaningfulness of one's life ('my life is empty and hollow'), and partly because of the *absence* of a single report of existential psychoses in the literature.

THE STUDY

Beyond alleging the symptoms and falsifying name, vocation and employment, no further alterations of person, history or circumstances were made. The significant events of life history, relationships with parents and siblings, spouse and children, work colleagues and people at school (consistent with the above-mentioned exceptions) were described as they were or had been. Frustrations and upsets were described along with joys and satisfactions. If anything, these facts should have strongly biased the subsequent results in favour of detecting sanity, since none of their histories or current behaviours was seriously pathological in any way.

Immediately upon admission to the psychiatric ward, the pseudo-patient stopped simulating *any* symptoms of abnormality. In some cases, there was a brief period of mild nervousness, since none really believed that they would be admitted so easily; indeed, their shared fear was that they would be immediately exposed as frauds and greatly embarrassed. Many had never visited a psychiatric ward before. So their nervousness was quite appropriate to the novelty of the hospital setting and abated rapidly.

Apart from this short-lived nervousness, the pseudo-patients behaved 'normally' on the ward, speaking to patients and staff as they might ordinarily. Because there is uncommonly little to do on a psychiatric ward, they tried to engage others in conversation. When asked by staff how they were feeling, they indicated that they were fine and no longer experienced symptoms. They responded to instructions from attendants, to calls for medication (which was not swallowed), and to dining hall instructions. Beyond the activities that were available on the admissions ward, they spent their time writing down their observations about the ward, its patients and staff. Initially this was done 'secretly', but it soon became clear that no one much cared, so it was subsequently done quite openly, in such public places as the dayroom.

The pseudo-patient, very much as a true psychiatric patient, entered hospital with no foreknowledge of when he would be discharged. Each was told that he would have to get out by his own devices, essentially by convincing the staff that he was sane. The psychological stresses associated with hospitalization were considerable, and all but one of the pseudo-patients wished to be discharged almost immediately after admission. They were, therefore, motivated not only to behave sanely, but to be paragons of cooperation. Nursing reports, obtained for most of them, all indicate that they were 'friendly', 'cooperative' and 'exhibited no abnormal indications'.

THE NORMAL ARE NOT DETECTABLY SANE

Despite their public 'show' of sanity, the pseudo-patients were never detected. Except in one case, they were admitted with a diagnosis of schizophrenia, and discharged with a diagnosis of schizophrenia 'in remission'. The label 'in remission' in no way indicates that the pseudo-patient had been suspected of simulating mental illness; indeed the evidence is rather strong that, once labelled schizophrenic, the label stuck, so that if he was to be discharged, he must naturally be 'in remission', not sane, nor, in the institution's view, had he ever been sane.

Although there were considerable variations between the hospitals, several were considered excellent. Length of hospitalization ranged from seven to 52 days (average 19 days), so there was plenty of opportunity for them to be carefully observed, although, in fact, they were not.

Pseudo-patients' daily visitors could detect no serious behavioural consequences of hospitalization, nor could other patients; indeed, it was quite common for the patients to 'detect' their sanity. During the first three hospitalizations, when accurate accounts were kept, 35 out of 118 patients on the admissions ward voiced their suspicions, some vigorously: 'You're not crazy. You're a journalist, or a professor [referring to the continual note-taking]. You're checking up on the hospital'. While most of the patients were reassured by the pseudo-patients' insistence that he had been sick before he came in, but was fine now, some continued to believe that he was sane throughout the hospitalization. So are patients better at detecting normality than psychiatrists?

Perhaps doctors are strongly biased towards Type-two errors (Scheff, 1966), i.e. they are more inclined to call a healthy person sick (a false positive) than a sick person healthy (a false negative, Type-one error). It is clearly more dangerous to misdiagnose illness than health, so it is better to err on the side of caution. However, what holds for medicine does not hold equally well for psychiatry.

Medical illnesses, while unfortunate, are not usually pejorative, but psychiatric diagnoses carry with them personal, legal and social stigmas (Cumming & Cumming, 1965; Farina & King, 1965; Freeman & Simmons, 1963; Johannsen, 1969; Linsky, 1970). It was therefore important to see whether the tendency toward diagnosing the sane insane could be reversed. An experiment was arranged at a research and teaching hospital whose staff had heard these findings, but doubted that such an error could occur in their hospital. They were informed that at some time during the next three months, one or more pseudo-patients would attempt to be admitted into the hospital. Each staff member was asked to rate on a 10-point scale each patient who presented himself at admissions or on the ward as to the likelihood that he was a pseudo-patient.

Judgements were obtained on 193 patients submitted for psychiatric treatment. All staff who had had sustained contact with, or primary responsibility for, the patient – attendants, nurses, psychiatrists, doctors and psychologists – were asked to make judgements. 41 patients were confidently judged to be pseudo-patients by at least one staff member, 23 were suspected by at least one psychiatrist, and 19 were suspected by one psychiatrist *and* one other staff member. In fact, all patients during this period were genuine.

The experiment indicates that the tendency to designate sane people as insane can be reversed when the stakes are high (prestige and diagnostic acumen). But were the 19 people suspected of being 'sane' by one psychiatrist and another staff member truly 'sane', or was it that, in trying to avoid the Type-two error, the staff tended to make more Type-one errors? There is no way of knowing, but one thing is certain: any diagnostic process which lends itself so readily to massive errors of this sort cannot be a very reliable one.

THE STICKINESS OF PSYCHODIAGNOSTIC LABELS

Beyond the tendency to call the healthy sick – a tendency which accounts better for diagnostic behaviour on admission than after a lengthy period of exposure – the data indicate the massive role of labelling in psychiatric assessment. Having been labelled schizophrenic, there is nothing the pseudo-patient can do to remove it, and it profoundly colours others' perceptions of him and his behaviour.

These findings are consistent with Gestalt psychology's emphasis on the meaning given to elements by the context in which they occur, and with Asch's (1946) findings that there are powerful 'central' personality traits (e.g. 'warm' vs. 'cold') which markedly colour the meaning of other information when forming an impression of another person. 'Insane', 'schizophrenic', 'manic-depressive' and 'crazy' are probably some of the most powerful of such central traits; indeed, many of the pseudo-patients' normal behaviours were entirely overlooked or profoundly misinterpreted. As far as I can determine, diagnoses were in no way affected by the rela-

Left margin: THE STUDY

tive health of the circumstances of a pseudo-patient's life. Rather, the reverse occurred: the perception of his circumstances was shaped entirely by the diagnosis. For example, one pseudo-patient had had a close relationship with his mother, but was rather remote from his father during early childhood. But during adolescence and beyond, his father became a close friend, while his relationship with his mother cooled. His present relationship with his wife was close and warm; apart from occasional angry exchanges, friction was minimal. The children had rarely been spanked. Surely there is nothing especially pathological about such a history; but observe how it was translated in the psychopathological context (the case summary prepared after the patient's discharge):

> This white 39-year-old male . . . manifests a long history of considerable ambivalence in close relationships, which begins in early childhood. A warm relationship with his mother cools during his adolescence. A distant relationship to his father is described as becoming very intense. Affective stability is absent. His attempts to control emotionality with his wife and children are punctuated by angry outbursts and, in the case of the children, spankings. And while he says that he has several good friends, one senses considerable ambivalence embedded in these relationships also. . .

The facts of the case were unintentionally distorted by the staff to achieve consistency with a popular theory of the dynamics of a schizophrenic reaction. If there were any ambivalence in his relationships, it was probably no greater than is found in all human relationships. Clearly, the meaning given to his verbalizations (i.e. ambivalence, affective instability) was determined by the diagnosis of schizophrenia. An entirely different meaning would have been attached if it were known that the man was 'normal'.

All pseudo-patients took extensive notes, publicly, and this raised questions in the patients' minds, as you would expect. Indeed, it seemed so certain that the notes would arouse suspicion, that elaborate precautions were taken to remove them from the ward each day. However, the closest any staff member came to questioning these notes occurred when one pseudo-patient asked about his medication, and began to write down the response; 'You needn't write it', he was told gently by the doctor. 'If you have trouble remembering, just ask me again'.

Nursing records for three pseudo-patients indicate that the writing was seen as an aspect of their pathological behaviour. 'Patient engages in writing behaviour' was the daily nursing comment on one of the pseudo-patients who was never questioned about his writing. Given that the patient is in hospital, he must be psychologically disturbed, and given that he is disturbed, continuous writing must be a behavioural manifestation of that disturbance, perhaps a subset of the compulsive behaviours sometimes correlated with schizophrenia.

Pseudo-patients' notes are full of patient behaviours which were misinterpreted by well-intentioned staff as stemming from within the patient, rather than the complex of environmental stimuli surrounding him. For example, one kindly nurse found a pseudo-patient pacing the long hospital corridors. 'Nervous, Mr X?', she asked. 'No, bored', he said. Again, not uncommonly, a patient would go 'beserk', because he had, wittingly or unwittingly, been mistreated by, say, an attendant. A nurse coming upon the scene would rarely inquire even cursorily into the possible environmental causes, but assumed that his upset stemmed from his pathology. Occasionally, a relative who had recently visited, or another patient might be suspected of triggering the outburst, but never a member of staff or the structure of the hospital. And a psychiatrist described a group of patients sitting outside the cafeteria half an hour before lunchtime as displaying the oral-acquisitive nature of the syndrome.

Just as Zigler and Phillips (1961) have shown that there is enormous overlap in the symptoms presented by patients with various diagnoses, so there is enormous overlap in the behaviours of the sane and the insane. We all lose our tempers 'for no good reason', feel depressed or anxious occasionally, again for no good reason, and find it difficult to get on with some other person. Conversely, the pseudo-patients felt that the bizarre behaviour upon which patients' diagnoses were allegedly based constituted only a small fraction of their total behaviour. If it makes no sense to label ourselves as permanently depressed on the basis of occasional depression, then it takes better evidence than is currently available to label all patients insane or schizophrenic based on bizarre behaviours or cognitions. It seems more useful, as Mischel (1968) has suggested, to discuss *behaviours*, the stimuli which provoke them, and their correlates.

THE EXPERIENCE OF PSYCHIATRIC HOSPITALIZATION

'Mental illness' is a recent term, and was coined by people who, for humanitarian reasons, wanted to change the status of the psychologically disturbed from that of witches and 'crazies' to one akin to the physically ill. But while their treatment has improved, they are still not seen in the same way as the physically ill; for example, mental illness supposedly lasts forever, and public attitudes are characterized by fear, hostility, aloofness, suspicion and dread (Sarbin & Mancuso, 1970; Sarbin, 1967; Nunnally, 1961). The mentally ill are society's lepers.

More disconcerting is the observation that these attitudes affect mental health professionals, who, while insisting that they are sympathetic to the mentally ill, probably experience an exquisite ambivalence towards psychiatric patients which includes negative attitudes. These attitudes are the natural offspring of the labels patients wear, and the places in which they are found. In the typical psychiatric hospital, staff and patients are strictly segregated, having their own dining facilities, bathrooms and assembly places. Staff emerge from the glassed quarters (which the pseudo-patients came to call the 'cage') mainly for caretaking purposes: to give medication, conduct a therapy or group meeting, instruct or reprimand a patient. Otherwise, staff keep to themselves, almost as if the disorder which afflicts their charges is somehow catching.

Doctors, especially psychiatrists, were even less available than nurses and attendants. They were rarely seen on the wards. Often they would be seen only when they arrived and departed, with the remaining time being spent in their offices or in the cage. Stanton and Schwartz (1954) have commented on the hierarchical organization of the psychiatric hospital, but its hidden meaning is worth noting again. Those with the most power have least to do with patients, and those with the least power have most to do with them, i.e. the attendants. However, insofar as they learn from their superiors' behaviour, they still spend as little time with the patients as they can, being seen mainly in the cage, which is where the models, the action and the power are.

THE STUDY

In four hospitals, the pseudo-patient approached a staff member with a request which took the following form: 'Pardon me, Mr [or Dr or Mrs] X, could you tell me when I will be presented at the staff meeting?' (or '. . . when am I likely to be discharged?'). While the content of the question varied according to the appropriateness of the target and the pseudo-patient's (apparent) current needs, the form was always a courteous and relevant request for information. Care was taken never to approach a particular staff member more than once a day (so as not to arouse their suspicions or irritate them), and the behaviour was neither bizarre nor disruptive. The data from these experiments are shown in Table 20.1. Small differences between the four institutions were overshadowed by the degree to which staff avoided continuing contacts which patients had initiated. By far their most common response was either a brief reply to the question while they were 'on the move' and with head averted, or no response at all. Often the reply was 'Good morning [Dave]. How are you today?' (moves off without waiting for an answer).

Table 20.1 also includes data recently obtained from Stanford University, where a young lady approached individual faculty members who seemed to be walking purposefully to a meeting or teaching engagement, and asked them six questions, including how to get to various parts of the campus. Without exception, all the questions were answered, no matter how rushed they were, all the respondents maintained eye contact and stopped to talk. Similar results were found in the University medical centre; except that when the young lady indicated that she was looking for a psychiatrist, she received less cooperation than when she indicated that she was looking for an internist.

Table 20.1

SELF-INITIATED CONTACT BY PSEUDO-PATIENTS WITH PSYCHIATRISTS, NURSES AND ATTENDANTS COMPARED TO CONTACT WITH OTHER GROUPS

Contact	Psychiatric hospitals		University campus (non-medical)	University medical centre physicians		
	(1) Psychiatrists	(2) Nurses & attendants	(3) Faculty	(4) 'Looking for a psychiatrist'	(5) 'Looking for an internist'	(6) No additional comments
Responses Moves on, head averted (%)	71	88	0	0	0	0
Makes eye contact (%)	23	10	0	11	0	0
Pauses and chats (%)	2	2	0	11	0	10
Stops and talks (%)	4	0.5	100	78	100	90
Mean number of questions answered (out of six)	*	*	6	3.8	4.8	4.5
Respondents (No.)	13	47	14	18	15	10
Attempts (No.)	185	1283	14	18	15	10

* Not applicable.

POWERLESSNESS AND DEPERSONALIZATION

Absence of eye contact and verbal contact reflect avoidance and depersonalization. I have records of patients who were beaten by staff just for having initiated verbal contact, as well as other kinds of punishment which seemed psychiatrically totally unjustifiable, but which seemed to go unquestioned. But neither anecdotal nor 'hard' data can convey the overwhelming sense of powerlessness which invades the individual as he is continually exposed to the depersonalization of the psychiatric hospital, whether this is public or private.

THE STUDY

Powerlessness was evident everywhere. The patient is deprived of many of his legal rights by virtue of his psychiatric commitment (Wexler & Scoville, 1971), his freedom of movement is restricted, he cannot initiate contact with staff, but only respond to their overtures, personal privacy is minimal, his personal history is available to any staff member (including volunteers) who chooses to read his file, and toilets may have no doors. Sometimes pseudo-patients felt that they were invisible, as when the initial examination was taken in a semi-public room, where staff members went about their business as if we were not there. On the ward, attendants gave out verbal and occasionally serious physical abuse to patients in the presence of other observing patients, some of whom (the pseudo-patients) were writing it all down, but it stopped quite abruptly when other staff members were known to be coming. Staff are credible witnesses, patients are not.

THE SOURCES OF DEPERSONALIZATION

The ambivalent attitude, which was discussed above, leads to avoidance, while the hierarchical structure of the psychiatric hospital facilitates depersonalization. There is also genuine underfunding, which means staff shortages, and it is usually patient contact that is sacrificed. But the addition of more staff would not necessarily improve patient care in this respect, since, even during hard times, staff meetings and record keeping are given higher priority than patient contact. The heavy reliance on psychotropic drugs tacitly contributes to depersonalization by convincing staff that treatment is indeed being conducted and that further patient contact may not be necessary. And why is there such a reliance on drugs in the first place?

THE CONSEQUENCES OF LABELLING AND DEPERSONALIZATION

Rather than confessing that we don't know, or are just embarking on understanding, we continue to label patients 'schizophrenic' etc., as if in those words we had captured the essence of understanding. But we have known for a long time that diagnoses are often not useful or reliable, and that we cannot distinguish insanity from sanity. How many people have been needlessly stripped of their privileges of citizenship, right to vote and drive and handle their own accounts? How many have feigned insanity in order to avoid the criminal consequences of their behaviour and, conversely, how many would rather stand trial than live interminably in a psychiatric hospital, but are wrongly thought to be mentally ill? A Type-two error in psychiatric diagnosis does not have the same consequences it does in medical diagnosis: a misdiagnosed cancer is a cause for celebration, but psychiatric diagnoses are rarely found to be in error because the label sticks, a mark of inadequacy forever.

Finally, how many patients might be 'sane' outside the psychiatric hospital, but seem insane in it; not because craziness resides in them, but because they're responding to a bizarre setting? Goffman (1961) calls the process of socialization to such institutions 'mortification', which includes depersonalization.

■ S U M M A R Y   A N D   C O N C L U S I O N S

It is clear that we cannot distinguish the sane from the insane in psychiatric hospitals, which themselves impose a special environment in which the meanings of behaviour can easily be distorted. Patients suffer powerlessness, depersonalization, segregation, mortification and self-labelling, all undoubtedly counter-therapeutic.

However, some promise seems to come from two sources; (*i*) the proliferation of community mental health facilities, crisis intervention centres, the human potential movement and behaviour therapies which avoid psychiatric labels, focus on specific problems and behaviours, and retain the individual in a relatively non-pejorative environment; (*ii*) the need to increase the sensitivity of mental health workers and researchers to the catch-22 position of psychiatric patients.

Our overwhelming impression of the staff was of people who really cared, were committed and were uncommonly intelligent. Where they failed, as they sometimes did painfully, it would be more accurate to attribute those failures to the environment in which they, too, found themselves than to personal callousness. In a more benign environment, one less attached to global diagnosis, their behaviours and judgements might have been more benign and effective.

EVALUATION

Theoretical issues

The medical model, including the classification of mental disorders/abnormality, has been fiercely attacked and defended during the past 40 years or so. During the 1960s, what became known as the 'anti-psychiatry' movement emerged, a group of psychiatrists and psychotherapists, among them R.D. Laing, Aaron Esterson, David Cooper and Thomas Szasz. Schizophrenia became the focus for their attack.

Perhaps one of the best known and most controversial challenges to the medical model is that of Szasz (1972), who argued that the distinction between organic and functional disorder is really one between 'disease of the brain' (*not* the mind) or neurophysiological disorder, and 'problems in living'. Bailey (1979) makes a similar distinction between *physical* illness and *disorders of psychosocial* or *interpersonal functioning*. This way, the concept of *mental* illness is, effectively, got rid of.

The debate has taken place at many different levels, often less 'fundamental' than challenging the very concept of mental illness itself. In defence of classification, Kendell (1983) claims that every psychiatric patient has attributes at three levels:

(A) those shared with *all* other psychiatric patients;
(B) those shared with *some* other psychiatric patients;
(C) those that are unique to them.

Classification is feasible provided there are attributes at level (B): the shared attributes are what constitutes one category as distinct from another. The value of classification depends on the relative size in importance of the attributes at (B) compared with (A) and (C). According to Miller & Morley (1986), most psychologists and psychiatrists believe that there *are* important attributes at level B.

However, just how reliable is psychiatric classification? This question really lies at the heart of Rosenhan's experiment, since he was trying to show that psychiatrists cannot be 'trusted' to identify people correctly as genuine psychiatric patients as distinct from pseudo-patients. Reliability is usually investigated by measuring the diagnostic agreement between two or more psychiatrists who have examined the *same* patients. Generally, agreement is quite high when discriminating between organic and functional disorders but can be very poor for specific diagnoses.

Early studies consistently showed poor reliability: psychiatrists varied widely in how much information they elicit at interview, as well as in their interpretations of that information. Variations were also found between groups of psychiatrists trained in different countries. For example, the US–UK Diagnostic Project (Cooper *et al.*, 1972) found that New York psychiatrists shown videotaped clinical interviews were twice as likely to diagnose schizophrenia as their London counterparts (shown the same videotapes). The International Pilot Study of Schizophrenia (WHO, 1973) confirmed that American psychiatrists (and those in the former USSR) had unusually broad concepts of the disorder.

However, little attempt was made in any of these reliability studies to ensure that the different psychiatrists used agreed criteria (Cooper, 1983).When attempts are made to construct special instruments or interview procedures for reaching a diagnosis based on operational criteria, and psychiatrists are trained to use them, then fairly impressive levels of reliability are achieved (especially for schizophrenia and psychotic depression). Such instruments include the Present State Examination (Wing *et al.*, 1979), the Feighner Criteria (Feighner *et al.*, 1972), Research Diagnostic Criteria (Spitzer *et al.*, 1978), and Schedule for Affective Disorders and Schizophrenia/SADS (Endicott & Spitzer, 1978).

The second and third of these helped to shape DSM-III (1980), which addressed itself largely to the whole problem of unreliability, especially unclear criteria. It covered a broader range of disorders, gave more specific categories, and used more precise language than earlier versions. The use of check lists helped to increase reliability,

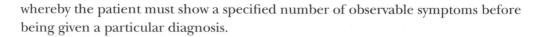

whereby the patient must show a specified number of observable symptoms before being given a particular diagnosis.

Significantly, it was DSM-II which was in use at the time of Rosenhan's study. It seems much less likely that psychiatrists using any of the later versions of DSM would have been misled by pseudo-patients, since a characteristic hallucination must be repeated on several occasions, whereas Rosenhan's colleagues basically made one such report! (Sarbin & Mancuso, 1980). However, despite the undoubted improvements in reliability since the publication of DSM-III (1980), aided by the use of 'decision trees' and computer programs that lead the psychiatrist through the tree (Holmes, 1994), problems remain (Davison & Neale, 1994).

Methodological issues

Although various types of reliability are applicable to abnormal psychology, the most relevant is *inter-rater reliability* (which is what the early reliability studies were concerned with). However, Rosenhan's study was not, technically, looking at this type of reliability, since each pseudo-patient was only assessed by one psychiatrist. Nevertheless, his findings have significant implications for the reliability of psychiatric diagnosis: if mental health professionals cannot distinguish between the mentally ill and healthy, the question of whether they can distinguish between different varieties of mental illness seems premature and, perhaps, even pointless (Lilienfeld, 1995).

In defence of those psychiatrists involved in Rosenhan's study, Kety (1974) poses the following (rather unsettling) scenario (cited in Sarbin & Mancuso, 1980):

> If I were to drink a quart of blood and, concealing what I had done, had come to the emergency room of any hospital vomiting blood, the behaviour of the staff would be quite predictable. If they labelled and treated me as having a bleeding peptic ulcer, I doubt that I could argue convincingly that medical science does not know how to diagnose that condition.

But as Sarbin & Mancuso (1980) point out, Kety does not go on to ask what the doctors would say when no bleeding was observed the next day, and all the tests proved negative. Would they discharge the patient with a diagnosis of 'Bleeding peptic ulcer, in remission'? This, of course, is meant to parallel the situation Rosenhan's pseudo-patients were in once they had been admitted.

One of Rosenhan's fiercest critics, Spitzer (1976), notes that the diagnosis 'Schizophrenia in remission' is extremely rare. In addition to his own New York hospital, he examined the records of discharged schizophrenic patients for 12 other US hospitals, and found that in 11 cases 'in remission' was either never used or used for only a handful of patients each year. Spitzer concluded from this that Rosenhan's pseudo-patients were given a discharge diagnosis which is rarely given to *real* patients with an admission diagnosis of schizophrenia, and that, therefore, the diagnoses were a *function* of the pseudo-patients' behaviours and *not* of the setting (psychiatric hospital) in which the diagnoses were made (as Rosenhan claims). In other words, these psychiatrists successfully recognized that the individuals who showed symptoms of a disorder that rarely disappears completely, had in fact experienced 'remission'. Thus, far from condemning diagnostic reliability, Rosenhan's study suggests that mental health professionals *can* actually distinguish psychotic from non-psychotic individuals with surprisingly high levels of accuracy (Lilienfeld, 1995). (See below).

Applications and implications

A separate issue, but one that is related to reliability, concerns the effect of *diagnostic labelling*, which Rosenhan discusses at great length. His results demonstrate dramatically what several prominent authors (e.g. Scheff, 1966) have hypothesised, namely that psychiatric labels tend to become *self-fulfilling prophecies*. Not only do psychiatric labels stick in a way that (other) medical labels do not, but, more seriously, *everything* the patient says and does is interpreted in accordance with the diagnostic label once it has been applied (e.g. the 'writing behaviour' of the pseudo-patients). According to Lilienfeld (1995), the study:

> . . . provides a sorely needed reminder of the human mind's propensity to rearrange or reframe facts to achieve consistency with preexisting beliefs . . .

Rosenhan is arguing that mental illness is a purely social phenomenon, the consequence of a labelling process.

A very relevant study here is one by Lindsay (1982). He obtained videotape recordings of participants alleged to have schizophrenia and of normal controls. He showed the tapes to a sample of ordinary people (patients in a general hospital), who acted as raters. One group was told nothing about the people in the video being rated, but two other groups were told either correctly or incorrectly, who were the schizophrenics and who were not. What would Rosenhan have predicted?

(*i*)   Where information about the person's psychiatric status was withheld, ratings should not differ according to whether s/he was actually a patient or not (especially as the tapes were carefully collected in order not to contain certain expressions of overt symptoms);

(*ii*) for the other two groups, ratings should emerge as more abnormal for the people identified as schizophrenic, *regardless* of whether this attribution was correct.

Although there was a small effect attributable to labelling, Lindsay found that the overwhelming thrust of the results was that the schizophrenic patients were rated as more abnormal regardless of whether any information was provided or its accuracy. These results 'strongly indicate that the label is far from wholly an empty one, and that there is a reality of some kind behind it' (Miller & Morley, 1986). Miller and Morley also point out that the patients taped by Lindsay were all fairly new cases, and so had not had long to adapt to the label and change their behaviour accordingly, as an extreme supporter of labelling would argue. They believe that to argue for 'labelling' as against the 'medical model' is a false dichotomy.

According to MacLeod (1998), *labelling theory* is an example of a theory that fitted the practices of a particular time and place. For example, the theory seems to be especially applicable to *involuntary* hospital admissions. When Scheff carried out his American research in the 1960s, a full 90% of all psychiatric hospital admissions were involuntary. When Bean (1979) replicated Scheff's study in the UK, the figure was found to be 18%. Not only will there be national/cultural differences in admission rates, but the figure for the USA is also likely to have fallen in that time.

What labelling theory and Rosenhan's study have usefully highlighted is how people labelled as mentally ill are treated. However, what they cannot account for is why someone begins to show deviant behaviour in the first place (MacLeod, 1998). Similarly, if the effects of labels like 'schizophrenia' (or more global psychological judgements, such as 'mentally ill') are so powerful, why were the genuine patients not deceived by them? It seems that the pseudopatients' actual behaviours overpowered whatever adverse effects the labels assigned to them may have exerted on these observers' perceptions (Lilienfeld, 1995).

Neisser (1973), in support of Rosenhan, refers to the 'irreversibility' of diagnostic labels. Instead of the pseudopatients being discharged with a diagnosis of 'normal' or 'normal: initial diagnosis in error', they received the discharge diagnosis of 'schizophrenia in remission'. It is almost as if the psychiatrist can never be wrong: it is a 'heads I win, tails you lose' situation, immunizing diagnostic practices from being proved wrong. However, Lilienfeld (1995) argues that the diagnosis 'schizophrenia in remission' communicates useful information, because schizophrenia tends to be a chronic disorder that often reappears following periods of remission (see above). This makes it more informative than 'normal': only 'in remission' indicates the increased risk of subsequent schizophrenic episodes. (Similarly, with, say, 'leukemia in remission'). Lilienfeld (1995) concludes by saying:

> . . . psychiatrists' unwillingness to reverse a diagnosis, although sometimes a self-serving refusal to admit error, can also be viewed as a prudent and calculated diagnostic decision to err on the side of patient safety.

Finally, Spitzer (1976) points out that Rosenhan, as a professor of law and psychology, should know that the terms 'sane'/'insane' are *legal*, not psychiatric, concepts, and no psychiatrist makes a diagnosis of 'sanity'/'insanity'. This is ironic in view of Rosenhan's condemnation of the use of psychiatric labelling.

Exercises

1. Why was it important to use a range of hospitals, and in what respects did they differ?

2. The admitting psychiatrists in Rosenhan's study uniformly made *Type-two errors*. He admits that this is often justifiable in medical diagnosis, but not in psychiatric diagnosis.

   (a) What are *Type-one* and *Type-two errors* in this context?
   (b) How do they differ here from how they are usually defined in relation to hypothesis testing in psychology?

3. If Rosenhan had used control groups in the two experiments, what might they have been?

4. Is there anything ethically unacceptable about the concealment of the true identity of the pseudo-patients and the inevitable deception involved?

5. List some of the major criteria for making the traditional distinction between neurosis and psychosis.

21 A case of multiple personality

Corbett H. Thigpen and Hervey Cleckley (1954)

Journal of Abnormal and Social Psychology, 49, 135–51

BACKGROUND AND CONTEXT

According to the tenth Revision of the International Classification of Diseases (ICD-10, 1992), Mental Disorders Section, *multiple personality disorder* (MPD) falls under the heading of 'Neurotic, Stress-Related and Somatoform Disorders'. This classification is used in the UK, and like all systems of classification is based on Kraepelin's original 1913 claim that certain groups of signs and symptoms occur together sufficiently often to merit the designation 'disease' or syndrome; he then described the diagnostic indicators associated with each syndrome.

In the USA, the American Psychiatric Association's official classification system (also used in the UK) is the Diagnostic and Statistical Manual of Mental Disorder (DSM). Originally published in 1952, the current edition is DSM-IV (1994). The category 'neurosis' is dropped and neurotic disorders are dispersed among several categories, such as Anxiety Disorders, Somatoform Disorders, and Dissociative Disorders. The last of these includes MPD, which is also known as *dissociative identity disorder* (DID).

Dissociative neurosis involves psychological rather than physical dysfunction (although Eve White did suffer also from terrible headaches), that is, it is characterized by disturbances in identity, memory, perception and awareness. It takes the form of a separation, or dissociation, of one part of the self from the other parts. (This has led to the common confusion between multiple personality and schizophrenia, in which a splitting occurs, but of a different kind from that involved in MPD).

MPD involves two or more integrated personalities or personality states residing simultaneously within the same individual, each having its own relatively stable pattern of relating to, and interpreting, the world. In addition, at least two of the personalities/personality states seize control of the individual's behaviour on a repeated basis (Apter, 1991). It is this co-existence of multiple distinct personalities/states that most clearly distinguishes MPD from schizophrenia and other disorders (Lilienfeld, 1995).

In addition, the 'original' personality (in this case Eve White) is usually not aware of the other (alternate) personalities (Eve Black, Jane), though these may be aware of the first – and of each other. Often, the other personalities embody parts of the first personality which have become repressed, and so have remained unexpressed.

In the literature, the number of reported personalities within a single individual range from 2 to over 100, with about half having 10 or more. These often differ in stated gender, age, family of origin, even race. They have even been reported to differ in eyeglass prescriptions, handedness, allergies, susceptibility to alcohol, and IQ (Lilienfeld, 1995). Often, they are polar opposites (as in the present case).

MPD is often accompanied by fugue ('flight'), a kind of extension of amnesia, in which the patient flees from home and self by wandering off on a journey, not knowing how s/he got there and unable to recall his/her true identity. The person assumes a new identity but, unlike many amnesic patients, does not experience confusion or disorientation. It is usually a brief episode, lasting hours or days rather than weeks. In the case of MPD, the fugue will usually be a period of time during which one of the alternate personalities was in control, leaving the 'original' personality unable to account for his/her actions (such as the spending spree which made Eve White's husband so angry!).

Note that DSM-IV does not specify amnesia as a defining characteristic of MPD. But Coons (1984, cited by Aldridge-Morris, 1989) argues that amnesia is an absolutely essential criterion for diagnosing MPD. Clearly, as with all other categories of mental disorder, there is no universally accepted definition, even within the American psychiatric profession.

The 'original' case was the fictional *Dr Jekyll and Mr Hyde* by Robert Louis Stevenson. A more recent, real-life case, even more dramatic and remarkable than the present one, is that of Sybil (Schreiber, 1973), who had 16 separate personalities! (see **Theoretical issues** below).

AIM AND NATURE OF THE STUDY

The article is an account of the psychotherapeutic treatment of a 25-year-old woman referred to the authors (who are psychiatrists: medically qualified professionals concerned with helping those with psychological problems), because of 'severe and blinding headaches'. It soon became clear that Eve White was experiencing marital problems and personal frustrations (probably the cause of her headaches), but the receipt of a letter marked the beginning of what the article is really about, namely, a case of MPD. Eve Black could at first only be 'contacted' through hypnosis, but this then became no longer necessary. The major method of treatment seemed to be simply talking to one or other Eve (there is no reference to drug therapy, for example), especially trying to encourage them to talk about childhood memories and events.

The case-study includes the report by an independent expert who gave the two Eves four psychological tests: the Wechsler-Bellevue Intelligence Scale (now known as the

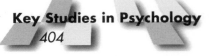

Wechsler Adult Intelligence Scale: WAIS), the Wechsler Memory Scale, Drawings of Human Figures, and the Rorschach ('Ink Blot') test, in which the testee has to say what a series of ambiguous drawings (ink blots) represent. (The Rorschach is a *projective* test, in which the testee supposedly projects unconscious feelings and wishes onto the images in the drawings.)

After eight months of treatment, Eve White suffered a major setback: her original symptoms returned, but were more intense and frequent, and this was the prelude to the appearance of a third personality, Jane, (hence 'The three faces of Eve'). An independent expert this time was asked to run EEG (electroencephalogram) tests (which measure the brain's electrical activity in the form of brain waves) on all three personalities, with the outcome showing Eve White and Jane to be indistinguishable and normal, but Eve Black to be borderline normal/psychopathic personality.

THE STUDY

The psychiatric manifestation called multiple personality has been extensively discussed. So too have the unicorn and the centaur. Nevertheless, like the unicorn and centaur in some respects, *multiple*, or *dual personality*, despite vivid appearances in popularized books on psychology (Allen, 1937), is not commonly encountered in the full reality of life (Alexander, 1930; McDougall, 1926; Morgan, 1932). Nearly all those perplexing reports of two or more people in one body, so to speak, are reports of observations made in a relatively distant past. The most significant manifestations of this sort discussed in the current literature occurred in patients studied half a century or more ago (William James, 1890, Morton Prince, 1906). It is scarcely surprising that psychiatrists today, never having directly observed such things as Morton Prince found in Miss Beauchamp, might be rather sceptical, especially as, in Prince's case, he used hypnosis, which may have '. . . moulded the course of its development to a degree that cannot be determined . . .' (McDougall, 1926).

Significantly, the studies of Prince and others on multiple personality are not even mentioned in some leading textbooks of psychiatry used in medical schools today (Muncie, 1948; Strecker *et al.*, 1951); if mentioned at all, the subject is usually dismissed with a few words (Henderson & Gillespie, 1947; Noyes, 1948). Freud apparently showed no appreciable interest in the disorder, Erickson and Kubie (1939) could find only one brief reference to the problem (in 'Collected Papers', 1946).

Our direct experience with a patient has forced us to review the subject of multiple personality. It has also provoked in us the reaction of wonder, sometimes of awe.

One of us had, for several months, been treating a 25-year-old married woman referred because of 'severe and blinding headaches'. At the first interview, she also mentioned 'blackouts' following the headache. Her family was not aware of anything that would suggest a real loss of consciousness or serious mental confusion.

During a series of irregular interviews (the patient had to travel from some distance), several important emotional difficulties were revealed and discussed. Although encouraging symptomatic improvement occurred, it was clear that her major problems had not been resolved. Eve White (as we shall call her) seemed to be an ordinary case with commonplace symptoms and a relatively complex, but familiar, set of marital conflicts and personal frustrations. We were puzzled during therapy about a recent trip for which she had no memory. Hypnosis was induced, and the amnesia quickly cleared up. Several days after a visit to the office, a letter was received (Figure 21.1).

What was the meaning of such a letter? Though unsigned, the postmark, the content, and the familiar penship in most of the message revealed that this had been written by Eve White. However, it raised puzzling questions. Had some child found the uncompleted page, scribbled those words, and, perhaps as a whim, mailed it in an already addressed envelope? Perhaps. The handwriting of the last paragraph certainly suggested the work of a child. Could Eve White herself, as a puerile prank, have decided to disguise her characteristic handwriting and added this inconsequential note? And if so, why? She seemed to be a circumspect, matter-of-fact person, meticulously truthful and consistently sober and serious about her grave troubles. It was rather difficult to imagine her becoming playful, or being moved by an impulse to tease, even on a more appropriate occasion. The 'black-outs' which she had rather casually mentioned, but which did not seem to disturb her very much, suggested, of course, that somnabulism or brief fugue might have occurred.

On her next visit, she denied sending the letter, though she recalled having begun one which she never finished; she thought she had destroyed it. During this interview, Eve White, usually an excessively self-controlled woman, began to show signs of distress and agitation. Apprehensively and reluctantly, she at last asked: did the occasional impression of hearing an imaginary voice indicate that she was 'insane'?

This information was startling. Nothing about Eve White suggested even an early schizoid change, and her own attitude toward what she now reported was in no way like that of patients experiencing 'ordinary' auditory hallucinations. Yet she insisted with painful embarrassment, that she had, on several occasions over the last few months, heard briefly, but distinctly, a voice, addressing her. Before the therapist could reply, an abstruse and inexplicable expression came over her face, apparently involuntarily. As if seized by pain, she put both hands to her head. After a tense moment of silence, her hands dropped. There was a quick, reckless smile and, in a bright voice that sparkled she said, 'Hi there, Doc!' Instead of the retiring and conventional, figure of Eve White, there was in this newcomer a childishly daredevil air, an erotically mischievous glance, a face marvellously free from the usual signs of care, seriousness and underlying distress, so long familiar in her predecessor. This new, and apparently carefree, girl spoke casually of Eve White and

THE STUDY

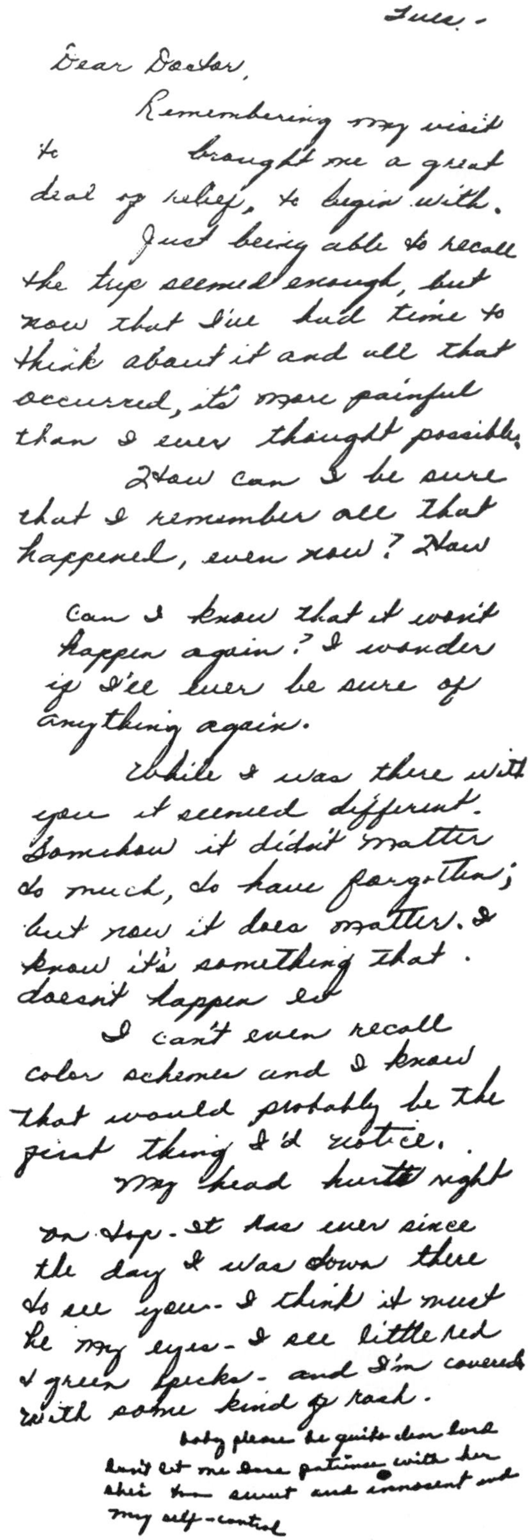

Tues.

Dear Doctor,

Remembering my visit to _____ brought me a great deal of relief, to begin with.

Just being able to recall the trip seemed enough, but now that I've had time to think about it and all that occurred, it's more painful than I ever thought possible.

How can I be sure that I remember all that happened, even now? How can I know that it won't happen again? I wonder if I'll ever be sure of anything again.

While I was there with you it seemed different. Somehow it didn't matter so much, to have forgotten; but now it does matter. I know it's something that doesn't happen...

I can't even recall color schemes and I know that would probably be the first thing I'd notice.

My head hurts right on top. It has ever since the day I was down there to see you. I think it must be my eyes. I see little red & green specks - and I'm covered with some kind of rash.

baby please be quite dear lord don't let me lose patience with her she so sweet and innocent and my self-control

Figure 21.1. This letter in retrospect was the first intimation that our patient was unusual. The dramatic and unexpected revelation of the second personality shortly followed.

her problems always using *she* or *her* in every reference, always respecting the strict bounds of separate identity. When asked her own name she immediately replied, 'Oh, I'm Eve Black'

A thousand minute alterations of manner, gesture, expression, posture, of nuances in reflex or instinctive reaction, of glance, of eyebrow tilting and eye movement, all argued that this could only be another woman. It is impossible to say just what all these differences were.

Over a period of 14 months, during a series of interviews totalling approximately 100 hours, extensive material was obtained about the behaviour and inner life of Eve White and Eve Black. How can the different personalities be called out? After the original spontaneous appearance of Eve Black, Eve White at first had to be hypnotized in order for us to talk with Eve Black. How Eve Black could 'pop out' of her own accord at unpredictable times, and yet could not come out on request, we do not know. After a few hypnotic sessions, we merely had to request Eve White to let us speak to Eve Black. Then we called Eve Black's name, and Eve Black would come out. The reverse was true when Eve Black was out, and we wished to speak to Eve White. Hypnosis was no longer necessary for obtaining the changes. This made things simpler for us, but complicated Eve White's life considerably, because Eve Black found herself able to 'take over' more easily than before.

Eve Black, so far as we can tell, has enjoyed an independent life since Eve's early childhood. She is not a product of disruptive, emotional stresses suffered during recent years. Eve White had no knowledge or suspicion of the other's existence until some time after she appeared unbidden before the surprised therapist. Though Eve White has learned that there is an Eve Black during the course of therapy, she does not have access to the latter's awareness. When Eve Black is 'out', Eve White remains functionally in abeyance, quite oblivious of what the coinhabitant of her body does, and apparently unconscious. However, Eve Black preserves awareness while absent, able to follow the actions and thoughts of her spiritually antithetical twin, but clearly not participating in them. For example, Eve Black regards Eve White's genuine and natural distress about her failing marriage as silly, and her warm, genuine, consistent and impressive love and concern for her four-year-old daughter as trite, bothersome, insignificant and 'something pretty corny'.

Eve White and her husband are temporarily separated, and the four-year-old child is living with her grandparents in a village, while Eve works and lives in a city about 100 miles away. She endures the loneliness, frustration and grief of separation from her warmly loved daughter, and she fears that, as the years pass, she will become little more than a coolly accepted stranger. But the vulnerable and delicately feminine Eve typically preserves a quiet dignity about personal sorrow. Under hypnosis, her unhappiness became clearer, but even then there is no frantic weeping or outbursts of self-pity; her quiet voice remains level as she discusses matters which leave her cheeks at last wet from silent tears.

THE STUDY

Eve Black has little or no real compassion for her. Nor does she seem in any important sense actively, or purposefully, cruel. She seems to be immune to major affective events in human relations, equally free of mercy and hatefulness.

Eve Black freely tells of episodes in childhood when she emerged, usually to engage in acts of mischief or disobedience, but she lies glibly and without compunction, so her account alone can never be taken as reliable evidence. Although Eve White has no access to her 'twin's' awareness or memory, her own memory has afforded considerable indirect evidence of Eve Black's stories through confirmation of reports of punishments she received and accusations made against her for deeds unknown to her, but described to us by Eve Black. Some stories have been substantiated by the patient's parents and her husband, who have all been interviewed.

Eve Black's adult behaviour is characterized by irresponsibility and a shallowly hedonistic desire for excitement and pleasure. She succeeded in concealing her identity not only from the other Eve, but also from her parents and husband. She herself denies marriage to this man, whom she despises, and any relation to Eve White's little girl, except that of an unconcerned bystander. Though she had often 'come out' in the presence of all these people, she went unrecognized until she agreed to reveal herself to them in the therapist's office. They had accounted for her ill will, harshness and occasional violence in terms of unaccountable fits of temper in a woman habitually gentle and considerate.

During her longer periods 'out', she avoids her family and close friends, and seeks the company of strangers or those insufficiently acquainted with her alternate to evaluate accurately the stupendous transformation. It seemed to us at first scarcely possible that she could for so long have concealed her separate identity from others. But who is likely to reach a conclusion which is inconceivable? Her parents and husband observed the same changes that we have observed, but, unlike ourselves, they have not had the hypothesis of multiple personality. Eve Black meant to remain unrecognized: when it suits her, she deliberately and skilfully acts so as to pass herself off as Eve White, imitating her usual tone of voice, gestures and attitudes.

Psychometric and projective tests were conducted on the two Eves by a well-qualified expert.

PSYCHOLOGICAL CONSULTATION REPORT

The patient is the oldest of three siblings, having twin sisters. She quit school two months before graduation from high school. She worked as a telephone operator. She has been married six years and has a four-year-old girl. She reports that she

THE STUDY

did things recently she cannot remember having done, and expresses serious concern about this condition. The following psychological tests were administered to both the predominant personality, Mrs White and the secondary personality, Miss Black: Wechsler-Bellevue Intelligence Scale, Wechsler Memory Scale, Drawings of Human Figures and Rorschach.

TEST BEHAVIOUR

Patient was neat, friendly and cooperative. However, while Mrs White was more serious, conscientious and anxious, Miss Black seemed rather less anxious, and gave more superficial responses. Still the basic behaviour pattern was very similar in both personalities. Speech was coherent, and there were no distortions in ideations or behaviour according to the assumed personality. No psychotic deviations were observed.

TEST RESULTS

Mrs White obtained an IQ of 110 and Miss Black 104 on the Wechsler-Bellevue Intelligence Scale. Both scores are lowered by anxiety and tenseness, and superficiality and slight indifference to success, respectively. Miss Black's memory function is on the same level as her IQ, while Mrs White's is far above her IQ, although she complained of a disturbance in memory. The only difficulty experienced by both is on recall of digits, an ability on which telephone operators usually excel! The Rorschach record of Miss Black is by far healthier than that of Mrs White. Miss Black has a hysterical tendency, while Mrs White's shows anxiety, obsessive-compulsive traits, rigidity and an inability to deal with her hostility.

PERSONALITY DYNAMICS

The projective tests indicate repression in Mrs White and regression in Miss Black. The dual personality appears to be the result of a strong desire to regress to an early period of life, namely the one before marriage. Miss Black is actually the maiden name of Mrs White. Therefore, these are not two different personalities with completely dissimilar ideation, but rather one personality at two stages of her life. As is characteristic for this type of case, the predominant personality is amnesic for the existence, activities or behaviour of the secondary one, while the latter is aware and critical of the predominant personality's activities and attitudes.

Mrs White admits difficulty in her relationship with her mother, and her performance on the Rorschach and drawings indicate conflict and resulting anxiety in her roles of wife and mother. Only with strong conscious effort can she compel herself to subject herself to these roles, which in turn increases the hostility. But she cannot accept this hostility, and regresses so as to avoid guilt feelings. By playing the role of Miss Black, she is able to discharge some of her hostility towards Mrs White. Miss Black has regained her previous freedom from marital and maternal conflicts, and so has escaped from the insoluble situation Mrs White found herself in through her marriage; she can also avert the – in her conviction – inevitable spiritual loss of her child. Not surprisingly, she shows contempt for Mrs White, who allowed herself to get into such a situation, because of lack of foresight and lack of courage to forcefully solve the dilemma.

Actually, the problem started much earlier in life, with a strong feeling of rejection by her parents, especially after the birth of her twin sisters; Mrs White loves them dearly, Miss Black despises them. Miss Black relates an episode in which she (i.e. Mrs White), having quit school to help support the family, sent home money to buy overcoats for her twin sisters, denying herself a badly wanted wristwatch. When the money was spent on two wristwatches instead, she reacted with strong, but repressed, hostility. Significantly, she removed her wristwatch while examined as Mrs White, stating that she doesn't like jewellery. There are several examples of her strong sense of rejection as well as sibling rivalry in her records.

Miss Black once recklessly bought several expensive and unneeded new dresses and two luxurious coats. On discovering this, Eve White's husband lost his temper and abused his wife for wantonly plunging him into debt. Her innocent denials could not reduce his anger, but her wholehearted agreement that it would be disastrous for them to run up such a bill, and her promptness in returning all the garments to the store did. Although Eve Black does not apparently regularly go out of her way to make trouble between them, her typical behaviour often adds to the genuine difficulties they already have. 'When I go out and get drunk', Eve Black with an easy wink once said to us, '*she* wakes up with the hangover. She wonder's what in the hell's made her so sick'.

In contrast with the case reported by Erickson and Kubie (1939), Eve Black has shown anything but a regular desire to help the other with her problems; often she has, by ingenious lies, misled the therapist into believing she was cooperating, when in fact her behaviour was particularly detrimental to Eve White's progress. However, one valuable means of influencing her is in the therapist's hands. Although Eve Black has apparently been able, since childhood, to disappear at will, the ability to displace Eve White's consciousness, and emerge to take control has always been limited: sometimes she could 'get out', sometimes not. Once Eve White, during treatment, learned of the other's existence, it has become clear that her willingness to step aside and 'release the imp' plays an important part in the alternate's ability to appear and express herself directly. Eve White cannot keep her suppressed permanently, but together with the therapist, Eve Black can be persuaded to avoid the more serious forms of misconduct by being allowed more time 'out'.

Even when invisible and inaccessible, she, apparently, has means of disturbing Eve White. She tells us she causes those severe headaches that brought the latter to us as a patient; her unsuccessful struggle to get out often produces this symptom in the other plus the (quasi-) hallucinatory voice which Eve White heard before the other Eve disclosed herself to us as her deliberate work.

From the two Eves during many interviews, and from her husband and parents, we obtained a great deal of information about the patient, and concluded that we had a reasonably complete and accurate history of her life since early childhood. So we were astonished by the report of a distant relative, who insisted that, a few years before she met her present husband, a previous marriage had taken place. Eve White denied this, and has never yet shown any knowledge of it, but Eve Black also maintained that we had been misinformed; however, under the persistent pressure of evidence, the latter admitted that she, and only she, had been the bride. No record of a legal union has been obtained, but there is considerable evidence that she did co-habit with such a man as she describes; she insists some sort of 'ceremony' was performed, saying that it was not formally recorded, and may have been a ruse. Eve Black was predominantly in control during this period, almost constantly present.

She claimed she had no desire for sex, but often enjoyed frustrating her supposed husband by denying herself to him. In turn, he beat her savagely, but she avoided most of the pain by 'going in', and leaving Eve White to feel the blows. But if this were the case, why did Eve White not remember them? Eve Black contends that she can, through great effort, 'pick out' or erase from Eve White's reach certain items of memory, and she did this with memory of the beatings. Several experiments by the therapist indicated that this claim is correct.

After approximately eight months of treatment, Eve White seemed to have made encouraging progress. For a long time she had not had headaches or 'blackouts', the imaginary voice had not been heard since the other Eve revealed herself to the therapist. Mrs White worked well at her job, and had progressed financially; she was hopeful of eventually reaching some acceptable solution to her marital problems, seemed to find some comfort in her successful efforts to provide for her daughter, and had made friends, with whom she occasionally enjoyed simple recreations.

Meanwhile, Eve Black had generally been causing less trouble. She seldom 'came out' to make errors or to indulge in pranks while Eve White was at work, but in leisure hours she often mixed with bad company, picked up dates and flirted.

At this point, the situation changed for the worse. The headaches returned, grew worse and more frequent, and so did the 'blackouts'. Eve Black denied all responsibility. She did not experience the headaches but, surprisingly, seemed now to participate in the blackouts and could give no account of what happened during them. Two or three times the patient was found lying unconscious on the floor by her room-mate, something which had not occurred during the previous blackout

THE STUDY

episodes. It became difficult for her to work effectively, she became less accessible during interviews and increasingly distressed.

Under hypnosis, Eve White occasionally re-experienced considerable emotion in recalling events from childhood, but we have never been able to hypnotize Eve Black. Some time after the return of headaches and blackouts, with Eve White's maladjustment gradually getting worse, a very early recollection was being discussed, concerning a painful injury she had sustained when scalded by water from a wash basin. As she spoke her eyes shut sleepily, her words soon stopped, her head dropped back on the chair. After two minutes, her eyes opened, blankly staring about the room, trying to orient herself. When her eyes finally met those of the therapist, slowly, with an unknown husky voice and immeasurable poise, she said, 'Who are you?'.

It was immediately and vividly apparent that this was neither Eve White nor Eve Black. We have gradually established that this third personality lacks Eve Black's obvious faults and inadequacies, is far more mature, vivid, boldly capable and interesting than Eve White. She calls herself Jane and only superficially can she be described as a compromise between the others.

Some weeks after Jane emerged, all three personalities were given Electroencephalogram tests.

REPORT OF ELECTROENCEPHALOGRAM: SUMMARY

All three personalities show alternate periods of alpha rhythm and low voltage fast activity, presumably due to alternate periods of mental relaxation and tenseness. The greatest amount of tenseness is shown by Eve Black, Eve White next, and Jane least. Eve Black shows a basic alpha rate of 12½ cycles per second, as compared with 11 cycles per second from Eve White and Jane. This places Eve Black's tracing on the borderline between normal and slightly fast (FI). Slightly fast records are sometimes (but not consistently) associated with psychopathic personality. Eve Black's record also shows evidence of restlessness and muscle tension, her EEG is definitely distinguished from the others, and could be classified as borderline normal. Eve White's and Jane's EEG cannot be distinguished: both are clearly normal.

For several months now there have been three patients to work with. Jane has awareness of what both Eves do and think, but incomplete access to their stores of knowledge and memories prior to her appearance on the scene. Through her, the

THE STUDY

therapist can determine when Eve Black has been lying. Jane feels free from Eve White's responsibilities and attachments, but is capable of compassion and, probably, of devotion and genuine love. She has cooperated with sincerity, and with judgement and originality beyond that of the others. She has learnt to take over many of Eve White's tasks at work and home in efforts to relieve and help her. She shows great wisdom and compassion towards Eve White's little girl. As time passes, she 'stays out' more and more. She emerges only through Eve White, and has not yet found a way to displace Eve Black, or to communicate through her. Could Jane remain in full possession of that integrated human functioning called personality, we believe our patient would probably regain full health, adjust satisfactorily and find her way to a happy life.

DISCUSSION

What is the meaning of the events we have observed and reported? Some, no doubt, will conclude that we have been thoroughly hoodwinked by a skilful actress. But we think it is unlikely that someone consciously acting could, over a period of months, avoid even one telling error or imperfection. But it is not impossible.

Have we been taken in by what is no more than superficial hysterical tomfoolery? There does seem to be something more, and something different from ordinary hysterical conversions and dissociations. Could it be due to a process of disintegration as in schizophrenia? None of the three personalities shows any signs of schizophrenia. Are we justified in claiming that our three performers have become split off from a once unified whole? Or is it possible that the functional elements composing each have never in the past been really or completely unified?

Obviously, the differing manifestations we have observed in one woman's physical organism do not, in all senses of the term, indicate three quite separate people. So what do we mean by the term *multiple personality*? This, of course, begs the question of what we mean by *personality*. For all these questions, there is no simple or single answer.

Whatever progress may or may not have been made by psychology and psychiatry during the last half century, we suggest that further direct study of multiple personality and careful reappraisal of Morton Prince's generally neglected studies may provide some promising clues which may eventually yield insight we need but lack today.

EVALUATION

Theoretical issues

Traditionally, reported cases of MPD have been considered to be extremely rare, with Morton Prince's (1906) Miss Beauchamp, the present case of Eve, and Sybil (Schreiber, 1973) being the most commonly cited. However, there seems to have been an 'epidemic' in MPD diagnosis in the USA during the last few decades. According to Lilienfeld (1995), between 1934 and 1971, there were only 12 reported cases, but several investigators have recently reported that they have seen 50 cases or more. According to Greaves (1980, cited by Aldridge-Morris, 1989), while only 14 cases were reported between 1944 and 1969 (six of them by Dr Cornelia Wilbur, Sybil's therapist), at least 50 cases were reported during the 1970s, followed by an explosion of reported cases during the 1980s. Coincidentally, MPD was included in DSM for the first time in 1980 (DSM-III), and this marked the turning point in its incidence and significance. Before 1980, there were just 200 cases in the entire world literature – by 1984, there were more than 1000 documented cases in the USA alone (Mair, 1999). This explosion has continued and extends far beyond the USA, including Holland, Germany, Switzerland, Turkey, South America, and Japan (Cohen, 1995).

One reason for the generally very low reported frequency of such cases (prior to 1980) is that often the existence of alternate personalities is discovered, initially, only through hypnosis, which no more than 10% of psychotherapists use. (This was not the case with Eve, where Eve Black made her first appearance quite spontaneously; but for a good while following this, she could only be 'summoned' hypnotically (Altrocchi, 1980.) Critics have argued that, instead of additional personalities being 'discovered' through hypnosis, they might be *created* by it! (Fahy, 1988; Lilienfeld, 1998)

What is quite evident in this recent 'epidemic' is that new cases seem to be confined to relatively few clinicians or investigators whose names constantly recur (Aldridge-Morris, 1989). How can we account for such dramatic changes?

(*i*)   The rise and fall of reported cases seems to be correlated with the impact of Freud's psychoanalytic theory (at least among psychotherapists and psychiatrists in the USA where the 'epidemic' has mainly occurred). Freud was an *anti-Realist* as far as MPD was concerned: he rejected the 'received view' (current during the late nineteenth and early twentieth centuries and which grew out of French psychiatry, especially the work of Janet) which claimed that the distinct personalities are separate, unique, persons having their own identities. As Freud's theories and psychoanalytic therapy became less widespread and influential from the mid-twentieth century, so the 'received view' resurged (Apter, 1991).

(*ii*) Apter (1991) also believes that the surge of reported cases of child sexual abuse (CSA) has contributed to the MPD epidemic. Child abuse (in general) has always featured very prominently in the MPD literature, and there are some horrendous examples from the histories of these patients (Sybil being a very 'good' example). Some regard MPD as being *caused* by abuse. For example, Kluft (1979, cited by Aldridge-Morris, 1989) in addressing the American Psychiatric Association, claimed that:

> I see multiple personality as a syndrome which follows child abuse. Most multiples, as children, have been physically brutalized, psychologically assaulted, sexually violated and affectively overwhelmed. A small number may have only experienced one of these forms of personal desecration.

Indeed, the view that adults diagnosed with MPD/DID started dissociating in early childhood, as a response to trauma which usually involved CSA, is currently the most popular, especially among US psychiatrists. According to Mair (1999), this view has only emerged in the last 20 years or so, and seems to have been greatly influenced by the publication of a single book, *Sybil* in 1973. The way that MPD is manifested has also changed since the publication of this book. Mair notes that later cases tend to have more alternate personalities (an average of 12; Sybil had 17), are more likely to be female, are more likely to be depressed or suicidal, and far more likely to report increasingly extreme and bizarre abuse (including ritual abuse that involves gang rape, torture, bestiality, human sacrifice and cannabilism). Rieger (1998) claims that Sybil's alternate personalities were created during therapy by a therapist who gave substance to her different emotional states by giving them names.

It is ironic, and perhaps also highly significant, that the decline of psychoanalytic theory and the surge in reported sexual abuse should both contribute to the MPD epidemic, in view of the claim that Freud rejected his own 'seduction theory' of neurosis (see Chapter 19).

(*iii*) MPD could be regarded as a largely North American phenomenon of the twentieth century (particularly the second half). Aldridge-Morris (1989) wrote to the British Psychological Society (BPS) and the Royal College of Psychiatrists in 1987, asking whether British professionals had experience of MPD comparable to their American counterparts. Of the very few replies received, only four came from professionals who believed they might have seen such patients (a total of six between them), and even these were very tentative. Aldridge-Morris (1989) states that:

> . . . it is clear that some therapists have an astronomically higher probability of meeting such patients than their colleagues and the vast majority (dare one say 'all'?) are in the United States.

One of these replies received by Aldridge-Morris came from Tony Armond, a consultant psychiatrist, who stated that:

In the UK, we react to any suggestions by patients or relatives that there are two or more personalities by immediately saying that there are two or more aspects to one personality, and asserting that the individual must take responsibility for both of these aspects. It works.

Aldridge-Morris (1989) goes on to say that MDP is unknown in the Czech Republic (CSSR), New Zealand, Australia, and India (but see above). So what features of US culture might be conducive?

Varma *et al.* (1981, cited in Aldridge-Morris, 1989) believe that there exists a fascination with role-playing among twentieth-century Western people, largely created, and certainly reinforced, by show business/the entertainment industry in general, and movies in particular. These include portrayal of cases of MPD, such as *The Three Faces of Eve, Sybil* and *When Rabbits Howl*. Such films provide 'stage directions' about such role enactment, with the therapist providing additional direction, as well as encouragement and, perhaps, most importantly, 'official validation' for the different identities enacted, especially when one of the personalities is enlisted as a 'therapeutic ally'.

Family and friends are also likely to be involved in legitimizing the adoption of such roles, with everybody concerned believing in the reality of the various alternate personalities (or alter egos). There is no suggestion of conscious deception or fabrication (Spanos *et al.*, 1986). Overall, there is much greater awareness of MPD in the USA than in the UK, more source data to provide role models, and, more generally, a greater acceptance/love of psychiatrists, psychotherapists and psychologists, together with a 'de-stigmatization' of psychotherapy – at least among the educated middle class (Aldridge-Morris, 1989).

(iv) So, isn't it plausible that the epidemic reflects an increase in the public's awareness of, and thus the ability to mimic, the symptoms of MPD? (Lilienfeld, 1995).

(v) Altrocchi (1980) also points out the preponderance of female patients, which is consistent, he claims, with the repressive lifestyle still experienced by women in Western culture.

Subsequent research

During several months of therapy following Jane's appearance, Eve White (real name Chris) learnt about the other two. A crucial moment was when Eve White was able to recall and deal with her feelings about a traumatic incident at age six, when her aunt forced her to kiss her dead grandmother. By then, Eve and her first husband had divorced, and Jane had married Don Sizemore, her (Chris's) present husband. During a crisis in Jane's life, a fourth personality appeared, Evelyn. She had all the memories of the other three, accepted responsibility for their actions, and seemed to be a much more mature and complete person than any one of them.

For almost 20 years, except for the movie *The Three Faces of Eve*, the public knew nothing more about the case. Then, on January 9th, 1975, Mrs Chris Sizemore of Fairfax, Virginia, revealed that she had been not only both Eves, Jane and Evelyn (all fictitious names), but many others besides, both before and after 1954, at least nine before Eve Black and approximately 22 altogether. Chris had had role models for denial, repression and dissociation while growing up. For example, her grandmother often refused to recognize something that displeased her, and tended to faint at times of stress, such as funerals. Chris also fainted at times of distress, and repressed memory of events such as her grandfather's funeral. Also, one of her personalities was blind, suggesting that a *conversion* reaction process (related to *somatoform disorders*) was part of her make-up.

Chris believes she began to develop separate personalities as a safety valve mechanism as young as two. By then she had seen a man drown, and another cut into three pieces by a saw at the lumber mill. (Her personalities tended to exist in groups of three!) In a personal communication to Altrocchi (1980), she describes the time she witnessed her mother cut her arm badly: Chris could not cope with this, and thought she was going to die. She ran to bed, stuck her head under the pillow, and felt herself receding into space, watching 'the other little girl' go get her father: 'It wasn't me, I was watching'.

She was always unusually sensitive, and unable to deal effectively with her kaleidoscopic emotions (Altrocchi, 1980). Chris Sizemore and her cousin, Elen Pittillo, together wrote '*I'm Eve*' (Sizemore & Pittillo, 1977), and they say this:

> Paradoxically, to survive intact, she splintered; she created other selves to endure what she could not absorb, to view what she could not comprehend, to do what she had been forbidden, to have what she had been denied.

When the pain became unbearable, Chris disappeared, and someone else took her place. But this produced the fugues and amnesias which made her even more inhibited and withdrawn, and did not help her to develop a coherent and acceptable self-concept.

She decided to reveal herself as the famous Eve as part of her therapy with Dr Tsitos, whose major strategy was to deal only with Chris, and to make it difficult for the others to come out. Over the years, as a personality died, she assimilated aspects of it. With the support of family, friends, and the public, she has successfully withstood her father's death, the tensions of public-speaking engagements, and national TV interviews.

Methodological issues

Some mental health workers are sceptical about MPD. Thigpen and Cleckley themselves ask if they have been hoodwinked by a skilful actress, and others have suggested that the behaviour is a combination of hypnotic suggestions and deliberate role playing (see **Theoretical issues** section above). Is there any evidence independent of the case-study itself for the separate existence of MPD as a form of mental disorder?

(*i*)   At the suggestion of McV. Hunt (then editor of the Journal in which the present article appeared), Thigpen and Cleckley gave the Semantic Differential attitude scale (Osgood, 1952, Osgood *et al.*, 1957) to Eve. Then Osgood and Luria subjected the resulting test scores to a blind analysis.

Each of the three main personalities (Eve White and Black, and Jane) was tested twice, at two-monthly intervals. Eve White emerged as socialized, construing the world 'normally' but showing an unsatisfactory attitude towards herself. Eve Black achieved a 'violent kind of adjustment', saw herself as perfect and perceived the world 'abnormally'; her construct system was the least stable over time. Finally, Jane had the most 'healthy' perception of the world and the most satisfactory self-evaluation.

Correlations of each personality with itself were regularly higher than the correlations between personalities (except for Eve White and Jane on the first testing). Osgood and Luria took this to be quantitative evidence that the Semantic Differential did show Eve White, Eve Black and Jane to be distinct personalities.

(*ii*)   London *et al.* (1969, in Thigpen & Cleckley, 1984) analysed, frame by frame, a 30-minute film of Eve, made by Thigpen and Cleckley, looking for possible facial regularities and other transformations of expressive behaviour. All three personalities 'appeared' in the film and all showed transient microstrabismus (the deviation of one eye from the axis of the other, such as one moving to the left, the other to the right, or one moving while the other doesn't). What is significant, is that each personality showed a different pattern of microstrabismus.

(*iii*)   Putnam *et al.* (1982, cited in Aldridge-Morris, 1989) studied 11 patients diagnosed with MPD and 11 controls (matched for age and gender). The visual evoked potentials (VEPs) to four intensities of light for the alter egos of the patients and simulated alternate personalities of the controls were compared. While no significant differences were found between the simulated personalities, the alter egos showed significantly lower correlations in both the amplitude and latency of their VEPs (i.e. they were more different from each other than were the simulated personalities).

While this (and other) objective data might seem quite convincing, some fundamental criticisms of the use of tests (especially, but not exclusively, psychological tests) have been made by Orne *et al.* (1984):

(a) When a blind tester is given a set of test scores for 'different' individuals, it is 'natural' to assume that they are, indeed, from separate testees. This reflects a 'normal' mental set, particularly as the hypothesis of MPD is such an unlikely one. Equally, to be told that they all come from a single testee will bias the tester towards perceiving common characteristics. What this all means is that the *objectivity* of the blind tester is always in doubt: we cannot take the assessment of 'separate personalities' at face value because of the assumption being made by the tester.

(b) The tests used can hardly be used diagnostically, since norms only exist for 'normal' populations, not for MPD populations.

(c) There needs to be control group data, allowing a demonstration of clinicians' ability to distinguish between test data derived from 'genuine' patients and that from participants who are faking or simulating. The Putnam *et al.* (1982) study cited above represents the kind of study which Orne *et al.* are advocating, but there are precious few studies of this kind.

Fahy (1988) argues that MPD is often difficult to distinguish from other dissociative disorders, somatoform disorders, borderline personality disorders, or malingering. There is no compelling evidence of specific physiological changes during the transitions between personalities: what changes are observed can be attributed to generalized differences in *arousal* between personalities. Alternatively, they could be attributed to short-lived mood changes (mood differences between different personalities: Lilienfeld, 1995).

Spanos *et al.* (1985) showed that college students could be hypnotically induced to display some MPD characteristics, when provided with proper instructions and cues from the experimenter (which might appear to invalidate the existence of MPD). However, they also point out that individuals predisposed to MPD may have a tendency towards suggestibility and fantasy, making them especially susceptible to cues from others (including psychotherapists). This same tendency may also confer a talent for adopting or enacting roles. From this perspective, the role-taking explanation does not necessarily mean that MPD does not exist. Rather,

> . . . patients with MPD can perhaps be conceptualized as uniquely capable of creating and entering a fantasy world inhabited by their own imaginary identities. (Lilienfeld, 1995)

Similarly, Davison & Neale (2001) point out that to demonstrate that role-play is possible does not in itself mean that this is what goes on in diagnosed cases of MPD.

Applications and implications

How does a diagnosis of MPD stand as a legal defence of criminals? Altrocchi (1980) cites the case of Arthur D. Wayne Bicknall, who was acquitted by a Californian judge, in 1976, of drunk driving after his psychiatrist, Allison, testified that one of the accused's other personalities ('Johnnie') was the true criminal. Allison actually summoned, under hypnosis, two of Bicknell's other personalities as character witnesses! Similarly, a Californian jury, in 1978, acquitted Ester Minor of forgery after three psychiatrists (including Allison) and two psychologists had testified that it was 'Raynell Potts' who had actually carried out the crimes without Ester's knowledge.

The whole status of expert witnesses is problematical, and different US States have different legal and judicial systems. But such cases highlight the concept of 'moral responsibility'. At the very least, one has to be performing the criminal act *knowingly*, and in the case of MPD this 'one' means the original personality. But if we went out and got drunk, and committed a crime 'under the influence' couldn't we all plead 'not guilty'? Presumably, however, getting drunk would have been done *knowingly*. By contrast, the person with MPD cannot knowingly switch personalities in order to escape responsibility. This, of course, presupposes that (conscious) role playing, acting, hypnotic suggestion and so on have been ruled out!

The 'received view' of MPD (see **Theoretical issues** above) is the belief that the alternate personalities satisfy the basic criteria for personhood: they are conscious, with thoughts, beliefs and (perhaps) their own body schema (Apter, 1991). Put another way, there is someone *who* the secondary selves are. But who? The original person all over again – or someone else? This, in turn, raises a number of fascinating questions: Do secondary personalities have the right to life? Is hypnotic merging ('fusion') of personalities under sodium amobarbital the death of those personalities? Should people with MPD have more than one vote? Do they have the right to a fair and just trial? (Apter, 1991). The last question, of course, relates to the issue of moral/criminal responsibility. In practice, at least, it is only ever the original or 'host' personality who is actually put on trial, under oath.

According to Saks (1997), an American lawyer, MPD should be regarded as a special case in mental health law. She argues that a new legal principle should be established, namely, 'irresponsibility by virtue of multiple personality disorder'. A major part of her argument centres around defining personhood (*What is a person?*). Unlike most individuals, for the person with MPD there is a discrepancy between 'me' and 'my body', and Saks believes that the law should be interested in the body *as a container for the person*. It is the person who may/may not be guilty, not the body, so that if the alternate personality that is put on trial is different from the one that occupied the body at the time the crime was committed, the former should not be held responsible. However, if the former was aware of the latter's criminal intentions and did nothing to try to prevent the crime, then the former would be complicit in the crime and would be at least partly responsible for it.

The reality of MPD is consistent with Double Brain Theory (DBT), according to which:

> . . . the human brain is essentially a 'double' brain consisting of a left and right hemisphere. 'Multiple personality' involves the alternate functioning of these hemispheres. The answers to the question, 'Who is the second personality?' was, 'the second personality is one of the cerebral hemispheres'. (Apter, 1991)

DBT originated at the same time as the Dissociationist school in French psychiatry and persists today in the context of split-brain patients (see Chapter 30). Accordingly, we all have two 'minds', we are all two persons, but it is only under extreme conditions (e.g. commissurotomy, where the two hemispheres are separated, or extreme stress or trauma) that the existence of these two selves becomes apparent, both subjectively and behaviourally. The former example describes split-brain patients, the latter multiple personalities.

Thigpen & Cleckley (1984) point out that, since Eve, they have come across only *one* case of MPD among the tens of thousands of patients they saw in the ensuing 30 years of practice. They argue that:

> While there are degrees of dissociation, some of which may be serious enough to require treatment, we urge that the diagnosis of multiple personality disorder be reserved for those very few persons who are truly fragmented in the most extreme manner.

Given that many more familiar and less controversial syndromes can coexist with MPD (e.g. schizophrenia, sociopathic personality, temporal lobe epilepsy), and given how extraordinarily complex the diagnosis of MPD is, Thigpen & Cleckley (1984) believe that MPD represents the false positive: *it* is more likely to be diagnosed than these other disorders.

Crellin (1998) cites a book by Hacking (*Rewriting the Soul*, 1995), which used MPD as a case example of the development of a 'symptom syndrome'. Hacking linked the so-called MPD 'epidemic' to (a) the development of a team of experts in the USA who had much to gain from promoting acceptance of the existence of a genuine disorder to which the label referred, and (b) the publication of 'first person accounts' by MPD sufferers. These were widely available and may have offered others a new way of making sense of their own particular form of experience. Hacking argues that people describe their experience of distress in ways which vary over time, according to the changing assumptions and models of expression available within the prevailing culture.

Both the British Psychological Society (1995) and the Royal College of Psychiatrists (1997) have warned of the ease with which therapists may unwittingly encourage *false memories* of childhood abuse. They should be particularly aware of the unreliability of

memories reported by patients suffering from dissociation. Even some of those who most strongly support the 'abuse theory' of MPD (e.g. Kluft, 1996; Ross, 1997) acknowledge that false memories present a problem. Mollon (1998) warns that dissociation involves pretence, and therapists have to admit to uncertainty about the truth of these clients' accounts. But he still insists that their pretence and fantasy is caused by childhood trauma.

A major problem with the 'abuse theory' is corroborating the claims of childhood abuse (Mair, 1999). While it is likely that some adults with MPD have suffered such abuse, the presence of a known history of abuse may sometimes be used as a basis for the diagnosis! The abuse may well have contributed to the patient's present problems, but this does not mean that *only* the abuse is responsible, or that the mechanisms involved are properly understood. According to Mair, the view that MPD is caused by severe childhood trauma:

> . . . rests on extremely shaky foundations and can neither be proved nor disproved. It is dogma, not science.

Exercises

1. Do you think that psychologists and psychiatrists should be used as expert witnesses in criminal cases?

2. Do you believe, if the testimony of an expert witness is accepted as showing that the defendant has MPD, that this should, necessarily, lead to a verdict of 'not guilty'?

3. Are there any advantages which the Thigpen and Cleckley case-study has over Freud's way of working with his patients (e.g. Little Hans, see Chapter 19)?

4. Name two important differences between MPD and schizophrenia.

5. (*i*) What is meant by a 'blind tester'?
    (*ii*) What advantages are usually claimed for using a blind tester?

6. Briefly describe the Semantic Differential attitude scale.

22 The effects of psychotherapy: an evaluation

H.J. Eysenck (1952)

Journal of Consulting Psychology, 16, 319–24

BACKGROUND AND CONTEXT

All forms of psychotherapy originate from Freud's psychoanalysis, and Eysenck was always one of Freud's most outspoken critics, both of his theory of personality and techniques of psychotherapy (which are intimately connected). Eysenck was a leading advocate of methods of treatment based on classical learning theory (i.e. conditioning), in particular those methods based on classical (Pavlovian) conditioning, known as *behaviour therapy*. From this perspective:

(*i*) all behaviour, whether adaptive or maladaptive, is acquired by the same principles of classical conditioning;

(*ii*) according to Eysenck & Rachman (1965), the case of Little Albert (see Chapter 16) exemplifies how *all* phobias are acquired (i.e. through classical conditioning), although they have both modified their views since then;

(*iii*) the medical model of psychological abnormality is completely rejected, including any distinction between 'symptoms' and underlying pathology. According to Eysenck (1960), if you 'get rid of the symptoms . . . you have eliminated the neurosis': what you see is what there is. However, MacKay (1975) observes that some behaviour therapists do use the formal diagnostic categories ('syndromes'), and try to discover which techniques are most effective with particular diagnostic groups. Key figures in this *nomothetic* approach ('*behavioural technology*') are Eysenck, Rachman and Marks;

(*iv*) the emphasis is on *current* behaviour and environmental influences: psychological problems are behavioural problems which need to be *operationalized* in terms of observable behaviours before any attempt can be made to change them.

Freud and Eysenck actually share the view that the same principles are involved in the development of both normal and abnormal behaviour; however, the principles themselves are rather different. So, for example, neurotic symptoms and dreams (which have much in common 'structurally') and defence mechanisms are all compromises between the opposing demands made on the ego by the id and superego. Neuroses are maladaptive solutions to the individual's problems, but involve

essentially the same compromises (especially defence mechanisms) involved in adaptive behaviour (e.g. phobias involve repression, as do all neuroses, displacement and projection: see Chapter 19).

Also like Eysenck, Freud rejected the medical model. Although he distinguished between 'symptoms' and 'underlying pathology', the latter is conceived in psychological (not genetic or biochemical) terms, and he was concerned with the individual and not the disorder. For example, a phobia is only the conscious, overt, manifestation of an internal, unconscious conflict. The phobic object has become symbolically associated with the underlying source of conflict and anxiety. Although he used diagnostic labels, he did so as linguistic conveniences rather than as an integral part of his theories, and he focused on understanding the patient's problems in their life context rather than on clinical labelling (Mackay, 1975).

Unlike Eysenck, Freud emphasized *past events*, particularly early childhood ones of a sexual nature, and *unconscious* (and other internal) factors; the latter, at best, can only be inferred from the patient's recollections, dreams and so on.

AIM AND NATURE OF THE STUDY

Eysenck (1992) claims that, prior to his 1952 article, the *outcome problem* (trying to assess, empirically, whether psychotherapy actually *works*) had never been properly addressed by clinical psychologists. So, the study represents the first major, scientific attempt to assess the effectiveness of psychotherapy.

The study is a survey of a large number of studies dealing with the improvement of neurotic patients following psychotherapy (either psychoanalytic or eclectic, i.e. 'mixed', a combination of different therapeutic techniques, not based on one particular school, such as psychoanalysis). Its aim is to test the hypothesis that 'psychotherapy facilitates recovery from neurotic disorder', that is, increases the chances of recovery. Eysenck does this by comparing those patients who have received psychotherapy (the 'experimental' group) with a 'control' group of patients who had been hospitalized for 'neurosis' in state mental hospitals (Landis, 1938) or treated only by their GPs with sedatives, tonics, suggestion and reassurance (Denker, 1946).

These control groups provided a 'baseline' of spontaneous recovery ('remission') against which to compare the patients who received psychotherapy, and 66% was the 'figure to beat'. Eysenck's article is largely responsible for the explosion of research into the effects of psychotherapy (Oatley, 1984).

THE STUDY

The recommendation of the committee on Training in Clinical Psychology of the American Psychological Association regarding the training of clinical psychologists in the field of psychotherapy has been criticized by this author in a series of papers (1949, 1950). The most cogent argument presented in favour of the Committee's policy is perhaps that which refers to the social need for the skills possessed by the psychotherapist. In view of the importance of the issues involved, it seemed worthwhile to examine the evidence regarding the actual effects of psychotherapy.

BASELINE AND UNIT OF MEASUREMENT

In the only other previous attempt to carry out such an evaluation, Landis (1938) has pointed out that 'before any sort of measurement can be made, it is necessary to establish a baseline and a common unit of measure. The only unit of measure available is the report made by the physician, stating that the patient has recovered, is much improved, is improved or unimproved. This unit is probably as satisfactory as any type of human subjective judgement, partaking of both the good and bad points of such judgements'. For a unit, Landis suggests 'that of expressing therapeutic results in terms of the number of patients recovered or improved per 100 cases admitted to the hospital'. As an alternative, he suggests 'the statement of therapeutic outcome for some given group of patients during some stated interval of time'.

Landis realized quite clearly that, in order to evaluate the effectiveness of any form of therapy, data from a control group of non-treated patients is necessary in order to compare the effects of therapy with the spontaneous remission rate. In the absence of anything better, he used the improvement rate in state mental hospitals for patients diagnosed under the heading of 'neuroses'. He points out the objections to using such patients as a control group.

> The fact that psychoneurotic cases are not usually committed to state hospitals unless in a very bad condition; the relatively small number of voluntary patients in the group; the fact that such patients do get some degree of psychotherapy, especially in the reception hospitals; and the probably quite different economic, educational and social status of the State Hospital group compared to the patients reported from each of the other hospitals; all argue against the acceptance of [this] figure . . . as a truly satisfactory baseline, but in the absence of any other better figure, this must serve.

Actually, the various figures quoted by Landis agree very well. The percentage of neurotic patients discharged annually as recovered or improved from New York state hospitals is 70 (for the period 1925 to 1934); for the USA as a whole, it is 68 (1926 to 1933). The percentage discharged as recovered or improved within one year of admission is 66 for the USA (1933) and 68 for New York (1914). The consolidated improvement rate of New York state hospitals (1917 to 1934) is 72 per cent, and this is the one chosen by Landis and which is accepted here. So, by and large, we may say that, of severe neurotics receiving mainly custodial care, and very little of any psychotherapy, over two-thirds recovered or improved to a considerable extent. 'Although this is not, strictly speaking, a basic figure for "spontaneous recovery", still any therapeutic method must show an appreciably greater size than this to be seriously considered' (Landis, 1938).

Another estimate of the required 'baseline' is provided by Denker (1946):

> 500 consecutive disability claims due to psychoneurosis, treated by general practitioners throughout the country, and not by accredited specialists or sanatoria, were reviewed. All types of neurosis were included, and no attempt made to differentiate the neurosthenic, anxiety, compulsive, hysteric, or other states, but the greatest care was taken to eliminate the true psychotic or organic lesions, which in the early stages of illness so often simulate neurosis. These cases were taken consecutively from the files of the Equitable Life Assurance Society of the United States, were from all parts of the country, and all had been ill of a neurosis for at least three months before claims were submitted. They, therefore, could be fairly called 'severe', since they had been totally disabled for at least a three-month period, and rendered unable to carry on with any 'occupation for remuneration or profit' for at least that time.

These patients were regularly seen and treated by their own doctors with sedatives, tonics, suggestion, and reassurance, but in no case was any attempt made at anything but this most superficial type of 'psychotherapy', which has always been the stock-in-trade of the GP.

Repeated statements, every three months or so, by their doctors, as well as independent investigations by the insurance company, confirmed the fact that these people were not actually engaged in productive work during the period of their illness, when they received disability benefits. Denker points out that this fact of receiving benefit may have actually prolonged the total period of disability, and acted as a disincentive to recovery. Therefore, the therapeutic results would not be expected to be as favourable in such a group as in other groups, where there was a financial incentive for the patient to adjust to his neurotic illness. The cases were all followed up for a least a five-year period, and often up to ten years, after the period of disability had begun. The criteria of 'recovery' used by Denker were as follows: (*i*) return to work, and ability to carry on well in economic adjustments for at least five years; (*ii*) complaint of no further or very slight difficulties; (*iii*) making successful social adjustments. Using these criteria, which are very similar to those normally used by psychiatrists, Denker found that 45 per cent of the patients recovered after one year, another 27 per cent after two years, making 72 per cent in all. Another ten, five and four per cent recovered during the third, fourth and fifth years, respectively, making a total of 90 per cent recoveries after five years.

This sample contrasts in many ways with that used by Landis. The former cases were probably not quite as severe, they were all voluntary, non-hospitalized patients and came from a much higher socio-economic background, mostly clerical workers, executives, teachers and professionals. In spite of these differences, the recovery figures for the two samples are almost identical. The most suitable figure to choose for Denker's sample is probably that for the two-year recovery rate, since follow-up would overestimate the efficiency of this 'baseline' procedure. The figure of 72 per cent for two-year recovery rate agrees exactly with that given by Landis. We may, therefore, conclude with some confidence that our estimate of two-thirds of severe neurotics showing recovery or considerable improvement without the benefit of systematic psychotherapy is not likely to be very far out.

EFFECTS OF PSYCHOTHERAPY

The results of 19 studies, covering over 7000 cases, and dealing with both psychoanalytic and eclectic types of treatment, are shown in Table 22.1. An attempt has been made to report results under four headings: (*i*) cured, or much improved; (*ii*) improved; (*iii*) slightly improved; (*iv*) not improved, died, discontinued treatment, etc. It was usually easy to reduce additional categories given by some writers to these basic four; some gave only two or three, and in those cases it was, of course, impossible to subdivide further, and the figures for combined categories are given. (In one or two cases, where patients who improved or improved slightly were combined by the original author, the total figure has been divided equally between the two categories.) A slight degree of subjectivity inevitably enters into this procedure, but it is unlikely to have caused much distortion. Rather more subjectivity is probably implied in the writers' judgement as to which disorders and diagnoses should be categorized as 'neurosis'. Schizophrenic, manic-depressive and paranoid states have been excluded, while organ neuroses, psychopathic states and character disturbances have been included. The number of cases where there was genuine doubt is probably too small to make much difference to the final figures, however they are allocated.

A number of studies have been excluded because of such factors as excessive inadequacy of follow-up, partial duplication of cases with others included in the table, failure to indicate types of treatment used, and other reasons which made the results useless for our purposes. Their inclusion would not have altered our conclusions to any considerable degree, although, as Miles *et al.* (1951) points out: 'When the various studies are compared in terms of thoroughness, careful planning, strictness of criteria and objectivity, there is often an inverse correlation between these factors and the percentage of successful results reported'.

Certain difficulties have arisen from the inability of some writers to make their column figures agree with their totals, or to calculate percentages accurately. Again, the writer has used his judgement as to which figures to accept. In certain

THE STUDY

Table 22.1

SUMMARY OF REPORTS OF THE RESULTS OF PSYCHOTHERAPY

	n	Cured; much improved	Improved	Slightly improved	Not improved; died; left treatment	% cured; much improved; improved
(A) Psychoanalytic						
1 Fenichel (1920–1930)	484	104	84	99	197	39
2 Kessel & Hyman (1933)	34	16	5	4	9	62
3 Jones (1926–1936)	59	20	8	28	3	47
4 Alexander (1932–1937)	141	28	42	23	48	50
5 Knight (1941)	42	8	20	7	7	67
All Cases	760		335	425		44
(B) Eclectic						
1 Huddleson (1927)	200	19	74	80	27	46
2 Matz (1929)	775	10	310	310	145	41
3 Maudsley Hospital Report (1931)	1721	288	900	533	69	
4 Maudsley Hospital Report (1935)	1711	371	765	575	64	
5 Neustatter (1935)	46	9	14	8	15	50
6 Luff & Garrod (1935)	500	140	135	26	199	55
7 Luff & Garrod (1935)	210	38	84	54	34	68
8 Ross (1936)	1089	547	306	236	77	
9 Yaskin (1936)	100	29	29	42	58	
10 Curran (1937)	83	51	32	61		
11 Masserman & Carmichael (1938)	50	7	20	5	18	54
12 Carmichael & Masserman (1939)	77	16	25	14	22	53
13 Schilder (1939)	35	11	11	6	7	63
14 Hamilton & Wall (1941)	100	32	34	17	17	66
15 Hamilton et al. (1942)	100	46	5	17	32	51
16 Landis (1938)	119	40	47	32	73	
17 Institute Med. Psychol. (quoted Neustatter)	270	58	132	55	25	70
18 Wilder (1945)	54	3	24	16	11	50
19 Miles et al. (1951)	53	13	18	13	9	58
All Cases	7293	4661		2632		64

cases, writers have given figures of cases where there was a recurrence of the disorder after apparent cure or improvement, without indicating how many patients were affected in these two groups respectively; all recurrences of this kind have been subtracted from the 'cured' and 'improved' totals, taking half from each. The total number of cases involved in all these adjustments is quite small.

We may now turn to the figures as presented. Patients treated by means of psychoanalysis improve to the extent of 44 per cent; patients treated eclectically improve to the extent of 64 per cent; patients treated only custodially or by GPs improve to the extent of 72 per cent. Thus there appears to be an inverse correlation between recovery and psychotherapy: the more psychotherapy, the smaller the recovery rate. This conclusion requires certain qualifications.

In the psychoanalytic results, we have classed those who stopped treatment as 'not improved'. It seems reasonable to regard someone who fails to finish treatment as a therapeutic failure, and the same rule has been followed with the data summarized under 'eclectic' treatment, except when the patient was definitely classified as 'improved' by the therapist. However, in view of the peculiarities of Freudian procedures it could be argued that it is more just to class those cases separately, and deal only with the percentage of successful completed treatments. Approximately one-third of the psychoanalytic patients listed broke off treatment, so that the percentage of successful treatments who finished treatment is approximately 66 per cent, approximately the same as under eclectic treatment and slightly worse than under a GP or custodial treatment.

Two further points require clarification: (*i*) are patients in our 'control' groups (Landis & Denker, 1948) as seriously ill as those in our 'experimental' groups? and (*ii*) are standards of recovery perhaps less stringent in our 'control' than in our 'experimental' groups? Although it is difficult to answer these questions definitely, from a close scrutiny of the literature it seems that the 'control' patients were probably at least as seriously ill as the 'experimental' patients, and possibly more so. As regards standards of recovery, those in Denker's study are as stringent as most of those used by psychoanalysts and eclectic psychiatrists, but those used by the State Hospitals in the Landis study are very probably more lenient.

What general conclusions can be drawn from these data? They fail to prove that psychotherapy, Freudian or otherwise, facilitates the recovery of neurotic patients; roughly two-thirds of a group of neurotic patients will recover or improve to a marked extent within about two years of the onset of their illness, whether they receive psychotherapy or not. This figure seems to be remarkably stable from one study to another, regardless of type of patient treated, standard of recovery used, or method of therapy used. From the point of view of the neurotic, these figures are encouraging; from the psychotherapist's point of view, they can hardly be called very favourable to his claims.

THE STUDY

The results do not necessarily disprove the possibility of therapeutic effectiveness. There are obvious shortcomings in any actuarial comparison, and these are particularly serious when there is so little agreement among psychiatrists regarding even the most fundamental concepts and definitions. Definite proof would require a special investigation, carefully planned and methodologically more adequate than these *ad hoc* comparisons. But even so, the results should make us seriously question the justification of giving an important place in the training of clinical psychologists to a skill whose existence and effectiveness is still unsupported by any scientifically acceptable evidence.

These results and conclusions will no doubt contradict the strong feeling of usefulness and therapeutic success which many psychiatrists and clinical psychologists have. In the absence of agreement between fact and belief, there is urgent need for a decrease in the strength of belief and an increase in the number of facts available. Until such facts as may be discovered in a rigorous analysis support the prevalent belief in therapeutic effectiveness of psychological treatment, it seems premature to insist on the inclusion of training in such treatment in the curriculum of the clinical psychologist.

SUMMARY

A survey was made of reports on the improvement of neurotic patients after psychotherapy, and the results compared with the best available estimates of recovery without benefit of such therapy. The figures fail to support the hypothesis that psychotherapy facilitates recovery from neurotic disorder. In view of the many difficulties associated with such actuarial comparisons, no further conclusions could be drawn from the data, whose shortcomings highlight the necessity of properly planned and executed experimental studies of this important field.

EVALUATION

Theoretical issues

Where Freud and Eysenck disagree, they do so fundamentally. This is seen most clearly when we ask how to assess the effectiveness of psychotherapy, the crux of Eysenck's famous 1952 paper. The criteria Eysenck refers to in the article (used by Denker) are:

(*i*) return to work and ability to carry on well in economic adjustments for at least five years;

(*ii*) complaint of no further or very slight difficulties;

(*iii*) making successful social adjustments.

These are all fairly tangible indicators of improvement, and even more so are the behaviour therapist's criteria that cure is achieved when patients no longer manifest the original maladaptive behaviour (e.g. the fear of spiders is eliminated). If these more stringent (or more easily measured) criteria of actual behaviour change are required before the therapist can be viewed as successful, then behaviour therapists *do* seem to be more effective than psychoanalysts or humanistic therapists (with cognitive approaches in between: Rachman & Wilson, 1980; Shapiro & Shapiro, 1982).

But are these criteria appropriate for assessing 'cure' or improvement as applied to psychoanalysis? According to Jacobs (1984), the goals of therapy are limited by what the client consciously wants to achieve and is capable of achieving, together with his/her motivation, ego strength, capacity for insight, ability to tolerate the frustration of gradual change, financial cost and so on. These factors, in turn, determine how cure is defined and assessed.

In practice, psychoanalysis ranges from 'psychoanalytical first aid' (Guntrip, 1968) or symptom relief, to different levels of more intense work. However, Storr (1966) believes that a quick, complete 'cure' is very much the exception rather than the rule, and most people who undergo psychoanalysis cannot expect their symptoms to disappear easily or (even if this should happen) that they will be freed of emotional problems. This is because of what we noted earlier (see **Background and context**) about neurotic symptoms being merely the outward and visible signs of an inner, less visible conflict. Exploration and analysis of the symptoms inevitably lead to an analysis of the whole person, his/her development, temperament and character structure. Symptom analysis, therefore, is usually just the *beginning* of the analytic process, and most patients do not have clear cut symptoms anyway! (Storr, 1966).

Psychoanalytic therapists may answer the question 'Does therapy work?' by saying it is a misleading question, like asking whether friendship 'works'. It is an activity that people take part in, which is important to them, affects, moves, even transforms them (Oatley, 1984). But for Eysenck, if it cannot be empirically demonstrated that it has well-defined beneficial effects, then it is worthless. Because he is interested in comparing recovery rates (measured statistically), his assessment of the effects of therapy is purely *quantitative*. By contrast, psychoanalysts and those who adopt other non-behavioural approaches (e.g. Rogers' client-centred therapy) are likely to be much more concerned with the *qualitative* aspects of therapy: *how* does it work, what is the nature of the therapeutic process, what is the role of the relationship between client and therapist, what are the important qualities of the therapist? and so on. The point here is that there are different *kinds* of questions one can ask by way of trying to assess the effects of psychotherapy.

Methodological issues

In Eysenck's own terms, there are important limitations to his study which are acknowledged in the article itself:

(*i*) If the many patients who drop out of psychoanalysis are not counted as 'failures' or 'not cured', the figure for those who do benefit rises from 44% to 66%. Elsewhere, Eysenck (1985, *Decline and Fall of the Freudian Empire*) argues that the large number of patients who drop out should be considered *failures*, rather than being omitted from the statistics. He also claims that the effectiveness of psychoanalysis always seems to be far lower than you would expect it to be (even allowing for the 'drop-outs' not counting as failures).

He states that patients who undergo psychoanalysis are nearly always YAVIS (young, attractive, verbal, intelligent and successful). These people tend to have a favourable prognosis regardless of treatment. Selection criteria exclude extremely disturbed people (including sexual deviants and alcoholics), those who do not request a 'talking therapy' and those not considered suitable for psychotherapy for other reasons.

> By thus excluding the most difficult and recalcitrant neurotic patients, and concentrating on those most likely to improve in any case, psychoanalysts would seem to have loaded the dice in their favour. Failure to do better than no treatment or eclectic forms of psychotherapy, where no or few patients are excluded, seems to suggest, if anything, that psychoanalysis does *less* well than eclectic psychotherapy or no treatment at all. (Eysenck, 1985)

He does not present any evidence regarding these claims of selectivity for psychoanalysis, although it is widely accepted that the nature of the therapy, together with its duration and expense, make it accessible only to the privileged few, namely the well-educated, articulate and reasonably well-off middle classes.

(*ii*) Landis (1938) points out a number of differences between psychotherapy patients and those state hospital patients he used as a control group to provide the baseline. He concludes by saying that these differences

> all argue against the acceptance of [this] figure . . . as a truly satisfactory baseline, but in the absence of any other better figure this must serve.

Eysenck (1985) says that it was *because* of the poverty of the evidence that in his 1952 article he did *not* say that psychoanalysis/psychotherapy had been proven to be useless; to have done so would have involved going far beyond what the evidence justified. What he did conclude, was that the psychoanalysts had failed to prove their claim that their methods were superior to no treatment at all. (By implication, the onus is on them to prove it, rather than on others to disprove it: a case of 'guilty until proven innocent'?)

However, he quotes at length from Rachman & Wilson's (1980) *The Effects of Psychological Therapy*:

> our reviews of the evidence that has accumulated during the past twenty-five years does not put us in a position to revise Eysenck's original estimate [of 66% spontaneous remission]. (Rachman & Wilson, 1980)

They go on to make two further points:

(*i*)   the figure of 66% needs to be revised for specific categories of neurotic disorder (e.g. obsessive disorders seem to have a much lower rate of spontaneous remission than anxiety disorders, with hysterical symptoms in between);

(*ii*) there is a serious lack of controlled evaluations of the effects of psychoanalysis.

Subsequent research

According to Garfield (1992), both the quantity and quality of psychotherapy research have increased since Eysenck's 1952 article, especially since the 1970s. Bergin (1971) reviewed some of the papers included in Eysenck's review, and concluded that, by choosing different criteria of 'improvement', the success rate of psychoanalysis could be raised to 83%. Bergin also cites certain studies (not included in Eysenck's review) which showed a 30% spontaneous remission rate.

However, again referring to Rachman & Wilson's (1980) review, Eysenck (1985) points out some curious features in Bergin's review which makes his conclusions unacceptable. First, the data from the new studies are treated separately from those on which Eysenck based his estimate: they should have been combined with, or at least considered in the light of, the original studies. Second, he omitted several studies which are more relevant to the question of spontaneous recovery than those actually included. Third, some of the studies he cites to support his 30% estimate do not actually deal with spontaneous remission of neurotic disorders at all (but, for example, deal with physical disease, such as ulcerative colitis). Eysenck concludes that Bergin's widely cited figure of 30% should be disregarded, because it is based on inadequate evidence. But is it any more inadequate than that on which Eysenck's own 66% was originally based?

Bergin & Lambert (1978) reviewed 17 studies of untreated 'neurotics', and found a median spontaneous remission rate of 43%. They also found that the rate of spontaneous remission varies a great deal depending on the disorder. For example, generalized anxiety and depression are much more likely to 'cure themselves' than phobias or obsessive-compulsive disorders. Here, at least, Eysenck and Bergin are in agreement. Eysenck (1985) makes no reference to this later study by Bergin and Lambert.

Smith & Glass (1977) reviewed 400 studies of a wide variety of therapies (including psychodynamic, Gestalt, client-centred therapy, transactional analysis, systematic desensitization, and eclectic) and concluded that all were more effective than no treatment. For example, the 'average' client who had received therapy scored more favourably on the outcome measures than 75% of those in the untreated control groups. Furthermore, there seemed to be no significant differences between behavioural and non-behavioural therapies. Luborsky *et al.* (1975) also found all forms of therapy to be equally effective.

Smith *et al.* (1980) extended the earlier study to include 475 studies (an estimated 75% of the published literature). Strict criteria for admission into their 'meta-analysis' included the comparison between a treated group (given a specified form of therapy) with a second group (drawn from the same population) given either no therapy, put on a waiting list, or given some alternative form of therapy. Again, therapy was shown to have a significant effect: the average client was better off than 80% of the control groups on the outcome measures. Smith *et al.* confirmed their earlier finding that, overall, neither behaviour therapy nor psychoanalytic therapy was superior, but different treatments did seem to be more effective with different kinds of mental/behavioural disorder.

Once again, Eysenck (1985) is very critical of the Smith *et al.* (1980) study. In their assessment of 18 different types of therapy, and using effect size (ES) scores (as an equivalent measure to the percentages quoted above), systematic desensitization emerged with an ES of 1.05, psychodynamic therapy with 0.69, and placebo treatments 0.56. Eysenck (1985) argues that instead of regarding placebo treatment as a treatment, it is more appropriately seen as a proper control against which to compare other, real treatments. On this basis, the difference between the psychodynamic and placebo 'treatments' is negligible, undermining the argument that psychodynamic therapy is beneficial.

Furthermore, there was no evidence in the Smith *et al.* (1980) study that better trained or more experienced therapists increased the chances of successful outcomes, or that the longer the therapy lasted, the more successful it was likely to be. On all counts, Eysenck says, the psychodynamic approach is undermined: surely, training, experience and duration of therapy should all influence the outcome of therapy but, apparently, these variables don't seem to make any difference! Eysenck (1985) concludes by saying:

> Even now, 30 years after the article in which I pointed out the lack of evidence for therapeutic effectiveness, and some 500 extensive investigations later, the conclusion must still be that there is no substantial evidence that psychoanalysis or psychotherapy have any positive effect on the course of neurotic disorders, over and above what is contributed by meaningless placebo treatment.

Some independent support for Eysenck comes in the form of a German study (Wittmann & Matt, 1986), originally designed as a replication – and extension – of the

Smith *et al.* (1980) study. The major finding was that the effects of psychotherapy based on German-language studies were less than half the size of those reported by Smith *et al.* In the light of this, Matt (1993) asks whether English – and German – language psychotherapies really do differ in their effectiveness, or are these differences due to other substantive and methodological differences between the two bodies of research? Matt describes the Smith *et al.* study as the most comprehensive meta-analysis of psychotherapy outcomes to date, and then defines meta-analysis as:

> . . . a type of literature review that makes explicit use of quantitative methods to sum up a body of separate but similar studies (i.e. primary studies) for the purpose of integrating the findings.

The Smith & Glass (1977) study was one of the first large-scale examples of this method, and in the field of psychotherapy outcome research alone, there have been more than 50 since 1983. Whether being discussed in a cross-cultural context or not, the central question according to Matt (1993) in all meta-analysis is: how can we be sure that outcome differences are due to the different treatments or interventions being used, rather than the effects of variables such as the subject populations (differences in the nature of the people receiving treatment), research design, meta-analytic techniques (e.g. differences in selection of studies, calculation of effect sizes) and contextual variables (e.g. social and political factors affecting the funding of research into psychotherapy outcomes, and editorial policies for accepting/rejecting research for publication)?

Compared with Smith *et al.*'s 0.85 average effect size (based on 1766 separate outcome comparisons), Wittmann & Matt (1986) found an average 0.39, based on 76 studies and 426 separate outcome comparisons. Matt (1993) compared the two studies and concluded that:

> . . . there are likely to be no major differences in effect magnitude between English and German psychotherapy. Instead, the type of disorders, therapeutic interventions, outcome measures, and the meta-analytic review itself appear to have differentially influenced the effect estimates obtained for the two bodies of research.

These differences probably led Smith *et al.* to *over*estimate, and Wittmann and Matt to *under*estimate, the benefits of psychotherapy. The study is important because it shows that the average effect estimates for psychotherapy outcomes studies, 'depend on, and have to be interpreted in, the cultural context in which the research is being conducted and reviewed' (Matt, 1993).

Svartberg & Stiles (1991) conducted a meta-analysis of 19 studies (conducted between 1978 and 1988), in which short-term psychodynamic psychotherapy (STPP) was compared with no-treatment controls (NT) and alternative treatments (AP). They claim that STPP has become the most popular form of short-term psychotherapy. While originating from psychodynamic or psychoanalytic theory, its use extends

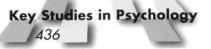

beyond less disturbed neurotics with specific problems to the severely depressed, addicts, mild and even severe personality disorders. Overall, STPP showed a small but significant superiority to waiting-list patients immediately following treatment, but small and significant inferiority to AP six months after treatment which increased during the next six months. It was therapies other than STPP which showed increasing benefits during the post-treatment period (the 'incubation' effect, which is usually claimed for psychodynamic therapy, although there may be an incubation effect in *long-term* psychodynamic therapy).

Therapies other than STPP were found to be superior in treating depressed patients, and cognitive behaviour therapy, especially, is effective with major depression (see Chapter 28). However, STPP seems to rival AP when treating mixed neurotic patients, unless they are young or the therapist is inexperienced. Similarly, STPP is less successful relative to NT when the patients are female or the therapist is experienced or specifically trained, and relative to AP when experienced therapists treat young neurotics.

According to Lilienfeld (1995), the question 'Is psychotherapy effective?' could be seen as remarkably complex in some respects, but also too simple in others. As Paul (1966) observes, what we need to ask is '*What* treatment, by *whom*, is most effective for *this* individual, with what specific problem, and under *which* set of circumstances? This is to do with the matching of client, therapy and setting, and the question still haunts psychotherapy research and disturbs therapists (Wilson & Barkham, 1994).

Applications and implications

We noted earlier (see **Subsequent research**) that when discussing Smith *et al.*'s (1980) meta-analytic study, Eysenck (1985) stated that neither better trained nor more experienced therapists increased the chances of successful outcome. He used this as a further criticism of psychotherapy in general, and psychoanalysis in particular, claiming that

> . . . if there were no positive effects of psychoanalysis as a therapy, then it would be completely unethical to apply this method to patients, to charge them money for such treatment, or to train therapists in these unsuccessful methods . . . (Eysenck, 1992)

These are, clearly, extremely important issues which need to be taken very seriously. Do therapists' credentials matter? Smith *et al.* concluded that the therapist's qualifications, training and length of experience were irrelevant, and several other reviews have reached the same conclusion (e.g. Christensen & Jacobson, 1994). Dawes (1994) claims that any sensitive person can do insight-oriented psychotherapy, provided s/he shows empathy, just as all that is needed to perform behaviour therapy is some knowledge of behavioural principles.

A study by Strupp & Hadley (1979) appears to support Dawes. A sample of students with mild neurotic problems were allocated to (a) a trained, highly experienced psychoanalytically-oriented therapist or (b) a college lecturer (in English, History, Maths or Philosophy) known by students to be a sympathetic listener. Meetings took place twice weekly for 18 sessions, at the end of which both groups were doing better than a control group (who received no specific help) in terms of emotional well-being, nor did they differ from each other. However, the study has been criticized for several reasons. For example, Strupp (1996) points out that while the college lecturers were selected for certain qualities, the therapists were chosen in a much more random way. Also, the therapists were not specialists in time-limited therapy, and would have been more used to longer-term therapy. Strupp also points out some important differences between professional therapists and non-professionals:

(*i*) training enhances common factors such as warmth, listening skill, and commitment to patients' welfare;
(*ii*) training equips the therapist to be better able to manage the way patients' problems manifest themselves in the therapeutic relationship (such as hostility, dependence, and idealization) and to avoid playing a complementary role (such as becoming responsible for a dependent patient).

More generally, professional psychologists, compared with non-professionals, are likely to be more effective with the full range of different patients and disorders (Wilson *et al.*, 1996). Seligman (1996) similarly argues that trained expertise becomes important when the patient's problem is more complex, when there is no training manual to follow, and when clinical judgement is needed, as in formulating the problem in the first place.

The value of training in psychotherapy is, perhaps, the most important *specific* factor involved in the effectiveness of therapy (MacLeod, 1998), and is related more to *process research* (*how* does therapy work?) than to outcome research (which was always Eysenck's primary concern). Strupp (1996) estimates that about 85% of the variability in therapeutic outcomes can be attributed to *common* factors (such as the therapist's personality, his/her ability to help patients gain understanding of their problems, and encouraging patients to face up to things they find difficult).

According to Westen & Morrison (2001), the greatest innovation in clinical training and practice in the past decade has been the expectation that treatment for mental disorder (as for medical trials) should be empirically validated or supported (i.e. evidence-based). As advocates of traditional psychotherapies retire, they have largely 'passed the torch' to younger, more empirically informed colleagues. Westen and Morrison carried out a meta-analysis of 34 studies of the efficacy of psychotherapy in three common disorders – depression, panic, and generalized anxiety disorder (GAD). The studies were reported in nine clinical psychology and psychiatric journals between 1990 and 1999. To be included in the meta-analysis, they had to test the efficacy of a specific psychosocial (i.e. non-medical) treatment against a waiting-list control group and an alternative therapy, have a follow-up of at least 12 months (only four followed up for two years), to include valid measures of outcome, and be experimental in nature.

Westen and Morrison found that the average patient who received an active treatment was substantially better off than control patients at the end of treatment. However, most did not show sustained improvement after one or two years, especially those who were depressed or generally anxious. The long-term treatment success for panic disorder was good, but the depressed or anxious patient maintained mild to significant levels of symptoms after treatment. Psychotherapy was most successful in treating panic disorder (46% showed sustained improvement), compared with depression or GAD. Acknowledging some of the limitations of their meta-analysis, Westen and Morrison conclude by saying that:

> The reality is that we do not know whether the small number of treatments tested in the laboratory fare better or worse in actual clinical practice than many of the interventions currently used by clinicians . . . [one approach is to develop] experimental treatments through controlled clinical trials, and, ultimately, test them on larger, more generalizable naturalistic samples.

Exercises

1. Name three of the differences (or possible differences) between the patients receiving psychotherapy and the control groups Landis used to establish a baseline. Which of the two control groups (Landis and Denker) is more reliable?

2. Why was it necessary to establish a baseline at all?

3. What are the three basic techniques used in psychoanalysis?

4. Briefly describe the differences between systematic desensitization, implosion and flooding as forms of behaviour therapy.

5. What is meant by 'symptom substitution'?

6. Explain the difference between (a) *psychodynamic* and (b) *psychoanalytic* theory/therapy.

7. In **Subsequent research**, Eysenck (1985) is cited as claiming that placebo treatment is more appropriately seen as a proper control against which to compare other, real, treatments.

   (a) What is meant by a 'placebo effect'?
   (b) Describe what the placebo condition in a drug trial might be.
   (c) Is it possible to devise a placebo control in a study of therapeutic effectiveness in the way Eysenck suggests?

23 A nation of morons

Stephen Jay Gould (1982)

> [This article is an edited extract from *The Mismeasure of Man* (1981)]
> *New Scientist,* May 6th, 349–52.

BACKGROUND AND CONTEXT

An early and striking example of the 'tenacity of unconscious bias and the surprising malleability of "objective" quantitative data in the interest of a preconceived idea' (Gould, 1981) is Binet's discovery of a positive correlation between head size and intelligence. When he first decided to study intelligence, it was 'natural' that Binet should use craniometry (the measurement of skulls, first used by Paul Broca). But he suspected that he would, unconsciously and unknowingly, distort the actual measurements so that they produced the results he expected, a clear case of *experimenter bias.*

It was to his credit that he realized the danger, and subsequent studies confirmed his original suspicions. This led him to conclude that, 'The idea of measuring intelligence by measuring heads seemed ridiculous' (Binet, 1900, quoted in Gould, 1981).

In 1904, Binet was commissioned by the French minister of public education to perform a study for a specific, practical, purpose, namely, to develop ways of identifying those children whose lack of success in normal classrooms suggested the need for some form of special education. Consequently, he brought together a large series of short tasks, related to everyday life problems (e.g. counting coins, assessing the 'prettier' face), but supposedly involving such basic reasoning processes as 'direction (ordering), comprehension, invention and censure (correction)' (Binet, 1909, quoted in Gould, 1981).

The result of his efforts was the first recognized test of intelligence in 1905, with tasks arranged in ascending order of difficulty. In 1908, the concept of Mental Age (MA) was introduced, and a child's general intellectual level was calculated as Chronological Age (CA) *minus* MA. Children whose MA was sufficiently behind their CA could then be identified for special education. Finally, it was the German psychologist, Stern, who, in 1912, pointed out that *division* is more appropriate than subtraction, since it is the *relative* (not the absolute) size of the difference that matters, hence MA/CA × 100/1 (multiplying by 100 gives a whole number). The IQ (Intelligence Quotient) was born.

Although he wanted to remove the superficial effects of clearly acquired knowledge, Binet refused to speculate on the *meaning* of the score assigned to each child. Intelligence is too complex to capture with a single number: it is the average of many performances, *not* an entity with an independent, objective, existence. Not only did he refuse to label IQ as a measure of innate intelligence, he also rejected it as a general device for ranking *all* pupils in terms of mental ability (as opposed to those needing special education).

Also, whatever the cause of poor school performance, the aim was to identify these children in order to help and improve, *not* to label in order to limit. It is this, rather than belief in/denial of innate intellectual differences, which represents the essential difference between strict hereditarians and their opponents (Gould, 1981: see Chapter 24). Ironically, many American school boards have come full circle, and now use IQ tests only as Binet originally recommended: as instruments for assessing children with specific learning problems (Gould, 1981).

However, returning to the early part of the twentieth century, and crossing from France to America, it was H.H. Goddard who first introduced Binet's scale to America, translated Binet's articles into English, applied his tests and advocated their general use. While agreeing with Binet that the tests worked best in identifying people just below the normal range, he regarded the scores as measuring a single, innate, entity, and his purpose in using tests was to recognize people's limits so that they could be segregated, to curtail breeding so as to prevent further deterioration of the endangered American stock, which was already threatened by immigration from without and by prolific reproduction of the feeble-minded from within (Gould, 1981).

Two categories of mental deficiency were already well established at this time: *idiots* (MA below 3) and *imbeciles* (MA between 3 and 7). But what about those whose MA was 8–12, 'high-grade defectives' who could be trained to function in society? Goddard called them *morons* (from the Greek for 'foolish'). This, of course, explains the title of Gould's article: the average MA of white, American adults was found, by Boring (in his analysis of Yerkes's 1921 data) to be 13, just above the upper limit of moronity.

AIM AND NATURE OF THE STUDY

It is important to be aware that the article is an edited extract from Gould's (1981) book *The Mismeasure of Man*, in which he traces the history of the measurement of human intelligence, from nineteenth century craniometry to today's highly technical and sophisticated methods of IQ testing. (Incidentally, the book won the [American] National Book Critics' Circle Award for 1982. A second edition was published in 1996.)

More importantly, the book is an attempt to expose the fundamental problems involved in the attempt to measure intelligence (problems which, by implication, apply to other aspects of complex, human, functioning, such as personality), and so offers an extremely thorough and lucid critique of intelligence testing. As a biologist, Gould is in a very sound position when arguing against one of the fundamental beliefs on which the IQ testing movement is based: the view that differences in IQ are largely determined by biological (i.e. genetic) differences between people, differences which cannot be modified. This belief that 'biology is destiny' is commonly referred to as the *genetic* or *hereditarian theory of intelligence* and the book as a whole is devoted to a refutation and rejection of this theory – both because of its scientific/methodological inadequacies, and (perhaps more critically) because of the racist social policies which it breeds and reinforces.

The IQ test can be regarded as an ideological weapon, used by a white-dominated society to oppress minority groups, especially (but by no means exclusively) American Blacks (African Americans) and people of Afro-Caribbean origin in the UK. As scientists, psychologists responsible for the construction and use of IQ tests are meant, and are seen by society at large, to be objective and value-free. But, as Gould convincingly demonstrates, their theories and instruments have too often been dangerous reflections of their own personal motives and racial, class, and sexual prejudices. (See Chapter 27 for a discussion of scientific colonialism.)

THE STUDY

The intelligence tests introduced in America for army recruits during the First World War were seen as the way to bring the respectability that psychology yearned for as a new science. But the tests produced some surprising results, and influenced the decision to restrict immigrants in the 1920s.

Robert M. Yerkes, about to turn 40, was a frustrated man in 1915. He had been on the faculty of Harvard University since 1902. He was a superb organizer of men, and an eloquent promoter of his profession. Yet psychology still wallowed in its reputation as a 'soft' science, if a science at all. Yerkes wished, above all, to establish his profession by proving that it could be as rigorous a science as physics. Along with most of his contemporaries, he equated rigour and science with number and quantification. The most promising source of copious and objective numbers, Yerkes believed, lay in the embryonic field of mental testing.

But mental testing suffered from inadequate support and its own internal contradictions. It was, first of all, practised extensively by poorly trained amateurs whose manifestly absurd results were giving the enterprise a bad name. In 1915, at the annual meeting of the American Psychological Association in Chicago, a critic reported that the mayor of Chicago had scored as a moron on one test. Yerkes joined with critics in discussions at the meeting and proclaimed: 'We are building up a science, but we have not yet devised a mechanism which anyone can operate.' Furthermore, available scales gave markedly different results even when properly applied. And support had been too inadequate, and coordination too sporadic, to build up a pool of data sufficiently copious and uniform to compel belief.

THE STUDY

Wars always generate their retinue of camp followers with ulterior motives. Many are simply scoundrels and profiteers, but a few are spurred by higher ideals. As the First World War approached, Yerkes got one of those 'big ideas' that propel the history of science: could psychologists possibly persuade the army to test all its recruits? If so, the philosopher's stone of psychology might be constructed: the copious, useful and uniform body of numbers that would fuel a transition from dubious art to respected science. Yerkes proselytized within his profession and within government circles, and he won his point. As Colonel Yerkes, he presided over the administration of mental tests to 1.75 million recruits during the First World War.

Yerkes brought together all the major figures from the hereditarian school of psychology – those who believed that everything important about intelligence and, indeed behaviour, is inherited and on the whole unaffected by the environment.

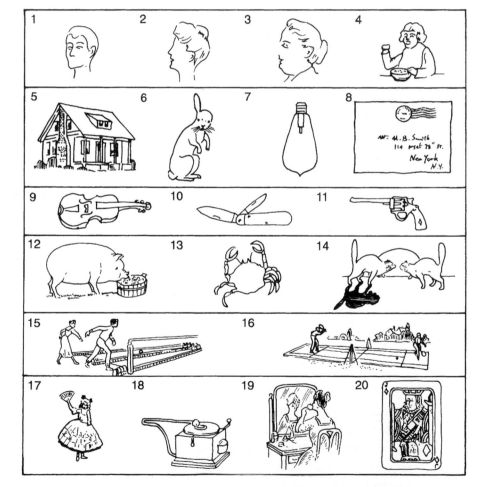

Figure 23.1. The Army Beta for testing innate intelligence. But were recent immigrants familiar with phonographs, tennis courts and light bulbs? Could they spot the missing rivet in the knife (10) or the ball in the right hand of the man (15)?

From May to July, 1917, he worked with Lewis Terman, H. H. Goddard and other colleagues at Goddard's Training School in Vineland, New Jersey, writing the army mental tests.

Their scheme included three types of tests. Literate recruits would be given a written examination, called the Army Alpha. Illiterates and men who had failed Alpha would be given a pictorial test, called Army Beta. Failures in Beta would be recalled for an individual examination. Army psychologists would then grade each man from A to E (with pluses and minuses) and offer suggestions for proper military placement. Yerkes suggested that recruits with a score of C – should be marked as 'low average intelligence – ordinary private'. Men of grade D are 'rarely suited for tasks requiring special skill, forethought, resourcefulness or sustained alertness'. D and E men could not be expected 'to read and understand written directions'.

The Alpha test included eight parts, the Beta seven; each took less than an hour and could be given to large groups. Most of the Alpha parts presented items that have become familiar to generations of test-takers ever since: analogies, filling in the next number in sequence, and so forth. This similarity is no accident; the Army Alpha was the granddaddy, literally as well as figuratively, of all written mental tests.

These familiar parts are not especially subject to changes of cultural bias, at least no more so than their modern descendants. In a general way, of course, they test literacy, and literacy records education more than inherited intelligence. Moreover, a schoolmaster's claim that he tests children of the same age and school experience, and therefore may be recording some internal biology, did not apply to the army recruits – they varied greatly in access to education and recorded different amounts of schooling in their scores.

A few of the test items are amusing in the light of Yerkes's assertion that the tests 'measure native intellectual ability'. Consider the Alpha analogy: 'Washington is to Adams as first is to . . .'

But one part of each test is simply ludicrous in the light of Yerkes's analysis. How could Yerkes and company attribute the low scores of recent immigrants to innate stupidity when their multiple-choice test consisted entirely of questions like:

Crisco is a: patent medicine, disinfectant, toothpaste, food product?

The number of Kaffir's legs is: 2, 4, 6, 8?

Christy Mathewson is famous as a: writer, artist, baseball player, comedian?

Recruits had to be allocated to their appropriate test. Men illiterate in English, either by lack of schooling or foreign birth, should have taken examination Beta, either by direct assignment, or indirectly upon failing Alpha. Yerkes's corps tried

THE STUDY

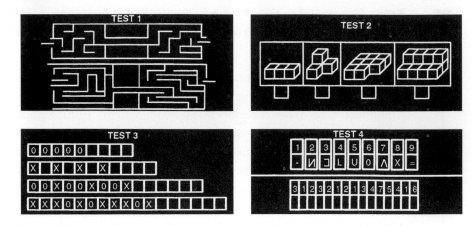

Figure 23.2. More examples from the Beta test for army recruits. Test 1: running a maze. Test 2: count the number of cubes. Test 3: find the next in the series. Test 4: translate the numerals into symbols. Remember, this was a test for illiterates – and they had to *write* their answers.

heroically to fulfil this procedure. But standards for the division between Alpha and Beta varied substantially from camp to camp. The problem cut far deeper than simple inconsistency among camps. The persistent logistical difficulties imposed a systematic bias that substantially lowered the mean scores of Blacks and immigrants. For two major reasons, many men took only Alpha and scored either zero or next to nothing, not because they were innately dumb, but because they were illiterate and should have taken Beta by Yerkes's own protocol. First, recruits and draftees had, on average, spent fewer years in school than Yerkes had anticipated. Lines for Beta began to lengthen and the entire operation threatened to clog at this bottleneck. At many camps, unqualified men were sent in droves to Alpha by artificial lowering of standards. Schooling to the third grade sufficed for Alpha in one camp; in another, anyone who said he could read, at whatever level, took Alpha.

Secondly, and more important, the press of time and the hostility of regular officers often precluded a Beta retest for men who had incorrectly taken Alpha. As the pace became more frantic, the problem worsened. The chief tester at Camp Dix complained, 'In June it was found impossible to recall a thousand men listed for individual examination. In July Alpha failures among Negroes were not recalled'. The stated protocol scarcely applied to Blacks who, as usual, were treated with less concern and more contempt by everyone. Failure on Beta, for example, should have led to an individual examination. Half the Black recruits scored D– on Beta, but only one fifth of these were recalled, the other four-fifths receiving no further examinations. Yet we know that scores for Blacks improved dramatically when the protocol was followed. At one camp, only 14.1 per cent of men who had scored D– on Alpha failed to gain a higher grade when retested on the Beta.

The effects of this systematic bias are evident in one of E.G. Boring's experiments with the summary statistics. Boring, later a famous psychologist himself, but then

Yerkes's lieutenant, culled 4893 cases of men who had taken both Alpha and Beta. Converting their scores to the common scale, he calculated an average mental age of 10.775 for Alpha and 12.158 for Beta. He used only the Beta scores in his summaries; Yerkes's procedure worked. But what of the myriads who should have taken Beta, but received only Alpha and scored abysmally as a result – primarily poorly educated Blacks and immigrants with an imperfect command of English, the groups whose low scores caused such a hereditarian stir later?

Academicians often forgot how poorly or incompletely the written record, their primary source, may represent experience. Some things have to be seen, touched and tasted. What was it like to be an illiterate Black or foreign recruit, anxious and befuddled at the novel experience of taking an examination, never told why, or what would be made of the results; expulsion, the front lines? In 1968, an examiner recalled his administration of Beta: 'It was touching to see the intense effort . . . put into answering the questions, often by men who never before had held a pencil in their hands.' Yerkes had overlooked, or consciously bypassed something of importance. The Beta examination contained only pictures, numbers and symbols. But it still required pencil work and, on three of its seven parts, a knowledge of numbers and how to write them.

The internal contradictions and an *a priori* prejudice thoroughly invalidated the hereditarian conclusions that Yerkes was to draw from the results. Boring himself called these conclusions 'preposterous' late in his career. But I had not understood how the Draconian conditions of testing made such a thorough mockery of the claim that recruits could have been in a frame of mind to record anything about their innate abilities. In short, most of the men must have ended up either utterly confused or scared shitless. I believe that the conditions of testing, and the basic character of the examination, make it ludicrous to believe that Beta measured any internal state deserving the label intelligence. Despite the plea for geniality, the examination was conducted in an almost frantic rush. Most parts could not be finished in the time allocated, but recruits were not forewarned.

Still, the tests did have a strong impact in some areas, particularly in screening men for officer training. At the start of the war, the army and national guard maintained 9000 officers; by the end, 200,000 officers presided, and two-thirds of them had started their careers in training camps where the tests were applied. In some camps, no man scoring below C could be considered for officer training.

But the major impact of Yerkes's tests did not fall upon the army. Yerkes may not have brought the army its victory, but he certainly won his battle. He now had uniform data on 1.75 million men, and he had devised, in the Alpha and Beta exams, the first mass-produced written tests of intelligence. Inquiries flooded in from schools and businesses. In his massive monograph on *Psychological Examining in the United States Army (1921)*, Yerkes buried a statement of great social significance in an aside. He spoke of 'the steady stream of requests from commercial

concerns, educational institutions and individuals for the use of army methods of psychological examining or for the adaptation of such methods to special needs.' Tests could now rank and stream everybody; the era of mass testing had begun.

Boring selected 160,000 cases from the files and produced data that reverberated through the 1920s with a hereditarian ring. The task was a formidable one. The sample, which Boring culled himself with the aid of only one assistant, was very large; moreover, the scales of three different tests (Alpha, Beta and individual) had to be converted to a common standard so that racial and national averages could be constructed from samples of men who had taken the tests in different proportions (few Blacks took Alpha, for example).

From Boring's ocean of numbers, three 'facts' rose to the top and continued to influence social policy in America long after their source in the tests had been forgotten:

● The average mental age of White American adults stood just above the edge of moronity at a shocking and meagre 13. Terman had previously set the standard at 16. The new figure became a rallying point for eugenicists who predicted doom and lamented our declining intelligence, caused by the unconstrained breeding of the poor and feeble-minded, the spread of Negro blood through interbreeding, and the swamping of an intelligent native stock by the immigrating dregs of Southern and Eastern Europe.

● European immigrants could be graded by their country of origin. The average man of many nations was a moron. The darker people of southern Europe and the Slavs of Eastern Europe were less intelligent than the fair people of Western and Northern Europe. Nordic supremacy was not jingoistic prejudice. The average Russian had a mental age of 11.34, the Italian, 11.01, the Pole, 10.74. The Polish joke attained the same legitimacy as the moron joke – indeed, they described the same animal.

● The Negro lay at the bottom of the scale with an average mental age of 10.41. Some camps tried to carry the analysis a bit further, and in obvious racist directions. For example, at Camp Lee, Blacks were divided into three groups based upon the intensity of skin colour; as might be expected, the lighter groups scored higher!

The grand average of 13 had political impact, but its potential for social havoc was small compared with Yerkes's figures for racial and national differences; for hereditarians could now claim that the fact and extent of group differences in innate intelligence had finally, once and for all, been established. Yerkes's disciple Carl Brigham, then an assistant professor of psychology at Princeton University, published in 1923 a book, short enough and stated with sufficient baldness (some would say clarity) to be read and used by all propagandists. *A Study of American Intelligence* became a primary vehicle for translating the army results on group differ-

Figure 23.3. The results of the Army intelligence tests influenced immigration policy in the States in the 1920s. The quotas were based on the arrivals before 1890. Immigrants up to that year were mainly Nordic, and supposedly more intelligent than the Southern and Eastern Europeans who arrived later.

ences into social action. Yerkes himself wrote the foreword and praised Brigham for his objectivity.

Once he had proved that the tests measure innate intelligence, Brigham devoted most of his book to dispelling common impressions that might threaten this basic assumption. The army tests had, for example, assessed Jews (primarily recent immigrants) as quite low in intelligence. Does this discovery not conflict with the notable accomplishments of so many Jewish scholars, statesmen, and performing artists? Brigham conjectured that Jews might be more variable than other groups; a low mean would not preclude a few geniuses in the upper range. In any case, he added, we probably focus unduly on the Jewish heritage of some great men because it surprises us: 'The able Jew is popularly recognized not only because of his ability, but because he is able and a Jew.' 'Our figures, then, would rather tend to disprove the popular belief that the Jew is highly intelligent.'

One persistent correlation threatened Yerkes's hereditarian convictions, and his rescuing argument became a major social weapon in later political campaigns for restricting immigration. Test scores had been tabulated by country of origin, and Yerkes noted the pattern so dear to the hearts of Nordic supremacists. He divided recruits by country of origin into English, Scandinavian and Teutonic on one side, and Latin and Slavic on the other, and stated, 'the differences are considerable (an

Figure 23.4. Jews came out badly in the tests. Notable Jews were explained by the fact that the public noticed the few great ones (for example, Einstein) because they were so rare.

extreme range of practically two years mental age)', favouring the Nordics, of course.

But Yerkes acknowledged a potential problem. Most Latins and Slavs had arrived recently and spoke English either poorly or not at all; the main wave of Teutonic immigration had passed long before. According to Yerkes's protocol, it should not have mattered. Men who could not speak English suffered no penalty. They took Beta, a pictorial test that supposedly measured innate ability independent of literacy and language. Yet the data still showed an apparent penalty for unfamiliarity with English. Yerkes had to admit, 'there are indications to the effect that individuals handicapped by language difficulty and illiteracy are penalized to an appreciable degree in Beta compared with men not so handicapped.'

Another correlation was even more potentially disturbing. Yerkes found that average test scores for foreign-born recruits rose consistently with years of residence in America. Did this not indicate that familiarity with American ways, and not innate intelligence, regulated the differences in scores? Yerkes admitted the possibility, but held out strong hopes for a hereditarian salvation. The Teutonic supremacists would soon supply that decision: recent immigration had drawn the dregs of Europe, lower-class Latins and Slavs. Immigrants of longer residence belonged predominantly to superior northern stocks. The correlation with years in America was an artefact of genetic status.

The army data had their most immediate and profound impact upon the great immigration debate, then a major political issue in America, and ultimately the greatest triumph of eugenics. Restriction was in the air, and may well have occurred without scientific backing. But the timing, and especially the peculiar character of the 1924 Restriction Act, clearly reflected the lobbying of scientists and eugenicists, and the army data formed their most powerful battering ram.

Henry Fairfield Osborn, trustee of Columbia University and president of the American Museum of Natural History, wrote in 1923 in a statement that I cannot read without a shudder when I recall the gruesome statistics of mortality for the First World War:

> I believe those tests were worth what the war cost, even in human life, if they served to show clearly to our people the lack of intelligence in our country, and the degrees of intelligence in different races who are coming to us in a way which no one can say is the result of prejudice . . . We have learned once and for all that the Negro is not like us. So in regard to many races and sub-races in Europe we learned that some which we had believed possessed of an order of intelligence perhaps superior to ours [read Jews] were far inferior.

Congressional debates leading to passage of the Immigration Restriction Act of 1924 continually invoked the army data. Eugenicists lobbied not only for limits to immigration, but for changing its character by imposing harsh quotas against nations of inferior stock – a feature of the 1924 Act that might never have been implemented, or even considered, without the army data and eugenicist propaganda. In short, Southern and Eastern Europeans, the Alpine and Mediterranean nations with minimal scores on the army tests, should be kept out. The eugenicists battled and won one of the greatest victories of scientific racism in American history. The first Restriction Act of 1921 had set yearly quotas at 3 per cent of immigrants from any nation then resident in America. The 1924 Act, following a barrage of eugenicist propaganda, reset the quotas at 2 per cent of people from each nation recorded in the 1890 census. The 1890 figures were used until 1930. Why 1890 and not 1920 since the Act was passed in 1924? 1890 marked a watershed in the history of immigration. Southern and Eastern Europeans arrived in relatively small numbers before then, but began to predominate thereafter. Cynical, but effective. 'America must be kept American', proclaimed Calvin Coolidge as he signed the bill.

Brigham had a profound change of heart six years after his book, but he could not undo what the tests had accomplished. The quotas stood and slowed immigration from Southern and Eastern Europe to a trickle. Throughout the 1930s Jewish refugees, anticipating the holocaust, sought to emigrate, but were not admitted. The legal quotas, and continuing eugenical propaganda, barred them even in years when inflated quotas from Western and Northern European nations were not filled. Estimates suggest that the quotas barred up to six million Southern, Central and Eastern Europeans between 1924 and the outbreak of the Second World War in 1939 (assuming that immigration had continued at its pre-1924 rate). We know what happened to many who wished to leave, but had nowhere to go. The paths to destruction are often indirect, but ideas can be agents as sure as guns and bombs.

EVALUATION

Theoretical issues

Terman, working at Stanford University, was the figure mainly responsible for standardizing Binet's (1911) test for use in America. From 1916 onwards, the *Stanford-Binet* became the standard for virtually all IQ tests that followed, including most of the written (group) tests. The Army Alpha and Beta marked the beginning of mass testing in the USA, which soon became a multimillion dollar industry.

Like Goddard, Terman agreed with Binet that the tests worked best in identifying 'high-grade defectives', and also like Goddard, but contrary to Binet's views, Terman emphasized people's limits in order to restrict their freedom to reproduce. Yerkes was the central figure in the Army Alpha and Beta tests, and together with Goddard and Terman, was the leading hereditarian of his day in the USA. The Army tests had been constructed to measure innate intelligence and so, by definition, there was no room for the role of environmental influence (Gould, 1981).

> As pure numbers, these data carried no inherent social message. They might have been used to promote equality of opportunity and to underscore the disadvantages imposed upon so many Americans. Yerkes might have argued that an average mental age of 13 reflected the fact that relatively few recruits had the opportunity to finish or even to attend high schoool. He might have attributed the low average of some national groups to the fact that most recruits from these countries were recent immigrants who did not speak English and were unfamiliar with American culture. He might have recognized the link between low Negro scores and the history of slavery and racism. But scarcely a word do we read through 800 pages of any role for environmental influence. (Gould, 1981)

This quote from Gould seems to illustrate very clearly how dogma can determine the way that data are interpreted in order to produce scientific 'fact': once a theorist has formulated a view of something, in this case the explanation of intellectual differences between national, ethnic, and racial groups, all the data are moulded to fit the theory and, hence, apparently, to support it. The often claimed objectivity of science is sacrificed on the altar of a theory which the scientist must 'prove' at all costs.

Yerkes, Goddard, and Terman were already committed hereditarians before they came together to work on the Army tests, and Gould gives some striking examples of the dogmatic nature of Yerkes's thinking:

(*i*)   He found a correlation of 0.75 between test score and years of education for 348 men who scored below the mean on Alpha. Only one had ever attended college, four had graduated from high school, and only 10 had ever attended high school. But Yerkes argued that men with more innate intelligence spend more time in school: that is *why* they spend more time in school.

The strongest correlations of test scores with schooling came from black–white differences. Once again, the fact that blacks spend relatively little time in school compared with whites is explained in terms of a disinclination on the part of blacks, based on low, innate intelligence.

How can you argue against such reasoning? Yerkes seems to be illegitimately inferring a *cause* from a correlation, since (*a*) it may be lack of schooling which causes the low IQ scores, and (*b*) there may be some third factor which accounts for *both* the low IQ scores and the short period of schooling, such as racial segregation (at that time officially sanctioned, if not mandated), poor conditions in black schools, economic pressures to leave school and find work among the poor (which blacks usually are). You can only infer which of two correlated factors is the cause of the other based on some theory about how they are related (Deese, 1972); in Yerkes's case, this is the hereditarian theory. So Yerkes is presenting data to support a theory, but for that to work, the data must first be interpreted according to that very theory: a classic example of *circular reasoning*!

(*ii*) Yerkes found that half the blacks from Southern states had not attended school beyond the third grade (age nine), while half those from Northern states had reached the fifth grade (age 11). Again, in the North, 25% completed primary school, compared with only 7% from the South, and the percentage of Alphas was very much smaller and the percentage of Betas very much larger in the Southern than the Northern group. Why? You can probably anticipate the explanation which Yerkes gave based on (*i*): only the best Negroes had been smart enough to move North!

> Even by standards of their own era, the American hereditarians were dogmatists. But their dogma wafted up on favourable currents into realms of general acceptance, with tragic consequences. (Gould, 1981)

Those tragic consequences were the immigration laws which condemned an estimated six million Europeans to the holocaust.

As a footnote, Gould points out that Brigham, Yerkes's disciple, whose 1923 book was a major influence on the 1924 Restriction Act, had a profound change of heart (1930), when he rejected the Army data as worthless as measures of innate intelligence. It seemed that the tests, after all, measured familiarity with American language and culture, *not* innate intelligence.

Methodological issues

Yerkes and his team had blindly assumed that the Army tests were not biased (they did not favour one national or racial group more than another). Indeed, this assumption is essential to the hereditarian argument: test results can only reflect innate differences in intelligence if the tests themselves are unbiased.

In 'modern times', it was initially Arthur Jensen in the USA who revived the 'race and IQ' debate with a highly controversial article, published in 1969 (*How much can we boost IQ and scholastic achievement?*). In it, he claimed that the failure of preschool compensatory programmes (such as Operation Headstart) was due to the innate inferiority of Black children.

This was followed, in 1980, by his 800-page book entitled *Bias in Mental Testing*, in which (a little perversely given the title) he argued that IQ tests are *not* biased, consistent with the hereditarian position of his predecessors, Yerkes *et al.* Gould (1987) reviewed Jensen's book and makes some incisive critical points. Jensen bypasses the whole issue of heritability, and he seems to advocate dropping discussion of what causes differences on test scores. But the question of causation is the motivating theme of the 1969 article, and is *implicit* throughout the 1980 book. The crucial question here is, what exactly does Jensen mean by 'bias'?

Gould (1987) distinguishes two meanings, one technical, one non-technical (or vernacular). Our ordinary understanding of the term, in the present context, is that the poorer performance of blacks is the result of environmental deprivation relative to whites. It is linked to the idea of fairness, and maintains that blacks have received a 'poor shake' for reasons of education and upbringing, rather than nature. This is the non-technical meaning of bias (or V-Bias: see **Applications and implications**).

The second, technical, sense of 'bias' is completely different and far narrower in its meaning, and Jensen addresses himself exclusively to this statistical or S-Bias. An IQ test is S-Biased if the *same* IQ score predicts *different* school grades (or some other performance criterion) for blacks and whites (*intercept bias*). As shown in Figure 23.5 below, both groups have the *same slope* but whites have a higher y-intercept (i.e. the same IQ score predicts *higher* school grades for whites than for blacks).

As Gould points out, 'No sensible tester wants to construct an instrument in which the same score means different things for different kinds of people.' Jensen devotes most of his book to showing that S-Bias does not affect mental tests and that it can be corrected when it does. But in showing that tests are unbiased, all Jensen has managed to show is that the lower black and higher white average scores lie on the same line, as shown in Figure 23.6 below.

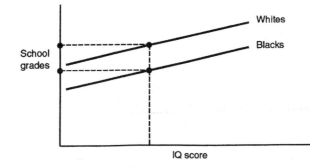

Figure 23.5. A test with S-Bias (from Gould, 1987).

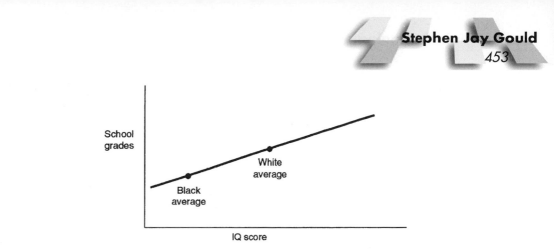

Figure 23.6. A test without S-Bias (from Gould, 1987).

While acknowledging the difference between this and V-Bias, Jensen argues that the culture-fairness of a test (or its degree of 'culture-loadedness': its V-Bias), cannot be defined objectively, and so S-Bias is the only kind of bias that should be discussed. In doing this, he seems to be undermining the hereditarian position since, as we saw above, only by *assuming* that tests have no V-Bias can differences in IQ scores be taken to reflect innate, genetic, differences. But if V-Bias cannot be defined or measured objectively, it cannot be ruled out, nor can it be shown *not* to affect test scores.

> In short, the primary content of this book is simply irrelevant to the question that has sparked the IQ debate and that Jensen himself addressed in his 1969 article: what does the lower average score of Blacks *mean*? His concept of bias (S-Bias) does not address the issue. (Gould, 1987)

In the second edition of *The Mismeasure of Man* (1996), Gould claims that this same basic mistake (confusing S- and V-bias and explicitly addressing only the former) is made by Herrnstein & Murray (1994) in their *The Bell Curve*. This is just one of several recent books promoting the hereditarian argument and right-wing social policies of a strongly racial nature (Howe, 1997).

Even more overtly racial is Rushton's *Race, Evolution, and Behaviour* (1995) and *The g Factor* (Brand, 1996), which achieved the rare notoriety of being withdrawn by its British publisher after Brand had announced that he was 'perfectly proud to be a racist in the scientific sense' (see Gross *et al.*, 1997).

Applications and implications

While Jensen (1980) dismisses the question of the culture-fairness of a test (V-Bias) as opposed to its S-Bias, others would regard it as crucial for interpreting black–white differences. Indeed, as we have seen, the hereditarian argument *depends* upon the fairness of tests being established.

According to Segall *et al.* (1999), for example, IQ tests are biased against those whose cultural background differs from that of the test's original normative sample. They

argue that all the attempts at constructing 'culture-fair' or 'culture-free' tests have failed: 'clearly, culturally mediated experience always interacts with test content to influence test performance'.

Frijda & Jahoda (1966) distinguish between culture-free and culture-fair tests. *Culture-free* tests are those which actually measure some inherent quality of human capacity equally well in all cultures. Clearly, no such test is possible. By contrast, a *culture-fair* test:

(*i*) could be a set of items which are equally unfamiliar to all possible persons in all possible cultures, so that everyone would have an equal chance of passing (or failing) the items; or

(*ii*) could comprise multiple sets of items, modified for use in each culture to ensure that each version of the test would contain the same amount of familiarity. This would give members of each culture about the same chance of being successful with their respective version.

While (*i*) is a virtual impossibility, (*ii*) is possible in theory, although in practice very difficult to construct (Segall, *et al.*, 1999). This seems to touch on the very concept of intelligence itself. For Gardner (1993), *contextualization* is all important:

> Rather than assuming that one would possess a certain 'intelligence' independent of the culture in which one happens to live, many scientists now see intelligence as an interaction between, on the one hand, certain proclivities and potentials and, on the other, the opportunities and constraints that characterize a particular cultural setting.

This can be seen as an anti-hereditarian argument, since Jensen, Yerkes, *et al. do* assume that intelligence can be measured separately from its cultural expression, because it is largely *biological* in nature. Another anti-hereditarian argument is to show that black–white differences are more to do with culture than race:

> The genetic differences between the classically described races of man [European, African, Indian, East Asian, New World, and Oceanian] are on the average only slightly greater [10 per cent] than those which exist between nations within a racial group [6 per cent], and the genetic differences between individual human beings within a population are far larger than either of these [84 per cent]. (Fernando, 1991)

In other words, if we are discussing black–white American differences, it is very difficult to do so in terms of *racial* differences, since this would account for only a small fraction of the *genetic* difference needed by the hereditarian argument to explain the large 15-point difference in IQ. According to Boyd & Richardson (1985, cited in Segall *et al.*, 1990), the action of biological evolution (Darwinian selection) is very slow: there has been virtually no biological evolution to speak of since the beginning of *homo sapiens*. However, the action of 'cultural evolution' ('the inheritance of acquired characteristics', through writing, instruction, ritual, tradition, and so on: Gould, 1981), is fast, so that differences between groups is likely to be more cultural than genetic in origin (Segall *et al.*, 1990).

The importance of culture can be seen in the *cultural psychology perspective*, according to which culture influences which behaviours are considered to be intelligent, the processes underlying intelligent behaviour, and the direction of intellectual development (Miller, 1997). While not rejecting all use of psychometric tests, Miller argues that:

> . . . all measures of intelligence are culturally grounded, with performance dependent, at least in part, on culturally based understandings. Thus, even in the controlled conditions of the experimental laboratory, intellectual performances reflect individuals' interpretations of the meaning of situations and their background presuppositions, rather than pure *g*.

Psychological theories of intelligence must offer generalizations that are *relative* to a particular time and context, but the hereditarians (such as Yerkes, Terman, Jensen, Herrnstein and Murray) argue for a universal, culture-free, unchanging, objectively measurable, biologically determined property called 'g' or general intelligence (Miller, 1997). Furthermore, these 'universal' theories are associated with right-wing social philosophy and policy, which their advocates are not afraid of concealing. For example, the Preface to *The Bell Curve* begins;

> This book is about differences in intellectual capacity among people and groups and what these differences mean for America's future. (Herrnstein & Murray, 1994)

Later, they claim that 'Affirmative action [positive discrimination], in education and the workplace alike, is leaking poison into the American soul'; and 'It is time for America once again to try living with inequality, as life is lived . . . .'

According to Kamin (1995),

> . . . This kind of sentiment, I imagine, is what led *New York Times* columnist Bob Herbert to the conclusion that *The Bell Curve* 'is just a genteel way of calling somebody a nigger'. Herbert is right. The book has nothing to do with science.

Exercises

1. Yerkes is also famous for other research he was involved in. What was it?

2. To defend the use of the Army Alpha and Beta tests as a measure of innate intelligence, they would have to be seen as measuring *aptitude* as opposed to *attainment*. Explain the difference and say why the distinction may not be valid.

3. What is a *eugenicist*?

4. Is it ethically acceptable to restrict people's ability to reproduce?

5. How did Yerkes explain the correlation between the average test score for foreign-born recruits and length of residence in the USA in a way that was consistent with the hereditarian theory?

24 Familial studies of intelligence: a review

Thomas J. Bouchard Jr and Matthew McGue (1981)

Science, 212, 1055–9

BACKGROUND AND CONTEXT

The relative influences of nature and nurture/heredity versus environment constitute the most controversial issue in the behavioural sciences, and:

> . . . nowhere are the weapons more poised to be fired than with respect to the question of the extent to which measured intelligence is a product – wholly or in large measure – of genetic endowment . . . (Gardner et al., 1996)

The nature-nurture/heredity-environment debate has raged on for most of psychology's history. Some of the major figures in this controversy (especially hereditarian theorists, who favour the nature/genetic side) are discussed in Chapter 23. According to Sternberg & Grigorenko (1997), virtually all researchers accept that:

(a) both heredity and environment contribute to intelligence;
(b) heredity and environment interact in various ways;
(c) extremely poor, as well as highly enriched, environments can interfere with the realization of a person's intelligence, regardless of his or her heredity.

However, there is little agreement beyond these very general beliefs.

Arguably, one of the stickiest aspects of the whole debate is the attempt to separate out the effects of heredity and environment: given agreement about (a) above, the question becomes 'how *much* does each contribute?' Most of the major attempts to 'parcel out' these two types of influence (twin studies, adoption studies, and other 'family resemblance' studies) have been conducted by *behaviour-genetic theorists* (leading examples of whom include Thomas Bouchard and Robert Plomin).

Behaviour-genetic theory, derived from evolutionary theory, focuses on the causes of individual *variation* in intelligence and other characteristics in populations. According to Scarr (1997), behaviour-genetic theorists regard four major sources of variation as crucial for explaining individual differences in intelligence:

(1) *Additive genetic effects:* these are the combined effect of many genes (the *genotype*), each contributing a small amount to differences in measured intelligence (the *phenotype*).

(2) *Non-additive genetic effects:* these include the effect of dominant genes and other major gene effects, and genotype-environment correlations and interactions (see **Evaluation** below).

(3) *Between-family non-genetic effects:* these refer to psychosocial environmental differences between one family and another, making siblings more similar than children reared in different families. Examples include social class and parental differences in child-rearing styles.

(4) *Within-family non-genetic variance:* these refer to those aspects of the environment, both biological and social, that make siblings in the same family different from one another. Examples include both pre-and post-natal influences that affect one sibling differently from another.

At a general level, behaviour-genetic theory claims that genetic differences are a major source of intellectual differences among children, regardless of parental rearing styles, unless parents are abusive or seriously neglectful (Scarr, 1992, 1993). Specific predictions focus on observations of intellectual resemblance among family members. Similarity in intelligence is predicted to the extent that parents and children, and siblings, are genetically related, with little/no similarity among those who are genetically unrelated, even if they are reared together. Observations of families with different degrees of genetic and environmental relatedness provide critical tests of these predictions (Scarr, 1997).

AIM AND NATURE OF THE STUDY

The article reports the findings of a comprehensive survey of the world literature on familial resemblance and measured intelligence, that is, IQ correlations between relatives. It is an update of an earlier and much cited review by Erlenmeyer-Kimling & Jarvik (1963). Not only have several new studies been reported since that review (59 in all), but also Burt's twin-study data have been *removed* (following the revelation in the 1970s that he fabricated many of his results: the whole debate about Burt's results has since been reopened by Joynson, 1989).

Altogether, 140 relevant studies were found, but the application of explicit selection criteria (see **Evaluation** below) reduced these to 111. The median correlation for each degree of blood-tie was found, and overall the results are consistent with those of Erlenmeyer-Kimling & Jarvik (1963). Although the review is not explicitly intended to support behaviour-genetic theory, *implicitly* it is. The explicit aim is to update the earlier review, which is certainly used more to support the genetic theory than oppose it. However, overall the results of both surveys would seem to be equally supportive of both the genetic *and* the environmentalist views, with the important exception of studies of separated identical or monozygotic (MZ) twins and adoption studies.

THE STUDY

A summary of 111 studies identified in a survey of the world literature on familial resemblances in measured intelligence reveals a profile of average correlations consistent with a polygenic mode of inheritance. There is, however, a marked degree of heterogeneity of the correlations within familial groupings, which is not moderated by sex of familial pairing or by type of intelligence test used.

In 1963, Erlenmeyer-Kimling and Jarvik published a summary of the world literature on IQ correlations between relatives. Their finding that the pattern of correlations averaged over independent studies was consistent with the pattern predicted by a polygenic theory of inheritance has been widely cited as strong evidence for some genetic determination of IQ (Matarazzo, 1972). Although the accumulation of a great many new studies, as well as the discrediting of Burt's important study on monozygotic (MZ) twins reared apart (Hernshaw, 1979; Dorfman, 1978), has outdated that review, the authors' summary or slightly modified versions of it (Jarvik & Erlenmeyer-Kimling, 1967) continue to be widely reproduced (Vernon, 1979). Plomin and DeFries (1980) have recently reported a comparison of those summary data with the results of several large, recent familial studies of IQ. They conclude that, in general, the recent studies show less resemblance between relatives than the Erlenmeyer-Kimling and Jarvik data. However, the summary is not comprehensive and it does not identify the factors which distinguish the two bodies of data. Roubertoux and Carlier (1978) have also published a recent review, but it contains only 37 per cent of the studies cited here.

The purpose of this report is to provide a comprehensive summary of the world literature on the IQ correlations between relatives. We have updated the 1963 summary, adding recent data and deleting several studies included in the earlier review which do not meet our methodological criteria for inclusion. Although the pattern of averages reported here and in earlier reviews is remarkably consistent with polygenic theory, the individual data points are quite heterogeneous. Therefore, we have also assessed the extent to which the reported correlations are heterogeneous, and have attempted to identify some factors contributing to this.

In our survey of the literature, we found 140 relevant studies. These were reduced to 111 by the application of explicit selection criteria. The 111 studies, which include 59 reported in the 17 years since the Erlenmeyer-Kimling and Jarvik summary, yielded 526 familial correlations based upon 113,942 pairings. Figure 24.1 shows correlation between relatives, biological and adoptive, in the 111 studies. The median correlation in each distribution is indicated by a vertical bar, and the small arrow indicates the correlation that would be predicted by a genetic model with no domi-

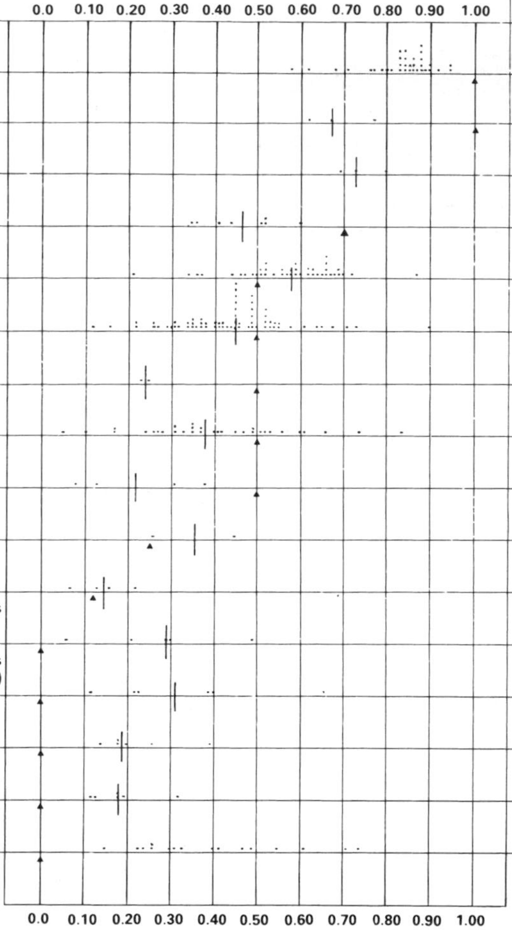

THE STUDY

	0.0 0.10 0.20 0.30 0.40 0.50 0.60 0.70 0.80 0.90 1.00	No. of correlations	No. of pairings	Median correlation	Weighted average	χ^2 (d.f.)	$\frac{\chi^2}{d.f.}$
Monozygotic twins reared together		34	4672	.85	.86	81.29 (33)	2.46
Monozygotic twins reared apart		3	65	.67	.72	0.92 (2)	0.46
Midparent–midoffspring reared together		3	410	.73	.72	2.66 (2)	1.33
Midparent–offspring reared together		8	992	.475	.50	8.11 (7)	1.16
Dizygotic twins reared together		41	5546	.58	.60	94.5 (40)	2.36
Siblings reared together		69	26,473	.45	.47	403.6 (64)	6.31
Siblings reared apart		2	203	.24	.24	.02 (1)	.02
Single parent–offspring reared together		32	8433	.385	.42	211.0 (31)	6.81
Single parent–offspring reared apart		4	814	.22	.22	9.61 (3)	3.20
Half-siblings		2	200	.35	.31	1.55 (1)	1.55
Cousins		4	1.176	.145	.15	1.02 (2)	0.51
Non-biological sibling pairs (adopted/natural pairings)		5	345	.29	.29	1.93 (4)	0.48
Non-biological sibling pairs (adopted/adopted pairings)		6	369	.31	.34	10.5 (5)	2.10
Adopting midparent–offspring		6	758	.19	.24	6.8 (5)	1.36
Adopting parent–offspring		6	1397	.18	.19	6.64 (5)	1.33
Assortative mating		16	3817	.365	.33	96.1 (15)	6.41

0.0 0.10 0.20 0.30 0.40 0.50 0.60 0.70 0.80 0.90 1.00

Figure 24.1. Familial correlations for IQ. The vertical bar in each distribution indicates the median correlation; the arrow, the correlation predicted by a simple polygenic model.

nance, no assortative mating, and no environmental effects. Although researchers do not subscribe to such a simple model, it provides a noncontroversial pattern against which to compare the results of various familial groupings. Different investigators will no doubt fit different models to the data.

In general, the pattern of average correlations in Figure 24.1 is consistent with the pattern of correlations predicted on the basis of polygenic inheritance, i.e. the higher the proportion of genes two family members have in common, the higher the average correlation between their IQs.

The data set contains considerable heterogeneity, as indicated by the χ^2 statistics. In an attempt to identify the factors contributing to the heterogeneity, we subdivided the familial groupings into opposite-sex and same-sex pairings (Figure 24.2)

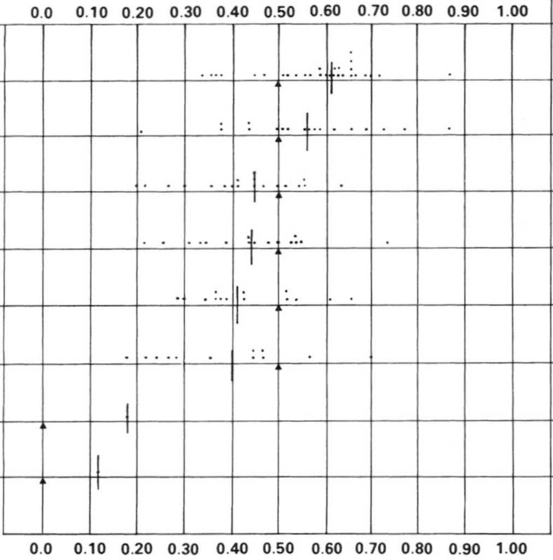

	No. of correlations	No. of pairings	Median correlation	Weighted average	χ^2(d.f.)	$\chi^2 \div$ d.f.
Same sex dizygotic twins	29	3670	.61	.62	68.14 (28)	2.43
Opposite sex dizygotic twins	18	1592	.565	.57	58.6 (17)	3.45
Same sex siblings pairs	19	6098	.45	.48	84.65 (17)	4.98
Opposite sex sibling pairs	16	5127	.445	.49	70.4 (14)	5.03
Same sex parent–offspring pairings	14	4648	.41	.40	55.4 (13)	4.26
Opposite sex parent–offspring pairings	12	4476	.40	.39	70.1 (11)	6.37
Same sex adopting parent–offspring pairings	1	460	.18	.18		
Opposite sex adopting parent–offspring pairings	1	461	.12	.12		

Figure 24.2. Familial correlations for IQ organized by opposite-sex and same-sex pairings.

THE STUDY

and male and female pairings (Figure 24.3). Among dizygotic (DZ) twins, the IQs of same-sex twins are more similar than those of opposite-sex twins. This may reflect a social-environmental effect (parents may treat same-sex twins more similarly than opposite-sex twins). The difference between non-twin same-sex and opposite-sex siblings and between same-sex and opposite-sex parent–offspring pairings is negligible. The male–female comparison does not yield consistent trends. For example, the average correlations are larger in male than female twins, but the reverse is true for other siblings. The absence of any demonstrable sex effect is consistent with a polygenic theory of inheritance, which does not posit the existence of sex linkage. Environmental theories which emphasize the importance of sex-role effects on general cognitive development are not supported by these results.

Another possible source of heterogeneity is the intelligence test used. We found great diversity in test selection. For example, the 34 correlations for MZ twins reared together were based on results from 22 different tests, the 41 DZ twin correlations upon results from 25. We do not have sufficient data to determine whether the size of the familial correlation is moderated by the specific test used. We did investigate whether individually administered tests and group-administered tests produced different correlations: (*i*) for the MZ twins reared together, the 24 correlations calculated on group tests produced a weighted average of 0.86, and the ten calculated on individual tests a weighted average of 0.84; (*ii*) for the DZ twins reared together, the weighted average of 32 correlations based on group tests is 0.60, and of nine correlations based on individual tests it is 0.61. In neither case was the difference significant.

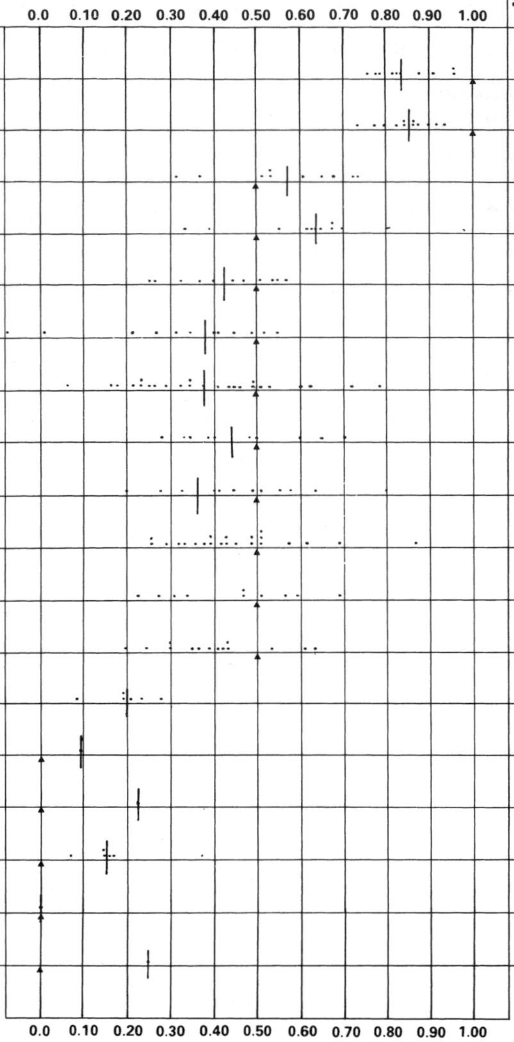

THE STUDY

	No. of correlations	No. of pairings	Median correlation	Weighted average	χ^2 (d.f.)	$\chi^2 \div$ d.f.
Female mz twin pairs	10	869	.835	.86	26.35 (8)	3.29
Male mz twin pairs	12	1,013	.86	.86	24.4 (10)	2.44
Female dz twin pairs	10	730	.58	.61	14.73 (8)	1.84
Male dz twin pairs	11	964	.64	.65	20.32 (9)	2.26
Female sibling pairs	11	1,986	.42	.50	28.34 (9)	3.15
Male sibling pairs	12	2,321	.38	.47	54.69 (10)	5.47
Mother–offspring reared together	25	5,660	.38	.41	119.02 (24)	4.96
Mother–daughter reared together	10	1,804	.44	.43	36.80 (9)	4.09
Mother–son reared together	12	2,802	.37	.39	38.52 (11)	3.50
Father–offspring reared together	22	5,497	.43	.41	141.17 (21)	6.72
Father–daughter reared together	10	1,658	.46	.39	33.08 (9)	3.68
Father–son reared together	14	2,843	.40	.38	36.86 (13)	2.84
Adopting mother–offspring	6	1,393	.195	.20	4.28 (5)	0.86
Adopting mother–daughter	1	212	.10	.10		
Adopting mother–son	1	247	.22	.22		
Adopting father–offspring	6	1,279	.155	.18	10.1 (5)	2.02
Adopting father–daughter	1	214	.00	.00		
Adopting father–son	1	248	.25	.25		

Figure 24.3. Familial correlations for IQ organized by male and female pairings.

The 34 correlations reported on 4672 MZ twin pairs reared together produce a weighted average correlation of 0.86, which is very close to those reported in earlier reviews, and is approximately the same for male and female pairs. Although the test of homogeneity yields a significant χ^2 value ($p < 0.02$), the degree of heterogeneity is not extreme, and from a few rather low correlations. The two most extreme values are the 0.58 reported by Blewett (1954) and the 0.62 reported by Nichols (1970); in both cases, the sample sizes are small (26 and 36 pairs respectively). The observation that 79 per cent of the reported correlations lie above 0.80 convincingly demonstrates the remarkable similarity of MZ twins.

After deleting the Burt data, we are left with results on just 65 pairs of MZ twins reared apart, as reported in three separate studies. The weighted average of 0.72 is much less than that for the MZ twins reared together, the difference suggesting the importance of between-family environmental differences. At the same time, the size of the correlation would be difficult to explain on the basis of any strictly environmental hypothesis.

Three studies give mid-parent–mid-offspring correlations, the weighted average being 0.72. In this case, the genetic expectation would depend upon the number of offspring which define mid-offspring value, and is thus indeterminate. The correlation between mid-parent and individual offspring does have a determinate simple genetic expectation of 0.707. The observed weighted average is only 0.50, a discrepancy discussed below.

The weighted average of the 41 correlations in DZ twin pairs is 0.60, considerably larger than for non-twin siblings, and same-sex DZ pairs show somewhat greater similarity than opposite-sex DZ pairs (0.62 vs. 0.57), with males being slightly more similar than females (0.65 vs. 0.61). As with the MZ twins, the test of homogeneity is significant ($p < 0.01$), although 75 per cent of the correlations fall within the narrow range 0.50 to 0.70. The two extreme values were reported in old studies on rather small samples, the lowest being the 0.21 reported by Wingfield (1928) on 26 pairs, the highest the 0.87 reported by Merriman (1924) on 51 pairs. The greater similarity of DZ twins is usually interpreted as reflecting greater environmental similarity, but it is also likely that bias in the recruitment of DZ twins is in the direction of increasing psychological similarity (Lykken *et al.*, 1978).

The weighted average for siblings reared together is 0.47 which, although close to the simple expectation of 0.50, is based upon 69 values, with a range of correlations from 0.13 to 0.90. Opposite-sex and same-sex siblings yield almost identical weighted averages (0.49 vs. 0.48), as do female and male siblings (0.50 vs. 0.47). The sibling correlations are based on over 25,000 pairs: one large representative study by Record *et al.* (1969) showed a correlation of 0.55 for over 5000 pairs.

While there is a wealth of data on siblings reared together, there is a dearth of information on siblings reared apart. Only 203 such pairs have been studied, in two investigations, yielding a weighted average of 0.24, much less than the expected value for such pairs and the average value for siblings reared together.

The weighted average correlation between individual parent and individual offspring is 0.42, based upon 32 correlations. There is a marked degree of heterogeneity, as evidenced not only by a significant χ^2 value ($p < 0.01$), but also by the broad range of the correlations. This cannot be attributed to a sex effect, since opposite-sex and same-sex pairings yield equivalent averages, or to a maternal effect, the average correlation of mother and offspring being the same as that of father and offspring. Although the large discrepancies between expected and observed correla-

THE STUDY

tions for parent and offspring reared in the parental home (reared together) may be easily interpreted as a result of a generational (social-environmental) effect, we cannot discount the role of biological factors: characteristics which are affected very little by the social environment, such as height and total fingerprint ridge count, show similar generational differences.

Similarly, correlations for parent and separated offspring are quite heterogeneous; the weighted average is 0.22, much less than the simple expectation of 0.50. McAskie and Clarke (1976) suggest that one possible explanation could be that parents and offspring are given different tests. In fact, roughly half our intergenerational correlations were based upon data from cases in which this did happen.

Two pairings which are rarely studied are half-siblings and cousins. Two half-sibling correlations, both reported by Nichols (1970) produce a weighted average of 0.31. The four reported correlations for cousins are quite homogeneous, the average being 0.15, very similar to the simple genetic expectation.

A number of recent adoption studies have added considerable knowledge, and enough studies are available to permit comparison of adopted/natural sibling pairs and adopted/adopted sibling pairs. The adopted/natural correlation should be higher, since it would contain a component for the covariance of genotype and environment (Plomin *et al.*, 1977). The present review in fact finds the reverse (see Figure 24.1).

The weighted average correlation of adoptive mid-parent and offspring is 0.24, and that of adoptive parent and offspring is 0.19. Genetic theory requires the biological mid-parent–offspring correlation to exceed the biological single parent–offspring correlation, and it does, although not by much (0.50 vs. 0.42). Some environmental theories predict the same effect (McAskie & Clarke, 1976); the failure to find any difference in the adoptive case must be considered surprising from an environmental point of view.

Unlike natural families, adopted offspring are rather more similar to the same-sex adoptive parent than to the opposite-sex adoptive parent (see Figure 24.2). However, this conclusion is based on a single study (Horn *et al.*, 1979). Overall, adoptive mothers are no more like their adopted children than adoptive fathers are.

The weighted average of 0.33 for correlations between mates is much smaller than the 0.50 sometimes reported (e.g. Jensen, 1978). The marked heterogeneity of the distribution indicates the sample-specific nature of these measures.

As in the earlier review, the pattern of averaged correlations is remarkably consistent with polygenic theory. This is not to discount the importance of environmental factors; MZ twins reared apart are far from perfectly correlated, DZ twins are more similar than other biological siblings, and adoptive parents' IQs show a consistent relation with the IQs of their adoptive offspring. However, we found no evid-

ence for two factors: sex-role and maternal effects, sometimes thought to be important. It is indisputable that the data support the inference of partial genetic determination of IQ, but it is doubtful whether they tell us about the precise strength of this effect. Certainly the large amount of unexplained variability within degrees of relationship suggests that any models used to explain the data should be used cautiously.

EVALUATION

Theoretical issues

Behaviour-genetic theorists mostly take it for granted that IQ tests are reliable and valid measures of intelligence. However, there are good reasons for challenging this assumption:

(*i*)   It is possible for two IQ tests, A and B, to have different standard deviations (a measure of dispersion of scores around the mean, and the usual way in which IQ scores are expressed), and therefore for the same individual to score differently on the two tests. This suggests that while intelligence is a *psychological* concept, IQ is a purely *statistical* concept. If it is possible for the same characteristic to be assigned different values according to which test is used to measure it, then perhaps instead of asking 'How intelligent is this individual?', we should ask 'How intelligent is this individual as measured by this particular test?' (Gross, 2001).

This is relevant in discussing the present study: Bouchard and McGue point out the diversity of tests used in the 111 studies they review. We cannot just assume the scales are equivalent, which makes the procedure of finding the median correlation for different studies far from straightforward.

(*ii*) Because intelligence is expressed as a number, the impression is created that IQ tells us in some absolute way about an individual's intellectual ability (in the same way as metres and centimetres tell us about their height). But whereas height is measured on a *ratio scale* (and by implication an interval scale too), many psychologists believe that intelligence can only be measured on an *ordinal scale*. IQ can tell us only how intelligent we are *relative* to others (higher or lower), but we cannot be more precise about the size of those differences (Ryan, 1972).

The idea that intelligence is hereditary (i.e. *differences* in IQ are inherited) is deeply built into the theory of IQ testing itself, because of its commitment to the measurement of something intrinsic and unchangeable. From the very beginning of the American and British mental testing movement, it was assumed that IQ was biologically heritable (Rose *et al.*, 1984: see Chapter 23). Rose *et al.* point out what they

consider to be certain mistaken senses of 'heritable' as used by psychometricians, which are mixed up with the geneticist's technical meaning of the term, and which contribute to false conclusions about the consequences of heritability:

(*i*)   *genes do not determine intelligence:* there is no one:to:one correspondence between the genes inherited from one's parents and even physical characteristics. What we inherit is the *genotype*, the genes which are involved in the development of a particular trait, while the *phenotype* is the actual trait itself as it manifests itself in the organism. While the former is fixed, the latter develops and changes constantly. The first principle of developmental genetics is that every organism is a unique product of the interaction between genes and environment at every stage of life;

(*ii*) even allowing that genes alone do not determine the phenotype, it is claimed that *they determine the effective limits of the phentotype:* genes determine capacity or potential. However, Ryan (1972) rejects the whole idea of innate potential on the grounds that it is impossible to measure potential separately from actual behaviour/performance.

Rose *et al.*'s first point is related to one of the areas of agreement among all researchers identified in the **Background and context** section above, namely that there is interaction between heredity and environment. For Wahlsten & Gottlieb (1997), the complex sequence of bidirectional and interacting causes makes it almost impossible to assign a definite role to the genotype unless a major gene can be identified. But the prevalent model in human behaviour-genetics assumes that heredity and environment are *additive*, separately acting causes whose contributions to any characteristic can be neatly separated statistically. Wahlsten and Gottlieb see this assumption as biologically unrealistic given our present state of knowledge.

Methodological issues

In general, *heritability* is estimated from the correlation of a trait between relatives (Rose *et al.*, 1984). However, most of the results of studies of family resemblance (or concordance studies) can be interpreted as supporting *either* the genetic *or* the environmentalist theory. This is because relatives resemble each other not only in terms of their genes, but also in terms of their environments, and the greater the degree of blood (genetic) relationship, the greater the likelihood that they will share the same environment. This is why psychologists and behaviour-geneticists take advantage of the 'natural experiments' of twin studies (particularly the separation of MZs) and adoption studies. Here is the opportunity to study the relative influence of the two (normally inseparable) variables: heredity and environment.

With Burt's twin studies no longer included in the survey, the three remaining studies of separated MZs are (presumably): (*i*) Newman *et al.* (1937); (*ii*) Shields (1962); and (*iii*) Juel-Nielsen (1965). One of the criteria for selection used by Bouchard and McGue (in 'Notes') was that:

> . . . the procedure for zygosity determination was both objective and valid. Use of a validated questionnaire was considered an acceptable procedure.

In other words, it should be possible to establish objectively whether or not any of the volunteers are MZs or DZs. But this was clearly *not* so in the case of the Newman *et al.* study (see, e.g. Kamin, 1977): in 1937 there was no reliable/valid medical test for zygosity which, surely, is the only kind of test that *should* be used!

Perhaps more seriously, the whole rationale of these studies is that MZs are reared separately (in truly uncorrelated environments). But this is also flawed, since several kinds of correlated environments can occur for supposedly separated MZs, such as the pre-natal and early post-natal environments. They are wombmates, and selective placement after separation is likely to produce low to moderate correlations of their childhood environments. In addition, there may be similarity of adult environments if and when the twins are reunited prior to psychological testing (as in the Minnesota Twin Study – see **Subsequent research** below – where testing took place on average 10 years following reunion!). This is an unacceptable confounding of the two factors (Wahlsten & Gottlieb, 1997).

Howe (1997) also argues that being separated at birth *is not the same* as being reared *completely* apart, which is, of course, impossible:

> . . . no two individuals who began life in the identical uterus can be said to have been reared apart to the extent that would be essential in order for an investigation based on separated twins to yield entirely unambiguous evidence about the effects of genes on intelligence. In practice, however, separation at birth is the best that can be done.

To share a womb is to share nine crucial formative months of one's life, and differences in pre-natal environments can have powerful effects on post-natal development. For example, maternal smoking and drinking during pregnancy can adversely affect the child's intelligence.

The problem with early *adoption studies* (e.g. Burks, 1928; Leahy, 1935) was that adoptive families differ, as a group, in a variety of ways from the 'matched control group' of ordinary biological families (see Kamin, 1977). The obvious improvement on this 'classical' design is to study adoptive parents who also have a biological child of their own. Here, the two children will have been reared in the same environment by the same parents, although they will be genetically unrelated to each other, and, of course, the adopted children will be genetically unrelated to the adoptive parents.

Scarr & Weinberg (1977, 1983) and Horn *et al.* (1979), used this new design, the former involving transracial adoptions (the mother and her biological child were white, while the adopted child was black). In both studies, there was no significant

difference between (*i*) the correlation of the mother's IQ and her biological child's IQ; and (*ii*) the correlation of her IQ with that of her adopted child's IQ. According to Rose *et al.* (1984):

> The child's race, like its adoptive status, had no effect on the degree of parent–child resemblance in IQ. These results appear to inflict fatal damage to the notion that IQ is highly heritable . . . children reared by the same mother resemble her in IQ to the same degree, whether or not they share her genes.

While behaviour-geneticists have taken the results of adoption studies, along with those of twin studies, as demonstrating the greater influence of genetics, there are other possible interpretations of the data. For example, according to the French adoption researchers (Duyme & Capron, 1992; Roubertoux & Capron, 1990), the adoption method is a good design for studying the importance of different post-natal environments, but cannot teach us about the role of genes (Wahlsten & Gottlieb, 1997).

Similarly, Howe (1997) argues that the adoptive homes involved in adoption studies have tended to be very similar in the degree to which they provide environments that succeed in stimulating intellectual development, It is, therefore, possible that the data may have under-represented the range of differences that can occur between children's everyday experiences. Had the adoptive parents varied more, the conclusions might have given more weight to the role of environmental factors and less to genetic ones.

Subsequent research

The most recent study, the Minnesota Twin Study (Bouchard *et al.*, 1990), has been going on since 1979, accumulating pairs of separated MZs (MZAs) during that time, with the latest figure standing at 56 (including two sets of male triplets). They have also studied 30 pairs of separated DZs, but the data is presented almost exclusively in terms of MZAs compared with MZTs (MZs reared together). (This represents a different 'methodology' from earlier studies, where the crucial comparisons are between MZAs and DZTs (of the same sex). In either case, the aim is to separate the two normally interrelated variables of heredity and environment.

Once recruited, twins were subjected to a week (50 hours) of intensive physiological and psychological assessment, being given multiple measures of personality and temperament, occupational and leisure-time interests and social attitudes, as well as intelligence. It is the most 'international' twin study to date, recruiting from all over the USA, the UK, Australia, Canada, New Zealand, China, Sweden and (the former West) Germany.

As far as IQ is concerned, Bouchard *et al.* found a *heritability estimate* of 70%: 70% of the variance between the IQ scores of individuals is attributable to genetic factors. As they point out, this is higher than the 47–48% heritability estimates proposed by Bouchard and McGue (in the present study) and by Loehlin (1989) and Plomin & Loehlin (1989). However, virtually the whole literature on IQ similarity in twins and siblings is limited to studies of children and adolescents. The mean age of the MZAs in the Minnesota study was 41 years (with a range of 19–68).

In the present study (Bouchard & McGue, 1981), the average median/weighted average IQ correlations for MZTs is 0.86 (based mainly on children and adolescents) compared with 0.72 for MZAs (Bouchard *et al.*, 1990), based mainly on adults (0.72 is also the figure for MZAs in the present study). If the mean MZT correlation were maintained into adulthood, its difference from the MZA correlation would suggest that being brought up together increases the similarity of IQ in twins (and siblings). But it appears to *decline* with age, due, for example, to accumulating non-shared environmental effects (McCartney *et al.*, 1990, cited in Bouchard *et al.*, 1990). This implies that the correlation for MZTs would move closer to that for MZAs which, in turn, means that common rearing has little influence on adult IQ.

Summarizing their findings as a whole, Bouchard *et al.* (1990) claim that adult MZs are about equally similar on most physiological and psychological traits regardless of rearing status: whether brought up together or apart, MZs are strikingly similar, because they are genetically identical. They rule out the significant effect of socio-economic status (SES) or other environmental variables on twins' IQ scores, but some of their methods for measuring environmental variables are dubious, to say the least. For example, as an 'index of cultural and intellectual resources', they provided a checklist of available household facilities such as power tools, sailboat, telescope, unabridged dictionary and original artwork.

Horgan (1993) points out some additional criticisms which have been made of the Minnesota study:

(*i*)   Rose, an American psychologist involved in a large-scale Finnish twin study (Langainvaimio *et al.*, 1984, cited by Bouchard *et al.*, 1990), claims that some of the 'eerie', 'bewitching' and 'remarkable' parallels between some of the reunited twins have been greatly exaggerated. If you bring together genetically unrelated people born on the same day in the same country, and ask them to find some similarities between them, you may find a lot of seemingly astounding coincidences. For example, Oskar was raised in (the former) Czechoslovakia as a Nazi, while his twin, Jack, was raised as a Jew in Trinidad, yet both wore shirts with epaulettes when they were brought together in 1979, both flushed the toilet before and after using it, and both enjoyed deliberately sneezing in order to startle people in lifts! Two British women wore seven rings and named their firstborn sons Richard Andrew and Andrew Richard!

(*ii*)   Kaprio, one of the Finnish psychologists involved in the Finnish study, believes that the method used to select twins may be biased. In the Finnish study, researchers comb the birth registers and send questionnaires to identified twins. But in the Minnesota study, much reliance is put on media coverage, with 'self-referrals' or relatives and friends telling twins about the study. The study has attracted considerable publicity, both in the USA and in other parts of the world, and Kaprio believes that it has attracted people who like publicity, making them an atypical sample of twins (let alone of people in general). He believes that this self-selection effect may help explain the higher heritability estimate compared with other studies (although Eysenck, 1973 and Jensen, 1969, give 80% as the heritability estimate, based primarily on twin and adoption studies).

(*iii*) Kamin asks whether the MZAs may, in fact, have had more extensive contact with each other while growing up than at least the media make out. Mean time together prior to separation is given as 5 months (range 0–49 months) and time apart before first reunion is 30 years (range 0.5–65 years). The two pairs referred to above are supposed to have met for the first time when they arrived in Minnesota for the study – but both had, in fact met previously.

According to Bouchard *et al.* (1990), any shared experiences the MZAs may have had as adults is unimportant, because they had already passed through the early 'formative years' (critical or sensitive period) for intelligence. However, many aspects of brain and behaviour retain significant plasticity in adults. According to Wahlsten & Gottlieb (1997),

> . . . The distinction between hardware and software that is so obvious in a computer is not present in the living brain, where experience continues to alter the connections throughout life. If brain structure can be altered significantly in adult animals, it seems likely that the intelligence of adult humans is also modifiable.

Children can sometimes recover dramatically from several years of extreme early privation (see Chapter 15), and adult IQ can fluctuate by up to 20 points over a period of years (Tyler, 1972). This evidence challenges the credibility of a critical period for human measured intelligence (Wahlsten & Gottlieb, 1997).

Applications and implications

More important than the specific size of the heritability estimate is the fact that it is *not* a fixed value, but a *relative* index referring to a particular population at a particular time. If everybody's environment were to become very similar, the higher the heritability estimate would become: relatively more of the variance between people's IQ scores would be attributable to genetic differences. This is another way of regarding heredity and environment as interacting variables, and it may be much more fruitful to try to understand *how* and *in what ways* they act to produce the phenotype of intelligence, than it is to measure *how much* each affects it.

Bouchard *et al.* (1990) suggest what the mechanism might be by which 'the genes affect the mind'. It is likely to be *indirect*, involving the 'effective psychological environment' of the developing child. Active infants and toddlers have different experiences from their passive siblings, partly because they elicit different parenting responses, partly because they will seek out different environments which match their temperaments. (These are examples of *gene-environment covariance* or *correlation*). When different individuals pay different attention and respond differently to the same objective experience, *gene-environment interaction* is taking place. Bouchard *et al.* propose that:

> The proximal cause of most psychological variance probably involves learning through experience, just as radical environmentalists have always believed. The effective experiences, however, to an important extent are self-selected, and that selection is guided by the steady pressure of the genome (a more distal cause). We agree with Martin *et al.* [1986] who see 'humans as exploring organisms whose innate abilities and predispositions help them select what is relevant and adaptive from the range of opportunities and stimuli presented in the environment. The effects of mobility and learning, therefore, augment rather than eradicate the effects of the genotype on behaviour.

If this view is correct, then the developmental experiences of MZs is more similar than those of DZs, again as environmentalist critics of twin research have argued. But even MZAs tend to elicit, select, seek out or create very similar effective environments and, to that extent, the impact of these experiences is counted as a genetic influence. If the genome (genotype) impresses itself on the psyche largely by influencing the characteristics, selection and impact of experiences during development (nature *via* nurture), then intervention is not ruled out even for highly heritable traits, but should be the more effective when tailored to each specific child's talents and inclinations (Bouchard *et al.*, 1990).

These views are echoed to some extent by Gould (1981), ironically, a major critic of the genetic theory of intelligence (see Chapter 23). What he calls the '*hereditarian fallacy*' is not the simple claim that IQ is to some degree 'heritable' (which it undoubtedly is, since all broad aspects of human performance or anatomy involve some heritable component). It is equating 'heritable' with 'inevitable' that is mistaken (see **Theoretical issues** above). Equally serious, and equally mistaken, is the confusion of *within-* and *between-group heritability*. This fallacy consists in assuming that if heredity explains a certain percentage of variation among individuals *within* a group (e.g. white Americans), it must also explain a similar percentage of variation *between* groups (e.g. white and black Americans) on the trait in question (e.g. IQ):

> . . . variation among individuals within a group and differences in mean values between groups are entirely separate phenomena. One item provides no licence for speculation about the other. (Gould, 1981)

Twin studies and adoption studies provide the heritability estimate for *within*-group differences, which have then been used by hereditarian theorists like Jensen (1969) to explain *between*-group differences in the same genetic terms.

Howe (1997) distinguishes between the direct and indirect influences of genetics on intelligence. These are often confused, but they have vastly different *practical* implications for human lives. Genetic or hereditarian theorists believe in *direct* influence, seeing an individual's intelligence as relatively fixed from birth, so that IQ cannot be greatly modified by environmental influences or interventions. However, *indirect* influence would mean that change is possible and that a particular IQ is not determined once and for all at birth. The former view implies that it is pointless trying to increase people's intelligence: only population control measures (*eugenics*) can restrain the burgeoning of a permanent underclass of people with low IQs (Herrnstein & Murray, 1996). By contrast, belief in indirect influence implies that it may be no more difficult to change IQ than those mental skills known to be acquired through experience and learning; in turn, this is consistent with the view that there is nothing unique or fundamental about those abilities which determine a person's performance on an intelligence test (Howe, 1998).

Gardner (1993) agrees with Bouchard *et al.* (1990) by arguing that, while there is considerable plasticity and flexibility in early development, they are mediated by strong genetic constraints which guide development along some paths rather than along others. However, he challenges one of the basic assumptions on which the hereditarian argument is based:

> Genetics has made its greatest progress in accounting for simple traits in simple organisms . . . But when it comes to more complex human abilities – the capacities to solve equations, to appreciate or create music, to master languages . . . we are still woefully ignorant about the genetic component and its phenotypical expression . . . rather than being related to a specific gene or a small set of genes, any complex trait reflects many genes, a fair number of which will be polymorphic (allowing a number of different realizations across a range of environments). Indeed, when it comes to capacities as broad (and vague) as human intelligence, it is questionable whether one ought to speak of 'traits' at all. (Gardner, 1993)

Segall *et al.* (1999) say that, as cross-cultural psychologists, they find Boyd & Richardson's (1985) 'dual inheritance' theory very useful. According to Segall *et al.*:

> . . . Dual inheritance theory shows that the nature *versus* nurture (or genetics *versus* culture) controversy is an inappropriate conceptualization of the relationship between biological and cultural forces. While they may have different outcomes, and involve different processes, they are parallel rather than competing forces. And, they interact with each other when applied to any particular individual human being.

Exercises

1. What is meant by a *polygenic* theory of intelligence?

2. What is meant by genetic '*dominance*'?

3. What is meant by assortative mating?

4. Why would the median be chosen as the 'average'?

5. In the Tables, what does each of the column headings mean:

   (*i*)   weighted average
   (*ii*) χ^2 (*d.f.*)
   (*iii*) $\chi^2 \div d.f.$

6. What is the difference between Individual and Group tests of intelligence? Give at least one example of each.

25 The measurement of psychological androgyny

Sandra L. Bem (1974)

Journal of Consulting and Clinical Psychology, 42 (2), 155–62

BACKGROUND AND CONTEXT

Prior to the 1970s, the prevalent view (both within psychology and in society at large) was that an individual could be *either* masculine *or* feminine. It was assumed that people who achieved a good fit with their sex type/sex role (i.e. a masculine male and a feminine female) were better adjusted psychologically/psychologically healthier than those who did not (Moghaddam, 1998).

According to Brown (1986), many widely used psychological tests (developed between the 1930s and 60s) had this conception built into them. Because of the way they were designed and scored, it was impossible for an individual to register as both highly masculine and highly feminine: they were seen as *mutually exclusive*, in the sense that the nearer the masculine end of the scale you scored, the further away from the feminine end you were. So it was impossible to find any *androgynous* people, i.e. individuals who display *both* masculine *and* feminine characteristics ('andro' = male, 'gyne' = female). ('Mutually exclusive' usually implies 'either/or', i.e. one *category* or another).

For example, Terman & Miles' (1936) scale saw masculinity–femininity as a single bipolar dimension, the core of personality rooted somehow in sexual anatomy/physiology and relatively fixed. They selected items which would best differentiate between male and female. It was impossible for the same individual to obtain high or low scores on *both* masculinity and femininity.

Other tests, including those of Gough (1952), Guilford & Guilford (1936), Hathaway & McKinley, (1943) and Strong (1943) all shared this bipolar view. When scores on the tests were factor analysed (tested for intercorrelations between different parts of the test), the same temperamental factors kept emerging: (*i*) independent, assertive, dominant and instrumental (masculine) and (*ii*) interpersonal sensitivity, compassion and warmth (feminine). These corresponded closely with sociological (Parsons & Bales, 1955) and anthropological (Barry, Bacon & Child, 1957) ideas of what might be universal masculinity and femininity, and until the early 1970s defined the dimensions most worth measuring (Brown, 1986).

By the early 1970s, several researchers had challenged this traditional view: the same individual could be high on both, low on both, or medium on both, since masculinity and femininity were *independent* dimensions. This shift in perspective owed a great deal to the feminist movement, including feminist psychologists, such as Sandra Bem. To 'discover' androgyny, it was necessary to incorporate this new conception into a new sort of test which would produce two logically independent scores: the Bem Sex-Role Inventory (BSRI) was the first and most influential of these tests (Moghaddam, 1998).

AIM AND NATURE OF THE STUDY

The article describes the development of a new sex-role inventory, the Bem Sex-Role Inventory (BSRI), a questionnaire designed to measure a person's degree of masculinity, femininity, or androgyny. The study describes how the questionnaire items were selected, how it is scored, psychometric analyses of internal consistency, and test–retest reliability, correlations with other measures of masculinity and femininity, data for normative samples (standardization), as well as the problem of social desirability response set.

The 'judges' (participants) rated about 400 personality characteristics, on a seven-point scale (1 = 'Not at all desirable'; 7 = 'Extremely desirable'). Each judge rated all the items just once, *either* 'for a man' *or* 'for a woman'; no judge rated both.

The judges were 40 Stanford University undergraduates (who completed the questionnaires in 1972), and an additional 60 (in 1973). In both samples, half were male and half were female.

The 'method' is the construction of a questionnaire, so there are no independent and dependent variables.

■ T H E ■ S T U D Y ■

This article describes the development of a new sex-role inventory that treats masculinity and femininity as two independent dimensions, thereby making it possible to characterize a person as masculine, feminine, or 'androgynous' as a function of the difference between his or her endorsement of masculine and feminine personality characteristics. Normative data are presented, as well as the results of various psychometric analyses. The major findings of conceptual interest are: (*i*) the dimensions of masculinity and femininity are empirically, as well as logically independent; (*ii*) the concept of psychological androgyny is a reliable one; (*iii*) highly sex-typed scores do not reflect a general tendency to respond in a socially desirable direction, but rather a specific tendency to describe oneself in accordance with sex-typed standards of desirable behaviour for men and women.

THE STUDY

Both in psychology and society at large, masculinity and femininity have long been conceptualized as bipolar ends of a single continuum, such that a person has had to be either masculine or feminine, but not both. This sex-role dichotomy has served to obscure two very plausible hypotheses; (*i*) that many individuals might be 'androgynous', i.e. they might be *both* masculine *and* feminine, *both* assertive *and* yielding, instrumental *and* expressive (depending on the situational appropriateness of these various behaviours); conversely, (*ii*) that strongly sex-typed individuals might be seriously limited in the range of behaviours available to them as they move from situation to situation. Both Kagan (1964) and Kohlberg (1966) believe that the highly sex-typed individual is motivated to keep his/her behaviour consistent with an internalized sex-role standard, presumably by suppressing any behaviour thought to be sex-inappropriate or undesirable. Thus, a narrowly masculine self-concept might inhibit behaviours which are stereotyped as feminine (and similarly for a narrowly feminine self-concept and masculine behaviours), whereas a mixed, or androgynous, self-concept might allow an individual to freely engage in both kinds of behaviour.

Before the current research could begin, it was first necessary to develop a new type of sex-role inventory which would not automatically build in an inverse relationship between masculinity and femininity, and this article describes such an inventory.

The Bem-Sex Role Inventory (BSRI) contains a number of features which distinguish it from other, commonly used, masculinity–femininity scales, e.g. the Masculinity–Femininity scale of the California Psychological Inventory (Gough, 1957): (*i*) it includes both a Masculinity scale and a Femininity scale, each of which contains 20 personality characteristics (see Table 25.1, below); (*ii*) because the BSRI

Table 25.1

ITEMS ON THE MASCULINITY, FEMININITY AND SOCIAL DESIRABILITY SCALES OF THE BSRI

Masculine items	Feminine items	Neutral items
46 Aggressive	32 Compassionate	9 Conscientious
55 Competitive	26 Sensitive to the needs of others	30 Secretive
1 Self-reliant	2 Yielding	57 Tactful

Note (i): The number before each item refers to the position of each adjective as it actually appears on the inventory.
Note (ii): Due to copyright reasons, the above 9 items represent only a sample of the 60 items (20 per scale) constituting the BSRI as a whole.

was founded on a conception of the sex-typed person as someone who has internalized society's sex-typed standards of desirable behaviour for men and women, these personality characteristics were selected as masculine or feminine on the basis of sex-typed social desirability, and not on the basis of differential endorsement by males and females as most other inventories have done; i.e. a characteristic qualified as masculine if it was judged to be more desirable in American society for a man than for a woman, and, similarly, feminine if judged to be more desirable for a woman than a man; (*iii*) the BSRI characterizes a person as masculine, feminine or androgynous as a function of the difference between his/her endorsement of masculine and feminine personality characteristics. So a person is sex-typed, whether masculine or feminine, to the extent that this difference score is high, and androgynous to the extent that it is low; (*iv*) the BSRI also includes a Social Desirability scale which is completely neutral with respect to sex; it was used during the development of the BSRI to ensure that the inventory was not simply tapping a general tendency to endorse socially desirable traits (see Table 25.1).

ITEM SELECTION

Both historically and cross-culturally, masculinity and femininity seem to have represented two complementary domains of *positive* traits and behaviours (Barry, Bacon & Child, 1957; Erikson, 1964; Parsons & Bales, 1955). In general, masculinity has been associated with an instrumental orientation, a cognitive focus on 'getting the job done', while femininity has been associated with an expressive orientation, an affective concern for the welfare of others.

Accordingly, as a preliminary to item selection for the Masculinity and Femininity scales, a list was compiled of approximately 200 personality characteristics that seemed to the author and several students to be both positive in value and either masculine or feminine in tone; this list served as the pool from which the masculine and feminine items were ultimately chosen. Similarly, an additional list of 200 characteristics was compiled which seemed to be neither masculine nor feminine in tone, half positive and half negative in value, from which the Social Desirability scale was chosen.

Because the BSRI was designed to measure how much a person divorces himself from those characteristics that might be considered more 'appropriate' for the opposite sex, the final items were selected if they were judged to be more desirable in American society for one sex than for the other. Specifically, judges used a seven-point scale, ranging from 1 ('Not at all desirable') to 7 ('Extremely desirable'), to rate the desirability of each of the approximately-400 personality characteristics mentioned above. (For example, 'In American society, how desirable is it for a man [woman] to be truthful [sincere]?'.) Each judge rated the desirability of all 400 characteristics either 'for a man' or 'for a woman'; no judge rated both. The judges were 40 Stanford undergraduates, who completed the question-naires during the winter of 1972, and an additional 60 who did so the following summer. In both samples; half were male and half were female.

A personality characteristic qualified as masculine if it was independently judged by both males and females in both samples to be significantly more desirable for a man than for a woman ($p<0.05$, for a two-tailed t-test); similarly, for feminine personality characteristics. Of those characteristics which met these criteria, 20 were chosen for the Masculinity scale and 20 for the Femininity scale (see Table 25.1). A neutral personality characteristic was one which (*i*) was independently judged by both males and females to be no more desirable for one sex than for the other ($t<1.2, p>0.2$), and (*ii*) did not produce significantly different desirability judgements by male and female judges ($t<1.2, p>0.2$). Ten positive and ten negative characteristics met these criteria, and were chosen for the Social Desirability scale in accordance with Edwards' (1964) finding that an item must be quite positive or quite negative in tone if it is to evoke a social desirability response set.

Once all the individual items had been selected, mean desirability scores were computed for the masculine, feminine and neutral items for each of the 100 judges. As Table 25.2 shows, for both males and females, the mean desirability of the 60 masculine and feminine items was significantly higher for the 'appropriate' sex, whereas the mean desirability of the neutral items was no higher for one sex than the other. These results are, of course, a direct consequence of the criteria used for item selection.

THE STUDY

Table 25.2

MEAN SOCIAL DESIRABILITY RATINGS OF THE MASCULINE, FEMININE AND NEUTRAL ITEMS

Item	Male judges			Female judges		
	Masculine item	Feminine item	Neutral item	Masculine item	Feminine item	Neutral item
For a man	5.59	3.63	4.00	5.83	3.74	3.94
For a woman	2.90	5.61	4.08	3.46	5.55	3.98
Difference	2.69	1.98	0.08	2.37	1.81	0.04
t	14.41*	12.13*	0.17	10.22*	8.28*	0.09
* $p<0.001$.						

Table 25.3

MEAN SOCIAL DESIRABILITY RATINGS OF THE MASCULINE AND FEMININE ITEMS FOR ONE'S OWN SEX

Item	Male judges for a man	Female judges for a woman
Masculine	5.59	3.46
Feminine	3.63	5.55
Difference	1.96	2.09
t	11.94*	8.88*
* $p < 0.001$.		

Table 25.3 separates out the desirability ratings of the masculine and feminine items for male and female judges rating their *own* sex; this seems to best represent the desirability of these items as perceived by men and women when asked to describe *themselves* on the BSRI. Not only are 'sex-appropriate' characteristics more desirable for both sexes than 'sex-inappropriate' characteristics, but men and women are nearly equal in their perceptions of the desirability of sex-appropriate and sex-inappropriate characteristics and the differences between them ($t < 1$ in all three comparisons).

SCORING

The BSRI asks a person to indicate on a seven-point scale how well each of the masculine, feminine and neutral personality characteristics describes him/herself. The scale ranges from 1 ('Never or almost never true') to 7 ('Always or almost always true') and is labelled at each point. Each person receives a Masculinity score, a Femininity score and, most important, an Androgyny score; in addition, a Social Desirability score can also be calculated.

The Masculinity and Femininity scores indicate how much a person endorses masculine and feminine personality characteristics as self-descriptive. Masculinity equals the mean self-rating for all endorsed masculine items and Femininity equals the mean self-rating for all endorsed feminine items; both can range from 1 to 7 and the two scores, remember, are logically independent.

The Androgyny score reflects the relative amounts of masculinity and femininity that the person includes in his or her self description and, as such, it best characterizes the nature of the person's total sex role. Specifically, the Androgyny score is defined as students' t-ratio for the difference between a person's masculine and feminine self-endorsement; i.e. the difference between masculinity and femininity normalized with respect to the standard deviations of his or her masculinity and femininity scores. The use of a t-ratio (instead of a simple difference score) has two conceptual advantages; (i) it allows us to ask whether a person's endorsement of masculine characteristics differs significantly from his or her endorsement of feminine ones and, if it does ($|t|^2 2.025$, *d.f.*$=38$, $p<0.05$), to classify that person as significantly sex-typed; (ii) it allows us to compare different populations in terms of the percentage of significantly sex-typed individuals present within each. (In the absence of computer facilities, one can use the simple Androgyny difference score, Femininity–Masculinity, as the index of androgyny. Empirically, the two indices are virtually identical ($r=0.98$), and one can approximate the t-ratio value by multiplying the Androgyny difference score by 2.322: this conversion factor was derived empirically from the combined normative sample of 917 students at two different colleges.)

The greater the absolute value of the Androgyny score, the more the person is sex-typed or sex reversed, with high positive scores indicating femininity and high negative scores indicating masculinity. A 'masculine' sex role thus represents not only the endorsement of masculine characteristics, but the simultaneous rejection of feminine ones; similarly, with a 'feminine' sex role. By contrast, the closer the Androgyny score is to zero, the more the person is androgynous; an 'androgynous' sex role thus represents the equal endorsement of both masculine and feminine characteristics.

The Social Desirability score indicates how much a person describes him/herself in a socially desirable way on items which are neutral with respect to sex; it can range from 1 to 7, with 1 indicating a strong tendency to describe oneself in a socially undesirable direction and 7 indicating a strong tendency to describe oneself in a socially desirable direction.

P S Y C H O M E T R I C   A N A L Y S E S

The BSRI was administered to 444 male and 279 female introductory psychology students at Stanford University, and to 117 male and 77 female paid volunteers at Foothill Junior College. Their data represent the normative data for the BSRI and serve as the basis for all of the analyses which follow.

INTERNAL CONSISTENCY

In order to estimate the internal consistency of the BSRI, coefficient alpha was calculated separately for the Masculinity, Femininity and Social Desirability scores of the subjects in both normative samples (Nunnally, 1967). The results showed all three scores to be highly reliable, both in the Stanford sample (Masculinity $\alpha=0.86$; Femininity $\alpha=0.80$; Social Desirability $\alpha=0.75$), and in the Foothill sample (0.86, 0.82 and 0.70 respectively). Because the reliability of the Androgyny *t*-ratio could not be calculated directly, coefficient alpha was computed for the highly correlated Androgyny difference score (Femininity–Masculinity), and was found to be 0.85 for the Stanford sample and 0.86 for the Foothill sample.

RELATIONSHIP BETWEEN MASCULINITY AND FEMININITY

These are logically independent scores, and the results of the two normative samples show them to be empirically independent as well (Stanford male $r=0.11$, female $r=-0.14$; Foothill male $r=-0.02$, female $r=-0.07$).

SOCIAL DESIRABILITY RESPONSE SET

Because the masculine and feminine items are all relatively desirable, even for the 'inappropriate' sex, it is important to verify that the Androgyny score is not simply tapping a social desirability response set. Accordingly, product-moment correlations were calculated between the Social Desirability score and the Masculinity, Femininity and Androgyny scores for the two samples separately. They were also calculated between the Social Desirability score and the absolute value of the Androgyny score. The correlations are shown in Table 25.4. As expected, both Masculinity and Femininity scores were correlated with Social Desirability, while near-zero correlations between Androgyny and Social Desirability confirm that the Androgyny score is not measuring a general tendency to respond in a socially desirable direction. Rather, it is measuring a very specific tendency to describe oneself in accordance with sex-typed standards of desirable behaviour for men and women.

THE STUDY

Table 25.4

CORRELATION OF MASCULINITY, FEMININITY, AND ANDROGYNY WITH SOCIAL DESIRABILITY

Sample	Masculinity with social desirability		Femininity with social desirability		Androgyny with social desirability		|Androgyny| with social desirability	
Stanford	0.42	0.19	0.28	0.26	0.12	0.03	0.08	−0.10
Foothill	0.23	0.19	0.15	0.15	−0.07	0.06	−0.12	−0.09
Stanford and Foothill combined	0.38	0.19	0.28	0.22	0.08	0.04	0.03	−0.10

TEST–RETEST RELIABILITY

The BSRI was administered for a second time to 28 males and 28 females from the Stanford normative sample, approximately four weeks after the first. Subjects were told we were interested in how their responses on the test might vary over time, and more explicitly instructed not to try to remember how they had responded originally. Product-moment correlations were calculated between the first and second administrations for all four scores which all proved to be highly reliable (Masculinity, $r=0.90$; Femininity, $r=0.90$; Androgyny, $r=0.93$; Social Desirability, $r=0.89$).

Table 25.5

CORRELATION OF THE MASCULINITY–FEMININITY SCALES OF THE CALIFORNIA PSYCHOLOGICAL INVENTORY (CPI) AND GUILFORD-ZIMMERMAN SCALE WITH THE MASCULINITY, FEMININITY AND ANDROGYNY SCALES OF THE BSRI

Scale	CPI		Guilford-Zimmerman	
	Males	Females	Males	Females
BSRI Masculinity	−0.42	−0.25	0.11	0.01
BSRI Femininity	0.27	0.25	0.04	−0.06
BSRI Androgyny	0.50	−0.04	0.04	−0.06

CORRELATIONS WITH OTHER MEASURES OF MASCULINITY– FEMININITY

During the second administration of the BSRI, subjects were also asked to complete the Masculinity–Femininity scales of the California Psychological Inventory and the Guilford-Zimmerman Temperament Survey, both of which have been used quite often in previous research on sex roles. As can be seen from Table 25.5, the Guilford-Zimmerman scale is not at all correlated with any of the Masculinity, Femininity and Androgyny scales of the BSRI, whereas the California Psychological Inventory is moderately correlated with all three. The reason for this difference is

Table 25.6

THE STUDY

Sex Differences on the BSRI

Scale score	Stanford University			Foothill Junior College		
	Males (n = 444)	Females (n = 279)	t	Males (n = 117)	Females (n = 77)	t
Masculinity						
M	4.97	4.57		4.96	4.55	
SD	0.67	0.69	7.62*	0.71	0.75	3.86*
Femininity						
M	4.44	5.01		4.62	5.08	
SD						
Social desirability						
M	4.91	5.08		4.88	4.89	
SD	0.50	0.50	4.40*	0.50	0.53	ns
Androgyny t-ratio						
M	−1.28	1.10		−0.80	1.23	
SD	1.99	2.29	14.33*	2.23	2.42	5.98*
Androgyny difference score						
M	−0.53	0.43		−0.34	0.53	
SD	0.82	0.93	14.28*	0.97	0.97	6.08*

* $p < 0.001$.

not clear, but the fact that none of the correlations is particularly high indicates that the BSRI is measuring an aspect of sex roles which is not directly tapped by either of these other two scales.

N O R M S

Table 25.6 presents the mean Masculinity, Femininity and Social Desirability scores separately by sex for both normative samples, together with means for both the Androgyny *t*-ratio and the Androgyny difference score. As can be seen, males scored significantly higher than females on the Masculinity scale, and females scored significantly higher than males on the Femininity scale, in both samples. On the two measures of Androgyny, males scored on the masculine side of zero, and females on the feminine side; this difference is significant in both samples and for both measures. On the Social Desirability scale, females scored higher than males at Stanford, but not at Foothill; however, this sex difference is quite small, even at Stanford.

Table 25.7 shows the percentage of subjects within each normative sample who qualified as masculine, feminine or androgynous as a function of the Androgyny *t*-ratio. Subjects are classified as sex-typed (whether masculine or feminine) if the

.Table 25.7

Percentage of Subjects in the Normative Samples Classified as Masculine, Feminine and Androgynous

Item	Stanford University		Foothill Junior College	
	Males ($n = 444$)	Females ($n = 279$)	Males ($n = 117$)	Females ($n = 77$)
% feminine ($t \geqslant 2.025$)	6	34	9	40
% near feminine ($1 < t < 2.025$)	5	20	9	8
% androgynous ($-1 \leqslant t \leqslant +1$)	34	27	4	38
% near masculine ($-2.205 < t < -1$)	19	12	17	7
% masculine ($t \leqslant -2.205$)	36	8	22	8

THE STUDY

Androgyny t-ratio reaches statistical significance ($|t|^2 2.025$, *d.f.*=38, $p<0.05$), and as androgynous if the absolute value of the t-ratio is $^3 1.00$. Table 25.7 also shows the percentage of subjects who fall between these various cut-off points.

CONCLUDING COMMENT

Hopefully, the development of the BSRI will encourage investigators in the area of sex differences and sex roles to question the traditional assumption that it is the sex-typed individual who typified mental health, and to begin focusing on the behavioural and societal consequences of more flexible sex-role self-concepts. In a society where rigid sex-role differentiation has already outlived its usefulness, perhaps the androgynous person will come to define a more human standard of psychological health.

EVALUATION

Theoretical issues

As we saw in **Background and context** above, the BSRI made it possible to measure androgyny by logically and empirically separating scores on masculinity and femininity: it comprises two *independent* scales. For large samples (male and female), the mean score on masculinity is higher for males and the mean score for femininity is higher for females (the scales really do differentiate the sexes). Where all participants are either male or female, individual masculinity and femininity scales are *uncorrelated*, which means the two dimensions are empirically/factually (and not just logically) independent (Brown, 1986).

According to the concept of androgyny, women were no longer expected or encouraged to restrict their behaviours to traditional gender-role-specific traits. Bem (1977), together with other feminist psychologists (e.g. Maracek, 1978), prescribed androgyny as a liberating force, leading women to fuller lives. However, while clearly an improvement over the traditional view that masculinity and femininity are opposites and mutually exclusive, the androgynous perspective still maintains that personality comprises feminine and masculine elements. Further, it implies that feminine and masculine elements are *equivalent*, when, in fact, masculine traits are more highly valued (Doyle & Paludi, 1991). As Hare-Mustin & Maracek (1988) argue:

> . . . when the idea of counterparts implies symmetry and equivalence, it obscures differences in power and social value . . . Arguing for no differences between women and men, however, draws attention away from women's

special needs and from differences in power and resources between women and men.

So, while the concept of androgyny is in some ways very radical, it retains aspects of the traditional view: masculinity and femininity are still implicitly seen as inherent characteristics of individuals, rather than socially determined categories. This focus on individuals (who may be androgynous regardless of biological sex or gender) detracts from considering women's special needs, and social and political inequalities between gender groups (Paludi, 1992).

Bem herself seems to have taken some of these criticisms into account in her later work (see discussion of *gender schema theory* in **Applications and implications** below). For example, in 1981 she wrote:

> . . . the concept of androgyny is insufficiently radical from a feminist perspective because it continues to presuppose that there is a masculine and a feminine within us all, that is, that the concepts of masculine and feminine have an independent and palpable reality rather than being themselves cognitive constructs derived from gender based schematic processing. A focus on the concept of androgyny thus fails to prompt serious examination of the extent to which gender organizes both our perceptions and our social world.

Eichler (1980, cited in Wetherell, 1997) saw androgyny as a meaningless ideal. If our society was actually androgynous, the concept itself would not exist, because sex (apart from its strictly biological sense) would be considered an irrelevant variable and defunct as a term of reference for social organization. It is illogical to aim towards achieving androgyny while simultaneously regarding it as the combination of highly desirable feminine and masculine qualities. While conceding this point, Bem's gender schema theory implies that gender conventions persist because they are internalized by individuals. Wetherell (1997) suggests an alternative interpretation, namely, that they persist because of their role in the reproduction of 'patriarchical social forms'. She argues that Bem's type of social psychology has effectively *decontextualized* sex: gender identity in the BSRI is viewed in the abstract, quite independent of the situations to which they might relate. In effect, a set of 'imaginary identities' is produced: the stereotypes or social consensus reflected by a small group of students become, in the BSRI, reified into a normative standard, invariant across contexts, culture or history.

> . . . Bem's attempt to discover gender as a literal state rather than to treat it as a metaphorical device could thus serve to bolster up the very ideological practice she hoped to defuse (through the concept of androgyny) . . . (Wetherell, 1997)

In other words, the BSRI, as with other psychometric tests (whether of personality or intelligence) claims to show what people are 'like'. The human 'subject' is unitary, coherent, consistent across situations, an 'individual' separated from, but influenced by, the rest of society. The BSRI encourages the view that androgyny, femininity and masculinity are built-in traits which one either has or doesn't have:

This impression, however, is an illusion . . . A snapshot of a constrained either/or type of response at one moment in time is generalised to become a permanent psychological feature . . . (Wetherell, 1997)

Methodological issues

Although the BSRI is the most widely used measure of sex-role stereotyping in adults (Hargreaves, 1986), and probably the most popular modern socio-psychological method for measuring gender identity (Wetherell, 1997), is not the only test of androgyny. Quite independently of Bem, Spence *et al.* (1975) devised the *'Personal Attributes Questionnaire'* (PAQ), which comprises instrumental (masculine) and expressive (feminine) trait terms (largely derived from the stereotypes described by Broverman *et al.*, 1972), which produces two essentially independent scores.

However, the PAQ did not assess androgyny in the same way as the BSRI, and this underlined a major problem with the BSRI, to do with the very concept of androgyny itself. By defining androgyny as the student *t*-ratio for the difference between a person's masculinity and femininity scores, Bem (unwittingly, of course) allowed for the *same* androgyny score (*t*-ratio of near zero) to be obtained in two very *different* ways: either by an individual who scores *high* on both scales or *low* on both. But surely two such individuals are likely to be very different kinds of people, in which case what do their same androgyny scores mean? (Note that what Bem calls the *t*-ratio is what is more commonly referred to as, simply, the *t*-test statistic.). By contrast, PAQ allowed for four cateogires of persons:

(*i*)   the highly sex-typed male: *high* masculinity, low femininity;
(*ii*) the highly sex-typed female: low masculinity, *high* femininity;
(*iii*) the androgynous person: *high* masculinity *and high* femininity;
(*iv*) the 'undifferentiated' person: *low* masculinity *and low* femininity.

The crucial difference is that Bem did not distinguish between (*iii*) and (*iv*); she confounded them. Consequently, she compared her original (1974) results with those of Spence *et al.* and concluded that the four categories (2×2) was superior: androgyny was now defined as only *high in both* masculinity and femininity (not low in both too). Her revised, and shortened, version of the BSRI (1977) is considered to be equivalent to PAQ (Lubinski *et al.*, 1983).

Hargreaves *et al.* (1981) believe this four-way classification produces its own difficulties (e.g. the loss of information when participants are divided into groups on the basis of median splits). They proposed that androgyny is most economically assessed as the *product* of an individual's masculinity and femininity scores: they are conceptually distinct but *interacting* variables (Hargreaves, 1986).

Subsequent research

Does the research evidence support the predictions made on the basis of the BSRI? Essentially, there are two: (*i*) scores on the BSRI will predict certain kinds of behaviour preference; and (*ii*) androgyny is a good predictor of psychological well-being/mental health.

(*i*)   Bem's research strategy is to assess sex-typing by means of the BSRI, then to relate this to behaviour in real-life situations. For example, Bem & Lenney (1976) asked participants to indicate which of a series of paired activities they would prefer to perform, for payment, while being photographed. Twenty activities were stereotypically masculine (e.g. nail two boards together), 20 were stereotypically feminine (e.g. iron cloth napkins) and 20 were neutral (e.g. play with a yo-yo). Sex-typed participants expressed a clear preference for sex-appropriate as opposed to sex-inappropriate activities, even though such choices paid less money than cross sex-typed activities.

(*ii*) Bem (1975) found that androgynous individuals show sex-role adaptability across situations, that is, they will behave as the situation requires, even though this means behaving in a sex-inappropriate way. Lubinski *et al.* (1981) reported that they express greater subjective feelings of emotional well-being, and Spence *et al.* (1975) found that they show higher levels of self-esteem. However, it is by no means clear that androgyny is a good predictor of psychological well-being. In fact, a review by Taylor & Hall (1982) suggests that masculinity in both males *and* females may be a *better* predictor than certain measures of androgyny, and Taylor (1986) makes the point that traditional sex roles are, on the whole, advantageous for men but disadvantageous for women. Spender (1980) has called the general tendency for 'masculine' attributes and occupations to be valued, while 'feminine' ones are derogated or downgraded, the 'plus male, minus female' phenomenon. According to Hefner *et al.* (1975, quoted in Taylor, 1986):

> . . . both men and women are trapped in the prisons of gender . . . but the situation is far from symmetrical; men are the oppressors and women are the oppressed.

Psychological well-being (measured by, for example, self-esteem, adjustment, relative absence of anxiety, depression, and psychosomatic symptoms) is generally more strongly related to masculinity than femininity on the BSRI, and seems not to distinguish reliably between sex-typed and androgynous individuals (Taylor, 1986).

The BSRI does distinguish between male and female test-takers (Bem, 1974, 1977), as does the PAQ (Spence & Helmreich, 1978; Storms, 1979); although the differences in means are usually small, they are significant. As might be predicted, when samples of gays (at the University of Texas) were compared with unselected male students, the former were found to be significantly lower on masculinity and higher on femininity, and the reverse pattern was found for lesbians, using PAQ (Spence & Helmreich, 1978). Larson (1981) found similar results using the BSRI.

However, Pedhazur & Tetenbaum (1979), after carrying out a large-scale factor analysis of BSRI scores, found that masculinity and femininity emerged as a distinct factor, independent of instrumentality and expressiveness. It seems that the relationship between these two temperaments and the popular understanding of masculinity and femininity is slight (Brown, 1986), and, as a result of the study, Bem dropped the latter from her revised, shorter BSRI (1977). PAQ had never included them.

So, what do PAQ and the BSRI really measure? According to Spence (1983), they primarily measure instrumentality and expressiveness, and can no longer legitimately be characterized by the all-encompassing 'masculinity' and 'femininity'. It follows that androgyny is also inappropriate, and any attempt to link mental health with androgyny should be much more cautious, linking socially desirable instrumentality/ expressiveness with, mainly, high self-esteem. Clifton *et al.* (1976) have shown that, if people are asked to give descriptions of various types of woman (carer, bunny, athlete, housewife, club), then only the image for 'housewife' matches that for femininity (using the BSRI). This illustrates the narrow realm from which Bem's gender stereotypes are drawn (Wetherell, 1997).

Applications and implications

During the 1980s, Bem (e.g.1984) reformulated her ideas as *gender schema theory*. Schemas are the internal (mental) conceptual frameworks an individual builds up, through past experience, which impose some order on the world, making an otherwise overwhelming range of apparently diverse events and objects predictable. In our everyday lives, we perceive the world *through* these schemas, such that the world as we know it is composed of the categories represented by our schemas (Edley & Wetherell, 1995).

The male/female distinction is one of the most important classification systems in human social life (Bem, 1987). The social world that children grow up in is thoroughly gendered and gender differentiation is everywhere imposed from 'outside' (toys, clothes, hairstyles, socialization practices, the media, and so on). Consequently, children soon learn to interpret their experiences through this same set of categories, including, importantly, their own sense of self. However, Bem proposes that not all children do this to the same degree. While some see themselves as entirely defined by a particular gender category (so that self and gender are almost synonymous), others imagine there to be at least some degree of difference between self and one's gender. Clearly, the former are strongly sex-typed compared with the latter (as measured by the BSRI).

Bem believes that the BSRI and PAQ *are* adequate measures of sex-typing and androgyny. Sex-typing essentially involves spontaneously thinking of things in sex-typed terms, whereas androgyny is a disposition to process information in accordance with relevant non-sex principles. In deciding whether a particular attribute on the BSRI is (not) self-descriptive, the sex-typed person does not reflect on individual behaviour, but quickly 'looks up' the attribute in his/her gender schemas, and responds accordingly. The essential difference between these two kinds of people is one of *cognitive* style. It no longer seems reasonable to expect androgynous *behaviour* in a sex-typed culture to be a mode of mental health, but Bem still believes that information-processing freed of the tyranny of sex-typing (i.e. androgyny) is desirable (Brown, 1986).

Another important qualification that should be made of the concept of androgyny is related to *age*. Hyde & Phillis (1979) gave the BSRI to 13- to 85-year-olds, and Sinnot (1982) tested a large sample of 60- to 90-year-olds (comparing them with Bem's 1974 student sample). Both studies found some evidence of reduced sex-typing in older men, who were likely to be more androgynous, less masculine and more feminine than younger men. But in older women, sex-typing was stronger. Sinnott also found that androgyny was generally associated with better physical and mental health (based mainly on self-reports), compared with highly sex-typed females and undifferentiated individuals. Allowing for income differences, masculinity scores were also overall associated with good mental health (Taylor, 1986).

Finally, what would be the consequences of Bem's goal of an androgynous society? If a society were to give meaning to behaviour in a way which ignored the actor's gender, the very notions of masculinity and femininity would cease to have significance (as we noted earlier). To the extent that we are currently able to specify the limits of masculinity and femininity, then we are able to measure androgyny. As Bem (1979) says:

> When androgyny becomes a reality, the *concept* of androgyny will have been transcended.

Archer & Lloyd (1985) seriously doubt that there will ever be an androgynous society, because some form of group differentiation seems essential to human social organization. Early gender awareness aids the child in organizing the social world, and reflects the child's understanding of it. Gender awareness arises partly through interaction with adults in his/her society, who are themselves moulded by their membership of gender groups. Nurture becomes second nature, and, as Bem herself argues, gender identity becomes an important schema in mental life. At the same time, Archer and Lloyd advocate that changes in the *content* of gender roles (and that of gender stereotypes) will continue as they have over the last 50 years. But they firmly expect gender categories to continue to exist in some form.

One such change may occur in relation to women's occupational roles, particularly in professional occupations. According to Nicolson (2000):

. . . The dilemma for many professional women is how to negotiate and give meaning to their sense of femininity and gender identity in the world of power and intellect, when that world has defined them as outside the main professional arena.

In order to survive in senior roles, women need to (re)claim their *right* to the world of intellect, power, and authority denied to them under social practices that define the normal woman as 'emotional', 'nurturing', and 'passive'. Being child-bearers, as well as child-carers, women who aspire to traditionally male occupational status run the risk of either being seen as 'unfeminine' (they have to 'toughen up' to succeed in male strongholds: Nicolson, 2000) or having to make terribly difficult choices between family and career which men do not have to face – except perhaps the few truly androgynous ones! (See Chapter 17.)

Exercises

1. Why was it important to have an equal number of male and female judges when deciding on items for the BSRI?

2. What level of measurement is used by the BSRI?

3. What is meant by the 'internal consistency' of a psychological test? What is it a measure of?

4. In the assessment of test–retest reliability, why was it important that participants didn't remember their answers on the original test?

5. The Pearson product-moment correlation was used to measure the degree of test–retest reliability:

   (*i*) is it parametric or non-parametric?
   (*ii*) what is the other most commonly used test of correlation?

6. When the BSRI scores are correlated with scores on the CPI and Guilford-Zimmerman Temperament Survey, the validity of the BSRI is being assessed.

   (*i*) What kind of validity is it?
   (*ii*) Name the other main kinds.

7. Can you name a famous test of personality which has a Social Desirability Scale built into it?

8. Explain why it is important to have a set of normative data for any psychological test, as in Table 25.6 (page 483).

26 Black is beautiful: a reexamination of racial preference and identification

Joseph Hraba and Geoffrey Grant (1970)

Journal of Personality and Social Psychology, 16 (3), 398–402

BACKGROUND AND CONTEXT

As the title makes clear, this study is concerned with racial (or ethnic) preference and identification, which are both related to *ethnic awareness.* These are, in turn, related to other aspects of social development, in particular racial/ethnic prejudice and discrimination, and self-esteem. The study represents the interaction (at the level of the individual) between the developmental and social aspects of ethnic awareness and these related processes: how do prejudice and discrimination (usually discussed as part of social psychology) affect the *self-perception* (including self-esteem) of members of minority groups?

Regarding *ethnic awareness,* by age four to five, children can make basic discriminations (such as black and white), and during the next few years more difficult ones (such as Anglo-American and Hispanic). By eight or nine, they understand that ethnic identity remains constant despite age changes or superficial attributes such as clothing. *Ethnic idenitity* involves awareness of one's own ethnicity and closely parallels developing awareness of others' ethnicity. It has been assessed mainly by using dolls or photos and asking children to point to one that looks most like them. Generally, children of four and over choose appropriately, although this is not always the case (Aboud, 1988).

Ethnic preference (measured, for example, by children's choice of a doll or photo that they would like to play with) is the main concern of the present study.

According to Phinney (1990), a child's construction of an ethnic identity involves several components. *Self-identification* refers to the ethnic label a child applies to itself (and corresponds to ethnic identity above), while *evaluative attitude* refers to the child's feelings (positive or negative) about being a member of a particular group (related to ethnic preference). A *sense of belonging* and *ethnic involvement* refer to having strong bonds with and participating in the social life/cultural practices of one's ethnic group respectively.

Most is known about self-identification and evaluative attitude, and most of the research has involved African-American children's self-concept. Starting with studies by the African-American couple Kenneth and Mamie Clark (1939, 1947), research up to the 1960s showed that black American children compared themselves unfavourably to whites and grow up feeling 'inferior'. Attitudes held by the majority towards one's ethnic group seemed to be consistently reflected in the child's developing attitude towards itself: the concept of *self-hatred* was even used to describe how such children reacted to the prejudice and discrimination they experienced (Allport, 1954).

> . . . it is no wonder that children from minority groups become highly self-conscious about their status. Belonging to a particular social group, and being able to define oneself in terms of that group, may have many advantages for a child, but when that group is subject to adverse discrimination and is looked down upon by the rest of society there may be unfortunate consequences for the way in which children define and evaluate themselves. (Schaffer, 1996)

While the idea of self-hatred originated in attempts to explain the characteristics of the Jewish community in the USA (Lewin, 1935, 1941), it has survived in the form of 'black negative self-identity'. It has stimulated a mass of research, with doll studies being the most popular. But despite the long history of research in this field, there is little conclusive evidence regarding what exactly constitutes an identity problem in the black child (Owusu-Bempah & Howitt, 2000: see **Theoretical issues** below).

According to Social Identity theory (see Chapter 12), a major need in a competitive society like ours is to understand the complexity of the social world and locate oneself at an acceptable station within it. Identification with a particular childhood category membership is a highly desirable goal. While negative racial attitudes may fulfil this function for the majority-group child in a multi-racial society, by definition they cannot do so for the minority group. This can be seen in the phenomenon of *misidentification* (black children choosing a white doll when asked to select one that looks like them), as demonstrated by Clark and Clark in their doll studies.

On the basis of these studies (among other things), the USA anti-segregationist movement influenced the US Supreme Court's 1954 decision that school segregation (educational apartheid) was not only detrimental to black children, but also unlawful. In the history of post-Second World War race relations, this was an event of monumental importance, and has to be classed as one of psychology's major (vicarious) achievements (regardless of the adequacy or otherwise of the doll studies generally) (Owusu-Bempah & Howitt, 2000).

This *self-denigration* by minority groups was addressed by civil rights and black politico-cultural movements in the USA during and beyond the 1960s, encouraging a positive connotation about blackness. This was captured in slogans such as 'Black is Beautiful'.

THE AIM AND NATURE OF THE STUDY

The study is a replication ('duplication') of Clark and Clark's (1939) famous 'doll study', which provided a means of assessing ethnic preference and identification that served as a blueprint for much subsequent research (Bennett *et al.*, 1991). (Note that their 1947 study is perhaps the more commonly cited of the two and is referred to in the introduction. However, Table 26.1 (page 497) makes it clear that Hraba and Grant's study is a replication of the 1939 study.)

The *independent variable* is the child's ethnic group membership ('race'), namely, white or black, with the latter being sub-divided into light, medium or dark. Participants are *selected* for these characteristics (race cannot, of course, be *manipulated*) and, by the same token, they cannot be randomly allocated to different conditions. So the method involved is a quasi-experiment (rather than a true experiment).

There are several *dependent variables*. Three of these were the ones assessed by Clark and Clark in the original study: racial preference (as measured by items 1–4: Give me the doll that you want to play with/Give me the doll that is a nice doll/Give me the doll that looks bad/Give me the doll that is a nice colour); racial awareness (as measured by items 5–7: Give me the doll that looks like a white child/Give me the doll that looks like a coloured child/Give me the doll that looks like a Negro child); racial self-identification (as measured by item 8: Give me the doll that looks like you). In addition, Hraba and Grant tried to identify the behavioural consequences of racial preference and identification by asking the children (and their teachers) to name and indicate the race of their best friends.

Asking children to choose a white or black doll is called a *forced-choice technique* (see **Evaluation** for criticism of this).

Hraba and Grant made two comparisons: (a) between their (Lincoln) sample with Clark and Clark's sample (this constitutes the basic replication); (b) between black and white children in the Lincoln sample, with whites providing a bench mark. The main findings were that, unlike the Clarks' sample, most of the black children preferred black dolls, just as the majority of the white children showed same-race preferences.

THE STUDY

> This study examined the racial preferences of black children in an interra-
> cial setting. The Clark and Clark doll study was duplicated in Lincoln,
> Nebraska, during May, 1969. Unlike the Clarks, the present authors found
> that the majority of the black children preferred the black dolls. Like the
> blacks, the majority of the white children preferred the doll of their own
> race. The racial identifications of both black and white children are

reported. Furthermore, the effects of age and skin colour upon racial preference and identification are compared with those reported by Clark and
Clark. A control for the race of interviewers showed that this variable did
not have a significant effect upon the dependent variable. The correspondence between doll choice and friendship was ambiguous. Interpretations of
all the results are given.

THE STUDY

Clark and Clark (1947) found that black children preferred white dolls and rejected
black dolls when asked to choose which were nice, which looked bad, which they
would like to play with, and which were a nice colour. This implies that black is not
beautiful.

This observation has been repeated, using a variety of methods and in a variety of
settings (Asher & Allen, 1969; Frenkel-Brunswik, 1948; Goodman, 1952; Greenwald
& Oppenheim, 1968; Landreth & Johnson, 1953; Morland, 1958, 1966; Radke, Trager,
& Davis, 1949; Trager & Yarrow, 1952).

However, Gregor and McPherson (1966) found that Southern, urban black children,
6 and 7 years old, generally preferred a black doll. Their procedures were identical
to Clark and Clark's, except only two dolls were presented. They proposed that
black children's preference for white stems from their contact with whites;
" . . . Negro children tend to be more outgroup oriented the more systematically
they are exposed to white contact." Clark and Clark did find that black children in
interracial nursery schools were more pronounced in their prefernce for white dolls
than those in segregated nursery schools. However, Morland (1966), using a picture
technique, found just the opposite.

Still, Clark, Clark and Goodman (1952), when using similar techniques, found that
black children in interracial settings preferred objects representing whites.
However, Johnson (1966) found 18 black youths (mean age of 12) in a Harlem
freedom school rated black equal to white. He concluded that his "study presents
evidence that not all Negroes have negative self-attitudes . . .". Perhaps, but the
techniques used by Johnson and Clark and Clark differ. Johnson had groups of
respondents rate black and white on four semantic differential scales. Furthermore,
the samples are not comparable on age and social setting. Possibly techniques,
sampling, and attitudes are confounded in a comparison of these two studies.

The thesis that for black children interracial contact engenders preference for
white cannot be overlooked in this literature. Some have advocated this interpretation (Gregor, 1963; Armstrong & Gregor, 1964; Gregor & McPherson, 1966). Unfortunately, any comparison of the evidence confounds time, techniques, sampling,
and setting with the dependent variable. The present study will test this thesis in an
interracial setting by duplicating the Clark and Clark doll study.

METHOD

PROCEDURE

The procedures used by Clark and Clark were followed as closely as possible. The respondents were interviewed individually using a set of four dolls, two black and two white, identical in all other respects. The same items used by the Clarks were used. They are as follows:

1. Give me the doll that you want to play with.
2. Give me the doll that is a nice doll.
3. Give me the doll that looks bad.
4. Give me the doll that is a nice colour.
5. Give me the doll that looks like a white child.
6. Give me the doll that looks like a coloured child.
7. Give me the doll that looks like a Negro child.
8. Give me the doll that looks like you.

Clark and Clark claimed that Items 1–4 measure racial preference, Items 5–7 measure racial awareness or knowledge, and Item 8 measures racial self-identification.

In an attempt to identify the behavioural consequences of racial preference and identification, we asked the children to name and indicate the race of their best friends. We also asked the teachers for the same information.

SAMPLE

Respondents were 4–8 years of age. Five public schools provided a sampling frame containing 73% of the correct age black children in the public school system of Lincoln, Nebraska. The total sample consisted of 160 children, 89 blacks, or 60% of the eligible blacks attending Lincoln public schools. The 71 white children were drawn randomly from the classrooms containing black respondents. The interviews were completed at the five schools during May 1969.

Previous research has controlled for race of interviewer (Asher & Allen, 1969; Morland, 1966). Although Morland reported that race of interviewer does not significantly affect respondents' choices, we controlled for race of interviewer by assigning the respondents to both black and white interviewers.

SETTING

Blacks comprise approximately 1.4% of the total population of Lincoln. The five public schools reflected this fact. Blacks accounted for 3% of the enrollment of three schools, and 7% and 18% of the other two schools. Furthermore, 70% of the black sample reported that they had white friends.

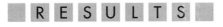

R E S U L T S

RACIAL PREFERENCE

The Clarks' finding that the majority of the black children preferred a white doll has been interpreted that they would rather be white. This was one of the Clarks' important findings and is the focus of this paper.

Table 26.1

A COMPARISON OF THE PRESENT RESULTS WITH THE CLARK AND CLARK (1939) DATA

Item	Clark & Clark[a] (1939) blacks	Lincoln sample (1969) blacks	χ^2 (1939–1969) blacks	Lincoln sample (1969) whites
1 (Play with)				
White doll	67 (169)	30 (27)	36.2**	83 (59)
Black doll	32 (83)	70 (62)		16 (11)
Don't know/ no response				1 (1)
2 (Nice doll)				
White doll	59 (150)	46 (41)	5.7*	70 (50)
Black doll	38 (97)	54 (48)		30 (21)
3 (Looks bad)				
White doll	17 (42)	61 (54)	43.5**	34 (24)
Black doll	59 (149)	36 (32)		63 (45)
Don't know/ no response		3 (3)		3 (2)
4 (Nice colour)				
White doll	60 (151)	31 (28)	23.1**	48 (34)
Black doll	38 (96)	69 (61)		49 (35)
Don't know/ no response				3 (2)

Note: Data in percentages. *N*s (number of participants) in brackets.
[a] Individuals failing to make either choice not included, hence some percentages add to less than 100.
* $p < 0.02$.
** $p < 0.001$.

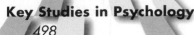

THE STUDY

Table 26.1 provides two comparisons. First, the differences in racial preference of the Clark and Clark (1939) sample and the Lincoln sample of 1969 are striking. On all the items the difference reaches statistical significance using chi-square.

Secondly, the sample of white children was collected to provide a bench mark against which to compare the racial preferences of black children. Gregor and McPherson (1966) and Morland (1966) have found that white children are more likely to prefer their own race than are black children. Table 26.1 shows that black and white children preferred the doll of their own race. The white children were significantly more ethnocentric on Items 1 and 2, there was no significant difference on Item 3, and the black children were significantly more ethnocentric on Item 4 using chi-square.

Age. The Clarks found that black children preferred white dolls at all ages (3–7), although this decreased with age. We found that a majority of the black children at all ages (3–8) preferred a black doll, and this preference increased with age. With white children there was a similar age trend except on Item 4.

Skin colour. The Clarks classified their subjects by skin colour into three categories: light (practically white), medium (light brown to dark brown), and dark (dark brown to black). The same criteria were used here. The Clarks found that the children of light skin colour showed the greatest preference for the white doll and the dark children the least. We did not find this trend. The light-skinned children were at least as strong in their preference for a black doll as the others.

RACIAL IDENTIFICATION

Items 5–7 measured knowledge of racial differences, while Item 8 measured racial self-identification. On Items 5 and 6 the Clarks found that a majority of their respondents correctly identified white and "coloured " dolls (94% and 93%, respectively). Our black sample was comparable. 90 % correctly identified a white doll and 94% correctly identified a coloured doll. On Item 7, more of our respondents made the correct identification (86% compared with 72%).

Age. Like the Clarks, we found an inverse relationship between misidentification (Items 5–8) and age. This relationship also held for whites.

Skin colour. Like the Clarks, we found insignificant differences in misidentification (Items 5–7) among black children by skin colour. However, on Item 8 the Clarks had found that more black children with light skin colour misidentified themselves (80%). Adding a mulatto [mixed race/offspring of white and black parents] doll, Greenwald and Oppenheim (1968) reduced the misidentification for these respondents to 11%. Fifteen per cent of our black respondents with light skin colour misidentified themselves. However, there was no significant difference in misidentification on Item 8 by skin colour.

Race of interviewer. Race of interviewer was not related to choice of doll on any of the items for both black and white children.

Race of respondents' friends. For both black and white children there was no apparent relationship between doll preference and race of friends. The sociometric information agreed and were combined. If a relationship were to be found, it would be most pronounced for those who preferred dolls of their own race without exception. Furthermore, only these respondents showed reliability in their doll preferences. 23 black and 20 white children made the choices favourable to their own race on all 4 items (1–4).

Even for these children there appears to be no relationship between doll preference and race of friends. Twenty (87%) of the 23 black children had white friends. Twelve (60%) of the 20 white children had all white friends. However, 41% of all white children had all white friends.

D I S C U S S I O N

DOLL PREFERENCE

These results indicate that black children in interracial settings are not necessarily white oriented. We will offer possible interpretations. First, times may be changing. That is, Negroes are becoming Blacks proud of their race. If change is occurring, previous research indicates that it is not at a universal rate across the country (Asher & Allen, 1969; Gregor & McPherson, 1966).

A second interpretation is that even 30 years ago black children in Lincoln, unlike those in other cities, would have chosen black dolls. This interpretation cannot be examined. A third and more reasonable interpretation is that conditions indigenous to Lincoln have mediated the impact of the "Black Movement". Johnson (1966) suggested that local organizations in black communities disseminate black pride. During the past two years a black pride campaign, sponsored by organizations which are black conscious, has been directed at adolescents and young adults in Lincoln. Black children through interaction with kin and friends may be modelling these attitudes.

The fourth interpretation is that interracial contact may engender black pride. Pettigrew (1967) proposed that interracial acceptance mediated the effect of interracial contact on the academic performance of blacks. Perhaps it influences black pride. The fact that 70% of the black sample had white friends and 59% of the white sample had black friends, given the racial composition of the schools, suggests this interpretation.

DOLL PREFERENCE AND FRIENDSHIP

The above interpretations have assumed that doll choice corresponds with interpersonal behaviour. Our findings suggest that such correspondence cannot be presumed. Three explanations of the lack of relationship between doll choice and friendship will be offered. They are predicated on two assumptions, one about the doll technique and the other about the meaning of "Black is beautiful".

The first explanation assumes that children will use the same criteria in friendship and doll choice. "Black is beautiful" is assumed to mean a rejection of whites. Combining these two assumptions, we expected those black children who without exception preferred black dolls to have all black friends. This expectation was not realized. However, being pupils of predominantly white schools, these respondents may have found it impractical to have all black friends despite their preferences.

The second explanation makes the same assumption about the doll technique, but it assumes that "Black is beautiful" translates into an acceptance of and by whites. Combining these we expected black children who without exception preferred black dolls to have both black and white friends. This expectation was nearly realized. More black children who had friends of both races preferred black dolls (except on Item 4) than those who had all black friends. This relationship approached statistical significance.

The third explanation does not assume doll choice corresponds with interpersonal behaviour. First, in the experimental setting, four dolls which were identical except for race, were presented to the respondent. Although black children may prefer a doll of their own race when race is the only cue that differentiates it from other dolls, they may consider other criteria more important in friendship. Perhaps race is not salient in friendship at this age (Criswell, 1937; Moreno, 1934). Secondly, Piaget has observed that children before 11 or 12 years of age cannot detect conceptual self-contradictions (Hunt, 1961; Maier, 1969). The fact that a majority of the respondents who were consistent in their choice on the four preference items (1–4) did not clearly reflect the bases for their doll preferences in their friendships suggests this possibility. Furthermore, the fact that a majority (73%) of all the respondents were inconsistent on Items 1–4 supports this suggestion.

EVALUATION

Theoretical issues

As we noted in **Background and context**, the Hraba and Grant study is really concerned with the self-perception of minority group children within the context of a racist society. One aspect of self-perception is self-esteem, the value or worth that an individual attaches to him or herself.

According to Wilson (1978), despite the 'Black is beautiful' revolution, American racism remains, as evidenced by the continuing preference for white, including 'belief in its inherent rightness and the hatred of black and belief in its inherent wrongness'.

In the USA, the Joint Commission on Mental Health of Children (1970) published a report indicating that discrimination can have damaging effects on the psychological adjustment and self-esteem of young children and adolesecents. In particular, through racial prejudice, the black child is subjected to derogatory views and negative self-images. As an early experience, this provides for the child's growing knowledge of how the black American is viewed (Powell-Hopson & Hopson, 1992).

According to Gopaul-McNichol (1992):

> . . . The total volume of what enters into the formation of attitudes by way of social inheritance is much greater than the child's personal experience at home . . .

However, in contradiction of this view, Schaffer (1996) maintains that:

> . . . How children make sense of their membership of a minority group is . . . not just a reflection of the majority view in their society; more immediate experiences in the family constitute a more powerful source of influence. It is thus perfectly possible for minority children to be aware of their underprivileged status in society and yet not internalize these values as part of their self-concept . . .

We need to distinguish between *group identity*, assessed by so-called preference measures indicating children's evaluation of their group, and *personal identity*, as assessed by self-esteem measures (see **Subsequent research** below).

According to Owusu-Bempah & Howitt (2000), the notions of black self-hatred and identity conflict inevitably imply that black children will typically have low self-esteem. But they claim that there is little historical or contemporary support for this, and, indeed, they claim that it is a myth. For over 20 years now, research has shown that black people's self-esteem is no different from that of white people, but still the myth lives on (see **Subsequent research** below).

Subsequent research

Milner (1975) studied five- to eight-year-old children (white, black and South Asian) in the UK, using very similar procedures to the Clarks. He used three dolls of different skin tones (white, black and South Asian), and when asked 'Which doll looks the most like you?', all the white children chose the white doll, 76% of the Asian children chose the Asian doll, while only 52% of the African-Caribbean children chose the black doll. The figures for racial misidentification were: white 0%, Asian 24%, and African-Caribbean 48%. When asked which of the dolls they would rather be, all the white children, 66% of the Asian children, and 80% of the African-Caribbean children, chose the white doll. Milner interpreted these findings as apparently showing that they would rather be white than a member of their own racial group. Essentially, the results duplicated those of the Clarks in the USA.

However, a later study (Milner, 1983) failed to find the same trend among black children, as did another UK study by Davey & Mullin (1982). These British studies, together with Hraba and Grant's American study, might have encouraged the belief that blacks growing up in a racist society could still like their race and themselves. However, further American studies gave cause for concern. For example, Powell-Hopson & Hopson (1988) studied the choices of black youngsters between black and white cabbage-patch dolls. About 66% of the black children preferred the white doll. Similar results were obtained in a study comparing children in the USA and Trinidad (Gopaul-McNichol, 1988). This last finding is particularly surprising, given that Trinidad is a predominantly black country. According to Owusu-Bempah & Howitt (2000), one obvious explanation for these contradictory findings is that the misidentification studies (including the Clarks') are seriously flawed (see **Methodological issues** below).

If racial prejudice is learnt through observation, imitation, reward for discrimination, and direct teaching (Wilson, 1978), then it should be possible to *reduce* prejudice and discrimination through these same learning processes. Powell-Hopson (1985) used the Clark and Clark doll test *plus* a treatment intervention which involved modelling, reinforcement, and learning colour meaning word associations. Based on a pre-test, the 35% of black children who chose a black doll to play with were reinforced (verbally praised) and allowed to sit up front with the researchers. The 65% who chose a white doll had to sit at the back. The researchers chose a black doll themselves and modelled pro-black responses to the preference items. A story was read depicting black children positively, and the children were asked to hold up black dolls and repeat 'pretty, nice, handsome, clean, smart, good' and 'we like these dolls the best'. The dolls were never referred to as black or white.

Later, having put the dolls away, they had to choose a doll to play with (post-test). This time, 68% chose a black doll. Only 27% of black children chose the black doll as 'looks bad' (compared with 76% on the pre-test).

While the study did *not* show that the black children wished they were white, it did indicate their awareness of society's preferences. These preferences are the result of conditioning and are susceptible to change through intervention. The use of black role models (the researchers) seemed to have a definite positive impact on children's attitudes and choices (Powell-Hopson & Hopson, 1992).

Studies which have looked specifically at black children's self-esteem, compared with white children, have produced conflicting results, as have studies looking at the relationship between racial preferences/attitudes and self-esteem (Clark, 1992). For example, McAdoo (1973, 1978) reported black children holding negative own-race attitudes ('We') but positive self-concepts ('Me'/'I'), both general and specific. Black children apparently compartmentalize their racial attitudes and prevent them from influencing self-evaluation. Similar results were reported by Rosenberg (1979).

According to Clark (1992), these results (a) raise serious doubts about the construct validity of instruments used to measure racial preference/attitude (such as the doll tests), making them poor predictors of self-concept/self-esteem (see below); (b) are contrary to the 'Black self-hatred doctrine' encouraged by so many previous studies. They contradict the belief that blacks who internalize negative racial group attitudes from the larger white society would inevitably possess negative self-evaluations (see the quote from Schaffer, 1996, above).

Moghaddam (1998) maintains that this belief arose from the research tradition pioneered by Clark and Clark (even though they were not directly testing self-esteem). Although it is possible to show a strong black doll preference and at the same time have low self-esteem, Hraba and Grant's results (which do not include a direct measure of self-esteem) are consistent with more recent research showing that ethnic minorities, as well as other minorities (including women, homosexuals, and the physically disabled) do not generally have lower self-esteem than other groups (Crocker & Major, 1989).

Methodological issues

As we noted in the **Aim and nature of the study** section above, the doll test represents a *forced-choice technique.* This technique has been criticized by several researchers (e.g. Aboud, 1988; Milner, 1981) on the following grounds:

● It fails to provide a measure of the *intensity* with which an attitude is held. When a child chooses a black doll, for example, it is unclear whether the preference is slight or very strong.

● It confounds *acceptance* of one group with *rejection* of another. If a child prefers the white doll, this does not necessarily mean he or she is rejecting the black doll. The child may marginally prefer the white (and so this is related to attitude intensity).

- It provides no indication of the *salience* of race in children's everyday social categorizations.

In connection with salience of racial categorization, Bennett *et al.* (1991) studied British 8- and 11-year-olds, both white and from a number of ethnic minorities. When asked to indicate liking/disliking for photos of children of various ethnic groups (a non-forced-choice technique), the older children showed a weaker ethnocentric bias and used a greater number of categorization strategies than the younger children. The single most important finding was the generally greater significance given to *individual* than ethnic differences among the older children (Bennett *et al.*, 1991).

Owusu-Bempah & Howitt (2000) argue that a major flaw of doll studies is the *age* of the children typically involved (four- to eight-year-olds in the Hraba and Grant study). The problem is that such young children are not capable of experiencing racial self-hatred, because they don't adequately grasp the concept of race. Indeed, what they appear to do is classify people in terms of their literal skin colour. For example, only people with very dark skin would be classified as black, while light-skinned blacks and Southern Asians would be classified as white (Alejandro-Wright, 1985). Consistent with this, in the Clark & Clark (1947) study, 20% of the light-skinned children, 73% of the medium-skinned, and 81% of the dark-skinned children said they were like the black doll. This suggests that a concept such as black self-hatred is unnecessary for explaining their doll choices, and it is not until 8–10 years that children begin to construe race in adult-related ways. The concept of race is extremely complex and socially variable, but below the age of eight it has little/no social meaning for them (Owusu-Bempah & Howitt, 2000).

Applications and implications

According to Schaffer (1996), it is primarily in adolescence that the issue of ethnic identity assumes importance and may become the focus of acute self-consciousness. The main challenge of ethnicity lies in the formation of an identity appropriate to one's group. This can cause difficulties when the group forms a social minority, and

> . . . when the child is of mixed race and, so to speak, has a foot in each camp, the strains will be even greater . . . (Schaffer, 1996)

So, while a concept of ethnic identity can be applied to all individuals, it has been studied almost exclusively as a phenomenon of relevance to ethnic minority group members, and furthermore, to be mixed race means that ethnic identity will have even greater salience.

> Mixed-race individuals have often been insultingly referred to as 'mulatto', 'half-caste' or 'half-breed', and throughout their history, mixed race children in Britain

have aroused strong feelings in the people around them. Attitudes have ranged from 'common-sense' doubt to extreme persecution, but they have never been indifferent. (Wilson, 1987, cited in Bradding, 1995)

Tizard & Phoenix (1993) studied a group of 58 14–17-year-olds, each with one white and one black (usually Caribbean) parent, all British born, living in London. Less than half thought of themselves as 'black', most of the rest describing themselves as 'mixed' or 'brown', and a few as 'more white than black'. However, these were not fixed identities: many seemed to switch back and forth between identifications often depending on the particular situation. Most resisted the pressure to be either black or white, because they felt *both*. They also did not want to alienate a parent by choosing one or other, therefore settling for something in between.

However, compared with a group both of whose parents were black, twice as many wished they were another colour. While some thought their status was interesting or exotic, others referred to the hostility they sometimes met from both blacks and whites, which confused and upset them. The stress involved in their identity formation was, thus, even greater than for the minority black group.

Despite the negative, unpleasant effects of racism encountered by this group of young people, they nonetheless seem to 'surface' during adolescence as well balanced, emotionally healthy individuals.

> Using our fairly stringent criteria, 60% of our sample were classed as having a positive racial identity . . . 20% intermediate, i.e. they expressed more anxieties about their status; 20% were considered to have a 'problematic' identity, responses indicating unhappiness and/or confusion. (Tizard & Phoenix, 1993).

The mixed race adolescent inhabits both a minority and majority society in a very complex, dynamic fashion. In terms of Social Identity theory (see Chapter 12), the extreme societal responses evoked by mixed race individuals may be due to the fact that they

> . . . strike at the very heart of a racist system. They threaten its existence by calling into question the categories upon which it is based. (Wilson, 1987, cited in Bradding, 1995)

Another group for whom racial identity is both especially salient and potentially difficult to establish are black children/adolescents growing up in a white family (*transracial placements*). Own-race adoption/fostering has been advocated as the ideal arrangement in both the USA and the UK (where the policy is fully embraced by the 1989 Children Act), but it continues to be debated, both among professionals and in the public domain (Owusu-Bempah & Howitt, 2000).

One of the arguments identified by Gill & Jackson (1983) as commonly proposed against transracial adoption is that such children will have problems identifying

themselves as either black or white, and that this confusion will induce low self-esteem. Their study of mixed race adolescent adoptees (mainly of Anglo-Asian origin) found that the overwhelming majority had no particular problems at school, most were above average ability, and many were actually amongst the most able. Both this and the Tizard and Phoenix study showed that the children had no problems recognizing the physical differences between themselves and others (they accurately identified their skin tone), just as minority children do. Overall, they were satisfied with their physical appearance and racial identity.

However, in a review of both British and American research, Rushton & Minnis (1997) conclude that transracial placements continue to be difficult because the social context is a racist one. Therefore, despite the fact that the limited research evidence tends to lend positive support for transracial placements, ethnically matched placements will be in the best interests of both the child and the community in most cases.

In order to help black children, professionals and all concerned must carefully distinguish between children's personal identity (and their 'private domain self-esteem') and their feelings about the black community in general (and their 'public domain self-esteem') (Owusu-Bempah & Howitt, 2000). They argue that:

> . . . Racism may negatively affect their perception or beliefs about their own race, but this does not automatically, nor necessarily, affect their sense of self-worth. Rather, it is their life chances which are restricted by racism . . . Institutional racism thwarts their efforts and aspirations, and very likely makes them embittered and angry. Our focus, therefore, must be on the racist system, rather than the individual psychology of the children.

But surely the problem needs to be tackled on *both* fronts. As Reicher (1999) says:

> The dangers of focusing on the systemic to the exclusion of the individual are every bit as serious as those of treating the individual to the exclusion of the systemic – and every bit as fatal to the fight against racism.

Exercises

1. What is a semantic differential (referred to just before the **Method** section)?

2. Why was it important to control for race of interviewer?

3. What does 'bench mark' mean (when referring to the sample of white children)? Why was it necessary to have a bench mark?

4. What does 'ethnocentric' mean?

5. Why should the preference for white (Clark and Clark) or black (Lincoln) dolls increase with age?

6. Regarding *Racial identification: Age*, explain what is meant by 'Like the Clarks, we found an inverse relationship between misidentification (Items 5–8) and age . . .'

7. Regarding *Racial identification: Race of respondents' friends*, explain what is meant by 'sociometric information'.

8. In the Introduction (just before **Method**, page 495), what is meant by '. . . any comparison of the evidence confounds time, techniques, sampling, and setting with the dependent variable . . .'?

9. The two white and two black dolls were identical in all respects apart from colour. Why was this (*i*) an important aspect of experimental control, and (*ii*) something that could potentially confound the results?

10. Explain why chi-square is the appropriate statistical test for analysing the data.

27 Extended self: rethinking the so-called negro self-concept

Wade W. Nobles (1976)

Journal of Black Psychology 2 (2), Feb. 15–24

BACKGROUND AND CONTEXT

The 'scientific colonialism' discussed by Nobles is very clearly manifested in *cross-cultural psychology*, defined as 'the scientific study of the ways in which social and cultural forces shape human behaviour' (Segall *et al.*, 1990). It involves the study by (mostly) Western psychologists of members of non-Western cultural populations, populations which are (usually), by definition, different from their own.

It is perhaps inevitable (if not justifiable) that when a Western psychologist studies members of some other culture, s/he will use theories and measuring instruments which have been developed in the 'home' culture. These can be used for studying *both* cross-cultural *differences* and *universal* aspects of human behaviour (the 'psychic unity of mankind', a phrase popular in the early twentieth century). For example, aggression is a cultural universal, but how it is expressed may be culturally specific.

The distinction between culture-specific and universal behaviour is one version of what has come to be known in cross-cultural psychology as the '*emic–etic*' distinction, which also refers to problems inherent in the cross-cultural use of instruments developed in a single culture (Segall *et al.*, 1999). The terms 'emic' and 'etic' were first used by Pike (1954), an anthropologist, and were based on the distinction made in linguistics between *phonemics* (the study of sounds as they contribute to the meaning of a particular language) and *phonetics* (the study of universal sounds used in human language, regardless of their relationship to meaning).

According to Pike (1967), the terms should be thought of as designating two different viewpoints regarding the study of behaviour:

> . . . the etic viewpoint [which] studies behaviour as from outside of a particular system, and as an essential initial approach to an alien system . . . [and] the emic viewpoint [which] results from studying behaviour as from inside the system.

Both viewpoints are part of cross-cultural psychology, but does the distinction have any real bearing on how research is actually conducted? According to Berry (1969), research must begin somehow and usually involves an instrument or observational technique necessarily rooted in the researcher's own culture (an *emic* for that culture). When such an emic is brought in from an outside culture, is assumed to be valid in the alien culture and so is taken to be valid for comparison purposes, an *imposed etic* is being used. This is a major hazard of cross-cultural research and is defined as:

> . . . the importation or exportation of a theory of human behaviour which has been developed in one culture (typically the US) to be tested in another cultural context where its application may be inappropriate. (Segall *et al.*, 1990)

An etic approach, in general, seeks to identify *universal* behavioural phenomena and is more likely to be used since the theories and measuring instruments already exist. But, as we have already seen, it is the approach which involves the much greater risk of the researcher imposing his or her own cultural biases and classification system on the behaviour of a different cultural group. One manifestation of this imposition is a view of other cultures as not merely differing from the 'home' culture but viewing these differences as *deficiencies* ('*we* are superior, *they* are inferior'): this evaluation of cultural differences is called *ethnocentrism*. The term 'ethnocentrism' was coined by Sumner (1906), who noted the strong tendency to use one's own group's standards as *the* standard when viewing other groups, to place one's group at the top of a hierarchy and to rank all other groups as lower (Berry *et al.*, 1992).

As compensation for the ethnocentric approach, an *emic* approach emphasizes the *uniqueness* of every culture by focusing on culture-specific phenomena, such as the behaviours, values, customs, and traditions of a particular society. This is the approach typically used in ethnographic anthropological research. *Ethnography* refers to 'fieldwork' carried out in particular cultures, producing ethnographic reports, which are a rich source of information and which serve as an important foundation for cross-cultural psychology (Berry *et al.*, 1992). The emic approach typically involves participant observation, the use of local people to serve as informed observers, and local test construction in an attempt to tap the culture's own indigenous system of classification or 'subjective culture' (Triandis, 1972).

However, like most distinctions, the emic/etic distinction does not involve a mutually exclusive dichotomy. A number of researchers recommend a combined emic/etic approach (Berry, 1969; Triandis, 1978; Hui & Triandis, 1985). Bringing together the researcher's own emic and the alien culture's emic, and seeking the features they have in common, the research might then emerge with a *derived etic* (Segall *et al.*, 1990).

AIM AND NATURE OF THE STUDY

This is a critical review article, in which Nobles offers insights into the psychology of being a Black person living in a society dominated by Whites. The central aim is to draw a fundamental distinction between the Black and White self-concept, and this is

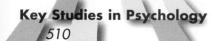

discussed within the context of a more general issue, namely the domination by White, Western societies (colonialism or imperialism) of Black, non-Western societies.

The imposition of Western psychological theories and concepts onto the experience of people from different sociocultural/sociopsychological groups, together with the 'taking of data' from those groups by Western psychologists for their own ends (and not for the benefit of the groups concerned), are both features of 'scientific colonialism'. This, in turn, is a manifestation of the more general (and more literal) political and economic colonialism, which has been (and remains) such a dominant feature of world history. The primary dimension along which both Western nations and Western psychologists differ from those they 'colonize', is power.

The article was originally presented to the National Association of Black Psychologists convention in America, in August, 1974. That Association was established in 1968 and one of its major goals is 'to develop an approach to psychology that is consistent with the experience of Black people.' It has played an important role in stimulating and contributing to the body of literature on the psychology of African Americans (Burlew *et al.*, 1992). The *Journal of Black Psychology*, from which the article comes, was founded in 1974.

■THE■STUDY■

For the oppressed to be really free, he must go beyond revolt, by another path he must begin other ways, conceive of himself and reconstruct himself independently of the Master. (Memmi, 1967)

It is indeed that in this society the subjects of social and psychological studies are in some capacity the powerless. It is, in fact, the powerful who study the powerless. Social scientists of all disciplines have traditionally occupied positions of economic, political, and psychological superiority over the people they select to study. In a very real sense, the position of the social scientist is similar to that of the colonial master and his subject people. In this regard, Lewis (1973) has noted the relationship between colonialism and anthropology; and like Galtuny (1967), she has recognized the parallels between the exploitation by social scientists (in terms of data and the creation of information) and the political and economic exploitation by colonists (in terms of natural resources and wealth). Both Galtuny and Lewis note that to exploit data from a country or community for processing into manufactured goods such as books and articles, is no different from exporting raw materials and wealth from a colony for the purposes of 'processing' into manufactured goods. Galtuny argues that in the academic arena this process is no less than 'scientific colonialism', whereby the 'centre of gravity for the acquisition of knowledge about a nation is located outside the nation itself.' We note, in this analogy, that just as the colonial power felt it had the right to claim and use for its benefit any product of commercial value in the colonies, so too the major aspects of scientific colonialism

Table 27.1

COMPARATIVE COLONIALISMS

Colonialism manifested by:	Political colonialism	Scientific colonialism
1. Removal of wealth:	Exportation of raw materials and wealth from colonies for the purpose of 'processing' it into manufactured wealth and/or goods.	Exporting raw data from a community for the purpose of 'processing' it into manufactured goods (i.e., books, articles, wealth, etc.).
2. Right of access and claim:	Colonial power believes it has the *right of access* and use for its own benefit anything belonging to the colonized people.	Scientist believes he has unlimited *right of access* to any data source and any information belonging to the subject population.
3. External power base:	The centre of power and control over the colonized is located outside of colony itself.	The centre of knowledge and information about a people or community located outside of the community or people themselves.

THE STUDY

is the 'idea' of unlimited *right of access* to data and the creation of information (see Table 27.1).

Nowhere has social science been more guilty of scientific colonialism than in the disciplines of psychology and anthropology. Psychology especially has contributed most clearly to the domination and continued oppression of peoples of colour. In fact it has become the single most powerful tool of oppression and its single most effective technique has been to place itself, its conceptions and formulations, as the standard by which all peoples of the world are to be understood.

Following the 'scientific colonialism' model further, one can see where psychologists and social scientists in general, like other colonialists, have historically reaped huge economic and political benefits in the form of better jobs, ease of publication, and recognition and fame, and like many anthropologists who returned from the 'bush', the psychologists who returned from our communities to create information on the lives and people of the ghetto, most often found a 'prestigious' institution of learning as a consequence of their trek into the 'unknown'.

Western psychology as a tool of oppression and domination is probably best seen in this country in the scientific investigation of 'Negro' intelligence and self-conception. The remainder of this paper will, however, address itself to only the scientific investigation of the so-called 'Negro' self-concept.

THE NEGRO SELF-CONCEPT AND SCIENTIFIC COLONIALISM

THE STUDY

Clearly, the assessment of the 'Negro' self-concept literature and its creators, in terms of (1) data being exported from the community to foreign shores (i.e. the university) for processing into manufactured goods (i.e. books and articles), (2) the centre of gravity for the acquisition of knowledge about 'Negro' self-concept being located outside of so-called 'Negroes' themselves, (3) the unlimited *right of access* to data and the creation of information, and (4) the profitable enterprise of studying and creating information about the lives and 'people of the ghetto', qualifies this literature as a prime example, almost by definition, of 'scientific colonialism'.

However, of the aspects which define this literature as a scientific colonialism, the understanding of how raw material (data) was *processed* is far more critical than the actual technique of raiding Black communities to capture the raw material. The process is critical solely because it is here that the scientist's own assumptions, guiding principles, ways of thinking and perceiving the world, are 'forged' with the raw material to produce the created information.

In terms of the so-called 'Negro' self-concept, the process by which information was created naturally reflected the thinking, perceptions, assumptions, and guiding principles of the investigators who conducted the studies. The 'process' is most clearly seen in the major philosophical and theoretical approaches of the study of the 'Negro' self-concept.

We contend that the 'process' factor (i.e. the philosophical/theoretical assumptions etc.) is directly related to the nature of the findings (i.e. the finished product) characteristic of the literature. The way in which information concerning self-conception, particularly the so-called 'Negro' self-concept, was 'processed' is indeed revealing given the above-mentioned relationship. The 'process' factor for the study of 'Negro' self-conception, like the self-concept literature in general, is characterized by four major philosophically based approaches (see Nobles, 1973).

It is this relationship (i.e. that between philosophy and scientific evidence or results) that Black psychologists particularly must be aware of. More directly, we need to recognize in what manner the literature created by non-African investigators represents a valid picture of Black reality. The key to this understanding is, of course, in the fact that the kinds of questions asked predetermine the types of answers possible (Clark, 1972). It is, however, the scientist's philosophy which determines the kinds of questions he will, in fact, ask. There is not only a clear and particular relationship between the kinds of questions you ask and the kinds of answers you will get, but there is also an even stronger relationship between one's guiding beliefs or philosophy and the kinds of questions one will ask. Thus, one can see that once you accept the a priori assumptions and subsequent questions (i.e. philosophical orientation) concerning a particular issue, one has at the same time predetermined the realm in which your answers may fall.

Answers are consistent with the questions asked. It is consistent, therefore, that if one asks a question (for instance, why are so-called 'Negroes' inferior to Whites?) that the question itself will predetermine the realm of the answer. That is, the answer can only relate to the already accepted assumption (philosophy or guiding belief of), in this example, the inferiority of Black people.

We contend, however, that the above mentioned characteristics of the so-called 'Negro' self-concept literature, combined with the philosophy–questions–answers relationship, require one to conclude that if you believe the Euro-American a priori assumptions and ask questions consistent with it, then one must, in turn, also accept the answers (results) characteristic of the research. That is, having accepted Euro-American assumptions about Black (African) reality, one's questions and answers about Black (African) people will be – in a predetermined manner – in response to the Euro-American reality.

The 'philosophical and theoretical assumptions' affecting the 'findings' relationship is particularly critical for understanding Western scholarship as it relates to African peoples. We contend that through the recognition of this relational aspect one can best illustrate (1) the fundamental relationship between the scientist's guiding principles (philosophy) and his scientific investigations (results), and (2) the point at which the scientist's guiding principles invalidate his analysis of a particular area or subject.

We note that the general characteristics of Euro-American philosophy or guiding principles are different from those of African philosophy and consequently, when African 'data' are processed by the guiding principles of Euro-Americans, the finished product (results) distorts the integrity of the original nature of the data. For instance, the European world view is tempered with the guiding principle of (1) 'survival of the fittest' and (2) 'control over nature'. These, in turn, naturally affect the nature of European values and customs. The emphasis on 'competition', 'individual rights', and the position of 'independence' and 'separateness' are clearly linked to the above mentioned guiding principles. Likewise, the overemphasis on 'individuality', 'uniqueness', and 'difference' in European-based psychobehavioural modalities is traceable to the values and customs characteristic of that community and the guiding principles reflected in it.

On the other hand, if one examines the African world view and compares it with the European, one can readily note the differences and their implications for understanding black self-conception. Rather than survival of the fittest and control over nature, the African world view is tempered with the general guiding principle of (1) survival of the tribe and (2) one with nature. In contrast with the European world view, the values and customs consistent with the African world view are characteristically reflective of the sense of 'cooperation', 'interdependence', and 'collective responsibility'. Similarly, the emphasis in African psychobehavioural modalities is not on individuality and difference but on 'commonality', 'groupness', and 'similarity' (see Figure 27.1).

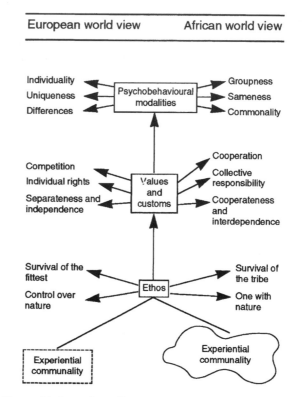

Figure 27.1. Comparative world view schematic.

The effects of these two different world views on the understanding of Black self-concept is critical. The nature of the 'processing' of data regarding Black people and our self-conceptions was, in fact, filtered through the European world view and to the extent that Black people are an African people, the 'process' has significantly distorted the validity of Black self-conception.

We have contended that African psychology is rooted in the nature of Black culture which is based on particular forms of African philosophical principles (Nobles, 1972). Consequently, the understanding of the psychology of Black people (more appropriately classified as Americanized Africans) must be African-based. Similarly, if we are to rid the literature of its scientific colonialism tone, the proper understanding of Black self-concept must be based on African assumptions and incorporate African-based analyses and conceptualizations. In this regard, we can clearly see the importance of understanding the African self-concept and its psychological basis for Black self-concept.

AFRICAN SELF-CONCEPT: THE EXTENDED SELF

When we examine the African philosophical tradition, particularly the ethosic orders of *survival of the people* and *one with nature*, we logically recognize that from this philosophical position an *extended* definition of self evolved. That is to say, the African self-concept was (is) by philosophical tradition the *we* instead of the *I*. Hence, in terms of self-conception, the African philosophical tradition, unlike Western philosophical systems, does not place heavy emphasis on the 'individual' or 'individuality'. It recognizes, rather, that only in terms of one's people does the 'individual' become conscious of one's own being (Mbiti, 1970). It is, in fact, only through others that one learns his duties and responsibilities toward himself and the collective self (tribe or people).

In terms of the African ethos, then, the first order or guiding belief (one with nature) suggests that African peoples believe themselves to be part of the natural rhythm of nature. The second order or guiding principle (survival of the tribe) suggests that African peoples believe in the cosmological and ontological importance of life, which in turn suggests that life never ends (Mbiti, 1970). Hence, the life of one's people is 'paramount' and 'permanent'. In accordance with the notions of *one with nature* and *survival of the tribe*, the African consequently thinks of experience as an intense complementary rhythmic connection or synthesis between the person and reality.

The cardinal point, therefore, in understanding the traditional African conception of self, is the belief that 'I am because we are, and because we are therefore I am' (Mbiti, 1970). Descriptively, we have defined this relationship (the interdependence of African peoples) as the 'extended self' (Nobles, 1972).

In recognizing that in terms of self-conception, the relationship of interdependence (the oneness of being) translates to an 'extended' definition, we note again that the African feels himself as part of all other African peoples or his tribe. One's self-definition is dependent upon the collective definition of one's people. In effect, the people definition *transcends* the individual definition of self, and the individual conception of self *extends* to include one's self and kind. The transcendent relationship (that between self and kind) is the *'extended-self'*.

The notion of the 'we' instead of the 'I' may become clearer through the following ontological analysis of the 'self'. It is generally safe to say that the establishment of self is achieved by (1) *recognizing* qualities or characteristics similar to one's own and/or (2) *denying* qualities and/or characteristics similar to one's own and/or other people. The self, therefore, can be considered the consequence of either of two processes – opposition and/or apposition. The way, however, in which African peoples are extended into themselves is not clear in this kind of simplistic distinction. One must distinguish between the levels and relativity of 'reality'.

The meaning that one has for being one *within* himself and his universe (The Oneness of Being) or what is felt as an inner feeling of oneness with oneself is the result of an interpretive process which evolved over the course of hundreds of millions of years. This inner 'something' which is called the self, is, in fact, the result of an evolutionary production which in the end left Man believing in the consistency of his own internalized organized system. The evolution and consistency of the internalized systems of varying groups of people is not, however, always the same.

The philosophical notion of the Oneness of Being, for instance, is predicated on Man being an integrated and indispensable part of the universe. For the African, the Oneness of Being suggests that Man participates in social space and elastic time as determined by the character of the universe. Hence, it is true, that *to be* is to be what *you are* because of your historical past as well as what you anticipate to be your historical future. In an existential manner, therefore, having recognized the historical grounding of one's being, one also accepts the collective and social history of one's people. African people, in turn, realize that one's *self* is not contained only in one's physical being and finite time. The notion of *interdependence* and *Oneness of Being* allows for a conception of self which transcends, through the historical consciousness of one's people, the finiteness of both the physical body, finite space, and absolute time.

Self-awareness or self-conception is not, therefore, limited (as in the Euro-American tradition) to just the cognitive awareness of one's uniqueness, individuality, and historical finiteness. It is, in the African tradition, awareness of self as the awareness of one's historical consciousness (collective spirituality) and the subsequent sense of 'we' or being 'One'.

It is in this sense that the self is portrayed as a 'transcendence into extendation'. That is, the conception of self transcends and extends into the collective consciousness of one's people.

BLACK SELF-CONCEPT

At this point in history, one cannot, however, talk about the African self-concept without talking about the effect of African peoples being dominated, oppressed, and subjugated by European peoples. In noting that the juxtapositioning of Africans and Europeans affected the traditions of both, we do not believe that the negative contact with Europeans resulted in the total destruction of things African. We do believe, however, that each system was different and that even now, after a relatively long period of contact, the systems of consciousness (i.e. self-knowledge) are still different.

For example, the European philosophical tradition bases the notion of self on the concept of independence (Brown, 1973). Consequently, the Euro-American self is believed to develop through the process of establishing one's 'uniqueness' and 'separateness' (i.e. 'I am (my) self by virtue of setting (my) self off and away from others, by opposing (my) self to others – Jasper, 1962). To 'discover' oneself, therefore, in this tradition is to establish one's 'individuality'.

In accordance with the African philosophical tradition, the analysis is different. Here, as discussed earlier, very little importance is given to 'individuality'. When one takes into account the notion of *interdependence* and the *Oneness of Being*, then one can see that a single person's conception of self and/or his self-identity is rooted in being whatever his people's definition is or was. Tribal or people membership, the 'we', in accordance with the extended definition of self, become the most fundamental and critical identity. One's conception of self is thus rooted in being an Ashanti, or Ibo, or Black, or African.

Clearly, the physical situation in which Africans – particularly in the Americas – find themselves involves the domination and imposition of a fundamentally European system of 'reality' on a non-European people. The situation naturally has caused psychological confusion because by nature of European 'reality', it denied the most compelling property (cosmological grounding of self in the collective, social, and spiritual sense of history) of the African conception of self.

This situation, it is suggested, produces the pseudo-identity referred to as the 'Negro'. The concept of 'Negro' refers to the African person who attempts to deny or is forced to (or convinced to) deny the philosophical basis of his Africanity, even though he cannot negate the recognizable properties (psychological facts) of his Africanity (Brown, 1973). This denial, it is believed, is due to the person being caught in the contradiction between the two philosophical systems (i.e. the African (black) and the Euro-American (white)). To be a 'Negro', therefore, is to be in a natural state of philosophical confusion (Muhammed, 1965).

The infliction of the Euro-American philosophical tradition, as it relates to self-conception (i.e. individuality, separateness, etc.) for African peoples, causes many of us to falsely believe that our natural temperament, tendencies and characteristic spirit were and are 'wrong' and/or 'uncivilized'. This confusion is fundamentally based on the fact that the Euro-American tradition denies the African his historical roots or the grounding of self into the collective and social definition of one's

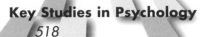

peoples, and that the so-called 'Negro' is taught (tricked) that the Euro-American culture is (1) the 'right' (only civilized) culture and (2) that he will or can be (under prescribed conditions) assimilated into it.

Hence, the Black self-concept is reflective of a situation Dubois (1903) described well over 70 years ago. It is, in fact, 'two warring idols in one dark body, one Negro and one American'. It is clearly the African in us that has never been acknowledged and until this aspect is shared the self-concept of the Black man will never be fully and accurately understood.

EVALUATION

Theoretical issues

Many of the general issues regarding cross-cultural psychology (comparing *different* cultures) can be related to the comparison of different cultural groups *within* the same culture:

> . . . there is a growing awareness that existing theories and research in psychology do not sufficiently consider the uniqueness of the experience of African Americans. One explanation for this phenomenon is the faulty assumption that Eurocentric psychological theories and research can be blindly applied across a variety of cultural groups. (Burlew *et al.*, 1992)

As if scientific colonialism were not objectionable enough, Nobles (and others) argues that psychology (and anthropology) is used as a tool of domination and oppression of 'peoples of colour', through its ethnocentric view of itself as the 'standard by which all peoples of the world are to be understood'. Given the close relationship between ethnocentrism and prejudice, it is not surprising that many writers (e.g. Fernando, 1991) have accused psychology of racism, especially in the areas of intelligence and mental health (e.g. Littlewood & Lipsedge, 1997; Owusu-Bempah & Howitt, 2000). Nobles himself identifies the study of 'Negro' intelligence and 'self-conception' as the 'best' examples of the abuse of psychology. (For a discussion of racism in relation to intelligence testing, see Chapter 23). It is to the 'Negro' self-concept that Nobles devotes the major part of his article.

An alternative to Eurocentric (mainly Anglo-Saxon) psychology is the Afrocentric paradigm (Myers, 1992). Many writers agree with Nobles that the self-concept of African-Americans is fundamentally different from that of white, European-Americans. The Eurocentric (Euro-American) world-view consists of the general guiding principles (*ethos*) of (1) survival of the fittest and (2) control over nature. In turn, these give rise to the fundamental *values and customs* of (*i*) competition, (*ii*) individual rights, and (*iii*) separateness and independence. In turn, these values and customs produce the *psychobehavioural modalities* of (a) individuality, (b) uniqueness, and (c) differences.

In contrast, the Afrocentric world-view involves (1) survival of the tribe and (2) one with nature, as its basic *ethos*, giving rise to the fundamental *values and customs* of (*i*) cooperation, (*ii*) collective responsibility, and (*iii*) cooperateness and interdependence, which, in turn, produce the *psychobehavioural modalities* of (a) groupness, (b) sameness, and (c) commonality. (This is a summary of Figure 27.1.) It is this world-view, rather than the Eurocentric, which, according to Nobles, is the appropriate one for understanding the psychology of black people, who are better described as Americanized Africans (or African-Americans).

What makes the African self-concept 'extended'? It is essentially the 'we' (as opposed to the Eurocentric 'I'), the experience of belonging to some greater whole (the tribe or people), and the belief that it is only through, and as part of, this greater whole, that one's self can be defined and experienced. (It is interesting to note here that one very influential Eurocentric theory of self, namely that of Gordon Allport (1955), makes reference to the extension of self, but it has a rather different meaning from Nobles's use of the term: see **Exercises** below.)

The notion of a person as a *bounded* individual has been central in Western philosophy and psychology, and, indeed, the description and understanding of the unique individual has been at the core of the psychological study of personality (Berry *et al.*, 1992). (This does *not* mean that all personality theories take an *idiographic* approach, only that *all* theories study people as separate entities, distinct from other individuals: this includes theories which adopt a *nomothetic* approach: see **Exercises** below).

This difference between the Eurocentric 'I' and the Afrocentric 'we' corresponds to the distinction between *Individualism* and *Collectivism*, as two major kinds of value-orientations. Triandis (1988) sees this dimension as referring to *group* differences (the social system), with an equivalent dimension at the individual level (personality), which he calls *idiocentric* and *allocentric* respectively. Similarly, the Eurocentric world-view reflects a 'culture of separateness', while the Afrocentric world-view reflects a 'culture of relatedness' (Kagitcibasi, 1985, cited in Berry *et al.*, 1992).

It is widely agreed that the Western concept of self denotes an individual who is separate, autonomous, atomized (composed of a set of discrete traits, abilities, values, and motives), and seeking separateness and independence from others (Markus & Kitayama, 1991). By contrast, in Eastern cultures, relatedness, connectedness, and interdependence are sought, rooted in the concept of self not as a discrete entity, but as inherently linked to others. The person is only made 'whole' when situated in one's place in a social unit (Berry *et al.*, 1992).

According to Cook & Kono (1977, cited in Myers, 1992), these concepts of self reflect an over-development of *one* aspect of being, and so represent two cultural extremes:

the West is materially advanced but spiritually bankrupt, while the East is spiritually developed but socially stagnant. African culture offers a middle ground or compromise between these two extremes: it displays a developed social consciousness and fluid social structure, but is relatively undeveloped materially. Myers argues that:

> . . . the fullest potential of what Africa can provide may be identified in contemporary times by her displaced children, African Americans. For it is they that are the inquiring offspring of the strongest 100,000,000 ancestors (some estimates range upwards to 200,000,000) torn from the motherland during over three hundred years of European slave trade. African Americans represent the union of opposites, culturally and racially.

Applications and implications

According to Myers (1992), the Afrocentric paradigm is truly *holistic:* it sees reality as both spiritual and material at the same time. 'Everything, including self, is the manifestation of one permeating essence that is the source of all things good' (Myers, 1992). Adopting this view results in the loss of a sense of an individualized ego/mind and the experience of an infinite mind or consciousness manifesting as oneself.

This conceptual system or paradigm is not exclusively African – nor could or should it be if the paradigm is valid. Rather, it seems to have *originated* in Africa and among Black people who, in the modern context, are likely to be labelled as of African descent. Equally important for Myers:

> . . . it is in the process of people of African descent (African Americans) rediscovering their heritage that this way of viewing life in total is recaptured, and is consequently termed *Afrocentric.*

Another feature of the *extended* African self-concept is the belief that the self includes all the ancestors and those yet-to-be-born: we have not 'died' until the last person who knew us by name has 'died'. Once this has happened, we enter the realm of ancestral spirits (universal consciousness). The self, as we have seen, also includes the entire people or community: 'I am because we are; we are, therefore I am'. Contrast this with the Eurocentric, 'I think, therefore I am' or *'cogito ergo sum'*, made famous by the French philosopher, Descartes, who used this argument to demonstrate the distinction between mind and body (or brain: see Chapter 30). This fundamental *dualism* can also be seen in other distinctions which are taken as 'givens' in Western culture, such as theory and practice, subject and object, knower and known, inside and outside, me and not-me. All these distinctions (or *dichotomies*) break down within the Afrocentric framework.

An interesting exception to this general rule is the Afrocentric 'the whole is contained in each of its parts' which has its counterpart in the Eurocentric, 'the whole is greater than the sum of its parts' (one of the major Gestalt principles of perceptual organization).

According to Watson (1973, cited in Fernando, 1991), Black Psychology is concerned with three main areas:

(1) providing a picture of black family life that is different from the one presented by conventional white wisdom, stressing the strengths within it and its way of making out in the world that blacks live in;

(2) highlighting the excessive numbers of black people being diagnosed as mentally ill and, in so doing, exposing white racism as the cause of black mental illness (see Littlewood & Lipsedge, 1997);

(3) questioning the validity for black people of established IQ tests (tests of intelligence) and devising new tests geared to black experience. These tests can be seen as a response to what was viewed as a growing racism, not just in society at large, but in the psychology profession itself (see Chapter 23).

In relation to the second of these, Owusu-Bempah & Howitt (2000) argue that:

> . . . the self and the community are only meaningfully separated and isolated within Western conceptions. The key point is that our understanding of what is psychologically healthy is conditioned by Western culture. Consequently we risk ignoring other possibilities and, worse still, see the alternatives as in some way faulty or pathological. If the selves of peoples beyond Western psychology are alien curiosities to Western Psychologists, how can psychology be in sympathy with these peoples?

If people from non-Western cultures are treated predominantly by practitioners (psychologists, therapists, psychiatrists, etc.) who are culturally Western, isn't there a good chance that the former will be misunderstood? At best, this might mean that they are not helped, at worst, they may be diagnosed as suffering from some mental disorder.

Owusu-Bemaph & Howitt (2000) ask if the recruitment of more black professionals would by itself improve the situation for black clients. While common sense would suggest 'yes', professionals disagree among themselves. In therapy, for example, 'Black-on-Black' does not automatically ensure that a therapist will deal successfully with black clients. As they say:

> . . . Simply because they are Black does not mean that they are regarded by the client as part of the Black community; the status of the practitioners may easily override racial considerations.

This is clearly illustrated by the experience of O'Brian (1990), a black male social worker cum family therapist, according to whom:

. . .: being a Black worker is not qualification enough to help a Black family; differences of class, position and status outweigh any similarity of skin colour.

As Owusu-Bempah & Howitt note:

. . . It is naïve, false, or even hypocritical, if not dishonest, for Black professionals to claim that they have not been affected by their Eurocentric primary and/or secondary socialization, their formal education and professional training.

A 'black' professional, in the eyes of many black clients, is one who does not focus exclusively on solving the client's problems, but who also regards 'the system' as in need of change. Teachers, social workers and other professionals need to recognize that race is just one of many factors impinging on their black clients: other social, psychological, political and economic factors may be more easily altered (Owusu-Bempah & Howitt, 2000).

A similar, but perhaps more radical position is adopted by Baldwin (1992). He sees black psychologists as perpetuating the domination of Eurocentric theories and models, either by applying them directly in trying to explain black people's psychological reality, or by trying to 'Blackenize' them to make them seem more relevant. Either way, he argues, black psychologists commit the fundamental 'self-destructive' error: failing to look to their own 'African' reality to give intellectual direction and inspiration to their own theoretical developments.

As for clinical psychology, the 'Eurocentric-oriented training' which black psychologists receive has virtually made them incapable of providing any type of truly culturally relevant mental health or psychological services to black people. Often, this takes the form of treating black people as if they were 'white people in black skin' (Baldwin, 1992).

Baldwin urges black psychologists to work towards the liberation of black people from Western oppression and to help them to move towards positive black mental health, the highest level of which is the vital psychological orientation called African self-consciousness.

In American psychiatry, black professionals have formed an association: the Black Psychiatrists of America (1973). Although there is some concern in the UK about racism in psychiatry, this has not led to the adoption of any particular strategies to counteract it. However, the Transcultural Psychiatric Society (UK) changed its constitution in 1985 to specify opposition to racism as a primary objective, and in 1987, the Royal College of Psychiatrists established a committee to consider 'problems of discrimination against trainees, other doctors in psychiatry and patients on the grounds of race'. Biennial Reports of the Mental Health Act Commission (1987, 1989 – a sort of Government inspectorate) have identified the needs of black and ethnic minorities as a priority, quoting the effects of racism on black people (Fernando, 1991).

Exercises

1. In **Theoretical issues**, a distinction is made between *idiographic* and *nomothetic* theories of personality. Briefly explain the difference between them and give *two* examples of each.

2. What is meant by 'self-concept' (in its Eurocentric sense)? Briefly describe each of its three main components.

3. When discussing the Negro self-concept in relation to scientific colonialism, Nobles talks about the processing of 'raw' material (data). Why does he see this as such a critical feature of scientific colonialism, and how does it relate to scientific practice in general?

4. In considering Figure 27.1, can you suggest any features of the Eurocentric world-view (other than those mentioned in **Theoretical issues**), either at the level of *ethos/values* or *customs/psychobehavioural modalities*, which are likely to have their opposite in the Afrocentric world-view?

5. In what respect does Allport's (1955) theory of self include an 'extended self'?

6. How does *ethnocentrism* relate to the concept of prejudice?

7. Nobles refers to Mbiti (1970), who says that African peoples believe in the 'cosmological and ontological importance of life, which in turn suggests that life never ends.' What are *cosmology* and *ontology*?

28 Cognitive, social and physiological determinants of emotional state

Stanley Schachter and Jerome E. Singer (1962)

Psychological Review, 69 (5), 379–99

BACKGROUND AND CONTEXT

Exactly what emotion is and how it can be explained has been a matter of controversy during most of psychology's history. It is useful to think of every emotion as comprising (a) a subjective experience (e.g. happiness, anger); (b) a set of physiological changes involving the nervous system and the endocrine system, over which we have little, if any, conscious control (although we may become aware of some of their effects, e.g. 'butterflies' in the stomach, sweating); and (c) associated behaviour (e.g. crying, running away, screaming).

Similarly, research interest has focused on four broad classes of emotional variable (Parkinson, 1987), namely, (*i*) cognitive appraisal of the situation (individuals react emotionally to stimulus events to the extent that they are perceived as relevant to their current goals/interests); (*ii*) the body's internal reaction (as in (b) above); (*iii*) overt behaviour (as in (c) above); (*iv*) facial expressions (which can be thought of as a subset of (*iii*)).

Although all the above are characteristic features of 'emotion', as understood by both psychologists and lay people, none is a necessary condition of emotional experience, so their presence cannot provide the material for a classical or logically exclusive definition (Parkinson, 1987). For example, Zajonc (1980) argues that emotion is possible without cognitive appraisal, Valins (1966) believes it is possible without physiological arousal, and Leventhal (1980) argues that it is possible without facial expression.

However, according to Schachter's (1964) *cognitive labelling theory* (or 'two-factor' theory) *both* physiological arousal *and* cognitive interpretation (or cognitive labelling) are necessary (and sufficient), but neither on its own is sufficient. The present study, which has been (and, to some extent remains) enormously influential, provides the cornerstone for that theory.

Cognitive labelling theory assumes that the physiological arousal associated with all emotional experiences is essentially the same, and this respresents one of the most controversial aspects of emotion theory and research, both before and since Schachter & Singer's (1962) study (see **Evaluation** section below). According to Hewstone *et al.* (1997),

> . . . the propositon that emotion arises from an interaction between a coarse type of global physiological arousal and finely differentiated cognitions appealed greatly to social psychologists who were becoming increasingly interested in the role played by cognition, and the study was quickly seized on by attribution theorists (e.g. Nisbett & Valins, 1972), who regarded it as evidence that attributions made for arousal helped to shape emotion.

AIM AND NATURE OF THE STUDY

The aim of the study is to test, experimentally, three propositions regarding the *interaction* between physiological and cognitive factors in the experience of emotion:

(1) If an individual experiences a state of physiological arousal for which s/he has no immediate explanation, s/he will 'label' this state and describe it in terms of the cognitions available. So precisely the same state of arousal could receive different labels (e.g. 'joy'/'anger'), depending on the cognitive aspects of the situation.

(2) If an individual experiences a state of physiological arousal for which s/he has a completely appropriate explanation (e.g. 'I've just been given an injection of adrenaline'), s/he will 'label' this state accordingly.

(3) Given the same circumstances, an individual will react emotionally, or describe his/her feelings as emotions, only to the extent that s/he experiences a state of physiological arousal.

These three propositions constitute the basic hypotheses being tested, by manipulating, separately:

(i) physiological arousal (epinephrine or placebo);

(ii) the extent to which participants have an appropriate explanation of their bodily state (*Epi Inf/ Epi Ign/ Epi Mis*); and

(iii) situations from which explanatory cognitions may be derived (angry or euphoric stooge). So participants in all four conditions (*Epi Inf/ Epi Ign/ Epi Mis/ Placebo*) encountered either a euphoric or an angry stooge.

(*Epi Inf* = given accurate account of effects of injection; *Epi Ign* = given no account; *Epi Mis* = given inaccurate account; *placebo* = given no account).

The design, therefore, was independent groups. In all conditions, participants (male college students studying introductory psychology) were told that the study was concerned with the effects of vitamin supplements (suproxin) on vision.

The dependent variable was the participant's emotional state, measured by:

(*i*) standardized observation through one-way mirror (during the experiment in company of stooge);

(*ii*) scores on a number of self-report scales (following the experiment but before the debriefing).

(Note that what is called 'epinephrine' in the USA is called 'adrenaline' in the UK: hence, the study is sometimes referred to as the 'adrenaline experiment').

THE STUDY

The problem of which cues, internal or external, permit a person to label and identify his own emotional state has been with us since James (1890) first proposed that 'the bodily changes follow directly the perception of the exciting fact, and that our feeling of the same changes as they occur *is* the emotion'. Since we are aware of a variety of emotional states, it should follow from James' proposition that the various emotions will be accompanied by a variety of distinguishable bodily states. James stimulated a formidable number of studies which searched for such bodily states, but almost all the early studies were negative; all the emotional states experimentally manipulated were characterized by a general pattern of excitation of the sympathetic nervous system, but there seemed to be no clear-cut physiological discriminators of the various emotions. Cannon (1929) concluded, by way of criticism of the James–Lange theory, that 'the same visceral changes occur in very different emotional states and in non-emotional states'.

More recent work, however, has suggested that there may be differentiators. Ax (1953) and Schachter (1957) found that fear and anger were both characterized by a high level of autonomic activation but also differed on several measures. Wolf and Wolf (1947) distinguished two patterns in the physiological responses of the stomach wall in a subject with a gastric fistula.

Whether or not there are physiological distinctions among the various emotional states must be considered an open question. Any differences which do exist are at best rather subtle, and the variety of emotion, mood and feeling states do not appear to be matched by an equal variety of visceral patterns.

This rather ambiguous situation has led Ruckmick (1936), Hunt *et al.* (1958), Schachter (1959) and others to suggest that cognitive factors may be major determinants of emotional states. It is suggested that one labels, interprets and identifies this general pattern of sympathetic excitation in terms of the characteristics of the precipitating situation; an emotional state may be considered a function of a state of physiological arousal and of a cognition appropriate to this state of arousal. The cognition, in a sense, exerts a steering function. Cognitions arising from the immediate situation as interpreted by past experience provide the framework within which one understands and labels his feelings; it is the cognition which determines whether the state of physiological arousal will be labelled 'anger', 'joy', 'fear', etc.

How would the two elements, physiological arousal and cognitive factors, interact? In most emotion-inducing situations, of course, both are completely interrelated. Imagine a man walking alone down a dark alley, a figure with a gun suddenly appears. The perception-cognition 'figure with a gun' in some way initiates a state of physiological arousal: this arousal is interpreted in terms of knowledge about dark alleys and guns, and the state of arousal is labelled 'fear'.

Sometimes, however, the two elements are, to some extent, independent. Marañon (1924) injected 210 of his patients with the sympathomimetic agent adrenalin, and then simply asked them to introspect. 71 per cent simply reported their physical symptoms with no emotional overtones, 29 per cent responded in an apparently emotional way, most of them describing their feelings in a way which Marañon described as 'cold' or 'as if' emotions (e.g. 'I feel *as if* I were afraid'). A very few cases apparently reported a genuine emotional experience, but even here, subjects had to be provided with an appropriate cognition, e.g. by speaking to the patients, while the injection was taking effect, of their sick children or dead parents. His results suggest that physiological arousal alone is insufficient to induce an emotion and have been replicated by Cantril and Hunt (1932) and Landis and Hunt (1932).

Marañon's subjects knew they were receiving an injection and probably knew that it was adrenalin and what its effects are. Consequently, they had a completely appropriate cognition or explanation as to why they underwent the physiological changes they did. This, we suggest, is why so few of Marañon's subjects reported any emotional experience.

Consider now a person in a state of physiological arousal for which no immediately explanatory or appropriate cognitions are available, e.g. they had been covertly injected with adrenalin or 'fed' a sympathomimetic drug, such as ephedrine. The person would be aware of palpitations, tremor, face flushing and most of the other symptoms associated with stimulation of the sympathetic nervous system (SNS), but, in contrast to Marañon's subjects, would be utterly unaware of why he felt this way. What would be the result of such a state?

Schachter (1959) suggests that 'evaluative needs' (Festinger, 1954) would be aroused, i.e. the need to understand and label his feelings, and he will do so in terms of his knowledge of the immediate situation. Should he at the time be with a beautiful woman, he might decide that he was madly in love or sexually excited, while should he be arguing with his wife, he might explode in fury and hatred. Again, should the situation be completely inappropriate, he could decide he was excited about something which had recently happened to him, or simply, that he was sick. In any case, it is our basic assumption that emotional states are a function of the interaction of such cognitive factors with a state of physiological arousal.

This line of thought leads to the following propositions:

THE STUDY

(*i*) Given a state of physiological arousal for which an individual has no immediate explanation, he will 'label' this state and describe it in terms of the cognitions available to him. Thus precisely the same state of arousal could be
labelled 'joy', or 'fury', or 'jealousy' or any of a great diversity of emotional
labels depending on the cognitive aspects of the situation.

(*ii*) Given a state of physiological arousal for which an individual has a completely appropriate explanation (e.g. 'I feel this way because I have just
received an injection of adrenalin'), no evaluative needs will arise and the
individual is unlikely to label his feelings in terms of the alternative cognitions available.

Now consider a person who is aware that he is in great danger (emotion-
inducing cognitions) but for some reason (drug or surgical) remains physio-
logically calm. Does he experience the emotion 'fear'? We believe that he
would not, which leads to:

(*iii*) Given the same circumstances, the individual will react emotionally or
describe his feelings as emotions, only to the extent that he experiences a
state of physiological arousal.

P R O C E D U R E

The experimental test of these propositions requires (*i*) the experimental manipulation of a state of physiological arousal, (*ii*) the manipulation of the extent to which
the subject has an appropriate explanation of his bodily state, and (*iii*) the creation
of situations from which explanatory cognitions may be derived.

In order to satisfy (*i*) and (*ii*), the experiment was presented as a study of the
effects of vitamin supplements on vision. As soon as a *S* arrived, he was taken to a
private room and told by *E*:

> In this experiment we would like to make various tests of your vision. We are particularly
> interested in how certain vitamin compounds and vitamin supplements affect the visual skills. In
> particular, we want to find out how the vitamin compound called 'Suproxin' affects your vision.
> What we would like you to do, then, if we can get your permission, is to give you a small
> injection of Suproxin. The injection itself is mild and harmless; however, since some people do
> object to being injected we don't want to talk you into anything. Would you mind receiving a
> Suproxin injection?

If the *S* agrees to the injection (and 184 out of 195 did), *E* continues with instructions
(see below), then leaves the room. After a few minutes, a doctor enters the room,
briefly repeats *E*'s instructions, takes *S*'s pulse and then injects him with Suproxin.

Depending upon conditions, *S* receives one of two forms of Suproxin: epinephrine or
placebo.

Epinephrine (adrenalin) is a sympathomimetic drug whose effects are almost always a perfect mimicry of stimulation of the SNS; shortly after injection, systolic blood pressure increases markedly, heart rate increases somewhat, cutaneous blood flow decreases, muscle and cerebral blood flow increase, blood sugar and lactic acid concentrations increase, and respiration rate increases slighty. The major subjective symptoms are palpitation, tremor and sometimes a feeling of flushing and accelerated breathing. Such effects usually begin within three to five minutes of injection and last anywhere from 10 to 60 minutes; for most *Ss*, these effects have subsided within 15 to 20 minutes after injection.

Ss in the *placebo* condition received the same quantity (½ cubic centimetre) of saline solution, which has no side-effects at all.

MANIPULATING AN APPROPRIATE EXPLANATION

By 'appropriate', we mean the extent to which the subject has an authoritative, unequivocal explanation of his bodily condition, i.e. a *S* who had been told that, as a direct consequence of the injection, he would feel palpitations, tremor, etc. A *S* who was told only that the injection would have no side-effects would have no appropriate explanation of his state.

Immediately after the *S* had agreed to the injection and before the doctor entered the room, *E* gave *S* one of three sets of information, depending on which condition the *S* had been assigned to:

(*i*)   *Epinephrine Informed (Epi Inf):* the *S* was told the actual side-effects of the injection, and that they would last for about 15 to 20 minutes. This information was reinforced by the doctor while she was actually giving the injection. So *Ss* here have a completely appropriate explanation of their bodily state: they know precisely what they will feel and why.

(*ii*)   *Epinephrine Ignorant (Epi Ign):* *E* said nothing about side-effects and simply left the room. The doctor told the *S* that the injection was mild and harmless and would have no side-effects, so *Ss* have no experimentally provided explanation for their bodily state.

(*iii*)   *Epinephrine Misinformed (Epi Mis):* *E* tells *S* that some subjects have experienced side-effects from Suproxin which last for about 15 to 20 minutes and involve the feet feeling numb, an itching sensation over parts of the body and a slight headache. Again, the doctor confirmed these symptoms. Of course, none of these is a symptom of epinephrine, and so *S* was being provided with a completely inappropriate explanation of his bodily condition. This represented a kind of control condition; if *Ss* in the *Epi Inf* became introspective, perhaps slightly troubled, then any differences between them and *Epi Ign Ss* on the dependent variable could be due to those factors rather than to differences in appropriateness.

THE STUDY

Ss in all the above conditions were injected with epinephrine. There was also a placebo condition in which *Ss* were injected with a saline solution and treated exactly the same as the *Epi Ign* condition.

PRODUCING AN EMOTION-INDUCING CONDITION

It was decided to manipulate emotional states which can be considered quite different: euphoria and anger. Schachter (1959) and Wrightsman (1960) have shown that people evaluate their own feelings by comparing themselves with others around them, and this is how emotional state is manipulated in this experiment.

Euphoria. Immediately after the *S*'s injection, the doctor left the room and *E* returned with a stooge, whom he introduced as another *S* and stated that both had had the Suproxin shot and that they had to wait for 20 minutes while the Suproxin was absorbed into the bloodstream, after which they would both be given the same tests of vision.

The room had been deliberately put into a state of mild disarray and, as *E* was leaving, he apologetically added that, if they needed any rough paper, rubber bands or pencils, they should help themselves. As soon as *E* had left, the stooge introduced himself again, made a series of standard icebreaker comments and began his routine. This was broken into a series of standard units, marked by a change in activity or a standard comment: (1) he starts doodling a fish on the rough paper; (2) crumples the paper and attempts to throw it into a wastebasket but misses and this leads to a 'basketball game'; gets up and does a jump shot; (3) if *S* has not joined in, he throws a paper ball to *S* saying, 'Here, you try it'; (4) continues his game; (5) continues but then gives up and decides to make paper airplanes instead; (6) fires plane, gets up and retrieves it, and fires again; (7) throws plane at *S*; (8) continues to fly plane; (9) tears off part of plane, screws up the paper and uses rubber band as sling and starts to shoot the paper; (10) continues shooting; (11) builds a tower of manilla folders and then shoots at it; (12) misses several times, finally hits and cheers as the tower falls; (13) while picking up the folders notices a pair of hula hoops and tries one; (14) twirls hoop wildly on arm, saying 'Hey, look at this – this is great'; (15) replaces hula hoop and sits down with feet on table. *E* returns shortly afterwards.

This routine was completely standard, and the only variations were those forced by the subject (e.g. introducing some nonsense of his own, asking the stooge to join in, making comments, etc.). *Ss* in all four conditions experienced this set-up; the stooge never knew which condition any particular *S* was in.

Anger. This began as the Euphoria condition did, but the *S* and stooge were asked to spend the 20 minutes waiting time answering questionnaires. Before looking at the questionnaires, stooge told *S* that he thought it unfair to be given injections, and that they should have been told when they were first called.

The five-page questionnaire started innocently enough, but then grew increasingly personal and insulting. The stooge, sitting opposite the *S*, paces his own answers so that at all times they are both working on the same question. At regular points, the stooge makes a series of standardized comments about the questions, starting off innocently enough, but growing increasingly querulous and finally he ends up in a rage; e.g. question 17 asks 'What is your father's average annual income?', and the stooge says, 'This really irritates me. It's none of their business what my father makes. I'm leaving that blank'. Question 28 reads: 'How many times each week do you have sexual intercourse?', to which the stooge responds, 'The hell with it! I don't have to tell them all this'. He rips up his questionnaire, crumples the pieces and hurls them to the floor, saying, 'I'm not wasting any more time. I'm getting my books and leaving', and he stamps out of the room.

Ss in the *Epi Ign*, *Epi Inf*, and *Placebo* conditions experienced this set-up, and the stooge never knew which condition any particular subject was in. The *Epi Mis* condition was not run in the Anger sequence because it was originally conceived as a control condition and it was felt that its inclusion in the Euphoria sequence above would suffice as a means of evaluating the possible artifactual effects of the *Epi Inf* instructions.

MEASUREMENT

Emotional state was measured in two ways; (*i*) standardized observation through a one-way mirror to assess *Ss*' behaviour, and (*ii*) self-report on a number of scales.

OBSERVATION

Euphoria. For each of the first 14 units on the stooge's standardized routine an observer kept a running record of what the *S* said and did; for each unit the observer coded *S*'s behaviour in one or more of the following categories:
Category 1: Joins in activity (e.g. made or flew airplanes, hula-hooped);
Category 2: Initiates new activity (e.g. threw open window and, laughing, hurled paper basketballs at passers-by);
Categories 3 and 4: Ignores or watches stooge.

Two observers independently coded two experimental sessions and they agreed completely on 88 per cent of the units.

Anger. For each of the units of stooge behaviour, an observer recorded *Ss*' responses and coded them according to the following category scheme:
Category 1: Agrees (e.g. 'I don't like that kind of personal question either') (Score of +2);
Category 2: Disagrees (e.g. 'Take it easy, they probably have a good reason for wanting the information') (Score of –2);

THE STUDY

Category 3: Neutral (noncommittal or irrelevant response to the stooge's remarks) (Score of 0);

Category 4: Initiates agreement or disagreement (e.g. 'Boy, I hate this kind of thing' or 'I'm enjoying this') (Score of +2 or–2);

Category 5: Watches (Score of 0);

Category 6: Ignores (Score of –1).

Two observers independently coded three experimental sessions; they agreed completely on 71 per cent of the units and their scores differed by a value of 1 or less for 88 per cent of the units (but always in the same direction).

SELF-REPORT OF MOOD AND PHYSICAL CONDITION

When *S*'s session with the stooge was completed, *E* returned, took pulses, and told them that there are many things besides Suproxin which affect performance on the vision tests, such as hunger, tiredness and mood at the time. The only way this information can be obtained is through questionnaires. He handed out a questionnaire which contained a number of mock questions about all these aspects of mental and physical state. To measure mood or emotional state, the following were the crucial questions:

1 How irritated, angry or annoyed would you say you feel at present?

I don't feel at all irritated or angry	I feel a little irritated and angry	I feel quite irritated and angry	I feel very irritated and angry	I feel extremely irritated and angry
(0)	(1)	(2)	(3)	(4)

2 How good or happy would you say you feel at present?

I don't feel at all happy or good	I feel a little happy and good	I feel quite happy and good	I feel very happy and good	I feel extremely happy and good
(0)	(1)	(2)	(3)	(4)

There were questions about the physical effects of epinephrine: (*i*) Have you experienced any palpitation (consciousness of your own heart beat)? and (*ii*) Did you feel any tremor (involuntary shaking of the hands, arms or legs)? To measure possible effects of the instructions in the *Epi Mis* condition, *Ss* were asked (*i*) Did you feel any numbness in your feet? (*ii*) Did you feel any itching sensation? (*iii*) Did you experience any feeling of headache? Answers to all these questions were given on a four-point scale (from 'Not at all' to 'An intense amount'). *Ss* were also asked two open-ended questions about other physical or emotional sensations. Pulse rate was taken immediately before the injections and immediately after the session with the stooge.

When *Ss* had completed these questionnaires, *E* announced that the experiment was over, explained the deception in detail, answered any questions and swore the *Ss* to secrecy. Finally, *Ss* answered a brief questionnaire about their experiences, if any, with adrenalin and their suspicion about the experimental set-up. None knew anything about the experiment beforehand, but 11 were so extremely suspicious of some crucial aspect of the experiment that their data were automatically discarded.

SUBJECTS

They were all male college students taking classes in introductory psychology at Minnesota University. 90 per cent of all such students volunteer for a subject pool for which they receive two extra points on their final exam for every hour they serve as subjects.

EVALUATION OF THE EXPERIMENTAL DESIGN

The disguised injection of Suproxin was far from ideal as a way of manipulating the absence of an immediate explanation of bodily state: some *Ss* would inevitably attribute their feelings to the injection regardless of what *E* told them. The effect of this would be to reduce differences between the several appropriateness conditions.

Although epinephrine unquestionably produces a state of physiological arousal, there is no question that a placebo does not prevent it. To the extent that the experimental situation produces sympathetic arousal, differences between epinephrine and placebo conditions will be reduced.

R E S U L T S

EFFECTS OF THE INJECTIONS ON BODILY STATE

Does the injection of epinephrine produce symptoms of sympathetic arousal compared with the placebo injection? On all items, *Ss* in the epinephrine conditions showed considerably more evidence of sympathetic arousal than those in placebo conditions, as measured by pulse rate and self-ratings on palpitation, tremor, numbness, itching and headache. (All comparisons showed a significant difference in excess of $p < 0.001$.) These results include data for five subjects who showed no relevant symptoms to the epinephrine, and these were automatically excluded from further calculation. *Ss* in the *Epi Mis* condition did not differ on numbness, itching and headache from *Ss* in any of the other experimental conditions.

EFFECTS OF THE MANIPULATIONS ON EMOTIONAL STATE

Euphoria. Self report: the scores in Table 28.1 are derived, for each *S*, by subtracting the value of the point he checks on the irritation scale from the value of the point he checks on the happiness scale, i.e. the higher the positive value, the happier the *S* reports himself as feeling.

Table 28.1

SELF-REPORT OF EMOTIONAL STATE IN THE EUPHORIA CONDITIONS

Condition	*n*	Self-report scales	Comparison	*p*
Epi Inf	25	0.98	Epi Inf vs. Epi Mis	<0.01
Epi Ign	25	1.78	Epi Inf vs. Epi Ign	0.02
Epi Mis	25	1.90	Placebo vs. Epi Mis,	
Placebo	26	1.61	Ign or Inf	*ns*
All *p* values reported throughout paper are two-tailed.				

Comparison of *Epi Mis* and *Epi Inf* makes it immediately clear that the experimental differences are not due to artefacts resulting from the instructions; in both conditions, *S* was warned to expect a variety of symptoms as a result of the injection, but in *Epi Mis*, self-report score is almost twice that in *Epi Inf* where the symptoms were completely appropriate to *S*'s bodily state.

Consistent with expectations, *Ss* were more susceptible to the stooge's mood, and consequently more euphoric, when they had no explanation of their own bodily states than when they did: the means of both *Epi Ign* and *Epi Mis* are considerably greater than the mean of *Epi Inf*.

Comparing placebo *Ss* to the epinephrine conditions, we note a recurring pattern, i.e. placebo *Ss* are less euphoric than either *Epi Mis* or *Epi Ign Ss* but rather more so than *Epi Inf Ss*. None of these differences is statistically significant.

Behaviour. To the extent that his mood has been affected, *S* should join in the stooge's manic activity and initiate similar activities of his own. The relevant data are shown in Table 28.2.

The activity index takes into account the degree of euphoria involved in different acts and the amount of time spent in each activity. On both behavioural measures (activity index and initiated acts), we find precisely the same pattern of relationships as those obtained with self reports: *Epi Mis Ss* behave somewhat more

Table 28.2

BEHAVIOURAL INDICATIONS OF EMOTIONAL STATE IN THE EUPHORIA CONDITIONS

Condition	*n*	Activity index	Mean number of acts initiated
Epi Inf	25	12.72	0.20
Epi Ign	25	18.28	0.56
Epi Mis	25	22.56	0.84
Placebo	26	16.00	0.54

p value			
Comparison		Activity index	Initiates*
Epi Inf vs. Epi Mis		0.05	0.03
Epi Inf vs. Epi Ign		*ns*	0.08
Placebo vs. Epi Mis, Ign or Inf		*ns*	*ns*

* Tested by comparison of the proportion of *Ss* in each condition initiating new acts.

euphorically than *Epi Ign Ss*, who in turn behave more euphorically than do *Epi Inf Ss*. On all measures, then, there is consistent evidence that a *S* will take over the stooge's euphoric mood to the extent that he has no other explanation of his bodily state.

Anger. Self report: anger, if manifested, is most likely to be directed at *E* and his annoyingly personal questionnaire. But *Ss* were afraid of endangering the extra points on their final exam by admitting their irritation to *E*'s face or spoiling the questionnaire. Though they were willing to express anger when alone with the stooge, they hesitated to do so on the mood self-rating and questionnaire which *E* might see, and only after the purposes of the experiment had been revealed were many of these *Ss* willing to admit to *E* that they had been annoyed. This pretty much forces us to rely on the behavioural measures derived from observation of *S*'s presumably private interaction with the stooge.

Behaviour. To calculate an 'Anger index', the numerical value assigned to a *S*'s responses to the stooge is summed together for the various units of stooge behaviour. A positive index value indicates that *S* agrees with the stooge's comment and is growing angry; a negative value indicates that *S* either disagrees with the stooge or

THE STUDY

Table 28.3

SELF-REPORT OF EMOTIONAL STATE IN THE ANGER CONDITIONS

Condition	n	Self-report scales	Comparison	p
Epi Inf	22	1.91	Epi Inf vs. Epi Ign	0.08
Epi Ign	23	1.39	Placebo vs. Epi Ign or Inf	ns
Placebo	23	1.63		

Table 28.4

BEHAVIOURAL INDICATIONS OF EMOTIONAL STATE IN THE ANGER CONDITIONS

Condition	n	Neutral units	Anger units
Epi Inf	22	+0.07	−0.18
Epi Ign	23	+0.30	+2.29
Placebo	22	−0.09	+0.79
Comparison for anger units		p	
Epi Inf vs. Epi Ign		<0.01	
Epi Ign vs. Placebo		<0.05	
Placebo vs. Epi Inf		ns	

ignores him. The stooge's routine has been divided into two phases: the first two 'neutral' units and the following 'angry' ones, the latter being the crucial ones as far as the prediction that *Epi Ign Ss* will be angrier than *Epi Inf Ss*. This is indeed the case (see Table 28.3).

CONFORMATION OF DATA TO THEORETICAL EXPECTATIONS

In both the euphoria and anger conditions, the emotional level in *Epi Mis* and *Epi Ign* conditions is considerably greater than that in the *Epi Inf* condition, as predicted. However, the results for the *Placebo* condition are ambiguous because they consistently fall between the *Epi Ign* and *Epi Inf Ss*. This is troublesome because it makes it impossible to evaluate unambiguously the effects of the state of physiological arousal. It is possible to account for the emotional restraint of the *Epi Ign* and *Epi Mis Ss*, namely, their attribution of their bodily state to the injection, thus making the stooge less of an influence. Some were clearly 'self-informed' (e.g. 'the shot gave me the shivers') and were not angry or euphoric at all. If these *Ss* are removed, the difference between the *Epi Ign* and the *Placebo Ss* becomes significant for anger ($p = 0.01$), and for euphoria, the difference between *Epi Mis*, *Epi Ign* and *Placebo Ss* is significant ($p = 0.03$).

How can we account for the consistent finding that *Placebo Ss* attain a higher emotional level (both reported and behavioural) than *Epi Inf Ss*? The assumption that there is no sympathetic arousal in the *Placebo* condition is completely unrealistic, for the injection is quite a dramatic situation and physiological arousal was produced. In both the anger and euphoria conditions, *Placebo Ss* who show signs of sympathetic arousal (pulse-rate increase or maintenance as opposed to decrease) show considerably more anger than *Ss* who show no such signs. Consistent with expectations, therefore, sympathetic arousal accompanies an increase in emotional level. Also, the emotional level of *Placebo Ss* showing no signs of arousal are very similar to that of *Epi Inf Ss*, implying that both factors (sympathetic arousal and appropriate cognition) are essential to an emotional state.

D I S C U S S I O N

Although the pattern of data falls neatly in line with theoretical expectations, the fact that we had to some extent to rely on internal analyses to partial out the effects of experimental artefacts makes our conclusions rather tentative. Consequently, a series of additional experiments, published elsewhere, was designed. In the first of these, Schachter and Wheeler (1962) used three experimental groups: epinephrine, placebo and chlorpromazine, a sympatholytic agent. Laughter at a slapstick movie was the dependent variable, and the evidence is good that amusement is a direct function of manipulated sympathetic arousal.

Two experiments with rats (Singer, 1961; Latané & Schachter, 1962) showed clearly that, when the self-informing tendency is eliminated, epinephrine, compared with a placebo, causes sympathetic arousal.

What are the implications of these findings, then, for the studies reviewed in the introduction, which have largely failed to differentiate between various emotional states? Perhaps they should be taken at face value, i.e. emotional states may, indeed, be generally characterized by a high level of sympathetic activation with few, if any, physiological distinguishers among the many emotional states. Although this study does *not* rule out the possibility of physiological differences, we have, through cognitive manipulation, produced in *Ss* the very disparate states of euphoria and anger, despite the same state of epinephrine-induced arousal. It may indeed be the case that cognitive factors are major determinants of the emotional labels we apply to a common state of sympathetic arousal.

'Activation theory' (Lindsley, 1951; Woodworth & Schlosberg, 1958) which sees emotional states as at one end of a continuum of activation defined by degree of autonomic arousal and EEG patterns, is clearly inadequate; this experiment shows that it is possible to have very high degrees of activation without a *S* either appearing to be, or describing himself as, 'emotional'. Cognitive factors seem to be indispensable elements in any theory of emotion.

S U M M A R Y

If emotional states are a function of a state of physiological arousal and of a cognition appropriate to this state of arousal, three propositions follow:

1   Given a state of physiological arousal for which an individual has no immediate explanation, he will label this state and describe his feelings in terms of the cognitions available to him. To the extent that cognitive factors are potent determinants of emotional states, it is predicted that precisely the same state of physiological arousal could be labelled 'joy' or 'fury' or 'jealousy' or any of a great diversity of emotional labels depending on the cognitive aspects of the situation.

2   Given a state of physiological arousal for which an individual has a completely appropriate explanation, no evaluative needs will arise, and he is unlikely to label his feelings in terms of the alternative cognitions available.

3   Given the same cognitive circumstances, the individual will react emotionally or describe his feelings as emotions only to the extent that he experiences a state of physiological arousal.

An experiment is described which, together with the results of other studies, supports these propositions.

EVALUATION

Theoretical issues

As we noted in **Background and context** above, a crucial assumption of Schachter's (1964) *cognitive labelling theory* is that the physiological arousal involved in different emotions is essentially the same. At the beginning of their article, Schachter and Singer state that James' (1890) theory (usually referred to as the 'James-Lange' theory) implies that different emotions '. . . will be accompanied by a variety of distinguishable bodily states . . .'. (It also implies that physiological arousal is *sufficient* for emotional experience.) They also point out that Cannon's (1929) theory (usually called the

'Cannon-Bard' theory) claims the *opposite*: 'the same visceral changes occur in very different emotional states . . . ' (Cannon, 1929).

According to Levenson (1994), it is a 'myth' that every emotion is autonomically different. It seems far more likely that reliable differences will only be found between emotions for which there are different associated typical behaviours, and even here it is quite unlikely that each will be unique (not sharing any features in common). For example, Levenson *et al.* (1990) have identified a small number of fairly reliable differences in patterns of autonomic nervous system (ANS) activity both between negative emotions (anger, disgust, fear and sadness) and between these and happiness.

These findings imply that we cannot draw general conclusions about the specificity of the body's response to emotional stimuli: it depends partly on which emotion (positive or negative, and which positive or negative emotion) we are talking about.

Pinel (1993) advocates a position falling between the extreme views represented by the James-Lange and Cannon-Bard theories: while there is insufficient evidence for the former's claim that every emotion has a distinct pattern of ANS activity, the latter's claim that the ANS responds in exactly the same way to all emotional stimuli is also clearly incorrect.

Dalgleish (1998) maintains that there is now good evidence that different emotions *are* associated with different physiological arousal patterns (which suggests that in the Schachter and Singer study, emotional 'selection' must have occurred, at least partly, at a pre-physiological stage). However, this evidence does not necessarily deal a death-blow to cognitive-labelling theory, which claims that physiological arousal is *necessary* but not *sufficient:* even if there are distinctive patterns of arousal, it is generally agreed that emotional experience can be modulated and refined by interpretations of arousal (Power & Dalgleish, 1997).

So, what evidence is there that there is more to emotional experience than just ANS arousal?

(*i*)   Most of Marañon's (1924) participants injected with adrenaline reported 'as if' emotions . The vital ingredient missing, according to Schachter and Singer, was the perception of an emotion-producing situation through which to interpret their arousal. They could explain their arousal in terms of the injection, and so did not have reason to label it as emotion.

(*ii*)   Hohmann's (1966) spinal-cord injured patients (paraplegics and quadriplegics) also reported 'as if' emotions, but this time because their injuries disrupted visceral responses and interfered with their emotional physiology. They described appropriate reactions to emotion-inducing situations, but didn't feel aroused: 'It's as if they're labelling a situation, not describing a feeling'. This strongly suggests that physiological arousal is necessary though not sufficient.

Obviously, this contrasting set of introspections is precisely what should be anticipated from a formulation of emotion as a joint function of cognitive and physiological factors (Schachter, 1964). However, these patients have various sources of information available to their central nervous system, including factual knowledge of the damage they have suffered, as well as that mediated via feedback from the periphery of their body (Reisenzein, 1983). Chwalisz et al.,(1988) reported intense emotional arousal in spinal cord injured patients, even where there was little feedback form the periphery.

(*iii*) Valins (1966) provided male participants with feedback of their supposed heart rate while watching slides of semi-nude 'Playboy' females. The heart rate was pre-recorded and programmed to increase in apparent response to presentation of half the slides, so that participants believed they were reacting to these pictures. These slides were rated as more attractive than those supposedly associated with unchanged heart rate. If people are prepared to *infer* emotion on the basis of information about their reactions to stimuli, this suggests physiological arousal is not necessary and that cognitive factors may be sufficient (Valins, 1966; Parkinson, 1987). One interpretation of these findings is that the men interpreted the manipulated feedback in the context of a lifetime of experiencing their own heart-beat (Toates, 2001). In Damasio's (1996) terms, Valins tapped into an 'as if' central nervous system emotional circuit that can operate with some independence from normal triggers and simulate peripheral arousal.

(*iv*) Similarly, Laird (1974) told participants that the activity of facial muscles was being measured by electrodes and that they should relax and contract certain muscles to allow accurate recording. In this way, he was able to induce smiles and frowns in the participants covertly. They evaluated slides according to their facial expression at the time: those seen while 'smiling' were rated more positively (even though there was no corresponding physiological arousal).

It is interesting to note that facial expressions are also related to (other) physiological responses. For example, extreme pleasantness of facial expression is associated with accelerated heart rate, while extreme unpleasantness is associated with decelerated heart rate (Fiske & Taylor, 1991). However, Laird (1974, 1984) claims that facial expressions are mediated by cognitive factors: we attribute particular emotional states to ourselves based on feedback from our facial muscles. Others (e.g. Izard, 1972, 1977) believe that this feedback directly affects emotional experience. However, any conclusions based on the study of *posed* facial expressions in the laboratory, rather than spontaneous, naturally occurring ones, must be tentative.

According to Schachter (1964), the Cannon-Bard theory was wrong in claiming that bodily changes and the experience of emotion are *independent,* and the James-Lange theory was mistaken in claiming that physiological changes *cause* the feeling of emotion. However, he shares the James-Lange belief that physiological changes *precede* the experience of emotion (but for different reasons). Emotional experience depends on *both* physiological change *and* the interpretation of those changes: we have to *decide* which particular emotion we are feeling and which label we attach to our arousal depends on what we *attribute* that arousal to. This is the 'two factor theory of emotion' (or cognitive labelling theory).

Methodological issues

Hilgard *et al.* (1979) make some important criticisms:

(*i*) epinephrine does not affect everyone in the same way, and Schachter and Singer in fact eliminated from their analysis five participants who later reported they experienced no physiological symptoms;

(*ii*) no assessment was made of participants' mood *before* the injections; presumably, someone in a better mood to begin with might respond more positively to a playful stooge;

(*iii*) how comparable are arousal states created by drugs and manipulated in the laboratory to naturally occurring, real-life emotions?

The results are usually cited as supporting the hypotheses (and, by implication, cognitive-labelling theory). Schachter and Singer themselves are a little more cautious: in the **Discussion** they say:

> Although the pattern of data falls neatly in line with theoretical expectations, the fact that we had to some extent to rely on internal analyses to partial out the effects of experimental artefacts makes our conclusion rather tentative . . .

They also cite other studies designed to address some of these 'artefacts', and at the very end of the article (the last sentence of the **Summary**), they state that:

> . . . An experiment is described which, together with the results of other studies, supports these propositions [hypotheses].

In other words, the present experiment *on its own* does *not* support the hypotheses, and this is particularly true of hypothesis (1). Specifically, the *self-report* data in the *anger* condition failed to support the hypothesis, and the authors conclude by saying:

> . . . This pretty much forces us to rely on the behavioural measures derived from observations of *S*'s presumably private interaction with the stooge.

The self-report means in the anger condition should have been on the *negative* side of the scale, but in fact they are all *positive* (see Table 28.3), suggesting that participants exposed to the angry stooge did not actually feel angry – regardless of their physiological state and the availability of a non-emotional explanation for their arousal (see **Exercises** below).

Similarly, support for hypothesis (3) is weak. To be consistent with this hypothesis, participants in the *placebo* condition should not have reacted emotionally to the anger or euphoria settings, and should, therefore, have scored significantly *lower* on measures of emotion than both the *Epi Mis* and *Epi Ign* participants. However, Tables 28.1 and 28.2 show there was no difference between any of these three groups (euphoria condition: self-report and behaviour), and Table 28.3 shows there was no difference between *placebo* and *Epi Ign* participants (anger condition: self-report).

This is acknowledged in the section before the **Discussion.**

Given that the unsupported hypothesis (1) is the most original aspect of Schachter and Singer's reasoning, it is somewhat surprising that their findings were so widely interpreted as providing good support for their predictions. According to Hewstone *et al.* (1997), the behavioural data in the anger condition cannot be compared directly with those from the euphoria condition: they are measuring quite different aspects of behaviour, thus making a direct test of hypothesis (1) impossible.

Subsequent research

A study by Wells & Petty (1980) suggests that Schachter was mistaken in believing that *both* arousal and the interpretation of that arousal are necessary, but that he is correct in his belief that cognitive factors are involved. Like Laird, Wells and Harvey showed that feedback from facial muscles (a form of non-verbal behaviour, of course) can influence our emotional experience. On the pretext that they were testing stereo headphones for 'comfort while you're moving', the researchers asked college students to either nod their heads ('Move your head up and down') or shake it ('Move your head back and forth') while listening to a radio broadcast. In between the music was a 90 second persuasive message about fees increases. Post-message opinion measures showed that the 'nodders' agreed significantly *more* with the message and the 'shakers' *less* compared with listen-only controls. None of the participants was the slightest bit suspicious that the head movements had had any effect on their attitudes.

Wells and Petty explain the results very simply: when we nod, we are almost always thinking positive thoughts and these associations are so well learned that 'nodding disagreement' is very difficult to do (the bodily and cognitive responses are incompatible). At the same time, compatible cognitive responses (in this example, agreeing) are augmented and increased.

According to Parkinson (1987), the focus of Schachter's model is an atypical state of affairs where the participant is unsure about the cause of arousal (*Epi Ign/Mis*). But Schachter (1964) admitted that usually we *are* aware of a precipitating situation prior to the onset of arousal (which takes approximately one to two seconds to reach consciousness), and so it is normally perfectly obvious to the person what aspects of the situation have initiated the emotion. However, even here the meaning of the emotion-inducing circumstances requires some cognitive analysis before the emotion can be labelled.

Schachter claims that, although the *quantitative* aspect of emotion can arise without cognitive mediation ('am I in a state of emotional arousal?'), the *qualitative* aspect requires prior cognition ('what emotion is it I am experiencing?'). According to Zajonc (1980), 'this view that affect is post cognitive is now probably the most popular attitude among emotion theorists'.

But are environmental cues as easily accepted as the basis for inferences about our own feelings as Schachter claims (Fiske & Taylor, 1991)? Using the original Schachter–Singer paradigm, several studies (e.g. Marshall, 1976; Maslach, 1979; Marshall & Zimbardo, 1979) have concluded that participants' efforts to understand an unexplained state of arousal is more extensive than a quick examination of salient cues in the surrounding environment. When trying to account for a current state of arousal, we often try to think of *past* occasions on which we felt like this. Others' behaviour may suggest or dictate how one should behave in that situation, but it does not provide information regarding why we feel as we do. At the very least, others' behaviour must, in some way, be *appropriate* (Weiner, 1992).

These researchers also found that such arousal is more likely to be interpreted *negatively* (as unease or nervousness similar to free-floating anxiety). This suggests that emotional lability is not as great as Schachter maintains. Also, if the dosage is high enough, adrenaline seems to produce an unpleasant mood, even in the *Epi Mis* condition, and in the presence of the euphoric stooge. In other words, unexplained arousal, rather than being a neutral state to which any emotional label can be applied, has a negative, unpleasant, quality about it.

Despite criticisms of their work, the real impact of Schachter and Singer's study was that it revived an old idea (implicit in the work of philosophers including Aritstotle, Descartes, and Spinoza), namely that emotions might be cognitive interpretations of situations (LeDoux, 1998). The view that cognition is an integral part of emotion is predominant in contemporary thinking in psychology (Dalgleish, 1998; LeDoux, 1998).

However, something was missing from Schachter and Singer's cognitive labeling theory. As LeDoux points out:

> . . . They tried to explain how we deal with emotional responses once they occur . . . but did not give an account of what generates the responses in the first place . . .

To take James's (1890) famous example of running away from a bear, both the James-Lange, and Schachter's cognitive labeling theories, fail to explain how the brain figures out that the bear is a source of danger. The significance of the stimulus (the bear) to the individual has to be determined, and it is this computed significance that '. . . starts the emotional ball rolling . . .' (LeDoux, 1998).

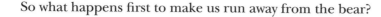

So what happens first to make us run away from the bear?

According to *cognitive appraisal* theorists (e.g. Arnold, 1960), we perceive the bear and appraise it unconsciously, and our conscious experience of fear results from the tendency to run. The response does not need to occur in order to have the feeling – a feeling only requires an action tendency. Emotions, therefore, differ from non-emotional states of mind by the presence of *appraisals* (the mental assessment of the potential harm or benefit of a situation: Arnold & Gasson, 1954) in their causal sequence: different emotions are distinguished from each other because different appraisals produce different action tendencies, which, in turn, produce different feelings.

The appraisal concept was adopted by other researchers in the 1960s, including Lazarus, a clinical psychologist who applied it to people's reactions to, and ways of dealing with, stressful situations (see **Applications and implications** section).

According to LeDoux (1998), appraisal remains the cornerstone of contemporary cognitive approaches to emotion, There are currently a number of appraisal theories (e.g. Frijda, 1988; Oatley & Johnson-Laird, 1996; Power & Dalgleish, 1997; Scherer, 1997), which are more similar than different (Oatley, 1998). Power & Dalgleish's (1997) approach tries to explain how it is that the same stimulus can have *emotional* meaning at one level, while simultaneously having *cold/factual* meaning at another. This can help explain more easily the dissociations in our experience, whereby we can either know something 'with the head' or 'with the heart' (Dalgleish, 1998). Although the evaluation of a situation is, clearly, the first step in the initiation of an emotional episode, and this usually happens unconsciously, LeDoux (1998) believes that:

> . . . in emphasizing cognition as the explanation of emotion, the unique aspects of emotion that have traditionally distinguished it from cognition are left behind.

Applications and implications

As we noted in **Background and context** above, one of the ways in which Schachter's work has influenced the cognitive approach to emotion is in the form of an *attributional theory* of emotion: the nature and/or intensity of an emotion seems to depend largely on the causes to which the individual attributes his/her physiological changes.

For example, Abramson & Martin (1981) grafted attribution principles onto Seligman's (1975) theory of learned helplessness in order to try to explain clinical depression. Clearly, the experience of the inability to control the outcome of one particular situation (helplessness) does not inevitably lead to clinical depression in most people. So what other factors are involved? Abramson and Martin believe that depression only occurs when people make certain attributions about their helplessness, specifically, when they believe it is caused by (*i*) *internal* factors (as opposed to environmental) which are perceived as (*ii*) *stable* (as opposed to variable), and when they are believed to reflect (*iii*) a *global deficiency* (as opposed to one specific to the kind of bad experiences which have happened). So, people get depressed when they conclude that helplessness is likely to pervade all aspects of their future lives.

Schachter's theory implies that emotional reactions induced by a threatening experience can be *reattributed* to a neutral or less threatening source. For example, if you blame some external stimulus rather than your own inadequacies, you may calm down sufficiently to break the vicious circle. One of the most important aspects of Schachter's work is the demonstration that our attributions for arousal are malleable (although, as we have seen above, not *as* malleable as he proposed). In other words, it is possible for us to mis-label our feelings and to draw mistaken conclusions about the causes of those feelings (the *mis-attribution effect*: Ross & Nisbett, 1991). This is clearly demonstrated in the present study: those in the *Epi Ign* and *Epi Mis* conditions all attributed their arousal to something other than the drug which was the actual cause.

A study by Nisbett & Schachter (1966) is a classic demonstration of the mis-attribution effect. Participants were given a sugar-pill placebo, which they were told was a drug, and which would affect them in one of two ways, either (*i*) tremors, shaky hands, pounding heart and other symptoms associated with fear arousal, or (*ii*) itching, headache, and other symptoms unrelated to fear. The 'drug' was administered just before undergoing a series of increasingly intense electric shocks: participants had to indicate at what point the shocks became painful and when they became intolerable.

As predicted, group (*i*) participants reported first experiencing pain at a *higher* shock level, and showed a *higher* tolerance level, than those in group (*ii*). Why? Because they *mis-attributed* their fear symptoms (which were, in fact, induced by the shock) to the drug, actually *reducing* the fear.

By inducing people to reattribute their arousal from a threatening source to a neutral or less threatening one, they can be helped to function more effectively in settings which currently induce anxiety (Fiske & Taylor, 1991). So what began as a laboratory based, experimental approach to emotional arousal (*the mis-attribution paradigm*: Valins, 1966), has profound clinical implications, since it provides the potential for a general model for the treatment of emotional disorders (Valins & Nisbett, 1972).

The mis-attribution effect has been criticized on several counts, which are summarized by Fiske and Taylor (1991). Some of these include:

(*i*)   it cannot be reliably replicated, and even when it is, it is not always clear that it is attribution which is the 'active ingredient';

(*ii*) the effect may only be temporary;

(*iii*) for mis-attribution to occur, the alternative source must be plausible, unambiguous and salient, while the actual cause must not be obvious and

participants must believe that the alternative source is having more impact on their arousal than it actually is;

(*iv*) laboratory studies seem to be more successful than actual clinical investigations. This could be because people with real problems already have a stable explanation for their arousal and do not search for alternatives, making them less vulnerable to mis-attribution effects. Alternatively, they may test out the alternative more fully than people with laboratory induced, short-term, problems.

In turn, this is related to stress. Cox (1978) argues that the experience of stress is usually described in ways associated with emotions: anger, anxiety, depression, fear, grief, guilt, jealousy and shame (the 'stress emotions': Lazarus, 1976). Agreeing with Schachter, Kagan (1975) believes that it is how an individual cognitively appraises the situation which shapes basic feelings into a specific emotion. This raises again the question of just how flexible/labile emotional experience is, and implies the crucial question as to how much stress can be reduced (or prevented) by changing people's cognitive appraisal of the situation.

A famous study by Speisman *et al.* (1964) involved showing participants a film on anthropology ('*Subincision in the Arunta*'), in which the penises of aboriginal boys are seen being cut with a jagged flint knife as part of a puberty rite. This normally causes high levels of stress. However, the sound track was manipulated, so that:

(*i*) the pain, jaggedness of the knife and so on were emphasized ('trauma');

(*ii*) the boys' anticipation of entering manhood was stressed ('denial');

(*iii*) the emotional elements were ignored and the traditions of the tribe were stressed ('intellectualization'); or

(*iv*) there was no commentary at all ('silent' control).

As predicted, arousal (measured by GSR) was highest in (*i*), next highest in (*iv*) and lowest in (*ii*) and (*iii*). What we tell ourselves about external situations influences the level of arousal we experience. But we should also ask if the converse is true: does the level of arousal influence how we appraise the situation? (This relates to the replications of the Schachter and Singer study discussed above).

Exercises

1. What scale of measurement is being used on the euphoria and anger scales (*self report of mood and physical condition*)?

2. In Table 28.1, what statistical test is likely to have been used?

3. In Table 28.2, the *Epi Mis* participants were somewhat (but not significantly) more euphoric than the *Epi Ign* participants. How could you account for this?

4. The participants were all male, as were the stooges. Can you think of any reasons why these results would not generalize to females? And what would be the effect of having an opposite-sex stooge?

5. How do Schachter and Singer account for the failure to find the predicted differences in the anger (self-report) condition?

6. All the tests used are two-tailed. What does this mean, and could one-tailed tests have been used?

7. Is it ethically acceptable to mislead participants about the side-effects of the injection (either *Epi Mis* or *Epi Ign*)?

8. In **Subsequent Research**, Ledoux (1998) criticizes appraisal theories for their failure to capture the unique aspects of emotion that make them different from cognition. He also says that they have based their understanding of appraisal processes largely on self-reports, that is, people's introspective verbal reflections. Why do you think he sees this as a (further) limitation of appraisal theories?

29

The relation of eye movements during sleep to dream activity: an objective method for the study of dreaming

William Dement and Nathaniel Kleitman (1957)

Journal of Experimental Psychology, 53, (5), 339–46

BACKGROUND AND CONTEXT

Dreaming has always fascinated human beings, although it is only very recently that it (and its relationship to sleep) has been studied scientifically. Although theories of sleep and theories of dreaming have been proposed separately, it is difficult to discuss one without the other. Sleep deprivation is a common way of studying the normal function of sleep, and the findings are often expressed in terms of how the dreaming process is disrupted. Similarly, as in the Dement and Kleitman study, dreaming is often studied using objective, physiological correlates or indicators (eye movements and EEG patterns in particular) as these occur during *rapid eye movement* (REM) sleep.

Starting with sleep, it is true that all mammals, reptiles, amphibians and fish have periods of sleep (or sleeplike periods), and different species also have different cycles of sleep and wakefulness. The human cycle is *monophasic* (one period of sleep/waking per 24-hour cycle), while rats, rabbits and other rodents are *polyphasic*. Human infants are also polyphasic to begin with, but they gradually adopt the monophasic pattern. Sleeping, therefore, is part of our *circadian rhythm* (*circa dies* = about one day), a daily cyclical change in body temperature, blood pressure, blood-plasma volume, hormone secretions and so on (Moor-Ede & Czeisler, 1984). We normally sleep during the low point of the temperature cycle.

What are the effects of disrupting the circadian rhythm? One common type of study involves shift workers who often report experiencing insomnia, digestive problems, irritability, fatigue, even depression. Workers who rotate shifts each week also have more accidents at work and lower productivity. Blakemore (1988) cites a study of workers at the Great Salt Lake Mineral and Chemical Corporation in Utah, USA, who worked a three-weekly shift cycle: day shift (week 1), night shift (week 2), evening shift (week 3) and so on. This is the worst possible arrangement as far as bodily rhythms are concerned: Blakemore likens it to travelling constantly from west to east and never quite overcoming the resulting jet lag (the Utah workers were forced to rotate their biological clock *backwards* by eight hours per week).

Because their sleep–wake cycle was *abruptly* disrupted (they did not have a chance to adapt to their shift before it changed again), the temperature cycle may have continued to adhere to old rhythms for a while. This can (at least partly) account for why psychological functioning and general well-being are adversely affected: it is not lack of sleep but disruption of the circadian rhythm which is the critical variable. This also applies to jet lag.

So what about studies of people actually being deprived of sleep (without a disruption of the circadian rhythm)? Webb & Bonnet (1979) limited participants to two hours sleep on one particular night. They suffered no ill effects the following day, but that night they fell asleep more quickly and slept longer than usual. Longer periods of sleep deprivation may result in some unpleasant psychological effects, but people are remarkably able to do without sleep. Webb and Bonnet gradually reduced the length of sleep in a group of volunteers from eight to four hours per night over a two-month period with no detectable effects.

However, when sleep is *abruptly* reduced (as, say, in the case of hospital doctors who may be on duty for up to 72 hours at a stretch), the effects are rather more serious: irritability, intellectual inefficiency, and an intense fatigue and need for sleep. Interestingly, these are more or less the same effects as are produced by depriving people of approximately two hours of REM sleep (but otherwise allowing them to sleep normally). The following night there is an increase in REM sleep, to compensate for the previous night's loss (the *REM rebound*: Webb & Bonnet, 1979).

When volunteers are able to get by on greatly (but *gradually*) reduced amounts of sleep, it is apparently because they pack their two hours of REM sleep tightly into the sleeping time they do have (thus reducing the amount of NREM sleep in between their dreams). When sleep is *abruptly* reduced, there is no time to adopt this alternative dreaming–sleep pattern.

So we may have found a crucial link between sleep and dreams: deprivation of REM sleep seems to be much more damaging (at least in the short-term) than loss of *non-rapid-eye movement* (NREM) sleep, and this seems to be because of the loss of dream time associated with REM sleep.

AIM AND NATURE OF THE STUDY

The study reports the results of a rigorous testing of the relationship between eye movements and dreaming. Three main hypotheses were being tested:

(*i*)   there is a significant association between REM/NREM sleep and dreaming, such

that (based on previous research) REM sleep is associated with dreaming and NREM is not;

(*ii*) there is a significant positive correlation between the subjective estimate of the duration of dreams and the length of eye-movement period prior to awakening;

(*iii*) there is a significant association between the pattern of eye movement and the content of the dream, such that the former actually reflects the visual experience of the dream.

Participants (seven adult males and two adult females) were studied under controlled laboratory conditions. They spent a night in the laboratory, being woken at various intervals during the night and during which physiological recordings were made of (*i*) changes in corneoretinal potential fields as the eyes moved, and (*ii*) brainwaves.

This was done by attaching (*i*) two/more electrodes near the eyes and (*ii*) two or three electrodes to the scalp. Why the study is so important is that it represents a way of objectively measuring physiological indicators of dreaming, although, as Dement and Kleitman say, ultimately the only 'proof' that dreaming has occurred is that the dreamer reports having dreamt.

■THE■STUDY■

The study of dream activity and its relation to physiological variables during sleep requires a reliable method of determining precisely when dreaming occurs. Ultimately, this knowledge always depends upon the subjective report of the dreamer, but becomes relatively objective if such reports can be significantly related to some physiological phenomena which in turn can be measured by physical techniques.

Such a relationship was reported by Aserinsky and Kleitman (1955), who observed periods of rapid, connected eye movements during sleep and found a high incidence of dream recall in *Ss* awakened during these periods and a low incidence when awakened at other times. The occurrence of these characteristic eye movements and their relation to dreaming were confirmed in both normal *Ss* and schizophrenics (Dement, 1955), and they were shown to appear at regular intervals in relation to a cyclic change in the depth of sleep during the night, as measured by the EEG (Dement & Kleitman, 1955).

This paper presents the results of a rigorous testing of the relation between eye movements and dreaming. Three approaches were used: (*i*) dream recall during rapid eye-movement or quiescent periods was elicited without direct contact between *E* and *S*, thus eliminating the possibility of unintentional cueing by *E*; (*ii*) the subjective estimate of the duration of dreams was compared with the length of eye-movement periods before awakening, reasoning that there should be a positive correlation if dreaming and eye movements were concurrent; (*iii*) the pattern of the eye movements was related to the dream content to test whether they represented a specific expression of the visual experience of dreaming or merely a random motor discharge of a more active central nervous system.

▪ M E T H O D ▪

The *Ss* for the experiments were seven adult males and two adult females. Five were studied intensively while data from the other four were minimal, the main intent being to confirm the results of the first five.

In a typical experiment, *S* reported to the laboratory a little before his usual bedtime. He was instructed to eat normally but to abstain from alcoholic or caffeine-containing drinks on the day of the experiment. Two or more electrodes were attached near the eyes for registering changes in the corneoretinal potential fields as the eyes moved, two or three were attached to the scalp for recording brain waves as a criterion of depth of sleep. *S* then went to bed in a quiet, dark room. All electrode lead wires were further attached to the top of the head and from there to

THE STUDY

Table 29.1

SUMMARY OF EXPERIMENTS

Ss	Night slept	Awakenings	Average nightly awakenings	Average sleeping time
DN	6	50	8.3	7:50
IR	12	65	5.4	4:20
KC	17	74	4.4	6:00
WD	11	77	7.0	6:30
PM	9	55	6.1	6:20
KK	2	10	5.0	6:00
SM	1	6	6.0	6:40
DM	1	4	4.0	7:00
MG	2	10	5.0	6:10
Totals	61	351	5.7	6:00

the lead box at the head of the bed in a single cord to minimize the possibility of entanglement and allow *S* a free range of movement. The potentials were amplified by a Model III Grass Electroencephalograph in an adjoining room; it was run continuously throughout the sleep period at a paper speed of 3 or 6 mm per second which allowed easy recognition of eye-movement potentials. A faster speed (3 cm/sec) was used for detailed examination of the brainwaves, although the slower speed permitted at least an approximate estimation of the gross pattern.

At various times during the night *Ss* were awakened to test their dream recall. It usually took less than five minutes to return to sleep after such awakening. Table 29.1 summarizes the experiments, showing the number of nights each *S* slept, and the number of awakenings. In all, 21 per cent of the awakenings fell in the first two hours of sleep, 29 per cent in the second two, 28 per cent in the third two, and 22 per cent in the fourth two.

R E S U L T S

THE OCCURRENCE OF RAPID EYE MOVEMENTS (REM)

Discrete periods during which their eyes showed rapid movements were observed in all nine *Ss* every night they slept, and were characterized by a low-voltage, relatively fast EEG pattern. In between the REM periods, EEG patterns indicating deeper sleep were either predominantly high-voltage, slow activity, or frequent, well-defined sleep spindles with a low-voltage background. No REMs were ever observed during the initial onset of sleep, although the EEG always passed through a stage similar to that accompanying the REM periods occurring later in the night. These findings were identical with previous observations on uninterrupted sleep (Dement & Kleitman, 1955).

REM periods which were not terminated by awakening varied between three and 50 minutes with a mean of about 20 minutes, and they tended to increase the later in the night they occurred. The eyes were not constantly in motion during such periods; rather, the activity occurred in bursts of one or two, up to 50 or 100 movements. A single movement generally took 0.1 to 0.2 seconds and was followed by a fixational pause of varying duration. The amount, pattern and size of the movement varied irregularly from period to period.

The REM periods occurred at fairly regular intervals throughout the night. The frequency of occurrence seemed to be relatively constant and characteristic for the individual: DM and WD averaged one eye-movement period every 70 minutes and 75 minutes respectively, KC 104 minutes; the other *Ss* fell between these extremes. The average for the whole group was one REM period every 92 minutes.

Despite the considerable disturbance of being awakened a number of times, the frequency and regularity with which REM periods occurred was almost exactly comparable to that found in an earlier study of uninterrupted sleep (Dement & Kleitman, 1955). If the awakening occurred during a period of no rapid eye movements (NREM), the return to sleep was never associated with REMs, nor was the time of onset of the next REM period markedly changed from what would have been expected in the absence of awakening. An awakening during an REM period generally terminated the REMs until the next period, and the sequence of EEG changes (excluding the brief period of wakefulness) was the same as that following an REM period which ended spontaneously. Exceptions did occur when *S* was awakened during an REM period in the final hours of sleep, when it was likely to be quite long if uninterrupted; the REMs sometimes started up again when *S* fell asleep. It seemed as though a period of heightened CNS activity had not run its normal course and, although *S* was able to fall asleep, he continued to dream.

EYE-MOVEMENT PERIODS AND DREAM RECALL

The arousing stimulus was the ringing of an ordinary doorbell placed near the bed and sufficiently loud to ensure immediate awakening in all levels of sleep. *Ss* then spoke into a recording device near the bed. They were instructed to first state whether or not they had been dreaming and then, if they could, to relate the content of the dream. When *S* had finished speaking, *E*, who could hear their voices, occasionally entered the room to question them further on some detail of the dream. There was no communication between *S* and *E* until *S* had definitely committed himself, and was considered to have been dreaming only if he could relate a coherent, fairly detailed description of dream content; assertions that he had dreamed without recall of content, or vague fragmentary impressions of content, did not count.

The awakenings were done either during REM periods or at varying intervals of time after the cessation of eye movements during the interspersed periods of NREMs. *Ss*, of course, were never told when awakened whether or not their eyes had been moving.

Table 29.2 shows the results of the attempts to recall dreams after the various awakenings. The REM and NREM awakenings for PM and KC were chosen according to a random numbers table to eliminate any possibility of intentional pattern. For DN, a pattern was followed, namely, three REM awakenings followed by three NREM awakenings, and so on. WD was told he would be awakened *only* when the recordings indicated he was dreaming, but REM and NREM awakenings were interspersed randomly. IR was awakened at the *E*'s whim.

Ss uniformly showed a high incidence of dream recall following REM awakenings and a very low incidence following NREM awakenings, regardless of how the awak-

Table 29.2

INSTANCES OF DREAM RECALL AFTER AWAKENINGS DURING PERIODS OF REMs
OR PERIODS OF NREMs

S	Rapid eye movements		No rapid eye movements	
	Dream recall	No recall	Dream recall	No recall
DN	17	9	3	21
IR	26	8	2	29
KC	36	4	3	31
WD	37	5	1	34
PM	24	6	2	23
KK	4	1	0	5
SM	2	2	0	2
DM	2	1	0	1
MG	4	3	0	3
Totals	152	39	11	149

THE STUDY

enings were chosen. DN was no more accurate than the others although there was a pattern he might have learned, and WD was no less accurate for being deliberately misled to expect to have been dreaming every time he was awakened. Over a narrow range, some *Ss* seemed better able to recall dreams than others.

Table 29.3 compares the results of the first half of the series of REM awakenings with the last half; practice was certainly not a significant factor as only one *S* showed any degree of improvement on later nights compared with early ones.

The incidence of dream recall dropped dramatically almost immediately upon cessation of REMs. In 17 NREM awakenings done within eight minutes of the end of an REM period, five dreams were recalled; although small, this was a much higher incidence than occurred when the NREM awakenings followed the end of REM periods by *more* than eight minutes (six dreams recalled in 132 awakenings).

In general, *Ss* were best able to make an emphatic statement that they had not been dreaming when the NREM awakenings were done during an intermediate stage of sleep, as indicated by a brainwave pattern of spindling with a low-voltage

Table 29.3

COMPARISON OF FIRST HALF OF SERIES OF REM AWAKENING WITH SECOND HALF

S	First half		Second half	
	Dream recall	No recall	Dream recall	No recall
DN	12	1	5	8
IR	12	5	14	3
KC	18	2	18	2
WD	19	2	18	3
PM	12	3	12	3
Totals	73	13	67	19

background. When aroused during a deep stage of sleep characterized by high-voltage, slow waves, *Ss* often awoke rather bewildered, and often felt that they must have been dreaming although they could not remember the dream. They often described feelings of pleasantness, anxiety, detachment, etc. but could not relate them to any specific dream content.

When *Ss* failed to recall following REM awakenings, this was usually early on in the night. Nineteen out of 39 such instances occurred during the first two hours, 11 during the second two hours, five in the third and four in the last.

LENGTH OF REM PERIODS AND SUBJECTIVE DREAM – DURATION ESTIMATES

At first, *Ss* were awakened at various intervals of time after the REMs had begun and were asked to estimate to the nearest minute the amount of time they had been dreaming. This proved too difficult, and a series was then done in which *Ss* were awakened either five or 15 minutes after the onset of REMs and were required on the basis of their recall of the dream to decide which was the correct duration. The two durations were chosen on the basis of a random series. Table 29.4 shows the results: all *Ss* were able to choose the correct dream duration very accurately except DN who could only recall the latter part of the dream and so underestimated its length.

In addition to the actual dream length, the lengths of the dream narratives were influenced by factors such as *Ss* talkativeness. However, the narrative length still

Table 29.4

RESULTS OF DREAM DURATION ESTIMATES AFTER 5 OR 15 MINUTES OF REMs

S	Five minutes		15 minutes	
	Right	Wrong	Right	Wrong
DN	8	2	5	5
IR	11	1	7	3
KC	7	0	12	1
WD	13	1	15	1
PM	6	2	8	3
Totals	45	6	47	13

showed a significant relationship to the duration of REM periods before awakening. Table 29.5 shows the correlation between minutes of REMs and lengths of dream narratives for each *S*. Length was measured by the number of words. Narratives for dreams recalled after 30 to 50 minutes of REMs were not a great deal longer than those after 15 minutes, although *Ss* had the impression of having been dreaming for an unusually long time. This was perhaps due to inability to remember all the details of very long dreams.

Table 29.5

CORRELATION BETWEEN DURATION OF REM PERIODS IN MINUTES AND NUMBER OF WORDS IN DREAM NARRATIVES

S	Number of dreams	r	p
DN	15	0.60	<0.02
IR	25	0.68	<0.001
KC	31	0.40	<0.05
WD	35	0.71	<0.001
PM	20	0.53	<0.02

SPECIFIC EYE-MOVEMENT PATTERNS AND VISUAL IMAGERY OF THE DREAM

The quality and quantity of the REMs themselves showed endless variation. Although the movements occurred in bursts of activity separated by periods of relative inactivity, the brainwave pattern during the whole period remained the same, whether there was much or little movement at any given moment of the period.

It was hypothesized that the movements represented the visual imagery of the dream, i.e. they corresponded to where and at what the dreamer was looking. It was impossible for *Ss* to state chronologically in what direction he had gazed during the dream. Instead, *Ss* were awakened as soon as one of four predominant patterns of movement had persisted for at least one minute, and were asked to describe in detail the dream content just before awakening. The four patterns were: (*i*) mainly vertical eye movements, (*ii*) mainly horizontal; (*iii*) both vertical and horizontal; (*iv*) very little or no movement.

Altogether, 35 awakenings were collected from the nine *Ss*. Periods of either pure vertical or horizontal movements were extremely rare but three such periods of vertical movements were seen. One *S* dreamed of standing at the bottom of a tall cliff operating some sort of hoist and looking up at climbers at various levels, and down at the hoist machinery. Another dreamed of climbing up a series of ladders looking up and down as he climbed. The third *S* dreamt of throwing basketballs at a net, first shooting and looking up at the net, and then looking down to pick another ball off the floor. In the only instance of pure horizontal movement, the dreamer was watching two people throwing tomatoes at each other. On ten occasions, *Ss* were awakened after one minute of little or no eye movement, and in all cases the dreams involved the dreamer watching something at a distance or just staring fixedly at some object. In two of these cases, about one minute of ocular inactivity was followed by several large movements to the left just a second or two before the awakening. The corresponding dream content was almost identical for both *Ss*: in one dream, *S* was driving a car, staring at the road ahead and as he approached an intersection was startled by the sudden appearance of a car speeding at him from the left; in the other, the dreamer was also driving a car, staring at the road ahead, when he saw a man on the left side of the road, and hailed him as he drove past.

In the 21 awakenings after a mixture of movements, *Ss* were always looking at people or objects close to them, e.g. talking to a group of people, looking for something, fighting with someone. There was no recall of distant or vertical activity.

In order to confirm the meaningfulness of these relationships, 20 naïve *Ss* as well as five of the experimental *Ss* were asked to observe distant and close-up activity while awake. Eye-movement potentials, as measured by electrodes, were in all cases comparable to those occurring during dreaming, both in amplitude and pattern. Furthermore, there was virtually no movement when viewing distant activity but much while viewing close-up activity.

D I S C U S S I O N

The results of these experiments indicate that dreaming accompanied by REMs and a low-voltage EEG occurred periodically in discrete episodes during the course of a night's sleep. The lack of dream recall, plus the fact that the brainwaves were at the lightest level of sleep only during REM periods and at deeper levels at all other times, suggests that dream activity does not occur at other times. The few instances of dream recall during NREM periods are best explained by assuming that the memory of the preceding dream persisted for an unusually long time; most such instances did, in fact, occur very soon (within eight minutes) after the end of REM periods.

Other workers have tried to relate dreaming to physiological phenomena during sleep. Wada (1922) believed that dreaming and gastric contractions occurred simultaneously, but this conclusion was based on only seven awakenings in two *Ss*, one of whom could not recall dream content. Scantlebury *et al.* (1942) also studied gastric activity, but did not draw any firm conclusions. McGlade (1942) suggested that dreaming occurs during a series of foot twitches immediately after the onset of sleep but the dreams were recalled on the morning after the experiments, and only three out of 25 *Ss* actually exhibited foot twitches.

Incidental observations have been made on the occurrence of dreaming by investigators studying brainwaves during sleep (Blake *et al.*, 1939; Davis *et al.*, 1938; Henry, 1941; Knott *et al.*, 1939; Loomis *et al.*, 1937). All stages of brainwaves were related to dreaming in these five papers, but no mention was made of whether or not actual dream content was recalled, and the number of reports by sleepers was generally very small.

In other studies of dreaming, excellently reviewed by Ramsey (1953), attempts were made to localize dream activity by simply awakening *Ss* at various times during the night. In general, it was found that dreams might be recalled at any time during the night, but that most were recalled in the later hours of sleep. This would correspond to the statistical incidence of REMs as previously reported by Aserinsky and Kleitman (1955) and Dement (1955) and is also consistent with the finding here that, even when the awakenings occurred during REM periods, recall was still more difficult earlier in the night.

We found that all *Ss* showed periods of REMs *every* night they slept, and so did Dement and Kleitman (1955), involving 16 *Ss* over 43 nights. It appears that periods of REMs and dreaming and the regularity of their occurrence are an intrinsic part of normal sleep. So why did Aserinsky and Kleitman (1955) and Dement (1955) find

THE STUDY

occasional subjects without REMs? One explanation could be that the recording was done by sampling rather than continuously, so that shorter-than-usual REM periods could have occurred between the samples, thus escaping observation. Alternatively, a lower amplification of the REM potentials was used which failed to record very small movements. A third possibility is that these *Ss'* dreams happened to be of the kind (e.g. watching distant activity) in which eye movements were at a minimum.

Rather than occurring instantaneously or with great rapidity, it seems that dreams progress at a rate comparable to a real experience of the same sort. An increase in the length of REM periods was almost always associated with a proportional increase in the length of the dream.

It seems reasonable to conclude that an objective measurement of dreaming may be achieved by recording REMs during sleep. This contrasts sharply with the forgetting, distortion and other factors involved in the reliance on the subjective recall of dreams. It thus becomes possible to study objectively the effect on dreaming of environmental changes, psychological stress, drugs, and a variety of other influences.

S U M M A R Y

Regularly occurring periods of REMs were observed during every night of experimental sleep in nine adult *Ss*. A high incidence of dream recall was obtained from *Ss* when awakened during REM periods, and a very low incidence when awakened at other times. A series of awakenings was done either five or 15 minutes after the REMs (dreaming) had begun, and *Ss* judged the correct dream duration very accurately. The pattern of the REMs was related to the visual imagery of the dream, and the eye movements recorded in analagous situations while awake corresponded closely in amplitude and pattern to those observed during dreaming.

EVALUATION

Theoretical issues

In humans, waking to sleep is a transition from where thought is strongly influenced by external sources to a mainly endogenous (internal) generation of mental activity in dreaming (Hobson, 1990). To some psychologists, sleep might be considered as 'non-behaviour', while to others the cognitive richness of dreaming makes sleep a prime candidate for investigation (Toates, 2001). Indeed, one of psychology's most famous

controversies concerns what interpretation, if any, should be placed on dreaming, and thereby what is thee function of sleep (see **Subsequent research** and **Applications and implications** below). It is widely accepted that sleep is *not* a passive process (a 'default state') that corresponds to neuronal fatigue (Dement, 1994). Indeed, in REM sleep the nervous system can display as much activity as during waking. Sleep is an active process, the output of specific activity in specific neuronal pathways (Hobson, 1986; Moruzzi, 1966). According to Mueller & Roberts (2001):

> . . . Few topics in psychology have aroused as much interest as dreams, and yet it is true that there are few which illustrate better the gulf . . . between what lay people expect from psychology and what scientific psychology delivers to them . . .

Be that as it may, there has been a good deal of support for the *REM rebound* phenomenon. For example, Dement (1960) woke volunteers from their REM sleep on five successive nights (while a control group was only woken during their NREM sleep). As well as becoming nervous, irritable and unable to concentrate, Dement also reported that the the REM-deprived tended to become paranoid, attributing sinister motives to the researcher, developing all kinds of unreasonable suspicions and even hallucinating.

However, he later maintained that these symptoms were *not* really caused by the lack of REM sleep, but were more likely to have been caused by the researcher's expectations, communicated (ironically) through concern for their welfare: Dement had told his participants what he thought the probable results would be, and that a psychiatrist would be on duty all the time. After the third day, little sleep at all was being had, since they had more frequent REM periods, and so were being woken more frequently. The symptoms were the combined effects of total lack of sleep and suggestion (i.e. *demand characteristics*: see Chapters 21 and 31).

Dement replicated his study in 1965 and found no evidence of symptoms of psychiatric disturbance with REM sleep deprivation (Empson, 1993). When allowed to sleep normally (without interruption), participants did 60% more dreaming until they had made up their lost REM time. For as many as five nights following their REM deprivation, they spent more time in REM than usual, and on some nights doubled their REM time. These results were consistent with the idea that REM sleep and the dreaming associated with it are especially important, perhaps representing the most important function of sleeping (Empson, 1993: see **Subsequent research** below). Many drugs, including alcohol and various sleeping pills, suppress REM sleep without affecting NREM sleep.

Methodological issues

Is it possible that the difference between REM and NREM sleep regarding the dreaming which goes on is actually an artefact of the ability to *recall* dreams following the 'rude awakening'?

Beaumont (1988) argues that being woken from NREM (or S-sleep) may lead to the dream being forgotten before *the participant* is sufficiently awake to report it. This is a deeper kind of sleep in which the brain is much less active, and shows EEGs very different from the waking state. By contrast, being woken from REM (or D-sleep) may allow the ongoing dream to be remembered and then reported (the brain is much more active and EEGs are much like those of the waking state).

Clearly, if this is so, then we have stumbled upon a major confounding variable which challenges the very basis of the sleep/dream research of Dement and Kleitman. Herman *et al.* (1978, cited in Smith *et al.*, 1986) claim that an appreciable amount of mental activity occurs during NREM sleep, and there are no completely consistent differences between dream reports obtained when participants are woken from either kind of sleep. According to Foulkes (1960), dream reporting can be obtained (although less frequently) from NREM sleep, and it is also now established that dreaming occurs not only in the lighter levels of NREM sleep but also in the hypnagogic period of sleep onset, as well as in 'daydreaming' as studied under laboratory conditions (Foulkes, 1993).

However, if people are woken from REM sleep, they commonly report that they were dreaming (Hobson, 1999), and dreaming is associated primarily with REM sleep (McCarley, 1995). According to Mueller & Roberts (2001), dream reports from REM sleep have maintained their position as the principal focus of empirical investigations of dreaming. The evidence regarding REM rebound, together with that concerning the actual eye-movements in REM and how these are related to the dream's content, would seem to represent support for the view of REM sleep as dream-state sleep independently of the sleeper's report of having dreamed (or not).

Subsequent research

So why are dreams so important? When Freud wrote his *Interpretation of Dreams* in 1900, the physiology of sleep was unknown. Since then, dreaming has come to be understood as part of a biologically determined sleep cycle (Winson, 1997).

Ornstein (1986) believes that REM sleep and dreaming may be involved in the reorganization of our schemas (mental structures), so as to accommodate new information. People placed in a 'disturbing and perplexing' atmosphere for four hours just before sleep (asked to perform difficult tasks with no explanation) will spend longer in REM sleep than normal. REM sleep time also increases after people have had to learn complex tasks. This may explain why REM sleep decreases with age: newborns spend half their 18 hours of sleep in REM sleep (nine hours), while adults usually spend only a quarter of their eight in REM sleep (two hours). It has been

suggested (consistent with Ornstein's proposal) that babies' brains need to process and assimilate the flood of new stimuli pouring in from the outside world and this is (partly) achieved through REM sleep (Oswald, 1966). REM sleep in early development might represent a 'test-run' of the information processing circuits that will be used later on (Toates, 2001).

According to the *activation-synthesis model* (Hobson & McCarley, 1977; McCarley, 1983; Hobson, 1988; Mamalek & Hobson, 1989), REM sleep results from activation of the 'REM-ON' area located in the pontine reticular formation (at the apex of the spinal column at the base of the brain). This prevents most sensory stimulation from reaching the brain. Although the motor cortex is highly active, generating activity which would normally produce movement, these commands do not reach the skeletal muscles that control the limbs, but are 'switched off' at a relay station at the top of the spinal column. This means that we are effectively *paralyzed* during REM sleep, which explains the loss of tone in the neck muscles under the chin (another defining characteristic of REM sleep: Empson, 1993). So, in the absence of motor output and sensory input, the brain is virtually isolated during REM sleep. Parts of the brain that control emotions and store memories may also be activated. This may occur either directly, via the REM-ON system, or indirectly, via activation of motor or sensory systems. In this way, aspects of the dreamer's personality become part of the dream.

When these simultaneously activated systems are synthesized, dreaming takes place. This process of *synthesis* is no different from what occurs in the waking brain. During wakefulness, available sensory and motor information is integrated with information on the current affective state, and memories of similar experiences and related meanings are then drawn on in order to make sense of it (Moorcroft, 1993). Sensory and motor information are strongly linked and seem 'normal'. Our perception usually flows smoothly, because the sequence of sensory and motor activations follow one another in an orderly way (Mueller & Roberts, 2001). But when we are asleep, what is activated at one moment may not be related to what is activated the next, resulting in bizarre shifts that are characteristic of dreams. So:

> . . . the difference between dreaming and being awake, is not the process of activation and synthesis, but the source of the activation – more external (and sequential) when awake, and almost entirely internal (somewhat random) when in REM sleep. (Mueller & Roberts, 2001)

Dreams normally arise from activity within the visual system (McCarley, 1995), and dream content is primarily visual and involves movement (Hobson, 1986). Many dreams do involve vigorous physical activity, such as running, jumping, struggling (see *Specific eye-movement patterns and visual imagery of the dream* in Dement and Kleitman's study, page 557). Again, many common dream experiences can be thought of as an *interpretation* of the body's physical states. For example, being chased, locked up or frozen with fear, may well reflect the blocked motor commands to our muscles during REM sleep. Floating, flying and falling experiences may reflect vestibular activation.

The sexual content of dreams may reflect vaginal engorgement and penile erection (Ornstein, 1986).

Perhaps there is also a sense in which we dream *instead* of acting (maybe suggesting the need for rest/restoration of the body): neural mechanisms in the brain stem block nerve impulses from the brain to the skeletal muscles ('paralysis'). Cats with brain stem injury act out their dreams by, for example, chasing the mouse of their dream, while ignoring a real mouse in their cage (Morrison, 1983, cited by Smith *et al.*, 1986).

Based partly on the activation-synthesis model, Crick & Mitchison (1983) proposed the idea of *reverse learning*. According to this idea, we dream in order to forget! A complex associational network such as the neocortex might become overloaded by vast amounts of incoming information, leading to the formation of false or 'parasitic' thoughts. These are interpretations which, whatever their origin, have no place in our latest view of the world, and which are redundant but persistent.

Accordingly, REM sleep serves to erase these false associations ('unlearning') on a regular basis. This is essential for the orderly functioning of memory, and in humans, dreams are a running record of these parasitic thoughts. Trying to remember our dreams, so crucial as far as psychodynamic theorists like Freud and Jung are concerned (see below), may *not* be such a good idea, since they are the very patterns of thought the system is trying to tune out. In their 1986 revision of the model, the erasure of parasitic thoughts now accounted *only* for bizarre dream content: nothing could be said about dream narrative (the more coherent, sequential, 'story-like' content). Furthermore, dreaming to forget was better expressed as dreaming to reduce fantasy or obsession.

However, does the truth of the activation synthesis model (and other *neural* models) *exclude* other theories of dreams? Not necessarily. While neural models may account for 'where dreams come from', (by focusing on the 'activation' component), they fail to address the issue of 'what dreams are for'. *Psychological* theories of dreaming focus on the synthesis component of the model, and try to explain its significance for the dreamer: dreams are inherently *meaningful*. But do neural accounts necessarily dismiss dreams as inherently meaningless? Perhaps Crick and Mitchison are focusing on the function of dreams (at least the bizarre, nonsensical aspects) *for the brain*, while Hobson and McCarley argue that motivational states, memories, emotions, and even the movement patterns activated in the brain during REM sleep are products of the *individual's experience and personality*. As they say, synthesis occurs in both dreams and waking life, and personality characteristics determine the meaning attached to a specific stimulus, whether its source is external or internal. Thus dreams may contain information that is relevant and revealing about the dreamer. However, they warn that this should not be taken too far: it does not follow that each element of a dream has symbolic meaning.

Freud, like Jung, saw symbolism as of central importance, taking the view that dreams can put the dreamer in touch with parts of the self usually inaccessible during waking life. According to Hall (1966), dreams are 'a personal document, a letter to oneself' and, like Jung, he advocated the study of dream *series* rather than single, isolated, dreams.

Applications and implications

Winson (1997), a neuroscientist, argues that neural and psychological theories of dreams are *not* mutually exclusive; for him, the key to understanding the meaning and function of dreams is the *theta rhythm*. This was originally detected in the hippocampus of rabbits when they were apprehensive of some environmental stimulus, and was subsequently recorded in other species, including rats and cats. While it was consistently observed in awake animals, it was then discovered in their REM sleep.

Awake animals seem to show theta rhythm when engaged in behaviours most crucial to their survival (*not* genetically encoded, such as feeding and sexual behaviour), such as predatory behaviour in cats, prey behaviour in rabbits, and exploration in rats (all involving a response to changing environmental stimulation). Further, because the hippocampus is involved in memory processing, the presence of theta rhythm in REM sleep in that region might be related to that activity: theta rhythm might reflect a neural process, whereby information essential to a species' survival (acquired during the day) was processed into memory during REM sleep.

Winson claims that there is considerable neuroscientific evidence (based mainly on rats) that theta rhythm does, indeed, encode memories during REM sleep. Other evidence comes from investigation of the *evolution* of REM sleep.

The emergence of a neural mechanism to process memory in REM sleep suggests differences in brain anatomy between mammals that have that aspect of the sleep cycle and those that don't. Such differences clearly do exist between three species of mammal: echidna (spiny-anteater), marsupials, and placentals. The echidna has a large, convoluted prefrontal cortex, larger in relation to the rest of its brain than in any other mammal (including humans). This is needed to perform a dual function: to react appropriately to incoming information based on past experience, and to evaluate and store new information to aid in future survival.

Without theta rhythm during REM sleep, the echidna would be unable to process information while asleep. For higher abilities to develop, the prefrontal cortex would have to become increasingly large (beyond the capacity of the skull), unless some other mechansim evolved. REM sleep could have provided this new mechanism, allowing memory processing to occur 'off-line'.

Coincident with the apparent development of REM sleep in marsupial and placental mammals was a remarkable neuro-anatomical change: the prefrontal cortex was dramatically reduced in size. Far less of it was needed to process information and it could develop to provide advanced perceptual abilities in higher species.

The nature of REM sleep supports this evolutionary argument. To maintain sleep, locomotion had to be suppressed by inhibiting motor neurons, but suppressing *eye movements* wasn't necessary because this does not disturb sleep. With the evolution of REM sleep, each species could process the information most needed for its survival, such as the location of food, and means of predation or escape: the very activities during which theta rhythm is present. In REM sleep, this information may be accessed again and integrated with past experience to provide an ongoing strategy for behaviour.

Although theta rhythm has not yet been detected in primates (including humans), the brain signal provides a clue to the origin of dreaming in humans:

> . . . Dreams may reflect a memory-processing mechanism inherited from lower species, in which information important for survival is reprocessed during REM sleep. This information may constitute the core of the unconscious. (Winson, 1997)

Because animals have no language, the information processed during their REM sleep is necessarily *sensory*. Consistent with our early mammalian origins, our dreams are also sensory (primarily visual: see above): they do *not* take the form of verbal narration. However, while there is no functional need in non-human species for this material to become conscious, there is no reason for it *not* to become conscious in humans: we *can* remember our dreams. Consistent with evolutionary and neuroscientific evidence, plus people's reports of their dreams:

> . . . dreams reflect an individual's strategy for survival. The subjects of dreams are broad-ranging and complex, incorporating self-image, fears, insecurities, strengths, grandiose ideas, sexual orientation, desire, jealousy and love. (Winson, 1997)

Dreams clearly have a deep psychological core. Although the topic 'chosen' for consideration during a night's sleep is unpredictable, certain of life's difficulties so engage psychological survival that they are selected for REM processing. Consistent with this is the finding that we tend to dream more when under stress, which suggests that dreams provide an endless variety of ideas and options (Panksepp, 1998a). Freud's dream theory contains a profound truth: there *is* an unconscious and dreams are indeed the 'royal road' to its understanding. However, the characteristics of the unconscious and associated processes of brain functioning are very different from Freud's ideas. Rather than a cauldron of untamed passions and destructive wishes,

> . . . the unconscious is a cohesive, continually active mental structure that takes note of life's experiences and reacts according to its own scheme of interpretation. Dreams are not disguised as a consequence of repression. Their unusual character is a result of the complex associations that are called from memory. (Winson, 1997)

On a more practical note, it is generally accepted that a characteristic symptom of mood disorders is sleep disturbances (typically, depressed patients fall asleep easily but wake early and are unable to get back to sleep). Kupfer (1976) reported that depressed people tend to enter REM sleep sooner than non-depressed, and spend increased time in it during the last half of sleep. Vogel *et al.* (1980) deprived depressed patients of REM sleep over a period of several weeks and found, remarkably, that this reduced their depression relatively permanently (Carlson & Buskist, 1997).

Exercises

1. Does it matter that seven of the nine participants were males and only two were females?

2. Why were participants asked to abstain from alcoholic or caffeine-containing drinks on the day of the experiment?

3. REM periods not terminated by awakening varied from 3 to 50 minutes, the *mean* being about 20 minutes. Would an alternative measure of central tendency be justified?

4. Why was it important that participants were never told, after wakening, whether their eyes had been moving or not?

5. Different participants were woken according to a variety of schedules:

   (*i*)   random number tables ($\times 2$);
   (*ii*) three REM, three NREM etc. ($\times 1$);
   (*iii*) told only woken from REM but actually woken from REM and NREM randomly ($\times 1$);
   (*iv*) at *E*'s whim.

   Why was this done? Why weren't random number tables used for all participants?

6. What statistical test would be used *re*: Tables 29.2, 29.3 and 29.4? Why?

7. In Table 29.5,

   (*i*) what test of correlation was used;
   (*ii*) were there any correlation coefficients that were not significant (at or below the 5 per cent level)?

30 Hemisphere deconnection and unity in conscious awareness

R.W. Sperry (1968)

American Psychologist, 23, 723–33

BACKGROUND AND CONTEXT

According to Ornstein (1986), the cerebral cortex appeared in our ancestors quite recently, about 50 million years ago. It performs the functions which have greatly increased our adaptability as a species. A feature of all primate brains is its division into hemispheres, *but* only with the human brain are they specialized for different functions (*lateral specialization* or *functional lateralization*). This represents the most recent development in human evolution (less than four million years old) and is uniquely human.

According to Bogen (1969, in Ornstein, 1986), scientists have been trying to characterize the nature of the left and right hemispheres for well over 100 years, and Sperry's work has made a tremendous contribution to our understanding of functional lateralization. The great physiologist Hughlings Jackson (1864) distinguished between the expressive nature of the left (its use of language as propositional) and the perceptual nature of the right. Zangwill (1961) proposed that the left is predominantly symbolic while the right is predominantly visuospatial. Similarly, Bogen & Gazzaniga (1965) regarded the left as verbal and the right as visuospatial. Again, Levy-Agresti & Sperry (1968) concluded that the:

> . . . mute, minor hemisphere is specialized for Gestalt perception, being primarily a synthesist in dealing with information input. The speaking, major hemisphere, in contrast, seems to operate in a more logical, analytic, computer-like fashion . . .

Ornstein (1986) summarizes the differences like this:

(*i*)   the left is specialized for *analytic and logical thinking* (breaking things down into their component parts), especially in verbal and mathematical functions, processes information *sequentially* (one item at a time) and its mode of operation is primarily *linear* (straight-line);

(*ii*) the right is specialized for *synthetic thinking*, (bringing different things together to form a whole), particularly in the area of spatial tasks, artistic activities, crafts, body image and face recognition, processes information more *diffusely* (several items at once) and its mode of operation is much less linear (more *holistic*).

A dramatic experimental breakthrough in the study of hemisphere specialization came when a new surgical technique for treating some forms of epilepsy was developed. Epileptic seizures are caused by a sort of electrical storm that spreads across the cortex, causing many millions of neurons to fire. A typical pattern of convulsions identified as a seizure occurs when this wave of electricity sweeps over the centres that control various parts of the body, producing violent spasms, and, eventually, loss of consciousness. In some patients, *both* hemispheres are involved, each amplifying the action of the other and contributing to the seizure (Coren, 1992).

Some clinical observers had noticed that, if a patient had suffered damage to the pathways connecting the two hemispheres (the corpus callosum), the frequency and severity of the seizures were often reduced. This led to the surgical procedure in which this connecting tissue was cut (the *split-brain operation*). Sometimes, as well as cutting the corpus callosum, the surgery involves cutting through the smaller anterior and hippocompal *commissures*, and in some cases the massa intermedia, as well. These more drastic operations are called *commissurotomies* (Coren, 1992).

The first commissurotomy on a human being was performed by two neurosurgeons in California, Vogal and Bogen. They began a series of such operations, involving 24 patients. Not only were the medical benefits quite dramatic (the epilepsy was eliminated or markedly reduced), the surgery did not appear to have any noticeable effects on personality, measured intelligence, ability to converse, perceptual ability or motor performance, or coordination of the two halves of their body in performing skilled tasks (Coren, 1992; Stevens, 1998).

Sperry, a neuropsychologist at the nearby California Institute of Technology, had developed a split-brain operation for use with non-humans in the early 1950s, which allowed testing of each hemisphere separately. He realized that such testing in humans might provide the definitive answer as to whether there are any differences between the abilities of the two hemispheres. Sperry's laboratory began extensive testing of Vogel and Bogen's patients (in 1961), and the present article reports the findings of one such study. For this work on 'split-brain' patients, Sperry was awarded the Nobel Prize in 1981.

AIM AND NATURE OF THE STUDY

The study is one of a series published by Sperry and his colleagues (e.g. Gazzaniga) in which they report their findings concerning the 'functional outcome' of commissurotomy: the behavioural, neurological and psychological effects of having the two cerebral hemispheres disconnected.

It is important to point out (although it should be clear enough from the article, and

Background and context above) that in no way was this surgery performed *as part of* psychological research: Sperry's participants were patients suffering from severe epilepsy, which could not be controlled in any less drastic way (e.g. drugs). He then took the opportunity to study these 'split-brain' patients: what better way to study the functioning of the two cerebral hemispheres than to present tasks to each hemisphere separately in people whose hemispheres cannot 'communicate' with each other?

In this way, Sperry's investigations are a kind of 'natural experiment', whereby the experimental manipulation is either done literally by nature (e.g. someone is born without a corpus callosum) or in the 'natural' course of the person's life (e.g. epileptics undergoing surgery for their epilepsy which disconnects the two halves of their brain).

This also means that the studies are clinical studies (as are studies of brain-damaged patients and memory, for example). The tasks are presented to participants under carefully controlled laboratory conditions.

THE STUDY

The following article is a result of studies my colleagues and I have been conducting with some neurosurgical patients, all advanced epileptics, in whom an extensive midline section of the cerebral commissures had been carried out in an effort to contain severe epileptic convulsions, not controlled by medication. In all these patients the surgical sections included division of the entire corpus collosum, plus division of the smaller anterior and hippocampal commissures, plus in some cases the massa intermedia. So far as I know, this is the most radical disconnection of the cerebral hemispheres attempted to date in human surgery. All the sections were performed in a single operation.

No major collapse of mentality or personality was anticipated as a result of this extreme surgery: earlier clinical observations on surgical section of the corpus callosum in man, as well as the results from dozens of monkeys on which I had performed exactly the same surgery, suggested that the functional deficits might very well be less damaging than some of the more common forms of cerebral surgery, such as frontal lobotomy, or even some of the unilateral lobotomies performed more routinely for epilepsy.

The first patient on whom this surgery was tried had been having seizures for over ten years with generalized convulsions that continued to worsen despite treatment. At the time of surgery, he had been averaging two major attacks per week, each leaving him debilitated for another day or so. Episodes of *status epilepticus* (recurring seizures which fail to stop, and represent a medical emergency with a fairly high mortality risk) had also begun to occur at two- to three-month intervals. Since leaving the hospital following his surgery over 5½ years ago, this man has not had a single generalized convulsion (according to latest reports). His level of medication has been reduced and his overall behaviour and well-being have improved (see Bogen & Vogel, 1962).

The second patient, a housewife and mother in her 30s has also been seizure-free since recovering from her surgery, more than four years ago (Bogen *et al.*, 1965). Even her EEG has regained a normal pattern. The excellent outcome in the initial, apparently hopeless, last resort cases led to further application of the surgery to some nine more individuals to date, most of whom are too recent for therapeutic evaluation. Although two patients are still having seizures (but much less severe and frequent, and largely confined to one side), the results overall continue to be predominantly beneficial and the outlook remains promising for selected severe cases.

Our own work has been confined entirely to an examination of the functional outcome, i.e. the behavioural, neurological and psychological effects of this surgical disruption of all cross-talk between the hemispheres. Initially, we were concerned as to whether we would be able to find in these patients any of the numerous symptoms of hemisphere deconnection shown in the so-called 'split-brain' animal studies of the 1950s (Myers, 1961; Sperry, 1967a,b). The historic Akelaitis (1944) studies had set the prevailing doctrine of the 1940s and 1950s, namely that no important functional symptoms are found in man following even complete surgical section of the corpus callosum and anterior commissure, provided that other brain damage is excluded.

These observations have been confirmed to the extent that the most remarkable effect of sectioning the neocortical commissures is the apparent lack of effect on ordinary behaviour. However, in contradiction of the earlier Akelaitis doctrine, we know today that with appropriate tests it is possible to demonstrate a large number of behavioural symptoms which correlate directly with the loss of the neocortical commissures in man and in animals (Gazzaniga, 1967; Sperry, 1967a,b; Sperry *et al.*, 1968). Collectively, these symptoms may be referred to as the syndrome of the neocortical commissures/forebrain commissures, or, less specifically, of hemisphere deconnection.

One of the more general and also more interesting and striking features of this syndrome may be summarized as an apparent doubling in most realms of conscious awareness. Instead of the normally unified single stream of consciousness, these patients behave in many ways as if they have two independent streams of conscious awareness, one in each hemisphere, each cut off from, and out of contact with, the mental experiences of the other, i.e. each hemisphere seems to have its own separate and private sensations, perceptions, concepts and impulses to act, with related volitional, cognitive and learning experiences. Following surgery, each hemisphere also has its own chain of memories which become inaccessible to the recall processes of the other.

THE STUDY

This presence of two minds in one body, as it were, is manifested in a large number and variety of test responses which I will try to review here very briefly, and in a rather simplified way.

Most of the main symptoms can be described for convenience by referring to a single testing set-up (shown in Figure 30.1). Principally, it allows for the lateralized testing of the right and left halves of the visual field, separately or together, and the right and left hands and legs with vision excluded. The tests can be arranged in different combinations, and in association with visual, auditory and other input, while eliminating unwanted stimuli. In testing vision, the subject with one eye covered centres his gaze on a designated fixation point on the upright translucent screen. The visual stimuli on 35mm transparencies are arranged in a standard projector equipped with a shutter and are then back-projected at $\frac{1}{10}$ of a second or less, too fast for eye movements to get the stimulus into the wrong half of the visual field. Figure 30.2 shows that everything seen to the left of the vertical meridian through either eye is projected to the right hemisphere and vice versa, without significant gap or overlap (Sperry, 1968).

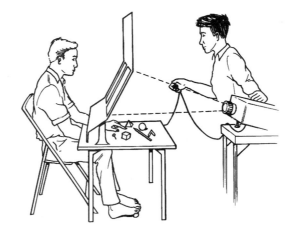

Figure 30.1. Apparatus for studying lateralization of visual, tactual, lingual and associated functions in the surgically separated hemispheres.

When the visual perception of these patients is tested under these conditions, they seem to have two separate visual inner worlds, one serving the right visual field and the other serving the left, each, of course, in its respective hemisphere. This doubling in the visual sphere shows up in many ways; e.g. after a projected picture of an object has been identified and responded to in one half-field, it is recognized again only if it reappears in the same half of the visual field; if it reappears in the opposite half, the subject responds as if he had no recollection of the previous exposure. Each half of the visual field in commissurotomized patients has its own train of visual images and memories.

Another example relates to speech and writing, the cortical mechanisms for which are centred in the dominant hemisphere. Visual material projected to the right half of the field – and hence to the hemisphere system of the typical right-handed patient – can be described in speech and writing in an essentially normal way. However, when the same material is projected into the left half of the field, and hence to the right hemisphere, the subject consistently insists that he did not see anything, or that there was only a flash of light on the left side. The subject acts as if blind or agnostic for the left half of the visual field. If, however, instead of asking the subject to tell you what he saw, you instruct him to use his left hand to point to a matching picture or object presented among a collection of other pictures or objects, he has no trouble, usually, in pointing out consistently the very item he has just insisted he did not see. Everything indicates that the hemisphere which is talking to the tester genuinely did not see the left-field stimulus, and so had no recollection of it. But the non-lingual right hemisphere did see it, and can recognize it, as indicated by pointing out selectively the matching item; like a deaf mute or some aphasics, this hemisphere cannot talk about the perceived object and, worse still, cannot write about it either.

If two different figures are flashed simultaneously to both visual fields, (e.g. a dollar sign on the left and a question mark on the right) and the subject is asked to draw what he saw using the left hand out of sight, he regularly reproduces the figure seen on the left half of the field, i.e. the dollar sign. If we now ask him what he has just drawn, he tells us without hesitation that what he drew was the question mark (or whatever it was presented to the right half of the field); i.e. one hemisphere does not know what the other hemisphere has been doing.

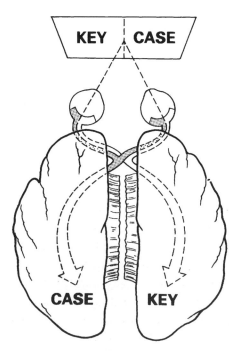

Figure 30.2. Things seen to the left of a central fixation point with either eye are projected to the right hemisphere and vice versa.

When words are flashed partly in the left field and partly in the right, the letters on each side of the midline are perceived and responded to separately. In the 'key case' example in Figure 30.2, the subject might first reach for and select with the left hand a key from among a collection of objects, indicating perception through the minor (right) hemisphere. With the right hand he might then spell out the words 'case', or he might speak the word if asked to give a verbal response. When asked what kind of 'case' he was thinking of, the answer coming from the left hemisphere might be something like 'in *case* of fire', or 'the *case* of the missing corpse', or 'a *case* of beer', etc., depending on the particular mental set of the left hemisphere at the time. Any reference to 'key case' under these conditions would be purely fortuitous, assuming that visual, auditory and other cues have been properly controlled.

In tests of stereognostic or other somaesthetic discriminations, objects put in the right hand for identification by touch are readily described or named in speech or writing, whereas if the same objects are placed in the left hand, the subject can only make wild guesses and may often seem unaware that anything at all is present. But again, if one of these objects is taken from the left hand and placed in a grab bag or scrambled among a dozen other test items, the subject is then able to search out and retrieve the initial object even after a delay of several minutes. However, unlike normal subjects, these people are obliged to retrieve the object with the same hand with which it was initially identified; they fail at cross-retrieval, i.e. they cannot recognize with one hand something identified only moments before with the other hand. Again, the second hemisphere does not know what the first hemisphere has been doing.

When the subjects are first asked to use the left hand for these stereognostic tests, they commonly complain that they cannot 'work with that hand', that 'the hand is numb', that they 'just can't feel anything or can't do anything with it' or 'don't get the message from that hand'. If they successfully retrieve a series of objects which previously they claimed they could not feel, and if this contradiction is then pointed out to them, they say things like 'Well, I was just guessing' or 'Well, I must have done it unconsciously'.

If two objects are placed simultaneously, one in each hand, and then are removed and hidden for retrieval in a scrambled pile of test items, each hand will hunt through the pile and search out selectively its own object. In the process, each hand may explore, identify and reject the item for which the other hand is searching. It is like two separate individuals working with no cooperation between them; indeed the interpretation of this, and many similar findings, is less confusing if we try to think of the commissurotomy patient not as a single individual but in terms of the mental faculties and performance capacities of the two hemispheres separately. Mostly it is the dominant, i.e. left, hemisphere which is in control, but in some tasks, particularly when these are forced in testing procedures, the minor hemisphere seems able to take over temporarily.

THE STUDY

When you split the brain in half anatomically, you do not divide in half its functional properties. In some respects cerebral functions may be doubled as much as halved because of the extensive bilateral redundancy in brain organization, whereby, particularly in sub-human species, most functions are separately and rather fully organized on both sides. Probably neither of the separated visual systems senses or perceives itself to be cut in half or even incomplete, just as the hemianopic patient who, following accidental destruction of an entire visual cortex of one hemisphere may not even notice the loss of the entire half sphere of vision until it is pointed out to him in specific optometric tests. Commissurotomy patients continue to watch TV and to read with no complaints about peculiarities in the perceptual appearance of the visual field.

Although intelligence, as measured by IQ, is not much affected and personality is little changed, commissurotomy patients do seem to be intellectually handicapped in ways that are probably not revealed in the ordinary tests. They all have marked short-term memory deficits, especially during the first year, have orientation problems and fatigue more quickly in reading and other tasks requiring concentration. Studied comparisons of the upper limits of performance before and after surgery are still needed.

Much of the foregoing is summarized in Figure 30.3. The left hemisphere in the right-handed patient is equipped with the expressive mechanisms for speech and writing, and with the main centres for the comprehension and organization of

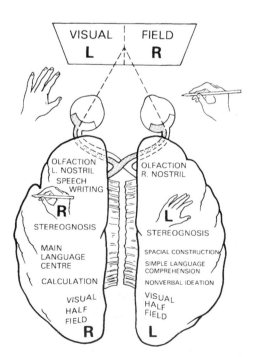

Figure 30.3. Schematic outline of the functional lateralization evident in behavioural tests of patients with forebrain commissurotomy.

language. It can communicate about the visual experiences of the right visual field and about the somaesthetic and volitional experiences of the right hand and leg, and right half of the body generally. Also, but not shown in Figure 30.3, it communicates, of course, about all the more general, less lateralized, cerebral activity that is bilaterally represented and common to both hemispheres. On the right side we have the mute aphasic and agraphic hemisphere, which cannot express itself verbally but which shows non-verbally that it is not agnostic; mental processes are indeed present and centred around the left visual field, hand, leg and half of the body.

To try to find out what goes on in that speechless agraphic minor hemisphere has always been one of the main challenges in our research. Does it really possess a true stream of conscious awareness, or is it just an agnostic automaton carried along in a reflex or trancelike state? This is related to many problems to do with lateral dominance and specialization in the human brain, the functional roles of the neocortical commissures and similar aspects of cerebral organization.

Clearly, the minor hemisphere can perform intermodal or cross-modal transfer of perceptual and mnemonic information at a characteristically human level. For example, after a picture of some object, such as a cigarette, has been flashed to the minor hemisphere via the left visual field, the subject can retrieve the item pictured from a collection of objects using blind touch with the left hand, which is mediated through the right hemisphere. However, unlike the normal person, the commissurotomy patient is obliged to use the corresponding hand (i.e. the left, in this case) for retrieval, and fails when asked to search out the same item with the right hand (see Figure 30.4). Using the right hand, the subject recognizes and can call off the names of each object that he comes to, but the right hand or its hemisphere does not know what it is looking for, and the hemisphere that can recognize the correct

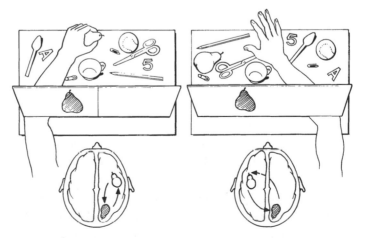

Figure 30.4. Visuo-tactile associations succeed between each half of the visual field and the corresponding hand. They fail with crossed combinations in which visual and tactual stimuli are projected into opposite hemispheres.

answer gets no feedback from the right hand. Hence, the two never get together, and the performance fails. Speech and other auditory cues must be controlled.

It also works the other way round, i.e., if the subject is holding an object in the left hand, he can then point out a picture of this object or the printed name of the object when these appear in a series presented visually. But again, these latter must be seen through the corresponding half of the visual field; an object identified by the left hand is not recognized when seen in the right half of the visual field. Intermodal associations of this kind have been demonstrated between vision, hearing and touch and, more recently, smell, in various combinations within either hemisphere but not across from one hemisphere to the other. This transfer is of special theoretical interest, since it is extremely difficult or impossible for the monkey brain, i.e. the right hemisphere may be animal-like in not being able to talk or write, but in other respects it shows mental capacities which are definitely human.

Other responses suggest the presence of ideas and a capacity for mental associations, and at least some simple logic and reasoning. In the same visuo-tactual test described above, the minor hemisphere, instead of selecting objects which match exactly the pictured item, seems able to select related items or ones which 'go with' the particular visual stimulus. For example, if we flash a picture of a wall clock and the nearest item that can be found tactually by the left hand is a toy wrist-watch, this is chosen. It is as if the minor hemisphere has an idea of a timepiece and is not just matching sensory outlines. Again, if the picture is of a hammer, the subject may choose a nail or a spike after checking out and rejecting all other items.

The minor hemisphere can also perform simple arithmetical problems. After a correct left-hand response has been made by pointing or by writing the number, the major hemisphere can then report the same answer verbally, but only after the left-hand response. If an error is made with the left hand, the verbal report contains the same error. If two different pairs of numbers are flashed to right and left fields simultaneously, the correct sum or product may be signalled separately by both hands. But when verbal confirmation of correct left-hand signals is required, the speaking hemisphere can only guess, showing again that the answer must have been obtained from the minor hemisphere.

In contradiction to the traditional belief that the disconnected minor hemisphere becomes 'word blind', 'word deaf' and 'tactually alexic', we found in commissurotomy patients that it is able to understand both written and spoken words to some extent, although it cannot express the understanding verbally (Gazzaniga & Sperry, 1967; Sperry, 1966; Sperry & Gazzaniga, 1967). If a word such as 'eraser' is flashed to the left visual field, the subject is able to search out an eraser from among a collection of objects using only touch with the left hand. But if he is asked what the item is after correct selection has been made, his answers show that he does not know what he is holding in his left hand, as is the general rule for left-hand stereognosis. This means, of course, that the *talking* hemisphere does not know the correct answer so the minor hemisphere must, in this situation, have read and understood the test word.

Again, if asked to find a 'piece of silverware', the subject may explore the array of test items and pick up a fork; if asked what it is he has chosen, he is just as likely to reply 'spoon' or 'knife' as fork. Both hemispheres have heard and understood the word 'silverware', but only the minor hemisphere knows what the left hand has actually found and picked up. Other tests show that the minor hemisphere can understand fairly complex spoken definitions like 'shaving instrument' (razor), 'dirt remover' (soap) and 'inserted in slot machines' (quarter).

It can also sort objects into groups by touch on the basis of shape, size and texture, and is superior to the major in tasks which involve drawing spatial relationships and performing block design tests.

The minor hemisphere demonstrates appropriate emotional reactions, as, for example, when a pin-up of a nude is interjected unexpectedly among a series of geometric shapes flashed to the right and left fields at random. The subject typically denies seeing anything, but a sneaky grin and perhaps blushing and giggling on the next couple of trials or so belies the verbal answer of the speaking hemisphere; apparently, only the emotional effect gets across, as if the cognitive component cannot be articulated through the brainstem. Similarly, Gordon and Sperry (1968) find that when odours are presented through the right nostril to the minor hemisphere, the subject cannot name it but can often indicate whether it is pleasant or unpleasant, whether verbally or by exclaiming (like 'phew!'). The specific information which fails to reach the major hemisphere is implied by the subject's correct selection, through left-hand stereognosis, of corresponding objects associated with the given smell. The minor hemisphere also expresses genuine annoyance at the errors made by its 'better', speaking, half in ordinary testing situations, when it knows the correct answer but cannot say it.

It seems, then, that in the right hemisphere we deal with a second conscious entity which is characteristically human and runs along in parallel with the more dominant stream of consciousness in the major hemisphere (Sperry, 1966). The quality of mental awareness in the minor hemisphere is perhaps comparable to that which survives in some types of aphasic patients following damage to the motor and main language centres. The dominant hemisphere may, under most ordinary conditions, be unaware of the presence of the minor one.

The more we see of these patients and the more of them we see, the more impressed we become with their individual differences and with the consequent qualifications that must be made to the general picture of the deconnection symptoms described.

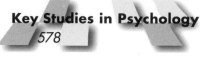

EVALUATION

Theoretical issues and subsequent research

One of the difficulties associated with generalizations in psychology (even with something as 'biological' as cerebral function) is the existence of *individual differences*. Some people seem to have much more lateralized brains than others; others have language more or less equally represented on both sides (*bilateral representation*: Beaumont, 1988).

As far as the left hemisphere being dominant for language, this seems to be true for 95% of right-handed patients, while only 5% had their right hemisphere dominant. But with left-handers, things are much less clear-cut: 75% had their left hemisphere dominant, none had the right dominant but 25% showed bilateral representation (based on a review by Satz (1979) of all studies between 1935 and 1975, cited in Beaumont, 1988). The best way to determine which side of the brain is dominant for language is to carry out the *Wada test*. A patient about to undergo brain surgery, which might affect a language area, is given a short-acting anaesthetic, first in one carotid artery and then, when the effects have worn off, in the other. This anaesthetizes each hemisphere in turn and if the patient can still engage in a normal conversation when, say, the right hemisphere is anaesthetized (but not the left), then the left hemisphere is judged to be dominant for language (Carlson, 1992).

Over and above this left-right handed difference, is the finding that women show less lateralization than men: the two hemispheres are more symmetrical in women than in men, such that damage to one side will, on average, affect a woman's performance less than a man's. It would follow that left-right specialization is most prevalent in right-handed men (and not 'all people': Ornstein, 1986).

However, Kimura (1992, 1999) believes that the issue of sex differences is more complex than has been previously claimed. Her own research (and that of others) has shown that, on average, men perform better than women at most spatial tasks, in particular mental rotation of an object or manipulating it in some other way, mathematical reasoning tests, navigation through a route, and target-directed motor skills (i.e. guiding or intercepting projectiles). However, women were superior at a certain kind of object-location task (but not other spatial tasks).

Women, on average, excel on tests that measure word recall, require finding words beginning with a specific letter, rapidly identifying matching items, and performing certain precision manual tasks (e.g. placing pegs in designated holes on a board). However, some of the average sex differences in cognition vary from slight to quite large, and:

> . . . men and women overlap enormously on many cognitive tests that show

average differences . . . On the whole, variation between men and women tends to be smaller than deviations within each sex, but very large differences between the groups do exist – in men's high level of visual-spatial targeting ability, for one. (Kimura, 1999)

A long history of research involving people with damage to one hemisphere indicates that in most people the left hemisphere is critical for language, and the right hemisphere for certain perceptual and spatial functions. As far as sex differences are concerned, it has been widely assumed that the two hemispheres are *more asymmetrically organized* (less symmetrical) for speech and spatial abilities in men than in women (Kimura, 1992, 1999). She has studied the ability of patients with damage to one hemisphere to rotate objects mentally. As expected, damage to the right hemisphere produced lower scores for *both* sexes than damage to the left. Also as expected, women did less well overall than men on a block rotation task. But, contrary to expectations, women were at least as much affected as men by damage to their right hemisphere. In other words, men and women seemed to be equally 'asymmetrical' as far as right-side damage interfering with spatial ability is concerned. What this suggests is that normal sex differences on such tasks are *not* caused by the dominance of the right hemisphere, but that some other brain system(s) must be involved in male superiority.

Men incur *aphasia* (impairment of the ability to produce speech) from left hemisphere damage more often than women do. The implication here is that speech must be more *bilaterally organized* (more symmetrical) in women. This would mean that women with right-side damage are almost as likely to be aphasic as women with left-side damage. However, in over 20 years of working with brain-damaged patients, Kimura has not found this to be the case. Why?

She has discovered another striking sex difference in brain organization for speech and related motor function. Women are more likely to suffer aphasia after damage to the *anterior* (towards the front) part of the brain. Because restricted damage within a hemisphere more often affects the posterior (towards the back) regions, in both sexes, women are usually better 'protected'. Speech functions are, therefore, less likely to be affected in women, *not* because they are more bilaterally organized, but because the critical/vulnerable area is less often affected.

Although she has found no evidence of sex differences relating to functional brain asymmetry for basic speech or spatial rotation ability, Kimura believes there may be a difference on more abstract verbal tasks. For example, while women seem to be equally affected by damage to either hemisphere on a vocabulary test, men only seem to suffer after left hemisphere damage. Kimura (1999) maintains that:

> . . . These findings suggest that when using more abstract verbal skills, women do use their hemispheres more equally than men do. But we have not found this to be true for all word-related tasks; for example, verbal memory appears to depend just as much on the left hemisphere in women as in men.

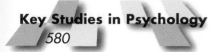

Ornstein (1986) refers to the work of De Lacoste and her colleagues in which they are beginning to be able to identify the male and female corpus callosum by sight alone. They are, it seems, as 'dimorphic' as are male and female arms: women's are larger overall and larger towards the back of the brain. According to Kimura (1992), the evidence regarding this alleged difference in the size of the back part of the corpus callosum (the splenium) is inconclusive. This may be due partly to variations in the shape of the corpus callosum associated with age, as well as different methods of measurement. The significance of the finding is the assumption that the size of the corpus callosum may indicate the number of fibres connecting the two hemispheres, such that the more fibres, the more efficient the communication between them. However, it is not clear whether it is the number of fibres which is the crucial male–female difference, and sex differences in cognitive functioning have yet to be related to a difference in callosal size (Kimura, 1992). Bogen (1969) believes that we must not let the 'rich diversity of natural phenomena obscure our recognition of the common and representative types'; in other words, the similarities still outweigh the differences.

fMRI and PET scans (see Chapter 33) have produced interesting, yet at times, apparently conflicting results (Kimura, 1999). Some research has shown greater differences in activity between the hemispheres of men than of women during certain language tasks (such as judging if two words rhyme, or creating past tenses of verbs), while other research has failed to find sex differences in functional asymmetry. This inconsistency may be due partly to the use of different language tasks in different studies, perhaps showing that the sexes may differ in brain organization for some language tasks, but not others. They may also reflect the complexity of these scanning techniques. The brain is always active to some degree, so for any activity (such as reading aloud) the comparison activity (here, reading silently) is intended to be very similar. We then 'subtract' the brain pattern that occurs during silent reading to find the brain pattern present while reading aloud:

> . . . Yet such methods require dubious assumptions about what the subject is doing during either activity. In addition, the more complex the activity, the more difficult it is to know what is actually being measured after subtracting the comparison activity. (Kimura, 1999)

While male superiority in visuospatial tasks (especially ones requiring mental rotation) is the most commonly cited intellectual difference between males and females (see above: Martin, 1998), Brosnan (1998) has offered an alternative interpretation of this common finding. Sixth-form students were given a standard test of visuospatial ability (the embedded figures test) but it was presented in one of two ways: either (a) in the traditional way; or (b) as a test of 'empathy'. Participants' levels of masculinity or femininity were also measured. Whereas the description of the tests did not affect the boys' performance, the girls underperformed when the test was described in the traditional way (as an explicit test of visuospatial ability).

Those girls scoring high in masculinity also scored more highly than those scoring high in femininity. Brosnan interprets these results as indicating that some sex differences may be attributable to 'psychological gender differences' which determine an individual's motivation. This *psychological* explanation contrasts sharply with *biological/neuropsychological* explanations that focus on differences in brain anatomy.

Methodological issues

Although there are only a few of them, split-brain patients offer the advantage of being able to target information to one hemisphere in the absence of communication with the other, via the corpus callosum. By projecting sensory information to one or other hemisphere, the mode of processing by that hemisphere can be studied in what is as near to controlled within-participant conditions as could be hoped for (Toates, 2001: see **Exercises**).

The brain damage is under surgical control and targets a defined, circumscribed area of the brain (Kosslyn *et al.*, 1999). However, Toates argues that any conclusions from such studies should be considered in the light of the following qualifications:

- The role of either hemisphere might be different when information is projected to both and there is communication between them.

- Behaviour is normally the product of an interaction between the hemispheres (Sperry, 1974). The performance of one in isolation might be deceptive regarding its role prior to surgery when interacting with the opposite hemisphere. As Toates states: '. . . There might be reorganization of processing systems following surgery (particularly if the patient is young), so that the performance of a hemisphere is changed.'

- The surgery is a last resort after years of suffering and failed medication (Kosslyn *et al.*, 1999). These patients cannot be assumed to be like controls in all other respects.

- Even split-brain patients would normally not act in such a way that information is projected solely to one hemisphere.

A certain amount of the tactile information arising from either hand is projected to *both* hemispheres, and so is available to both hemispheres even in split-brain patients. But in the absence of inter-hemispheric communication, the fine-grained processing of detail by the somatosensory cortex (as in object discrimination) is available only to the contralateral (opposite side) hemisphere. Hence, the experimenter can project visual information to one hemisphere and tactile information to the other, and spilt-brain patients are unable to integrate these two sources (Kosslyn *et al.*, 1999). Unfortunately, the nature of sound, the ear, and the fact that auditory information is projected to both hemispheres, means that a comparable procedure for targeting auditory information to one hemisphere only is not possible (Toates, 2001).

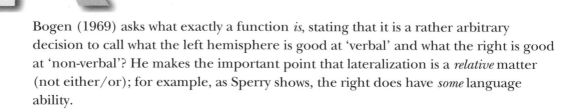

Bogen (1969) asks what exactly a function *is*, stating that it is a rather arbitrary decision to call what the left hemisphere is good at 'verbal' and what the right is good at 'non-verbal'? He makes the important point that lateralization is a *relative* matter (not either/or); for example, as Sperry shows, the right does have *some* language ability.

Ornstein (1986) points out that some studies have shown that the primary factor in hemisphere lateralization is *not* the type of information (words or pictures versus sounds or shapes) which is processed, but *how* it is processed. For example, participants were given a technical passage and two folk tales. There was no change in the level of activity in the left hemisphere, but the right was more activated while the participant was reading the stories than while reading the technical material.

Much of what we know about normal brain function in general (and lateralization in particular) is based upon the study of those who have suffered brain damage or, in the case of split-brain patients, undergone drastic surgery for epilepsy. In the case of the former, we assume that the damaged area has stopped working correctly but that the rest of the brain carries on more or less as normal. This may or may not be a reasonable assumption (Beaumont, 1988). In the case of the latter, long-standing pre-surgical pathology might have caused an abnormal reorganization of their brains so that generalizing to normal brains may be invalid (Cohen, 1975: see Toates' qualifying points on page 581).

Cohen cites a study by Kinsbourne in which the left hemisphere of aphasic patients was anaesthetized. They continued to speak fluently, although unintelligibly, suggesting that the abnormal speech is produced by the right hemisphere. This, according to split-brain studies, has some language understanding but is supposed to be *mute*.

However, Ornstein (1986) and others cite many studies of 'normal' brains which seem to support the lateralization findings from split-brain studies (e.g. Kimura 1961, 1964). Cohen is also critical of these, since she believes the two hemispheres do not function in isolation but form a highly integrated system. Most everyday tasks involve a mixture of 'left' and 'right' skills, such as listening to speech (in which we analyse both the words *and* the pattern of intonation) and reading (which requires both analysis of visual shapes and linguistic knowledge). Far from 'doing their own thing', the two hemispheres work very much together (Cohen, 1975). Similarly, Fernald (1997) claims that the terms 'right- and left-brained' are grossly inaccurate when used in the same way as 'handedness'. The hemispheres are *integrated*, separate but complementary information-processing sub-systems.

Carlson (1992) points out that damage to the right hemisphere will result in difficulties in reading maps, perceiving spatial relationships and recognizing complex geometrical forms. But such patients will also have trouble *talking* about things like maps and complex geometrical forms, as well as understanding others' speech, which

involves recognition of emotion in the tone of the voice. Clearly, *both* hemispheres have a contribution to make to language abilities.

According to Kosslyn *et al.* (1999);

> . . . some popular dichotomies, such as the left hemisphere being analytic and verbal whereas the right is holistic, artistic, creative and perceptual need careful qualification . . .

Applications and implications

One striking example of the dominance of the right hemisphere for manipulation of spatial patterns comes from a black-and-white film made by Gazzaniga and Sperry. It features W.J., the first patient operated on by Vogel and Bogen. He was given a fairly standard test of spatial ability (*block design* and the *Koh blocks test)*, in which a pattern has to be constructed from a set of cubes.

W.J. is shown a pattern and quickly assembles the blocks needed to match it with his left hand (under the control of the right hemisphere). When the same task is given to the right hand (under the control of the left hemisphere), his behaviour changes dramatically. He hesitates, moves slowly and hesitantly, and is clearly making some major errors. As his frustration level increases, suddenly from the lower edge of the screen his left hand darts into the picture to make a grab for the blocks and to try to assemble them. Only a quick intervention by Gazzaniga, grasping W.J.'s hand and gently but firmly removing it from the table, prevents the left hand from taking over.

The left hand was impelled to step in because the right hemisphere, which knows it is proficient and can do this kind of task, was getting frustrated and annoyed watching the bumbling actions of the right hand (controlled by the spatially inept left hemisphere). Eventually, W.J. resorted to sitting on his left hand to stop the interference! (Coren, 1992).

One fascinating hypothesis suggests that the right hemisphere's greater ability to process and mentally manipulate visual images may form the underpinning for other, more complex functions. For example, individuals with right hemisphere damage often report an inability to dream, which is also mentioned by split-brain patients. However, when talking to a split-brain patient, you are speaking only to the left hemisphere. Perhaps this statement from the left hemisphere ('I cannot dream') should be interpreted as meaning that the *left hemisphere doesn't dream*: it is possible that the right hemisphere still does but is unable to talk about it. This is sensible, since dreams are predominantly a sequence of thoughts dominated by visual imagery (Coren, 1992; see Chapter 29).

This leads on to what is perhaps both the most interesting and the most controversial of all the issues relating to lateralization and, in particular, split-brain patients: do the two halves of the brain represent two kinds of consciousness (two minds)?

Ornstein (1986) refers to reports of an entire hemisphere being removed for the treatment of certain kinds of epilepsy (hemispherectomy), after which the 'person' remained, no matter which hemisphere was removed. So if possession of a 'mind' requires only one hemisphere, does having two hemispheres make possible the possession of two minds? Indeed, do split-brain patients have two minds, two separate, distinct modes of consciousness? Ornstein and Sperry certainly think so.

For example, Sperry claims that 'when the brain is bisected, we see two separate 'selves' (essentially a divided organism with two mental units, each with its own memories and its own will) competing for control over the organism (Sperry, 1964, quoted in Apter, 1991). Does this mean that the normal role of the corpus callosum is to keep the two hemispheres in exact synchrony, so that we normally have one, unified, mind? Ornstein asks if cerebral commissurotomy produces a splitting or doubling of the mind, or is it more correctly considered a manoeuvre which helps to manifest the duality there all the time?

While Sperry and Gazzaniga seem to believe the former, Bogen (1969) and Pucetti (1977, cited in Apter, 1991) take the latter view. Pucetti, for example, argues that split-brain patients are not special in having two minds, because even when the hemispheres are joined, we are two minds. These two conscious selves, each in its own hemisphere, are subjectively and behaviourally connected, so that their separate existence is undetectable: under 'normal' circumstances we appear to be unified and synchronized beings. The commissurotomy makes apparent the duality that is there all the time (Apter, 1991). This argument is an instance of *Double Brain Theory* which essentially 'reduces' the mind (or the 'self' or personality) to a hemisphere of the brain, and it is also used to explain the phenomenon of multiple personality disorder (Apter, 1991; see Chapter 21).

According to Mackay (1987) there is no reason in principle to object to the science fiction speculation that if a human nervous system could be *completely* bifurcated and each half left in working order, that the resulting structure might embody two distinct persons (as in Siamese Twins). However, in the real world of split-brain patients, he doubts whether any of the evidence to date requires or justifies such a drastic interpretation of their condition.

Mackay (1978) and Mackay & Mackay (1982) spent several months, courtesy of Sperry and Gazzaniga, in New York and Passadena, testing a variety of split-brain patients in an attempt to engage the two hemispheres in a dialogue with each other. The most ambitious tests were performed on a cooperative and intelligent patient, J.W., aged 27 (not to be confused with the W.J. shown in the film).

The results show that a form of low-level dialogue, exchanging information by question and answer, could be sustained between the two hemispheres (Mackay, 1987). But they did nothing to answer the question as to whether the two half-participants had the kind of 'independence of will' possessed by two normal human players on opposite sides of a guessing game. How *could* it be answered? What about the capacity to *bargain*? An attempt to do this with J.W. led Mackay (1987) to conclude that all the existing evidence (including his) is insufficient to justify claims that the two hemispheres *do* embody 'two free wills':

> . . . it would seem more parsimonious to describe a split-brain patient not as 'two people' or 'two free wills' but as one person who is liable in certain circumstances to show a peculiarly elaborate form of absent-mindedness . . .

and again,

> It is only if the neural equipment for self-supervisory normative activity were known to be completely duplicated (in *each* hemisphere), at cortical levels normally linked by the corpus callosum that we could plausibly regard split-brain patients as two people. (Mackay, 1987)

Parfit (1987) agrees that, while the split-brain patient does have two streams of consciousness, we should not regard them as constituting two persons, because, in a sense, there is *none*. He distinguishes the *ego theory* (of what persons are) from the *bundle theory*, which explains the unity of consciousness by claiming that ordinary people are, at any time, aware of having several different experiences. This can easily be extended to cover split-brain cases: at any time, there is not one state of awareness of several different experiences, but two such states (*not* two separately existing egos). Split-brain cases have great theoretical importance because they 'challenge some of our deepest assumptions about ourselves' (Parfit, 1987).

Based on his work with split-brain patients, Gazzaniga (1998) has proposed the concept of 'the interpreter'. This refers to a capacity, or set of mechanisms, residing in the left hemisphere of human brains. Its function is to enable us to make inferences and to form beliefs about both interior events (internal bodily states) and external events, including our own actions and other people's. The interpreter frees us from the immediacy of the present environment; it allows us to remember and to plan, and to do so in inventive and unique ways.

In the case of a split-brain, the left hemisphere, when presented with information that is properly contextualized only by what is presented to the right hemisphere, will recontextualize and make good sense of that information in terms of a scene presented to the left hemisphere. In one experiment, the left hemisphere is visually presented with a picture of a chicken claw, and the right hemisphere with a scene involving snow. The patient is then asked to pick out from an array of pictures images that are associated with the presented pictures. As expected, with his right hand (controlled by the left hemisphere) the patient points to a chicken, and, with his left hand (controlled by the right hemisphere) to a snow shovel. When asked to explain why he chose those items, he responds: 'Oh, that's simple. The chicken claw goes with the chicken, and you need a shovel to clean out the chicken shed' (Gazzaniga, 1998).

The reasonable interpretation which makes sense out of a piece of information that has its proper context registered in the right hemisphere (the shovel) is fully generated in the left hemisphere.

In normal, non-split brains, of course, the contextualized information from the right hemisphere is delivered to the interpreting mechanism in the left hemisphere across the corpus callosum. The interpreter integrates that information and generates rational coherence in relation to other aspects of current and remembered experience. What we find, then, in the left hemisphere, is what the ancient Greek philosophers, such as Plato and Aristotle, would have called the rational part of the soul. Agreeing with them, Gazzaniga regards this capacity for rational invention as what distinguishes the human from the non-human animal (Gallagher, 1998).

The interpreter is essential not only for making sense of the perceptual world, but also for interpreting our self. It represents an aspect of brain function that allows for unique development on the basis of personal experience and culturally relative contexts. The individual self is the product of an inventive brain working within a matrix of unique perspectives provided by culturally structured experience (Gallagher, 1998).

Exercises

1. Referring to the **Methodological issues** (see page 581), why should there be a difference between the two hemispheres in their respective responses to the technical passage and the stories?

2. Ornstein (1986) reports an experiment in which brain activity was recorded while participants mentally rotated objects in space. They were then asked to count the number of boxes. Which hemisphere would be mainly involved in each case?

3. In what way could split-brain patients be considered unrepresentative of adult participants in general?

4. Why can split-brain experiments not be considered *true* experiments?

5. What does Toates (2001) mean when he says that split-brain studies come as close to controlled within-participant conditions as you might hope for?

6. Explain the difference between (a) *localization* and (b) *lateralization* of brain function.

31 Hypnosis, motivation and compliance

Martin T. Orne (1966)

American Journal of Psychiatry, 122, 721–6

BACKGROUND AND CONTEXT

A crucial distinction in the discussion of hypnosis is made between (*i*) the 'state'/'special process' view and (*ii*) the 'non-state'/social psychological view (Wagstaff, 1987, 1995). This corresponds to what Orne (in the present article) refers to as (a) the subjective experience theory of hypnosis, and (b) the motivational theory of hypnosis respectively. The 'state'/'subjective experience' theory is commonly referred to as the 'traditional' approach.

According to Wagstaff, this controversy as to the nature of hypnosis has raged since the late eighteenth century. Although it was once thought that hypnosis is a special sort of sleep (the Greek 'hypnos' = sleep), not all modern state theorists subscribe to this view. However, they continue to see hypnosis as an altered state of consciousness with various depths, the assumption being that the deeper the hypnotic state, the more likely it is that the hypnotized person will manifest hypnotic phenomena (Hilgard, 1978; Bowers, 1983).

The state of hypnotic trance (supposedly qualitatively different from a normal waking state) is usually brought about through *induction procedures* (e.g. eye-fixation and vocal suggestions for sleep and relaxation). In academic research, susceptibility to hypnosis is usually measured by means of standardized scales, including the Stanford Hypnotic Susceptibility Scale, Form C (referred to by Orne) (plus forms A and B), and the Harvard Group Scale of Hypnotic Susceptibility. These typically suggest to the individual that 'your hand is heavy and falling' (hand lowering), 'you cannot bend your arm' (arm rigidity) or 'you will find it difficult to remember' (amnesia), and sometimes 'there is a fly buzzing round your head' (hallucination).

The traditional view also makes two fundamental assumptions:

(a) hypnotized people experience their responses as 'happening to them' (Bowers, 1983) or involuntary 'happenings' (as implied by the instructions given during the induction procedure); and

(b) individuals will be able to do things while hypnotized of which they would be incapable in the waking state (or at least their performance is superior), including the ability to control pain (Hilgard & Hilgard, 1984), and distinctive abilities in displays of amnesia and hallucinations (Orne, 1979; Kihlstrom, 1980; Bowers, 1983).

However, most academic state theorists do *not* accept the claims that 'hypnotized' people can actually be regressed back to before their birth and former lives in Roman Britain or Medieval York. Nevertheless, the state view has dominated the popular conception of hypnosis, partly perhaps because of the popularity of 'media hypnotists', such as Paul McKenna, and partly because of the dramatic nature of many hypnotic phenomena (both alleged and actually demonstrated), such as tolerating surgery without pain and becoming deaf and blind. But is there an alternative, non-state explanation for all these phenomena?

Non-state theorists are mainly social and cognitive psychologists (Wagstaff being the UK's leading exponent of this view), who see the hypnotic situation as a *social–psychological interaction*. The hypnotist and participant act out social roles: the participant's role is to act according to previous expectations and to cues provided by the hypnotist and to try very hard to act *as if* 'hypnotized'. Non-state theorists question the basic assumptions made by state theorists.

Both state and non-state theorists recognize the problem of compliance or faking, largely as a result of the pioneering work of Orne (starting in 1959). He stressed the extent to which participants in *any* experimental context may modify their behaviour in an attempt to please the experimenter, save themselves embarrassment, or bolster self-image. For example,

(*i*) Milgram (1974) claims that the desire not to commit a social impropriety and not to ruin an experiment can be extremely powerful (more than we realize: see Chapter 7);

(*ii*) Sheridan & King (1972) found that 72% of ordinary people were prepared to give high levels of *real* shock to a *real*, innocent, puppy;

(*iii*) Orne (1962) himself found that participants will agree to ridiculous requests if the context is appropriate. For example, he asked participants to perform additions on sheets filled with random numbers (224 additions per sheet × 2000 sheets) and told them to continue working while he was away, but that he would return eventually. Five and a half hours later it was Orne who had to give up! The participants were quite willing to go on for hour after hour rather than let the experimenter down.

Similar pressures apply in the hypnotic situation. In addition, the participant may be genuinely curious and wish to experience hypnosis. Having started, it may be difficult to back out; having finished, it may be difficult to understand why they did it. However, to some non-state theorists, far from being mere annoyance, compliance is an integral component of much hypnotic responding (Spanos, 1991; Wagstaff, 1991).

AIM AND NATURE OF THE STUDY

This is primarily a review article in which Orne attempts to reconcile what seems to be the contradictory findings from (*i*) experimental studies of hypnosis and (*ii*) clinical experience (the use of hypnosis with patients in a therapeutic setting).

While presenting data from his own studies, he also discusses the findings of several other researchers and clinicians, and so no one study is looked at in any great detail. He suggests two alternative ways of looking at hypnosis:

(*i*) it involves a change in the individual's motivation to please the hypnotist, making him/her unusually compliant (the non-state approach);
(*ii*) it involves a change in the individual's subjective experience (the state approach).

As far as (*i*) is concerned, he cites a number of studies (including his own) which argue against the hypothesis that 'being susceptible to hypnosis leads to a generalized tendency to comply with requests from the hypnotist'.

Regarding (*ii*), the criteria used by trained observers for establishing that a participant is actually hypnotized all focus on the critical variable of his/her ability to respond to suggestions (ideomotor/challenge/hallucinations and memory distortions/post-hypnotic behaviour). Although this suggestibility refers at one level to overt behaviour, more importantly, at another level, it refers to an assumed change in the individual's experience:

> a subject is genuinely hypnotized not because he is willing to report certain things, but because his report really describes his personal subjective experience.

(e.g. a *compulsion* to carry out the post-hypnotic suggestion regardless of whether s/he actually recalls it). Further, the wider the range of distortions in his/her perception or memory which can be induced by appropriate cues, the more deeply the individual is said to be hypnotized.

THE STUDY

Recent research findings have indicated the need to reconsider what had appeared to be reasonable assumptions about the nature of hypnosis. At first sight, the implications of these studies seem to be at variance with clinical experience and common sense, but careful consideration actually allows us to reconcile clinical and experimental findings in a more satisfactory way than has been possible in the past.

It has been widely held that hypnosis alters the relationship between subject and hypnotist by changing the subject's motivation; one of the more extreme versions of this view was proposed by Orne (1954, 1959) based on White (1941). It was assumed that the hypnotic state increases the subject's motivation to please the

THE STUDY

hypnotist, i.e. it makes him unusually compliant. This assumption seems soundly based on the behaviour of hypnotized individuals who certainly *appear* to do things that they would not normally do. Nevertheless, a careful evaluation has failed to uncover any evidence for increased compliance in hypnosis, which is how the hypnotic state has usually been defined. To reconcile this finding with the effectiveness of hypnosis in clinical practice, it has been necessary to clarify the definition of hypnosis itself.

The alternative view of hypnosis is that, rather than it representing a change in the degree of compliance, it is a change in the subjective experience of hypnotized individuals. This latter definition can encompass adequately the kinds of phenomena usually subsumed under the concept of hypnosis, and suggests that the observed compliance of hypnotized subjects, and especially their responsiveness to therapeutic suggestions, may not be an intrinsic part of hypnosis itself.

The motivational view of hypnosis seems compelling because hypnotized subjects are quick to comply with the hypnotist's requests even when unusual or bizarre behaviour is requested. However, the source of the subject's motivation in such cases need not be the hypnotic state itself. In lecturing to college students about hypnosis, I often illustrate this point with a simple demonstration: I ask a number of students to perform certain actions, e.g. one to take off his right shoe, another to exchange his tie with his neighbour, another to give me his wallet and so on. After these things have been done, I point out that if the same behaviour had occurred after a hypnotic induction, it would have seemed that the students were under hypnotic control, i.e. while all the behaviours were admissible requests in a hypnosis situation, it is unusual for lecturers to make such 'unreasonable' requests and, therefore, it is tempting to assume – incorrectly – that only hypnotized persons would comply with them.

An experimental demonstration of this point is provided by Orne and Evans (1965), replicating studies by Rowland (1939) and Young (1952), which appeared to prove that subjects can be compelled to carry out antisocial and self-destructive acts under hypnosis. The earlier studies had shown that deeply hypnotized subjects can be compelled to pick up a rattlesnake, lift a penny out of fuming nitric acid and throw the acid at an assistant. Orne and Evans confirmed these findings but also found that this behaviour could be obtained equally well from non-hypnotized individuals in the waking state. The waking subjects were fully aware that the behaviour they were being asked to perform would normally be highly self-destructive, antisocial and dangerous but, in a post-experimental interview, they revealed that they were convinced (correctly) that appropriate safeguards would be taken to protect them and the assistant from any real harm.

So far it has not been possible to find any behaviour which subjects will perform under hypnosis which they will not perform in the waking state. This does not necessarily mean that hypnosis may not increase the range of behaviours that people are willing to perform, but it shows that subjects tend to do anything that might conceivably be required of them in an experimental setting. Any behaviour which subjects might *not* carry out is well beyond the range that an experimenter could afford to request, a point underlined by Milgram's (1963) studies in which subjects continued to give what seemed to be extremely high and dangerous levels of electric shock to another person in the context of a learning experiment.

EFFECT ON PERFORMANCE OF DIFFICULT TASKS

Rather than examining the range of tasks that subjects will perform, one can study the effect of hypnosis on performance quantitatively by using difficult, fatiguing tasks. If the subject is used as his own control, he may indeed perform much better in hypnosis than when awake; however, experimental subjects are extremely compliant, even without being hypnotized. If they think that the experimenter is trying to prove that hypnosis increases performance, they may easily provide him with supporting data; not necessarily by *increasing* their hypnotic performance, but by *decreasing* their waking performance (Evans & Orne, 1965; Orne, 1959). Moreover, Orne (1954, 1959), Barber and Calverley (1964) and Levitt and Brady (1964) have shown that with proper motivation, waking subjects can surpass their own hypnosis performance. In these studies, however, no attempt was made to equate instructions in the two conditions, so that subjects were motivated very differently during waking and hypnosis. Consequently, they shed no light on whether hypnosis alone increases the subjects' motivation to comply with the hypnotist's requests.

To answer this question, *identical instructions* would have to be given in both conditions, e.g. asking a subject to hold a kilogram weight at arm's length as long as possible; performance would be a measure of the degree of compliance induced by identical instructions in different states. A serious methodological problem involved in such experiments is the difficulty, if not the impossibility, of giving instructions to a hypnotized subject in the same way as to a waking subject. While the 'lyrics' may remain constant, the 'melody' is usually drastically altered, and therefore the total communication is quite different, so any differences in performance (which are to be expected) could be due either to how the instructions are given or the presence of hypnosis.

An ingenious experimental design by London and Fuhrer (1961) gets around this difficulty. A large number of subjects are given an initial test of susceptibility to hypnosis and from them, the extreme responders and non-responders are selected. They are all told that they are sufficiently deeply hypnotizable for the purposes of the experiment. In the main part of the experiment, a very neutral, relaxing form of trance induction is used and subjects are tested on a motor task. A comparison is then made between performance of good and poor hypnotic subjects; if hypnosis

Side text: THE STUDY

makes subjects more compliant, the performance of the former should be superior to that of the latter. But in several studies, London and Fuhrer (1961) and Rosenhan and London (1963a, b) found that, if anything, it was the poor hypnotic subjects who performed better under hypnotic conditions. In a detailed replication, Evans and Orne (1965) found *no* difference between good and poor subjects. It certainly seems as though hypnotizable subjects are not more motivated to comply with the wishes of the hypnotist than the others.

Evans and Orne have carried out a great deal of experimental work involving not only excellent hypnotic subjects, but also essentially unhypnotizable ones used as controls. Retrospectively, it occurred to us that the number of cancelled appointments and actual drop-outs in the highly hypnotizable group was greater than in the non-hypnotizable group, so we began to record subjects' time of arrival for experimental sessions and correlated their punctuality with their hypnotic performance. We found a modest but significant *negative* relationship: the good subjects tended to arrive late for the experiments while the poor subjects tended to arrive early. Whatever the explanation for these findings, they are not what would be expected if good hypnotic subjects are especially motivated to please the hypnotist.

Similarly, Shor (1964) asked subjects to choose the highest level of shock they would be willing to tolerate, prior to an experiment involving electric shock; the poor hypnotic subjects chose significantly higher shock levels than the good ones.

All these findings argue against the hypothesis that being susceptible to hypnosis leads to a generalized tendency to comply with requests from the hypnotist. No such tendency appears when the requests are not directly relevant to the hypnotic situation, i.e. a subject who carries out hypnotic suggestions may not necessarily be more likely to carry out other requests.

CRITERIA FOR HYPNOSIS

In order to understand these results, it is necessary to examine the definition of hypnosis itself. What criteria do we have in mind when we say that someone is hypnotized? Observers watching a subject respond to suggestions usually agree on whether he is hypnotized, and how deeply. The most widely used objective scale of hypnotic depth is probably the Stanford Hypnotic Susceptibility Scale, Form C (Weitzenhoffer & Hilgard, 1962), and is used in most of the empirical work done today. Scale scores agree very well with the judgements of trained observers.

But what criteria do observers actually use? What must a subject do to achieve a high score on the scale? Clearly, the critical variable is the subject's ability to respond to suggestions, but hypnotic suggestions are not all of the same kind. They can be classified into four groups: (*i*) ideomotor; (*ii*) challenge; (*iii*) hallucinations and memory distortions (of which amnesia is a special example) and (*iv*) post-hypnotic behaviour. Such a classification has received empirical support from the factor analytic results of Evans (1965).

In a classic ideomotor suggestion, such as the sway test, the subject is told that he is falling backwards, and is told what to experience: 'You are falling backward . . . you feel yourself falling further and further backward'. The response is defined as positive by the extent to which the subject actually falls but it is implicitly assumed that he falls *because he feels himself drawn backward* rather than because of the conscious volitional decision: 'I will fall backward', which would not count as an ideomotor response. The experimenter is not trying to measure behavioural compliance as such, but rather the behavioural manifestations of a subjective experience. If one were measuring only behavioural compliance, one would use the simple instruction, 'Fall backward now'; in an experimental context, anyway, compliance would be almost total.

The challenge suggestion (e.g.'Your eyes are tightly glued together; you cannot open them. Try to open them. You cannot') is also scored behaviourally, on the basis of the subject's failure to open them. Here too it is hoped that this behaviour accurately reflects a subjective inability to open the eyes, rather than mere compliance with the hypnotist's wish. While these two possibilities are difficult to distinguish operationally, the response measures 'depth of hypnosis' only in so far as it reflects an *experienced* inability on the part of the subjects to open his eyes, i.e. the extent to which a subject *cannot* comply even when he is challenged to do so.

Suggestions dealing with hallucination, amnesia or other memory distortions are also designed to produce responses which reflect a presumed change in the subject's experience; a subject is genuinely hypnotized not because he is willing to report certain things, but because his report really describes his personal subjective experience.

POST-HYPNOTIC PHENOMENON

This is most difficult to deal with in this context, because the usual criterion is purely behavioural: does the subject carry out the suggestion? Nevertheless, the response is subjectively quite different from simple compliance, for it is presumed that subjects experience a *compulsion* to carry out the suggested behaviour, regardless of whether they actually recall the suggestion. Evans (1965) has tried to measure separately the compulsion and recall elements of typical post-hypnotic suggestions, and found them to be only moderately correlated. Orne (1965) summarized data on post-hypnotic behaviour and concluded that, despite this subjective compulsion, a post-hypnotic suggestion is likely to be less effective than a simple request to carry out the behaviour. These quantitative and qualitative differences provide convincing evidence that post-hypnotic suggestion is not merely a matter of behavioural compliance.

So the criteria for determining whether a subject is hypnotized do not focus primarily on whether he does what he is told, but are attempts to measure the extent to which distortions in his perception or memory can be induced by appropriate cues. If a wide range of distortions can easily be induced, the subject is said to be deeply hypnotized. Thus the essence of hypnosis is not so much a way of manipulating a person's behaviour (as it is often portrayed in popular literature and patients' fantasy) as of creating distortions of perception and memory; this explains why it does not necessarily increase compliance or obedience as such, especially in experimental contexts which already predispose subjects to a very high degree of compliance.

If we take this experiential definition of hypnosis, a simple motivational theory cannot be sustained and has been repeatedly contradicted by experimental findings. Tasks which could, in principle, be carried out by non-hypnotized individuals are not carried out better under hypnosis; the hypothetical 'increased motivation to please the hypnotist' which ought to manifest itself in performance on such tasks, apparently does not occur.

In a clinical context, the therapist is often more interested in changing the patient's behaviour than in studying his experience. So-called 'hypnotic' therapy has been found useful in changing habit patterns and in suppressing a wide range of neurotic symptoms. Therapists have often decided that a patient was successfully hypnotized whenever his behaviour was changed by the therapist's suggestion, and a suggestion is 'hypnotic' if it follows a trance-induction procedure and has successful results, even without any evaluation of depth of hypnosis by the usual means. This definition is clearly different from the subjective criterion discussed above. It is quite possible that patients fail to enter hypnosis in the experiential sense, and yet respond to a therapeutic suggestion; conversely, other patients may be *deeply hypnotized and fail to respond to such a suggestion*. The clinical procedure which defines 'hypnosis' *post hoc* would, by its nature, fail to recognize such a situation.

It is highly probable that hypnotizability in our sense does not correlate highly with response to therapeutic suggestion, as indicated by the puzzling phenomenon of 'light hypnotic trance', which may be sufficient to produce therapeutically marked changes in behaviour. Two recent patients were totally unable to manifest hypnotic phenomena, and did nothing more than close their eyes in response to a request to do so. By any of the usual criteria they were not hypnotized at all, yet therapeutic suggestions produced dramatic positive responses.

It is possible that a hypnotic trance-induction procedure may fail to induce hypnosis itself, and yet make the patient more responsive to therapeutic suggestions. We should separate two aspects of the therapeutic situation using trance induction: (*i*) the effect of suggestions made during a situation defined by doctor and patient as 'hypnosis' and (*ii*) the classic state of hypnosis in which the patient responds to suggestions from the hypnotist by distorting reality. Susceptibility to (*ii*) may be different from susceptibility to (*i*), which often involves no cognitive distortion.

The necessary and sufficient conditions for the classic subjective phenomena of hypnosis are as yet unclear, but the hypothesis that it is essentially a matter of compliance seems untenable. Even the more plausible hypothesis that it depends on an increased motivation to carry out any tasks requested by the hypnotist must be rejected, or at least restricted to apply only to tasks involving cognitive distortions. If so, how can we understand the clinical effectiveness of the hypnotic induction procedure? This procedure does seem to change the existing transference relationship, and 'hypnotic' suggestions do often change symptoms which resisted other forms of suggestion.

EFFECT ON ROLE RELATIONSHIP

Such therapeutic effects may not be primarily a function of hypnosis itself, but may result from the changed relationship which exists when a therapist assumes the role of 'hypnotist', and shares with the patient the expectation that hypnosis involves unlimited compliance. This is certainly a different role relationship from the usual therapeutic one: not only are magical powers ascribed to the therapist by the patient, but the therapist's behaviour tends to reinforce these fantasies. Also, therapists encourage regressive behaviour, and allow an intense closeness which they might otherwise be unwilling to tolerate. These changes in the doctor–patient relationship may be among the sufficient conditions for evoking a real hypnotic state.

Perhaps the increased response to suggestions usually attributed to hypnosis relates more to these relationship changes than to the hypnotic potentiality for distorted perceptions. Even in individuals for whom this relationship fails to evoke hypnosis, the relationship as such may still alter the patient's motivation, and dramatically affect his response to certain types of suggestion. If this were true, it would help to explain many of the apparent contradictions about hypnosis, including the vastly differing reports by different hypnotists about the percentage of hypnotizable individuals in the population, and the lack of correlation between hypnotizability and compliance.

THE STUDY

EVALUATION

Theoretical issues

Are the state and non-state views mutually exclusive (can only *one* be true)? State theorists do not reject social psychological factors. Indeed Orne (1959, 1966, 1970, 1979) is actually a state theorist who has been a major experimentalist trying to tease out the effects of simple compliance or sham behaviour to see what is left. However, non-state theorists argue that it is unnecessary to propose any unique/special hypnotic process over and above compliance, imagination, relaxation and other 'normal' processes.

The most popular contemporary state theory is *neo-dissociation theory* (Hilgard, 1974, 1977, 1978, 1979; Bowers, 1983). Basically this maintains that we have multiple systems of control, not all conscious at the same time, but which can be brought into consciousness 'under hypnosis'. This is best illustrated by Hilgard's demonstration of the 'hidden observer' phenomenon. The individual is hypnotized and then given the following instruction:

> When I place my hand on your shoulder, I shall be able to talk to a hidden part of you that knows things are going on in your body, things that are unknown to the part of you to which I am now talking. The part to which I am now talking will not know what you are telling me or even that you are talking . . . You will remember that there is a part of you that knows many things that are going on that may be hidden from either your normal consciousness or the hypnotized part of you. By doing this, you can contact another system of control or 'part' of you, which will then speak, unaware of the normal 'waking part' or 'hypnotized part'.

Neo-dissociation theory provides a powerful explanation of *trance-logic*, which is discussed in **Methodological issues** below.

Arguably, the *pièce de résistance* of hypnosis is hypnotic analgesia (the control/elimination of surgical and non-surgical pain through hypnosis alone). Laboratory studies induce pain by plunging the individual's hand into ice-cold water or applying a pressure stimulus, and it seems undeniable that hypnotic techniques can be useful in this way (e.g. Hilgard & Hilgard, 1984).

However, does this in itself prove conclusively that it is a special state which is responsible? While non-state theorists are not arguing that all hypnotic phenomena are faked, pain relief *could* occur for a variety of reasons other than the inducement of a special state (e.g. relaxation and distraction). Wagstaff (1987, 1995) points out that:

(a) pain is a complex psychological sensation and can be alleviated through relaxation, reduction of stress and anxiety, and the use of strategies such as distraction and reinterpretation of the noxious (painful) stimulus. All of these are often used in cases of hypnotic surgery (e.g. Spanos & Chaves, 1989);

(b) many surgical procedures are less painful than might be commonly predicted. For example, many internal organs are insensitive to pain, and it's not true that the deeper you cut into the body the more it hurts – but pulling and stretching of damaged tissue is painful;

(c) cases of surgery with hypnosis alone are rare, and there are important individual differences in pain thresholds.

Non-state theorists point out that many apparently supportive studies have tended to use the same participants in *both* the hypnotic and the non-hypnotic conditions, making interpretation of the results more difficult (see **Exercises** below). For participants who are not hypnotically susceptible, hypnotic suggestions may actually be *less* effective than other pain-reducing strategies, such as distraction (Spanos, 1986a, 1989). Nevertheless, some state theorists continue to report that hypnotic suggestions are superior to non-hypnotic interventions (Bowers & Davidson, 1991).

Some of the most interesting results have come from 'hidden observer' reports (e.g Hilgard, 1986). Non-state theorists argue that these reports simply reflect what participants think they are expected to say as implied by experimental instructions (Spanos, 1989; Wagstaff, 1981a). For example, Spanos has found that 'hidden observers' will report greater, the same, or less pain than the ordinary 'hypnotized' part, if these expectations are conveyed to them.

According to Wagstaff (1995), disagreements about the mechanisms involved in hypnotic pain control are as rife as ever, but perhaps the most fascinating outcome of research in this area is the realization that human beings have a considerable capacity to control and tolerate pain without chemical analgesics.

Do some people have a particular susceptibility to, or talent for, hypnosis? (Mollon, 1998). According to Bliss (1986), the capacity for hypnosis depends on ability in *self-hypnosis*. This might involve a vivid imagination, a capacity for absorption in fantasy, or for directing attention to fantasy as opposed to external reality. Spiegel (1974) identified certain people who are unusually suggestible, easily hypnotized and self-hypnotized (the 'grade 5 syndrome').

A number of researchers have studied fantasy proneness as a personality trait and found that highly fantasy-prone people were more likely to report severe physical abuse in childhood, and were also more lonely and isolated as children. This suggests that the capacity for fantasy and imagination may be developed *defensively* in certain people in compensation for childhood abuse or loneliness: but these people are also more likely to invent and distort accounts of abuse (Mollon, 1998).

Both 'camps' seem to agree that the tendency to become absorbed in imagination (through activities such as reading, listening to music, and daydreaming) is one of the main correlates of hypnotic susceptibility (Nash, 2001). For state theorists, this reflects a capacity to *dissociate* (which they see as lying at the heart of hypnosis: e.g. Bowers,

1983), while non-state theorists argue that a tendency to fantasize would facilitate the role of 'hypnotized' individual. Not only is there no need to see the hypnotic state as an altered state of consciousness over-and-above a state of fantasy, but hypnotic susceptibility is also correlated with social conformity, acting skills, and the possession of appropriate attitudes and expectancies (Spanos, 1986b; Wagstaff, 1991).

Methodological issues

Most experiments have compared groups of hypnotic participants (those given a hypnotic induction procedure) with various control groups, set up to test alternative, non-state explanations. One commonly used control group is the *simulating group* (Orne, 1959, 1979), in which participants are told to fake hypnosis but not told *how* to do it.

Other control groups include 'task-motivated' groups, instructed, for example, to try hard to imagine and experience suggestions (but they are not given a formal hypnotic induction procedure: Barber, 1969). The rationale here is that if hypnotic participants respond no differently from non-hypnotic controls, then there is no need to postulate a special state to explain the behaviour of the former. Conversely, if controls *cannot* reproduce the behaviours of hypnotic participants, then it seems that hypnosis *does* involve an additional, unique, element.

So, do hypnotized participants show *physiological changes* not shown by controls? Many measures have been used, including EEG, blood pressure, blood-clotting time, breathing rate, skin temperature and oral temperature. None of these consistently differentiates between hypnotic participants and controls. Although these responses may *change* when a person is given hypnotic induction, equivalent changes are shown when a person is asked to close their eyes, relax or imagine various effects. Nor are hypnotic physiological changes equivalent to people when asleep or sleepwalking (e.g. Spanos, 1982; Wagstaff, 1981a). Most researchers of both 'camps' now seem to agree that the search for a unique correlate of the hypnotic state has not been very successful (Wagstaff, 1995). Physiological differences are discussed further in **Subsequent research** below.

Are hypnotized participants capable of extraordinary feats of which controls are incapable (the question of *transcendent properties*)? Not only do many state theorists deny that hypnotic participants can transcend normal human capacities, but there is no conclusive evidence that they are superior on a whole variety of tasks (see **Background and context** above), assuming that the controls are motivated to try hard and take the task seriously (e.g. Wagstaff, 1981a, 1982b, 1984).

Indeed, some studies have shown that simulators may overplay their role and actually outperform the hypnotic participants (e.g. picking up a poisonous snake, throwing acid at the experimenter (both tricks!), peddling heroin, mutilating the Bible and committing slanders: Wagstaff, 1981a, 1982b). Hypnosis does *not* increase memory for the details of crimes any more than instructing people to relax or vividly imagine events (Wagstaff, 1984: see **Applications and implications** below), and simulators are just as capable as hypnotized participants of giving the impression that painful stimuli do not hurt (Hilgard *et al.*, 1978: see **Theoretical issues** above).

But are there any more subtle measures of hypnotic responding? Wagstaff (1987) believes that probably the most significant demonstration of the differences between hypnotic ('real') and simulating behaviour is what Orne (1959, 1979) calls *'trance-logic'*. Four phenomena in particular have been identified as key examples:

(1) If it is suggested to hypnotic participants ('reals') that they cannot see an object actually in front of them (e.g. a chair), although some will claim they cannot see it, they will still walk around it rather than bump into it. By contrast, simulators tend to bump into it while claiming they cannot see it. Again, if shown a chair and asked to hallucinate a man sitting in it, 'reals' will tend to report that the image is transparent (they can still see the chair through the man!). But simulators tend to report it as opaque (not transparent), and so cannot see the chair through the man.

(2) If 'reals' view a person and, at the same time, receive a suggestion to hallucinate that person standing in a different location, they tend to report seeing *both* the actual person and the hallucinated image. Hardly any simulators do this. Orne (1959) called this the 'double hallucination' response.

(3) When given a suggestion to regress back to childhood, some 'reals' will report, alternately or simultaneously, that they felt *both* like an adult and a child.

(4) Unlike a child, 'reals' will correct a complex sentence, while simulators tend to report feeling like a child all the time and will write the sentence incorrectly (as would a child).

According to the state view, 'reals' have little need for logical consistency and can tolerate illogical responses: this is 'trance-logic'. Trance-logic can now be explained in terms of dissociated 'parts': the 'part' which does not see the chair is dissociated from the 'part' which knows it is there and walks round it. Also, the 'part' which sees the man in the chair is dissociated from that which does not. So both the man *and* the back of the chair are reported at the same time. These 'parts' are unaware of each other because they are separated by 'amnesia barriers', but they can break through simultaneously, so that participants report incongruities and logical inconsistencies.

One of the appeals of the theory is its ability to reinterpret some results which otherwise would seem to support the non-state view. For example, some hypnotic participants instructed to go deaf, when asked 'Can you hear me?' will answer 'No, I can't hear you' (Barber *et al.*, 1974). Instead of falling for a simple trick (non-state view), the 'part' which answers is dissociated from the 'part' which cannot hear (*neo-dissociation theory*). (Although, as Wagstaff says, it would make more sense if the 'hidden part' said, 'Yes, I *can* hear you'!) Wagstaff (1987) concludes that, ultimately, it's a question of parsimony as to which is the 'true' explanation: is it *necessary* to postulate dissociative processes and amnesic barriers when more 'normal' factors will do?

Subsequent research

According to Concar (1998), some of the latest experiments (in Boston, USA) have involved the collaboration of Spiegel, a neuropsychologist and doctor, and imaging experts (including Kosslyn), using PET scanning to measure blood flow changes linked to hypnosis (see Chapter 33). In one experiment, after a hypnotist had tried to put participants in a trance, they were told to manipulate in their mind's eye pieces of artwork shown on a computer screen inside the scanner. They either had to 'colour in' grey images or become 'colour blind', seeing only in shades of grey when faced with images containing real colours. Both instructions involve hallucinations that hypnotized people are supposed to be able to achieve at will.

Some were unable to experience colour hallucinations, but others reported more success. The early indications are that the hallucinations are real. The scans of those who claimed success with colour manipulation were different from those who failed, and some of the differences were in specific and highly relevant parts of the brain. Among those who claimed they had become 'colour blind', there was *reduced* blood flow to a part of the occipital lobe, while it *increased* in those who claimed they could colour-in grey images. Someone who was faking could not produce such distinctive brain changes. Rainville *et al.* (1997, cited in Nash, 2001) tried to locate the brain structures associated with the 'suffering' component of pain, as distinct from the sensory aspects. They hypnotized eight susceptible volunteers, asking them to place a hand in a tub of painfully hot water. It was suggested that it was either more or less unpleasant than it really was. PET scans revealed that this produced large changes in their anterior cingulate gyrus (part of the limbic system involved in the control of attention, emotion and motivation), which sets the volume/tone of the emotional 'sound track' the brain attaches to thoughts and perceptions.

If hypnosis really helped participants to take the emotional sting out of the pain they felt, this would be the one brain area in which you would expect to detect changes. Blood flow *increased* when the suggestion was that it would be *more* unpleasant, and *decreased* when the suggestion was that it would be *less* so. More importantly, the blood flow changes correlated so well with what participants claimed to be feeling: the more the pain seems to hurt, the more this region 'lit up', and vice-versa. Crucially, the experimenter's suggestions made no difference to blood flow to their somatosensory cortex, where pain sensations are processed.

Concar (1998) argues that the hypnotic state is not one of sleep or dreaming, but rather involves the brain 'turning in on itself', losing track of time and interest in the external world, gaining the ability to treat products of the imagination as real and believable. According to Gruzelier (1998: at the Imperial College School of Medicine in London), hypnosis impairs verbal fluency and other skills linked to the left frontal lobe. Slowing down of the left frontal lobe might be one way to suspend the brain's logical, critical faculties (see Chapter 30).

The non-state interpretation of these PET findings is that the blood flow patterns are correlated *not* with trance states but with perfectly ordinary mental and physical changes (such as relaxation and increased concentration). According to Kirsch (1997), the brain-imaging studies simply support the idea that suggestions can radically alter our behaviour and experience. What they *don't* show is that hypnosis is necessary for suggestions to have such effects. No one has shown that the brains of hypnotizable people respond any differently to suggestions *after* they have been hypnotized compared with before: that is probably because hypnosis does not cause any differences. It merely singles out those who are already suggestible, and this is all that is being measured in hypnosis research.

Applications and implications

We noted in **Methodological issues** above that hypnosis does not appear to increase memory for the details of crimes compared with instructions to relax or vividly imagine events. For example, Erdleyi (1996) reviews several studies of non-traumatic memory and concludes that *hypnotic hypermnesia* (enhanced memory retrieval) is nothing but hypermnesia. While agreeing that hypnosis *does* improve retrieval of meaningful material (but not for meaningless material or recognition memory, as in identitification parades), he dismisses its use in police interrogation. Others disagree, such as Geiselman *et al.* (1985), who found that hypnotic interviews conducted by experienced practitioners produced 35% more correct facts than police interviews alone (see Chapter 5: **Applications and implications**).

Hammond (1995) describes hypnosis as a controlled dissociation. People who have been traumatized often spontaneously enter trance-like dissociative states during or after the trauma, so hypnosis may recreate the dissociated context of the original experience and hence aid memory retrievel.

According to Nash (2001), perhaps nowhere has hypnosis produced more controversy than in relation to *recovered memories* (the *false memory syndrome* controversy (see Chapter 19). A key cue that we seem to use in making the distinction between reality and imagination is the experience of effort. At the time of encoding a memory, a 'tag' cues us as to the amount of effort made: if the event is tagged as having involved a good deal of effort on our part, we tend to interpret it as something that we imagined, while if little effort is involved, we tend to interpret it as something that actually happened to us.

. . . Given that the calling card of hypnosis is precisely the feeling of effortlessness, we can see why hypnotized people can so easily mistake an imagined past event for something that happened long ago. Hence, something that is merely imagined can become ingrained as an episode in our life story. (Nash, 2001).

The hypothesis that beliefs *about* hypnosis influence its effects was supported by Wagstaff & Frost (1996). In participants who had been hypnotized and given a social psychological view of hypnosis (linking its effects to role-play rather than trance), hypnotic pseudomemories and posthypnotic amnesia were greatly reduced compared with controls who did not hear the social psychological account. According to Hammond (1995):

It is vitally important that therapists (and the public) view hypnosis realistically. Material evoked through hypnotic exploration may include accurate information, partially accurate information, and confabulation. Memory is not perfect, in or out of hypnosis, and is subject to being influenced by the processes of daily living, waking suggestions, peer influence, or any type of retrieval effort.

Regarding its role in pain control, there is a vast number of studies showing that hypnosis can effectively reduce pain from cancer and other chronic conditions, as well as in patients undergoing treatment for burn-wounds, children enduring bone-marrow procedures, and women in childbirth. Its pain-relieving effects may sometimes even exceed those of morphine (Nash, 2001). Nash also cites evidence that patients who receive a combination of cognitive behaviour therapy (CBT) and hypnosis for a range of problems (including obesity, insomnia, anxiety and hypertension) showed greater improvement than 70% of those who received only CBT. There is also strong evidence for its effectiveness as a component in the broader treatment of some types of asthma, some skin disorders, irritable bowel syndrome, haemophilia , and the nausea associated with chemotherapy. However, it seems to have little effect in the treatment of drug and alcohol dependence. *How* it works is currently unknown (Nash, 2001).

Exercises

1. In the *Criteria for hypnosis* section (pages 592–3), referring to the Stanford Hypnosis Susceptibility Scale, Orne writes 'Scale scores agree very well with the judgement of trained observers'.

    (*i*) What's another word for 'agree'?
    (*ii*) How would this agreement be measured statistically?

2. Orne refers to Form C of the above Scale. Wagstaff refers to Forms A and B. What is the purpose/advantage of having different forms of the same test? What are they used for?

3. In **Methodological issues**, it was noted that non-state theorists have criticised many studies of pain inducement on the grounds that the same participants are tested in both the hypnotized and non-hypnotized conditions.

    (a) Why is this a (potential) problem?
    (b) How can it be prevented?

4. Wagstaff's reference to Orne's (1962) findings (*re*: five and a half hours of adding up numbers etc.) can be explained in terms of what Orne calls 'demand characteristics'. What does this mean, and what is its importance for human psychological experiments in general?

5. Whereas the clinical use of hypnosis may be ethically quite as acceptable as any other therapeutic procedure, do you find anything wrong with the experimental use of hypnosis (e.g. when people may be asked to 'make fools of themselves')?

32 Visions from the dying brain: Near-death experiences may tell us more about consciousness and the brain than about what lies beyond the grave

Susan Blackmore (1988)

New Scientist, 1988, 5 May, 43–46

BACKGROUND AND CONTEXT

According to Greyson (2000), near-death experiences (NDEs) are:

> . . . profound psychological events with transcendental and mystical elements, typically occurring to individuals close to death or in situations of intense physical or emotional danger.

NDEs (and the related out-of-body experience/OBE) represent one type of *paranormal* phenomenon which, collectively, form the subject-matter of *parapsychology*. Colman (1987) defines parapsychology as

> . . . a branch of psychology devoted to examining and seeking to explain . . . apparently supernatural or paranormal (beside or beyond the normal) phenomena . . . .

Watt (2001) explicitly rejects any reference to 'supernatural' in her definition, because this implies that such phenomena are incompatible with scientific theorizing and investigation. She defines parapsychology as '. . . the scientific study of paranormal phenomena and experiences . . .', where 'paranormal' means that:

> . . . the phenomena appear to suggest that organisms can interact with the environment in ways that are not explicable within current scientific understanding. This does not mean that paranormal phenomena can never be understood, but it may mean that some of our present scientific knowledge and theories would need to be adjusted to accommodate them . . .

Two people almost entirely responsible for founding *experimental* parapsychology in the 1930s were the husband and wife biologists, J.B. and Louisa Rhine. They wanted to find evidence against a purely materialist view of human nature (i.e. the philosophical doctrine according to which only physical matter exists: everything in the universe – including thoughts and feelings – can be explained in terms of physical laws).

The origins of parapsychology are often traced back to *spiritualism,* a Christian faith with the added dimension of spirit communication (contact with the spirits of the dead through the 'agency' of mediums). Spiritualism, which flourished during the 1850s–1880s, presented a direct challenge to science. Physics was becoming enormously successful at this time, while Darwin's theory of evolution was seen as a direct threat to many people's religious beliefs. Evolution in particular, and materialism (an essential feature of science) in general were strongly opposed by the Church and some saw spiritualism as providing the evidence needed to refute them (Blackmore, 1995).

Scientists and other scholars began to take the claims of spiritualism seriously and to investigate them. In 1882, the Society for Psychical Research (SPR) was founded in London, and the *Journal of the Society for Psychical Research* shortly afterwards. Its objective was:

> to examine without prejudice or prepossession and in a scientific spirit those faculties of man, real or supposed, which appear to be inexplicable on any generally recognized hypothesis. (in Blackmore, 1995)

Despite having the same aims, the Rhines wished to dissociate themselves from spiritualism and bring their new science firmly into the laboratory. They popularized the term 'parapsychology' (taken from the German 'parapsychologie', a term already in use at this time), using it to distinguish their more scientific approach from the more common 'psychical research' that typically involved field work with mediums and psychics. The Rhines began to develop experimental methods, and defined their terms operationally.

In 1934, J.B. Rhine first descibed *extrasensory perception* (ESP), a general term used to cover three types of communication supposedly occurring *without the use of the senses*:

● *telepathy* involves picking up information from another person (or mind-to-mind communication).

● *clairvoyance* involves picking up information from distant objects or events.

● *precognition* involves picking up information from/about the future.

Also in 1934, the Rhines began another controversial step by investigating *psychokinesis* (PK), defined as '. . . the movement or change of physical objects by purely mental processes, without the application of physical force . . .' (Colman, 1987), a case of mind over matter.

ESP and PK, collectively, are called 'psi', which came to be used as a general term

covering any paranormal phenomenon or the hypothesized mechanism underlying them (Blackmore, 1995).

AIM AND NATURE OF THE STUDY

The 'study' is primarily a review article, in which Blackmore discusses NDEs and considers alternative explanations in terms of known or hypothesized *physiological processes*, in particular those relating to brain mechanisms. She argues in the opening paragraph that before interpreting such experiences as evidence of life-after-death, we need to rule out other explanations, both physiological and psychological: not only can we apply what we already know (about the brain) to these experiences, but they can also teach us much about the brain.

She cites research, both that of others and her own conducted in the Brain and Perception Laboratory at the University of Bristol medical school. However, the article is not an account of a specific study (unlike most of those that appear in this book).

■T H E ■ S T U D Y ■

Near-death experiences, reported by people who have been revived from apparent death, are deeply mysterious – or so we are led to believe. Many people think that they provide evidence for life after death or the inexplicability of our spiritual nature. Yet before we jump to such conclusions, we should see just how far physiological and psychological explanations can account for them, and how much near-death experiences, in turn, have to teach us about the brain.

After some 15 years of research, one thing is clear: when people come close to death and later recover they tend to describe a well-structured set of experiences. Here is a brief example sent to me by a woman from Cyprus:

> An emergency gastrectomy was performed. On the 4th day following that operation I went into shock and became unconscious for several hours . . . Although thought to be unconscious I remembered, for years afterwards, the entire, detailed conversation that passed between the surgeon and anaesthetist present . . . I was lying above my own body, totally free of pain and looking down at my own self with compassion for the agony I could see on the face; I was floating peacefully. Then . . . I was going elsewhere, floating towards a dark, but not frightning, curtain-like area . . . then I felt total peace . . . Suddenly it all changed – I was slammed back into my body again, very much aware of the agony again.

In 1975 Raymond Moody, a psychiatrist from Georgia, first published his collection of near-death experiences (*Life after Life*). His account included experiences of floating along a dark tunnel, leaving the body and being able to watch the proceedings from a distance. People also reported meeting a 'being of light' who helped them review their past lives. Finally, they felt as if they were passing into another

Figure 32.1.

THE STUDY

world where some final barrier marked the return from joy, love and peace to pain, fear or sickness.

Moody did no more than collect cases, and many people did not believe that his rather idealistic description would hold up to more thorough investigation. In fact it did. Kenneth Ring, of the University of Connecticut, interviewed 102 people who had come close to death through illness, accident or suicide attempts. Of these, almost half reported experiences which conformed in an obvious way to Moody's description (*Life after Death*, 1980). Ring categorized five stages of the near-death experience: peace, body separation, entering the darkness (or the tunnel), seeing the light, and entering the light. Not only did these five stages tend to unfold in order, but the first stage was more common (60% of his sample reported peace) and the last least common (10%).

This seemed to imply a kind of 'ready-made' experience waiting to unfold its later, deeper stages the closer one came to death. More recently, Bruce Greyson (1985), a psychiatrist from the University of Michigan Medical Centre, challenged this 'invariance hypothesis'. He found that near-death experiences are not entirely invariant.

Such experiences also tend to take somewhat different forms in different cultures. For example, in India people more often meet up with some kind of messenger who consults a list of names and concludes that the wrong person has been called up – a reprieve is given. For Christians, the being of light is sometimes seen as Jesus, the angel Gabriel or even St. Peter at his gates.

For anyone who finds it hard to imagine these experiences, I should emphasize how real they seem. The tunnel is so convincing that people often assume it is some 'real' passageway to the next life. The out-of-body experience is so realistic that people are convinced that their spirit has left their body and can see and move without it. The positve emotions are so strong that many do not want to 'come back'.

For those who reach the final stages, it often seems as though a conscious decision has been made to return to life and responsibilities rather than remain in bliss and peace. For many people, their life thereafter is quite different. They claim to be less materialistic and far more grateful for life and concerned with the welfare of others.

So how can we explain tunnels, out-of-body experiences and life transformations? In classic occult lore, the astral body is the vehicle for consciousness, separating from the physical body permanently at death, but also, temporarily, during life. So the out-of-body experience is really 'astral projection'. The tunnel is the transition between astral and etheric worlds; the blackness happens as consciousness is transferred from one to the other.

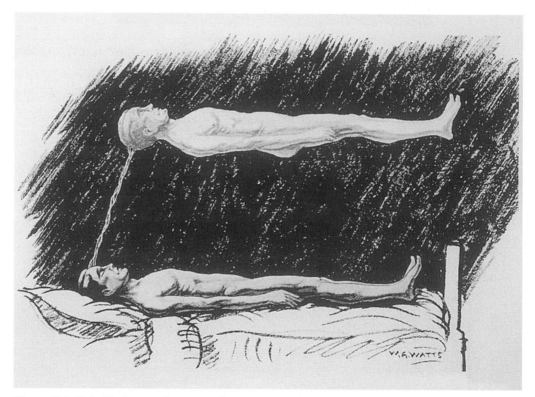

Figure 32.2. Out-of-body experiences convince many people that an 'astral body' leaves the corporeal body at death.

The problems with such an explanation are numerous. There is the question of what the astral is made of and how the astral and physical interact (indeed reflections of all mind-body problems). Then there is the problem of treating consciousness as some kind of 'stuff' to be carried about by bodies. But the worst problem is that such theories provide very few testable predictions. The main one is that the astral body should be detectable, and many brave attempts have been made to detect it. From ingenious experiments early this century, which involved weighing people as they died, to modern parapsychological experiments, there has always been the hope that new apparatus would finally reveal the astral body. But instruments of increasing sensitivity have demonstrated only a reduction in the size of any claimed effect. I have argued that these theories have failed to make any progress (*Beyond the Body*, 1982).

Nonetheless, such theories have great appeal because they seem, especially to the people who have had the experiences, to account for the phenomena. Dismissing near-death experiences as 'just imagination' or 'only an hallucination' is not a satisfactory explanation. If we are to provide better theories, we must not only criticize the occult ones effectively, but also produce alternatives that build on the rest of science, which make testable predictions and which also make sense to the people who have had near-death experiences. This is a tall order, but not impossible.

The astronomer Carl Sagan argued, and with much popular encouragement, that we can account for the universality of near-death experiences only by reference to the one experience we all share – birth. So the tunnel is 'really' the birth canal and the tunnel experience and the out-of-body experience are a reliving of one's birth. Similar arguments have produced the big business of 'rebirthing', regression and all sorts of other 'New Age' techniques. The problems here are rather obvious. The birth canal is not at all like a tunnel, even if the fetus were actually face first and open-eyed into it. The cognitive capacities of the newborn are not such that it would remember the experience in a way which would make sense to an adult 20 or 50 years later. Studies of so-called 'age-regression' under hypnosis show that subjects are generally inventing superficially plausible experiences. They greatly overestimate the capacities of young children.

The one redeeming feature of such a theory is that it is testable. If tunnels and out-of-body experiences are a rerun of birth, people born by Caesarean section should not have them. I gave a questionnaire to 254 people of whom 36 had been born by Caesarean. Both groups reported the same proportion of out-of-body and tunnel experiences. It could be that the experiences are based on the *idea* of birth *in general* but this drastically weakens the theory.

The weakest theory of all, though, must be the bald asserttion that the experiences are 'just hallucinations'. Although it is often held up as 'the scientific answer', it merely begs the questions: why those hallucinations? why a light at the end? why out-of-body experiences on the ceiling and not in the big toe? and why do they all seem so real? An effective approach must answer all these questions.

The tunnel seems to have a rather interesting origin in the structure of the visual system. It is not confined to near-death experiences but can occur in epilepsy or migraine; when falling asleep, meditating or just relaxing; with pressure on both eyes; or with certain drugs such as LSD, psilocybin, or mescaline. In the 1930s,

Heinrich Kluver at the University of Chicago noted it as as one of the four constant forms of drug-induced hallucinations; the others were the grating or lattice, the spiral and the cobweb. Why do all these different conditions produce the same hallucinations?

The visual cortex of the brain, which processes both vision and visual imagination, is usually in a stable state; it is kept that way to a large extent by some neurons inhibiting others. Many of the conditions that produce hallucinations are those which reduce or interfere with inhibition. LSD, for example, suppresses the action of the Raphe cells, which regulate activity in the visual cortex. Any interference with inhibition may produce a highly excitable state.

Jack Cowan, a neurobiologist from the University of Chicago, argued (1982) in an analogy with fluid mechanics, that such an increase in cortical excitability would destabilize the uniform state and induce stripes of activity which propagate through the visual cortex. So what kind of perception would these stripes produce? Visual space is first represented on the retina and then again in different areas of the brain's visual cortex. The centre of the visual field uses up far more neurons than the edges, and the whole 'picture' is mapped from the retina to brain by a complex mathematical function. Cowan shows that because of this mapping, the stripes of activity in the cortex would appear as though they were concentric rings, tunnels or spirals in the world outside. Movement of the stripes would produce expansion or shrinking.

So it seems that the tunnel is a natural consequence of the way in which the visual cortex represents the visual world. And the light at the end? Because the number of neurons devoted to any unit area is much higher in the centre of the visual field, you would still expect a much greater effect in the centre if all neurons were equally affected by the release from inhibition. Presumably, the more disturbed the system, the bigger the light ought to be, although no one has yet tested this idea.

Many questions remain, such as why one always seems to move forwards through the tunnel in near-death experiences, though not necessarily in other tunnel experiences. The most pressing question, however, is why, if it is an hallucination, it seems so real.

The answer to this may lie in asking what makes anything seem real. The distinction between 'out there' and 'in my mind' is not an easy one as far as the nervous system is concerned. Almost as soon as processing in vision or hearing starts, information from memory is mixed in with the sensory input. As the information passes through the multiple stages of processing, lines, edges, spaces and objects are represented in different ways. It seems unlikely that any simple tag could be attached which says 'this came from outside' or 'this is hallucination'. I suggest instead that the decision is made at a much higher level. The system simply takes the most stable model of the world it has at any time and calls that 'reality'.

In normal life there is one 'model of reality' that is overwhelmingly stable, coherent and complex. It is the one built up from sensory input. It is the model of 'me, here, now'. I am suggesting that this seems real only because it is the best model that the system has at the time.

But what about the dying system? What about a brain with massive disinhibition, beset with noise and in danger of failing altogether to produce a workable model of reality? It may well be that the stripes of activity in the visual cortex are the most stable model the system has. So naturally it seems real. It is, after all, real in exactly the same sense as anything ever is real – because it is the best model at the time. And because the processing of images also takes place in the visual cortex, it makes sense that other images, and even whole other worlds, will be incorporated into the tunnel perspective.

No sensible system will give up entirely at this point. So what should it do? The obvious objective is to get back to a model driven by sensory input – a stable representation of the world out there – as soon as possible. One way of doing this would be to rely on memory: to ask, as it were, 'Who am I? Where am I? What am I doing?' The answers will be there in memory, if enough capacity remains for processing. But we know something interesting about memory models. They are often in bird's-eye view.

So let us suppose that a dying woman's system constructs a model of what she knows should be happening; her body on the operating table, the surgeons around the bed, the lights above and the apparatus around. This may well be in a bird's-eye view, from the ceiling. It may be rather a good model. You need only think of the power of radio to invoke detailed visual images to realize just how good it could be. It may even incorporate some input, such as the sounds of the people talking or the clink of instruments on the trolley, not to mention the jolts of attempts of resuscitation. In this way a mental model could be produced which is not only convincing but actually contains some correct details about the events going on at the time – and is in a bird's-eye view.

If this model is the best the system has at the time, it will seem perfectly real. Again it is 'real' in exactly the same sense as anything ever is. This is, I suggest, how the out-of-body experience comes about.

From this approach come lots of testable predictions. For example, the people who have out-of-body experiences ought to be those who can more easily imagine scenes from a bird's-eye view, or more easily switch viewpoints in their imagination. I have confirmed this in several experiments (1987). They might also be those who recall things in bird's-eye view. Both myself and Harvey Irwin from the University of New South Wales, Australia, have found that people with out-of-body experiences tend to be those who recall dreams in a bird's-eye view, though not the events from waking life. The reason for this is not clear, but this approach already seems to be

THE STUDY

producing more progress than that based on the notion that something leaves the body.

There is one small piece of evidence which presents a big challenge to the view I have presented here. Michael Sabom, a cardiologist from Atlanta, Georgia, has claimed that patients have seen things during near-death experiences that they could not possibly have reconstructed from hearing or from what they previously knew of resuscitation techniques (*Recollections of Death*, 1982). Not only did he collect a few anecdotal tales, such as a shoe seen on an inaccessible window ledge, but he asked subjects to imagine going through a resuscitation procedure and to tell him what they 'saw'. What they saw was nothing like the detailed and correct descriptions of apparatus or the movement of needles on dials which people with near-death experiences saw from out of the body.

There are some problems with Sabom's work. A better control group would be made up of subjects who had actually been through the full procedure, and experienced the actions and conversations of staff. For this might all be heard during a near-death experience. The behaviour of the needles ought to be recorded precisely for comparison with the patient's account of the near-death experience. All this may be done in future research. Only then shall we know whether Sabom's data really challenge the view presented here and even whether they hold out any hope to those looking for 'something more' after death.

What, finally, of the reports of other worlds? Are they really the place where we shall meet again? Here we enter a much more tricky area with none of the predictability of the tunnel and the out-of-body experience. I think it is reasonable to suppose that the details of the other worlds depend upon one's expectation and prior experience, but the same process makes them seem real and unforgettable. The possible worlds will depend on the constraints of a failing information processing system, and as we learn more about the system's functioning those constraints should become more obvious. In any case, it is an extraordinary experience to be thrown out of the normal limits of the sensory world and have to face up to the limits of one's own mental models.

This, then, is why the near-death experience has such a profound and lasting effect on the people who experience it. It is devastating to find that other worlds, tunnels or flying out of the body can seem real. If we take the view that consciousness depends upon the mental models being constructed at any one time, these people's consciousness has been transformed. Even when they come back to normal and the 'real' world resumes its dominance, they cannot forget that for a time other worlds of imagination seemed real; that the body was trivial and for some there was even no self at all. It is a direct peek into the constructed nature of self and the world. They can never seem so solid or important again.

So the near-death experience may, after all, be transcendent and transforming, but

THE DEPARTURE OF THE ASTRAL BODY AT DEATH
According to clairvoyant vision of Andrew Jackson Davis.

Figure 32.3. Years of ingenious experiments have failed to detect a departing spirit.

not so very mysterious. It may tell us more about consciousness and the brain than about what may or may not happen after the grave. Its many components can be seen as changes in mental models brought about by disinhibition of the cortex and the breakdown of the normal model of reality driven by sensory input. But they should not be dismissed as 'just hallucinations'. They are life-transforming and important hallucinations and ones we would do well to try to understand.

EVALUATION

Theoretical issues

According to Alcock (1981), the development of definitions of ESP, PK and other terms (see **Background and context** above) was important, but the definitions themselves are problematic. They are all negative in the sense that they depend on ruling out 'normal' communication before the paranormal can be assumed.

Progression in parapsychology's experimental methods has necessarily been designed to exclude the 'normal' even more securely. However, this inevitably leaves it open for critics to argue for even more devious ways in which sensory communication or outright fraud might occur (Blackmore, 1995).

Another consequence of some definitions is that the field of parapsychology is ever-shrinking. For example, hypnosis, hallucinations and lucid dreams used to be considered part of parapsychology, until psychologists made progress in understanding them. As Boring (1966) said, a scientific success is a failure for psychical research. In other words, parapsychology is concerned with those phenomena that 'mainstream' or 'regular' psychology cannot explain, phenomena that cannot be accommodated by currently available models or theories. This is inevitable if parapsychology is defined as the study of the paranormal, and may be one reason that parapsychologists now prefer to define their subject-matter in terms of psychic *experiences*, without commitment to a particular explanation (Blackmore, 1995).

Blackmore's article can be seen in this context. She argues strongly and persuasively against the 'they are just imagination or hallucinations' dismissal of NDEs and OBEs. She sees them as real, powerful experiences which have a lasting impact on people's lives, such that they need to be taken seriously. However, she rejects 'non-scientific' interpretations (astral body leaving the physical body, glimpsing life-after-death, etc.) in favour of explanations in terms of brain function (neuropsychological explanations).

As she states, to provide 'better' theories than the occult (i.e. supernatural) ones, we must '. . . produce alternatives that build on the rest of science, which make testable predictions and which also make sense to the people who have had near-death experiences . . .' But don't such experiences have their impact precisely because those who have them believe in the truth of the occult theories? To reduce them to suppression of the normal inhibitory mechanisms in the visual cortex, and to stress what they have in common with other experiences, detracts from their special qualities (or does this beg the question?).

While she argues that these experiences should be taken seriously, Blackmore seems to be claiming that only a scientific explanation, allowing testable hypotheses, will do. As a consequence, she seems to have defined NDEs and OBEs as no longer paranormal. Indeed, she states (1995) that the study of OBEs is increasingly becoming part of psychology (as distinct from parapsychology). More recently – and more generally – she states that:

> . . . I do not know whether psi exists but I do know that the only way to find out is by imaginative, meticulous and open-minded research . . . (Blackmore, 1997)

This illustrates the paradox of parapsychology: if the explanations that are brought to bear are those already available in mainstream psychology, where does the 'para' come in? In Colman's (1987) definition (see **Background and context** above), the crucial word seems to be 'apparently'.

For Morris (1989), who holds the Koestler Chair of Parapsychology at the University of Edinburgh, parapsychology can be defined as 'the study of apparent new means of communication between organism and environment'. It, therefore, falls within *anomalistic* psychology: the study of anomalies or unusual experience and behaviour. It is heuristically useful (useful as a 'rule of thumb') to regard psychic ability in simple communication terms. In the case of ESP, the organism appears to be serving as a receiver in a communication system. Some aspect of the environment is acting as the source or sender, so that a message (or influence) appears to be conveyed from source to receiver. The only difficulty for psychic communication is that we cannot yet specifiy a channel or means of conducting the information from sender to receiver. As for PK, the direction of transfer of information or influence is reversed: the organism appears to be the source and some aspect of the environment the 'recipient' of the influence. Once again, no channels or physical means of conveying the influence have yet been specified.

According to this communication model of 'psi', someone observes that there has been a coincidence between events in an organism and events in the environment and attributes special meaning to that coincidence. The observer is saying: 'I observed two events that resembled each other and I cannot understand why this should be, unless somebody involved was being psychic'.

Morris (1989) considers the 'psychology of evaluating evidence for psi'. Coincidences do arise by chance, without meaningful causal connections of any sort. In a series of ingenious experiments, two eminent cognitive psychologists, Tversky and Kahneman (1973, 1986) showed that people in general have a very poor intuitive grasp of probability theory (the likelihood of classes of similar events occurring 'just by chance'). Even professional mathematical psychologists showed such deficits. People display biases of perception and judgement that contribute to their tendency to regard any given coincidence, noticed after the fact, as more unlikely than it really is. This, in turn, could help to explain people's readiness to attribute particular behaviour to psi or psychic abilities.

OBERs (or 'autoscopic' experiences) (like one Blackmore had in 1970 while listening to Pink Floyd) are reported by about 30% of people, and surveys show that over 50% of the population believes in the paranormal. Apart from simply wanting to believe in 'something more' (than earthly life), this poor ability to judge probabilities may contribute to such widespread belief in the paranormal (Blackmore, 1997).

Sceptical researchers (e.g. Alcock, 1981) have tended to characterize those who believe in the paranormal ('sheep') as being cognitively inferior to disbelievers ('goats'). Indeed, a substantial proportion of the empirical work generated by such researchers has been devoted to exploring the nature of this supposed deficiency. Irwin (1993) has coined the term 'cognitive deficits hypothesis' to describe the philosophy behind this research programme. However, the findings are inconsistent and, at best, provide only equivocal support for the cognitive deficits hypothesis.

Methodological issues

NDEs have been reported following resuscitation (after the person had been pronounced clinically dead), by people who actually died but were able to describe their experiences in their final moments, as well as by individuals who in the course of accidents or illnesses simply *feared* they were near to death (Greyson, 2000). According to Roe (2001), in all three types of case it could be claimed that the experience has more to do with the *process* of dying than with the end-point of death itself. Roe poses the crucial question: Are people who have NDEs really dead? The answer he gives is: 'It depends on how you define 'dead'.

Initially, doctors determined death by checking for pulse, respiration and pupil reaction to light. With the invention of the stethoscope, the focus shifted to the heart. With the advent of cardiopulmonary resuscitation, it became clear that people who had been pronounced dead could be brought back to life. Attention has, therefore, shifted to brain function. Yet a lack of cortical activity – and even brainstem quiescence – may only be symptomatic of *dying*, rather than an indicator of actual death. In each case, there may be a suspicion that some remnant of life may be going undetected which is capable of maintaining some kind of phenomenological experience.

These shifts in focus show how difficult it is to identify any single event as defining death. As Roe (2001) points out:

> . . . death is a process that takes time, and if the appropriate action is taken then the dying process can be reversed . . .

An extreme definition of death is given by Roberts & Owen (1988), involving an irreversible – and permanent – loss of organ functions. Accordingly, all NDE reports refer to the experiences of people who have remained alive. If NDEs genuinely indicate what happens after we die (as many who report them believe), then we might expect to find differences between those who were actually near death and those who merely *thought* they were. But there is little evidence to support this claim. For example, Greyson *et al.* (1990) compared NDEs in patients whom they believed would have died without medical intervention, and those who believed they were near death but in fact were not. The fact that virtually identical NDEs can be induced by perceived threat needs to be taken into account in any potential explanation (Roe, 2001: see **Subsequent research**).

By their very nature, NDEs and OBEs are *spontaneous* occurrences: people are unlikely to volunteer for experiments in which they are brought to the brink of death and most researchers would not think such experiments ethically acceptable even if such volunteers could be found!

According to Colman (1987), spontaneous cases are not generally regarded as scientific evidence for psi for three major reasons:

(1) They are unrepeatable, making it impossible for independent researchers to check them (unlike general psychology or experimental parapsychology). There is also a lack of theory as to when and where spontaneous psi should occur.

(2) It is impossible to *exclude* a normal explanation, i.e. some perfectly normal process (such as falling asleep and dreaming) could account for the apparently paranormal experience. The accumulation of similar cases does not necessarily strengthen the case for psi: there may be even more instances of apparitions, for example, that went unreported because they *did not* coincide with anything interesting. In 27 years of psychoanalytic work with patients, many of whom were firm believers in the paranormal, Freud never encountered a paranormal dream.

(3) Most importantly, cases of spontaneous psi inevitably rely on the testimony of those who report them. According to the philosopher Hume (1748/1902), in such cases there are three possibilities: (*i*) the report is true; (*ii*) the report is false (because the informant is mistaken); (*iii*) the report is false (because the informant is dishonest). One of these must be correct, but how do we choose between them? If the informant reports a paranormal event, it is literally contrary to the laws of nature, which implies that it is as unlikely as anything could be, therefore, it must be more likely that the informant is either mistaken or dishonest ((*ii*) or (*iii*), neither of which is contrary to any law of nature, is more likely than (*i*)). Consequently, there are never good grounds for believing the testimony. This argument also applies to first-hand experiences: even the testimony of one's own senses can be mistaken without violating any law of nature (Colman, 1995).

However, Hume's argument (which was originally concerned with testimony for miracles but which has been consistently presented as an argument against any parapsychological phenomenon) has itself been heavily criticized (Roe, personal communication). For example:

(a) whether psi phenomena violate any known laws is debatable and certainly cannot just be assumed;

(b) it presumes that existing knowledge is reliable – which is not supported by the history of science. In particular, it perversely implies that earlier testimony (which gave rise to such laws) is inherently superior to contemporary testimony: this claim would disallow any disagreements or anomalies (whether in parapsychology or 'mainstream' psychology);

(c) it presumes that existing knowledge is complete, that there are no special cases or conditions to which general laws may not apply.

In face of the criticisms of spontaneous cases identified by Colman above, the use of experimental, laboratory based studies assumes even greater importance than perhaps it does in general psychology. However, the history of parapsychology is '. . . disfigured by numerous cases of fraud involving some of the most "highly respected scientists", their colleagues and participants . . .' (Colman, 1987). For example, Soal (Soal & Bateman, 1954), a mathematician at Queen Mary College, London, tried to replicate some of the Rhines' telepathy experiments using ESP or Zener cards. Despite his rigid controls and the involvement of other scientists as observers throughout, accusations of fraud resulted in a series of re-analyses of the data. Marwick (a member of the Society for Psychical Research in London) finally proved (in 1978) that Soal *had* cheated (Blackmore, 1995).

Against this, it is misleading to suggest that experimenter fraud is rife in paranormal psychology, or even that it is more common here than in other disciplines. According to Roe (personal communication), books such as *Betrayers of the Truth* (Broad & Wade, 1982) show that fraud is more likely when the rewards are high and the chances of being caught (publicly exposed) are low. This characterizes mainstream science (especially medicine), and is certainly *not* characteristic of paranormal psychology.

Subsequent research

According to Blackmore (1995), apparitions at the moment of death, mediumistic communication, and other apparent forms of evidence for survival after death are still being investigated – but much less than in the early days of psychical research. One unresolved problem is the 'super-ESP' hypothesis! If the possibility of ESP or PK is admitted, then any evidence supposedly coming from a discarnate (disembodied) being could alternatively said to come from the psi powers of the living. This may have to entail ridiculously complex or powerful forms of ESP, unlike anything seen in the laboratory (hence 'super-ESP'). Nevertheless, it is always an alternative which makes finding evidence for survival next to impossible.

NDEs represent one kind of evidence. While originally thought to be rare, it is now suggested that up to one-third of people who come close to death have them (Roe, 2001). Although this may be an overestimate, it is certainly not an uncommon experience. This could reflect improvements in resuscitation methods, such that:

> . . . more people survive the kinds of close brush with death (e.g. heart attack, drowning, road traffic accident) that would previously have been fatal . . . (Roe, 2001)

Alternatively, it could just mean that the notion of NDE has become part of popular culture, and so may provide the basis for some fanatasized experience produced while unconscious or in crisis. Its portrayal in films such as *Flatliners* has made the classic NDE almost archetypal (Roe, 2001). (This has parallels with the 'epidemic' in reported cases of multiple personality disorder, especially by psychiatrists in the USA: see Chapter 21).

The term 'NDE' was coined by Moody in his book *Life After Life* (1975), based on his collection of over 150 cases. In it, he identified 15 key features, His main purpose was to convince researchers that the topic was worthy of serious study, and in that he was very successful (Roe, 2001). Not only is there now The International Association for Near-Death Studies and its *Journal of Near-Death Studies*, but more detailed research since Moody's pioneering study has confirmed that the experience takes a consistent form and is independent of its cause or any drugs taken at the time. For example, Ring (1980) took Moody's research a step further by using a structured interview and measurement scale with 102 survivors of life-threatening injuries or illnesses. Forty-nine (48%) met his criteria for deep or moderate NDE, the other 53 (52%) being 'nonexperiencers'. The great majority had suffered a sudden episode, such as coronary infarction (heart attack) or haemorrhage. Based on their accounts, Ring identified a 'core experience', comprising five stages (feelings of deep peace and well-being, a sense of separation from the body/OBE, entering darkness/passing through a tunnel, seeing the light, and entering the light/beautiful garden). The stages tended to occur in this order, with earlier stages being more common than later ones, but they are still better thought of as a trend, as opposed to a fixed sequence. Fenwick (1997) collected over 300 accounts, and his findings are strikingly similar to Ring's.

For the most part, 'survivors' are not reporting that death is a terrifyingly painful and horrible ordeal. Instead, they are reporting beautiful, peaceful feelings, OBEs, floating and moving anywhere at will. Returning to their bodies, these survivors report boldly changed lives, usually with no fear of death and many new values and spirituality (Bailey & Yates, 1996).

Yet according to Orbach (1999), it would be strange – and unbelievable – if all the NDEs reported were blissful. She argues that:

> . . . There must surely be a shadow side to the experience, but, although this is obviously true, not many distressing NDEs get reported . . . it could be a sense of shame that silences those who have caught glimpses of hell, the sinners' destination . . .

Orbach cites reports of negative NDEs by Evans-Bush & Greyson (1996), in which people are frightened by the prospect of entering the tunnel, experience an emptiness and loss of meaning, and a 'wailing and gnashing of teeth, grotesque sub-human creatures, tormented and tormenting'.

The blissful feelings associated with NDEs can be explained by the release of endorphins (the brain's natural pain killers) under stress, and (OBEs) can be understood in psychological terms, such as the defence mechanism of *depersonalization*, and the hallucinatory effect of terror (Blackmore, 1993, Nuland, 1994). Many of the phenomena are similar to those induced by stimulation of the temporal lobe.

Endorphins released at times of fear or stress are known to induce temporal lobe seizures. The few cases of people being able to see things they could not possibly have heard or known about are very hard to substantiate (Blackmore, 1993), and overall, evidence for survival, though often claimed, is elusive (Blackmore, 1995).

According to Nuland (1994), no sensible observer can discount the many tales from the 'almost-beyond' collected by reliable investigators interviewing credible survivors. Nuland maintains that NDE is the result of a few million years of biological evolution and has a life-preserving function for the species. He claims that:

> . . . The fact that it seems in some few instances to occur even when 'death' has been prolonged or relatively stress-free does not alter my expectation that it will one day be proven to be driven, if not specifically by endorphins, then by some similar biochemical mechanism . . .

Like Nuland, Kübler-Ross is a medical practitioner, internationally renowned for her work with terminally ill patients. Based on her own research, she takes a very different view of the nature and meaning of NDE from either Nuland or Blackmore (or, indeed, the vast majority of investigators). During the 1980s, she (and her colleagues) collected over 25,000 cases from a wide range of cultural and religious (and non-religious) backgrounds all over the world, including a two-year-old child and a 97-year-old man. Kübler-Ross (1991) concludes that:

> . . . At the moment of death, all of you will experience the separation of the real immortal You, from the temporary house, namely the physical body . . . the soul or the entity . . . the butterfly in the process of leaving the cocoon. When we leave the physical body there will be a total absence of panic, fear or anxiety . . .

Applications and implications

As a neurophysiologist and neuropsychiatrist, Fenwick (1997) argues that all thoughts and feelings result from neuronal activity in the brain. 'Mind' is merely a product of the brain, and '. . . certainly cannot act at a distance from it, or independently of it'. Agreeing with Blackmore, he believes that our models of the world are created in our brains from the messages that come in coded pulses via the sense organs. In deep unconsciousness, there can be no model building, no experiencing, and no memory. Yet NDEs are remarkably lucid and clearly remembered. How is this possible?

NDEs have much in common with mystical experiences, and the brain activity involved is probably the same in both cases (Orbach, 1999). Morse (1990) believes that understanding NDEs will be the first step in healing the gulf between science and religion. According to Corbett (1996):

The psychologist cannot definitively answer the question of whether consciousness is literally able to move out of the body into another realm of reality. But . . . to insist on a purely organic explanation of these events [NDEs] is to abandon true openness in the face of an unanswerable question.

For Orbach (1999):

When science can take us no further, we are left with the possibility of soul . . . Does the mind (or self) exist independently of the brain? In trying to find an answer we must look a little harder for a definition of who we are – both in life and death.

According to Jung (1967), there is a psychic reality beyond our narrow ego-consciousness. He speculated on its continuation after the individual death of our body. If we assume that life continues in some mysterious 'there', then since 'there' can have no location, the only way of continuing is in the psyche – free from the limits of space and time. Like Fenwick (1997), Jung was astonished at what happens when the cerebral cortex has stopped functioning. He had a NDE himself that produced a state of bliss, and he refers to cases of severe brain injury (syncope), during which there can be both dreaming and perception of the outside world. Against all the odds, some sort of consciousness seems to remain possible in apparent unconsciousness (Orbach, 1999).

No one theory of NDEs provides a comprehensive explanation. Where a theory is successful, it tends to focus selectively on particular features that can be explained, while ignoring or underplaying the importance of those that cannot. However, they may still be able to provide us with a rich source of speculative predictions that can be tested in future investigations (Roe, 2001). Although the evidence as it stands may be inadequate, it is premature to reject psychological or organic theories in favour of a spiritualist one. Roe concludes by stating that:

. . . we are still some way from developing an understanding of the nature and cause of NDEs, and further work is clearly necessary. Whatever the ultimate resolution . . . the NDE is an intriguing and powerful area of human experience that merits our continued interest.

Exercises

1. When discussing the 'astral projection' explanation of OBEs, Blackmore asks what the astral is made of and how it interacts with the physical (a basic problem with all theories of the *mind-body relationship*). What are some of the main theories of this relationship (sometimes called the *mind-brain* problem) and how do they tackle the issue of interaction between the physical and the non-physical?

2. When discussing Sagan's account of the tunnel component of NDEs in terms of reliving one's birth, Blackmore cites a study in which she found the same proportion of OBEs and tunnel experiences reported by people born normally and by Caesarean section. She takes this as evidence against Sagan's account.

   (*i*) Are the data consistent with her prediction?

   (*ii*) Are there different types of memory which could explain the link between the birth experience and tunnel experiences?

   (*iii*) Does Sagan's theory (and related 'New Age' techniques) necessarily overestimate the capacities of newborns?

3. What are LSD, psilocybin and mescaline? What properties do they share?

4. When discussing why experiences such as tunnel experiences, if they are hallucinations, seem so real, Blackmore states that the nervous system cannot easily distinguish between 'out there' and 'in my mind'. What other distinction, commonly made in cognitive psychology's discussion of information processing, does this correspond to?

5. Does Greyson's (1985) challenge to the 'invariance hypothesis' of NDEs have any parallels in other areas of psychology (such as developmental), and what implications might cross-cultural variations have for the 'reality' of NDEs?

6. What does it mean to say that Blackmore's explanation of NDEs and OBEs is *reductionist*? Does her account in terms of neuropsychological mechanisms necessarily exclude the 'occult theory', i.e. if the former is true, must the latter be false? More generally, is the scientific 'model of reality' inherently more 'true' than others (such as the occult model), and if so, by what criteria?

33

Brain abnormalities in murderers indicated by positron emission tomography

Adrian Raine, Monte Buchsbaum, and Lori LaCasse (1997)

Biological Psychiatry, 42, 495–508

BACKGROUND AND CONTEXT

Neuroscientists no longer have to rely on laboratory animals or brain-damaged patients requiring surgery to view what is going on inside the human brain as it occurs. We can now peer into a healthy brain and observe the moment-to-moment changes that occur in relation to mental activity (although this does *not* mean that we can literally look inside someone's *mind:* see **Exercises** and Chapter 30).

Recent technology (since the early 1970s: Raichle, 1998), in the form of *brain imaging* techniques, enables neuroscientists to (a) understand the relationship between specific areas of the brain and what functions they serve; (b) locate the areas of the brain that are affected by neurological disorders; and (c) develop new strategies for treating brain disorders.

A *computed* (or *computerized*) *tomography scan* (CT scan) involves a series of X-ray beams passed through the head, each producing a different 'shot'. These images are then assimilated by a computer, producing cross-sections ('slices') of the structure of the brain. CT scans are used mainly for the detection and diagnosis of brain injury and disease, and tell us nothing about the brain's function.

Magnetic resonance imaging (MRI) uses the detection of radio frequency signals produced by displaced radio waves in a magnetic field. It provides an anatomical view of the brain. The more recent *functional* magnetic resonance imaging (fMRI) detects changes in blood flow to particular areas of the brain, thus providing both an anatomical and a functional view of the brain.

In *positron emission tomography* (PET), a radioactively labelled substance (a tracer) is added to substances naturally used by the body (such as oxygen, fluorine, carbon, nitrogen or glucose). This is either injected or inhaled. When this material gets into the bloodstream, it goes to brain areas that use it. So, oxygen and glucose, for example, accumulate in brain areas that are metabolically active. When the radioactive material breaks down, it gives off a neutron and a positron. When a positron hits an electron, both are destroyed and two gamma rays are released. Gamma ray detectors record the brain area from where the gamma rays are emitted. This provides a functional view of the brain.

Since the late 1980s, *cognitive neuroscience* has emerged as a very important growth area in neuroscience as a whole, combining the experimental strategies of cognitive psychology with the imaging techniques described above (amongst others: Raichle, 1998). According to Gazzaniga (2000):

> The push to understand the mind and brain is now one of the biggest and most dynamic struggles in science . . .

Attempts to understand the mind while ignoring the brain have often 'died on the vine' (Gazzaniga, 2000). Churchland & Sejnowski (1988), speaking from the perspectives of a philosopher and theoretical neuroscientist respectively, argue that although the software of the brain might in principle be inferred from the hardware, this cannot tell you how the system actually works. Theorizing is crucial, but only neurobiological reality will provide the essential hints and allow the pruning of ideas that are obviously wrong.

Conversely, cognitive thinking helps ensure that neuroscientists are studying something interesting. Raichle (1998) believes that the new imaging techniques were seized upon by psychologists who had previously developed appropriate concepts and experimental approaches, and both functional imaging and psychologists were thus 'catapulted to stardom'.

PET scans pinpoint in brilliant colour the regions of the brain where neurons are working during a particular mental task. They have shed a new and exciting light onto many brain diseases and pathological conditions, including epilepsy, Parkinson's disease, Alzheimer's disease, Huntington's disease, and Down's syndrome. They are being used extensively in psychiatry, because PET is very sensitive to biological brain changes during episodes of schizophrenia, depression, and other psychological disorders (Sabbatini, 1997). Most recently, and perhaps most controversially, they are being used to study the brain in relation to criminal behaviour, particularly violent crime.

AIM AND NATURE OF THE STUDY

The aim of the study is to provide direct evidence for the claim that murderers pleading not guilty by reason of insanity (NGRI) have brain dysfunction. Using PET scans, glucose metabolism was measured in a variety of brain areas and structures while participants were engaged in a continuous performance challenge task. The significance of glucose metabolism is that glucose is the principal type of fuel used by neurons when transmitting information. So, the *lower* the glucose metabolism, the *less* the activity in any particular area of the brain.

Based on previous research (with both violent offenders and non-violent controls, and non-human animals), Raine *et al.* expected to find differences between the 41 murderers pleading NGRI and controls matched for age and sex, only in specific brain areas.

(a) As far as *cortical* areas are concerned, the murderers were expected to show *lower* glucose metabolism (and, hence, *less* activity) in the *prefrontal cortex* (lateral – away from the centre – and medial – in the centre), the *superior parietal gyrus* (a gyrus is the structure between two sulci or fissures, which refer to the folds characteristic of the cortex, and 'superior' denotes 'as seen from above': Toates, 2001), and the *left angular gyrus* (a region of the parietal lobe behind the posterior end of the lateral fissure). The murderers did, indeed, show significantly lower activity in these areas. No differences were expected – or found – in the *temporal lobe* or the *cingulate* (see **Evaluation**).

(b) As far as *subcortical* areas are concerned, the murderers compared with the controls showed reduced glucose metabolism in the *corpus callosum*. In addition, the former showed *abnormal asymmetries* in the *amygdala, thalamus*, and the *medial temporal lobe* (including the *hippocampus*). This means that there was reduced glucose metabolism in the left hemisphere compared with the right for these areas (that is, murderers showed a bias towards increased right hemisphere activity). Raine *et al.* suggest that processing of negative emotion (such as anger and aggression) might be subject to less inhibition from the left hemisphere. No differences were expected – or found – for the *caudate* (nucleus), *putamen* or *globus pallidus* (together comprising the *basal ganglia*), the *midbrain*, or the *cerebellum*.

Lower than normal activity in the prefrontal cortex (PFC), parietal cortex and corpus callosum suggests a deficit in the integration of information needed to modify and inhibit behaviour. For example, increased blood flow to the PFC usually occurs when people are engaged in planning some future behaviour. Luria (1973) found that patients with PFC damage were often unable to effect forward planning, living in the 'here and now', controlled by currently physically present stimuli and situations.

Abnormalities in the hippocampus and amygdala suggest deficiency in forming and utilizing emotionally coloured perceptions and memories (Toates, 2001). In the amygdala, for example, emotional significance is given to the cognitive processing about the world performed by the temporal cortex (to which it is connected) (LeDoux, 1998). The amygdala also receives, more directly from the senses, raw information about threats (such as loud noises), before elaborate processing takes place (LeDoux, 1989).

The areas where no differences were found or expected are all concerned with movement. For example, the cerebellum (along with the motor cortex, basal ganglia and some other regions) plays a role in the computation of the commands sent to effect motor action (Toates, 2001).

Raine *et al.* conclude that their preliminary findings:

> . . . provide initial indications of a network of abnormal cortical and subcortical brain processes that may predispose to violence in murderers pleading NGRI.

However, they also comment that:

> . . . these findings cannot be taken to demonstrate that violence is determined by biology alone; clearly, social, psychological, cultural and situational factors also play important roles in predisposing to violence . . .

A major reason for this qualification of their results is to do with the nature of the study. The independent variable (IV) is being a murderer (pleading NGRI) or not being a murderer (at all), while the dependent variable (DV) is glucose metabolism levels in various parts of the brain (both cortical and subcortical). Clearly, the IV is *selected for*, rather than manipulated, so we cannot be sure that any differences in brain activity actually *cause* the violent behaviour. To be able to make that sort of claim, a true experiment would be necessary, while this present study (as with all such studies) is a *quasi-experiment*.

Essentially, Raine *et al.* have found that certain brain abnormalities are *correlated* with certain types of violent behaviour. It remains possible that developing violent tendencies actually changes the function of certain brain areas, rather than vice-versa. Similarly, both the brain abnormalities and the violent behaviour could be the result of one or more social, psychological, cultural and situational factors that Raine *et al.* refer to (see **Evaluation** section and **Exercises**).

T H E   S T U D Y

> Murderers pleading not guilty by reason of insanity (NGRI) are thought to have brain dysfunction, but there have been no previous studies reporting direct measures of both cortical and subcortical brain functioning in this specific group. Positron emission tomography brain imaging using a continuous performance challenge task was conducted on 41 murderers pleading NGRI and 41 age- and sex-matched controls. Murderers were characterized by reduced glucose metabolism in the prefrontal cortex, superior parietal gyrus, left angular gyrus, and the corpus callosum, while abnormal asymmetries of activity (left hemisphere lower than right) were also found in the amygdala, thalamus and medial temporal lobe. These preliminary findings provide initial indications of a network of abnormal cortical and subcortical brain processes that may predispose to violence in murderers pleading NGRI.

INTRODUCTION

It has long been suspected that generalized brain dysfunction may predispose to violent behaviour. Studies using electroencephalographic (EEG), neurological, neuropsychological, and cognitive test techniques have repeatedly shown that violent offenders have poorer brain functioning than normal controls (Eichelman, 1993; Eysenck & Gudjonsson, 1989; Elliott, 1987; Lewis et al., 1988; Moffitt, 1988; Raine, 1993), but until recently it has not been possible to localize which brain areas in particular may be dysfunctional in violent offenders.

However, it has long been thought that dysfunction of the prefrontal cortex may disrupt the regulation of aggression, and this idea has been supported by neurological studies of patients with damage to the prefrontal cortex (Damasio et al., 1990; Weoger & Bear, 1988). Some neuropsychological and psychophysiological studies on violent and forensic populations have shown abnormalities in hemispheric asymmetries of function (Convit et al., 1991; Hare & McPherson, 1984; Raine et al., 1990a) and reduced EEG interhemispheric coherence (Flor-Henry et al., 1991), which may be linked to dysfunction of the corpus callosum (Nachshon, 1983; Yeudall, 1977), but this hypothesis has not been tested using direct measures of callosal functioning. Recent event-related potential mapping techniques have implicated dysfunction in the left angular gyrus in violent offenders as indicated by reduced slow-wave amplitudes (Barratt et al., in press). Experimental animal research, together with neurological studies of patients have further implicated limbic structures such as the amygdala and hippocampus in modulating aggression (Bear, 1990; Elliott, 1992; Gorenstein & Newman, 1980; Mirsky & Siegel, 1994; Watson et al., 1983a), while the thalamus also provides an important afferent source of the hypothalamic-induced attack in cats (Mirsky & Siegel, 1994). Although such research on animals and humans who have suffered brain insults is of key importance, it is one step removed from the question of whether severely violent offenders have brain dysfunction localized to specific brain areas.

The advent of brain imaging research has recently made it possible for the first time to directly assess brain functioning in violent individuals. Initial research in this area has again implicated frontal brain regions in addition to the temporal cortex (Goyer et al., 1994; Volkow & Tancredi, 1987). Although these important initial studies support the idea of localized brain dysfunction in aggressive patients, they have involved small samples in hospitalized patients and have focused on aggressive personality as opposed to seriously violent behaviour.

One particularly important group of violent offenders in forensic psychiatry consists of those who commit murder and plead not guilty by reason of insanity (NGRI). Although it is thought that such individuals have localized brain impairments, there has been no previous brain imaging research on this important population. In a preliminary report on a pilot sample of 22 such offenders compared to

22 normals, Raine *et al.* (1994) provided some initial support for the idea of pre-frontal dysfunction in this group. In the present study, the sample size is extended to 41 murderers and 41 controls, and analysis of subcortical structures is now undertaken. To our knowledge, this is the largest sample of violent offenders assessed on functional brain imaging. It is hypothesized that these seriously violent individuals have relatively localized brain dysfunction in the prefrontal cortex, angular gyrus, amygdale, hippocampus, thalamus, and the corpus callosum, brain areas previously linked empirically or conceptually to violence. Conversely, no dysfunction is expected in other brain areas (caudate, putamen, globus pallidus, midbrain, cerebellum), which have been implicated in other psychiatric conditions, but which have not been related to violence.

M E T H O D S

SUBJECTS

Murderers. The experimental group consisted of 41 subjects tried in the state of California (39 men, 2 women) with a mean age of 34.3 years (SD = 10.1), charged with either murder or manslaughter (labeled below as 'murderers' for ease of reference). They were referred to the University of California, Irvine (UCI) Imaging Centre to obtain evidence relating to a NGRI defence or to capability of understanding the judicial process (incompetence to stand trial), while some who had been found guilty were referred to obtain information for diminished capacity as an ameliorating circumstance in the sentence phase of the trial. Reasons for referral were very diverse and included schizophrenia (6 cases), history of head injury or organic brain damage (23), history of psychoactive substance abuse (3), affective disorder (2), epilepsy (2), history of hyperactivity and learning disability (3), and passive-aggressive or paranoid personality disorder (2). In 7 of the above cases, there were also unusual circumstances surrounding the crime that additionally led to the suspicion of some mental impairment. Offenders were not receiving regulated psychoactive medication at the time of positron emission tomography (PET) scans, and were instructed to be medication-free for the 2-week period preceding the brain scanning. All subjects were in custody during this period, and penal authorities agreed to refrain from administering medication. Urine screens at the time of PET scanning were negative for every murderer referred for study.

Controls. A control group was formed by matching each murderer with a normal subject of the same sex and age who had been tested using identical PET imaging procedures in the same laboratory. Six murderers (all men) had been diagnosed as schizophrenic by psychiatrists. These 6 were individually matched on age and sex with 6 schizophrenics from a larger psychiatric sample tested under identical procedures at the Brain Imaging Centre at the University of California, Irvine (Buchs-

THE STUDY

baum *et al.*, 1990). The resulting 41 controls (39 men, 2 women) had a mean age of 31.7 years (SD = 10.3), which did not differ from murderers ($p > 0.26$). Normal controls had been screened for health by physical exam., medical history, and a psychiatric interview. No subject was taking any medication, had a history of psychiatric illness in self or first-degree relatives, or had current significant medical illness. Those with a history of seizure disorder, head trauma, or substance abuse were excluded. They participated under protocols and consent forms approved by the Human Subjects Committee of University of California, Irvine.

PET TASK PROCEDURE

Fluorodeoxyglucose (FDG) was injected into a subject in the test room and taken up by the brain as a tracer of brain metabolic rate for a 32-min period, during which the subject completed the continuous performance task (CPT; Nuechterlein *et al.*, 1983). A degraded stimulus version of the CPT was used as the frontal challenge task, because it has been shown to produce increases in relative glucose metabolic rates in the frontal lobes in normal controls, in addition to increases in right temporal and parietal lobes. Full procedural details are reported in Buchsbaum *et al.*, (1990).

Ten minutes before the FDG injection, subjects were given practice trials on the CPT. Thirty seconds before injection, the task was started so that initial task novelty would not be FDG labeled. After 32 min of FDG uptake, the subject was transferred to the adjacent PET scanner room. An individually molded, thermosetting plastic head holder was used to hold the head still during the scan. Ten slices at 10-mm intervals parallel to the canthomeatal line were obtained. Scans started at the level of 80% of head height above the canthomeatal line (vertex to canthomeatal line, usually 12–14 cm) and step downward at 10-mm intervals.

Brain regions were identified using two techniques as follows:

Cortical Peel Technique (lateral areas). Surface cortical regions of interest were measured using a modification of the original cortical peel technique (Buchsbaum *et al.*, 1990) with the four lobes and four anatomical subdivisions of each identified sterotactically (Buchsbaum *et al.*, 1989). This technique has been used by at least nine different PET groups. Absolute glucose values for each region of interest were expressed as a measure relative to all other regions contained in that slice. Relative rates are more widely reported, have the advantages of removing whole brain metabolic rate, are more likely to be related to function in specific neuroanatomical systems (Fox & Mintum, 1989), and show greater reliability within subjects over time (Bartlett *et al.*, 1991). The following three prefrontal values (averaged across slices) for each hemisphere were extracted: superior frontal gyrus, middle frontal gyrus, and inferior frontal gyrus (see Figure 33.1). Bilateral temporal (superior, middle, inferior, and posterior), parietal (postcentral, supramarginal, superior parietal lobule, and angular gyrus), and occipital (area 19, area 17 superior, area 17 inferior, and area 18) measures averaged across slices were also taken (see Figure 33.1).

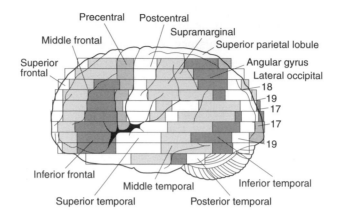

Figure 33.1 Lateral view of 10 stacked slices showing surface superior, middle, and inferior cortical prefrontal areas, precentral frontal cortex, and temporal, parietal, and occipital areas from cortical peel analysis. The top slice corresponds to slice #2, or 80% of head height in the brain atlas of Matsui and Hirano (1978).

Box Technique (medial areas). Medial cortical and subcortical regions of interest were located in PET slices by reference to stereotaxic coordinates as detailed in Buchsbaum *et al*. (1989). A 3 × 3 pixel region of interest box was placed on cortical and subcortical; structures at each level, according to a standard list (see Figure 33.2). As each pixel measured 2 × 2 mm, the size of the region of interest box was approximately one full-width half-maximum. Pre-frontal measures extracted from each slice level (given as a percentage of the distance from the external auditory meatus to the top of the head) according to a brain atlas (Matsui & Hirano, 1978, see Figure 33.2) were as follows: superior frontal gyrus (average of 80%, 74%, 68%, and 61% slice levels as shown in Figure 33.2), anterior medial frontal gyrus (68% level), medial frontal gyrus (average of 61%, 54%, and 47% levels), and orbital gyrus (21% level).

To assess stereotaxic error due to individual differences in structure location within the plane, we evaluated the stereotaxic frame based on the brain outline. Stereotaxic error could place boxes in the caudate into the ventricle, thereby diluting metabolic rates with cerebrospinal zero rates, but confidence limits based on application of the current system to magnetic resonance images confirm 2-SD limits within the caudate (Buchsbaum *et al*., 1992).

Subcortical regions theorized to relate to violence were as follows: corpus callosum (47% level, see Figure 33.2); medial temporal lobe, including the hippocampus (average of 34%, 28%, and 21%), amygdala (21%); thalamus (41%); and cingulate (61%, 54%, 41%, and 34%). Subcortical regions theorized not to be related to violence were extracted as follows: caudate (average of 41% and 34%), putamen

THE STUDY

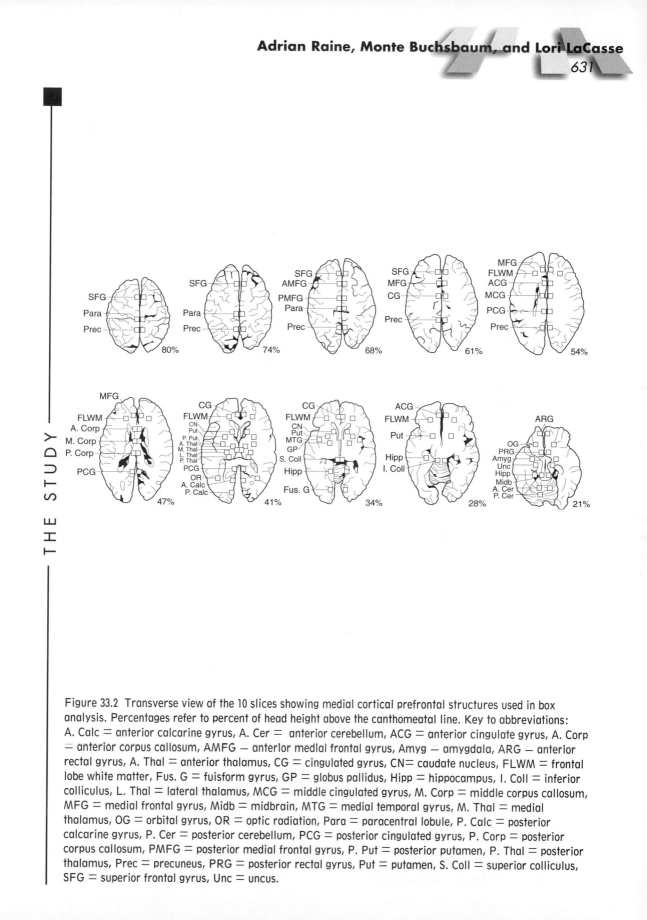

Figure 33.2 Transverse view of the 10 slices showing medial cortical prefrontal structures used in box analysis. Percentages refer to percent of head height above the canthomeatal line. Key to abbreviations: A. Calc = anterior calcarine gyrus, A. Cer = anterior cerebellum, ACG = anterior cingulate gyrus, A. Corp = anterior corpus callosum, AMFG – anterior medial frontal gyrus, Amyg – amygdala, ARG – anterior rectal gyrus, A. Thal = anterior thalamus, CG = cingulated gyrus, CN = caudate nucleus, FLWM = frontal lobe white matter, Fus. G = fuisform gyrus, GP = globus pallidus, Hipp = hippocampus, I. Coll = inferior colliculus, L. Thal = lateral thalamus, MCG = middle cingulated gyrus, M. Corp = middle corpus callosum, MFG = medial frontal gyrus, Midb = midbrain, MTG = medial temporal gyrus, M. Thal = medial thalamus, OG = orbital gyrus, OR = optic radiation, Para = paracentral lobule, P. Calc = posterior calcarine gyrus, PCG = posterior cingulated gyrus, P. Corp = posterior corpus callosum, PMFG = posterior medial frontal gyrus, P. Put = posterior putamen, P. Thal = posterior thalamus, Prec = precuneus, PRG = posterior rectal gyrus, Put = putamen, S. Coll = superior colliculus, SFG = superior frontal gyrus, Unc = uncus.

(average of 41%, 34%, and 28%), globus pallidus (34%), midbrain (21%), and cerebellum (21%).

R E S U L T S

For both cortical and subcortical analyses, values were averaged across slices and
two-way group (murderers and controls) × hemisphere (left and right) repeated
measures multivariate analyses of variance using the MANOVA approach (Vasey &
Thayer, 1987) were conducted. For some brain areas gyrus was added as a third
factor in a three-way MANOVA. All tests of significance for planned comparisons
(*t* tests) are two tailed. Means and SDs for all brain areas are shown in Table 33.1.

Table 33.1

GROUP MEANS AND STANDARD DEVIATIONS (IN PARANTHESES) FOR MURDERERS
AND CONTROLS FOR CORTICAL AND SUBCORTICAL RELATIVE GLUCOSE
METABOLISM

	Left hemisphere		Right hemisphere	
	Control	Murderers	Control	Murderers
Cortical				
Lateral prefrontal*	1.12 (0.05)	1.09 (0.06)	1.14 (0.05)	1.11 (0.06)
Medial prefrontal*	1.25 (0.09)	1.20 (0.11)	1.22 (0.10)	1.17 (0.12)
Parietal*	1.15 (0.10)	1.10 (0.11)	1.17 (0.10)	1.13 (0.11)
Occipital*	1.09 (0.10)	1.12 (0.11)	1.11 (0.10)	1.15 (0.10)
Temporal	0.90 (0.08)	0.90 (0.10)	0.93 (0.08)	0.94 (0.08)
Cingulate	0.99 (0.12)	0.96 (0.17)	0.94 (0.12)	0.92 (0.14)
Subcortical				
Corpus callosum*	0.68 (0.12)	0.56 (0.18)	0.67 (0.12)	0.56 (0.18)
Amygdala**	0.97 (0.14)	0.94 (0.17)	0.83 (0.14)	0.88 (0.16)
Medial temporal lobe and hippocampus**	0.95 (0.10)	0.91 (0.10)	0.93 (0.11)	0.96 (0.09)
Thalamus**	1.09 (0.14)	1.09 (0.12)	1.09 (0.16)	1.15 (0.14)
Caudate	1.19 (0.16)	1.18 (0.15)	1.27 (0.13)	1.27 (0.12)
Putamen	1.22 (0.12)	1.21 (0.13)	1.26 (0.11)	1.28 (0.10)
Globus pallidus	0.96 (0.18)	0.94 (0.13)	0.97 (0.15)	0.98 (0.16)
Midbrain	0.74 (0.12)	0.75 (0.13)	0.76 (0.11)	0.80 (0.12)
Cerebellum	1.01 (0.17)	1.05 (0.16)	1.03 (0.16)	1.10 (0.17)

* Main group effect
** Group × hemisphere interaction

THE STUDY

CORTICAL REGIONS

Prefrontal. As anticipated on the basis of the previous pilot data, the expanded group of 41 murderers had lower glucose metabolism relative to controls in both lateral and medial prefrontal cortical areas (see Table 33.1 and Figure 33.3). We repeated exactly the same analyses that we had previously conducted on a smaller sample (Raine *et al.*, 1994) and found from two separate group × hemisphere MANOVAs a main effect for both lateral [$F(1,80) = 5.6$, $p < .02$] and medial [$F(1,80) = 6.2$, $p < .02$] prefrontal areas, with no interactions for hemispheres ($p > .75$).

A more detailed breakdown of prefrontal subregions indicated that murderers had significantly lower glucose metabolism for left and right medial superior frontal

THE STUDY

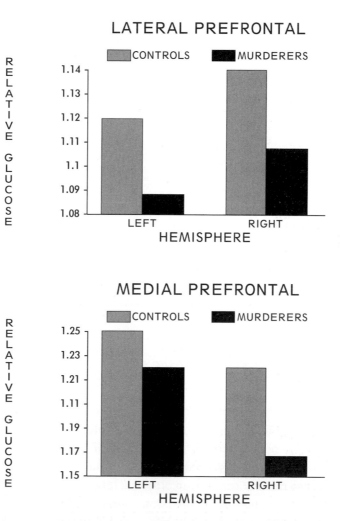

Figure 33.3 Relative glucose metabolic rates for murders and controls in lateral prefrontal cortex (above) and medial prefrontal cortex (below). Murderers have significantly lower lateral (p < .02) and medial (p < .02) prefrontal functioning in both hemispheres.

THE STUDY

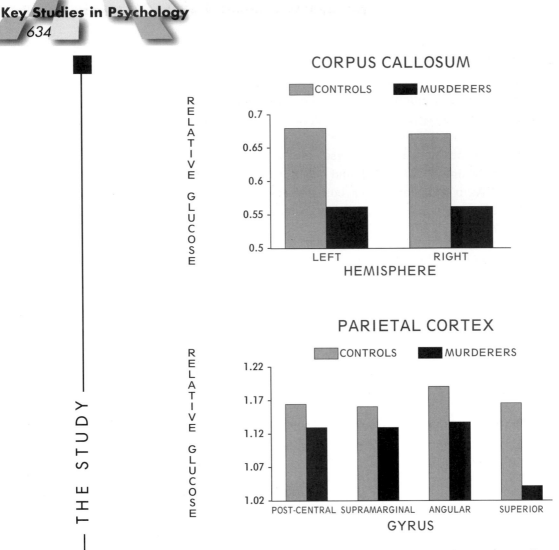

Figure 33.4 Relative glucose metabolic rates for murderers and controls in the corpus callosum and parietal cortex. Murderers have lower activity in the corpus callosum bilaterally (p < .001), in the superior parietal gyri bilaterally (p < .05), and also in the left angular gyrus (p < .06).

cortex (*t* = 2.6, *p* < .02), left anterior medial cortex (*t* = 3.1, *p* < .003), right orbitofrontal cortex (*t* = 2.1, *p* < .04), and lateral middle frontal gyri of both left (*t* = 2.1, *p* < .04) and right (*t* = 2.8, *p* < .007) hemispheres.

Parietal. Murderers had lower parietal glucose metabolism than controls, especially in the left angular gyrus and bilateral superior parietal regions. A three-way group × hemisphere × gyrus (angular, superior, supramarginal, and postcental gyri) MANOVA indicated a marginal main effect for group, $F(1,80) = 3.7$, $p < .06$, but also a significant group × gyrus interaction, $F(3,78) = 3.9$, $p < .02$. As indicated in the lower half of Figure 33.4, murderers had significantly lower glucose specifically in both left (*t* = 2.5, *p* < .02) and right (*t* = 2.0, *p* < .05) superior parietal gyri, with an additional trend for the left angular gyrus (*t* = 1.9, *p* < .06). No other effects involving group were significant ($p > .33$).

Temporal. Murderers were identical to controls on lateral temporal lobe glucose metabolism (see Table 33.1). A group × hemisphere × gyrus MANOVA revealed no significant main group effect ($p > .86$) or interaction involving group ($p > .20$).

Occipital. Murderers were found to show significantly *higher* occipital lobe glucose metabolism than normals (see Table 33.1). A group × hemisphere × area MANOVA revealed a main effect for group, $F(1,82) = 6.8$, $p < .02$, and a group × area interaction, $F(3,78) = 4.5$, $p < .006$. A breakdown of this interaction indicated that increased metabolism in murderers was especially marked bilaterally in areas 17 (inferior) ($t = 3.8$, $p < .0001$) and 18 ($t = 3.4$, $p < .001$). No other interactions with group were significant ($p > .11$).

SUBCORTICAL REGIONS

Corpus Callosum. Murderers had bilaterally lower glucose metabolism in the corpus callosum than controls (see upper half of Figure 33.4). A group × hemisphere MANOVA indicated a main effect for group, $F(1,80) = 11.6$, $p < .001$, with no interaction effect ($p > .10$).

Amygdala. Murderers had relatively reduced left and greater right amygdala activity compared with controls. A group × hemisphere MANOVA revealed no main group effect ($p > .83$), but instead showed a significant group × hemisphere interaction, $F(1,80) = 6.8$, $p < .02$. As indicated in Figure 33.5, murderers showed an abnormal asymmetry consisting of relatively reduced left amygdala activity, but relatively greater right amygdala activity. A laterality coefficient (computed using the formula left − right/left + right) indicated that murderers had relatively lower left than right amygdala activity (mean = 0.03, SD = .10) compared to controls (mean = 0.08, SD = .08) ($t = 2.5$, $p < .02$).

Medial Temporal Lobe Including The Hippocampus. Murderers had relatively reduced left and greater right activity. A group × hemisphere MANOVA revealed no main group effect ($p > .93$), but instead showed a significant group × hemisphere interaction, $F(1,80) = 8.4$, $p < .005$. As indicated in Figure 33.5, murderers showed an abnormal asymmetry consisting of relatively reduced left medial temporal/hippocampal activity, but relatively greater right activity. A laterality coefficient indicated that murderers had relatively lower left than right activity (mean = −0.03, SD = 0.06), compared to controls (mean = 0.01, SD = 0.07) ($t = 2.8$, $p < .006$).

Thalamus. Murderers had relatively greater right thalamic activity compared to controls. A group × hemisphere MANOVA revealed no main group effect ($p > .25$), but instead showed a significant group × hemisphere interaction, $F(1,80) = 4.4$, $p < .04$). As indicated in Figure 33.5, murderers showed an abnormal asymmetry

(left margin) THE STUDY

THE STUDY

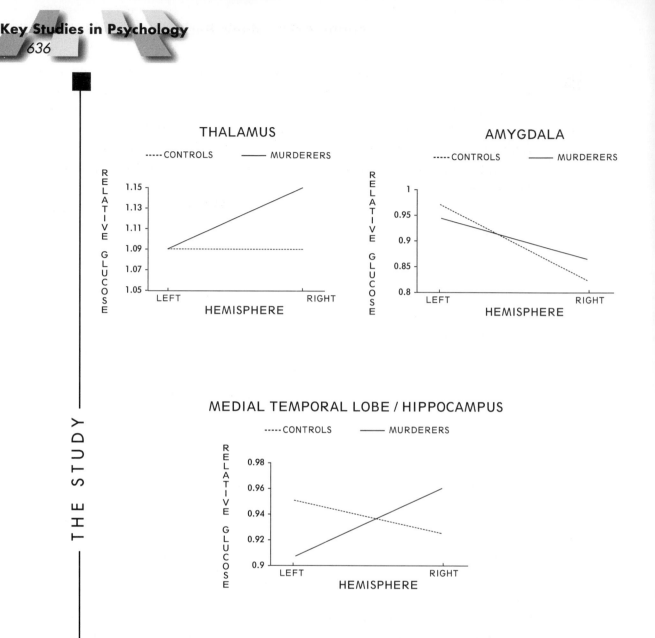

Figure 33.5 Significant group x hemisphere interactions for relative glucose metabolic rates for murderers and controls in the thalamus (p < .04), medial temporal lobe/hippocampus (p < .005), and amygdala (p < .02).

consisting of relatively greater right thalamic activity. A laterality coefficient indicated that murderers had relatively lower left than right activity (mean = −0.03, SD = 0.07) compared to controls (mean = 0.0, SD = 0.06) ($t = 2.0, p < .05$).

Cingulate. Murderers did not differ from controls on cingulated glucose metabolism (see Table 33.1). Both the group main effect and the group × hemisphere interaction were nonsignificant ($p > .29$).

Caudate, Putamen, Globus Pallidus, Midbrain, and Cerebellum. To assess specificity of subcortical findings, groups were compared on glucose metabolic activity in the above structures, which have characterized other mental disorders (see Discussion), but which have not been theorized to relate to violent crime. Means and SDs are given in Table 33.1. Group main effects for the caudate, putamen, globus pallidus, and midbrain were all nonsignificant ($p > .25$), as were all interactions involving group ($p > .17$). A trend was observed for murderers to have slightly higher (not lower) cerebellar glucose metabolic activity than normals ($t = 1.7$, $p < .10$). All interactions involving group were nonsignificant ($p > .30$).

BEHAVIOURAL PERFORMANCE ON THE CPT

Groups did not differ on any aspect of behavioural performance on the CPT. Averaged means and SDs (in parentheses) for the two groups (controls and murderers respectively) were as follows: d': 3.63 (0.73), 3.55 (0.74), $t = 0.5$, $p > .64$; true positives (correct hits): 37.1 (5.6), 36.7 (4.5), $t = .79$, $p > .42$; false negatives (errors of omission): 3.6 (5.0), 3.3 (4.5), $t = .24$, $p > .80$; false positives (errors of commission): 4.5. (8.4), 2.3 (3.9), $t = 1.5$, $p > .15$; true negatives (correct misses): 114.8 (8.4), 117.7. (3.9), $t = 1.3$, $p > .20$.

EFFECTS OF HANDEDNESS, HEAD INJURY, AND ETHNICITY

Although subjects were matched on gender, age, and schizophrenia, it was not possible to simultaneously match them on handedness, head injury, and ethnicity. Six of the murderers were left-handed. These were compared to right-handed murderers and the analyses described earlier for PET variables that produced significant group differences were repeated. All such analyses were nonsignificant, with the exception that left-handed murderers tended to have *higher* (not lower) medial prefrontal activity ($p < .08$), and had a significantly *less* abnormal amygdala asymmetry ($p < .002$) than right-handed murderers. Results indicate, therefore, that greater rates of left-handedness in the murderer group relative to controls cannot account for reduced prefrontal activity and the abnormal amygdala asymmetry.

Fourteen of the murderers were non-white. Analyses comparing them to white murderers on PET measures were nonsignificant ($p > .14$) in all cases, indicating ethnic status did not influence findings.

Twenty-three murderers had a history of head injury. They did not differ from murderers without a history of head injury on PET measures ($p > .27$), with the one exception of a trend for head-injured murderers to have lower activity in the corpus callosum ($p < .08$). than non-head-injured murderers. Although analyses suggest that history of head injury cannot account for most findings, the possibility that they account for group differences in the corpus callosum cannot be ruled out.

T H E   S T U D Y

DISCUSSION

KEY FINDINGS

The key findings from this preliminary study are that murderers pleading NGRI are characterized by a) reduced glucose metabolism in bilateral prefrontal cortex, the posterior parietal cortex (bilateral superior gyrus and left angular gyrus), and the corpus callosum, and b) abnormal asymmetries of activity (left hemisphere lower than right) in the amygdala, thalamus, and medial temporal gyrus including the hippocampus. These data both confirm deficits in the prefrontal cortex from our earlier pilot study, and also yield new findings. These in turn provide both some general support for preexisting biological theories of violence, and also suggest new perspectives for understanding the type of brain dysfunction that may predispose to violence in this specific group of offenders.

BIOSOCIAL PATHWAYS FROM BRAIN DEFICITS TO VIOLENCE

A key question concerns how these multisite deficits can translate into violence via neuropsychological, psychological, cognitive, social, and situational pathways. Regarding prefrontal deficits, damage to this region can result in impulsivity, loss of self-control, immaturity, altered emotionality, and the inability to modify behaviour, which can all in turn facilitate aggressive acts (Damasio, 1985; Damasio *et al.*, 1994; Moffitt & Henry, 1991; Stuss & Benson, 1986; Weiger & Bear, 1988). Regarding limbic deficits, the amygdala has been repeatedly associated with aggressive behaviour in both animals and humans (Bear, 1989; Mirsky & Siegel, 1994; Weiger & Bear, 1988). The amygdala, hippocampus, and prefrontal cortex make up part of the limbic system governing the expression of emotion, while the thalamus relays inputs from subcortical limbic structures to the prefrontal cortex (Fuster, 1989; Mirsky & Siegel, 1994). The hippocampal formation is thought to modulate aggression in cats through its action on the lateral hypothalamus via the lateral septal area (Mirsky & Siegel, 1994; Siegel & Flynn, 1968), and together with the septal area and prefrontal cortex forms the neurobiological basis of the behavioural inhibition system of Gray (1982), which is theorized to be dysfunctional in violent and psychopathic individuals (Gorenstein & Newman, 1980). The amygdala is believed to act on the medial hypothalamus through at least two pathways in the modulation of aggression in animals (Watson *et al.*, 1983b). The hippocampus, amygdala, and thalamus are also of critical importance to learning, memory, and attention; abnormalities in their functioning may relate to deficits in forming conditioned emotional responses and the failure to learn from experience displayed by criminal and violent offenders (Cleckley, 1976; Raine, 1993). The amygdala additionally plays a role in the recognition of affective and socially significant stimuli (Nishijo *et al.*, 1988), with destruction of the amygdala in animals resulting in a lack of fear (Bear,

1991) and in man a reduction in autonomic arousal (Lee *et al.*, 1988). Thus, abnormalities in the amygdala could be relevant to a fearlessness theory of violence based on psychophysiological findings of reduced autonomic arousal in offenders (Raine *et al.*, 1990b; Raine 1993).

The posterior parietal cortex (including superior and angular gyri) is centrally involved in the integration of sensory input and the formation of abstract concepts (Kolb & Wishaw, 1990), and in conjunction with its reciprocal connections with the dorsolateral prefrontal cortex (Goldman-Rakic *et al.*, 1983) may contribute to the cognitive and social information processing deficits observed in violent offenders (Dodge & Crick, 1990; Moffitt & Silva, 1988). Reductions in glucose metabolism in the left angular gyrus have been correlated with reduced verbal ability (Gur *et al.*, 1994), while damage to the left angular gyrus has been linked to deficits in reading and arithmetic. Such cognitive dysfunctions could predispose to educational and occupational failure, which in turn predispose to crime and violence. Learning deficits commonly occur in violent offenders who also have low verbal IQs (Quay, 1987; Raine, 1993).The more anterior parietal regions, which are involved in more basic somatic sensations and perceptions, are unaffected in murderers, indicating some specificity of dysfunction within the parietal region.

Although it has been speculated for many years that dysfunction to the corpus callosum may be a neurobiological predisposition to violence (e.g., Nachshon, 1983; Yeudall, 1977), until now there has been no direct evidence to support the claim. Although white matter metabolic values are only approximately 50% of grey matter values (thus biasing toward floor effects and nonsignificant results), we obtained our strongest group differences for this region. Callosal dysfunction and the consequent lack of interhemispheric integration could contribute to the abnormal asymmetries of function and reduced interhemispheric integration previously observed in antisocial and violent groups (Hare & McPherson, 1984; Flor-Henry *et al.*, 1991; Raine *et al.*, 1990a). We have previously hypothesized that the reduced lateralization for processing linguistic information observed in violent groups may arise from a reduction in the normal neurodevelopmental processes of hemispheric specialization. This process may be partly accounted for by dysfunction of the corpus callosum (Raine *et al.*, 1995).

Another potential implication of poor interhemispheric transfer is that the right hemisphere, which has been implicated in the generation of negative affect in humans (Davidson & Fox, 1989), may experience less regulation and control by left hemisphere inhibitory processes (Cook, 1986; Flor-Henry, 1987), a factor that may contribute to the expression of violence in predisposed individuals. Rats that are stressed early in life are right hemisphere dominant for mice-killing (Garbanati *et al.*, 1983). Severing the corpus callosum in these rats leads to an increase in muricide (Denenberg *et al.*, 1986), indicating that the left hemisphere inhibits the right hemisphere mediated killing via an intact corpus callosum. Both Sperry (1974) and

Dimond (1979) noted the inappropriate nature of emotional expression and the inability to grasp long-term implications of a situation in split-brain patients, giving pointers to the inappropriate emotional expression of violent offenders and their lack of long-term planning (Cleckley, 1976). Nevertheless, findings from animal research cannot be directly extrapolated to humans. Furthermore, callosal dysfunction as such is unlikely to cause aggression; it may instead contribute to violence in those with concurrent limbic and cortical abnormalities.

Findings of group differences in glucose metabolism in the posterior parietal cortex, amygdala, and medial temporal lobe including the hippocampus may be related. The amygdala may be part of a system for processing socially relevant information (Brothers & Ring, 1993), and functions in parallel with the object recognition system of the hippocampus and the spatial recognition system of the posterior parietal cortex (Kolb & Wishaw, 1990). Disruption of such a system could partly explain the socially inappropriate behaviour shown by some violent individuals (Cleckley, 1976) and the mis-recognition and mis-appraisal of ambiguous stimuli in potentially violent social situations (Dodge *et al.*, 1990; Nachshon & Rotenberg, 1977).

Findings of this study suggest that the neural processes underlying violence are complex and cannot be simplistically reduced to single brain mechanisms causing violence in a direct causal fashion. Instead, violent behaviour probably involves disruption of a network of multiple interacting brain mechanisms that predispose to violence in the presence of other social, environmental, and psychological predispositions (Eichelman, 1992; Earls, 1991; Lewis *et al.*, 1988). Nevertheless, attempts to 'network' findings from the individual brain sites in this study must proceed cautiously, because there are brain mechanisms relevant to aggression (e.g. septum and hypothalamus) that could not be imaged in this study. Consequently, this study cannot provide a complete account of the neurophysiology of violence in this specific and selected subgroup of violent offenders, although it does provide preliminary evidence that murderers pleading NGRI have different brain functioning compared to normals, and it also gives initial suggestions as to which specific neural processes may predispose to their violent behaviour.

POTENTIAL CONFOUNDS

There are five reasons we believe these are not mere chance findings. First, the sample size (41 in each group) is not small for PET research, and is substantially larger than other imaging studies of violent populations. Second, the strength of effects were not trivial, with a mean of 0.55 (range = 0.36 -0.80), which is viewed as medium (Cohen, 1988). Third, areas were selected for analysis on the basis of prior theorizing, and all but one of these produced significant effects. Fourth, to help limit the possibility of Type 1 errors, overall MANOVAs were conducted and two-tailed tests used throughout. Fifth, brain areas that have not been theoretically linked to violence but that have been linked to other mental disorders (caudate, putamen, globus pallidus, midbrain, cerebellum) did *not* yield group differences. This double dissociation lends some support to the relatively differential nature of the brain deficits in terms of both anatomy and mental condition. Nevertheless, some effects were marginal (e.g. left angular gyrus), and results must be treated cautiously, particularly those regarding subcortical laterality effects and increased occipital functioning, which were not predicted a priori.

The findings do not appear to be a function of group differences in age, gender, schizophrenia, handedness, ethnicity, or history of head injury. The greater rates of left handedness, head injury, and non-whites in the murderer group do not account for overall murderer versus control group differences. However, there was a trend ($p < .10$) for murderers with a history of head injury to have reduced glucose metabolism in the corpus callosum. This would be consistent with the idea that sheering of white nerve fibres during closed head injuries could contribute to damage to the corpus callosum (McAllister, 1992). In addition, because we did not have more extensive neurological and medical data to assess history of head injury, we cannot definitively rule out prior head injury as a possible contribution toward reduced brain activity in the murderers.

The fact that groups did not differ in behavioural performance on the CPT suggests not only that difference in brain functioning is not easily accounted for by motivational or attentional deficits in the murderers, but also that the significantly *greater* occipital activity (visual areas 17 and 18) in murderers may possibly represent compensation for the reduced activity in the prefrontal cortex, an area which is critical for the execution of this challenge task (Buchsbaum *et al.*, 1990). Cognitive parity between groups cannot be claimed, because no IQ data were available. Nevertheless, we do not believe that lower IQ in the murderer group can account for reduced glucose metabolism, because low IQ has been associated with *higher*, not lower, cerebral glucose metabolism (Haier *et al.*, 1988).

SPECIFICITY OF FINDINGS

Could comorbid psychiatric conditions in the murderers account for the PET findings? The most important psychiatric condition in murderers is schizophrenia, which was controlled for by matching six schizophrenic murderers with age-and sex-matched hospital schizophrenics. Differences in brain functioning in murderers show a different pattern to that observed in other mental disorders. Psychiatric patients show abnormalities in brain structures not found in the murderers, while murderers have abnormalities not previously reported in psychiatric patients. For example, whereas altered functioning has been found in schizophrenics for the lateral temporal cortex (Buchsbaum *et al.*, 1990 DeLisi *et al.*, 1989), basal ganglia (Buchsbaum, 1990; Early *et al.*, 1987; Gur & Pearlson, 1993), cingulated gyrus (Siegel *et al.*, 1993), caudate (Siegel *et al.*, 1993), and cerebellum (Volkow *et al.*,

1992), these structures were unaffected in murderers. Similarly, there is a growing consensus that affective disorder involves dysfunction to both frontal and temporal lobes (Baxter *et al.*, 1989; Cummings, 1993; George *et al.*, 1993). In contrast, although murderers have widespread bilateral reductions in prefrontal glucose utilization, they did not show the lateral temporal deficits observed in schizophrenics using the same methodology (Buchsbaum *et al.*, 1990), while depressives tend to have dysfunction lateralized to the left hemisphere (Baxter *et al.*, 1989; Bench *et al.*, 1993; Drevets *et al.*, 1992) and to the left dorsolateral prefrontal region in particular (Baxter *et al.*, 1989; Bench *et al.*, 1993), in contrast to the bilateral prefrontal findings for murderers. Furthermore, depressives have been reported to show additional involvement of the caudate nucleus (Cummings, 1993) and cingulate gyrus (George *et al.*, 1993), brain areas unaffected in murderers. Obsessive-compulsives show higher, not lower, glucose levels in orbitofrontal cortex (Baxter *et al.*, 1988; Benkelfat *et al.*, 1990), while symptom intensity in this group is associated with higher (not lower) functioning in the hippocampus and thalamus (McGuire *et al.*, 1994). With respect to substance abuse, acute cannabinol administration affects cerebellar functioning (Volkow *et al.*, 1991), whereas murderers showed normal cerebellar activity. Detoxified alcoholics show increased (not decreased) brain metabolism during detoxification, with persistent low metabolic levels being shown for the basal ganglia (Volkow *et al.*, 1994), a structure unaffected in murderers. Whereas cerebellar hypometabolism and degeneration has been observed in chronic alcoholics (Gilman *et al.*, 1990), murderers showed nonsignificantly higher, not lower, cerebellar activity.

Reduced prefrontal activity does not seem to be specific to severe violence, as this has also been observed in a variety of psychiatric conditions. On the other hand, there have been no previous reports in any psychiatric condition of left lower than right asymmetries in the amygdala, thalamus, and hippocampus coupled with dysfunction of the corpus callosum and left angular gyrus. For example, although there have been variable reports of either increased, decreased, or normal thalamic activity in schizophrenia (Buchsbaum *et al.*, 1987; Resnick *et al.*, 1988; Siegel *et al.*, 1993), the left lower than right asymmetries for these structures in murderers have not been previously reported. While prefrontal dysfunction may represent a deficit common to many forms of psychopathology, additional dysfunction to these other brain structures may lead to a pathway toward violence as opposed to other conditions. In drawing comparisons across imaging studies, it must be borne in mind that some studies have used exactly the same imaging methodology as in the present study (e.g. Buchsbaum *et al.*, 1990; Siegel *et al.*, 1993; DeLisi *et al.*, 1989), while others have used different methodologies (e.g. Baxter *et al.*, 1989; Volkow *et al.*, 1992). As such, strict comparisons across studies are not possible.

Although coexisting psychopathology may contribute to violence and should not be discounted as unimportant, such pathology per se cannot account for the specific network of brain dysfunction observed in this violent group. Nevertheless, although subjects constituted a relatively specific subgroup of violent offenders (all had committed homicide and were pleading NGRI), they do not constitute a homogeneous clinical group. Specifically, heterogeneity would contribute to a type II error and the failure to observe significant group differences in some brain regions of interest. As such, these initial findings must be viewed with caution.

STRENGTHS, LIMITATIONS, AND CONCLUSIONS

As with all initial findings, the current study has limitations, including relatively modest spatial resolution relative to the most advanced present-day PET techniques, the lack of standardized diagnostic and neuropsychological assessments, and the use of the canthomeatal line for slice placement, which has a variable orientation to brain landmarks, and which can lead to significant variability across subjects in the anatomical localization of regions of interest. Limitations such as the absence of psychiatric control groups have also characterized the first brain imaging studies of other conditions, such as schizophrenia, as well as some current studies. In addition, findings apply only to a select subgroup of severely violent offenders and cannot be generalized at this stage to violence per se. Furthermore, findings for subcortical asymmetries and the occipital cortex were not predicted a priori and need to be replicated in an independent study.

However, the study also had a number of strengths. These include by far the largest sample of seriously violent offenders ever imaged, matching for age, sex, and schizophrenia, ruling out confounds of handedness, ethnicity, and head injury, and establishing group equivalence on behavioural performance of the challenge task and psychopharmacologic control over medication and illegal drug use in weeks prior to scanning. Such strengths are not common in this field, which is hampered by multiple obstacles to research. Despite some limitations in the research, we nevertheless felt it appropriate to report these findings, because they constitute the first to document multiple but selective brain deficits assessed using PET in a group of severely violent offenders who are of particular importance in forensic psychiatry, and because they provide both theoretical directions and a critical empirical base upon which future brain imaging studies of violent offenders may build. At the same time, the need for caution in interpreting findings due to their preliminary nature, and the need for independent replication, must be reemphasized.

It is critically important to document what this study does and does not indicate. First, these findings cannot be taken to demonstrate that violence is determined by biology alone; clearly, social, psychological, cultural and situational factors also play important roles in predisposing to violence (Eichelman, 1992; Elliott, 1987, 1988). Second, these data do not demonstrate that murderers pleading NGRI are not responsible for their actions, nor do they demonstrate that PET can be used as a diagnostic technique. Third, our findings cannot address the issue of the cause (genetic or environmental) of the brain dysfunction, nor do they establish causal direction. Fourth, findings cannot be generalized at the present time from NGRI murder cases to other types of violent offenders. Fifth, specificity to violence as opposed to crime per se has not been established, as this requires the inclusion of nonviolent criminal control group, which was not available. However, these initial findings do show that as a group, murderers pleading NGRI have statistically significant differences in glucose metabolism in selected brain regions compared to normals. They also suggest, but do not conclusively demonstrate, that reduced activity in the prefrontal, parietal, and callosal regions of the brain, together with abnormal asymmetries of activity in the amygdala, thalamus, and medial temporal lobe including the hippocampus, may be one of many predispositions toward violence in this specific group. As with all initial findings in the field, future independent replication, refinement, and extension to less select populations of violent offenders are greatly needed.

EVALUATION

Theoretical issues

It is likely that at least some of those murderers in Raine *et al.*'s study would be diagnosed as having *antisocial personality disorder* (APD: DSM-IV, 1994) or *dissocial personality disorder* (ICD-10, 1992). (These labels refer to what used to be called *psychopathic personality disorder* or *psychopathy*.) Those judged to have APD:

- act violently towards their marriage partners, and their children;

- are impulsive and fail to strive consistently towards a goal, lacking a purpose in life;

- have low tolerance of frustration and have a tendency towards violence, which often results in repeated criminal offences. This may begin with petty acts of delinquency, but progresses to callous, violent crimes. Their lack of guilt and failure to learn from experience leads to behaviour that persists despite serious consequences and legal penalties;

- commit a disproportionate number of violent crimes.

Hare (1991) has identified two distinct, but correlated, factors involved in APD. *Factor 1* refers to affective and interpersonal characteristics, including superficial charm, pathological lying, manipulation, lack of empathy, shallow affect, and lack of guilt. *Factor 2* refers to a chronic and versatile antisocial lifestyle, including proneness to boredom, a parasitic lifestyle, impulsivity, juvenile delinquency, and a violation of release conditions.

According to Mitchell & Blair (2000), displaying the full APD seems to involve a complex interaction between social environment and biological predispositions. In particular, social environment (such as socio-economic status/SES) influences factor 2, while factor 1 is unrelated to SES. This suggests that biological make-up determines whether individuals show emotional difficulties, but these emotional factors are only *risk factors:* an adverse social environment provides the conditions needed for the disorder to develop.

While there is some evidence that the earlier a juvenile begins engaging in delinquent behaviour the more likely s/he is to become a violent offender, only 50% will do so (Gibbs, 1995). Other risk factors include drug dependence and alcoholism, family dysfunction, childhood behavioural problems, deviant peers, poor school performance, inconsistent parental supervision and discipline, separation from parents, poverty, childhood abuse, low verbal IQ, and witnessing violent acts.

However, these experiences are all far more common than the incidence of violence, which makes it very difficult to determine which factors are causes of, and which are merely correlated with, violent crime (see **Aim and nature of the study** above). Similarly, these non-biological risk factors cannot explain or predict which individuals who experience one or more of them actually becomes violent. This brings us back to the issue of biological predisposition (Hare's factor 1). According to Raine (cited in Gibbs, 1995):

> . . . Research in the past 10 years conclusively demonstrates that biological factors play some role in the etiology of violence. That is scientifically beyond doubt.

However, the precise importance of that role is still very much in doubt. As with sociological risk factors, no biological abnormality has been shown to actually *cause* violence – nor is that likely except in cases of extreme psychiatric disorder (Gibbs, 1995).

The fact that murderers are overwhelmingly male (as both perpetrators and victims), combined with the observation that males are the more aggressive sex in nearly all mammals, has led many to suppose that men are unavoidably aggressive and that murder is a natural consequence of male biology (Nisbett & Cohen, 1999).

Studies in the late 1960s claimed to show that many violent criminals had an extra Y chromosome and thus an extra set of 'male' genes. For example, in a special hospital in Scotland one patient in 35 was found to be XYY, compared with about 1:700 among newborn males in Scotland as a whole. However, most XYY men are psychologically normal, non-violent non-offenders (Shields, 1976).

Also, the variation in murder rates among different societies makes it clear that, whatever men's biological predispositions may be, cultures have a great influence on the likelihood that a man will kill. For example, Columbia's rate is 15 times that of Costa Rica, and the rate for the USA is 10 times that of Norway (Nisbett & Cohen,

1999). Nisbett and Cohen also note that there are marked differences *within* the USA. In small Southern towns the murder rate for white males is about double the rest of the country. They attribute this difference to a 'culture of honour' in the Southern states, according to which men think it is justifiable to kill to protect one's property or to meet insults with violence. This is reflected in laws and social policies, which are more likely to exonerate people who shoot another person for 'property' reasons. According to Nisbett and Cohen, this North/South difference:

> . . . shows that violence is a matter of nurture as much as one of nature. Whether a man reaches for his gun or his civility when insulted is a matter of culture.

So, if men are not inevitably and necessarily violent, but biological factors unquestionably play a part in violent behaviour, what might be the potential biological basis of APD? According to Damasio (1996), damage to the orbitofrontal cortex (a small area of the frontal cortex located roughly behind and a little below the centre of your forehead) causes severe behaviour problems. In particular, these patients often have rage attacks and may become aggressive ('acquired sociopaths': Damasio, 1994).

However, their aggression tends to be *reactive*, that is, they react angrily to things that provoke or frustrate them, while that of APD sufferers tends to be *instrumental* (it is a means to an end, such as obtaining some material gain). These two groups also differ in their emotional responding. Whereas damage to the orbitofrontal cortex produces reduced autonomic activity in response to various social signals, those with APD show reduced autonomic activity only in response to sad or fearful expressions and during fear conditioning (but see Raine *et al.*'s research in **Subsequent research**).

Another major candidate is the amygdala, which is at the centre of the 'emotional brain' (LeDoux, 1998: see **Aim and nature of the study** above). Mitchell & Blair (2000) believe that this functions atypically from an early age in people with APD *and* that this actually *leads to* the disorder. It has been known for a long time that the amygdala is a crucial component in brain systems that mediate fear. So, animals (human or non-human) with a damaged amygdala will not show normal fear conditioning, or startle reflex potentiation (LeDoux, 1998).

More recently, the amygdala has been shown to be involved in human emotional response to sad facial expressions. In one experiment, Blair *et al.* (1999) used PET to show that the sadder a sad face shown to normal participants, the greater the activity in the amygdala and connected brain areas. Damage to the amygdala can, therefore, account for the lack of empathy shown by those with APD. According to Mitchell & Blair (2000):

> . . . We therefore believe that amygdala dysfunction may very well be a biological risk factor for the development of this serious disorder.

Raine *et al.* (2000) present evidence for the involvement of the prefrontal cortex in APD (see **Subsequent Research** below).

Methodological issues

Raine *et al.* present their results in terms of significant differences between murderers and controls for different brain areas, both cortical and subcortical. But these are sometimes referred to as a *main group effect* and sometimes as a *group × hemisphere interaction.*

All the findings were based on the use of repeated measures multivariate analyses of variance (MANOVA), in which two-way group (murderers and controls) × hemisphere (left and right) analyses were performed. So, in the case of the prefrontal lobe, for example, the difference in glucose metabolism between murderers and controls was due entirely to which group participants belonged to. However, in the case of the amygdala, medial temporal lobe (including the hippocampus), and thalamus, the differences were due to the joint effects of the group *and* one or other hemisphere exerting a greater effect. As we saw above, murderers showed a bias towards greater activity in the *right* hemisphere relative to the left (asymmetry).

PET scans depend on tracing the location of radioactive material. So, as McGhee (2001) points out, we need to be sure that sufficient radioactive material was injected in the first place for it to appear during a scan. This is especially important if we are looking at a small area of the brain or low activity processes. If we predict activity in brain area X, but not in Y, we need to be sure that if we do see this pattern on the scan it is because of different neural activity levels, *not* because there was insufficient radioactive material injected to show up at Y.

A problem shared by PET, MRI and fMRI is the sheer computational load involved (McGhee, 2001). High-powered computers are needed to collect, store and present the data gathered from successive scans. Special software is available to ensure that successive images are matched together correctly to produce accurate displays over time, without compromising the structural detail. Nevertheless, the faster images are captured, the greater the amount of 'noise' which threatens to obscure the signal (Menon & Kim, 1999).

A further problem is that different studies identify different 'hot spots' (areas of greatest neural activity) for the same task. Farah & Aguirre (1999), for example, found that 17 separate studies indicated between them no fewer than 84 different candidates for the precise brain region involved in object recognition.

Gabrielli (1998) has identified some additional technical and conceptual issues in the interpretation of neuroimaging:

(a) The images generated by PET and fMRI scans *are not* images of neural activity as such, but of nearby (local) blood flow or metabolic changes (such as glucose metabolism) which are *indicative* of neural activity. With fMRI techniques, some aspects of the response to the magnetic field depend on blood-oxygen levels. It is

often unclear just what the activity around neurons is actually indicative of.

(b) Neuroimaging studies often compare the activity levels in response to two or more tasks. Some tasks are not only different in kind, but also in difficulty or duration. Consequently, the observed differences in the scan might be due to the different processing being carried out *or* to different levels of effort required *or* to slightly longer processing times.

(c) Both PET and fMRI need to allow the activation levels to 'clear' before the next trial can begin. This can lead to complications, as participants anticipate future trials or keep on thinking about earlier trials.

(d) Residual activity can be found in parts of the brain that are severely damaged. These traces may be of processes not directly involved in those being studied, but merely correlated with it. It could be that in undamaged brains, much of the activity we observe is nothing to do with the critical processes that actually produce the behaviour the participant is engaging in.

According to McGhee (2001):

> . . . scans can only describe brain activity, not brain function. To describe brain function requires further interpretation of the stimuli presented to the subject and of the patterns of responses to those stimuli over several trials . . .

Some specific methodological limitations of the Raine *et al.* study are mentioned in the **Aim and nature of the study** section above.

Subsequent research

Major damage to grey and white matter in the prefrontal cortex and autonomic deficits have been found to produce pseudo-psychopathic personality in patients with neurological disorders. While it is true that the social inappropriateness of patients with adult-onset prefrontal damage tends not to include violent and criminal behaviour, their altered social behaviour in many ways resemble that of lifelong developmental sociopathic individuals (Damasio, 2000). However, until recently no researcher actually studied those with APD (who have no discernable brain trauma) to see if they have subtle prefrontal deficits.

Raine *et al.* (2000) used MRI to study the brains of 21 volunteers with APD, comparing them with 34 healthy participants (control group), 26 with substance dependence (substance-dependent group), and 21 psychiatric controls. Autonomic activity (skin conductance and heart rate) were also assessed during a social stressor in which participants gave a videotaped speech on their faults and failures. All the participants were male.

What Raine *et al.* found was that the APD group showed an 11.0% reduction in prefrontal grey matter volume in the absence of any obvious brain lesions (but no difference in white matter volume), as well as reduced autonomic activity during the stressor (they sweated less and showed lower heart rate). These deficits predicted group membership independently of psychosocial risk factors. The researchers conclude that their findings provide the first evidence for a structural brain deficit in APD. This prefrontal structural deficit may underlie the low arousal, poor fear conditioning, lack of conscience, and decision-making deficits associated with antisocial, psychopathic behaviour.

According to Damasio (2000) the fact that the APD group did not show the autonomic responses commonly seen in a normal population is evidence of the selective emotional disturbance of these individuals. This disturbance sets in at the level of secondary emotions, such as embarrassment and guilt. This disturbance is comparable with what Damasio and his colleagues have found in neurological patients with selective prefrontal damage.

However, Damasio warns against falling into the 'phrenological trap' set behind every new identification of a brain area with some supposed role. As he points out:

> . . . the normal or pathologic effects associated with that certain area can be properly understood only in the context of multicomponent neural systems . . . the normal or pathologic effects related to a given area are quite often the result of actions elsewhere in the brain . . .

In the case of APD, the malfunction of prefrontal circuits is probably accompanied by malfunction in various subcortical areas (such as the amygdala and brainstem) and in higher-order association areas of the cortex outside the frontal area. But not only must we take into account the operation of these large-scale systems, we must also consider the many factors likely to shape the assembly and eventual operation of these systems:

> . . . Those factors range from the level of molecules and neurons to the level of social and cultural phenomena that impinge on the life of whole individuals. (Damasio, 2000)

(See **Theoretical issues** above.)

Applications and implications

If it can be demonstrated that people with APD have a brain disorder, in the form of reduced grey matter in their prefrontal cortex, then isn't it reasonable to explain their violent conduct – including murder – in terms of that brain deficit? In other words, the violence can be blamed on the brain deficit, absolving the offender of blame and responsibility ('He couldn't help himself – his relative lack of grey matter in his prefrontal cortex prevented him from controlling his behaviour as normal people can': see Chapter 21). This is obviously relevant to the NGRI plea made by the 41 murderers in the Raine *et al.* (1997) study.

Clearly, this is an extremely important moral and legal issue. To use this as a legal defence, it would first have to be shown to be a scientifically reliable finding – the defendant really does have this brain deficit. But even here some doubts have been raised. Mayberg (cited in Fillon, 2000), a professor of psychiatry and neurology in Canada, argues that using evidence based on PET (or other) scans in the courtroom are moves led by defence attorneys and not by doctors:

> Anyone who is facing murder charges will be depressed when the PET scan is taken, and that [depression] might very well show up [during the test] . . . But there isn't enough evidence to show what their brain looked like at the time of the crime. It's not scientific. (Mayberg, in Fillon, 2000)

Mayberg also claims that we have a long way to go before she will accept the link between brain disorder and violent crime. Society and the legal and medical professions are a long way from using PET scans as a predictive tool. We have enough trouble reaching simple solutions for diseases that are clearly organic.

Second, such a defence assumes that the brain deficit actually *caused* the violent behaviour. However, as we have seen above, even Raine and Damasio, two of the leading researchers in the field, acknowledge the role of non-biological factors in violent behaviour. At the very least, the defence would have to demonstrate that the brain abnormality was the *major* contributor, but this would seem to be impossibly difficult to do. In addition, there are cases (at least in the UK) where accepting evidence of psychiatric disorder does not necessarily result in a 'diminished responsibility' verdict. Peter Sutcliffe, the 'Yorkshire Ripper', was convicted of the murder of several prostitutes despite his paranoid schizophrenia. Similarly, it does not necessarily follow that evidence of reduced prefrontal grey matter will absolve someone with APD of legal (and moral) responsibility for their crime.

The accumulating evidence regarding the prefrontal cortex and APD raises a complex ethical (and legal) dilemma. Raine (in Gibbs, 1995) asks us to imagine that we are the parent of an eight-year-old boy:

> . . . I could say to you, 'Well, we have taken a wide variety of measurements, and we can predict with 80 percent accuracy that your son is going to become seriously violent within 20 years. We can offer you a series of biological, social and cognitive intervention programs that will greatly reduce the chance of his becoming a violent offender.

> What do you do? Do you place your boy in those programs and risk stigmatizing him as a violent criminal even though there is a real possibility that he is innocent? Or do you say no to the treatment and run an 80 percent chance that your child will grow up to (a) destroy his life, (b) destroy your life, (c) destroy the lives of his brothers and sisters, and, most important, (d) destroy the lives of innocent victims who suffer at his hands?

While such a choice is purely hypothetical, many people (especially in the USA) are calling for the screening of potential violent criminals (Gibbs, 1995). Raine (1993) himself, for example, advocates a medical approach to crime control based on screening, diagnostic prediction, and treatment. One worry with this is that voluntary screening for the good of the individual child might lead to compulsory screening for the protection of society.

It is ethically one thing to convict someone of an offence and then compel them to do something, and another to require someone who hasn't committed any offence to undergo the same treatment/screening (Gibbs, 1995). Even the former case is an ethical minefield. As Gibbs argues:

> Unravelling the mysteries of human behaviour . . . creates a moral imperative to use that knowledge. To ignore it – to imprison without treatment those whom we define as sick for the behavioural symptoms of their illness – is morally indefensible. But to replace a fixed term of punishment set by the conscience of a society with forced therapy based on the judgement of scientific experts is to invite even greater injustice.

Gibbs believes that, as a result of political pressures, researchers seem to have been intimidated into not including members of minority groups in any violence studies with a biological bias – and from collecting medical data in multiracial studies. While there is no reason to suspect any genetic link between race and antisocial behaviour, Gibbs fears that supposedly objective biological research could inadvertently reinforce racial stereotypes.

■ Exercises ■

1. At the beginning of the **Background and context** section, the point is made that being able to look into someone's brain is not the same as being able to look into their mind. What do you understand by this distinction? What do you consider the relationship between mind and brain to be?

2. In the **Aim and nature of the study** section, it is claimed that Raine *et al.*'s evidence is essentially *correlational*: brain abnormalities in the murderers could be *caused by* their violent behaviour, just as easily as their violence is caused by their abnormal brains. Can you think of any other examples like this from abnormal psychology?

3. What do you understand by the terms 'aggression' and 'violence'?

4. In **Theoretical issues**, reference is made to brain abnormalities as a biological predisposition towards violence, with psychological, social, cultural and situational risk factors operating as potential triggers for actual violence. What account of schizophrenia is this similar to?

5. In **Methodological issues**, Gabrielli's (1998) point (b) is a way of questioning the *internal validity* of some neuroimaging studies (McGhee, 2001). What do you understand by the term 'internal validity', and what is Gabrielli claiming about it in relation to neuroimaging studies?

6. At the end of **Subsequent research**, how does the Damasio (2000) quote relate to the issue of *reductionism*?

7. Debate the moral dilemma posed by Raine in **Applications and implications**.

8. Why do you think Gibbs (1995) is concerned that studying whites only in the context of violence will reinforce racial stereotypes (at the end of **Applications and implications**)?

Answers to Exercises

CHAPTER 1 (MILLER, 1969)

1. It seems impossible to live among people without trying to understand (explain), predict and control their behaviour to some degree (as well as trying to understand our own!). In interpersonal perception, for example, the *attribution process* refers to the ways the lay person attributes causes to others' (and his/her own) behaviour (see Chapter 11), and *stereotypes* are one kind of 'implicit personality theory'. (Also, see Kelly's, 1955, *personal construct theory*, in which a central notion is 'man the scientist'.)

2. According to Orne (1962), social situations involve mutual expectations by the participants, and this includes psychology experiments. On the participant's side, s/he is trying to ascertain the true purpose of the experiment, and to respond in a way which will support the hypothesis being tested. In this context, any cues which convey an experimental hypothesis become important determinants of the participant's behaviour: '*demand characteristics*' are the sum total of these cues. The central point is that the participant is not a passive responder, but actively tries to work out what is going on and how to perform. The situation is very different from that in which a human experimenter investigates some part of the physical world: people are not inanimate objects but animate, conscious, thinking beings. (The role of demand characteristics recurs throughout the book.)

3. Legge (1975) and others distinguish between formal and informal psychology. Our common sense, intuitive or 'natural' understanding is unsystematic, and does not constitute a body of knowledge. Part of the aim of formal psychology is to provide such a systematic body of knowledge. While he believes that most psychological research should be aimed at demonstrations of 'what we already know' (common sense), it should aim to go one step further: only the methods of science can provide us with the public communicable body of knowledge we need.

4. I will let you struggle with this one yourself!

5. According to Jones & Elcock (2001), popular psychology makes claims about intra- and inter-personal psychology ('the mind' and our social interactions, respectively) that are specifically tailored to a lay audience/the general public. These are often presented in the form of 'how to' books, such as those that deal with communication and sexual difficulties between men and women (and relationship problems more generally) and how to improve these, that claim to teach you to read body language, and that claim to help you gain greater self-knowledge and hence improve the quality of your life.

While this is relevant to Miller's advocacy of 'giving psychology away', there is a greater risk of unfounded speculation and individual prejudices being published as 'popular psychology' (and, in turn, influencing everyday psychology) than in scientific psychology (Jones & Elcock). As we saw in **Evaluation**, scientific psychology arose partly as an attempt to keep such speculation and prejudice in check: scientific claims have to be based on the use of scientific methods and have to be presented in a way which allows others ('peers') to check them and interpret them for themselves, often by (trying to) replicate them. These 'rules' do not apply to popular psychology. (But we should be aware that the use of scientific methods cannot prevent prejudices – see Chapters 23 and 27 – and the whole idea of 'objectivity' in psychology is problematic, as we saw in **Evaluation**.)

CHAPTER 2 (DEREGOWSKI, 1972)

1. (*i*)   BINOCULAR (Retinal) DISPARITY: because our eyes are (approximately) 6cm apart, they each receive slightly different retinal images, and the superimposition of these two images is *stereoscopic vision*. Convergence is related to this.

   (*ii*)   MOTION PARALLAX: this is the major *dynamic* depth cue, and refers to the speed of apparent movement of objects nearer or further away from us. Generally, objects further away seem to move more slowly than nearer objects.

2. (*i*)   RELATIVE BRIGHTNESS: brighter objects normally appear to be nearer.

   (*ii*)   AERIAL PERSPECTIVE: objects at a great distance appear to have a different colour (e.g. the hazy, bluish tint of distant mountains).

   (*iii*)   HEIGHT IN THE HORIZONTAL PLANE: when looking across a flat expanse (e.g. across the sea), objects which are more distant seem 'higher' (i.e. closer to the horizon) than nearer objects, which seem 'lower' and closer to the ground.

   (*iv*)   LIGHT and SHADOW: 3-D objects produce variations in light and shade (e.g. we normally assume that light comes from above).

   (*v*)   ACCOMMODATION: refers to the change in the shape of the lens of the eye depending on the distance of the object. It flattens for distant objects and thickens for closer ones.

   (*vi*)   CONVERGENCE: refers to the simultaneous orienting of both eyes towards the same object. When looking at a distant object (25 feet or more), the line of vision of our two eyes is parallel, but the closer the object, the more our eyes turn inward towards each other.

3. *Monocular* cues are those which can be detected with one eye only and so (*i*) are not primarily dependent on biological processes (except accommodation) and (*ii*) are mainly *pictorial*, i.e. they are features of the visual field itself. (*Binocular* cues – retinal disparity and convergence – are *non-pictorial*.)

4. If the participant takes note of depth cues, and makes the 'correct' interpretation of the relationship between the parts when asked 'What is the man doing?' and 'What is closer to the man?', s/he is judged to be a 3-D perceiver.

5. Participants were asked to build a model of a drawing of two squares. Most 3-D perceivers (on Hudson's test) built a 3-D model, while most 2-D perceivers built a flat (2-D) model.

6. Concurrent validity.

7. There will be a significant positive correlation between participants' response to the Hudson pictures and the kind of model (3-D or flat) which they build of a drawing of two squares.

CHAPTER 3 (BARON-COHEN *ET AL.*, 1985)

1. Smith *et al.* (1998) discuss a general methodological issue that arises whenever people with learning difficulties are tested, namely, finding an appropriate *control group*. In the case of autistic children, for example, it is usual to compare them with other children who have the same MA (but who are not autistic). However, if, say, we compared a group of autistic children (MA of 6) with a group of normal children (also with a MA of 6), while the latter's CA would be about 6, the former's might be, say, 12, representing a big difference in their experience.
   To overcome this, some researchers use children with *other* learning difficulties, such as Down's syndrome, as control group (additional to normal children). This is what Baron-Cohen *et al.* did in the 1985 study. Others (e.g. Leslie & Frith, 1988) used children with specific language impairments: since autism is often most conspicuous as a language and communicative disorder, such children are a better match than Down's children (Mitchell, 1997).

2. They were used to ensure that any failure on the critical false belief question couldn't be interpreted as either a failure to (a) recognize where the marble *actually* was now (Reality question) or (b) remember where the marble had been before (Memory question). (See **Aim and nature of the study**).

3. After the experimenter introduced the dolls, the child was asked to name them (Naming question). This was used to ensure that the child could correctly identify the dolls. The subsequent questions presuppose that the child can do this: otherwise, responses to those questions would be difficult to interpret.

4. (*i*)   As Bryant (1998) observes (see **Theoretical issues**), Piaget's concept of egocentrism represents a domain-*general* approach, while ToM represents a domain-*specific* approach. For Piaget, the general lack of reversibility in children below 7 accounts for their egocentrism, which is also often discussed in terms of *centration* (or a failure to de-centre: the child can only focus on *one* aspect of an object or situation at a time, in this case, its own particular viewpoint, to the exclusion of other possible viewpoints).
           By contrast, underlying ToM is an independent mental module (ToMM),

which is *specialized* for representing *mental* representations (Leslie, 1987, 1994; Leslie & Roth, 1993).

(*ii*)   While ToM deficiency implies egocentrism, egocentrism does not imply ToM deficiency. It is 'normal' for children under seven to be egocentric, but autistic children (if, indeed, their underlying cognitive deficiency is lack of ToMM) will *remain* 'egocentric'.

(*iii*)   The critical age in normal children for the appearance of ToM is four (see **Theoretical issues**), while, according to Piaget, egocentrism continues up to 7. This suggests that they are not one and the same.

(*iv*)   In the **Discussion**, Baron-Cohen *et al.* distinguish between *conceptual* and *perceptual* perspective-taking. The former is what is being tested by their false-belief task, while the latter is tested by the 'three mountains' task (Piaget & Inhelder, 1956) and Hughes & Donaldson's, 1979, variation of this (the 'policeman-doll' task).

The 'three mountains' task is a test of *egocentrism*, which, in terms of their distinction, involves only visuo-spatial skills (seeing things from another's perspective), while ToM involves attributing beliefs to other people (such that their beliefs may sometimes differ from one's own). Evidence that autistic children are successful on perceptual perspective-taking tasks, but unsuccessful on conceptual perspective-taking tasks, indicates very clearly that the two types of task are testing quite different abilities/skills.

5.   To the extent that the children were *selected* because they were either autistic, Down's syndrome or normal, the design was *independent groups/samples*. In that each child was tested twice (trials 1 and 2), the design was (also) *repeated measures*. This explains why χ^2 was used for testing *between*-group differences, while the Binomial test was used for testing *within*-group differences (consistency of responses on trials 1 and 2).

6. (*i*)   'Position preference' means that the child would have pointed to the *same* (wrong) location on each trial. If a child had pointed to the box on trial 2 (as s/he did on trial 1), this could be due *either* to a 'preference' for that location *or* a failure to grasp that Sally's belief might differ from his/her own as to the location of the marble. In other words, position preference would have confounded the results.

(*ii*)   'Negativism' usually refers to a resistance to doing what others suggest or request we do. Here, it would denote a tendency to give the wrong answer- almost for the sake of it ('being awkward' or 'bloody-minded'). This was clearly *not* the case with the Reality and Memory Questions.

CHAPTER 4 (CRAIK & LOCKHART, 1972)

1. An algorithm is a procedure which guarantees a solution to a given problem by systematically testing every alternative in turn, until the correct response is

produced and verified (e.g. a flow diagram or decision chart). By contrast, heuristics do *not* guarantee a solution, but drastically reduce the amount of 'work' that must be carried out, by selecting the most likely options from a possible set.

2. If you are asked to name the *colour of the ink* in which a word is written, there is an interference effect produced if the word is the name of a *different* colour (e.g.'blue' written in red ink). The Stroop effect is also demonstrated if you are asked to state *the number of digits* in an array (e.g.'4444' is easier than '444')

3. Trace decay; interference.

4. Trace decay; prevention of consolidation; interference; motivated forgetting (repression); cue-dependent forgetting. (The last three all represent a failure to retrieve.)

5. It is a way of reducing a larger amount of unrelated items of information to a smaller number of meaningful items, e.g. letters into words/words into sentences/numbers into historical dates.

6. (*i*) recall (*ii*) recognition

7. In the Hyde & Jenkins (1973) study, five orienting tasks were used:
    (*i*)   rating words for pleasantness (semantic/deep processing);
    (*ii*)   estimating the frequency with which words are used in English (semantic/deep);
    (*iii*)   detecting the number of 'e's and 'g's in the words (non-semantic/shallow);
    (*iv*)   deciding the part of speech appropriate to each word (non-semantic/shallow);
    (*v*)   deciding whether or not the word fitted various sentence frames (non-semantic/shallow).

8. Incidental learning takes place when the participant is not expecting to be tested on the learned material: they are not *trying* to remember, because they are not expecting to be given a memory test (but it is retained despite this). In LOP experiments, it is the *orienting task* which is being manipulated, and nothing else is meant to influence retention (such as deliberate attempts to remember).

CHAPTER 5 (LOFTUS & PALMER, 1974)

1. (a)   The overall design was *independent groups/samples*, because different groups were asked different forms of the critical question (the *independent variable*). However, each group watched (the same) seven films (which varied from 5–30 seconds), with the overall speed estimate for each group (the *dependent variable*) being the mean estimate for all seven films. This represents a form of *repeated measures* (see (b)).

   (b)   Presumably, this was done in order to ensure that *order effects* did not influence the speed estimate. Participants may have become more accurate in their estimation of speed over the course of the seven films (*practice effect*), or they may have mentally tired (*fatigue*). These possible effects need to be controlled for, since they may contaminate the effect of the independent variable.

(c) The order of films for each group was, presumably, *randomly* determined.

(d) There was *no* control condition as such. All five groups were given a different form of the critical question, that is, each contained a different verb relating to how the cars 'touched'. The mean speed estimates were compared *with each other*, rather than with a baseline (control) condition. This is perfectly legitimate; not all experiments have a (true) control condition, in the sense of a condition in which there is no manipulation of the IV.

Can you think of what a control condition might have been?

2. Again, this is to prevent *order effects* from contaminating the results. The critical 'broken glass' question needed to be no more or less 'conspicuous' than any of the non-critical questions, otherwise the 'yes' or 'no' response may have reflected the order of the question as much as the influence of the original speed-related critical question. By randomly determining where the 'broken glass' question appeared in the list, its position was prevented from becoming a confounding variable.

3. This is an easier question to ask than to answer.

The meaning of words comprises both *connotation* (they evoke associations and feelings) and *denotation* (they *refer* to things). The 'touch'-related verbs used in the critical question evoke different associations and feelings, so that, for example, 'contacted' connotes something quite gentle and non-violent compared with, say, 'smashed'.

We're likely to hear reports of a 'car smash', but not a 'car contact', because it is only serious accidents that tend to get reported in the first place. This illustrates how we *learn* the connotations of words, which are often *implied* rather than made explicit. What words *denote* is more likely to be explicit than implicit, which is why it is easier to *define* some words than others.

4. In the *warnings technique,* participants are given false, misleading information, then warned that it is false and should be disregarded. This is essentially what happens when jurors hear the evidence of a witness, who is later discredited, and are then instructed to disregard his/her testimony. It seems they cannot to this. Experiments have shown that participants who are warned to disregard false information do no better than those who aren't warned (Cohen, 1993).

In the *second guess technique,* participants whose initial response is influenced by the misleading information are given a second opportunity to report what they saw. Again, they are usually unable to retrieve the 'original' memory.

Both these techniques are designed to challenge the substitution hypothesis, by showing that the original memory *can* be recovered (the co-existence hypothesis). But overall the evidence for the recoverability of the original memory is very slight, so there is little support for the co-existence hypothesis and the substitution hypothesis is more likely to be correct (Cohen, 1993).

5. According to Pezdek & Roe (1996), the false memory was implanted by an older sibling who, in principle, could have been there at the time, providing a plausible

basis for Chris to assume Jim might remember, even if Chris didn't at first. Also, getting lost in a shopping mall isn't a remarkable event and most children would probably have a pre-existing schema for a shopping mall, which could then be activated by the suggestion of a particular instance of getting lost. By contrast, 'It is hardly likely that most children would have a pre-exisiting schema for sexual abuse' (Pezdek & Roe, 1996).

However, Freud made us aware of the possible universal existence of childhood fantasies of incest. Moreover, the incest *barrier* (or taboo) is surely a very deep, pre-existing schema:

> . . . It could also be argued that in some therapeutic, 'recovery movement' and survivorship settings which are focused on abuse, the incoming participants do develop 'pre-existing' schemata of abuse prior to remembering abuse. (Mollon, 1998)

(See Chapter 19.)

CHAPTER 6 (GARDNER & GARDNER, 1969)

1. **(a)**   Language implies communication – but not vice-versa.
    (b)   While many non-human species are, like human beings, able to communicate, many critics of studies like those of Gardner and Gardner argue that *language* is unique to humans (it is a human *species-specific* behaviour).
    (c)   Non-human communication systems are quite inflexible and, although usually well adapted to a particular habitat, can become inaccurate when the environment changes. By contrast, human language can be modified by experience and is adaptable to novel situations.
    (d)   Communication involves a two-way process, whereby a message (or signal) is conveyed from a sender to one/more recipient: its reception is denoted by a change in the recipient. Communication, therefore, requires a *deliberate* attempt by a sender to impart information to others (Clamp & Russell, 1998).
    (e)   Language is an arbitrary system of symbols, '. . . which taken together make it possible for a creature with very limited powers of discrimination and a limited memory to transmit and understand an infinite variety of messages and to do this in spite of noise and distraction' (Brown, 1965).

2. The tendency to attribute human characteristics (motives, feelings and so on) to non-human animals.

3.

Washoe	Children
1 She was relatively old when training began. 2 She was raised in an unnatural environment. 3 She was deliberately taught to sign, which chimpanzees don't do spontaneously (i.e. language *training*). 4 Only signs were taught (*not* grammar). The debate concerns whether chimps sign 'grammatically'.	1 They are exposed to language from birth. 2 They are (usually) raised in natural environments. 3 They don't (usually) have to be deliberately taught language, because it is spontaneous (i.e. language *acquisition*). 4 *Both* words that denote objects, actions etc. *and* purely grammatical terms are acquired spontaneously (although early telegraphic speech involves only the former).

4. Deaf children learning ASL (Carroll, 1986).

5. Direct comparisons between studies can only be made if the same (or very similar) methods are used. For example, it's much easier to use signs spontaneously than, say, plastic symbols, so when evaluating a study's data regarding spontaneity (compared with children's spontaneous speech) this must be taken into account.

6. To some extent this is a matter of opinion; I'll let you think about this one.

7. It could be argued that, in some ways, rearing chimps 'as children' and training them to use language (usually in isolation from other chimps) is as unacceptable as raising them in laboratories. Is it 'mental or emotional cruelty' for the sake of 'science' or for the sake of meeting some need in the scientist (such as identifying 'human nature')?

CHAPTER 7 (MILGRAM, 1963)

1. (*i*)   Proximity of the participant to the experimenter: when the experimenter left the room halfway through, the obedience rate dropped to zero. When he was never seen, but all instructions were given via a tape recorder, it was 22%.

   (*ii*)   Proximity of the participant to the learner: when in the same room and 1½ feet away, obedience rate was 40%, when the participant held the learner's arms down on the shock plate, it was 30%.

   (*iii*)   The presence of another 'participant' who actually threw the switch: 92.5% obedience.

2. I will let you sort this out for yourself. It is something which would lend itself well to a formal debate in class. [One point worth pursuing is whether it is an adequate defence for Milgram to say he didn't anticipate the results, however sincerely. Isn't it like pleading ignorance of the law, which is usually *not* an acceptable *legal* defence?]

3. They were volunteers, answering advertisements in a newspaper and direct mail advertisements. Although clearly not a random sample, Milgram claims they represented a wide range of occupations (postal clerks, high-school teachers,

salesmen, engineers and labourers) and they had a wide range of educational experience.

However, those who went on obeying up to 450 volts seemed to have a stronger authoritarian character and a less advanced level of moral development. But this was a matter of degree only. Rosenthal & Rosnow (1966), amongst others, have found that people who volunteer for experiments are considerably *less* authoritarian than those who do not.

4. (*i*)   Conformity refers to group pressure exerted by one's peers (equals), while obedience refers to the demands made by an authority figure (someone with greater power/higher status). Another difference is that group pressure is implicit (no overt demands are made by the group), whereas in obedience the authority figure *orders* the person to behave in a particular way (and so the influence is overt and explicit).

   (*ii*)   They are both forms of *social influence*, in which there is an 'abdication of individual initiative in the face of some external social pressure' (Milgram, 1992): people deny the responsibility for their own behaviour which they 'normally' accept.

CHAPTER 8 (HANEY, BANKS & ZIMBARDO, 1973)

1. (*i*)   The 'prisoners' remained in the prison 24 hours per day.

   (*ii*)   They wore a uniform (loose-fitting smock), with an identification number on front and back.

   (*iii*) They were allowed no personal belongings, and were issued only minimum necessities for personal hygiene, etc.

   (*iv*)   They were stripped, sprayed, given uniforms, had a 'mug shot' taken, etc. upon arrival.

   (*v*)   There was a clear difference in power and status between prisoners and guards ('staff'), and 'social distance' was maximized.

2. *Qualitative* means that there are no numbers presented which could be subjected to statistical analysis (*quantitative* data) but, instead, the findings are presented in the form of an account of the behaviour of the prisoners and guards and the meaning of that behaviour in the context of the mock prison. (The behaviour *is* being analysed – but in a non-statistical way.)

   (It seems that quantitative data *were* collected – see question **5** below – but these are not presented in this article.)

3. The fundamental attribution error (FAE: see Chapter 11).

4. They mean that it isn't possible to separate the effects of the prison environment from those of the prisoner and guard characteristics, when trying to explain their behaviour. The two sets of factors get 'mixed up', and only an experimental study is capable of 'pulling them apart'.

5. The *independent variable* is the role of prisoner or guard.

The *dependent variables* are:

(*i*) transactions between and within each group of participants, recorded on video and audio tape, as well as directly observed; (*ii*) individual reactions on questionnaires, mood inventories, personality tests, daily guard shift reports, and post-experimental interviews.

6. *Mundane realism* (or 'ecological validity') means the relevance of the findings to real life/to what extent they can be generalized beyond the context in which they were obtained; in this case, to real (rather than mock) prisons.

7. Independent groups/samples.

8. They can be analysed after the study is completed, without the pressures of needing to move quickly on to the next period of observation (as in direct observation): there is no danger of any relevant behaviour being 'missed' while earlier behaviour is being recorded/analysed.

9. (*i*)   Any prior familiarity with other participants would mean that interactions are not determined exclusively by the *roles* to which they have been assigned;

   (*ii*) the experience of participating in the study together could adversely affect the relationship which existed prior to the study (especially in the case of those allocated to *different* roles).

10. This is something you might like to debate in class, or prepare as a seminar paper. According to Reicher, while the participants know they are on television, they can only self-monitor for so long. They cannot consistently behave for the camera. Also, volunteers were selected who understood that this was a serious piece of research, not a way into TV presenting:

> . . . It is not personality-led. Other reality television programmes try to create characters; we are doing the exact opposite – studying the group. We won't have versions of Big Brother's Craig and Anna. We won't have the same tabloid appeal. (Reicher, in Brockes, 2001)

Against this, Zimbardo (in *The Psychologist*, 2002) argues that:

> It is vital to remember that these made-for-TV experiments can never be valid as studies hypothesis testing as are those in scientific laboratories. All generalizations from them are constrained by the fact the 'subjects' are acting for the camera, volunteering to become celebrities, to be seen by their friends and family and public, changes how they act. We do learn about behaviour under these special circumstances, but we must be cautious about the applicability of any findings beyond this television setting.

CHAPTER 9 (PILIAVIN, RODIN & PILIAVIN, 1969)

1. *Independent variables*: (*i*) type of victim (drunk/ill); (*ii*) race of victim (white/black); (*iii*) presence/absence of model.
   Dependent variables: (*i*) latency of helping response; (*ii*) race of helper; (*iii*) number of helpers; (*iv*) movement out of the 'critical area'; (*v*) spontaneous comments.

2.

	Advantages	Disadvantages
Field experiments	**1** Results can be much more easily generalized (high ecological validity). **2** Participants not normally aware of participating in an experiment and so 'demand characteristics' not a problem.	**1** Much more difficult to control extraneous variables. **2** Much more difficult to replicate. **3** More time-consuming and expensive. **4** Ethical issues associated with 'unsolicited' participants.
Laboratory experiments	**1** Much greater control over extraneous variables. **2** Much easier to replicate. **3** Less time-consuming and expensive. **4** Participants can easily be debriefed.	**1** Problems in generalizing to real-life situations, because of their artificial nature (low ecological validity). **2** Participants' more likely to be influenced by 'demand characteristics'.

3. Natural and quasi (the latter sometimes being called 'pseudo' or '*ex post facto*' experiments. The important point here is that the independent variable has not been manipulated as in 'true' experiments. When participants are chosen because of their gender, race, intelligence (or on the basis of any other source of *individual differences*) they cannot be randomly allocated to control/experimental groups which characterize 'true' experiments. (See Coolican, 1999.)

4. The level of measurement is *nominal*: each time someone helped, they were *either* of the same race as the victim *or* of a different race, the victim was *either* ill *or* drunk, and so on. So, 'events' were being put into one category or another. The design was independent groups.

5. If you look at the results for black victims (Table 9.3), the numbers are very small (0), making it likely that the expected frequencies (E) will be below 5 in two or more cells. This means that the ordinary χ^2 cannot be used, so Fisher's exact test is used instead. The test is also known as the Fisher–Yates test. (Yates is the person responsible for 'Yates's correction' as used in a 2×2 Chi-squared test and wherever there is one degree of freedom.)

6. In its most general sense, a *heuristic* is a strategy for solving problems which helps to select actions most likely to lead to a solution, but which (unlike an *algorithm*) cannot guarantee a solution. In the context of 'a model of response to emergency situations', it refers to a set of theoretical assumptions about the kinds of variables likely to determine the probability of a bystander going to the assistance of a victim.

7. *Pluralistic ignorance* is one of the ways in which the presence of other people can inhibit an individual's tendency to offer assistance to a victim. It occurs when two or more individuals define a situation as a non-emergency after seeing that everyone else is apparently calm and not showing any signs of alarm. ('It can't be an

emergency if everyone is behaving calmly . . .'). The crucial point is that everyone is trying to look calm, because no one wants to be seen as the odd one out!

8. On each trial, a team of four student confederates boarded the train. The female confederates sat outside the critical area and recorded data as unobtrusively as possible during the journey, while the male model and victim remained standing (see **Procedure**). The females were (like the model and victim) just 'other passengers' as far as the real passengers were concerned.

9. **(a)** Prosocial behaviour is a label for a wide variety of actions 'defined by society as generally beneficial to other people and to the ongoing political system' (Piliavin *et al.*, 1981).

   (b) '. . . an action that has the consequences of providing some benefit or improving the well-being of another person . . . ' (Schroeder *et al.*, 1995).

   (c) '. . . behaviour intended to help another without regard for benefit to oneself . . .' (Moghaddam, 1998).

10. The participants cannot give their *consent*, let alone their *informed consent*, because they are not even aware that an experiment is taking place. They are being *deceived* (they don't know that it isn't a genuine emergency) but cannot be *debriefed* (as usually happens in laboratory experiments). This, in turn, increases the chances that psychological ill-effects (guilt, distress, anxiety, etc.) will be more prolonged.

CHAPTER 10 (FESTINGER & CARLSMITH, 1959)

1. Independent groups (or independent measures).

2. Unrelated *t*-test. This is a parametric test which requires *interval* data. But were the rating scales true interval scales? The alternative would have been the Mann–Whitney *U*.

3. Hypothesis **2** says 'The *larger* the pressure . . . the *weaker* will be . . .'. This suggests a one-tailed (directional) prediction. (Hypothesis **1** just talks about a 'tendency to change', and so is two-tailed/non-directional.)

4. It removes experimenter bias, so that the interviewer cannot be influenced by knowledge of what condition the participant was tested under as to how he *ought* to have rated the task. Since the participant is also ignorant as to the purpose of the experiment, this represents a double-blind technique.

5. The independent variable = the size of reward ($1 or $20). The dependent variable = the degree of attitude change (how enjoyable the task was rated).

6. Correlation.

7. Yes: they were male psychology students, who have to spend a certain number of hours participating as participants (i.e. it is a course requirement).

8. When participants believed the pill would relax them, the dissonance arising from the high-choice condition was still sufficient to produce attitude change (and it is contrary to what they expect to feel, so the 'discomfort/tension' must be due to their counter-attitudinal behaviour).

When given no information, the situation is no different from the Festinger and Carlsmith $1 situation.

But when told the pill would make them feel tense, the tension is attributed to the pill rather than the counter-attitudinal behaviour (and so the question of high/low choice becomes irrelevant).

9. One possibility is that someone other than the experimenter might ask the participant to 'tell the lie'; another is that the 'favour' is asked in a non-face-to-face way (e.g. in writing). You may be able to think of other possibilities.

CHAPTER 11 (NISBETT, CAPUTO, LEGANT & MARACEK, 1973)

1. 'Organized whole', 'pattern' or 'configuration';
    Wertheimer, Köhler and Koffka.
2. The value of *t* is less than 1, not (or non-) significant.
3. Since *t*-tests are parametric tests, and since parametric tests require the use of an interval (or ratio) scale of measurement, the rating scale is taken to be using interval level data to measure estimates of the actor volunteering for a similar task.
4. Not real and unlikely to be found in real-life situations.
5. (*i*)   'emphasize the role of properties of the chosen object . . . be more likely to . . . emphasize the role played by dispositions and traits . . .'.
    (*ii*)   'It was anticipated that participants would explain their own choices and their friends' similar choices differently, by emphasizing either the role of properties of the chosen object or the role played by dispositions and traits of the choosing individual.'
    (*iii*) 'directional' (one-tailed), 'non-directional' (two-tailed).
6. *p* is greater than 0.10 but less than 0.15: the probability of obtaining a *t* value of 1.63 by chance alone (the significance level) is between 0.10 and 0.15.
7. (*i*)   The *independent variable* is the person whose behaviour is being explained (a paragraph on why my best friend chose his college major, etc.); the *dependent variable* is the actual attributions made (entity versus disposition).
    (*ii*)   Repeated measures.
    (*iii*) Essentially by a form of *content analysis*. The paragraphs were scored using a coding system, which identified each reason as either a pure entity or as invoking some dispositional property of the actor.
    (*iv*)   If a reason referred in any way to the person doing the choosing (e.g. 'I need someone I can relax with'), and included any which could be described as entity × disposition interaction reasons (e.g. 'We can relax together').
8. (*i*)   *Parallel* forms.
    (*ii*)   Reliability (specifically, *internal consistency*).
    (*iii*) The other major measure of internal consistency is the *split-half* method. *Test–retest reliability* is a measure of consistency over time.
9. (*i*)   Counterbalancing.

(*ii*) To ensure that the order in which participants completed the questionnaires did not bias the way they attributed trait. In particular, to ensure that the order in which they completed the sheet for self did not influence the tendency to attribute more traits to others than to self.

10. Participants were equally consistent in their tendency to attribute more traits to others, regardless of which trait dimensions were involved and which target persons were being assessed.

11. It could be argued that to see ourselves as acting in accordance with 'the demands and opportunities of each new situation as it arises' involves an *illusion of freedom* (see Chapter 10). If our traits and dispositions are the exclusive 'causes' of our behaviour, then to this extent we are not free either (i.e. we cannot help but act in a particular way because 'that's the kind of person we are').

CHAPTER 12 (TAJFEL, 1970)

1. Prejudice is an attitude, discrimination is a form of behaviour. Prejudiced attitudes are not a very reliable predictor of discriminatory behaviour, largely because the latter is more directly a function of the objective social situation than of individual attitudes.

2. (*i*) How obvious it is how one can benefit a member of the in-group relative to an out-group member.

(*ii*) *Fairness* or *even-handedness*: awarding an equal number of points to any two individuals, regardless of the groups they belong to; *Maximum Generosity*: awarding points in a way which discriminates in favour of the out-group; *Maximum In-group Favouritism*: awarding points in a way which discriminates in favour of the in-group.

(*iii*) Fairness or even-handness: 7/8: 8/7
Maximum Generosity: 1/14:14/1
Maximum In-group Favouritism: 14/1:1/14

3. *Intra*group choices involve two members of the *same* group (*intra* = 'within'), either two members of the in-group *or* of the out-group. *Inter*group choices involve one member of the in-group *and* one member of the out-group (*inter* = 'between'). Generally, when making intragroup choices, fairness prevailed: the same overall mean was found (7.5), whether the choice was between two in-group or two out-group members. However, (*i*) when making intergroup choices, significantly more points were awarded to in-group members (mean over 9), and (*ii*) when choosing between two in-group members, participants tended to favour the largest total sums (maximum joint profit/MJP), while when choosing between two members of the out-group, they tended to favour smaller total sums (thereby indirectly conferring a relative advantage on the in-group).

4. (*i*) This was done to control the variables of transparency and nature of choice (i.e. in-group/out-group, in-group/in-group, out-group/out-group), to ensure that

there was no interaction effect. For example, if all or most of the in-group/out-group choices had involved very transparent matrices, this may have biased the results in the direction of ingroup favouritism, thus constituting a *confounding variable*. Tajfel was only interested in-group membership (this was the manipulated independent variable) as an influence on points allocation, so all other variables likely to affect the outcome had to be kept constant.

CHAPTER 13 (SAMUEL & BRYANT, 1984)

1. (*i*)   Counterbalancing.
   (*ii*)   To reduce the impact of order effects (e.g. practice or fatigue as a result of doing one task before another). This is an inherent problem in a repeated measures design.
   (*iii*)   Using the initial letter of each material (*M* = mass, *N* = number, *V* = volume), the following could have been used: MNV, NVM, VNM, such that one third of the children within each age group and within each condition were tested in each of these three, predetermined, orders.
2. As Samuel and Bryant say, it was used to check that children who answered the post-transformation question correctly in the other two conditions did so by bringing over information from the pre-transformation display. It was, therefore, serving as a *control* condition.
3. A child may have mastered all kinds of classification but not all kinds of conservation. So vertical decalage refers to inconsistencies *between* different abilities or operations.

CHAPTER 14 (BANDURA, ROSS & ROSS, 1961)

1. The earlier studies did not test generalization of imitative responses to new settings in which the model is absent. Bandura *et al.* consider this to be a more crucial test of imitative learning.
2. If a child has been reinforced in the past for imitating male or female models, the child will be more likely to imitate such a model in the future.
3. (*i*)   Matched pairs (or participants).
   (*ii*)   It controls the crucial participant variable of the child's 'natural' level of aggression.
   (*iii*)   Independent groups (or samples).
   (*iv*)   It counts as a *related* design, and so the appropriate statistical test is one that is suitable for a related design (see question **6** below).
4. (*i*)   The scale was measuring aggression at an *interval* level, since this is required by the parametric Pearson test.
   (*ii*)   Spearman's rank order correlation coefficient is the non-parametric equivalent of Pearson.

5. To ensure that they were 'under some degree of instigation to aggression', since (*i*) observation of other people's aggression tends to reduce aggression in the observer, and (*ii*) if participants in the non-aggressive condition expressed little aggression in the face of appropriate instigation, this would indicate the presence of an inhibitory process.

6. It is a test used for *related* designs, when there are more than two conditions; in this case, there are *three*: two experimental (aggressive/non-aggressive), and one control. The symbol for the test is χ^2_r (see Table 14.2, page 262). Since it involves ranks, and the assumption of homogeneity of variance could not be made, the test must be non-parametric.

7. It is the binomial sign test used when there are three or more conditions. Like the 'standard' (two conditions) binomial test, it is used with nominal data.

8. 'Extremely skewed' tells us that the scores are not normally distributed, suggesting that they have not been drawn from a normally distributed population. This is the other assumption made by parametric tests (see question **6** above).

9. (*i*) Positive reinforcement (*ii*) Shaping (*iii*) Operant conditioning.

10. It seems that mere observation may be sufficient for *learning* of the model's behaviour, but for reproduction (i.e. actual imitation) of that behaviour to occur, reinforcement of the observer's behaviour (or of the model's) may be necessary.

11. Deliberately exposing children to aggressive behaviour could be objected to, because they are learning how to act in a socially undesirable way. Equally, subjecting the children (in all three groups) to 'mild aggression arousal' (see question **5** above) by deliberately frustrating them is objectionable by its very nature. However, the study as a whole could be defended if it is seen as contributing to our knowledge of the harmful effects of the media: it is a case of balancing the need to protect individual participants against the need to carry out socially beneficial research.

CHAPTER 15 (HODGES & TIZARD, 1989)

1.

	Cross-sectional	Longitudinal
Advantages	**1** Relatively simple and quick: it's a short-term study, so is relatively inexpensive. **2** Requires no continuity of the research team. **3** Data needn't be 'frozen' over long time period until participants have completed their development. **4** Provides age-related norms.	**1** No cohort problem (same participants are being compared with themselves). **2** Smaller number of participants required. **3** Sensitive to changes in behaviour which occur quickly (assuming the intervals between successive observations are fairly short). **4** Provides individual growth curves (as well as age-related norms).
Disadvantages	**1** *Cohort effect*: if widely different age-groups/cohorts are compared, any differences could be due *either* to actual change in the variables under investigation *or* the fact that they represent different generations. **2** Participants need to be matched on relevant variables, which is time-consuming and expensive. **3** Larger number of participants required. **4** Can *describe* behaviour changes over time, but *not* explain them.	**1** Time-consuming and expensive. **2** Requires continuity of research team. **3** The participants who 'survive' may be affected in some way by repeated testing over the years: this may make them a less representative sample than they originally were.

2. (*i*) A natural experiment takes place in the normal course of events, and is not due to any kind of interference on the psychologist's part: the changes which occur would have occurred anyway.

(*ii*) Because the psychologist is not randomly allocating participants to the experimental/control conditions, there is no control over participant variables (and so the experiment is not a true, but a 'quasi' experiment).

3. The original 30 London working-class children no longer seemed appropriate for the mainly middle-class adopted group, or the restored group who lived in mainly disadvantaged homes. A comparison 16-year-old was found, therefore, for each of the ex-institution adolescents, matched on sex, one- or two-parent family, occupational status of main breadwinner, and position in family.

4. Without it, it would be impossible to know if it was the institutional experience, rather than something else, which affected the adolescents' relationships (e.g.'they might have turned out like that anyway'). This is the basic principle of *all* control (comparison) groups.

5. This is a way of studying young children's attachments to their parents (in particular, the mother) devised by Ainsworth *et al.* (1971, 1978). It comprises a sequence of eight episodes in which the mother (and/or the father) and a stranger come and go from the room, each episode lasting about three minutes. Trained observers record the child's attachment behaviour in the mother's presence, when she leaves and returns, how the child responds to the stranger, and how its play is affected throughout.

CHAPTER 16 (WATSON & RAYNER, 1920)

1. (*i*)   'In the 1920s' should be '1920'.
   (*ii*)   'J.B. Watson' should be 'J.B. Watson and R. Rayner'.
   (*iii*) 'did a series of experiments with children' should be 'initiated some laboratory experiments with an infant, Albert B'.
   (*iv*) 'how emotional responses can be conditioned and deconditioned': no mention of 'deconditioning' in the original (the emphasis very much on conditioning).
   (*v*)   'an eight-month-old orphan, Albert B.' should be 'nine-month-old Albert B., whose mother was a wet-nurse in a children's hospital'.
   (*vi*) 'who happened to be fond of rabbits, rats, mice and other furry animals' should be 'none of these induced a fear response'.
   (*vii*) 'toy rabbit' should be 'white rat' (a real one).
   (*viii*) 'Then the rabbit was displayed to Albert, and, half a second or so later, Watson made a sudden loud noise' should be 'joint presentations' (of the rat and hammer on steel bar).
   (*ix*) 'crashing metal plates together' should be 'hammer on steel bar'.
   (*x*)   '. . . it spread to other stimuli . . . such as a glove, a towel, a man's beard, a toy and a ball of wool' should be 'rabbit, dog, fur coat, cotton wool, Watson's hair, and a Santa Claus mask'.
   (You can work out the others for yourself.)

2. It can be thought of as a whole series of *repeated measures*, and any one measure may depend, in subtle or complex ways, on the measures previously taken. If we know that the successive scores obtained from a participant are independent of each other, then there is no *statistical* objection to single-participant designs (Robson, 1973).

3. Stimulus generalization.

4. Discrimination.

5. Extinction and spontaneous recovery.

CHAPTER 17 (LEVINSON, 1986)

1. A hierarchical progression means that each stage in the developmental sequence is more advanced than the one before; e.g. concrete operations represent a higher level of cognitive development than pre-operational intelligence (or sensorimotor intelligence).

2. *Décalage* (both horizontal and vertical). A child who can conserve number but not weight is displaying *horizontal* décalage; a child who can conserve number but is still egocentric is displaying *vertical* décalage.

3. *Longitudinal* research involves the study of the same group of individuals over a period of time (usually years), while *cross-sectional* research involves the comparison of different age groups at more or less the same point in time. Major advantages of the latter include the fact that it is quicker, cheaper, and generally easier to carry out. (See answers to Chapter 15.)

4. Generativity vs. stagnation (the seventh of the *Eight Ages of Man*, middle adulthood or maturity, 20s–50s).

5. The Social Readjustment Rating Scale comprises 43 Life Events, each assigned a mean value (from 100 for 'death of spouse' to 11 for 'minor violations of the law'). The amount of life stress a person has experienced in a given time period (usually one year) is measured by the total life change units (LCUs): these are obtained by adding up the mean values of the Life Events (life changes) which the person has experienced in that time period.

6. *Gerontology* is the scientific study of the ageing process (from the Greek words *geron/ontos*, meaning 'old man'). It is an inter (multi-) disciplinary field of study, including psychology, sociology and medicine and so is *not* a field of psychology.

7. *Geriatrics* (*geras/iatros*, meaning 'old age'/'physician') is a branch of medicine concerned with the diseases and care of the elderly.

CHAPTER 18 (FERNALD, 1985)

1. The aim of the study was to establish whether babies prefer listening to motherese as opposed to 'normal' adult-adult speech. If so, it should not make any difference who is speaking it (familiar mother's voice or unfamiliar stranger's voice).

2. No: motherese is not defined in terms of a female voice. However (as shown in **Subsequent research**), women's higher pitched voices, together with the baby's early preference for the mother's voice, make it more likely that preference for motherese will be manifested in response to a female voice.

3. (a) No: the eight-second bursts of speech were played *regardless* of what the baby did or in which direction it turned its head.

   (b) Yes: the baby's turning left or right *caused* motherese or adult-adult speech to be played (motherese was a reinforcer for turning in *that* direction).

4. One-tailed (or directional, *literally* in this case: the prediction specifies that 'infants would make significantly more head-turns in the direction required to produce *motherese*'). (Note that a *two-tailed t* test was used to compare the mean number of head-turns in the motherese direction and the expected chance performance: this appears to be a contradiction).

5. (a) Counterbalancing: Group 1:   Left/First
                                           Group 2:   Right/First
                                           Group 3:   Left/Second
                                           Group 4:   Right/Second.

   (b) This could have been determined *randomly* for each baby. But (a) *guarantees* that all combinations are covered to exactly the same extent (12 babies per group).

6. This provides an objective definition/measure, which can then be applied by any number of experimenters/observers: subjective definitions or interpretations are effectively ruled out, thus providing greater reliability.

7. Two stimuli (such as a checkerboard pattern and a plain square of the same size) are presented simultaneously. If more time is spent looking at one, it can be inferred that (*i*) the baby can perceive the difference (can discriminate) between them, and (*ii*) the baby prefers the one it looks at longer.
   In the Fernald study (experimental trials), *neither* stimulus (motherese or adult-adult speech) is presented *unless* the baby behaves in a pre-determined way (30 degree head-turn),

CHAPTER 19 (FREUD, 1909)

1. The investigator has little or no control over variables (making it impossible to infer cause-and-effect), it involves an individual (or family), and so cannot be replicated, it often involves the interpretation of the participant's behaviour from a particular theoretical perspective, and the investigator cannot be objective due to his/her role as a therapist/psychiatrist in a helping role (as opposed to scientist role).
   [All these points are a matter of degree, especially 'objectivity'. See, for example, Gross (2001).]

2. The case-study is really Freud's interpretation of Hans's father's interpretation of his son's phobia: not the most direct connection between Freud and his patient (whom he actually saw on only one or two occasions). But Freud and the father were of one mind anyway regarding the Oedipal theory, and so would have probably reached the same interpretation, but the 'price' paid for this agreement is fitting Hans's behaviour, dreams and so on *into* the theory.

3. Qualitative data = non-statistical, not involving any measurement, but rather description and interpretation.
   Quantitative data = statistical, based on (precise) measurement. Can much more easily be 'checked out' by another investigator.

4. This is one you might want to debate in the class. Remember, Bowlby's interpretation, like Freud's, is made from a particular theoretical perspective, namely attachment theory; Fromm's is more objective in this sense.

CHAPTER 20 (ROSENHAN, 1973)

1. In order to be able to generalize the results: the hospitals used should be representative of USA psychiatric hospitals in general.
   They were in different States, on both coasts, both old/shabby and new, research-orientated and not, well staffed and poorly staffed (staff: patient ratio), 11 state, one private, federal or university funded.

2. Psychiatrists are more likely to call a healthy person sick (a false positive, Type-two error) than a sick person healthy (a false negative, Type-one error).
   In psychology, we make a Type-one error when we incorrectly reject the Null hypothesis (i.e. we should have accepted it), and a Type-two error when we incorrectly accept the Null hypothesis (i.e. we should have rejected it).

3. For example:
   (*i*) Pseudo-patients trying to gain admission but *without* complaining of hearing voices, or with different symptoms.
   (*ii*) Telling staff the results of the first experiment, but not telling them to expect any pseudo-patients.

4. However distasteful such concealment is, it was a necessary first step:

   . . . Without concealment, there would have been no way to know how valid these experiences were; nor was there any way of knowing whether whatever detections occurred were a tribute to the diagnostic acumen of the staff or to the hospital's rumour network . . . I have respected their [individual staff and hospitals] anonymity, and have eliminated clues that might lead to their identification. (Rosenhan, 1973: Notes)

5.

Neurosis	Psychosis
1 Only a *part* of the personality is involved/affected.	1 The *whole* personality is involved/affected.
2 Contact with reality is maintained.	2 Contact with reality is lost – inability to distinguish between subjective experience and external reality.
3 The neurotic has *insight* (recognition that there is a problem).	3 The psychotic lacks *insight*.
4 Neurotic behaviour is an exaggeration of 'normal' behaviour (there is only a *quantitative* difference).	4 Psychotic behaviour is discontinuous with 'normal' behaviour (they are *qualitatively* different).
5 Often begins as a response to a stressor.	5 Usually there is no precipitating cause.
6 Related to patient's personality prior to onset of illness.	6 Unrelated to the patient's personality prior to onset of illness.
7 Treated mainly by *psychological* methods.	7 Treated mainly by *physical* methods.

CHAPTER 21 (THIGPEN & CLECKLEY, 1954)

1. and **2.** These can both be debated (perhaps together) in your psychology class.

3. (*i*)   They have no particular theoretical 'axe to grind', so there is much less chance of bias in their interpretations.

(*ii*)   They asked independent experts to give a variety of tests: psychological and neuro-physiological, objective and projective.

(*iii*)   Thigpen and Cleckley could reach a diagnosis and interpretation together, while Freud had no co-worker with whom he could discuss his cases. (A noteworthy exception was, of course, Little Hans's father, but he was a 'Freudian' already; see **Evaluation** for Chapter 19.)

(*iv*)   Thigpen and Cleckley involved Eve's relatives to help verify certain recollections, and to add information, and in this way throw light on the case. (By contrast, Hans's father was also his major *psychoanalyst*!)

4.

Multiple personality disorder	Schizophrenia
1 Hearing voices is the only kind of hallucination, but it is not a major symptom. **2** Involves fugue and amnesia. **3** Is a form of dissociative disorder (traditionally *neurosis* – see answers to Chapter 19). **4** Usually treated *psychologically* (psychotherapy). **5** The different personalities/states are 'self-contained', although some are very specific/superficial. Each represents a 'part of the whole'.	**1** Auditory hallucinations are not the only kind, and are usually a major symptom. **2** Does not involve fugue and amnesia. **3** Traditionally, a major (functional) *psychosis*: see answers to Chapter 20. **4** Usually treated *physically* (major tranquilizers). **5** The personality as a whole is split. For example, there is a breakdown between self/reality, self/other, emotion/cognition.

5. (*i*)   A 'blind tester' is someone who assesses performance on a test without knowing whose scores they are (i.e. the tester does not know the identity of the personality: Eve White, Eve Black or Jane).

(*ii*)   The main advantage is that the tester will not be (unwittingly) influenced when assessing performance on the test by the knowledge of whose performance is being assessed: there will be no *experimenter bias* (no chance of the tester's expectations unconsciously biasing the way the test is scored).

6. The Semantic Differential is an attitude scale which comprises at least nine pairs of *bipolar* adjectives, for each of which there is a seven-point scale. The scale as a whole involves three factors: *evaluative* (e.g. 'good–bad'), *potency* (e.g. 'strong–weak'), *activity* (e.g. 'active–passive'). The attitude object is usually denoted by a single word, rather than a statement.

CHAPTER 22 (EYSENCK, 1952)

1. (*i*) Psychoneurotic cases are not usually committed to state hospitals unless in a very bad psychological state;

   (*ii*) there were relatively few voluntary patients in the hospital group;

   (*iii*) such patients do receive *some* degree of psychotherapy;

   (*iv*) there were probably quite important differences between the two groups *re* economic, educational and social status.

   Denker's: his group was receiving no psychotherapy, came from all over the USA, displayed a wide range of neuroses and had a higher socio-economic status. *But* they were probably more incapacitated than the psychotherapy group.

2. The baseline represents the rate of spontaneous recovery (recovery without any treatment); if psychotherapy works, it must aid recovery *beyond* the baseline.

3. (*i*) Dream interpretation;

   (*ii*) free association;

   (*iii*) transference.

4. (*i*) Systematic Desensitization (SD) involves a step-by-step exposure to the phobic object (usually by imagining it), while simultaneously relaxing.

   (*ii*) Implosion involves exposing the patient to what, in SD, would be at the top of the hierarchy (a list of least to most feared contact with the phobic object), without any relaxation.

   (*iii*) Flooding is exposure which takes place *in vivo* (e.g. with an actual spider, rather than imagining it), but is otherwise more like Implosion than SD.

5. This refers to the replacement of a removed symptom (e.g. phobia) by another symptom (e.g. another phobia). It is what psychoanalytic theorists believe happens when *only* the behaviour itself (the fear), and not the underlying conflict, is dealt with (as in behaviour therapy). (See **Background and context**.)

6. *Psychodynamic* is a more general term than *psychoanalytic*. 'Psychodynamic' implies the *active* forces within the personality, the inner causes of behaviour, which include feelings, conflicts, drives, and especially a variety of *unconscious* motivational factors. Freud's psychoanalytic theory was the first such theory and all *depth psychology* stems, more or less directly, from psychoanalytic principles. The theories (and therapies) of, for example, Jung and Adler, are psychodynamic, but not psychoanalytic.

7. (**a**) This refers to the patients' *expectation* of success or improvement. When we call a change a placebo effect, we usually mean that it was brought about by some means other than that intended in a particular treatment.

   (**b**) In drug trials, a placebo denotes an inactive/inert substance (usually a sugar pill) which takes account of the psychological (as opposed to pharmacological) influences on physiological change. So, in drug trials, the placebo condition is the *control* condition.

(c) It is quite appropriate in drug trials to use an *intentional placebo* (as opposed to an inadvertent one), that is, a treatment *designed* to have no effect, in itself, on a particular disorder. However, their use in psychotherapy research is a misapplication of drug trial methods: in psychotherapy, the expectation is part of the treatment (Mair, 1992).

This makes 'placebo' an unfortunate term, since it clearly does not denote something inactive/inert. Even non-placebo controls (such as delayed treatment or no treatment controls) will produce expectations specific to that particular condition (e.g. disappointment and rejection respectively: Barkham & Shapiro, 1992).

CHAPTER 23 (GOULD, 1982)

1. Yerkes was one of the pioneers of modern primatology (the study of primates).
2. *Aptitude* tests are intended to measure someone's *capacity/potential* to achieve in a particular skill or occupation or academic subject; they claim to reduce to a minimum the effect of specific learning and experience. *Attainment* (or achievement) tests measure how much a person knows about a specific subject or the person's current level of performance (e.g. reading ability). IQ tests have always claimed to be aptitude tests. However,
   (*i*) they rely on reading/arithmetic or other acquired skills to assess capacity or potential;
   (*ii*) they can only measure capacity or potential by assuming cultural fairness;
   (*iii*) capacity or potential does not exist separately from some actual performance or behaviour.
3. A eugenicist believes that people with socially undesirable characteristics (such as low intelligence or criminal tendencies) should be prevented from producing offspring, in order to prevent the spread of these characteristics. (This is part of a broader belief in the need to *breed* human beings in order to achieve a 'better' society, based, of course, on the assumption that socially important abilities and behaviours are largely genetically determined.) In practice, this would be done through sterilization and/or institutionalizing certain individuals.
4. This clearly lends itself to a class debate/seminar discussion. It centres around the fundamental ethical conflict between the rights of the individual versus the rights of others ('society'), a conflict which has surfaced on occasions in relation to AIDS and 'safe sex', and is usually involved in debates about banning smoking from public places.
5. Recent immigration had drawn the dregs of Europe: lower-class Latins and Slavs (these were of naturally inferior intelligence). Those immigrants of longer residence belonged predominantly to superior (i.e. of naturally higher intelligence) Northern stocks. In other words, the positive correlation between years spent in the USA and IQ score was attributable to 'genetic stock', *not* to increased absorption of American culture.

Ironically, this demonstrates the principle of not inferring cause and effect from a correlation. Although, without question, years spent in the USA *did* increase IQ scores (i.e. there was a cause-and-effect relationship), this anti-hereditarian argument was shown to be invalid by the argument that the two variables (length of residence/IQ score) both stemmed from a *third* variable (genetic stock). Yerkes, therefore, used a valid form of reasoning to reach what is, almost certainly, an invalid conclusion.

CHAPTER 24 (BOUCHARD & MCGUE, 1981)

1. The view that many pairs of genes are involved in the inheritance of intelligence (not just a single pair, as in eye-colour, for example).
2. Some genes are more powerful than others. For example, the brown-eye gene is dominant over the blue-eye gene, such that if someone inherits one of each (genotype) they will actually have brown eyes (phenotype).
3. The tendency for organisms (including human beings) to select as mates/sexual partners those with characteristics similar to their own.
4. If a range of values includes some scores which are extreme in one direction only, then the mean will be distorted and the median will be a more 'typical' score.
5. (*i*)   A figure which takes sample size (the number of pairings) into account as a weight, which makes the different studies more comparable.
   (*ii*)   A measure of heterogeneity (dissimilarity) between the median correlations within each category. d.f. is, of course, determined by the number of studies in a set.
   (*iii*) χ^2 divided by its d.f. has an expectation of 1.0 under the homogeneity (similarity) hypothesis, and can be used to compare the relative heterogeneity of different categories (i.e. between categories).

6.

Individual tests (e.g. Stanford-Binet/Wechsler Intelligence Scale for Children/WISC)	Group tests (e.g. Raven's Progressive Matrices, British Ability Scales/BAS)
1 Used primarily as diagnostic tools in a clinical setting (e.g. disruptive behaviour at school).	1 Used primarily for purposes of selection (e.g. the 11-plus examination in England and Wales) and research.
2 Involves a one-to-one situation between the psychologist administering the test and the person being tested.	2 As many people are tested at one time as is practical (e.g. the number of tables and chairs in the room).
3 A face-to-face situation, in which it is important to put the testee at ease before testing proper begins.	3 Presented in the form of written questions (like an examination).
4 No standardized instructions as such.	4 Standardized instructions.
5 May/may not be timed.	5 Timed.
6 Usually involves some *performance* items.	6 No performance items.
7 Some scope for interpretation by the psychologist of the testee's answers.	7 No scope for interpretation. They are *objective* tests (only one answer can be accepted as correct), usually marked by computer.

CHAPTER 25 (BEM, 1974)

1. The criterion for selecting an item was that it should be independently judged, by males and females, to be significantly more desirable for men or for women. The implication is that males and females will have different ideas about what's desirable for the same and opposite sex, so that only where they do agree can an item be reliably considered sex-typed (and, hence, included).

2. It comprises a seven-point scale, each with a verbal description. It is taken to represent an *interval* scale because a *t*-test is used, which is parametric and requires an interval scale. (The androgyny score is expressed as a *t*-ratio, i.e. the *t*-test statistic.)

3. It is a measure of the test's *reliability*. Each item should be measuring the same variable and to the same extent (i.e. all items should contribute equally to the overall score). A common method for assessing internal consistency is the split half method. (Bem expresses the internal consistency of the BSRI as a coefficient alpha: a.)

4. Because if they had, it wouldn't have been a measure of the *reliability* of the test, but of the participants' memory.

5. (*i*)   parametric;
   (*ii*)   Spearman's rank-order correlation.

6. (*i*)   concurrent;
   (*ii*)   face/predictive/construct.

7. Eysenck Personality Questionnaire (EPQ); the Social Desirability scale is known as the 'Lie Scale'.

8. A test must be properly standardized, that is, tried out on a large, representative sample of the population for whom it is intended, in order to establish a set of norms for that population, so that any individual's score can be compared against those norms.

CHAPTER 26 (HRABA & GRANT, 1970)

1. See **Answers** to Chapter 21.

2. So that this was effectively ruled out as an influence on the child's behaviour. For example, black children interviewed by a white experimenter might have felt obliged to express a preference for white dolls: they may, in some way, have believed that this was the 'right' choice to make.

3. A 'baseline' or control (comparison) group.
   Without knowing white children's preference, black children's preference couldn't be meaningfully assessed. For example, if white children had preferred black dolls (for whatever reason), this would give a very different meaning to black children's preference for white dolls.

4. 'A view of things in which one's own group is the centre of everything, and all others are scaled and rated with reference to it . . . Each group . . . boasts itself superior . . . and looks with contempt on outsiders. Each group thinks its own folkways the only right one . . .' (Sumner, 1906). (See Chapter 27.)

5. Because children's ethnic awareness and ethnic identity become more sophisticated as they get older (see **Background and context**).

6. 'As children get *older,* they are *less* likely to misidentify dolls' racial idenitity'; **or** '*younger* children are *more* likely to misidentify dolls' racial identity compared with older children'.

7. This refers to Sociometry (Moreno, 1953), a method for assessing interpersonal attitudes (e.g. friendship choices) in 'natural' groups (e.g. at school, college, work). Choice of friends, for example, is represented as a *sociogram* which charts friendship patterns, revealing the popular and unpopular members, the likely leaders, the isolates, and so on.

8. It is difficult, if not impossible, to disentangle the effects of these variables on the dependent variable: we cannot tell which (if any) are actually influencing the outcome.

9. (*i*) The independent variable is the child's ethnic group membership, so the dolls must embody this characteristic (skin colour, as opposed to, say, size) and no other.

   (*ii*) If only skin colour differed, there could be a 'contradiction' between this and other racial/ethnic characteristics. So, the black doll might have 'white hair and features' and the white doll 'black hair and features'. This makes interpretation of the results potentially more difficult.

10. It is used to compare the results from the Clark & Clark sample and Hraba & Grant's Lincoln sample. The results for each sample are presented as the *proportions* of children choosing *either* the white *or* black doll. Since the two samples are *independent* of each other, χ^2 is the appropriate test to use.

CHAPTER 27 (NOBLES, 1976)

1. *Idiographic* theories maintain that every individual is *unique* and should be studied as such. They are also concerned with the *whole* person. Allport's (1961) trait theory and Kelly's (1955) personal construct theory are two examples.
   Nomothetic theories are concerned with the *comparison* of individuals and discovering the factors which constitute *personality in general.* They advocate the *measurement of particular aspects* of personality, through the use of standardized tests, as in Eysenck's EPQ (Eysenck Personality Questionnaire) and Cattell's 16 PF (Personality Factor) Questionnaire.

2. The self-concept can be thought of as the individual's beliefs about his/her personality, how the individual perceives his/her personality. It comprises:

(i)   *Self-image* (ego-identity): the kind of person we think we are, what we think we are like (essentially *descriptive*).

(ii)   *Self-esteem* (ego-identity): how much we like and accept or approve of ourselves, how worthwhile a person we think we are (essentially *evaluative*).

(iii)   *Ideal-self* (ego-ideal): the kind of person we would like to be.

3.   The fundamental point here is that all scientific 'observations' require some degree of *interpretation*. The 'data' constitute 'uninterpreted' observations, so that when 'African data' are interpreted or processed by the guiding principles of the Eurocentric-American world view, the finished product (results or 'facts') represents a distortion of the original. This is like Deese's (1972) view that *scientific facts = data + theory*: 'facts' do *not* exist objectively, independently of some theoretical interpretation.

4.   (i)   The Eurocentric concept of *time* is *linear:* it travels in a straight line from past, through present, to future, and it is measured objectively in discrete units. Individualist cultures also see time as a commodity, a precious resource which can be 'used', 'saved', 'bought', 'wasted', and which should be rationed and controlled through the use of schedules and appointments. In collectivist cultures, time is regarded as a limitless, 'elastic' resource, which enables individuals to meet their obligations to various members of the community to whom they are bound (Owusu-Bempah & Howitt, 2000).

(ii)   The notion of *individual responsibility* is central to much of Eurocentric (Western) philosophy (in particular, moral philosophy or ethics) and the legal/criminal code.

(iii)   The distinction between *us* and *them,* the categorization of oneself as belonging to this group and not that group, is fundamental to social perception in a Eurocentric world view (see Chapter 12). This distinction is central to *ethnocentrism* (see question **6** below).

5.   Allport identified eight major components of the 'proprium' (which 'includes all aspects of personality that make for inward unity; it refers to the sense of what is peculiarly ours'), one being *ego-extension*. This is part of the self-image which refers to those things and people (significant others) that are not literally the individual but which constitute, psychologically, part of the individual and which we call 'mine': *material possessions, love objects* (both *people and things*), and *non-material possessions* (e.g. *beliefs, attitudes, and values*).

6.   Ethnocentrism can be seen as a facet of prejudice (an extreme attitude), whereby we judge the behaviour and values of members of other cultural/ethnic/national groups using the standards and values which derive from our own membership groups. Other groups are not merely *different* but *inferior* if they deviate from our own group's standards and values.

7.   *Cosmology* is the study of (or belief in) the universe as an ordered whole. *Ontology* is a branch of philosophy (specifically metaphysics) concerned with the essence of things or the nature of existence.

CHAPTER 28 (SCHACHTER & SINGER, 1962)

1. Ordinal: 4 is higher than 3, but not necessarily to the same degree as 2 is higher than 1, as would be the case on an interval scale. It would be difficult to justify the claim that the difference between 'a little irritated and angry' and 'quite irritated and angry' is equivalent to the difference between 'very irritated and angry' and 'extremely irritated and angry'. An interval scale has to be much more precise than this.

2. Mann–Whitney *U*: a test of difference, using independent samples and ordinal data.

3. Perhaps being told about side-effects (the wrong ones) produced a higher level of arousal, which made them more sensitive to environmental cues about the meaning of their arousal. This is, of course, quite consistent with the hypotheses.

4. The kinds of variables which would need to be taken into account are:
   (*i*)   general susceptibility to the influence of other people;
   (*ii*) general sensitivity to drugs such as epinephrine;
   (*iii*) appropriateness of the stooge's behaviour *re*: sex roles;
   (*iv*) perceived attractiveness of the opposite-sex stooge, and its effect on the general level of arousal.

5. Anger, if manifested, is most likely to be directed at the experimenter and his annoyingly personal questionnaire. But participants were afraid of endangering the extra points on their final exam by admitting their irritation to the experimenter's face or spoiling the questionnaire. Though willing to express anger when alone with the stooge (*behavioural indications*, which they didn't realize were being observed), they hesitated to do so on the self-rating and questionnaire (which the experimenter might see).
   Only after they had been debriefed were many participants willing to admit to the experimenter that they had been annoyed.

6. It means that the *direction* of the results is *not* being predicted. But from the three propositions, it would seem quite reasonable to make one-tailed (directional) predictions.

7. As a general principle, deception is to be discouraged. But this experiment depended on it. What is perhaps more worrying is the (apparent) lack of any medical checks/precautions given when an injection was actually being given.

8. (This is something you might like to debate in class, or it could be the topic for a seminar.)
   LeDoux (1998) describes introspection as a '. . . blurry window into the workings of the mind . . .' If there is one thing we do know from introspection it is that we are often in the dark about why we feel as we do. There is considerable experimental evidence that much emotional processing occurs (or can occur) unconsciously. Also, people often find their emotions puzzling, and he claims that:

   > . . . Consciously accessible appraisal processes cannot be the way, or at least not the only way, the emotional brain works . . .

More generally, the 'debate' concerns what has been called 'privileged access'. According to Johnson-Laird (1988), for example, there is always more going on cognitively ('in the mind') than is available to consciousness. In other words, the individual does *not* have privileged access to how s/he makes decisions, forms attitudes, or why s/he acts in a particular way. (This is relevant, in turn, to Freud's psychoanalytic theory, and to the free will/determinism debate: see Gross, 2003 [*Themes*, 2nd ed.].) According to Nisbett & Wilson (1977), there is no direct access to cognitive processes at all. Rather, we only have access to the ideas and inferences that are the *outputs* resulting from such processes – *not* the processes themselves.

CHAPTER 29 (DEMENT & KLEITMAN, 1957)

1. Although there is no particular reason for thinking that there are sex differences regarding REM/NREM sleep, it is always desirable to have roughly equal numbers of males and females. Perhaps more important is the very small number of participants; individual differences were found *re*: ability to recall dreams, for example, so much larger samples (or replications) are needed before any generalizations can be made.

2. These drugs are known to affect normal sleep activity (e.g. alcohol suppresses REM sleep without affecting NREM sleep).

3. With such a wide range of scores, the mean could be distorted (by the high and low scores). So the *median* might have been more appropriate.

4. This information may have influenced their dream reports: if they (through 'demand characteristics') believed that they were 'meant' to report 'proper dreams' after REM sleep, they might not have given honest and 'objective' accounts of their dreams.

5. This was a way of ensuring that the differential dream reports for REM/NREM sleep were not 'contaminated' by the sequence of awakening. If a common pattern emerged even when, for example, one participant had been told he/she had only been woken from REM sleep, this would be a better test of the genuine difference between the two kinds of sleep.

6. Sign Test: looking for a difference (e.g. between REM and NREM periods), repeated measures design (all participants were woken from REM and NREM sleep), nominal data (recalled dream/didn't recall dream).

7. (*i*)   Pearson's Product Moment (interval data, parametric test).
   (*ii*)   No, they were all $p = 0.05$ or less.

CHAPTER 30 (SPERRY, 1968)

1. The technical material is almost exclusively logical, but in stories many things happen at once; the sense of a story emerges through a combination of style, plot

and evoked images and feelings. So, language *in the form of stories* can stimulate the right hemisphere (Ornstein, 1986).

2. Mentally rotating the object in space: right hemisphere (spatial abilities). Counting the boxes: left hemisphere (numerical/mathematical/symbolic/analytic abilities).

3. Not only have they undergone a commissurotomy, but they have had intractable epilepsy (i.e. it could not be cured by any less drastic treatment, such as drugs, which they have probably been taking for many years).

4. Split-brain patients have not been randomly allocated to the 'commissurotomy condition'; it's difficult to find volunteers for such studies! So, participants are chosen because they already have a split brain.

5. When studying split-brain patients, their two hemispheres are being compared with each other (through targeting information to each hemisphere separately). Participant variables (such as their history, temperament, intelligence) are held constant, since it is the *same* participant whose two hemispheres are being compared.

6. (a)   This refers to the fact that some specific functions and processes are controlled by relatively precise and circumscribed cortical regions. For example, language is controlled partly by Broca's area in the frontal lobe (damage to which causes difficulties in *producing* language) and partly by Wernicke's area in the temporal lobe (damage to which causes difficulty in *understanding* language).

   (b)   For most people, these cortical areas are found in *one or other* cerebral hemisphere. Broca's and Wernicke's areas are usually found in the *left* hemisphere. So, language is *both* localized *and* lateralized.

CHAPTER 31 (ORNE, 1966)

1. (*i*)   'Correlate'.

   (*ii*)   A test of correlation (either Pearson or Spearman).

2. They are used to assess the *reliability* of the Scale ('Alternative or Parallel Forms'), i.e. the *consistency* with which the test measures whatever it is measuring. There should be a significant positive correlation between scores on the different Forms if the test is reliable.

3. (a)   As in any repeated measures design, participants are likely to learn something about the hypothesis/purpose of the experiment from being tested in both conditions.

   (b)   Counterbalancing can be used to reduce this (and other kinds of order effects): half are tested 'hypnotized'/'non-hypnotized'; half are tested 'non-hypnotized'/'hypnotized'.

   However, the difference in conditions (especially the instructions given) are *so* different (it is, after all, the instructions that are the independent variable), that this 'precaution' may be insufficient to prevent the results from being confounded.

4. See the answer to **2** (Chapter 1).
5. Some of the questions you may want to consider are:
    (*i*)   Is the experimenter displaying gratuitous sadism?
    (*ii*) Does it serve a valid scientific purpose?
    (*iii*) Does it contribute towards the clinical use of hypnosis?
    (*iv*) Are participants properly debriefed?
    [Your answers to these questions may, of course, depend on whether you adopt a state or non-state view.]

CHAPTER 32 (BLACKMORE, 1988)

1. Theories fall into two main categories: *dualist* (which distinguish between mind and brain) and *monist* (which claim that only mind *or* physical matter is real). The question of *interaction* only arises, of course, in the case of dualist theories.
    (*i*)   According to Descartes' seventeenth century dualist theory (which first introduced the mind-body problem into philosophy), the mind can influence the brain, but not vice-versa. While *epiphenomenologists* see the mind as a kind of by-product of the brain (the mind has no influence on the brain), *interactionists* see the influence as two-way. So, according to this definition, Descartes was not a true interactionist: he saw the 'contact' between the mind and brain as taking place in the pineal gland.
    (*ii*) *Psychophysical parallelists* are dualists who believe that there is *no* mind-brain interaction at all: mental and neural events are merely perfectly synchronized or correlated.
2. (*i*)   She claims that if tunnels and OBEs are a return to birth, people born by Caeserean should not have them (i.e. *none*). However, of the two groups (36 born by Caeserean, 218 not), the *same proportion* reported these experiences. She does not give precise numbers, but if just *one* out of 36 born by Caeserean had such experiences, this would appear to invalidate her argument (unless 'same proportion' means zero in both groups, but then no conclusion could be drawn either way).
    (*ii*)   Usually, when we refer to memory (and especially when speaking of autobiographical memory/AM), we are concerned with conscious awareness of representations of past experience (*explicit memory*). But there are other forms of memory that aren't conscious. For example, classical and operant conditioning (and other forms of learning) clearly take place from birth but don't require conscious awareness. Also, we often form representations of early traumatic experiences which aren't available to conscious recall or expression in language, and which may be startlingly accurate. Both these examples illustrate *implicit memory* (or *behavioural/enactive* memory: Mollon, 1998).
    (*iii*) In *The Primal Scream* (1973), Janov describes how birth represents the primary

trauma in an individual's life from which all others stem and which, therefore, is the source of all anxiety. The aim of *primal therapy* is to help people overcome the defences built up against the intolerable pain associated with birth by experiencing the pain while re-enacting the birth process.

Janov claims that the body 'remembers' the trauma, such that adult medical problems (e.g. asthma) may reflect the individual's difficult birth (e.g. difficulty in breathing/lack of oxygen). This is a form of *implicit remembering*.

3. They are all hallucinogenic drugs (*hallucinogens*), which produce most profound effects on consciousness (perception, thought processes, and emotion). For this reason, they are sometimes called *psychedelics* ('mind-expanding' or 'mind-manifesting').

   Mescaline comes from the peyote cactus, while *psilocybin* is obtained from the mushroom *Psilocybe mexicana* ('magic mushroom'). *Lysergic acid diethylamide* (LSD) is chemically synthesized (i.e. manufactured).

4. According to the *top-down* (or *conceptually-driven*) approach, we make *inferences* about what things are like, drawing on our knowledge and expectations of the world (based on past experience). An example is Gregory's theory of *indirect* perception ('things are often *not* what they seem').

   According to the *bottom-up* (or *data-driven*) approach, we perceive things *directly*, based on sensory information (sense-data) presented to us (*no* inferences are involved: 'things *are* as they seem'). An example is Gibson's theory of perception.

5. Grief/grieving is a good example. Several writers (e.g. Freud, Engel, Parkes) have described the characteristic stages or phases of the grieving process: every individual passes through the same invariant ('fixed') sequence of stages. Others (e.g. Ramsay & de Groot, 1977) identify *components* of grief: these are not separate, discrete stages, may not be successive, and not everyone will necessarily experience each and every one. Some tend to appear earlier or later in the grieving process, but each individual may display a unique pattern.

   Cross-cultural variations suggest the possibility that there is some underlying 'core' experience (which is universal), while the form of that experience (messenger, Jesus, Gabriel, 'just a light') may be influenced by cultural, religious and individual factors. In other words, NDEs may be 'real' (the 'underlying' core experience may be explicable in neuropsychological terms), but the particular form of the experience is shaped by non-physiological factors.

6. One answer is provided by the answer to **5**. It suggests that there is *more* to NDEs than the neuropsychological processes/events that Blackmore proposes: they cannot be simply or completely explained in terms of such processes, which makes her attempt to do so *reductionist*.

   The wider issue of the 'truth' of different models of reality is something that could usefully be discussed in a seminar/tutorial (see Gross *et al.*, 1997).

CHAPTER 33 (RAINE, BUCHSBAUM & LACASSE, 1997)

1. While the brain is a physical organ of the body (which can be prodded, cut open, and removed from the skull), the mind is a shorthand for all those processes and operations ('thinking') which we do *with* our brain but which is not identical with the brain. However, not everyone would accept this distinction, and philosophers and others have been debating the relationship between mind and brain (or the 'mind-body relationship') for thousands of years (see, for example, Gross, 2003).

2. According to the *dopamine hypothesis*, schizophrenia is caused by an excess of the neurotransmitter dopamine. However, it is possible that schizophrenic symptoms cause the excess dopamine in the brains of patients showing those symptoms.

3. Ethologists consider aggression to be instinctive in all species and important in the evolutionary development of the species, allowing individuals to adapt to their environment. However, as applied to humans, there are different types of aggression (some positive, such as self-defence, some negative), and violence is a term that would only be applied to an extreme form of human aggression in which a deliberate attempt is made to inflict serious physical injury on another person. In **Theoretical issues**, a distinction is made between *reactive* and *instrumental* aggression.

4. According to the *diathesis-stress model* (e.g. Zubin & Spring, 1977), schizophrenics inherit a predisposition (diathesis) towards developing schizophrenic symptoms. Whether or not they actually develop them depends on environmental stresses (which may be biological, social or familial).

5. In general terms, *internal validity* refers to the extent to which the outcome of an experiment can be attributed to the variables that have actually been controlled (as opposed to extraneous, uncontrolled, variables). Gabrielli's point is that sometimes it may be unclear whether differences in brain activity (as revealed by brain imaging) reflect differences in the nature of the tasks, rather than other aspects of the tasks (such as their duration or the amount of effort required).

6. To claim that APD can be explained solely in terms of abnormalities in certain brain systems would be *reductionist*, because it would be leaving out of the picture both the micro-level factors (molecules and neurons) and macro-level factors (social and cultural phenomena) which affect an entire person. In other words, a person (with or without APD) cannot be *reduced* to these brain systems (see Gross, 2001).

7. Set up a class/group debate on the rights and wrongs of screening children for potential future violence and making it compulsory for someone found to be a potential violent offender to undergo intervention programs.

8. If research shows that violent behaviour is largely determined by biological factors, and if violent crime statistics reveal that blacks and other minority groups are over-represented (which they are), then it could be concluded that blacks have a biological predisposition towards violence. Unless the reasons for their being over-represented are explored in terms of social and cultural factors, the role of biological factors will appear to be all-important.

REFERENCES

Aboud, F. (1988) *Children and prejudice.* Oxford: Blackwell.

Abramson, L.Y. and Martin, D.J. (1981) Depression and the causal inference process. In J.H. Harvey, W.J. Ickes and R.F. Kidd (eds.), *New Directions in Attitude Research,* Vol. 3, Hillsdale, NJ: Lawrence Erlbaum.

Abse, D. (1974) The Dogs of Pavlov, cited in S. Milgram (1974) *Obedience to Authority.* New York: Harper & Row.

Adorno, T.W., Frenkel-Brunswick, E., Levinson, D.J. and Sanford, R.N. (1950) *The Authoritarian Personality.* New York: Harper & Row.

Ainsworth, M.D.S., Blehar, M.C., Waters, E. and Wall, S. (1978) *Patterns of Attachment: a Psychological Study of the Strange Situation.* Hillsdale, NJ: Lawrence Erlbaum.

Aitchison, J. (1983) *The Articulate Mammal* (2nd ed.). London: Hutchinson University Library.

Aitchison, J. (1998) *The Articulate Mammal* (4th ed.). London: Routledge.

Alba, J.W. and Hasher, L. (1983) Is memory schematic? *Psychological Bulletin, 93,* 203–31.

Alcock, J.E. (1981) *Parapsychology: Science or magic?* Oxford: Pergamon.

Aldridge-Morris, R. (1989) *Multiple Personality: an exercise in deception.* Hove and London: LEA.

Alejandro-Wright, M. (1985) The child's conceptions of racial classification: a socio-cognitive developmental model. In M.B. Spencer, G.K. Brookins, & W.R. Allen (eds.) *Beginnings: The Social and Affective Development of Black Children.* Hillsdale, NJ: Erlbaum.

Allison, R.B. (1974) A new treatment approach for multiple personalities. *American Journal of Clinical Hypnosis, 17,* 15–32.

Allison, R.B. (1977) Diagnosis and treatment of multiple personality. Paper presented at American Psychiatric Association, Toronto, July 1977. Cited in J. Altrocchi (1980) *Abnormal Behaviour.* New York: Harcourt Brace Jovanovich.

Allison, R.B. (1978) On discovering multiplicity. *Sven Tidskr Hypnos, 2,* 4–8.

Allport, G.W. (1954) *The Nature of Prejudice.* Reading, MA: Addison-Wesley.

Allport, G.W. (1955) *Becoming: Basic Considerations for a Psychology of Personality.* New Haven: Yale University Press.

Allport, G.W. and Pettigrew, T.F. (1957) Cultural influences on the perception of movement: the trapezoidal illusion among Zulus. *Journal of Abnormal and Social Psychology, 55,* 104–13.

Altrocchi, J. (1980) *Abnormal Behaviour.* New York: Harcourt Brace Jovanovich.

American Psychiatric Association (1980) *Diagnostic and Statistical Manual of Mental Disorders* (3rd ed.). Washington, DC: American Psychiatric Association.

American Psychiatric Association (1987) *Diagnostic and Statistical Manual of Mental Disorders* (3rd ed. revised). Washington, DC: American Psychiatric Association.

American Psychiatric Association (1994) *Diagnostic and Statistical Manual of Mental Disorders* (4th ed.). Washington, DC: American Psychiatric Association.

Anderson, J.R. (1995) *Learning and Memory: An Integrated Approach.* New York: John Wiley & Sons.

Anderson, J.R. and Reder, L. (1979) An elaborative processing explanation of depth of processing. In L.S. Cermak and F.I.M. Craik (eds.), *Levels of Processing in Human Memory.* Hillsdale, NJ: Lawrence Erlbaum.

Apter, A. (1991) The problem of Who: multiple personality, personal identity and the double brain. *Philosophical Psychology, 4*(2), 219–48.

Apter, T. (2001) *The Myth of Maturity.* New York: Norton.

Archer, J. and Lloyd, B. (1985) *Sex and Gender.* Cambridge: Cambridge University Press.

Arnold, M.B. and Gasson, J.A. (1954) Feelings and emotions as dynamic factors in personality integration. In M.B. Arnold and S.J. Gasson (eds.), *The Human Person,* New York: Ronald.

Arnold, M.B. (1960) *Emotion and personality.* New York: Columbia University Press.

Aronson, E. (1988) *The Social Animal* (5th ed.). New York: Freeman.

Aronson, E. (1992) *The Social Animal* (6th ed.). New York: W.H. Freeman & Co.

Aronson, E. and Carlsmith, J.M. (1963) Effect of the severity of threat on the devaluation of forbidden behaviour. *Journal of Abnormal and Social Psychology, 6,* 584–8.

Aslin, R.N. (1987) Visual and auditory development in infancy. In J.D. Osofsky (ed.), *Handbook of Infant Development.* New York: Wiley.

Asperger, H. (1944) Die 'Autistischen Psychopathen' in Kindesalter. *Archiv für Psychiatrie und Nervenkrankheiter, 117,* 76–136.

Atkinson, R.C. and Shiffrin, R.M. (1968) Human memory: a proposed system and its control processes. In K.W. Spence and J.T. Spence (eds.), *The Psychology of Learning and Motivation* (Vol. 2). London: Academic Press.

Atkinson, R.C. and Shiffrin, R.M. (1971) The control of short-term memory. *Scientific American, 224,* 82–90.

Baddeley, A. (1995) *Memory.* In C.C. French and A.M. Colman (eds.), *Cognitive Psychology.* London: Longman.

Baddeley, A. (1997) *Human Memory: Theory and Practice* (revised ed.). Hove, E. Sussex: Psychology Press.

Baddeley, A.D. (1999) *Essentials of Human Memory.* Hove: Psychology Press.

Bailey, C.L. (1979) Mental illness – a logical misrepresentation? *Nursing Times,* May, 761–2.

Bailey, L.W. and Yates, J. (1996) *The near-death experience: A reader.* New York: Routledge.

Baldwin, J.A. (1992) The role of Black psychologists in Black liberation. In A.K.H.

Burlew, W.C. Banks, H.P. McAdoo and D.A.Y. Azibo (eds.), *African American Psychology: theory, research and practice*. Newbury Park, Ca.: Sage Publications.

Baltes, P.B. (1987) Theoretical propositions of life-span developmental psychology: on the dynamics of growth and decline. *Developmental Psychology, 23*, 611–26.

Bandura, A. (1965) Influence of model's reinforcement contingencies on the acquisition of imitative responses. *Journal of Personality and Social Psychology, 1*, 589–95.

Bandura, A. (1973) *Aggression: a social learning analysis*. Englewood Cliffs, NJ: Prentice–Hall.

Bandura, A. (1977) *Social Learning Theory*. Englewood Cliffs, NJ: Prentice–Hall.

Bandura, A. (1978) On paradigms and recycled ideologies. *Cognitive Therapy and Research, 2*, 79–104.

Bandura, A. (1986) *Social Foundations of Thought and Action*. Englewood Cliffs, NJ: Prentice–Hall.

Bandura, A. (1989) Social cognitive theory. In R. Vasta (ed.) *Six Theories of Child Development*. Greenwich, CT: JAI Press.

Bandura, A., Blanchard, E.B. and Ritter, B. (1969) Relative efficacy of desensitization and modelling approaches for inducing behavioural, affective and attitudinal changes. *Journal of Personality and Social Psychology, 13*, 173–99.

Bandura, A., Ross, D. and Ross, S.A. (1963a) Imitation of film-mediated aggressive models. *Journal of Abnormal and Social Psychology, 66*, 3–11.

Bandura, A., Ross, D. and Ross, S.A. (1963b) Vicarious reinforcement and imitative learning. *Journal of Abnormal and Social Psychology, 67*, 601–7.

Banuazizi, A. and Movahedi, S. (1975) Interpersonal dynamics in a simulated prison: a methodological analysis. *American Psychologist, 30*, 152–60.

Barber, T.X. (1969) *Hypnosis: a Scientific Approach*. New York: Van Nostrand.

Barber, T.X., Spanos, N.P. and Chaves, J.F. (1974) *Hypnotism: Imagination and Human Potentialities*. New York: Pergamon.

Barkham, M. and Shapiro, D. (1992) Response to Paul Kline. In W. Dryden and C. Feltham (eds.), *Psychotherapy and its Discontents*. Buckingham: Open University Press.

Barnes, R.D., Ickes, W.J. and Kidd, R. (1979) Effects of perceived intentionality and stability of another's dependency on helping behaviour. *Personality and Social Psychology Bulletin, 5*, 367–72.

Baron, R.A. (1977) *Human Aggression*. New York: Plenum.

Baron, R.A. and Byrne, D. (1991) *Social Psychology* (6th ed.). Boston: Allyn and Bacon.

Baron-Cohen, S. (1987) Autism and symbolic play. *British Journal of Developmental Psychology, 5*, 139–48.

Baron-Cohen, S. (1988) Social and pragmatic deficits in autism: Cognitive or affective? *Journal of Autism & Developmental Disorders, 18*, 379–402.

Baron-Cohen, S. (1989) The autistic child's theory of mind: a case of specific developmental delay. *Journal of Child Psychology & Psychiatry, 30*, 285–97.

Baron-Cohen, S. (1990) Autism: A specific cognitive disorder of 'mind-blindness'. *International Review of Psychiatry, 2*, 79–88.

Baron-Cohen, S. (1993) From attention-goal psychology to belief-desire psychology: The development of a theory of mind and its dysfunction. In S. Baron-Cohen, H. Tager-Flusberg, and D.J. Cohen (eds.), *Understanding other minds: Perspectives from Autism*. Oxford: Oxford University Press.

Baron-Cohen, S. (1995) Infantile Autism. In A.A. Lazarus and A.M. Colman (eds.), *Abnormal Psychology*, London: Longman.

Baron-Cohen, S., Jolliffe, T., Mortimore, C., and Robertson, M. (1997) Another advanced test of theory of mind: evidence from very high functioning adults with autism or Asperger Syndrome. *Journal of Child Psychology & Psychiatry, 38* (7), 813–22.

Baron-Cohen, S., Wheelwright, S., Hill, J., Raste, Y., and Plumb, I. (2001) The "Reading the Mind in the Eyes" Test Revised Version: A Study with Normal Adults, and Adults with Asperger Syndrome or High-functioning Autism. *Journal of Child Psychology & Psychiatry, 42* (2), 241–251.

Barry, H., Bacon, M.K. and Child, I.L. (1957) A cross-cultural survey of some sex differences in socialization. *Journal of Abnormal and Social Psychology, 55*, 327–32.

Bartlett, F.C. (1932) *Remembering*. Cambridge: Cambridge University Press.

Bartsch, K. and Wellman, H. M. (1995) *Children talk about the mind*. Oxford: Oxford University Press.

Batson, C.D. (1987) Prosocial motivation: Is it ever altruistic? In L. Berkowitz (ed.), *Advances in Experimental Social Psychology* (vol. 20). New York: Academic Press.

Batson, C.D. (1991) *The altruism question: Toward a social psychological answer*. Hillsdale, NJ: Lawrence Erlbaum.

Batson, C.D. (1995) Prosocial motivation: Why do we help others? In A. Tesser (ed.), *Advanced Social Psychology*. Boston: McGraw-Hill.

Batson, C.D. (2000) Altruism: Why do we help others? *Psychology Review, 7*(1), 2–5.

Baumrind, D. (1964) Some thoughts on ethics of research: after reading Milgram's behavioural study of obedience. *American Psychologist, 19*, 421–3.

Bean, P. (1979) Psychiatrists' assessments of mental illness. *British Journal of Psychiatry, 135*, 122–8.

Beaumont, J.G. (1988) *Understanding Neuropsychology*. Oxford: Blackwell.

Bedell, G. (2002) Why don't we just grow up? *Observer Review*, 3 Feb., 4.

Bee, H. (1989) *The Developing Child* (5th ed.). New York: Harper & Row.

Bee, H. (1994) *Lifespan Development*. New York: HarperCollins.

Bee, H. (2000) *The Developing Child* (9th ed.) Boston: Allyn & Bacon.

Belli, R.F. (1989) Influences of misleading postevent information: information interference and acceptance. *Journal of Experimental Psychology: General, 118*, 72–85.

Bekerian, D.A. and Bowers, J.M. (1983) Eye-witness testimony: were we misled? *Journal of Experimental Psychology: Learning, Memory and Cognition, 9*, 139–45.

Bem, D.J. (1965) An experimental analysis of self-persuasion. *Journal of Experimental and Social Psychology, 1*, 199–218.

Bem, D.J. (1967) Self-perception: an alternative interpretation of cognitive dissonance phenomena. *Psychological Review, 74*, 183–200.

Bem, D.J. (1972) Self-perception theory. In L. Berkowitz (ed.), *Advances in Experimental Social Psychology*, 6, New York: Academic Press.

Bem, S.L. (1975) Sex role adaptability: one consequence of psychological androgyny. *Journal of Personality and Social Psychology, 31*, 634–43.

Bem, S.L. (1977) On the utility of alternative procedures for assessing psychological androgyny. *Journal of Consulting and Clinical Psychology, 45*, 196–205.

Bem, S.L. (1979) Theory and measurement of androgyny: a reply to the Pedhazur-Tetenbaum and Locksley-Cotten critiques. *Journal of Personality and Social Psychology, 37*, 1047–54.

Bem, S.L. (1981) Gender schema theory: A cognitive account of sex-typing. *Psychological Review, 66*, 354–64.

Bem, S.L. (1984) Androgyny and gender schema theory: a conceptual and empirical integration. In R.A. Dienstbier (ed.), *Nebraska Symposium on Motivation.* Lincoln: University of Nebraska Press.

Bem, S.L. and Lenney, E. (1976) Sex-typing and the avoidance of cross-sex behaviour. *Journal of Personality and Social Psychology, 33*, 48–54.

Bennett, M., Dewberry, C., and Yeeles, C. (1991) A reassessment of the role of ethnicity in children's social perception. *Journal of Child Psychology & Psychiatry, 32* (6), 969–82.

Berger, M. (1973) Early experiences and other environmental factors – an overview. In H.J. Eysenck (ed.), *Handbook of Abnormal Psychology* (2nd ed.). London: Pitman.

Bergin, A.E. (1971) The evaluation of therapeutic outcomes. In A.E. Bergin and S.L. Garfield (eds), *Handbook of Psychotherapy and Behaviour Change: an Empirical Analysis.* New York: Wiley.

Bergin, A.E. and Lambert, M.J. (1978) The evaluation of therapeutic outcomes. In A.E. Bergin and S.L. Garfield (eds), *Handbook of Psychotherapy and Behaviour Change: an Empirical Analysis* (2nd ed.). New York: Wiley.

Berkowitz, L. (1969) The frustration–aggression hypothesis revisited. In L. Berkowitz (ed.), *Roots of Aggression: a re-examination of the frustration–aggression hypothesis.* New York: Atherton Press.

Berkowitz, L. (1993) *Aggression: its causes, consequences and control.* New York: McGraw-Hill.

Berry, J.W. (1969) On cross-cultural comparability. *International Journal of Psychology, 4*, 119–28.

Berry, J.W., Poortinga, Y.H., Segall, M.H. and Dasen, P.R. (1992) *Cross-cultural Psychology: research and applications.* New York: Cambridge University Press.

Bettelheim, B. (1960) *The Informed Heart.* New York: Free Press.

Bickman, L. (1974) The social power of a uniform. *Journal of Applied Social Psychology, 1*, 47–61.

Billig, M. and Tajfel, H. (1973) Social categorization and similarity in intergroup behaviour. *European Journal of Social Psychology, 3*, 27–52.

Blackmore, S. (1993) *Dying to live: Science and the near-death experience.* London: Grafton.

Blackmore, S. (1995) Parapsychology. In A.M. Colman (ed.), *Controversies in Psychology*. London: Longman.

Blackmore, S. (1997) In search of the Paranormal. *Psychology Review, 3* (3), 2–6, Feb.

Blair, R.J.R., Morris, J.S., Frith, C.D., Perrett, D.I., and Dolan, R.J. (1999) Dissociable neural responses to facial expressions of sadness and anger. *Brain, 122*, 883–893.

Blakemore, C. (1988) *The Mind Machine*. London: BBC Books.

Blewitt, P. (1983) *Dog* versus *collie*. Vocabulary in speech to young children. *Developmental Psychology, 19*, 602–9.

Bliss, E. (1986) *Multiple Personality, Allied Disorders and Hypnosis*. New York: Oxford University Press.

Boas, F. (1927) Primitive art, cited in R. Serpell (1974) *Culture's Influence on Behaviour*. London: Methuen.

Bogen, J.E. (1969) The other side of the brain. In R. Ornstein, *The Psychology of Consciousness* (2nd revised ed.). Harmondsworth: Penguin.

Bogen, J.E. and Gazzaniga, M.S. (1965) cited in J.E. Bogen (1969).

Boring, E.G. (1966) Introduction. In C.E.M. Hansel (Ed) *ESP: A scientific evaluation*. New York: Scribners.

Botwinick, J. (1984) *Ageing and behaviour* (3rd ed.). NY: Springer.

Bouchard, T.J., Lykken, D.T., McGue, M., Segal, N.L., Tellegen, A. (1990) Sources of human psychological differences: the Minnesota study of twins reared apart. *Science, 250*, 223–8.

Bower, G.H. and Karlin, M.B. (1974) Depth of processing pictures of faces and recognition memory. *Journal of Experimental Psychology, 103*, 751–7.

Bowers, K.S. (1983) *Hypnosis for the Seriously Curious*. NY: Norton.

Bowers, K.S. and Davidson, T.M. (1991) A neo-disassociative critique of Spanos's Social Psychological model of hypnosis. In S.J. Lynn and J.W. Rhue (eds.). *Theories of hypnosis: Current models and perspectives*. Buffalo, NY: Prometheus.

Bowlby, J. (1951) *Maternal Care and Mental Health*. Geneva: World Health Organization.

Bowlby, J. (1969) *Attachment and Loss*, Vol. 1: Attachment, Harmondsworth: Penguin.

Bowlby, J. (1973) *Attachment and Loss*, Vol. 2: Separation-Anxiety and Anger, Harmondsworth: Penguin.

Bowler, D.M. (1992) 'Theory of mind' in Asperger's syndrome. *Journal of Child Psychology & Psychiatry, 33*, 877–93.

Boyd, R. and Richardson, J. (1985) *Culture and the evolution process*. Chicago: University of Chicago Press.

Bradbury, T.N. and Fincham, F.D. (1990) Attributions in marriage: Review and critique. *Psychological Bulletin, 107*, 3–33.

Bradding, A. (1995) Questions of identity in adolescents of mixed parentage. *Psychology Teaching*, New Series (No. 4), 53–66, Nov.

Brand, C. (1996) *The g Factor: General Intelligence and its Implications*. Chichester: Wiley.

Bransford, J.D., Franks, J.J., Morris, C.D. and Stein, B.S. (1979) Some general constraints on learning and memory research. In L.S. Cermak and F.I.M. Craik (eds.), *Levels of Processing in Human Memory*. Hillsdale, NJ: Lawrence Erlbaum.

Brehm, S. (1992) *Intimate Relationships* (2nd ed.). New York: McGraw-Hill.

Broadbent, D. (1958) *Perception and Communication*, Oxford: Pergamon.

Brockes, E. (2001) The experiment. *Guardian G2*, 16 Oct., 2–3.

Bromley, D.B. (1988) *Human Ageing – An Introduction to Gerontology* (3rd ed.). Harmondsworth: Penguin.

Bronfenbrenner, U. (1979) *The Ecology of Human Development: Experiments by Nature and Design*. Cambridge, MA: Harvard University Press.

Brosnan, M.J. (1998) The implications for academic attainment of perceived gender-appropriateness upon spatial task performance. *British Journal of Educational Psychology, 68,* 203–15.

Broverman, I.K., Vogel, S.R., Broverman, D.M., Clarkson, F.E. and Rosenkrantz, P.S. (1972) Sex-role stereotypes: a current appraisal. *Journal of Social Issues, 28,* 59–78.

Brown, H. (1985) *People, Groups and Society*. Milton Keynes: Open University Press.

Brown, R. (1965) *Social Psychology*. New York: Free Press.

Brown, R. (1970) The first sentences of child and chimpanzee. In R.Brown (ed.), *Psycholinguistics*. New York: Free Press.

Brown, R. (1973) *A First Language*. London: Allen and Unwin.

Brown, R. (1986) *Social Psychology* (2nd ed.). New York: Free Press.

Brown, R. (1988) *Group Processes*. Oxford: Blackwell.

Brown, R. (1996) Intergroup relations. In M. Hewstone, W. Stroebe, and G.M. Stephenson (Eds) *Introduction to Social Psychology* (2nd ed.). Oxford: Blackwell.

Bruce, V. (1998) Fleeting images of shade: Identifiying people caught on video. *The Psychologist, 11* (7), 331–7, July.

Bruner, J.S. (1983) *Children's talk: Learning to use language*. Oxford: Oxford University Press.

Bryant, P. (1998) Cognitive Development. In M. Eysenck (ed.). *Psychology: an integrated approach*. Essex: Adison Wesley Longman Ltd.

Brunswick, E. (1956) *Perception and the Representative Design of Psychological Experiments*. Berkeley: University of California Press.

Buber, M. (1937) *I and Thou*. Edinburgh: T. and T. Clark.

Buehler, R., Griffin, D., and Ross, M. (1995) It's about time: optimistic predictions in work and love. In W. Stroebe and M. Hewstone (eds.), *European Review of Social Psychology* (vol. 6). Chichester: J. Wiley.

Burks, B.S. (1928) The relative influence of nature and nurture upon mental development: a comparative study of foster parent–foster child resemblance and true parent–true child resemblance. *Yearbook of the National Society for the Study of Education, 27,* 219–316.

Burlew, A.K.H., Banks, H., McAdoo, H.P. and Azibo, D.A.Y. (eds.) (1992) *African American Psychology: theory, research and practice*. Newbury Park, Ca.: Sage Publications.

Burley, P.M. and McGuiness, J. (1977) Effects of social intelligence on the Milgram paradigm. *Psychological Reports, 40,* 767–70.

Burr, V. (2002) *The Person in Social Psychology*. Hove: Psychology Press.

Bushman, B. (1984) Perceived symbols of authority and their influence on compliance. *Journal of Applied Social Psychology, 14,* 501–8.

Buss, A.H. (1971) Aggression pays. In J.L. Singer (ed.), *The Control of Aggression and Violence.* New York: Academic Press.

Byrne, D. (1969) Attitudes and attraction. In L. Berkowitz (ed.), *Advances in Experimental Social Psychology,* 4, New York: Academic Press.

Caine, T.M. and Hope, K. (1967) *Manual of the Hysteroid–Obsessoid Questionnaire.* London: University of London Press.

Campbell, D.T. (1964) Distinguishing differences of perception from failures of communication in cross-cultural studies. In F.S.C. Northrop and H.H. Livingstone (eds.), *Cross-cultural Understanding.* New York and London: Harper and Row.

Campbell, H.J. (1973) *The Pleasure Areas.* London: Eyre Methuen.

Cannon, W.B. (1927) The James-Lange theory of emotions: a critical examination and an alternative theory. *American Journal of Psychology, 39,* 106–24.

Carlsmith, J.M., Collins, B.E. and Helmreich, R.L. (1966) Studies in forced compliance: 1. The effect of pressure for compliance on attitude change produced by face-to-face role-playing and anonymous essay-writing. *Journal of Personality and Social Psychology, 4,* 1–13.

Carlson, N.R. and Buskist, W. (1997) *Psychology: The Science of Behaviour* (5th ed.). Needham Hts., MA: Allyn & Bacon.

Carlson, N.R. (1992) *Foundations of Physiological Psychology* (2nd ed.). Needham Heights, MA: Allyn and Bacon.

Carroll, D.W. (1986) *Psychology of Language,* Monterey, CA: Brooks/Cole Publishing Company.

Ceci, S.J., Huffman, M.L.C., Smith, E., and Loftus, E.F. (1994) Repeatedly thinking about a non-event: Source misattributions among preschoolers. *Consciousness & Cognition, 3,* 388–407.

Chen, H., Yates, B.T., and McGinnies, E. (1988) Effects of involvement on observers' estimates of consensus, distinctiveness, and consistency. *Personality & Social Psychology Bulletin, 14,* 468–78.

Chisolm, K., Carter, M.C., Ames, E.W., and Morison, S.J. (1995) Attachment security and indiscriminately friendly behaviour in children adopted from Romanian orphanages. *Development & Psychopathology, 7,* 283–294.

Chomsky, N. (1957) *Syntactic Structures.* The Hague: Mouton.

Chomsky, N. (1959) Review of Skinner's *Verbal Behaviour. Langauge, 35,* 26–58.

Chomsky, N. (1965) *Aspects of the Theory of Syntax.* Cambridge, MA: MIT Press.

Chomsky, N. (1968) *Language and Mind.* New York: Harcourt Brace Jovanovich.

Chomsky, N. (1980) *Rules and Representations.* Oxford: Blackwell.

Christensen, A. and Jacobson, N.S. (1994) Who (or what) can do psychotherapy: The status and challenge of non professional therapies. *Psychological Science, 5,* 8–14.

Churchland, P. and Sejnowski, T.J. (1988) Perspectives on Cognitive Neuroscience. *Science, 242*(4879), 741–745.

Chwalisz, K., Diener, E., and Gallagher, D. (1988) Autonomic arousal feedback and emotional experience: evidence from the spinal cord injured. *Journal of Personality & Social Psychology, 54,* 820–828.

Clamp, A. and Russell, J. (1998) *Comparative Psychology.* London: Hodder & Stoughton.

Claridge, G. (1987) Schizophrenia and human individuality. In C. Blakemore and S. Greenfield (eds.), *Mindwaves.* Oxford: Blackwell.

Clarke, A. & Clarke, A. (2000) *Early Experience and the Life Path.* London: Jessica Kingsley.

Clark, K. and Clark, M. (1939) The development of consciousness of self in the emergence of racial identification in Negro pre-school children. *Journal of Social Psychology, 10,* 591–7.

Clark, K. and Clark, M. (1947) Racial identification and preference in Negro children. In T. Newcomb and E. Hartley (eds.), *Readings in Social Psychology.* New York: Holt.

Clark, M.L. (1992) Racial Group Concept and Self-Esteem in Black Children. In A.K.H. Burlew, W.C. Banks, H.P. McAdoo, and D.A.Y. Azibo (eds.), *African American Psychology: Theory, Research and Practice.* Newbury Park, CA: Sage Publications.

Clarke, A.D.B. (1972) Comment on Koluchova's 'Severe deprivation in twins: a case study'. *Journal of Child Psychology and Psychiatry, 13,* 103–6.

Clarke, A.M. and Clarke, A.D.B. (1976) *Early Experience: Myth and Evidence.* London: Open Books.

Clarke-Stewart, A. (1973) Interactions between mothers and their young children: Characteristics and consequences. *Monographs of the Society for Research in Child Development, 38* (Whole No. 153).

Clifton, A.K., McGrath, D. and Wick, B. (1976) Stereotypes of women: a single category? *Sex Roles, 2,* 135–148.

Cohen, D. (1995) Now we are one, or two, or three . . . *New Scientist, 146,* 14–15, June 17.

Cohen, G. (1975) Cerebral apartheid: a fanciful notion? *New Behaviour, 18* (September), 458–61.

Cohen, G. (1986) Everyday memory. In G. Cohen, M.W. Eysenck and M.E. Le Voi, *Memory: A Cognitive Approach.* Milton Keynes: Open University.

Cohen, G. (1993) Everyday memory and memory systems: The experimental approach. In G. Cohen, G. Kiss, & M. Levoi, *Memory: Current Issues* (2nd ed.). Buckingham: Open University Press.

Cohen, S. and Taylor, L. (1972) *Psychological Survival: the experience of long-term imprisonment.* Harmondsworth: Penguin.

Colman, A.M. (1987) *Facts, Fallacies and Frauds in Psychology.* London: Unwin Hyman.

Colman, A.M. (1995) Introduction. In A.M. Colman (ed.), *Controversies in Psychology.* London: Longman.

Concar, D. (1998) You are feeling very, very sleepy. *New Scientist, 159* (2141), 26–31, July.

Colligan, M.J., Frockt, W. and Tasto, D.L. (1978) Frequency of sickness, absence and worksite clinic visits as function of shift. *Journal of Environmental Pathology, 2,* 125–48.

Condon, W.S., Ogston, W.D. and Pacoe, L.V. (1969) Three faces of Eve revisited: a study of transient microstabismus. *Journal of Abnormal Psychology, 74,* 618–20.

Constantinople, A. (1979) Sex role acquisition: in search of the elephant. *Sex Roles, 5,* 121–33.

Coolican, H. (1990) *Research Methods and Statistics in Psychology.* London: Hodder and Stoughton.

Coolican, H. (1994) *Research Methods and Statistics in Psychology* (2nd ed.). London: Hodder & Stoughton.

Coolican, H. (1999) *Research Methods and Statistics in Psychology* (3rd ed.). London: Hodder & Stoughton.

Cooper, J.E. (1983) Diagnosis and the diagnostic process. In M. Shepherd and O.L. Zangwill (eds.), *Handbook of Psychiatry: 1. General Psychopathology.* Cambridge: Cambridge University Press.

Cooper, J. and Axsom, D. (1972) Effort justification in psychotherapy. In G. Weary and H.K. Mirels (eds.), *Integrations of Clinical and Social Psychology.* New York: Oxford University Press.

Cooper, J. and Fazio, R.H. (1984) A new look at dissonance theory. In L. Berkowitz (ed.), *Advances in Experimental Social Psychology,* Vol. 15. New York: Academic Press.

Cooper, R.P. and Aslin, R.N. (1990) Preference for infant-directed speech in the first month after birth. *Child Development, 61,* 1584–95.

Corbett, L. (1996) *The Religious Function of the Psyche.* London: Routledge.

Coren, S. (1992) *Left Hander.* London: John Murray.

Cornwell, D. and Hobbs, S. (1976) The strange saga of Little Albert, *New Society* (March), 602–4.

Cox, T. (1978) *Stress.* Basingstoke: Macmillan.

Craig, G.J. (1992) *Human Development* (6th ed.). Englewood Cliffs, NJ: Prentice–Hall.

Craik, F.I.M. and Tulving, E. (1975) Depth of processing and the retention of words in episodic memory. *Journal of Experimental Psychology: General, 104,* 268–94.

Crellin, C. (1998) Philosophy and the practice of therapy. *The Psychologist, 11* (4), 176–8, April.

Crews, F. (1997) *The Memory Wars: Freud's Legacy in Dispute.* London: Granta.

Crick, F. and Mitchison, G. (1983) The function of REM Sleep. *Nature, 304,* 111–14.

Crick, F. and Mitchison, G. (1986) REM sleep and neural nets. *Journal of Mind & Behaviour, 7,* 229–49.

Crocker, J. and Major, B. (1989) Social stigma and self-esteem: The self-protecting properties of stigma. *Psychological Review, 96,* 608–30.

Croyle, R.T. and Cooper, J. (1983) Dissonance arousal: physiological evidence. *Journal of Personality and Social Psychology, 45,* 782–91.

Croyle, R.T. and Loftus, E.F. (1995) Psychology and the Law. In A.M. Colman (ed.), *Controversies in Psychology.* London: Longman.

Cumberbatch, G. (1995) *Media Violence: Research Evidence and Policy Implications: Report prepared for the Council of Europe Directorate of Human Rights.* Strasbourg: The Council of Europe.

Curtiss, S. (1977) *Genie: a Psycholinguistic Study of a Modern-day 'Wild Child'.* London: Academic Press.

Dalgleish, T. (1998) Emotion. In M. Eysenck (ed.), *Psychology: an integrated approach.* Harlow: Addison Wesley/Longman Ltd.

Damasio, A.R. (1996) *Descartes' Error: Emotion, Reason, and the Human Brain.* London: Papermac.

Damasio, A.R. (2000) A Neural Basis for Sociopathy. *Archives of General Psychiatry, 57* (2) (see http://archpsyc.ama-assn.org/issues/v57n2/rfull/yem9457. html)

Davey, A.G. and Mullin, P.N. (1982) Inter-ethnic friendship in British primary schools. *Educational Research, 24,* 83–92.

Davis, K. (1940) Extreme social isolation of a child. *American Journal of Sociology, 45,* 554–65.

Davis, K. (1947) Final note on a case of extreme isolation. *American Journal of Sociology, 52,* 432–7.

Davison, G.C. and Neale, J.M. (1994) *Abnormal Psychology* (6th ed.). New York: John Wiley & Sons.

Davison, G.C. and Neale, J.M. (2001) *Abnormal Psychology* (8th ed.). New York: John Wiley & Sons Inc.

Dawes, R.M. (1994) *House of cards.* New York: Free Press.

DeCasper, A.J. and Spence, M. (1986) Newborns prefer a familiar story over an umfamiliar one. *Infant Behaviour & Development, 9,* 133–50.

Deese, J. (1972) *Psychology as Art and Science.* New York: Harcourt, Brace Jovanovich.

Dement, W. (1960) The effect of dream deprivation. *Science, 131,* 1705–7.

Dement, W.C. (1994) History of sleep physiology and medicine. In M.H. Kryger, T. Roth., & W.C. Dement (eds.) *Principles and Practice of Sleep Medicine.* Philadelphia: Saunders.

Denker, R. (1946) Results of treatment of psychoneuroses by the general practitioner. A follow-up study of 500 cases. *New York State Journal of Medicine, 46,* 2164–6.

Deregowski, J.B. (1968) Pictorial recognition in subjects from a relatively pictureless environment. *African Social Research, 5,* 356–64.

Deregowski, J.B. (1969) Preference for chain-type drawings in Zambian domestic servants and primary school children. *Psychologica Africana, 82,* 9–13.

Deregowski, J.B. (1970) A note on the possible determinants of split representation as an artistic style. *International Journal of Psychology, 5,* 21–6.

Deregowski, J.B., Muldrow, E.S. and Muldrow, W.F. (1972) Pictorial recognition in a remote Ethiopian population. *Perception, 1,* 417–25.

Deregowski, J.B. (1989) Real space and represented space: Cross-cultural perspectives. *Behaviour & Brain Sciences, 12,* 51–119.

Devlin Report (1976) *Report on the Secretary of State for the Home Department of the Departmental Committee on Evidence of Identification in Criminal Cases.* London: HMSO.

Donaldson, M. (1978) *Children's Minds.* London: Fontana.

Dovidio, J.F., Piliavin, J.A., Gaertner, S.L., Schroeder, D.A. and Clark, R.D. (1991) The arousal: cost–reward model and the process of intervention. In M.S. Clark (ed.),

Prosocial Behaviour: review of personality and social psychology (vol. 12). Newbury Park, CA: Sage Publications.

Doyle, J. and Paludi, M. (1991) *Sex and gender: The human experience.* Dubuque, IA: Wm. C. Brown.

Duck, S. (1991) *Friends for Life* (2nd ed.). London: Harvester Wheatsheaf.

Duck, S. (1992) *Human Relationships* (2nd ed.). London: Sage Publications.

Duncan, H.F., Gourlay, N. and Hudson, W. (1973) *A Study of Pictorial Perception among Bantu and White Primary School Children in South Africa.* Johannesburg: Witwatersrand University Press.

Dunn, J. (1994) Changing minds and changing relationships. In C. Lewis and P. Mitchell (eds.), *Children's early understanding of mind: Origins and development.* Hove: Lawrence Erlbaum Associates.

Durkin, K. (1995) *Developmental Social Psychology: From infancy to old age.* Oxford: Blackwell.

Duval, S. and Wicklund, R.A. (1973) Effects of objective self-awareness on attributions of causality. *Journal of Experimental Social Psychology, 9,* 17–31.

Duyme, M. and Capron, C. (1992) Socioeconomic status and IQ: what is the meaning of the French adoption studies? *European Bulletin of Cognitive Psychology, 12,* 585–604.

Eagly, A.H. (1987) *Sex Differences in Social Behaviour: a Social-Role Interpretation.* London: Lawrence Erlbaum.

Ebbinghaus, H. (1885) *Über das Gedachtnis.* Leipzig: H.Ruyer and C.E. Bussenius. Published in translation (1913) as *Memory.* New York: Teachers' College Press.

Edley, N. and Wetherell, M. (1995) *Men in Perspective: practice, power and identity.* Hemel Hempstead: Prentice-Hall/Harvester Wheatsheaf.

Eimas, P.D., Siqueland, E.R., Jusczyck, P., and Vogorito, J. (1971) Speech perception in infants. *Science, 171,* 303–6.

Eiser, J.R. and van der Pligt, J. (1988) *Attitudes and Decisions.* London: Routledge.

Eliot, L. (1999) *Early Intelligence.* Harmondsworth: Penguin.

Elms, A.C. (1972) *Social Psychology and Social Relevance.* Boston: Little, Brown.

Empson, J. (1989) *Sleep and Dreaming.* London: Faber and Faber.

Empson, J. (1993) *Sleep and Dreaming* (2nd, revised ed.). Hemel Hempstead: Harvester Wheatsheaf.

Endicott, J. and Spitzer, R.L. (1978) A diagnostic interview: the schedule for affective disorders and schizophrenia. *Archives of General Psychiatry, 35,* 837–44.

Engel, M., Nechlin, H., and Arkin, A.M. (1975) Aspects of mothering: Correlates of the cognitive development of black male infants in the second year of life. In A. Davids (ed.), *Child personality and psychopathology: Current topics* (vol. 2). New York: Wiley.

Erdelyi, M.H. (1996) *The Recovery of Unconscious Memories, Hypermnesia and Reminiscence.* Chicago: University of Chicago Press.

Erikson, E.H. (1950) *Childhood and Society.* New York: Norton.

Erikson, E.H. (1959) *Young Man Luther: a study in psychoanalysis and history.* London: Faber.

Erikson, E.H. (1963) *Childhood and Society* (2nd ed.). New York: Norton.

Erikson, M. (1968) The inhumanity of ordinary people. *International Journal of Psychiatry, 6,* 278–9.

Erlenmeyer-Kimling, L. and Jarvik, L.F. (1963) Genetics and intelligence: a review. *Science, 142,* 1477–9.

Esterson, A. (1998) Jeffrey Masson and Freud's seduction theory: a new fable based on old myths. *History of the Human Sciences, 11* (1), 1–21.

Esterson, A. (2001) The mythologizing of psychoanalytic history: deception and self-deception in Freud's accounts of the seduction episode. *History of Psychiatry, xii,* 329–352.

Etzioni, A. (1968) A model of significant research. *International Journal of Psychiatry, 6,* 279–80.

Evans-Bush, N. and Greyson, B. (1996) Distressing near-death experiences. In L.W. Bailey & J. Yates (eds.) *The Near Death Experience: A Reader.* New York: Villard.

Eysenck, H.J. (ed.) (1960) *Behaviour Therapy and the Neuroses.* Oxford: Pergamon.

Eysenck, H.J. (1973) *The Inequality of Man.* London: Temple Smith.

Eysenck, H.J. (1976) The learning theory model of neurosis – a new approach. *Behaviour Research and Therapy, 14,* 251–67.

Eysenck, H.J. (1985) *Decline and Fall of the Freudian Empire.* London: Viking Press.

Eysenck, H.J. (1992) The outcome problem in psychotherapy. In W. Dryden and C. Feltham (eds.), *Psychotherapy and its Discontents,* Buckingham: Open University Press.

Eysenck, H.J. and Rachman, S. (1965) *The Causes and Cure of Neurosis.* London: RKP.

Eysenck, M.W. (1979) Depth, elaboration and distinctiveness. In L.S. Cermak and F.I.M. Craik (eds.), *Levels of Processing in Human Memory.* Hillsdale, NJ: Lawrence Erlbaum.

Eysenck, M.W. (1984) *A Handbook of Cognitive Psychology.* London: Lawrence Erlbaum.

Eysenck, M.W. (1986) Working memory. In G. Cohen, M.W. Eysenck and M.E. Le Voi, *Memory: A Cognitive Approach.* Milton Keynes: Open University.

Eysenck, M. (1998) Memory. In M. Eysenck (ed.), *Psychology: an integrated approach.* Harlow: Addison Wesley Longman Ltd.

Eysenck, M. W. and Keane, M.J. (1995) *Cognitive Psychology: A Student's Handbook* (3rd ed.). Hove: Erlbaum.

Eysenck, M.W. and Keane, M.T. (2000) *Cognitive Psychology: A Student's Handbook* (4th ed.). Hove: Psychology Press.

Fahy, T.A. (1988) The diagnosis of multiple personality disorder: A critical review. *British Journal of Psychiatry, 153,* 597–606.

Fairbairn, G. (1987) Responsibility, respect for persons and psychological change. In S. Fairbairn and G. Fairbairn (eds.), *Psychology, Ethics and Change.* London: RKP.

Fairbairn, G. and Fairbairn, S. (1987) Introduction: psychology, ethics and change. In S. Fairbairn and G. Fairbairn (eds.), *Psychology, Ethics and Change.* London: RKP.

Fantz, R.L. (1961) The origin of form perception. *Scientific American, 204,* 66–72.

Farah, M.J. and Aguirre, G.K. (1999) Imaging visual recognition: PET and fMRI studies of the functional anatomy of human visual recognition. *Trends in Cognitive Sciences, 3,* 179–186.

Faris, J.C. (1972) *Nuba Personal Art.* London: Duckworth.

Farrar, M.J. (1992) Negative evidence and grammatical morpheme acquisition. *Developmental Psychology, 28,* 90–8.

Farrar, S. (2002) Screws get on with cons in TV experiment. *Times Higher Education Supplement,* 1 Feb., 3.

Fazio, R.H., Zanna, M.P. and Cooper, J. (1977) Dissonance and self-perception: an integrative view of each theory's major domain of application. *Journal of Experimental and Social Psychology, 13,* 464–79.

Fenwick, P. (1997) Is the near-death experience only N-methyl-D-aspartate blocking? *Journal of Near-Death Studies, 16,* 43–53.

Feighner, J.P., Robins, E., Guze, S.B., Woodruff, R.A., Winokur, G. and Munoz, R. (1972) Diagnostic criteria for use in psychiatric research. *Archives of General Psychiatry, 26,* 57–63.

Fernald, A. (1989) Intonation and communicative intent in mothers' speech to infants: is the melody the message? *Child Development, 60,* 1479–510.

Fernald, A. and Kuhl, P. (1985) Acoustic determinants of infant preference for motherese speech. *Infant Behaviour & Development, 10,* 279–93.

Fernald, A. and Mazzie, C. (1991) Prosody and focus in speech to infants and adults. *Developmental Psychology, 27,* 209–221.

Fernald, D. (1997) *Psychology,* Upper Saddle River, NJ: Prentice-Hall Inc.

Fernando, S. (1991) *Mental Health, Race and Culture.* Basingstoke: Macmillan/Mind Publications.

Ferry, G. (1984) A sense of purpose: behaviour and evolution. In G.Ferry (ed.), *The Understanding of Animals.* Oxford: Blackwell and New Scientist.

Festinger, L. (1954) A theory of social comparison processes. *Human Relations, 7,* 117–40.

Festinger, L. (1957) *A Theory of Cognitive Dissonance.* New York: Harper and Row.

Field, T. (1985) Neonatal perception of people: maturational and individual differences. In T.M. Field and N.A. Fox (eds.), *Social Perception in Infants.* Norwood, NJ: Ablex.

Fillon, M. (2000) Their Brains Made Them Do It: Do Abnormalities in Grey Matter Cause Violence? http://webmd.lycos.com/content/article/1728.59230

Fishbein, M. and Ajzen, I. (1975) *Belief, Attitude, Intention, and Behaviour: an introduction to theory and research.* Reading, MA.: Addison-Wesley.

Fiske, S. and Taylor, S. (1991) *Social Cognition* (2nd ed.). New York: McGraw-Hill.

Fonagy, P., Steele, H., Steele, M. and Holder, J. (1997) Attachment and Theory of Mind: Overlapping Constructs? In *Bonding and Attachment: Current Issues in Research and Practice,* Occasional Parers, No. 14, Association for Child Psychology & Psychiatry.

Fontana, D. (1982) Intelligence. In D. Fontana (ed.), *Psychology for Teachers.* London and Basingstoke: BPS and Macmillan Press.

Foulkes, D. (1960) Dream reports from different stages of sleep. *Journal of Abnormal & Social Psychology, 65,* 14–25.

Foulkes, D. (1993) Data constraints on theorising about dream function. In A. Moffitt,

A. Kramer, & R. Hoffmann (eds.) *The functions of dreaming*. New York: State University of New York Press.

Fox, D. and Prilleltensky, I. (1997) Introduction. In D. Fox and I. Prilleltensky (eds.), *Critical Psychology: An Introduction*. London: Sage.

Freedman, J. (1963) Attitudinal effects of inadequate justification. *Journal of Personality, 31*, 371–85.

Freedman, J. (1965) Long-term behavioural effects of cognitive dissonance. *Journal of Experimental and Social Psychology, 1*, 145–55.

Freud, S. (1905) *Three Essays on the Theory of Sexuality*, Pelican Freud Library, Vol. 7. Harmondsworth: Penguin.

Freud, S. (1922) *Postscript (to the Case of Little Hans)*, Pelican Freud Library, Vol. 8. Harmondsworth: Penguin.

Frijda, N. and Jahoda, G. (1966) On the scope and methods of cross-cultural psychology. *International Journal of Psychology, 1*, 109–27.

Frijda, N.H. (1988) The laws of emotion. *American Psychologist, 43*, 349–58.

Frith, U. (1989) *Autism: Explaining the enigma*. Oxford: Basil Blackwell.

Frith, U. (1993) Autism. *Scientific American, 268* (6), 78–84, June.

Fromm, E. (1970) *The Crisis of Psychoanalysis*. Harmondsworth: Penguin.

Fundudis, T. (1997) Young Children's Memory: How Good Is It? How Much Do We Know About It? *Child Psychology & Psychiatry Review, 2* (4), 150–8.

Gabrielli, J.D.E. (1993) Cognitive neuroscience of human memory. *Annual Reviews of Psychology, 49*, 87–115.

Gallagher, S. (1998) The Neuronal Platonist: Michael Gazzaniga in conversation with Shaun Gallagher. *Journal of Consciousness Studies, 5* (5–6), 706–717.

Gardner, B.T. and Gardner, R.A. (1971) Two-way communication with an infant chimpanzee. In A. Schrier and F. Stollnitz (eds.), *Behaviour of Non-Human Primates*, Vol. 4. New York: Academic Press.

Gardner, B.T. and Gardner, R.A. (1975) Evidence for sentence constituents in the early utterances of child and chimp. *Journal of Experimental Psychology: General, 104*, 244–67.

Gardner, B.T. and Gardner, R.A. (1980) Two comparative psychologists look at language acquisition. In K. Nelson, *Children's Language*, Vol. 2. New York: Gardner Press.

Gardner, H. (1993) *Frames of Mind* (2nd ed.). London: Fontana.

Gardner, H., Kornhaber, M.L., and Wake, W.K. (1996) *Intelligence: Multiple Perspectives*. Orlando, FA: Harcourt Brace & Co.

Gardner, R.A. and Gardner, B.T. (1978) Comparative psychology and language acquisition. In K. Salzinger and F. Denmark (eds.), *Psychology: the State of the Art, Annals of the New York Academy of Sciences, 309*, 37–76.

Garfield, S.L. (1982) Eclecticism and integration in psychotherapy. *Behaviour Therapy, 13*, 610–23.

Garfield, S. (1992) Response to Hans Eysenck. In W. Dryden & C. Feltham (eds.), *Psychotherapy and its Discontents*. Buckingham: Open University Press.

Garry, M., Loftus, E.F., and Brown, S.W. (1994) Memory: a river flows through it. *Consciousness & Cognition, 3,* 438–51.

Gathercole, S.E. (1998) The development of memory. *Journal of Child Psychology & Psychiatry, 39* (1), 3–27.

Gay, P. (1988) *Freud: a life for our time.* London: J.M. Dent and Sons Ltd.

Gazzaniga, M.S. (1998) *The Mind's Past.* Berkeley, CA: University of California Press (see http://www.imprint.co.uk/gazza_iv.htm)

Gazzaniga, M.S. (2000) Introduction to Part 1. In M.S. Gazzaniga (ed.) *Neuroscience: A Reader.* Oxford: Blackwell.

Gelder, M., Gath, D. and Mayon, R. (1989) *Oxford Textbook of Psychiatry* (2nd ed.). Oxford: Oxford University Press.

Geiselman, R.E., Fisher, R.P., MacKinnon, D.P., and Holland, H.L. (1985) Eyewitness memory enhancement in the police interview: cognitive retrieval mnemonics versus hypnosis. *Journal of Applied Psychology, 70,* 401–12.

Gibbs, W. Wayt (1995) Seeking the criminal element. *Scientific American, 272* (3), 76–83.

Gibson, J.J. (1950) *Perception of the Visual World.* Houghton: Mifflin.

Gill, O. and Jackson, B. (1983) *Adoption and Race: Black, Asian and Mixed Race Children in White Families.* London: Batsford.

Gleitman, L.R. and Wanner, E. (1988) Current Issues in Language Learning. In M.H. Bornstein and M.E. Lamb (eds.), *Perceptual, Cognitive and Linguistic Development.* Hove and London: Lawrence Erlbaum Associates.

Goffman, E. (1968) *Asylum: Essays on the Social Situation of Mental Patients and Other Inmates.* Harmondsworth: Penguin.

Gold, K. (1995) Here be dragons and treasure too. *Times Higher Education Supplement,* 18–19, August 18.

Gombrich, E.H. (1960) *Art and Illusion.* London: Phaidon.

Gopaul-McNichol, S.A. (1988) Racial identification and racial preference of black pre-school children in New York and Trinidad. *Journal of Black Psychology, 14,* 65–68.

Gopaul-McNichol, S.A. (1992) Racial identification and Racial Preference of Black Preschool Children in New York and Trinidad. In A.K.H. Burlew, W.C. Banks, H.P. McAdoo, and D.A.Y. Azibo (eds.), *African American Psychology: Theory, Research and Practice.* Newbury Park, CA: Sage Publications.

Gough, H.G. (1952) Identifying psychological femininity. *Educational and Psychological Measurement, 12,* 427–39.

Gould, R.L. (1978) *Transformations: growth and change in adult life.* New York: Simon and Schuster.

Gould, S.J. (1981) *The Mismeasure of Man.* New York: Norton.

Gould, S.J. (1987) *An Urchin in the Storm.* Harmondsworth: Penguin.

Gould, S.J. (1996) *The Mismeasure of Man* (Revised and expanded ed.). Harmondsworth: Penguin.

Graham, P. and Rutter, M. (1985) Adolescent disorders. In M. Rutter and L. Hersov (eds.), *Child and Adolescent Psychiatry: Modern Approaches* (2nd ed.). Oxford: Blackwell.

Greenwald, A.G. (1975) On the inconclusiveness of 'crucial' cognitive tests of dissonance versus self-perception theories. *Journal of Experimental and Social Psychology, 11*, 490–9.

Gregor, A.J. and McPherson, D. (1965) A study of susceptibility to geometric illusions among cultural out groups of Australian aborigines. *Psychologica Africana, 11*, 1–13.

Gregory, R. (ed.) (1987) *Oxford Companion to the Mind.* Oxford: Oxford University Press.

Greyson, B. (2000) Near-death experiences. In E. Cardena, S.J. Lynn & S. Krippner (eds.), *Varieties of anamolous experience: examining the scientific evidence.* Washington, DC: American Psychological Association.

Guilford, J.P. and Guilford, R.B. (1936) Personality factors, S. E. and M. and their measurement. *Journal of Psychology, 2*, 109–27.

Gross, R. (1995) *Themes, Issues and Debates in Psychology.* London: Hodder & Stoughton.

Gross, R. (2003) *Themes, Issues and Debates in Psychology* (2nd ed.). London: Hodder & Stoughton.

Gross, R., Humphreys, P., and Petkova, B. (1997) *Challenges in Psychology.* London: Hodder & Stoughton.

Gross, R. (2001) *Psychology: The Science of Mind and Behaviour* (4th ed.). London: Hodder & Stoughton.

Gruzelier, J. (1998) A Working Model of the Neurophysiology of Hypnosis: A Review of Evidence. *Contemporary Hypnosis, 15*, 5.

Gunter, B. and McAleer, J.L. (1990) *Children and Television: the one-eyed monster?* London: Routledge.

Gunter, B. and McAleer, J. (1997) *Children & Television* (2nd ed.). London: Routledge.

Guntrip, H. (1968) cited in M. Jacobs (1984), Psychodynamic therapy: the Freudian approach. In W. Dryden (ed.), *Individual Therapy in Britain.* London: Harper and Row.

Hall, C.S. (1966) *The Meaning of Dreams.* New York: McGraw Hill.

Hall, G.S. (1904) *Adolescence.* New York: Appleton and Co.

Hammond, D.C. (1995) Hypnosis, false memories, and gudelines for using hypnosis with potential victims of abuse. In J.L. Alpert (ed.), *Sexual Abuse Recalled.* Northvale, NJ: Aronson.

Happé, F. (1994a) *Autism: an introduction to psychological theory.* London: UCL Press.

Happé, F. (1994b) An advanced test of theory of mind: Understanding of story characters' thoughts and feelings by able autistic, mentally handicapped, and normal children and adults. *Journal of Autism & Developmental Disorders, 24*, 129–54.

Hare, R.D. (1991) *Manual for the Hare Psychopathy Checklist – Revised.* Toronto: Multi-Health Systems.

Hare-Mustin, R. and Maracek, J, (1988) The meaning of difference: Gender theory, postmodernism, and psychology. *American Psychologist, 43*, 455–64.

Hargreaves, C.D. (ed.) (1987) *Preventing Adolescent Pregnancy: an Agenda for America.* Washington, DC: National Academy Press.

Hargreaves, D.J. (1986) Psychological theories of sex-role stereotyping. In D.J. Hargreaves and A.M. Colley (eds.), *The Psychology of Sex Roles.* London: Harper and Row.

Hargreaves, D.J., Stoll, L., Farnworth, S. and Morgan, S. (1981) Psychological androgyny and ideational fluency. *British Journal of Social Psychology, 20*, 53–5.

Harré, R. (1989) Language games and the texts of identity. In J. Shotter and K.J. Gergen (eds.), *Texts of Identity*. London: Sage.

Harris, B. (1997) Repoliticizing the History of Psychology. In D. Fox and I. Prilleltensky (eds.), *Critical Psychology: An Introduction*. London: Sage.

Harrower, J. (1998) *Applying Psychology to Crime*. London: Hodder & Stoughton.

Harrower, J. (2001) *Psychology in Practice: Crime*. London: Hodder & Stoughton.

Hathaway, S.R. and McKinley, J.C. (1943) *The Minnesota Multiphasic Personality Inventory*. New York: Psychological Corporation.

Hayes, C.D. (ed.) (1987) Preventing adolescent pregnancy: an agenda for America, cited in M.Rutter (1989), Pathways from childhood to adult life. *Journal of Child Psychology & Psychiatry, 30* (1), 23–51.

Hayes, K.H. and Hayes, C. (1951) Intellectual development of a house-raised chimpanzee. *Proceedings of the American Philosophical Society, 95*, 105–9.

Hazan, C. and Shaver, P.R. (1987) Conceptualizing romantic love as an attachment process. *Journal of Personality and Social Psychology, 52*, 511–24.

Heather, N. (1976) *Radical Perspectives in Psychology*. London: Methuen.

Hebb, D.O. (1949) *The Organization of Behaviour*. New York: Wiley.

Hebb, D.O. *et al.* (1952) The effects of isolation upon attitudes, motivation and thought. *Fourth Symposium, Military Medicine, 1*, Defence Research Board, Canada.

Hefner, R., Rebecca, M. and Oleshansky, B. (1975) Development of sex-role transcendence. *Human Development, 18*, 143–58.

Heider, F. (1958) *The Psychology of Interpersonal Relations*. New York: Wiley.

Herman, J.H., Ellman, S.J. and Roffwarg, H.P. (1978) The problem of NREM dream recall re-examined. In A.M. Arkin, J.S. Antrobus and S.J. Ellman (eds.), *The Mind in Sleep: Psychology and psychophysiology*. Hillsdale, NJ: Lawrence Erlbaum.

Herrnstein, R.J. (1982) IQ testing and the media. *Atlantic Monthly* (August), 68–74.

Herrnstein, R.J. and Murray, C. (1994) *The Bell Curve: Intelligence and Class Structure in American Life*. New York: Free Press.

Herrnstein, R.J. and Murray, C. (1996) *The Bell Curve: Intelligence and Class Structure in American Life* (with a new afterword by Charles Murray). New York: Free Press.

Hetherington, E.M. and Baltes, P.B. (1988) Child psychology and life-span development. In E.M. Hetherington, R. Learner and M. Perlmutter (eds.), *Child Development in Life-Span Perspective*. Hillsdale, NJ: LEA.

Hewstone, M. and Antaki, C. (1988) Attribution theory and social explanations. In M. Hewstone, W. Stroebe, J.P. Codol and G.M. Stephenson (eds.), *Introduction to Social Psychology*. Oxford: Blackwell.

Hewstone, M. and Fincham, F. (1996) Attribution Theory and Research: Basic Issues and Applications. In M. Hewstone, W. Stroebe, and G.M. Stephenson (eds.), *Introduction to Social Psychology* (2nd ed.). Oxford: Blackwell.

Hewstone, M., Fincham, F., and Jaspars, J. (1981) Social categorization and similarity

in intergroup behaviour: a replication with penalties. *European Journal of Social Psychology, 11,* 101–7.

Hewstone, M., Manstead, A.S.R., and Stroebe, W. (1997) Emotion. In M. Hewstone, A.S.R. Manstead, and W. Stroebe (eds.), *The Blackwell Reader in Social Psychology.* Oxford: Blackwell.

Hilgard, E.R. (1974) Toward a neo-dissociationist theory: multiple cognitive controls in human functioning. *Perspectives in Biology and Medicine, 17,* 301–16.

Hilgard, E.R. (1977) *Divided Consciousness: Multiple Controls in Human Thought and Action.* New York: Wiley.

Hilgard, E.R. (1978) States of consciousness in hypnosis: divisions or levels? In F.H. Frankel and H.S. Zamansky (eds.), *Hypnosis at its Bicentennial: Selected Papers.* New York: Plenum.

Hilgard, E.R. (1979) Divided consciousness in hypnosis: the implications of the hidden observer. In E. Fromm and R.E. Shor (eds.), *Hypnosis: Developments in Research and New Perspectives* (2nd ed.). New York: Aldine.

Hilgard, E.R., Atkinson, R.L. and Atkinson, R.C. (1979) *Introduction to Psychology* (7th ed.). New York: Harcourt Brace Jovanovich.

Hilgard, E.R. and Hilgard, J.R. (1984) *Hypnosis in the Relief of Pain.* New York: Kaufmann.

Hilgard, E.R., Hilgard, J.R., Macdonald, J., Morgan, A.H. and Johnson, L.S. (1978) Covert pain in hypnotic analgesia: its reality as tested by the real-simulator. *Journal of Abnormal Psychology, 87,* 655–63.

Hilliard, A.G. (1992) IQ and the Courts: *Larry P.* v. *Wilson Riles* and *PASE* v. *Hannon.* In A.K.H. Burlew, W.C. Banks, H.P. McAdoo and D.A.Y. Azibo (eds.), *African American Psychology: theory, research and practice.* Newbury Park, Ca.: Sage Publications.

Hinde, R.A. (1982) *Ethology.* London: Fontana Paperback.

Hinde, R.A. (1987) *Individuals, Relationships and Culture: links between ethology and the social sciences.* Cambridge: Cambridge University Press.

Hinde, R.A. and Stevenson-Hinde, J. (eds.) (1988) *Relations within Families: mutual influences.* Oxford: Clarendon Press.

Hobson, A. (1988) *The Dreaming Brain.* New York: Basic Books.

Hobson, A. (1999) Sleep and Dreaming. In M.J. Zigmond, F.E. Bloom., S.C. Landis, J.L. Roberts, & L.R. Squire (eds.), *Fundamental Neuroscience.* San Diego, CA: Academic Press.

Hobson, J.A. and McCarley, R.M. (1977) The brain as a dream state generator: An activation-synthesis hypothesis of the dream process. *American Journal of Psychiatry, 134,* 1335–48.

Hochberg, J. and Gilper, R. (1967) Recognition of faces (1): an exploratory study. *Psychonomic Science, 12,* 619–20.

Hockett, C.D. (1960) The origin of speech. *Scientific American, 203,* 88–96.

Hofling, K.C., Brotzman, E., Dalrymple, S., Graves, N. and Pierce, C.M. (1966) An experimental study in the nurse–physician relationship. *Journal of Nervous and Mental Disorder, 143,* 171–80.

Hogg, M.A. and Vaughan, G.M. (1998) *Social Psychology* (2nd ed.). Hemel Hempstead: Prentice Hall Europe.

Hohmann, G.W. (1966) Some effects of spinal cord lesions on experienced emotional feelings. *Psychophysiology, 3*, 143–56.

Hollander, E.P. (1981) *Principles and Methods of Social Psychology* (4th ed.). New York: Oxford University Press.

Holmes, D.S. (1994) *Abnormal Psychology* (2nd ed.). New York: HarperCollins.

Holmes, T.H. and Rahe, R.H. (1967) The social readjustment rating scale. *Journal of Psychosomatic Research, 11*, 213–18.

Horgan, J. (1993) Eugenics revisited. *Scientific American, 286* (6) 92–100, June.

Horn, J.M., Loehlin, J.L. and Willerman, L. (1979) Intellectual resemblance among adoptive and biological relatives: the Texas adoption project. *Behaviour Genetics, 9*, 177–207.

Horwitz, M. and Rabbie, J.M. (1982) Individuality and membership in the intergroup system. In H. Tajfel (ed.) *Social Identity and Intergroup Relations.* Cambridge: Cambridge University Press.

Hosch, H.M., Leippe, M.R., Marchioni, P.M. and Cooper, D.S. (1984) Victimization, self-monitoring, and eye-witness identification. *Journal of Applied Psychology, 64*, 280–8.

Howe, M.J.A. (1980) *The Psychology of Human Learning.* New York: Harper and Row.

Howe, M.J.A. (1997) *IQ in Question: The Truth about Intelligence.* London: Sage.

Howe, M.J.A. (1998) Can IQ change? *The Psychologist, 11*(2), 69–71, Feb.

Hudson, W. (1960) Pictorial depth perception in sub-cultural groups in Africa. *Journal of Social Psychology, 52*, 183–208.

Hudson, W. (1962) Pictorial perception and educational adaptation in Africa. *Psychologica Africana, 9*, 226–39.

Hughes, M. and Donaldson, M. (1979) The use of hiding games for studying the coordination of viewpoints. *Educational Review, 31*, 133–40.

Hui, C.H. and Triandis, H.C. (1985) Measurement in cross-cultural psychology: a review and comparison of strategies. *Journal of Cross-Cultural Psychology, 16*, 131–52.

Hume, D. (1902) *Enquiry concerning human understanding* (edited by L.A. Selby-Bigge). Oxford: Oxford University Press. (Originally published 1748).

Hyde, J.S. and Phillis, D.E. (1979) Androgyny across the life span. *Developmental Psychology, 15*, 334–6.

Hyde, T.S. and Jenkins, J.J. (1973) Recall for words as a function of semantic, graphic and syntactic orienting tasks. *Journal of Verbal Learning and Behaviour, 12*, 471–80.

Hyman, R. (1985) The Ganzfield psi experiments: A critical appraisal. *Journal of Parapsychology, 49*, 3–49.

Irwin, H.J. (1993) Belief in the paranormal: a review of the empirical literature. *Journal of the American Society for Psychical Research, 87*, 1–39.

Izard, C.E. (1977) *Human Emotions.* New York: Plenum.

Israels, H. and Schatzman, M. (1993) The seduction theory. *History of Psychiatry, 4*, 23–59.

Jackson, G. (1992) *Women and Psychology – What Might That Mean?* Paper delivered at ATP Conference, July 1992.

Jackson, J.H. (1864) cited in J.E. Bogen (1969) The other side of the brain. In R. Ornstein (1986), *The Psychology of Consciousness* (2nd revised ed.). Harmondsworth: Penguin.

Jacobs, M. (1984) Psychodynamic therapy: the Freudian approach. In W.Dryden (ed.), *Individual Therapy in Britain.* London: Harper and Row.

Jacobs, M. (1992) *Sigmund Freud,* London: Sage Publications.

Jacoby, L.L. and Craik, F.I.M. (1979) Effects of elaboration of processing at encoding and retrieval: trace distinctiveness and recovery of initial context. In L.S. Cermak and F.I.M. Craik (eds.), *Levels of Processing in Human Memory.* Hillsdale, NJ: Lawrence Erlbaum.

Jacques (1965) cited in MacDaniels, J. (1997) *Mid-Life Crisis: Recent Research.* (see http://www.hope.edu/academic/psychology/335/webrep2/crisis.html)

Jahoda, G. (1966) Geometric illusions and environment: a study in Ghana. *British Journal of Psychology, 57,* 193–9.

James, W. (1884) What is an emotion? *Mind, 9,* 188–205.

James, W. (1890) *Principles of Psychology.* New York: Holt.

Janis, I.L., Kaye, D. and Kirschner, P. (1965) Facilitating effects of 'eating-while-reading' on responsiveness to persuasive communications. *Journal of Personality & Social Psychology, 1,* 181–6.

Janov, A. (1973) *The Primal Scream.* London: Sphere Books Ltd.

Jensen, A.R. (1969) How much can we boost IQ and scholastic achievement? *Harvard Educational Review, 39,* 1–123.

Jewitt, J. (1998) Unpublished D. Clin. Psych. Research Thesis. University College, London.

Johnson, R.F., Maher, B.A. and Barber, T.X. (1972) Artifact in the 'essence of hypnosis': an evaluation of trance logic. *Journal of Abnormal Psychology, 79,* 212–20.

Joint Commission on Mental Health of Children (1970) *Crisis in mental health: Challenge for the 70s.* New York: Harper & Row.

Jones, D. and Elcock, J. (2001) *History and Theories of Psychology: A Critical Perspective.* London: Arnold.

Jones, E.E. and Davis, K.E. (1965) From acts to dispositions: the attribution process in person perception. In L. Berkowitz (ed.), *Advances in Experimental Social Psychology, 2,* New York: Academic Press.

Jones, E.E. and Nisbett, R.E. (1971) *The Actor and the Observer: divergent perceptions of the causes of behaviour.* Morristown, NJ: General Learning Press.

Jones, M.C. (1924) The elimination of children's fears. *Journal of Experimental Psychology, 7,* 382–90.

Jones, M.C. (1974) Albert, Peter and J. B. Watson. *American Psychologist, 29,* 581–3.

Jones, R.A., Linder, D.E., Kiesler, C., Zanna, M. and Brehm, J.W. (1968) Internal states or external stimuli: observers' attitude judgements and the dissonance theory–self persuasion controversy. *Journal of Experimental and Social Psychology, 4,* 247–69.

Joynson, R.B. (1974) *Psychology and Common Sense.* London: RKP.

Joynson, R.B. (1989) *The Burt Affair.* London: Routledge.

Juel-Nielson, N. (1965) Individual and environment: a psychiatric and psychological investigation of monozygous twins raised apart. *Acta Psychiatrica et Neurologica Scandanavica,* Supplement 183.

Jung, C.G. (1967) *Memories, Dreams, Reflections.* London: Collins.

Kagan, A. (1975) Epidemiology, disease and emotion. In L. Levi (ed.), *Emotions, their Parameters and Measurement.* New York: Raven Press.

Kagan, J. (1984) *The Nature of the Child.* New York: Basic Books.

Kamin, L.J. (1977) *The Science and Politics of I.Q.* Harmondsworth: Penguin.

Kamin, L.J. (1995) Behind the Curve. *Scientific American, 272* (2), 82–6, Feb.

Kanner, L. (1943) Autistic disturbance of affective contact. *Nervous Child, 2,* 217–50.

Kay, H. (1972) Psychology today and tomorrow. *Bulletin of the British Psychological Society, 25,* 177–88.

Kebbell, M.R. and Wagstaff, G.F. (1999) The effectiveness of the cognitive interview. In D. Canter & L. Alison (eds.). *Interviewing and Deception.* Ashgate.

Kelley, H.H. (1967) Attribution theory in social psychology. In D.Levine (ed.), *Nebraska Symposium on Motivation,* 15, Lincoln, Na.: University of Nebraska Press.

Kelley, H.H. (1972) Causal schemata and the attribution process. In E.E. Jones, D.E. Kanouse, H.H. Kelley, R.E. Nisbett, S. Valins and B. Weiner (eds.), *Attribution: perceiving the causes of behaviour.* Morristown, NJ: General Learning Press.

Kellogg, W.N. and Kellogg, L.A. (1933) *The Ape and the Child.* New York: McGraw-Hill.

Kelly, G.A. (1955) *A Theory of Personality – The Psychology of Personal Constructs.* New York: Norton.

Kendell, R.E. (1983) The principles of classification in relation to mental disease. In M. Shepherd and O.L. Zangwill (eds.), *Handbook of Psychiatry: 1. General Psychopathology.* Cambridge: Cambridge University Press.

Kent, G. (1991) Anxiety. In W. Dryden and R. Rentoul (eds.), *Adult Clinical Problems.* London: Routledge.

Kety, S.S. (1974) From rationalization to reason. *American Journal of Psychiatry, 131,* 957–62.

Kihlstrom, J.F. (1980) Post hypnotic amnesia for recently learned material: interactions with 'episodic' and 'semantic' memory. *Cognitive Psychology, 12,* 227–51.

Kilbride, P.L., Robbins, M.C. and Freeman, R.B. (1968) Pictorial depth perception and education among Baganda school children. *Perceptual and Motor Skills, 26,* 1116–18.

Kilham, W. and Mann, L. (1974) Level of destructive obedience as a function of transmitter and executant roles in the Milgram obedience paradigm. *Journal of Personality & Social Psychology, 29,* 696–702.

Kimura, D. (1961) Some effects of temporal-lobe damage on adult perception. *Canadian Journal of Psychology, 15,* 156–65.

Kimura, D. (1964) Left-right differences in perception of melodies. *Quarterly Journal of Experimental Psychology, 16,* 355–8.

Kimura, D. (1992) Sex differences in the brain. *Scientific American*, 80–7, Sept. (Special Issue).

Kimura, D. (1999) Sex Differences in the Brain. *Scientific American Presents, 10* (2), 26–31.

Kirsch, I. (1997) Suggestibility or Hypnosis: What do our scales really measure? *The International Journal of Clinical & Experimental Hypnosis, 45*, 212, July.

Kline, P. (1988) *Psychology Exposed.* London: Routledge.

Kluft, R.P.(1996) Treating the traumatic memories of patients with dissociative identity disorder. *American Journal of Psychiatry, 153*, 103–110.

Knox, J.V., Morgan, A.H. and Hilgard, E.R. (1974) Pain and suffering in ischemia: the paradox of hypnotically suggested anaesthesia as contradicted by reports from the 'hidden observer'. *Archives of General Psychiatry, 30*, 840–7.

Koluchova, J. (1972) Severe deprivation in twins: a case-study. *Journal of Child Psychology & Psychiatry, 13*, 107–14.

Koluchova, J. (1976) The further development of twins after severe and prolonged deprivation: a second report. *Journal of Child Psychology & Psychiatry, 17*, 181–8.

Koluchova, J. (1991) Severely deprived twins after 22 years observation. *Studia Psychologica, 33*, 23–28.

Kosslyn, S.M., Gazzaniga, M.S., Galaburda, A.M., and Rabin, C. (1999) Hemispheric specialization. In M.J. Zigmond, F.E. Bloom, S.C. Landis, J.L. Roberts, & L.R. Squire (eds.), *Fundamental Neuroscience.* San Diego, CA: Academic Press.

Kraepelin, E. (1913) *Psychiatry* (8th ed.). Leipzig: Thieme.

Kreitman, N. (1961) The reliability of psychiatric diagnosis. *Journal of Mental Science, 107*, 876–86.

Kübler-Ross, E. (1991) *On Life After Death.* Berkley, CA: Celestial Arts.

Kupfer, D.J. (1976) REM latency: A psychobiologic marker for primary depressive disease. *Biological Psychiatry, 11*, 159–74.

Kurdika, N.K. (1965) Defiance of authority under peer influence. Unpublished doctoral dissertation, Yale University.

Kvale, S. (1992, ed.) *Psychology and Post-Modernism.* London: Sage.

Lahey, B.B. (1983) *Psychology – An Introduction.* Dubugue, Iowa: Wm. C. Brown Co.

Laird, J.D. (1974) Self-attribution of emotion: the effects of facial expression on the quality of emotional experience. *Journal of Personality & Social Psychology, 29*, 475–86.

Landis, C. (1938) Statistical evaluation of psychotherapeutic methods. In S.E. Hinde (ed.), *Concepts and Problems of Psychotherapy*, London: Heineman.

Larson, P.C. (1981) Sexual identification and self-concept. *Journal of Homosexuality, 7*, 15–32.

Latané, B. and Darley, J.M. (1970) *The unresponsive bystander: why does he not help?* New York: Appleton-Century-Croft.

Lazarus, R.S. (1976) *Patterns of Adjustment.* New York: McGraw-Hill.

Leahy, A.M. (1935) Nature–nurture and intelligence. *Genetic Psychology Monographs, 17*, 235–308.

LeDoux, J.E. (1989) Cognitive-emotional interactions in the brain. *Cognition & Emotion, 3,* 267–289.

LeDoux, J.E. (1998) *The Emotional Brain: The Mysteries Underpinnings of Emotional Life.* New York: Simon & Schuster.

Legge, D. (1975) *An Introduction to Psychological Science.* London: Methuen.

Lepper, M.R., Greene, D. and Nisbett, R.E. (1973) Undermining children's intrinsic interest with extrinsic reward: a test of the overjustification hypothesis. *Journal of Personality & Social Psychology, 28,* 129–37.

Leslie, A.M. and Frith, U. (1988) Autistic children's understanding of seeing, knowing, and believing. *British Journal of Developmental Psychology, 6,* 315–24.

Leslie, A.M. and Roth, D. (1993) What autism teaches us about metarepresentation. In S. Baron-Cohen, H. Tager-Flusberg, and D.J. Cohen (eds.) *Understanding other minds: Perspectives from autism.* Oxford: Oxford University Press.

Leslie, A.M. (1987) Pretence and representation: The origins of 'theory of mind'. *Psychological Review, 94,* 412–26.

Leslie, A.M. (1994) Pretending and believing: issues in the theory of ToMM. *Cognition, 50,* 211–38.

Levenson, R.W. (1994) The search for autonomic specificity. In P. Ekman and R.J. Davidson (eds.) *The nature of emotion: Fundamental questions.* New York: Oxford University Press.

Levenson, R.W., Ekman, P., and Friesen, W.V. (1990) Voluntary facial action generates emotion-specific autonomic nervous system activity. *Psychophysiology, 27,* 363–84.

Leventhal, H. (1980) Toward a comprehensive theory of emotion. *Advances in Experimental Social Psychology, 13,* 139–207.

Levinson, D.J., Darrow, D.N., Klein, E.B., Levinson, M.H. and McKee, B. (1978) *The Seasons of a Man's Life.* New York: A.A. Knopf.

Levinson, D.J. and Levinson, J.D. (1997) *The Seasons of a Woman's Life.* New York: Ballantine Books.

Levy-Agresti, J. and Sperry, R.W. (1968) Differential perceptual capacities in major and minor hemispheres. *Proceedings of National Academy of Sciences, 61,* 1151.

Lewin, R. (1991) Look who's talking now. *New Scientist, 130* (1766), 48–52.

Leyens, J.P. and Codol, J.P. (1988) Social cognition. In M. Hewstone, W. Stroebe, J.P. Codol and G.M. Stephenson (eds.), *Introduction to Social Psychology.* Oxford: Blackwell.

Liben, L.S. and Signorella, M.L. (1980) Gender-related schemata and constructive memory in children. *Child Development, 51,* 11–18.

Light, P.H., Buckingham, N. and Robbins, A.H. (1979) The conservation task as an interactional setting. *British Journal of Educational Psychology, 49,* 304–10.

Lilienfeld, S.O. (1995) *Seeing both sides: Classic controversies in abnormal psychology.* Pacific Grove, CA: Brooks/Cole Publishing Co.

Lilienfeld, S.O. (1998) *Looking Into Abnormal Psychology: Contemporary Readings.* Pacific Grove, CA: Brooks/Cole Publishing Company.

Linder, D.E., Cooper, J. and Jones, E.E. (1967) Decision freedom as a determinant of

the role of incentive magnitude in attitude change. *Journal of Personality & Social Psychology, 6*, 245–54.

Lindsay, G. (1995) Values, ethics and psychology. *The Psychologist, 8*, 493–8.

Lindsay, W.R. (1982) The effects of labelling: blind and non-blind ratings of social skills in schizophrenic and non-schizophrenic control subjects. *American Journal of Psychiatry, 139*, 216–19.

Littlewood, R. and Lipsedge, M. (1997) *Aliens and Alienists: Ethnic minorities and psychiatry* (3rd ed.). London: Routledge.

Locksley, A., Ortiz, V. and Hepburn, C. (1980) Social categorization and discriminatory behaviour: extinguishing the minimal intergroup discrimination effect, *Journal of Personality & Social Psychology, 39*, 773–83.

Loehlin, J.C. (1989) Partitioning environmental and genetic contributions to behavioural development, *American Psychologist, 44*, 1285.

Loftus, E.F. (1975) Leading questions and the eyewitness report. *Cognitive Psychology, 7*, 560–72.

Loftus, E.F. (1979) Reactions to blatantly contradictory information. *Memory and Cognition, 7*, 368–74.

Loftus, E.F. (1991) Made in memory: distortions in recollection after misleading information. In G.H. Bower (ed.), *The Psychology of Learning and Motivation*. New York: Academic Press.

Loftus, E.F. (1997) Creating False Memories. *Scientific American, 279*(3), 50–5, September.

Loftus, E.F., Freedman, J.L. and Loftus, G.R. (1970) Retrieval of words from subordinate and superordinate categories in semantic hierarchies. *Psychonomic Science, 21*, 235–6.

Loftus, E.F. and Hoffman, H.G. (1989) Misinformation and memory: the creation of new memories. *Journal of Experimental Psychology: General, 118*, 100–4.

Loftus, E.F. and Palmer, J.C. (1974) Reconstruction of automobile destruction: an example of the interaction between language and memory. *Journal of Verbal Learning and Verbal Behaviour, 13*, 585–9.

Loftus, E.F. and Zanni, G. (1975) Eye-witness testimony: the influence of the wording of a question. *Bulletin of the Psychonomic Society, 5*, 86–8.

Lubinski, D., Tellegen, A. and Butcher, J.N. (1981) The relationship between androgyny and subjective indicators of emotional well-being. *Journal of Personality & Social Psychology, 40*, 722–30.

Lubinski, D., Tellegen, A. and Butcher, J.N. (1983) Masculinity, femininity and androgyny. *Journal of Personality & Social Psychology, 44*, 428–39.

Luborsky, L., Singer, B. and Luborsky, L. (1975) Comparative study of psychotherapies: is it time that 'everyone has won and all must have prizes?' *Archives of General Psychiatry, 32*, 995–1008.

Ludwig, A.M., Brandsma, J.M., Wilbur, C.B., Bendfeldt, F. and Jameson, D.H. (1972) The objective study of a multiple personality: or, are four heads better than one? *Archives of General Psychiatry, 26*, 298–310.

MacFarlane, A. (1975) Olfaction in the development of social preferences in the

human neonate. In R. Porter and M. O'Connor (eds.), *Parent–Infant Interaction*. Amsterdam: Elsevier.

MacKay, D. (1975) *Clinical Psychology: Theory and Therapy*. London: Methuen.

MacKay, D. (1987) Divided brains – divided minds? In C. Blakemore and S. Greenfield (eds.), *Mindwaves*. Oxford: Blackwell.

MacLeod, A. (1998) Therapeutic interventions. In M. Eysenck (ed.), *Psychology: an integrated approach*. Harlow: Addison Wesley/Longman Ltd.

MacNamara, J. (1982) *Names for Things*. Cambridge, MA: Bradford MIT Press.

Main, M., Kaplan, N., and Cassidy, J. (1985) Security in infancy, childhood and adulthood: A move to the level of representation. In I. Bretherton & E. Waters (eds.), *Growing Points of Attachment: Theory and Research*. Chicago: University of Chicago Press.

Mair, K. (1992) The myth of therapist expertise. In W. Dryden and C. Feltham (eds.), *Psychotherapy and its Discontents*. Buckingham: Open University Press.

Mair, K. (1999) Multiple personality and child abuse. *The Psychologist, 12*(2), 76–80.

Malpass, R.S. and Devine, P.G. (1981) Eye-witness identification: line-up instructions and the absence of the offender. *Journal of Applied Psychology, 66*, 345–51.

Mamelak, A. and Hobson, A. (1989) Dream bizarreness as the cognitive correlate of altered neuronal behaviour in REM sleep. *Journal of Cognitive Neuroscience, 1*, 201–222.

Mandler, G. (1984) *Mind and Body: The Psychology of Emotion and Stress*. New York: Norton.

Mantell, D.M. (1971) The potential for violence in Germany. *Journal of Social Issues, 27*, 101–12.

Maracek, J. (1978) Psychological disorders in women: Indices of role strain. In I. Frieze, J. Parsons, P. Johnson, D. Ruble, and G. Zellman (eds.), *Women and sex roles: A social psychological perspective*. New York: Norton.

Marañon, G. (1924) Contribution à l'étude de l'action émotive de l'adrenaline. *Revue Française Endocrinol, 2*, 301–25.

Marcel, T. and Patterson, K. (1978) Word recognition and production. In J. Requin (ed.), *Attention and Performance*, 7, Hillsdale, NJ: Lawrence Erlbaum.

Markus, H. and Kitayama, S. (1991) Culture and the self: Implications for cognition, emotion and motivation. *Psychological Review, 98*, 224–53.

Marshall, G. (1976) cited by E.R. Hilgard, R.L. Atkinson and R.C. Atkinson (1979), *Introduction to Psychology* (7th ed.). New York: Harcourt Brace Jovanovich.

Marshall, G.D. and Zimbardo, P.G. (1979) Affective consequences of inadequately explained physiological arousal. *Journal of Personality & Social Psychology, 37*, 970–88.

Martin, N. (1998) Sex differences: Where and Why? *The Psychologist, 11*(8), 395, August.

Masataka, N. (1993) Motherese is a signed language. *Infant Behaviour & Development, 15*, 453–60.

Maslach, C. (1979) Negative emotional biasing of unexplained arousal. *Journal of Personality & Social Psychology, 37*, 953–69.

Maslow, A.M. (1954) *Motivation and Personality*. New York: Harper and Row.

Mason, M.K. (1942) Learning to speak after six and one half years of silence. *Journal of Speech & Hearing Disorders, 7,* 295–304.

Masson, J. (1992) *The Assault on Truth: Freud and child sexual abuse.* London: Fontana.

Matt, G.E. (1993) Comparing classes of psychotherapeutic interventions: a review and analysis of English- and German-language meta-analyses. *Journal of Cross-Cultural Psychology, 24*(1), 5–25.

McAdoo, H.P. (1973*) A different view of race attitudes and self-concepts in Black preschool children,* Urbana: University of Illinois.

McAdoo, H.P. (1978) Self-concept in Black preschool children. In W. Cross and A. Harrison (eds.), *Third Conference on Empirical Research in Black Psychology.* Washington, DC: NIE.

McAllister, M. (1998) Putting psychology in context. *The Psychologist, 11*(1), 13–15, Jan.

McArthur, L.Z. and Post, D. (1977) Figural emphasis and person perception. *Journal of Experimental Social Psychology, 13,* 733–42.

McCarley, R.W. (1983) REM dreams, REM sleep and their isomorphism. In M.H. Chase and E.D. Weitzman (eds.), *Sleep Disorders: Basic and Clinical Research,* Vol. 8. New York: Spectrum.

McCarley, R.W. (1995) Sleep, dreams and states of consciousness. In P.M. Conn (ed.) *Neuroscience in Medicine.* Philadelphia: J.B. Lippincott.

McDermott, M. (1993) On Cruelty, Ethics and Experimentation: Profile of Philip G. Zimbardo. *The Psychologist, 6*(10), 456–459.

McGarrigle, J. and Donaldson, M. (1974) Conservation accidents. *Cognition, 3,* 341–50.

McGhee, P. (2001) *Thinking Psychologically.* Basingstoke: Palgrave.

McGurk, H. and Jahoda, G. (1975) Pictorial depth perception by children in Scotland. *Journal of Cross Cultural Psychology, 6,* 279–296.

Meeus, W.H.J. and Raaijmakers, Q.A.W. (1986) Administrative obedience: Carrying out orders to use psychological-administrative violence. *European Journal of Social Psychology, 16,* 311–24.

Mehler, J., Bertoncini, J., Barrière, M. and Jassik-Gerschenfeld, D. (1978) Infant recognition of mother's voice. *Perception, 7,* 491–7.

Mehler, J. and Dupoux, E. (1994) *What Infants Know: the new cognitive science of early development.* Oxford: Blackwell.

Memon, A. (1998) Telling it all: The cognitive interview. In A. Memon, A. Vrij, & R. Bull (eds.) *Psychology and Law: Truthfulness, Accuracy and Credibility.* Maidenhead: McGraw-Hill.

Messer, D.J. (1981) Non-linguistic information which could assist the young child's interpretation of adults' speech. In W.P. Robinson (ed.), *Communication in Development.* London: Academic Press.

Milgram, S. (1970) The experience of living in cities. *Science 167,* 1461–8, March. Reprinted in S. Milgram (1992) *The Individual in a Social World* (2nd ed.). New York: McGraw-Hill.

Milgram, S. (1972) Interpreting obedience: error and evidence. In A.G. Miller (ed.), *The Social Psychology of Psychological Research.* New York: Free Press. Reprinted in S. Milgram (1992) *The Individual in a Social World* (2nd ed.). New York: McGraw-Hill.

Milgram, S. (1974) *Obedience to Authority*. New York: Harper Torchbooks.

Milgram, S. (1977) Subject reaction: the neglected factor in the ethics of experimentation. *The Hastings Centre Report*, Oct., 19–23. Reprinted in S. Milgram (1992), *The Individual in a Social World* (2nd ed.). New York: McGraw-Hill.

Milgram, S. and Hollander, P. (1964) The murder they heard. *The Nation*, *198*(25), 602–4. Reprinted as The Urban Bystander in S. Milgram (1992) *The Individual in a Social World* (2nd ed.). New York: McGraw-Hill.

Miller, A.G. (1986) *The Obedience Experiments: a case-study of controversy in social science.* New York: Paeger.

Miller, D.T. and Ross, M. (1975) Self-serving biases in the attribution of causality: fact or fiction? *Psychological Bulletin, 82*, 213–25.

Miller, E. and Morley, S. (1986) *Investigating Abnormal Behaviour*. London: Lawrence Erlbaum.

Miller, J.G. (1997) A cultural-psychological perspective on intelligence. In R.J. Sternberg and E. Grigorenko (eds.), *Intelligence, Heredity, and Environment*. New York: Cambridge University Press.

Milner, D. (1975) *Children and Race*. Harmondsworth: Penguin.

Milner, D. (1981) Racial prejudice and social psychology. In J. Turner and H. Giles (eds.), *Intergroup behaviour*. Oxford: Blackwell.

Milner, D. (1983) *Children and Race: Ten Years On*. London: Ward Lock Educational.

Mischel, W. (1968) *Personality and Assessment*. New York: Wiley.

Mischel, W. (1969) Continuities and change in personality. *American Psychologist, 24*, 1012–18.

Mischel, W. (1986) *Introduction to Personality: a new look* (4th ed.). New York: CBS Publishing.

Mitchell, D. and Blair, J. (2000) Psychopathy. *The Psychologist, 13*(7), 356–360.

Mitchell, J. (1974) *Psychoanalysis and Feminism*. Harmondsworth: Penguin.

Mitchell, P. (1997) *Introduction to Theory of Mind*. London: Arnold.

Moghaddam, F.M. (1998) *Social Psychology: Exploring Universals Across Cultures*. New York: W.H. Freeman & Co.

Mollon, P. (1998) *Remembering Trauma: A Psychotherapists's Guide to Memory and Illusion*. Chichester: John Wiley & Sons.

Moody, R. (1975) *Life after Life*. Covinda, GA: Mockingbird.

Moorcroft, W.H. (ed.) (1993) *Sleep, dreaming and sleep disorders*. Lanham, MD: University Press of America Inc.

Moore, C. and Frye, D. (1986) The effect of the experimenter's intention on the child's understanding of conservation. *Cognition, 22*, 283–98.

Moore-Ede, M.C. and Czeisler, C.A. (eds.) (1984) *Mathematical Models of the Circadian Sleep–Wake Cycle*. New York: Raven Press.

Moreno, J.L. (1953) *Who shall survive?* (2nd ed.). New York: Beacon.

Morris, C.D., Bransford, J.D. and Franks, J.J. (1977) Levels of processing versus transfer appropriate processing. *Journal of Verbal Learning and Verbal Behaviour, 16*, 519–33.

Morris, R.L. (1989) Parapsychology. In A.M. Colman and J.G. Beaumont (Eds) *Psychology Survey*, no.7. Leicester: British Psychological Society.

Morrison, A.R. (1983) A window on the sleeping brain. *Scientific American, 248*, 94–102.

Morse, M. (1990) *Closer to the Light: Learning from Children's Near-Death Experiences.* New York: Villard.

Moruzzi, G. (1996) The functional significance of sleep with particular regard to the brain mechanisms underlying consciousness. In J.C. Eccles (ed.) *Brain and Conscious Experience.* Berlin: Springer-Verlag.

Mueller, A. and Roberts, R. (2001) Dreams. In R. Roberts & D. Groome (eds.) *Parapsychology: The Science of Unusual Experience.* London: Arnold.

Mummendey, A., Simon, B., Dietze, C., Grunwert, M., Haeger, G., Kessler, S., Lettgen, S., and Schaferhoff, S. (1993) Categorization is not enough: intergroup discrimination in negative outcome allocations. *Journal of Experimental Social Psychology, 28*, 125–44.

Mundy-Castle, A.C. and Nelson, G.K. (1962) A neuropsychological study of the Knysma forest workers. *Psychologia Africana, 9*, 240–72.

Murphy, J., John, M. and Brown, H. (1984) *Dialogues and Debates in Social Psychology.* London: Lawrence Erlbaum/Open University.

Myers, D.G. (1998) Adulthood's Ages and Stages. *Psychology, 5*, 196–197.

Myers, L.J. (1992) Transpersonal psychology: the role of the Afrocentric paradigm. In A.K.H. Burlew, W.C. Banks, H.P. McAdoo and D.A.Y. Azibo (eds.), *African American Psychology: theory, research and practice.* Newbury Park, CA: Sage Publications.

Nash, M.R. (2001) The Truth and the Hype of Hypnosis. *Scientific American, 285*(1), 36–43.

Neisser, U. (1973) Reversibility of psychiatric diagnoses. *Science, 180*, 1116.

Newell, R. and Dryden, W. (1991) Clinical problems: an introduction to the cognitive behavioural approach. In W. Dryden and R. Rentoul (eds.), *Adult Clinical Problems.* London: Routledge.

Newman, H.H., Freeman, F.N. and Holzinger, K.J. (1937) *Twins: a study of heredity and environment.* Chicago: University of Chicago Press.

Nicholson, J. (1993) *Men and Women* (2nd ed.). Oxford: Oxford University Press.

Nicolson, P. (2000) Gender, Power and the Health Care Professions. In L. Sherr & J.S. St. Lawrence (eds.) *Women, Health and The Mind.* Chichester: John Wiley & Sons Ltd.

Nisbett, R.E. and Cohen, D. (1999) Men, Honour and Murder. *Scientific American Presents, 10*(2), 16–19.

Nisbett, R.E. and Schachter, S. (1966) Cognitive manipulation of pain. *Journal of Experimental Social Psychology, 2*, 227–36.

Nuland, S.B. (1994) *How We Die.* London: Chatto & Windus.

Oatley, K. (1984) *Selves in Relation: an introduction to psychotherapy and groups.* London: Methuen.

Oatley, K. (1998) Emotion. *The Psychologist, 11* (6), 285–8, June.

Oatley, K. and Johnson-Laird, P.N. (1996) The communicative theory of emotions:

Empirical tests, mental models, and implications for social interaction. In L.L. Martin and A. Tesser (eds.), *Striving and Feeling: Interactions among Goals, Affect and Self-Regulation*. Mahwah, NJ: Erlbaum.

O'Brian, C. (1990) Family therapy with black families. *Journal of Family Therapy, 12*, 3–16.

Olson, S.L., Bayles, K., and Bates, J.E. (1986) Mother-child interaction and children's speech progress: A longitudinal study of the first two years. *Merrill-Palmer Quarterly, 32*, 1–20.

Orbach, A. (1999) *Life, Psychotherapy and Death*. London: Jessica Kingsley.

Orne, M.T. (1959) The nature of hypnosis: artifact and essence. *Journal of Abnormal & Social Psychology, 58*, 277–99.

Orne, M.T. (1962) On the social psychology of the psychological experiment: with particular reference to demand characteristics and their implications. *American Psychologist, 17*, 776–83.

Orne, M.T. (1966) Hypnosis, motivation and compliance. *American Journal of Psychiatry, 122*, 721–6.

Orne, M.T. (1970) Hypnosis: motivation and the ecological validity of the psychological experiment. In W.J. Arnold and M.M. Page (eds.), *Nebraska Symposium on Motivation*. Lincoln, Nebraska: University of Nebraska Press.

Orne, M.T. (1979) On the simulating subject as quasi-control group in hypnosis research: what, why and how? In E. Fromm and R.E. Shor (eds.), *Hypnosis: Research Developments and Perspectives* (2nd ed.). New York: Aldine.

Orne, M.T., Dinges, D.F. and Orne, E.C. (1984) On the differential diagnosis of multiple personality in the forensic context. *International Journal of Clinical and Experimental Hypnosis, 32*, 118–69.

Orne, M.T. and Holland, C.C. (1968) On the ecological validity of laboratory deceptions. *International Journal of Psychiatry, 6*(4), 282–93.

Ornstein, R. (1986) *The Psychology of Consciousness* (2nd revised ed.). Harmondsworth: Penguin.

Osgood, C.E. (1952) The nature and measurement of meaning. *Psychological Bulletin, 49*, 192–237.

Osgood, C.E. and Luria, Z. (1957) Case Report: a blind analysis of a case of multiple personality using the semantic differential. In C.H. Thigpen, H. Cleckley, *The Three Faces of Eve*. New York: McGraw-Hill.

Osgood, C.E., Suci, G.J. and Tannenbaum, P.H. (1957) *The Measurement of Meaning*. Urbana, Ill: University of Illinois Press.

Osgood, C.E. and Tannenbaum, P.H. (1955) The principle of congruity in the prediction of attitude change. *Psychological Review, 62*, 42–55.

Oswald, I. (1966) *Sleep*. Harmondsworth: Penguin.

O'Toole, K. (1997) The Stanford Prison Experiment: Still powerful after all these years. http://www2.stanford.edu/dept/news/relaged/970108prisonexp.html

Otto, L.B. (1979) Antecedents and consequences of marital timing. In W.R. Burr, R.

Hill, F.I. Nye and I.L. Reiss (eds.), *Contemporary Theories about the Family*, Vol. 1. New York: Free Press.

Owens, J.E., Cook, E.W., and Stevenson, I. (1990) Features of 'near-death experience' in relation to whether or not patients were near death. *Lancet, 336*, 1175–1177.

Owusu-Bempah, K. and Howitt, D. (2000) *Psychology Beyond Western Perspectives*. Leicester: BPS.

Ozonoff, S., Pennington, B.F., and Rogers, S.J. (1991) Executive function deficits in high-functioning autistic individuals: relationship to theory of mind. *Journal of Child Psychology & Psychiatry, 32*(7), 1081–105.

Paludi, M.A. (1992) *The Psychology of Women*. Dubuque, IA: Wm. C. Brown.

Parfit, D. (1987) Divided minds and the nature of persons. In C. Blakemore and S. Greenfield (eds.), *Mindwaves*. Oxford: Blackwell.

Parkes, C.M. (1993) Bereavement as a psychosocial transition: processes of adaptation to change. In M.S. Stroebe, W. Stroebe and R.O. Hansson (eds.), *Handbook of Bereavement: theory, research and intervention*. New York: Cambridge University Press.

Parkin, A. (1998) Memory. In P. Scott and C. Spencer (eds.), *Psychology: A Contemporary Introduction*. Oxford: Blackwell.

Parkin, A.J. (1987) *Memory and Amnesia: an introduction*. Oxford: Blackwell.

Parkin, A.J. (1993) *Memory: phenomena, experiment and theory*. Oxford: Blackwell.

Parkin, A.J. (2000) *Essential Cognitive Psychology*. Hove: Psychology Press.

Parkinson, B. (1987) Emotion – cognitive approaches. In H. Beloff and A.M. Colman (eds.), *Psychology Survey*, No. 6, Leicester: British Psychological Society.

Parsons, T. and Bales, R.F. (1955) *Family Socialization and Interaction Process*. Glencoe, Ill.: Free Press.

Patterson, F.G. (1978) The gestures of a gorilla: language acquisition in another pongid. *Brain and Language, 5*, 72–97.

Patterson, F.G. (1980) Innovative uses of language by a gorilla: a case-study. In K. Nelson (ed.), *Children's Language*, Vol. 2. New York: Gardner Press.

Paul, G.L. (1966) *Insight versus desensitization in psychotherapy: An experiment in anxiety reduction*. Stanford, CA: Stanford University Press.

Pavlov, I.P. (1927) *Conditioned Reflexes*. London: Oxford University Press.

Pedhazur, E.J. and Tetenbaum, T.J. (1979) Bem Sex Role Inventory: a theoretical and methodological critique. *Journal of Personality & Social Psychology, 37*, 996–1016.

Pegg, J.E., Werker, J.F., and McLeod, P.J. (1992) Preference for infant-directed over adult-directed speech: evidence from 7-week-old infants. *Infant Behaviour & Development, 15*, 325–45.

Pennington, D. C., Gillen, K., and Hill, P. (1999) *Social Psychology*. London: Arnold.

Perner, J. and Wimmer, H. (1985) 'John thinks that Mary thinks that': Attribution of second-order beliefs by 5–10 year old children. *Journal of Experimental Child Psychology, 39*, 437–71.

Perner, J., Ruffman, T., and Leekam, S.R. (1994) Theory of mind is contagious: You catch it from your sibs. *Child Development, 65*, 1228–38.

Petitto, L.A. and Seidenberg, M.S. (1979) On the evidence for linguistic abilities in signing apes. *Brain and Language, 8,* 162–83.

Pezdek, K. and Roe, C. (1996) Memory for childhood events: how suggestible is it? In K. Pezdek and W.P. Banks (eds.), *The Recovered Memory/False Memory Debate.* London: Academic Press.

Phillips, J.R. (1973) Syntax and vocabulary of mothers' speech to young children: Age and sex comparisons. *Child Development, 44,* 182–5.

Phinney, J.S. (1990) Ethnic identity in adolescents and adults: Review of research. *Psychological Bulletin, 108,* 499–514.

Piaget, J. (1926) *The Language and Thought of the Child.* London: Routledge and Kegan Paul.

Piaget, J. and Inhelder, B. (1956) *The Child's Conception of Space.* London: Routledge & Kegan Paul.

Piaget, J. and Szeminska, A. (1952) *The Child's Conception of Number.* London: Routledge and Kegan Paul.

Pike, K.L. (1954) Emic and etic standpoints for the description of behaviour. In K.L. Pike (ed.), *Language in Relation to a Unified Theory of the Structure of Human Behaviour.* Part 1, Glendale, CA: Summer Institute of Linguistics.

Piliavin, J.A., Dovidio, J.F., Gaertner, S.L. and Clark, R.D. (1981) *Emergency Intervention.* New York: Academic Press.

Piliavin, J.A., Piliavin, I.M., Loewenton, E.P., McCauley, C. and Hammond, P. (1969) On observers' reproductions of dissonance effects: the right answers for the wrong reasons? *Journal of Personality & Social Psychology, 13,* 98–106.

Pinel, J.P.J. (1993) *Biopsychology* (2nd ed.). Boston: Allyn and Bacon.

Plomin, R. and Loehlin, J.C. (1989) Direct and indirect IQ heritability estimates: a puzzle. *Behavioural Genetics, 19,* 331–42.

Plutchik, R. and Ax, A.F. (1967) A critique of determinants of emotional state by Schachter and Singer (1962). *Psycho-physiology, 4,* 79–82.

Poole, D.A. and Lindsay, D.S. (1995) Interviewing pre-schoolers: Effects of nonsuggestive techniques, parental coaching, and leading questions on reports of nonexperienced events. *Journal of Experimental Child Psychology, 60,* 129–54.

Porpodas, C.D. (1987) The one-question conservation experiment reconsidered. *Journal of Child Psychology & Psychiatry, 28*(2), 343–9.

Potter, M.C. (1966) On perceptual recognition. In J.S. Brown, R.C. Olver & P.M. Greenfield (eds.), *Studies in Cognitive Growth.* New York: Wiley.

Powell-Hopson, D. (1985) *The effects of modelling, reinforcement, and colour meaning word associations on doll colour preference of Black preschool children and White preschool children.* Unpublished doctoral dissertation, Hofstra University.

Powell-Hopson, D. and Hopson, D.S. (1988) Implications of doll-colour preference among Black preschool children and white preschool children. *Journal of Black Psychology, 14,* 57–63.

Powell-Hopson, D. and Hopson, D.S. (1992) Implications of Doll Colour Preferences Among Black Preschool Children and White Preschool Children. In A.K.H. Burlew,

W.C. Banks, H.P. McAdoo, and D.A.Y. Azibo (eds.), *African American Psychology: Theory, Research and Practice*. Newbury Park, CA: Sage Publications.

Power, M.J. and Dalgleish, T. (1997) *Cognition and Emotion: From order to disorder*. Hove: Lawrence Erlbaum.

Premack, D. (1971) On the assessment of language competence in the chimpanzee. In A.M. Schrier and F. Stollnitz (eds.), *Behaviour of Non-human Primates*, Vol. 4. New York: Academic Press.

Premack, D. and Woodruff, G. (1978) Does the chimpanzee have a 'theory of mind'? *Behavioural & Brain Sciences, 4,* 515–26.

Price-Williams, D. (1966) Cross-cultural studies. In B.M. Foss (ed.), *New Horizons in Psychology*, 1. Harmondsworth: Penguin.

Prilleltensky, I. and Fox, D. (1997) Introducing Critical Psychology: Values, Assumptions and the Status Quo. In D. Fox and I. Prilleltensky (eds.), *Critical Psychology: An Introduction*. London: Sage.

Quinton, D. and Rutter, M. (1988) *Parental Breakdown: The Making and Breaking of Intergenerational Links*. London: Gower.

Rabbie, J.M. and Horwitz, M. (1969) Arousal of ingroup-outgroup bias by a chance win or loss. *Journal of Personality & Social Psychology, 13,* 269–77.

Rachman, S. and Wilson, G. (1980) *The Effects of Psychological Therapy*. Oxford: Pergamon.

Raichle, M.E. (1998) Behind the Scenes of Functional Brain Imaging: A Historical and Physiological Perspective. *Proceedings of the National Academy of Sciences, 95*(3), 765–772.

Raine, A. (1993) *The Psychopathology of Crime: Criminal Behaviour as a Clinical Disorder*. San Diego, CA: Academic Press.

Raine, A., Lencz, T., Bihrle, S., LaCasse, L., and Colletti, P. (2000) Reduced Prefrontal Grey Matter Violence and Reduced Autonomic Activity in Antisocial Personality Disorder. *Archives of General Psychiatry, 57*(2), 119–127 (see http://archpsyc.ama-assn.org/issues/v57n2/abs/yoa/9157.html)

Ramsay, R. and de Groot, W. (1977) A further look at bereavement. Paper presented at EATI conference, Upsala (cited in Hodgkinson, P.E. (1980) Treating abnormal grief in the bereaved. *Nursing Times*, 126–8, Jan.).

Rank, S.G. and Jacobson, C.K. (1977) Hospital nurses' compliance with medication overdose orders: a failure to replicate. *Journal of Health & Social Behaviour, 18,* 188–93.

Rappaport, J. and Stewart, E. (1997) A Critical Look at Critical Psychology: Elaborating the Questions. In D. Fox and I. Prilleltensky (eds.). *Critical Psychology: An Introduction*. London: Sage.

Regan, D. and Totten, J. (1975) Empathy and attribution: Turning observers into actors. *Journal of Personality & Social Psychology, 32,* 850–6.

Reicher, S. (1999) Differences, self-image and the individual. *The Psychologist, 12*(3), 131–133.

Reisenzein, R. (1983) The Schachter theory of emotion: two decades on. *Psychological Bulletin, 94,* 239–264.

Rieger (1998) cited in Davison & Neale (2001).

Ring, K. (1980) *Life after death: a scientific investigation of the near-death experience.* New York: Coward, McCann & Geoghegan.

Ring, K. (1980) *The invisible picture: A study of psychic experiences.* Jefferson, NC: McFarland.

Rivers, W.H.R. (1901) Visual spatial perception. In A.C. Haddon (ed.), *Reports of the Cambridge Anthropological Expedition to the Torres Straits*, Vol. 2(1). Cambridge: Cambridge University Press.

Roberts, G. and Owen, J. (1988) The near-death experience. *British Journal of Psychiatry, 153*, 607–617.

Robson, C. (1973) *Experiment, Design and Statistics.* Harmondsworth: Penguin.

Roe, C.A. (2001) Near-death experiences. In R. Roberts & D. Groome (eds.) *Parapsychology: The Science of Unusual Experience.* London: Arnold.

Rogers, R.W. and Deckner, C.W. (1975) Effects of fear appeals and physiological arousal upon emotion, attitudes and cigarette smoking. *Journal of Personality & Social Psychology, 32*, 222–30.

Rose, S., Lewontin, R.C. and Kamin, L.J. (1984) *Not in Our Genes: biology, ideology and human nature.* Harmondsworth: Penguin.

Rose, S.A. and Blank, M. (1974) The potency of context in children's cognition: an illustration through conservation. *Child Development, 45*, 499–502.

Rosenberg, M. (1979) Group rejection and self-rejection. In R. Simmons (ed.), *Research in community and mental health: An annual Compilation of research*, Vol.1. Greenwich, CT.: JAI Press.

Rosenhan, D. (1969) Some origins of concern for others. In P. Mussen, J. Langer and M. Covington (eds.), *Trends and Issues in Developmental Psychology.* New York: Holt, Rinehart and Winston.

Rosenthal, R. and Rosnow, R.L. (1966) Volunteer subjects and the results of opinion change studies. *Psychological Reports, 19*, 1183.

Ross, C.A. (1997) *Dissociative Identity Disorder: Diagnosis, Clinical Features and Treatment of Multiple Personality.* New York: Wiley.

Ross, L. (1977) The intuitive psychologist and his shortcomings. In L. Berkowitz (ed.), *Advances in Experimental Social Psychology*, 10. New York: Academic Press.

Ross, L. and Nisbett, R.E. (1991) *The Person and the Situation: perspectives of social psychology.* New York: McGraw-Hill.

Roubertoux, P.L. and Capron, C. (1990) Are intelligence differences hereditarily transmitted? *European Bulletin of Cognitive Psychology, 10*, 555–94.

Routtenberg, A. and Lindy, J. (1965) Effects of the availability of rewarding septal and hypothalamic stimulation on bar-pressing for food under conditions of deprivation. *Journal of Comparative & Physiological Psychology, 60*, 158–61.

Rumbaugh, D.M. (ed.) (1977) *Language Learning by a Chimpanzee: The LANA Project.* New York: Academic Press.

Rumbaugh, D. and Savage-Rumbaugh, S. (1994) Language and Apes. *APA Psychology Teacher Network*, 2–9, Jan.

Rumelhart, D.E. and Norman, D.A. (1983) Representation in memory. In R.C.

Atkinson, R.J. Herrnstein, B. Lindzey and R.D. Luce (eds.), *Handbook of Experimental Psychology*. New York: Wiley and Sons.

Rushton, A. and Minnis, H. (1997) Transracial family placements. *Journal of Child Psychology & Psychiatry, 38* (2), 147–59.

Rushton, J.P. (1991) Is altruism innate? *Psychological Inquiry, 2,* 141–3.

Rushton, J.P. (1995) *Race, Evolution and Behaviour*. New Brunswick, NJ: Transaction Publishers.

Rutter, M. (1981) *Maternal Deprivation Reassessed* (2nd ed.). Harmondsworth: Penguin.

Rutter, M. (1985) Infantile autism and other pervasive developmental disorders. In M. Rutter and L. Hersov (eds.), *Child and adolescent psychiatry*. Oxford: Basil Blackwell.

Rutter, M. (1987) Continuities and discontinuities from infancy. In J. Osofsky (ed.), *Handbook of Infant Development* (2nd ed.). New York: Wiley.

Rutter, M. (1989) Pathways from childhood to adult life. *Journal of Child Psychology & Psychiatry, 30*(1), 23–51.

Rutter, M. (and the English and Romanian Adoptees (ERA) study team) (1998) Developmental Catch-up, and Deficit, Following Adoption after Severe Global Early Privation. *Journal of Child Psychology & Psychiatry, 39*(4), 465–76.

Rutter, M. and Rutter, M. (1992) *Developing Minds: challenge and continuity across the life span*. Harmondsworth: Penguin.

Ryan, J. (1972) IQ – The illusion of objectivity. In K. Richardson and D. Spears (eds.), *Race, Culture and Intelligence*. Harmondsworth: Penguin.

Sabbatini, R.M.E. (1997) The PET Scan: A New Window Into the Brain. (see http://www.epub.org.br/cm/n01/pet/pet.htm)

Saks, E.R. (1997) *Jekyll on trial: Multiple personality disorder and criminal law*. New York: New York University Press.

Salmon, P. (1985) *Living in Time: a new look at personal development*. London: J.M. Dent and Sons Ltd.

Sarbin, T.R. and Mancuso, J.C. (1980) *Schizophrenia: medical diagnosis or moral verdict?* New York: Pergamon.

Savage-Rumbaugh, E.S., Murphy, J., Seveik, R.A., Williams, S., Brakke, K., and Rumbaugh, D.M. (1993) Language comprehension in ape and child. *Monographs of the Society for Research in Child Development, 58,* 3–4.

Savage-Rumbaugh, E.S., Rumbaugh, D.M. and Boysen, S.L. (1980) Do apes use language? *American Scientist, 68,* 49–61.

Savin, H.B. (1973) Professors and psychological researchers: conflicting values in conflicting roles. *Cognition, 2*(1), 147–9.

Scarr, S. (1992) Developmental theories for the 1990s: Development and individual differences. *Child Development, 63,* 1–19.

Scarr, S. (1993) Biological and cultural diversity: The legacy of Darwin for development. *Child Development, 64,* 1333–53.

Scarr, S. (1997) Behaviour-Genetic and Socialization theories of intelligence: Truth and reconciliation. In R.J. Sternberg and E. Grigorenko (eds.), *Intelligence, Heredity and Environment*. New York: Cambridge University Press.

Scarr, S. and Weinberg, R.A. (1977) Intellectual similarities within families of both adopted and biological children. *Intelligence, 1*, 170–91.

Scarr, S. and Weinberg, R.A. (1983) The Minnesota Adoption Studies: genetic differences and malleability. *Child Development, 54*, 260–7.

Scarr-Salapatek, S. (1976) An evolutionary perspective on infant intelligence: species patterns and individual variations. In M.Lewis (ed.), *Origins of Intelligence*. New York: Plenum.

Schachter, F.F. and Strage, A.A. (1982) Adults' talk and children's language development. In S.G. Moore and C.R. Cooper (eds.), *The young child: Reviews of Research* (vol. 3). Washington, DC.: National Association for the Education of Young Children.

Schachter, S. (1964) The interaction of cognitive and physiological determinants of emotional state. *Advances in Experimental Social Psychology, 1*, 49–80.

Schaffer, H.R. (1996a) *Social Development*. Oxford: Blackwell.

Schaffer, H.R. (1996b) Is the Child Father to the Man? *Psychology Review, 2*(3), 2–5.

Schaffer, H.R. (1998) Deprivation and its effects on children. *Psychology Review, 5*(2), 2–5.

Scheff, T.J. (1966) *Being Mentally Ill: A sociological theory*. Chicago: Aldine.

Scher, S.J. and Cooper, J. (1989) Motivational basis of dissonance: the singular role of behavioural consequences. *Journal of Personality & Social Psychology, 56*, 899–906.

Scherer, K. (1997) Profiles of emotion-antecedent appraisal: Testing theoretical predictions across cultures. *Cognition & Emotion, 11*, 113–50.

Schieffelin, B. and Ochs, E. (1988) A cultural perspective on the transition from prelinguistic to linguistic communication. In R.M. Golinkoff (ed.), *The Transition from Prelinguistic to Linguistic Communication*. Hillsdale, NJ: Lawrence Erlbaum.

Schiffman, R. and Wicklund, R.A. (1992) The minimal group paradigm and its minimal psychology. *Theory and Psychology, 2*(1), 29–50.

Schlenker, B.R. (1982) Translating action into attitudes: an identity-analytic approach to the explanation of social conduct. In L.Berkowitz (ed.), *Advances in Experimental Social Psychology*, Vol. 15. New York: Academic Press.

Schneider, K. (1959) Primary and secondary symptoms in schizophrenia. In S.R. Hirsch and M. Shepherd (eds.) (1974), *Themes and Variations in European Psychiatry*. New York: John Wright.

Schreiber, F.R. (1973) *Sybil*. Harmondsworth: Penguin.

Schroeder, D.A., Penner, L.A., Dovidio, J.F. and Piliavin, J.A. (1995) *The psychology of helping and altruism: Problems and puzzles*. New York: McGraw-Hill.

Segall, M.H., Campbell, D.T. and Herskovits, M.J. (1963) Cultural differences in the perception of geometrical illusions. *Science, 139*, 769–71.

Segall, M.H., Dasen, P.R., Berry, J.W. and Poortinga, Y.H. (1990) *Human Behaviour in Global Perspective: an introduction to cross-cultural psychology*. New York: Pergamon.

Segall, M.H., Dasen, P.R., Berry, J.W. and Poortinga, Y.H. (1999) *Human Behaviour in*

Global Perspective: An Introduction to Cross Cultural Psychology (2nd ed.). Needham Heights, MA: Allyn & Bacon.

Seligman, M.E.P. (1970) On the generality of the laws of learning. *Psychological Review, 77,* 406–18.

Seligman, M.E.P. (1975) *Helplessness: On Depression, Development and Death.* San Francisco: Freeman.

Seligman, M.E.P. (1996) The effectiveness of psychotherapy: the Common Reports study. *American Psychologist, 50,* 965–74.

Semin, G.R. and Fiedler, K. (1989) Relocating attributional phenoemena within a language-cognition interface: the case of actors' and observers' perspectives. *European Journal of Social Psychology, 19,* 491–508.

Serpell, R.S. (1976) *Culture's Influence on Behaviour.* London: Methuen.

Serpell, R. and Deregowski, J.B. (1980) The skill of pictorial perception: An interpretation of cross-cultural; evidence. *International Journal of Psychology, 15,* 145–180.

Shaffer, D.R. (1985) *Developmental Psychology: theory, research and applications.* Monterey, Ca: Brooks/Cole.

Shanab, M.E. and Yahya, K.A. (1978) A cross-cultural study of obedience. *Bulletin of the Psychonomic Society, 11,* 267–9.

Shapiro, D.A. and Shapiro, D. (1982) Meta-analysis of comparative therapeutic outcomes: a replication and refinement. *Psychological Bulletin, 92,* 581–604.

Shatz, M. (1978) Children's comprehension of question-directives. *Journal of Child Language, 5,* 39–46.

Shatz, M. and Gelman, R. (1973) The development of communication skills: Modifications in the speech of young children as a function of the listener. *Monographs of the Society for Research in Child Development, 38* (Whole No. 152).

Shaver, K.G. (1987) *Principles of Social Psychology* (3rd ed.). Hillsdale, NJ: LEA.

Shek, D.T.L. (1996) Mid-life crisis in Chinese men and women. *Journal of Psychology, 130,* 109–119.

Sheridan, C.L. and King, R.G. (1972) Obedience to authority with an authentic victim. *Proceedings, Eightieth Annual Convention, American Psychological Association,* Washington, DC: American Psychological Association.

Sherif, M. and Sherif, C.W. (1953) *Groups in Harmony and Tension.* New York: Harper Brothers.

Sherif, M., White, B.J. and Harvey, O.J. (1955) *Experimental Study of Positive and Negative Intergroup Attitudes Between Experimentally Produced Groups: Robber's Cave study.* Norman: University of Oklahoma.

Sherif, M., Harvey, O.J., White, B.J., Hood, W.R. and Sherif, C. (1961) *Intergroup Co-operation and Competition: the Robber's Cave experiment.* Norman: University of Oklahoma.

Shields, J. (1962) *Monozygotic Twins Brought Up Apart and Brought Up Together.* London: Oxford University Press.

Shields, J. (1976) Heredity and Environment. In H.J. Eysenck & G.D. Wilson (eds.), *A Textbook of Human Psychology.* Lancaster: MTP Press.

Shor, R.E. (1962) Physiological effects of painful stimulation during hypnotic analgesia under conditions designed to minimize anxiety. *International Journal of Clinical & Experimental Hypnosis, 10*, 183–202.

Shotter, J. (1975) *Images of Man in Psychological Research*. London: Methuen.

Shute, B. and Wheldall, K. (1995) The incidence of raised average pitch and increased pitch variability in British 'motherese' speech and the influence of maternal occupation and discourse form. *First Language, 15*, 35–55.

Simpson, J.C. (2000) It's All in the Upbringing. *Johns Hopkins Magazine*, April (http://www.jhu.edu/~jhumag/0400web/35.html)

Singer, P. (1993) The rights of ape. *BBC Wildlife Magazine, 11*(6), 28–32.

Sinnott, J.D. (1982) Correlates of sex roles of older adults. *Journal of Gerontology, 37*, 587–94.

Sizemore, C.C. and Pittillo, E.S. (1977) *I'm Eve*. Garden City, New York: Doubleday.

Skeels, H.M. (1966) Adult status of children with contrasting early life experiences: a follow-up study. *Monographs of Society for Research of Child Development, 31*, No. 103, 3.

Skinner, B.F. (1957) *Verbal Behaviour*. New York: Appleton-Century-Crofts.

Skuse, D. (1984) Extreme deprivation in early childhood – I Diverse outcomes for three siblings from an extraordinary family. *Journal of Child Psychology & Psychiatry, 25*(4), 523–41.

Skuse, D. (1984) Extreme deprivation in early childhood – II Theoretical issues and a comparative review. *Journal of Child Psychology & Psychiatry, 25*(4), 543–72.

Slater, A. (1994) Perceptual Development in Infancy. *Psychology Review, 1*(2), 12–16, Nov.

Smith, J.A., Harré, R., and Van Langenhove, L. (1995) Introduction. In J.A. Smith, R. Harré, and L. Van Langenhove (eds.), *Rethinking Psychology*. London: Sage.

Smith, P.B. and Bond, M.H. (1998) *Social Psychology Across Cultures* (2nd ed.). Hemel Hempstead: Prentice Hall Europe.

Smith, M.L. and Glass, G.V. (1977) Meta-analysis of psychotherapeutic outcome studies. *American Psychologist, 32*, 752–60.

Smith, M.L., Glass, G.V. and Miller, R.L. (1980) *The Benefits of Psychotherapy*. Baltimore, MD: Johns Hopkins University Press.

Smith, P.K. and Cowie, H. (1991) *Understanding Children's Development* (2nd ed.). Oxford: Blackwell.

Smith, P.K., Cowie, H., and Blades, M. (1998) *Understanding Children's Development* (3rd ed.). Oxford: Blackwell.

Smith, R.E., Sarason, I.G. and Sarason, B.R. (1986) *Psychology – The Frontiers of Behaviour* (3rd ed.). New York: Harper and Row.

Smith, V.L. and Ellsworth, P.C. (1987) The social psychology of eye-witness accuracy: misleading questions and communicator expertise. *Journal of Applied Psychology, 72*, 294–300.

Snow, C.E. and Ferguson, C.A. (1977, Eds) *Talking to children*. Cambridge: Cambridge University Press.

Soal, S.G. and Bateman, F. (1954) *Modern Experiments in Telepathy*. London: Faber.

Sokolov, J.L. (1993) A local contingency analysis of the fine-tuning hypothesis. *Developmental Psychology, 29,* 1008–123.

Solso, R.L. and Johnson, H.H. (1989) *Introduction to Experimental Design in Psychology* (4th ed.). New York: Harper and Row.

Sonderegger, T.B. (1970) Intracranial stimulation and maternal behaviour. *American Psychological Association Convention Proceedings 78th Meeting,* 245–6.

Sorokin, P.A. (1966) *Sociological Theories of Today.* New York: Harper and Row.

Spanos, N.P. (1982) A social psychological approach to hypnotic behaviour. In G. Weary and H.L. Mirels (eds.), *Integrations of Clinical and Social Psychology.* New York: Oxford University Press.

Spanos, N.P. (1986a) Hypnotic behaviour: A social psychological interpretation of amnesia, analgesia and trance logic. *Behavioural and Brain Sciences, 9,* 449–67.

Spanos, N.P. (1986b) Hypnosis and the modification of hypnotic susceptibility: A social psychological perspective. In P.L.N. Naish (ed.), *What is hypnosis?* Philadelphia, PA: Open University Press.

Spanos, N.P. (1989) Experimental research on hypnotic analgesia. In N.P. Spanos and J.F. Chaves (eds.), *Hypnosis: The cognitive-behavioural perspective,* Buffalo, NY: Prometheus.

Spanos, N.P. and Chaves, J.F. (1989) Hypnotic analgesia and surgery: In defence of the social-psychological position. *British Journal of Experimental & Clinical Hypnosis, 6,* 131–9.

Spanos, N.P., Weekes, J.R., and Bertrand, L.D. (1985) Multiple personality: A social psychological perspective. *Journal of Abnormal Psychology, 94,* 362–76.

Spanos, N.P., Weekes, J.R., Menary, E., and Bertrand, L.D. (1986) Hypnotic interview and age regression procedures in the elicitation of multiple personality symptoms: A simulation study. *Psychiatry, 49,* 298–311.

Speisman, J.C., Lazarus, R.S., Mordkoff, A.M. and Davidson, L.A. (1964) The experimental reduction of stress based on ego defence theory. *Journal of Abnormal & Social Psychology, 68,* 367–80.

Spence, J.T. (1983) Comment on Lubinski, Tellegen and Butcher 'Masculinity, femininity and androgyny viewed and assessed as distinct concepts'. *Journal of Personality & Social Psychology, 44,* 440–6.

Spence, J.T. and Helmreich, R.L. (1978) *Masculinity and Femininity. Their Psychological Dimensions, Correlations and Antecedents.* Austin: University of Texas Press.

Spence, J.T., Helmreich, R.L. and Stapp, J. (1975) Ratings of self and peers on sex role attributes and their relation to self-esteem and concepts of masculinity and femininity. *Journal of Personality & Social Psychology, 32,* 29–39.

Spender, D. (1980) *Man-Made Language.* London: Routledge & Kegan Paul.

Sperry, R.W. (1974) Lateral specialization in the surgically separated hemispheres. In F.O. Schmitt and F.G. Worden (eds.), *The Neurosciences Third Study Program.* Cambridge, MS: MIT Press.

Spiegel, H. (1974) The grade 5 syndrome: the highly hypnotizable person. *International Journal of Clinical & Experimental Hypnosis, 22,* 303–19.

Spinney, L. (1998) Liar! Liar! *New Scientist, 157* (2121), 22–26, Feb.14.

Spitzer, R.L. (1976) More on pseudoscience in science and the case for psychiatric diagnosis. *Archives of General Psychiatry, 33*, 459–70.

Spitzer, R.L., Endicott, J. and Robins, E. (1978) Research diagnostic criteria: rationale and reliability. *Archives of General Psychiatry, 35*, 773–82.

Stein, B.S., Morris, C.D. and Bransford, J.D. (1978) Constraints on effective elaboration. *Journal of Verbal Learning & Verbal Behaviour, 17*, 707–14.

Stenner, P. and Brown, S.D. (1998) Implications for research. *The Psychologist, 11* (4), 172–5, April.

Stephenson, G.M. (1988) Applied social psychology. In M. Hewstone, W. Stroebe, J.P. Codol and G.M. Stephenson (eds.), *Introduction to Social Psychology*. Oxford: Blackwell.

Stephenson, G.M. (1996) Applied social psychology. In M. Hewstone, W. Stroebe, and G.M. Stephenson (eds.), *Introduction to Social Psychology* (2nd ed.). Oxford: Blackwell.

Stern, D.N., Spieker, S., Barnett, R.K., and MacKain, K. (1983) The prosody of maternal speech: Infant age and context related changes. *Journal of Child Language, 10*, 1–15.

Sternberg, R.J. and Grigorenko, E. (1997) Preface. In R.J. Sternberg and E. Grigorenko (eds.), *Intelligence, Heredity and Environment*. New York: Cambridge University Press.

Stevens, R. (1983) *Erik Erikson*. Milton Keynes: Open University Press.

Stevens, R. (1998) Neuroscience. In P. Scott and C. Spencer (eds.), *Psychology: A Contemporary Introduction*. Oxford: Blackwell.

Storms, M.D. (1973) Videotape and the attribution process: reversing actors' and observers' points of view. *Journal of Personality & Social Psychology, 27* (2), 165–75.

Storms, M.D. (1979) Sex-role identification and its relations to sex-role attributes and sex-role stereotypes. *Journal of Personality & Social Psychology, 37*, 1779–89.

Storr, A. (1966) The concept of cure. In C. Rycroft (ed.), *Psychoanalysis Observed*. London: Constable.

Storr, A. (1987) Why psychoanalysis is not a science. In C. Blakemore and S. Greenfield (eds.), *Mindwaves*. Oxford: Blackwell.

Stratton, P. and Hayes, N. (1988) *A Student's Dictionary of Psychology*. London: Edward Arnold.

Stroebe, W. and Jonas, K. (1996) Principles of Attitude Formation and Strategies of Change. In M. Hewstone, W. Stroebe, and G.M. Stephenson (eds.), *Introduction to Social Psychology* (2nd ed.). Oxford: Blackwell.

Strong, E.K. (1943) *Vocational Interests of Men and Women*. Stanford, CA: Stanford University Press.

St Claire, L. and Turner, J.C. (1982) The role of demand characteristics in the social categorization paradigm. *European Journal of Social Psychology, 12*, 307–14.

Strupp, H.H. and Hadley, S.W. (1979) Specific versus non-specific factors in psychotherapy: a controlled study of outcome. *Archives of General Psychiatry, 36*, 1125–36.

Strupp, H.H. (1996) The tripartite model and the Common Reports study. *American Psychologist, 51*, 1017–24.

Sumner, W.G. (1906) *Folkways*. Boston: Ginn.

Svartberg, M. and Stiles, T.C. (1991) Comparative effects of short-term psychodynamic psychotherapy: a meta-analysis. *Journal of Consulting & Clinical Psychology, 59*(5), 704–14.

Szasz, T. (1972) *The Myth of Mental Illness.* London: Paladin.

Tajfel, H., Billig, M.G., Bundy, R.P. and Flament, C. (1971) Social categorization and intergroup behaviour. *European Journal of Social Psychology, 1,* 149–78.

Tajfel, H. and Turner, J.C. (1979) An integrative theory of intergroup conflict. In W.G. Austin and S. Worchel (eds.), *The Social Psychology of Intergroup Relations.* Monterey, Ca: Brooks/Cole.

Tajfel, H. and Turner, J.C. (1986) The social identity theory of intergroup behaviour. In S. Worchel & W.G. Austin (eds.) *Psychology of intergroup relations* (2nd ed.) Monterey, CA: Brooks/Cole.

Taylor, A. (1986) Sex roles and ageing. In D.J. Hargreaves and A.M. Colley (eds.), *The Psychology of Sex Roles.* London: Harper and Row.

Taylor, L. and Taylot, M. (2001) Why don't we have kids any more? *Observer Review,* 3 June, 1–2.

Taylor, M.C. and Hall, J.A. (1982) Psychological androgyny: theories, methods and conclusions. *Psychological Bulletin, 92,* 347–66.

Tedeschi, J.T. and Rosenfeld, P. (1981) Impression management theory and the forced compliance situation. In J.T. Tedeschi (ed.), *Impression Management Theory and Social Psychological Research.* New York: Academic Press.

Tedeschi, J.T., Schlenker, B.R. and Bonoma, T.V. (1971) Cognitive dissonance: private ratiocination or public spectacle? *American Psychologist, 26,* 685–95.

Terman, L.M. and Miles, C.C. (1936) *Sex and Personality.* New York: McGraw-Hill.

Terrace, H.S. (1979a) *Nim.* New York: Knopf.

Terrace, H.S. (1979b) How Nim Chimpsky changed my mind. *Psychology Today* (November), 65–76.

Terrace, H.S. (1987) Thoughts without words. In C. Blakemore and S. Greenfield (eds.). *Mindwaves.* Oxford: Blackwell.

The Psychologist (2002) Stanford revisited. *The Psychologist, 15*(3), 109.

Thigpen, C.H. and Cleckley, H. (1957) *The Three Faces of Eve.* New York: McGraw-Hill.

Thigpen, C.H. and Cleckley, H.M. (1984) On the incidence of multiple personality disorder. *International Journal of Clinical & Experimental Hypnosis, 32,* 63–6.

Tizard, B. and Phoenix, A. (1993) *Black, white or mixed race?* London: Routledge.

Toates, F. (2001) *Biological Psychology: An Integrative Approach.* Harlow: Pearson Education Ltd.

Totman, R. (1976) Cognitive dissonance and the placebo response. *European Journal of Social Psychology, 5,* 119–25.

Triandis, H.C. (1972) *The Analysis of Subjective Culture.* New York: Wiley.

Triandis, H.C. (1988) Collectivism *vs.* individualism: a reconceptualization of a basic concept in cross-cultural social psychology. In C. Bagley and G.K. Verma (eds.), *Personality, Cognition and Values.* London: MacMillan.

Tulving, E. (1972) Episodic and semantic memory. In E.Tulving and W. Donaldson (eds.), *Organization of Memory*. London: Academic Press.

Turner, E.A. and Wright, J. (1965) Effects of severity of threat and perceived availability on the attractiveness of objects. *Journal of Personality & Social Psychology, 2,* 128–32.

Turner, J.C. (1985) Social categorization and the self-concept: a social-cognitive theory of group behaviour. In E.J. Lawler (ed.) *Advances in group processes: theory and research*. Greenwich, CT: JAI Press.

Turner, J.C., Hogg, M.A., Oakes, P.J., Reicher, S.D., and Wetherell, M.S. (1987) *Rediscovering the Social Group: A self-categorization theory*. Oxford: Blackwell.

Turner, L.H. and Solomon, R.L. (1962) Human traumatic avoidance learning: Theory and experiments on the operant-respondent distinction and failures to learn. *Psychological Monographs, 76* (40, whole No. 559).

Turner, J.C. (1991) *Social Influence*. Milton Keynes: Open University Press.

Tversky, A. and Kahneman, D. (1973) Availability: A heuristic for judging frequency and probability. *Cognitive Psychology, 5,* 207–32.

Tversky, A. and Kahneman, D. (1986) Judgement under uncertainty: Heuristics and biases. In H. Arkes and K. Hammond (eds.), *Judgement and Decision Making*. Cambridge: Cambridge University Press.

Tyerman, A. and Spencer, C. (1983) A critical test of the Sherif's Robber's Cave experiment: intergroup competition and cooperation between groups of well-acquainted individuals. *Small Group Behaviour, 14*(4), 515–31.

Tyler, L.E. (1972) Human abilities. *Annual Review of Psychology, 23,* 177–206.

Vaillant, G. (1977) *Adaptation to Life: how the best and brightest come of age*. Boston: Little Brown.

Valins, S. (1966) Cognitive effects of false heart-rate feedback. *Journal of Personality & Social Psychology, 4,* 400–8.

Valins, S. and Nisbett, R.E. (1972) Attribution processes in the development and treatment of emotional disorders. In E.E. Jones, D.E. Kanouse, R.E. Kelley, R.E. Nisbett, S. Valins and B. Weiner (eds.), *Attribution: perceiving the causes of behaviour*. Morristown, NJ: General Learning Press.

Van Langenhove, L. (1995) The theoretical foundations of experimental psychology and its alternatives. In J.A. Smith, R. Harré, and L. Van Langenhove (eds.), *Rethinking Psychology*. London: Sage.

Vernon, M.D. (1962) *The Psychology of Perception*. Harmondsworth: Penguin.

Vogel, G.W., Vogel, F., McAbee, R.S. and Thurmond, A. (1980) Improvement of depression by REM sleep deprivation. *Archives of General Psychiatry, 37,* 247–53.

Wagstaff, G.F. (1981a) *Hypnosis, compliance and belief*. Brighton: Harvester.

Wagstaff, G.F. (1981b) Source amnesia and trance logic: Artifacts in the essence of hypnosis? *Bulletin of the British Society of Experimental & Clinical Hypnosis, 4,* 3–5.

Wagstaff, G.F. (1984) The enhancement of witness memory by 'hypnosis': a review and methodological critique of the experimental literature. *British Journal of Experimental & Clinical Hypnosis, 2,* 3–12.

Wagstaff, G.F. (1987) Hypnosis. In H. Beloff and A.M. Colman (eds.), *Psychology Survey No. 6*. Leicester: British Psychological Society.

Wagstaff, G.F. (1991) Compliance, belief and semantics in hypnosis: A non-state sociocognitive perspective. In S.J. Lynn and J.W. Rhue (eds.), *Theories of hypnosis: Current models and perspectives*. New York: Guilford.

Wagstaff, G.F. (1995) Hypnosis. In A.M. Colman (ed.), *Controversies in Psychology*. London: Longman.

Wagstaff, G.F. (2002) Eyewitness testimony. *Psychology Review, 8*(4), 28–31.

Wagstaff, G.F. and Frost, R. (1996) Reversing and breaching posthypnotic amnesia and hypnotically created pseudomemories. *Contemporary Hypnosis, 13*, 191–7.

Wahlsten, D. and Gottlieb, G. (1997) The invalid separation of effects of nature and nurture: Lessons from animal experimentation. In R.J. Sternberg and E. Grigorenko (eds.), *Intelligence, Heredity and Environment*. New York: Cambridge University Press.

Walker, S. (1984) *Learning Theory and Behaviour Modification*. London: Methuen.

Ward, I. (2001) *Phobia*. Cambridge: Icon Books.

Warr, P. (1987) *Work, Unemployment and Mental Health*. Oxford: Clarendon Press.

Watson, J.B. (1913) Psychology as the behaviourist views it. *Psychological Review, 20*, 158–77.

Watson, J.B. (1924) *Behaviourism*. New York: Norton.

Watt, C. (2001) Paranormal cognition. In R. Roberst & D. Groome (eds.) *Parapsychology: The Science of Unusual Experience*. London: Arnold.

Waugh, N.C. and Norman, D. (1965) Primary memory. *Psychological Review, 72*, 89–104.

Webb, W.B. and Bonnett, M.H. (1979) Sleep and dreams. In M.E. Meyer (ed.), *Foundations of Contemporary Psychology*. New York: Oxford University Press.

Weiner, B. (1979) A theory of motivation for some classroom experiences. *Journal of Educational Psychology, 71*, 3–25.

Weiner, B. (1985) An attributional theory of achievement motivation and emotion. *Psychological Review, 92*, 548–73.

Weiner, B. (1992) *Human Motivation*. Newbury Park, Ca: Sage Publications.

Wells, G.L. (1978) Applied eyewitness testimony research: System variables and estimator variables. *Journal of Personality & Social Psychology, 36*, 1546–1557.

Wells, G.L. and Petty, R.E. (1980) The effects of overt head movements on persuasion: Compatibility and incompatibility of responses. *Basic & Applied Social Psychology, 1*, 219–30.

Wells, G.L., Small, M., Penrpd, S., Malpass, R.S., Fulero, S.M., and Brimacombe, C.A.E. (1998) *Eyewitness Identification Procedures: Recommendations for Lineups and Photospreads*. Cited in *Encyclopaedia of Psychology* (1999). Washington, DC: American Psychological Association.
(see http://psych-server.iastate.edu/faculty/gwells/encyclopediaapentry.html

Wells, M. (2002) BBC halts 'prison experiment'. *Guardian*, 24 Jan., 5.

Werker, J.F., Pegg, J.E., and McLeod, P.J. (1994) A cross-language investigation of

infant preference for Infant-directed communication. *Infant Behaviour & Development, 17,* 323–33.

Westen, D. and Morrison, K. (2001) A multi-dimensional meta-analysis of treatments for depression, panic, and generalized anxiety disorder: An empirical examination of the status of empirically supported therapies. *Journal of Consulting & Clinical Psychology, 69,* 875–899.

Wetherell, M. (1997) Linguistic Repertoires and Literary Criticism: New Directions for a Social Psychology of Gender. In M.M. Gergen and S.N. Davis (eds.), *Toward a New Psychology of Gender: A Reader.* New York: Routledge.

Williams, B. (1999) Unpublished D. Clin. Psych. Research Thesis. South Thames (Salomons) University.

Wilson, A.N. (1978) *The developmental psychology of the Black child.* New York: United Brothers Communications System.

Wilson, G.T., Nathan, P.E., O'Leary, K.D., and Clark, L.A. (1996) *Abnormal Psychology: Integrating Perspectives.* Needham Hts., MA: Allyn & Bacon.

Wilson, J.E. and Barkham, M. (1994) A practitioner-scientist approach to psychotherapy process and outcome research. In P. Clarkson & M. Pokorny (eds.), *The handbook of psychotherapy.* London: Routledge.

Wilson, S.C. and Barber, T.X. (1983) The fantasy-prone personality: implications for understanding imagery, hypnosis and parapsychological phenomena. In A. Sheikh (ed.), *Imagery: Current Theory, Research and Application.* New York: Wiley.

Wimmer, H. and Perner, J. (1983) Beliefs about beliefs: representation and constraining function of wrong beliefs in young children's understanding of deception. *Cognition, 13,* 103–28.

Wing, J.K., Cooper, J.E. and Sartorious N. (1974) *Measurement and classification of psychiatric symptoms.* Cambridge: Cambridge University Press.

Winograd, E. (1976) Recognition memory for faces following nine different judgements. *Bulletin of the Psychonomic Society, 8,* 419–21.

Winson, J. (1997) The Meaning of Dreams. *Scientific American Mysteries of the Mind,* Special Issue, 7(1), 58–67 (originally published Nov. 1990).

Wittmann, W.W. and Matt, G.E. (1986) Meta-analysis as a method for integrating psychotherapeutic studies in German-speaking countries. *Psychologische Rundschau, 37,* 20–40.

Wohlwill, J.F. (1965) Texture of the stimulus field and age as variables in the perception of relative distance. *Journal of Experimental Child Psychology, 2,* 163–77.

Wolpe, J. (1958) *Psychotherapy by reciprocal inhibition.* Stanford, CA: Stanford University Press.

Wolpe, J. and Rachman, S. (1960) Psychoanalytic evidence: a critique based on Freud's case of Little Hans. *Journal of Nervous & Mental Diseases, 131,* 135–45.

World Health Organization (1973) *Report of the International Pilot Study of Schizophrenia,* Vol. 1, Geneva: W.H.O.

World Health Organization (1992) *The ICD-10 Classification of Mental and Behavioural Disorders: Clinical descriptions and diagnostic guidelines,* Geneva: W.H.O.

Yarrow, L.J. (1961) Maternal deprivation: toward an empirical and conceptual re-evaluation. *Psychological Bulletin, 58,* 459–90.

Yin, R. (1969) Looking at upside-down faces. *Journal of Experimental Psychology, 81,* 141–5.

Yuille, J.C. and Cutshall, J.L. (1986) A case-study of eye-witness memory of a crime. *Journal of Applied Psychology, 71,* 291–301.

Zajonc, R.B. (1980) Feeling and thinking: preferences need no inferences. *American Psychologist, 35,* 151–75.

Zaitchik, D. (1990) When representations conflict with reality: the preschooler's problem with false belief and 'false' photographs. *Cognition, 7,* 333–62.

Zangwill, O.L. (1961) cited in J.E. Bogen (1969), The other side of the brain. In R. Ornstein (1986) *The Psychology of Consciousness* (2nd revised ed.). Harmondsworth: Penguin.

Zanna, M.P. and Cooper, J. (1974) Dissonance and the pill. An attributional approach to studying the arousal properties of dissonance. *Journal of Personality & Social Psychology, 29,* 703–9.

Zebrowitz, L.A. (1990) *Social Perception.* Milton Keynes: Open University Press.

Zillmann, D. (1978) *Hostility and Aggression,* Hillsdale, NJ: LEA.

Zimbardo, P.G. (1969) The human choice: individuation, reason and order versus deindividuation, impulse and chaos. In W.J. Arnold and D. Levine (eds), *Nebraska Symposium on Motivation,* Lincoln: University of Nebraska Press.

Zimbardo, P.G. (1973) On the ethics of intervention in human psychological research with special reference to the 'Stanford Prison Experiment'. *Cognition, 2*(2), 243–55.

Zimbardo, P.G. (1975) Pathology of imprisonment. *American Psychologist,* October. Reprinted in D. Krebs (ed.), *Readings in Social Psychology: Contemporary Perspectives.* New York: Harper & Row.

Zimbardo, P.G. and Leippe, R. (1991) *The Psychology of Attitude Change and Social Influence.* New York: McGraw-Hill.

Zubin, J. and Spring, B. (1977) Vulnerability – a new view of schizophrenia. *Journal of Abnormal Psychology, 86,* 103–126.

Author Index

Subject Index

Note: page numbers in **bold** refer to diagrams, page numbers in *italics* refer to tables.